Upon These Shores

Upon These Shores

THEMES IN THE AFRICAN-AMERICAN EXPERIENCE

1600 TO THE PRESENT

Edited by

William R. Scott & William G. Shade

ROUTLEDGE

NEW YORK AND LONDON

Published in 2000 by
Routledge
29 West 35th Street
New York, NY 10001

Published in Great Britain by
Routledge
11 New Fetter Lane
London EC4P 4EE

Printed in the United States of America on acid-free paper
Design: Jack Donner

Library of Congress Cataloging-in-Publication Data

Scott, William R. (William Randolph), 1940–
    Upon these shores : themes in the African-American experience, 1600 to the present /
William R. Scott and William G. Shade
        p. cm.
    Includes bibliographical references and index.
    ISBN 0–415–92406–5 — ISBN 0–415–92407–3 (pbk.)
    1. Afro-Americans—History. 2. Afro-Americans—Historiography.
I. Shade, William G. II. Title.
E185 .S416 2000
973'.0496073—dc21

                                                                99–034688

To the students and staff
of the
United Negro College Fund
and
Andrew W. Mellon Minority Fellows Program

contents

Foreword

William H. Gray III

I T GIVES ME GREAT PLEASURE to write this foreword to an important and timely book on Americans of African descent. This anthology on various aspects of the black experience, past and present, appears toward the end of an era of enormous change in the status of America's largest racial minority. The essays in this collection are informed by a deep sense of the long journey our people have traveled since being forcibly brought to these shores in chains. It is fitting that this book should appear at the end of the twentieth century because these are both triumphant and troublesome times for black Americans. We must pause at this point and reflect on both our trials and our triumphs and how we must confront remaining challenges.

As we try to judge the position of African Americans in today's world and look toward reaching the goal of a truly color-blind society, we must begin with a clear view of the vibrant history of the African-American community and the diversity of African-American experience. When one looks at the images of black America carried around the globe by the miracle of television, it is easy to forget that these powerful images fail to represent the lives of the vast majority of African Americans and consequently who we really are.

During my lifetime legal segregation has ended and wide areas of opportunity have opened. In the last twenty-five years, for instance, African Americans gained far greater equal access to education. The result was more equitable opportunities in kindergarten, in elementary school, in junior high and high school that permitted considerably larger numbers of African Americans to earn college degrees. Yet in numerous ways, both large and small, white racism remains to constrict the aspirations of black Americans and cast a shadow on the American dream. The combination of economic and educational deprivation has had devastating consequences for African Americans—consequences that can't be erased in a few decades.

But we have come a mighty long way in the half century since I was born.

I can remember having to ride in the back of the bus. I can remember drinking from a "colored" water fountain. But when I recall the past, I marvel at how far we've come. Think: in the year I was born, more than 90 percent of all African Americans were living below the poverty line. As this decade began that level was about one-third. But that is still too high, particulary when the national average is less than 15 percent. We still have a long way to go.

African Americans make up 10 percent of the workforce—but comprise only 2 percent of the scientists and engineers. African-American seventeen years olds read, on average, at the level of white thirteen year olds. While African-Americans' scores on the college board exams went up 45 points in the 1980s, the total number earning bachelor's degrees fell 8 percent. The reason is no mystery. In the 1980s the cost of higher education increased 50 percent, but spending on support of education, at least at the federal level, decreased 50 percent. And African-American families, whose assets average a tenth of that of white families, simply can't afford to send their children to college without help.

Fortunately, the 1990s witnessed new and sustained growth in the black student population. African Americans continued to improve their SAT scores, and the gap between the scores of white students and black students narrowed considerably. In the first half of the decade the number of bachelor's degrees awarded, which had remained practically static in the 1980s, jumped by nearly 40 percent. Clearly some African Americans—primarily the black middle class—have benefited from the economic boom of the 1990s, and as we approach the end of the decade and the twentieth century, the number of African Americans enrolled in higher education—two-year and four-year colleges and graduate school—nears the two million mark.

Another figure captures the pathos and pain that many black Americans have experienced. In 1991, there were 136,000 African-American males between eighteen and twenty-four in prison, and 378,000 black males the same age in college. The number of black youths in higher education exceeds those in jail, but just think what the cost of such a high rate of incarceration means not to one community, but to this great society that must compete in a new world reality in the twenty-first century.

Looking at those trends, and also looking at where this country needed to go, I decided to leave government and devote my life to promoting black education. Historically black colleges still graduate one-third of all African Americans with baccalaureate degrees. At United Negro College Fund schools, forty-one of them private, enrollment has increased by 20 percent in the past five years—twice the national rate. Ninety percent of the UNCF students receive financial aid. But the average endowment per student at our colleges is only one-third the average for private four-year colleges.

And the cost of education has gone up across the board. Again, fortunately, the general economic situation and the support provided higher education by the recent administration has changed the picture. While unemployment has reached new lows, young black men continue to struggle. The inability to find work, often a direct result of poor primary education that plagues our hyper-segregated inner cities, blights the lives of too many and adds to the swelling prison population. Nonetheless, earlier reports turn out to have been exaggerated and the positive college enrollment trends of the 1990s have produced a situation in which the black male college population is two and a half times the black prison population. Aside from the increasing numbers of African Americans attending and graduating from colleges and universities (most of which are public institutions), a larger proportion are in four-year schools, and there is only a modest difference in the proportion going to graduate school, thanks in part to programs such as that sponsored by the Mellon Foundation at private black colleges and universities.

In the next century, we will face keen competition from abroad. A united European community has become a political reality. Economic goliaths on the Pacific rim will be our major economic competitors. America cannot afford to enter the twenty-first century without applying all of its brainpower. That means making sure that underprivileged, disadvantaged, and yes, the under-class, locked in our urban inner cities and in our rural poor areas, get a chance to become competent, productive, and contributing members of our society.

If we do not broaden our nation's opportunities, then we will fail in our mission. John Akers, president of IBM, has accurately stated, "If we are to be competitive in the next century we must have competent workers." And in the next century more than 80 percent of all the new workforce will come from three groups: women, minorities, and new immigrants. It just makes good sense to invest in education and provide opportunity for a new generation if we are to have growth and opportunity for all Americans.

There is a significant threat, though, to these institutions, and a threat to our society in working together to redress the past inequities of our society. It's what I call the "color-blind" argument, which goes something like this: we must have a color-blind society. Was that not the goal of the Civil Rights movement? Was that not the goal and the dream of Martin Luther King Jr., where all would be judged by individual merit and by "the content of their character"? Wasn't that the dream and the ultimate goal? Therefore, the argument says that today we must eliminate all race-conscious and race-specific remedies such as affirmative action and hiring goals for the private and public sectors. Code words, such as "quotas," are devised to imply that unfair advantages are being given to unqualified minority candidates.

The underlying assumption is that after three and one-half centuries of slavery and legalized segregation, in the last three decades enough progress has been made to balance the playing field and thus there is no longer need for any compensatory action. In fact, such compensatory actions may in and of themselves be the root cause of future discrimination. Well, most Americans believe that we should strive for a color-blind society. And all of us believe ultimately that should be the goal. But there is a question: Can we seriously believe that in thirty years we have been able to undo all the effects of more than three hundred and fifty years of degradation?

I want you to understand, I agree with Martin Luther King Jr. that our goal should be a color-blind society. But I also know that it was just thirty years ago when black citizenship rights were curtailed by law in this country simply because of skin color. And if all compensatory remedies are stopped today, you would still leave in place many of the centuries-old inequities. There are examples of progress, but the fact remains that if we stop struggling for justice, then we will fail to produce a society with true equality of opportunity and turn our backs on the promises of the Declaration of Independence.

One must recognize that it was only thirty-five years ago when Congress passed the public accommodations bill and made it possible for me to stay in the Holiday Inn in Mississippi. And it was not until 1965 when Congress guaranteed that someone of my color in Alabama could go to the polls and vote for elected officials. I think that it is obvious that you can not reverse three and a half centuries in one-quarter of a century. It takes time to redress past inequities.

Are there new methodologies that we may have to employ to make greater progress? Why, yes, we have to do that, and we have to work those out together as a people and not play upon the fears of one another. If we play upon the fears of each other, then we will allow those who've become battered and embittered in both of our communities to take center stage. That would be a great tragedy. We must reach a common agenda, an agenda that binds us as close as we were in the struggle for equal justice thirty and forty years ago. We may have disagreements on strategies, but we can never disagree on the ultimate goal of a color-blind society.

Within our country, working through the churches and schools, we need to build bridges of understanding between the diverse ethnic and religious communities that comprise the United States by educating each community about the other. Understanding is based upon education. We must learn another community's background if we are to understand its people. We must strive to appreciate their sufferings and achievements. We must hasten to comprehend both the simplicity and the complexity of their lives and open our minds to imagine seeing their world as they see it, whether they are rich or poor, or of high station in life or low. We must try to dream their dreams and suffer their disappointments and misfortunes.

This book offers the opportunity for knowledge, education, and understanding. It allows the opportunity for African Americans, my brothers and sisters, to look into their past and examine the complexity of their community and thus better understand themselves. It presents information and guidance for those from other communities and cultures that make up our vast multicultural nation to open their minds to our history, open their hearts to our afflictions, and open their eyes to our achievements.

These essays enable the readers to penetrate deeply into our experience by studying its profundity and its complexity. They will be able to confront the essentially paradoxical nature of the black condition expressed by W. E. B. DuBois as our "double consciousness." As he wrote, nearly a century ago in *The Souls of Black Folk*:

> The history of the American Negro is the history of this strife,—this longing to attain self-conscious manhood, to merge his double self into a better and truer self. In this merging he wishes neither of the older selves to be lost. He would not Africanize America, for America has too much to teach the world and Africa. He would not bleach his Negro soul in a flood of white Americanism, for he knows that Negro blood has a message for the world. He simply wishes to make it possible for a man to be both a Negro and an American, without being cursed and spit upon by his fellows, without having the doors of opportunity closed roughly in his face.

Chronology of African-American History

900	Rise in West Africa of the kingdom of Ghana.
1203	Conquest of Ghana by Sumanguru, king of the Sosso empire.
1230	Rise of Mali, the successor state to Ghana, and accession of Sundiata, who defeated the Sosso and ruled over the Sudanic area of West Africa until his death about 1260.
1305	Reports of expeditions sent across the Atlantic by Abu Bakari II, king of Mali.
1324–1325	Pilgrimage to Mecca of Musa I, the most renowned mansa of Mali.
1415	Portuguese military expedition captures Ceuta, the northern terminus of several trans-Saharan caravan routes in Morocco.
1442	Portuguese bring first African slaves to Europe.
1444	The first Portuguese contacts are made with sub-Saharan Africa initiating the seizure and enslavement of West Africans in Europe.
1450s	Portuguese establish trading posts along the West African coast.
1464	Accession of Sonni Ali of Songhai.
1468	Mali is conquered by Sonni Ali and absorbed by Songhai, the largest of the West African empires, which lasted from 1450 to 1800.
1486	The Portuguese start a settlement at São Tomé in the Gulf of Guinea and import African slaves as sugar plantation laborers.
1488	Bartholomeu Dias rounds the Cape of Good Hope.

1492	Columbus reaches the New World and claims it on behalf of Spain.
	An African, Pedro Alonso Nino, is among Columbus's crew. Other Africans later accompanied Balboa, Ponce De Leon, Cortez, Pizarro, and Menendez.
1493	Pope Alexander VI issues a proclamation dividing newly discovered lands in the Americas, Africa, and Asia between Spain and Portugal, which is ratified a year later by the Treaty of Tordesillas.
1501	Spanish merchants receive licenses from the Crown to import African slaves to the Caribbean island of Hispaniola, thus starting the slave trade to the Americas.
1538	Estevanico, an African employed in Spain's service, explores and claims for Madrid the area of the United States that is now Arizona and New Mexico.
1619	The first African slaves taken to Jamestown, Virginia, and sold as indentured servants.
1641	Massachusetts becomes first mainland colony in British North America to recognize slavery in its legal code. Connecticut followed in 1650; Virginia in 1661; Maryland in 1663; New York and New Jersey in 1664; South Carolina in 1682; Rhode Island and Pennsylvania in 1700; North Carolina in 1715; and Georgia in 1750.
1676	Bacon's Rebellion occurs in Virginia.
1688	Quakers and Mennonites in Germantown, Pennsylvania, make first antislavery protest in Western Hemisphere.
1712	Slaves revolt in New York City.
1739	Slaves rebel along the Stono River in South Carolina.
1741	Slave revolt scare in New York City leads to execution of thirty-one slaves and five whites.
1770	Crispus Attucks killed in the Boston Massacre.
1773	Phillis Wheatley's book, *Poems on Various Subjects, Religious and Moral*, published.
1775	Continental Congress bars Blacks from serving in Continental Army.
	Lord Dunmore offers freedom to slaves who will support the Crown.
	First American antislavery society is founded in Philadelphia.
1776	Continental Congress approves George Washington's order to encourage enlistment of free blacks in the Continental Army.

Declaration of Independence accepted after the Continental Congress removed Jefferson's protest against the slave trade.

1777 Vermont becomes the first state to abolish slavery; followed by Massachusetts in 1780 and New Hampshire in 1783. Connecticut and Rhode Island bar slavery in 1784.

1780 Pennsylvania provides for gradual emancipation. Similar gradual emancipation plans were adopted by New York in 1799 and New Jersey in 1804, although there were as a consequence still slaves in New Jersey when the Thirteenth Amendment was passed in 1865.

1787 Northwest Ordinance passed outlawing slavery in the territory north of the Ohio River.

Richard Allen and Absolom Jones found Philadelphia's Free African Society.

Prince Hall establishes African Lodge No. 459, the first Black Masonic Lodge in the United States.

United States Constitution written with no direct reference to slavery, but clauses providing that: the slave trade could exist until 1807; provision could be made for the rendition of fugitive slaves; and that three-fifths of the slaves would be counted in determining the number of delegates to the House of Representatives from each state and the number of presidential electors.

1791 Revolt led by Toussaint L'Ouverture begins in San Domingue to overthrow French rule.

1793 Eli Whitney invents the cotton gin making possible the development of the Cotton Kingdom of the Lower South.

Congress passes the first Fugitive Slave Law.

1794 Absolom Jones, the first black ordained Episcopal minister in America, founds First African Church of St. Thomas in Philadelphia.

Richard Allen and his followers organize Bethel African Methodist Episcopal Church in Philadelphia.

Zion Methodist Church established in New York City.

Boston African Society founded.

1800 Gabriel Prosser's slave conspiracy uncovered in Richmond, Virginia.

1804 Jean Jacque Dessalines proclaims the independence of Haiti as the second republic established in the Western Hemisphere.

Ohio enacts the first of the northern Black Laws, which restricted the rights and movement of free blacks.

1808   United States ends the legal importation of slaves.

1811   Largest slave revolt in the United States takes place in Louisiana.

1816   African Methodist Episcopal Church is organized at a general convention in Philadelphia.

The American Society for the Colonization of Free People of Color, commonly called the American Colonization Society, is organized in Baltimore to transport free blacks to Africa.

1820   Missouri Compromise admits Missouri as a slave state and Maine as a free state and prohibits slavery in that portion of the Louisiana Purchase above 36 30'.

1822   Denmark Vesey's slave conspiracy in Charleston, South Carolina, is uncovered and suppressed. The South Carolina legislature passes in response the first Negro Seamen's Act.

1827   *Freedom's Journal*, the first African-American newspaper, established in New York City.

1829   Publication of David Walker's *Appeal to the Coloured Citizens of the World*.

1830   First National Negro Convention meets at Philadelphia's Bethel Church.

1831   Abolitionists William Lloyd Garrison establishes *The Liberator*.

Nat Turner leads a slave revolt in Southampton County, Virginia, killing 56 whites. Turner was executed and skinned and over two hundred African Americans were killed.

1833   American Antislavery Society organized in Philadelphia.

Parliament passes the act abolishing slavery in the British Empire the following year.

1836   House passes the Gag Rule, which restricted debate on petitions relating to slavery. It was reenacted with each new congress until December, 1844.

1839   The Liberty Party, which was the only antebellum party dedicated to the abolition of slavery and the protection of the rights of free blacks, organizes in Warsaw, New York.

1845   Publication of the *Narrative of the Life of Frederick Douglass: An American Slave*.

1846   The Wilmot Proviso to restrict slavery from territory acquired as a result of the Mexican War is introduced into Congress.

1848   Free Soil Party organized in Buffalo, New York.

1850   Compromise of 1850 passes, bringing California into the Union as a free state and outlawing the slave trade in the District of Columbia, but also opening Utah and New Mexico territories to slavery and enacting a new pro-slavery fugitive slave law.

1851   Christiana "Riot" in Pennsylvania in which a slaveholder was killed attempting to apprehend several fugitive slaves under the new law.

1852   Publication of *Uncle Tom's Cabin* by Harriet Beecher Stowe.

1853   Publication of William Wells Brown's *Clotel: The President's Daughter*, the first novel published by an African American.

1854   Anthony Burns, a fugitive slave, is returned from Boston to Virginia by U.S. Army, Marines, and Navy under orders from President Franklin Pierce.

        Kansas-Nebraska Act repeals the Missouri Compromise and opens the Louisiana Purchase area to slavery.

1855   John Mercer Langston is elected clerk of Brownhelm Township in Lorain County, Ohio, the first African American elected to political office in the United States.

1857   *Dred Scott* v. *Sanford* denies that free blacks were ever citizens and declared the Missouri Compromise unconstitutional opening the territories to slavery.

1859   John Brown raids the Harper's Ferry arsenal in Virginia hoping to start a broad slave revolt. He was hanged for treason against the state.

1860   Abraham Lincoln elected president.

        South Carolina secedes from the Union.

1861   Confederate States of America is established following the secession of the other states of the Lower South.

        The Confederate government attacks Fort Sumter beginning the Civil War. Lincoln's call for troops to suppress the rebellion provokes the secession of Virginia, North Carolina, Tennessee, and Arkansas.

        Serfdom is abolished in Russia by Czar Alexander II.

1862   African-American soldiers enlisted in the Union Army.

        Slavery is abolished in the territories of the United States and the District of Columbia.

1863   Lincoln issues the Emancipation Proclamation freeing the slaves held in the areas in rebellion against the United States.

1865   Civil War ends.

The Bureau of Refugees, Freedmen, and Abandoned Lands (Freedmen's Bureau) established.

Black Codes passed by all-white governments of the southern states.

Thirteenth Amendment ending slavery in the United States is ratified.

1865–1866 The Ku Klux Klan, the most important of the several white, racist paramilitary groups created by ex-rebels is founded by ex-Confederate General Nathan Bedford Forrest in Pulaski,Tennessee.

1866 Congress passes Civil Rights bill over veto of President Andrew Johnson.

Congress passes Supplementary Freedmen's Bureau Act over veto of President Johnson.

Riots in Memphis and New Orleans.

1867 Congress gives Black men the vote in the District of Columbia.

Congress passes initial Reconstruction acts.

Constitutional conventions chosen by universal manhood suffrage meet in the former Confederate states. The proportion of black members of conventions ranged from 10 percent in Texas to 61 percent in South Carolina.

1868 House of Representatives impeaches Andrew Johnson. The Senate acquits him by one vote.

Arkansas, North Carolina, South Carolina, Louisiana, Alabama, and Florida readmitted to the Union.

Fourteenth Amendment nationalizing American citizenship and guaranteeing federal protection of the Freedmen's civil rights is ratified.

1870 The remaining ex-Confederate states—Virginia, Mississippi, Texas, and Georgia—are readmitted to the Union.

Hiram R. Revels of Mississippi becomes the first African-American U.S. Senator.

Fifteenth Amendment prohibiting the states from denying African Americans the vote is ratified.

The first of three acts—sometimes termed the Ku Klux Klan Acts—passed to enforce the Fifteenth Amendment.

Joseph H. Rainey of South Carolina becomes the first African American elected to the House of Representatives.

1872 Frederick Douglass presides over Colored National Convention.

1874   Democrats win a majority in the House of Representatives.

Gradually the white Democrats were taking over the ex-Confederate state governments and undoing Reconstruction in the South, achieving majorities in Tennessee (1869); Virginia (1869); North Carolina (1870); Georgia (1871); Texas (1873); Arkansas (1874); Alabama (1874); Mississippi (1875); South Carolina (1876); Louisiana (1877); and Florida (1877).

1875   The "Lame-Duck" Republican Congress passes the Civil Rights Act guaranteeing equal rights in public places and prohibiting restriction of African Americans from juries.

1876–1877   Republican Rutherford B. Hayes elected over Democrat Samuel Tilden in a disputed election marred by violence against Blacks in the South.

1877   Troops are withdrawn from South Carolina and federal attempts at Reconstruction ends.

1881   Tennessee passes the first Jim Crow railroad-car law.

1886   Slavery abolished in Cuba.

1888   Slavery abolished in Brazil.

1890–1908   Mississippi and South Carolina followed by Louisiana, North Carolina, Alabama, Virginia, Georgia, and Oklahoma amend constitutions with poll taxes, literacy tests, and property qualifications, effectively excluding blacks from political life in the South.

1895   Booker T. Washington delivers "Atlanta Compromise" speech at the Cotton States and International Exposition.

Black feminist and women's club leader Mary Church Terrell founds the National Association of Colored Women (NACW).

1896   In a landmark decision, *Plessy* v. *Ferguson*, the Supreme Court upholds the doctrine of separate but equal public facilities for whites and blacks.

1898   Black military contingents see service in the Spanish American War, distinguishing themselves in battle at El Caney, Las Guasimas, and San Juan Hill.

1900   The First Pan-African Congress is held in London, England.

1903   W. E. B. DuBois publishes the "Souls of Black Folk" and formally rejects the leadership of Booker T. Washington.

1905   The Niagara Movement, led by W. E. B. DuBois and Monroe Trotter, is established at Niagara Falls, New York, to renew public agitation for black constitutional rights.

1908   Race riot in Springfield, Illinois, on the 100th anniversary of
            Lincoln's birthday leads to founding in February 1909 of the
            National Association for the Advancement of Colored People
            (NAACP).

1911   The National Urban League is founded under the leadership of
            George E. Haynes and Eugene Kinkle Jones to improve condi-
            tions for urban blacks.

1914–1929   The great migration of nearly 500,000 black workers from the
            South to the North.

1915   Carter G. Woodson founds the Association for the Study of
            Negro Life and History and the "Journal of Negro History."

1916   Jamaican immigrant Marcus Garvey organizes the Universal
            Negro Improvement Association (UNIA) in Harlem, New
            York.

1917   The United States enters World War I; 370,000 black soldiers
            and 1,400 officers serve in the American Expeditionary Force.

1919   In the Red Summer of 1919, more than twenty-five race riots in
            which African Americans resort to armed defense erupt in
            major U.S. cities.

1920   The important literary and artistic movement called the
            Harlem Renaissance is born.

1923   Marcus Garvey is convicted of mail fraud and sentenced to five
            years imprisonment in Atlanta penitentiary. In 1927 he is
            released and deported to Jamaica.

1926   Carter G. Woodson inaugurates Negro History Week.

1930   Nation of Islam is founded in Detroit, Michigan.

1935   Educator Mary McLeod Bethune establishes the National
            Council of Negro Women.

            African Americans launch massive protests against Italy's inva-
            sion of Ethiopia.

1936   Jesse Owens wins four medals in track and field at Berlin
            Olympics.

1937   Joe Louis wins world heavyweight boxing championship.

1941   March on Washington Movement organized by A. Philip
            Randolph, president of the Brotherhood of Sleeping Car
            Porters, causes President Franklin Roosevelt to issue Executive
            Order 8802 barring discrimination in defense industries and
            creating a Fair Employment Practices Commission to
            investigate complaints of discrimination.

1942   The Congress of Racial Equality (CORE) is founded.

1943	President Roosevelt proclaims a state of emergency and sends troops to restore order in Detroit, site of the war period's most serious race riot.
1945	An estimated 1 million black men and women serve in U.S. armed forces during World War II.
1947	Jackie Robinson of the Brooklyn Dodgers integrates major league baseball.
1948	President Harry Truman desegregates armed forces.
1950	The Korean War of 1950–1953 is first U.S. war fought with full integration of the American military.
1954	The Supreme Court in *Brown* v. *Board of Education of Topeka* rules racial segregation in public schools unconstitutional, overthrowing *Plessy* v. *Ferguson*.
1955	Emmett Till, a 14-year-old black youth, is abducted and lynched in Money, Mississippi. Rosa Parks, a seamstress and civil rights activist, is arrested after refusing to give her seat to a white passenger sparking the Montgomery, Alabama bus boycott.
1957	The Southern Christian Leadership Conference (SCLC) is organized in New Orleans and names Martin Luther King Jr. president. Congress passes first federal Civil Rights Act since 1875, creating a federal civil rights commission and civil rights division in the U.S. Justice Department. President Eisenhower sends 1,000 federal troops to Little Rock, Arkansas, to prevent interference with the integration of Central High School.
1960	Students at North Carolina A & T in Greensboro, North Carolina, begin the "sit-in" movement against segregated lunch counters. The Student Nonviolent Coordinating Committee ("Snick") is organized at Shaw University in Raleigh, North Carolina. President Eisenhower signs Civil Rights Act that provides greater protection of black voting rights.
1961	CORE begins freedom bus rides throughout the South to challenge segregated interstate public transportation.
1962	Twenty-Fourth Amendment to U.S. Constitution bars poll tax in federal elections. Twelve thousand federal troops sent to University of Mississippi to ensure admission of James Meredith.

1963	Martin Luther King Jr. leads major civil rights protests in Birmingham, Alabama, to desegregate the city.
	Medgar Evers, local NAACP field secretary, is murdered in Jackson, Mississippi.
	Two hundred and fifty thousand participate in March on Washington, the largest civil rights demonstration in U.S. history.
1964	Riots in Harlem, Jersey City, Philadelphia, Rochester, Chicago.
	Martin Luther King Jr. is awarded Nobel Peace Prize.
	Three civil rights workers murdered in Philadelphia, Mississippi.
	Civil Rights Act bans discrimination in education, employment, and public accommodations.
1965	Malcolm X is assassinated at Audubon Ballroom in Harlem, New York.
	President Lyndon Johnson signs Voting Rights Act, which authorized intervention of federal examiners when state officials refused to register eligible black voters.
	The term "affirmative action" is developed as part of Executive Order 11246, which prohibited discrimination by firms doing business with federal government and gave federal agencies power to enforce minority hiring.
	Fifty thousand marchers, led by Martin Luther King Jr., participate in Selma-to-Montgomery civil rights march.
	A six-day riot erupts in the Watts section of Los Angeles.
1966	James Meredith is wounded leading a voter registration march from Memphis to Jackson, Mississippi.
	During continuation of the Meredith march, Stokely Carmichael, SNCC's leader, calls for "Black Power."
	Bobby Seale and Huey Newton found the Black Panther Party in Oakland, California.
	Edward Brooke, a Massachusetts Republican, becomes first African American elected to U.S. Senate since Reconstruction.
1967	Thurgood Marshall, the U.S. solicitor general, becomes first African American appointed to the Supreme Court.
	Riot in Newark, New Jersey, the worst outbreak of urban violence since Watts.
1968	Martin Luther King Jr. assassinated in Memphis, Tennessee.
1971	Congressional Black Caucus is formed.

1972	Shirley Chisholm, a black congresswoman from Brooklyn, runs for U.S. president.
1976	President-elect Jimmy Carter appoints Georgia house representative Andrew Young ambassador to the United Nations.
1977	A televised version of Alex Haley's novel, *Roots*, is viewed by more than 130 million Americans.
1978	Supreme Court's rules in *Regents of University of California* v. *Allan Bakke* that the University violated the equal protection clause of the Constitution, thus violating Bakke's civil rights, giving support to position that affirmative action constituted reverse discrimination.
1983	President Reagan signs bill making the third Monday in January a federal holiday honoring Martin Luther King Jr.
1984	TransAfrica's anti-apartheid protests at the South African Embassy in Washington lead to creation of nationwide Free South Africa Movement (FSAM).
	Jesse Jackson, head of Operation Push, seeks the Democratic Party nomination for U.S. president.
1986	U.S. Congress overrides presidential veto and passes the Comprehensive Anti-Apartheid Act (CAAA), mandating selective sanctions against South Africa.
1989	Douglas Wilder of Virginia is elected first black governor in the nation.
	General Colin Powell is appointed chairman of the armed forces Joint Chiefs of Staff.
	David Dinkins elected as the first African-American mayor of New York City.
1991	First African and African-American Summit, organized by Reverend Leon Sullivan, is held in Abidjan, Ivory Coast.
	Airing of the videotaped beating by Los Angeles police of black motorist Rodney King sparks national outrage.
	Judge Clarence Thomas is confirmed by Senate to fill the seat vacated by retiring Justice Thurgood Marshall.
1992	Carol Moseley Braun becomes first African-American woman to serve in U.S. Senate.
1993	President Clinton appoints five African Americans to his cabinet.
1995	At the call of minister Louis Farrakhan of the Nation of Islam, more than a million African-American men attend march in Washington, D.C.

introduction

The Long Rugged Road

William R. Scott and William G. Shade

> We are the children of the black sharecroppers, the first-born of the city
> tenements. We have tramped down a road three hundred years long. We
> have been shunted to and fro by cataclysmic social changes. We are a folk
> born of cultural devastation, slavery, physical suffering, unrequited long-
> ing, abrupt emancipation, migration, disillusionment, bewilderment, job-
> lessness, and insecurity—all enacted within a short space of historical
> time.
> —Richard Wright, *12 Million Black Voices* (1941)

MERICANS OF AFRICAN DESCENT have struggled a long time
since their ancestors arrived "upon these shores" to survive and
thrive in a democracy originally conceived by and for Americans
from Europe. Plagued by pervasive color proscriptions and prejudices since
their ancestors' forced passage to the New World nearly 400 years ago, black
Americans have persistently strived to overcome racial adversity and achieve
human harmony. Even now, after victories long ago over slavery and more
recently over segregation, vestiges of discrimination based on white power
and privilege persist and repress black progress. Likewise, demeaning racial
myths and stereotypes, dissent over welfare policy and affirmative action,
resistance in some urban and suburban neighborhoods to residential integration, and ghastly hate crimes committed by white supremacists continue to
fan the flames of racial antagonism. So does the alienation produced by dire
poverty and the reactionary rhetoric of black extremists who castigate whites
as a demon race and a variety of recent immigrant groups as racists.

The marked integration since the 1960s of blacks in fields such as business, law, education, entertainment, government, sports, television, and the
military—sometimes at top levels—suggests that despite the divisions caused
by continuing racial antipathy not an unsubstantial number of Americans have
outwardly and inwardly rejected racism—the belief in the superiority of one
race over another. As President Clinton's advisory board on race relations
found, racial attitudes among white Americans have improved steadily during
the past forty years. There exists, the panel concluded, "a deep-rooted
national consensus to the ideals of racial equality and integration." Debate
abounds, however, on the best means to achieve lasting racial peace and how

far the nation must still go to erase remaining barriers to black justice. There's no public accord on the distance we must still travel to reach the proverbial "promised land" where one will not be judged by the color of their skin but by the content of their character.

OUT OF AFRICA

W. E. B. DuBois, the prolific black scholar who left the United States at the age of ninety-three to live the end of his long life in exile in the newly independent African nation of Ghana, was one of the first historians of the black experience to note the longevity of the black presence in North America. In his classic work *The Souls of Black Folk*, DuBois recognized nearly a century ago that blacks had come to America's shores far in advance of the ancestors of most Americans. Records of the arrival in the seventeenth century of some twenty African captives at Jamestown, Virginia, caused him to observe that the Negro had as much claim to this land as the Anglo-Saxon, that Africans had reached British America even before the persecuted band of English Puritans had arrived at Plymouth Rock. "Before the Pilgrims landed aboard the Mayflower," declared DuBois, "we were here."

Few Americans are aware, even a century later, that the ancestors of the nation's 34 million African Americans, almost 13 percent of the population, crossed the Atlantic in chains in massive waves during the initial European colonization and conquest of the New World. Aside from scholars, the public is mostly unaware that the black presence in America antedated the migrations of the Scotch-Irish and Germans in the eighteenth century and long preceded the arrival of Catholic Irish and Germans in the mid-nineteenth century as well as the later migration of southern and eastern Europeans in the decades before World War I. As a result, we have commonly slighted facts that explain the vastly different historical experiences of black and white Americans.

It is true that a sizable number of white immigrants came to the New World in the seventeenth and eighteenth centuries as indentured servants or as convicts sentenced to overseas labor. But the majority of Europeans migrated voluntarily. And, although many endured prejudice and penury, all were extended—in relatively short order—the rights to life, liberty, and the pursuit of happiness eventually pronounced in America's Declaration of Independence. Africans, in contrast, arrived involuntarily and were commonly denied basic human rights. In fact, blacks were typically discriminated against in England's American colonies even before the legal codification of racial slavery. This drastic distinction between the early experiences of Americans from Africa and those from Europe, which prepared the pattern for future race relations, was driven by both economic and emotional factors. Among these was the decision of settler planters to build an agricultural economy based on enslaved black labor when farmers were faced with a critical shortage of white indentured servants in the last quarter of the seventeenth century. The pejorative perceptions of blackness prevalent in the culture of Elizabethan England and Enlightenment Europe also inspired a racial ideology that starkly divided the world into black and white.

In this volume, Joseph C. Miller reveals the African heritage of African Americans and the crucial connection between the rise of plantation economies in the New World tropics and the emergence there of racial slavery. He describes the appearance of a new trading system based on the sale of human beings between the fifteenth and eighteenth centuries, which brought Europe, Africa, and America together in a vast maritime and commercial network that produced far-reaching riches and ruin simultaneously. Miller also points out the derivations and destinations of the slaves. He notes that captured Africans were taken to the Americas from every inhabited part of Africa's Atlantic coast and that most—more than 85 percent—of those Africans who survived the ocean voyage found themselves laboring as slaves on the sugar islands of the Caribbean or in Portuguese Brazil. Only a small minority—about 6 or 7 percent of the total—were carried to British North America.

A notably controversial aspect of the slave trade is the number of Africans who were shipped across the Atlantic to the Americas from the European encounter in 1492 to about 1870, when the slave trade effectively ended in North America, and the number who expired in the course of capture and rupture from home. Estimates vary greatly, but scholars, led by historian Philip D. Curtin, now generally agree that between eleven and thirteen million Africans were seized and sold into transoceanic bondage. Students of the slave trade also speculate that about ten million survived the deadly oceanic crossing to the Americas known as the "Middle Passage," which typically took Portuguese, English, French, Spanish, Dutch, and American slave ships five to eight weeks to complete.

Another contentious point is the fact that the slave trade involved enterprise and exchanges between the agents of European merchants and monarchies and African princes and principalities. How could Africans, it is often asked, seize and sell other Africans for sale as slaves? How could they barter fellow Africans for European cloth, horses, metals, muskets, and liquor? A part of the answer is that African slave dealers usually shared no cultural ties with the people they sold. Victims of the slave trade were mostly kidnapped or captured in war and were normally from other ethnic groups who were viewed as aliens without legal rights. Until after the European domination of Africa in the nineteenth century, Africans held no transethnic or continental identity. Between the time of the first and final passage of captured persons across the Atlantic, Africans viewed themselves as they had for thousands of years, as members of specific kinship groups, rather than as an African people.

In 1619, African captives arrived in Jamestown, Virginia, the first permanent settlement in British North America. But it took about a century for a stratified biracial society based on black slavery to emerge among the English settlers. This early period of provincial America, as portrayed by Jean R.

Soderlund, witnessed the evolution of the legal status of chattel slavery—essentially new to the English common law—and its codification by colonial magistrates throughout Britain's American provinces. The evolving caste system of racial slavery led to the petrification in the colonies of previous English prejudices toward the lower classes, outsiders, and darker races and produced the emergence of white racism in the eighteenth century.

Initially, the black population of colonial society was small, amounting in 1660 to only about three thousand. It grew rapidly, however, at the end of the seventeenth century when the British actively entered the slave trade. By 1700 the number of Africans in North America had leapt to twenty-seven thousand—nearly all of whom were slaves and who constituted 11 percent of the English colonies' total population. The rising demand for forced labor to cultivate large-scale cash crops had led to the mass importation of African slaves mostly into the colonies of the Chesapeake Bay region and the lower South. These huge imports, combined with the natural increase of the slave population caused by lower death rates and the high birthrates of native-born slave women, produced a large black presence in provincial America.

By the middle of the eighteenth century, four different kinds of slave societies had emerged in colonial America: one in the North where slavery was part of a mixed economy; another in the Chesapeake Bay region where tobacco was the primary crop; another in the Carolina low country based on rice and indigo; and another in the lower Mississippi valley that featured sugar and, later, cotton production. The blacks enslaved within these sundry colonial economies constituted a critical part of the country's demography. The English colonies' total population of slightly more than one million included some 236,000 Americans of African descent, almost a quarter of the nation's inhabitants. And, in the fifteen years before the American Revolution, nearly 40 percent of the 222,000 immigrants who crossed the Atlantic to British North America arrived as slaves from Africa or the Caribbean. This swelling black presence along the North Atlantic seaboard played a crucial role in the development of a distinctly American society in the British colonies.

Peter H. Wood notes that in the English-controlled settlements Africans served as partners with Europeans in the construction of an evolving American culture. This world that the colonists—black and white, slave and free—subsequently "made together" in the areas of work, family, language, and spiritual life came to reflect a strong African ambience. Despite the enormous constraints of slavery, Africans had an immediate, varied, and lasting influence on the character of American culture through their numbers, broad geographic distribution, and customs they strove to remember and adapt to the alien world of the American plantation. Africans also had a strong impact on the psychology of the American ruling class, which became increasingly fearful of black resistance and revolt as the nation's black populace steadily grew.

The American Revolution freed England's thirteen colonies from control of the mother country but produced ambiguous results for the new republic's expanding black populace. As British critics of the rebellion often noted, those colonists most loudly protesting limitations of their own freedom within the Empire often owned slaves. And, while the war for independence was fought with the aid of five thousand black volunteers, the patriots' successful struggle for freedom never generated the broad emancipation of enslaved African Americans. The republican idealism that produced the rebellion led the northern states, where it was economically feasible, to adopt gradual emancipation plans in the two decades following the American colonists' victory. Elsewhere slavery remained pretty much untouched.

The southern states, where the economy was slave-based and 90 percent of the slaves resided, did little more than make voluntary manumission easier for liberal masters. Furthermore, the new Constitution of the United States, ratified in 1789, comprised contradictions and compromises on the issue of involuntary servitude. The Founding Fathers provided for, but delayed for twenty years, the termination of American participation in the international slave trade, assured federal support for the capture and return of fugitive slaves, and, through the famous three-fifths clause, guaranteed the political power of slaveholders by agreeing to count three-fifths of the slave population for the purpose of representation in Congress. When the first ten amendments known as the Bill of Rights were added to the Constitution in 1791, they provided for the protection of the rights of free men from encroachment by the federal government, but they left the control of slaves up to the individual states.

By the time of the election of the Virginia statesman and slaveholder Thomas Jefferson to the American presidency, the country's black population had grown to more than one million, just under 20 percent of the nation's entire population. Nine out of ten blacks were still enslaved, however, and lived below the Mason-Dixon line, which divided the North from the South. There, slaves built and tended the homes of their masters, tilled the fields, toiled in their workshops and factories, and worked as hired-out laborers on public works projects. Sometimes they bargained with slavemasters to produce extra food for themselves and their families by raising their own crops or livestock and marketing their own products. The result was an "internal economy" that reduced the drudgery of plantation life and boosted bondsmen's sense of autonomy.

The "peculiar institution" of slavery, which became an exclusively southern practice after abolition in the North, expanded with the development of the Cotton Kingdom in the early nineteenth century as the population of the southern states shifted to the south and west from the original areas of slave concentration around the Chesapeake Bay and the low country of South Carolina and Georgia. Three-quarters of the region's slaves were involved in agricultural labor, and by the mid-nineteenth century more than half worked in gangs on the cotton plantations of the lower South. Most of the slaveholders owned only a handful of slaves (five or fewer), but most slaves lived on plantations with more than twenty slaves.

In his examination of antebellum black plantation life, Norrece T. Jones explores the work, family, and religion of the masses of slaves and the ways forced black laborers struggled to survive and defy the power of the slaveocracy. He notes that a strong sense of community often surfaced in the slave quarters, a sequestered part of the plantation where resident whites rarely tarried. The semiautonomous world the slaves forged there, Jones writes, became a fertile ground for subtle and covert forms of day-to-day resistance as well as more dramatic kinds of defiance that included flight and revolt.

Large numbers of slaves ran away, only to be captured and flogged and frequently sold away from their families as punishment. Some who fled settled among Indians, like the Seminoles of Florida, with whom they intermarried. Perhaps as many as 100,000 fugitives successfully escaped slavery for freedom in the northern states or Canada with the aid of the "Underground Railroad," an informal network of free blacks and white abolitionists. Others, such as Gabriel Prosser, Denmark Vesey, and Nat Turner and their followers, took up arms to end slavery.

Studies of slave resistance have revealed some 250 slave revolts and conspiracies from the early seventeenth century through the Civil War. Unlike black rebels in the Caribbean or South America, however, rebellious North American slaves never had ample unity, numbers, weapons, or safe refuge to organize successful armed opposition to the slaveocracy. Furthermore, as scholars have shown, slaves in the American South were so widely dispersed and so carefully policed that rebellion was virtually impossible. In addition, owners carefully cultivated family formation and familial ties as a further means of control over potential rebels.

Southern slavery as constituted in either the Chesapeake Bay, the Carolina low country, or the lower Mississippi valley was never simply an agrarian institution. On the eve of the Civil War the slave population had grown to nearly four million. Of those between 160,000 and 200,000 slaves worked in industry and about 6 percent lived in cities and towns. In areas outside the countryside discipline was notoriously lax, however, undermining urban slavery and creating broad mingling of the races that produced large concentrations of racially mixed people known as mulattoes. Around Charleston, South Carolina, and New Orleans, Louisiana, manumitted and free-born mulattoes formed a separate caste and some, as the Federal censuses reveal, were even slaveholders, but most of the 260,000 legally free blacks living in the slave states were dirt poor.

Only a thin line separated freedom from slavery in antebellum America. William G. Shade contends that free blacks before the Civil War were only nominally free. A mostly destitute group, they were barred by law and custom from many of the rights that whites typically enjoyed. While some free persons of color prospered despite the prevalence of white prejudices, they were generally perceived by whites of all classes as social pariahs. As Chief Justice Roger B. Taney wrote in the majority opinion in the 1857 freedom suit of *Dred*

Scott v. Sanford, "negroes of the African race" could not be citizens and "had no rights which the white man was bound to respect."

Consequently, legally free African Americans, even those who lived north of slavery in states where human bondage was ended after the American Revolution, were regularly denied citizenship rights and frequently forced into separate black enclaves in the nation's cities. It was partly in response to the rising racial segregation they experienced in northern urban centers that free blacks built autonomous economic, social, and religious institutions. These associations—especially the black church, the convention movement, and abolitionist societies—not only fostered moral and social development but also provided the institutional basis in the free states for African-American resistance to slavery and discrimination.

UP FROM SLAVERY

The devastating Civil War that erupted in 1861 after decades of sectional dissension over the western expansion of slavery ended in defeat for the Confederacy and prompted ratification of amendments to the Constitution that ended the long nightmare of black bondage. By the war's end, the transplanted Africans who had endured slavery and grown in great numbers had been transformed as a body from assorted African identities into a new people—an amalgam of black, white, and red humanity. By the time of emancipation, most African Americans had ceased to dream of a return to their ancestral lands. They had become acculturated, absorbed with an American consciousness and attainment of the "American dream." The black masses and leaders—the politicians, ministers, teachers, independent farmers, and small businessmen—had become with the proclamation of their freedom quintessential advocates of the democratic principles passionately preached, but poorly practiced, by the larger society. Moved by the gospel of equality under God espoused by evangelical Christianity, to which many of them were converted in colonial times, and human rights tenets in the Constitution, African Americans embarked after captivity on a campaign to achieve complete equality in America and rejected periodic calls for either separatism or mass migration back to Africa.

Historians still contest, more than a century after its announcement, the importance of the Emancipation Proclamation issued by Abraham Lincoln in 1863. Because the order was restricted to slaves in rebel-controlled territory where it was rejected by Confederate authorities and left unaffected some 800,000 bondsmen in loyal border states, scholars dispute the proclamation's impact and Lincoln's credentials as the "great emancipator." To clarify its significance, Armstead L. Robinson discusses the edict's impact on black Americans of the war era. He shows that the proclamation, despite its limitations, temporarily filled most blacks—even those who had seriously considered emigration to another land—with faith in the promise of America. He reveals too that black hope gradually faded as new forms of white supremacy emerged.

With the passage of the Thirteenth Amendment to the Constitution, which formally ended slavery in 1865, and subsequent ratification of the Fourteenth and Fifteenth Amendments guaranteeing black citizenship and voting rights, African Americans held great hope that the day of "Jubilee" had arrived, that the dark night of racial degradation was forever over. These beliefs were buttressed by black participation first as Union soldiers in the war itself and then in the political process during Reconstruction when for the first time blacks were elected to public office at the local, state, and national levels.

Trust that they had been essentially relieved of racist repression was short-lived. The train of fatal events following passage of the Fifteenth Amendment and the readmission to the Union of the seceded southern states led relentlessly to the resurgence of race domination and the establishment of segregation throughout the South in the 1890s. The account of black advancement in the South after slavery and the subsequent revival of white supremacy constitutes a sad chapter in American history. In the postbellum era, the nation's white leadership grew tired of "the Negro question" and became far more committed to sectional reconciliation than the protection of African Americans' newly granted rights. Compromises made between white politicians in both sections of the country led to the end of Reconstruction in 1877 and the resumption in the former Confederacy of white "home rule."

As Gerald D. Jaynes shows, the four million newly emancipated slaves mostly remained in the rural South from the end of the Civil War until World War II and worked the land as sharecroppers and tenant farmers. The freedmen's hope was to achieve property and autonomy, but black economic independence based on landownership was frustrated as planters and their partners, resolved to reinstate white supremacy in the postbellum South, drove black workers from the political process and prevented African Americans from using collective efforts to improve their economic status. As black political power and economic development waned, the plight of rural labor worsened and many blacks abandoned agrarian life, first moving to the growing cities of the New South, which promised improved economic opportunities. Others looked west to Kansas and Oklahoma, and a few even considered migration and colonization in Africa. Eventually huge numbers turned to the urban centers of the industrialized North in search of the promised land.

Carole C. Marks stresses the significance of urbanization and migration at the time of World War I. These twin processes doubled the proportion of blacks living in cities between 1900 and 1940 and began the dramatic shift of the African-American population northward that would reach its pinnacle in the decades following World War II. The dramatic demographic shift of blacks from the farms and small towns of the South to the factories and sprawling cities of the North produced major consequences for African-American society, not the least of which involved the uneasy confrontation of the cultures of southern and northern blacks. This process was further complicated by the simultaneous arrival of thousands of blacks from the Caribbean who had come to the mainland in search of expanded economic opportunities. The two migrations and the rich mixture of subcultures that resulted precipitated the emergence in northern cities of a new urban black culture with distinctive regional traits, class structure, and community institutions formed in response to group needs and the de facto segregation and economic discrimination the migrants faced, whether they were from "down home" or the islands.

The social and economic changes accompanying the northern migration forced African Americans to form alternative racial strategies that formed a spectrum of attitudes and actions ranging from assimilation to separatism. As Wilson J. Moses writes, tension between these two positions characterized black protest thought from the 1890s through the two world wars into the 1960s. These divergent strands of thought were most evident in the philosophies, politics, and programs of the most influential African-American thinkers of this century—the conservative educator Booker T. Washington, who disavowed integration and preached accommodation; W. E. B. DuBois, the Marxist scholar, radical integrationist, and advocate of organized protest; Marcus Garvey, the Jamaican immigrant and pan-Africanist who supported selective black repatriation in Africa; the militant Christian social reformer, integrationist, and advocate of nonviolent protest Martin Luther King Jr.; and the unyielding Black Muslim separatist Malcolm X. Although only King was personally active in the "Second Reconstruction" following World War II, the theories and strategies associated with each of these thinkers affected the broad struggle for justice that emerged in the 1950s.

Edward P. Morgan traces the Civil Rights movement from its initial integrationist phase through the articulation of the somewhat separatist concept of Black Power. Key actors in the struggle that ended the long reign of Jim Crow in the South and led to the passage of major black rights legislation in the mid-1960s include Martin Luther King Jr., who emerged as the most forceful leader of the movement during the Montgomery, Alabama, bus boycott in 1955–1956, and the major black rights organizations of the era—the National Association for the Advancement of Colored People (NAACP), the Congress of Racial Equality (CORE), the Southern Christian Leadership Conference (SCLC), and the Student Nonviolent Coordinating Committee (SNCC). The crusade, waged with liberal white allies who were often Jewish groups and students, set the stage for the extensive integration of trained and talented blacks into the American mainstream.

An unforeseen result, however, of the campaign for black rights was that serious fragmentation of the movement occurred at the very moment of its greatest success with the passage of the Civil Rights Act of 1964 and the Voting Rights Act a year later. In the mid-1960s seething ghetto discontent erupted in bloody and costly riots across the country, black separatist ideologies gained mass appeal, the alliance of blacks and Jews was broken over strong political differences, and radical splinter groups such as the Black Panthers appeared to provoke violent reactions from the white establishment. A subsequent backlash among white voters elected Richard Nixon and a succession of conservative Republican presidents who sought to check the effects of the civil rights laws and liberal Democratic initiatives that comprised Lyndon Johnson's vision of a "Great Society."

AFRICAN-AMERICAN IDENTITY AND CULTURE

Studies of black folkways show that African Americans constructed from the savagery of slavery and segregation a distinctive and dynamic culture—evident in black spirituality, speech, humor, music, dance, and dress—a culture that sustained them psychologically through severe oppression and became deeply ingrained in American society. Scholar Henry Louis Gates Jr. has noted that the most striking change in twentieth-century America is the growing centrality of the black experience to the national culture of the United States. The black presence is pervasive, he writes, in artistic, cultural, and quasi-cultural endeavors of every kind from the frontiers of modern art through the written word to mass marketing exemplified by widespread images on billboards of basketball star Michael Jordan.

Any consideration nowadays of American black culture commonly leads to the subject of *Africanisms*, a term coined years ago by anthropologist Melville J. Herskovits to describe surviving remnants and influences of African culture in the Americas. In his seminal work *The Myth of the Negro Past*, Herskovits contends that slavery did not entirely destroy the African heritage of American blacks and that traces of tribal customs survived the strain of captivity. Moreover, some of the cultural traits that had endured had been transmitted to whites producing a kind of Africanization of the larger society. American culture has derived therefore not only from Europe and native America but also out of Africa.

At the time, most African-American intellectuals, led by the sociologist E. Franklin Frazier, vigorously rejected the persistence of Africanisms in contemporary black life. To these black thinkers, such notions sustained racist arguments that prevented black assimilation into American society and supported racial segregation. By the 1970s, however, the views of black scholars had shifted as Africanisms were embraced by leading African-American academics much affected by the actions of Black Power advocates to enhance group pride and extol the African roots of black culture in the United States. There exists broad public acceptance as well of the persistence of remnants of African aesthetics, cuisine, language, and music in modern African-American culture.

Across the color line, black culture has long fascinated white imaginations and, since the 1920s when white artists and audiences first started earnestly imitating jazz music and dance styles, successive segments of white youth have been drawn to black culture. Analysts, such as "Rap" expert Tricia Rose, have ascribed the allure of blackness among young whites to views of African-American culture as the consummate symbol of rebellion against social custom. In the broad borrowing by white teens of the styles of music, speech, and dress connected with hip-hop culture, urban scholars see the most pronounced sign presently of white absorption with black culture.

Adoption of black culture can probably be seen most clearly in the greatest contribution of the United States to the musics of the world, the African-American idiom known as jazz—a "creative creolization" of African-American and European-American strains that have spread their dominion across the whole world. Black musical traditions and genres, both sacred and secular, examined here by Waldo F. Martin, also project aspects of the African heritage. The spirituals, gospel, blues, along with jazz and black popular music—including rap—all embody sounds of blackness with an African base and beat. Yet the instrumentation, scales, and harmonies have been those shared with Europeans, and the creation and development of jazz has been until quite recently unique to American blacks among peoples of the African diaspora.

Like jazz, African-American writing is far more American than African. African themes have shaped the content of black prose and poetry, but the African heritage has not directly affected the artistic styles of black American authors. Rather their work has been distinguished by its focus on African-American subject matter and on analysis of race relations. A succession of major twentieth-century black writers—Langston Hughes in the 1910s and 1920s, Richard Wright in the 1930s and 1940s, Ralph Ellison in the 1940s and 1950s, and James Baldwin in the 1950s and 1960s—combined artistic brilliance with searing social criticism.

Since their works first appeared in the eighteenth century African-American writers have voiced distinctive strains, writes Gerald Early, which have deeply affected the tenor of American literature. From the writings of the young Phillis Wheatley of Boston, black authors have illuminated the African-American experience and frequently advanced a social agenda through the strong African-American oral tradition, the slave narratives, the literature of the Harlem Renaissance of the 1920s, the black aesthetic movement of the 1970s, and the present works of leading black writers—predominantly women, such as Toni Morrison (the first black American to receive the Nobel Prize for literature), Alice Walker, and Maya Angelou.

Whether vestiges of African culture are still considerably felt in contemporary African-American society, sizable numbers of American blacks are currently absorbed with the recovery of an African identity. Following many previous but sporadic cultural reclamation movements, after the decolonization of most of sub-Saharan Africa in the 1960s, African Americans began consciously to address the critical issues of culture, skin color, and identity. The rapid restoration of black power in the land of their ancestors produced among African Americans a wave of new awareness and appreciation of their African heritage.

From the revival of black rule in Africa appeared attempts by emergent

"Africanists" in communities across the United States to restore race pride based on reverence of their African roots. These proponents offered not only a new racial nomenclature but also the popularization of African culture and the use of African garb, hairstyles, languages, names, dances, art, religion, as well as African-derived value systems and celebrations. Most important, they have called for the study of black history from an Afrocentric perspective. Drawing upon earlier arguments advanced by earlier black scholars such as historian Carter G. Woodson, the new "Africanists" contend that construction of the past from a black point of view reflects the positive realities of African societies and develops pride in an ancient past.

Black history constructed from an "Afrocentric" view is currently at the center of sharp conflict over curriculum reform and scholarly debate over African contributions to Western civilization. Critics charge that the claims of such scholars as George M. James, Cheik Anta Diop, Yosef ben-Jochannan, and Martin Bernal, author of the controversial *Black Athena*, are false and such assertions that ancient Egypt was a black African civilization and Greek philosophy was stolen from the early Egyptians are egregiously wrong. While Afrocentrism is, in their view, a charismatic rather than an intellectual movement that teaches myth as history, others hold that it merely restores a great part of the African-American legacy that has been concealed.

RELIGION, CLASS, AND FAMILY

The history of Africans in America depicts remarkable perseverance and positivism. However dismal conditions have sometimes been, African Americans have generally been steadfast in the belief that they would overcome adversity. As Reverend Martin Luther King Jr. wrote in his "Letter from a Birmingham Jail," black Americans have displayed a bottomless ability to aspire, develop, and acclaim life while afflicted with brutal injustice and shameful humiliation. This ability to endure affliction, King suggested, sprang from a strong spirituality, a central feature of the rich and resilient culture created from experience in slavery and segregation.

Since the late eighteenth century, when the diverse African faiths gave way to mass conversions to evangelical Christianity spread by Baptist and Methodist preachers, African Americans have been among society's most religious groups. Reliance upon faith in God and steadfast belief in Christ as the rock of salvation provided strength to withstand enormous suffering in anticipation of divine deliverance. The conviction that the Lord would bless them mightily helped sustain belief in heavenly salvation and elevation of the black race. These themes constitute the thrust of Gayraud S. Wilmore's essay on black religion in America, which explores the central role the black church has played in African-American culture.

Since the 1960s, sizable numbers of African Americans have steadily taken advantage of expanded job possibilities created by the Civil Rights movement in producing federal legislation mandating equal employment opportunities. The effect of these advances in job opportunities has been an enlarged black bourgeoisie that is substantially larger and occupationally more diverse than the former black middle class acidly described by E. Franklin Frazier forty years ago. Whereas the old black middle class formed between the world wars was mainly restricted to schoolteachers and ministers but also included undertakers, real estate agents, and postal workers, the modern black middle class more closely resembles its white counterpart occupationally.

By 1993 nearly half (46 percent) of all employed blacks held white-collar positions; one-quarter of black families earned between $25,000 and $50,000, and 14 percent earned more than that amount. The number of college graduates was increasing faster for blacks than for whites and the proportion of African Americans enrolled in the nation's colleges and universities equaled the proportion of blacks in the total population. Robert Gregg discusses here the ways in which this recent flowering of the black middle class was made possible by changes in the American job market, government, civil service, the armed forces, industrial labor, and the universities.

But amid the opportunities now open to educated blacks, a downward turn in the economy could threaten the security of middle-class African Americans whose members continue to be substantially first generation with blue-collar roots. Moreover, racial prejudice still thwarts the mobility of blacks to move to the top levels of their professions. Surveys show that, because of racial bias confronted in the corporate world, the black bourgeoisie is more apprehensive about achieving the "American dream" than are many of the African-American poor whose position in society is far more perilous.

For many blacks poverty remains a devastating reality. Slightly fewer than one-third of all African-American families, but more than 40 percent of black children presently live at or below the "poverty line." From the ranks of the black poor there has emerged since the mid-1960s an expanding black underclass, mainly youths, who exist outside the occupational system, virtually trapped in permanent unemployment and inclined toward criminal behavior. Public policy prescriptions advanced thus far to address the needs of the black poor, especially when blue-collar work disappears, have experienced only modest success. Thirty years ago Daniel P. Moynihan, now a senator from New York, popularized the correlation between poverty and female-headed black households. Since then the "crisis" of the black family has been a topic of constant debate among scholars and policymakers. Walter R. Allen's study of black family structure and status questions some facile assumptions commonly reflected in the media about the quality of black life in modern America. He contends that characterizations of the black family headed by a single mother with several children living in a tenement tend to ignore the extensive regional, ethnic, and income differences among black families and distinctions in values and lifestyles.

Most black families, Allen shows, have escaped the cycle of deprivation and destruction, and the typical black family is middle class. Yet these families remain challenged by lingering effects of racism and the economic insecurity inherent in their newly attained status. In fact, the social and economic progress of blacks slowed between the mid-1970s and early 1990s. Thirty percent of America's black families have sunk deeper into poverty and become increasingly located outside the educational system, without jobs, consigned to high-crime areas, and facing limited futures. Moreover, according to the U.S. Census Bureau, the proportion of black families headed by married couples has continued to shrink, down from 50 percent in 1990 to 46 percent in 1998.

The present plight of poor black families is a product of multiple factors. Industrial decline in urban areas, the failure of the public school system, the proliferation of guns and illegal drugs, and massive unemployment are critical contributors to the crisis of impoverished black husbands, wives, and children. Beverly Guy-Sheftall suggests another is the distinctive place of African-American women in a society, where they have long been confronted with the challenge of a "woman question and a race problem." The power of both racism and sexism have made it doubly difficult, she shows, for black females to create successful and satisfying lives.

Some of the special tensions felt by black women are mirrored in the stress between white and black feminists in the women's movement. According to critics, sisterhood across racial boundaries has been undermined by hostility, jealousy, and competition. Even so, neither race nor gender alone can explain the complexity of the black female experience compelling black women to fight on both fronts. The examples of individuals like Sojourner Truth, the abolitionist and feminist, Ida Wells Barnett, the progressive social reformer and antilynching crusader, Mary McLeod Bethune, educator and New Deal official, and Pauli Murray, lawyer, minister, educator, and one of the founders of the National Organization for Women (NOW) provide dramatic proof of how black female leadership has linked liberation with freedom from both racism and patriarchy.

A DREAM DEFERRED

Color continues to pose a challenge as well for American education. The condition of black education in the United States since the 1954 Supreme Court decision in the case of *Brown v. Board of Education of Topeka, Kansas*, which declared the doctrine of "separate but equal" in education unconstitutional, presents a paradoxical pattern of improvement and deterioration. Stephen N. Butler's study of the struggles over desegregation, busing, and affirmative action as well as the quality of schooling reveals the country's recent achievements and failures in advancing black education.

On the positive side, nearly every indicator of educational improvement signaled in the decade or so after *Brown* that a revolution in schooling had taken place in black America. From the mid-1960s into the early 1970s most of the school districts in the South were successfully integrated. By 1980 the median years of school completed by African Americans was twice what it had been at the time of World War II and only slightly below that of whites. More than half of all black adults were high school graduates. The proportion of African Americans who were college graduates was higher than the proportion of high school graduates in 1940 and well above the percentage of whites who graduated from college in 1960. The proportion of black high school graduates enrolled in college had moved close to that of whites.

While such statistics suggested that blacks and whites were receiving comparable instruction, some data implied otherwise. The contrasting educational experiences of African Americans and other Americans has been starkly reflected in the outcomes of standardized academic achievement tests; black schoolchildren still score lower on such tests than most other students. This is due partly to racial bias in the tests. The difference in scores also closely correlates with the growing racial isolation of inner-city black youths in deteriorating public school systems. In just a decade from the late 1960s to the late 1970s, because of working- and middle-class flight among whites and African Americans, the urban core of the country's major metropolitan areas has become increasingly black, poor, isolated from opportunities, and populated by a growing underclass.

Despite positive changes made to remove racial bias in law enforcement agencies and the courts, skin color still affects equitable execution of the law and dispensation of justice. The disproportionately high rate of black arrests, convictions, incarcerations, and death penalties provides graphic proof of the role race still plays in the criminal justice system. At the same time, the public furor over recent verdicts in the widely publicized Rodney King case, where policemen were caught on camera brutally beating a black man suspected of drunken driving, and the murder trial of O. J. Simpson, where race was said to play a role in the prosecution, underscore the power color continues to exert in our courts.

Donald G. Nieman's review of key Supreme Court decisions since 1970 on racial discrimination and affirmative action—benign racial, ethnic, and gender preferences—provides telling examples of the racial division that still cuts deeply across American society. It shows that Americans are bitterly divided over employment, contractual, and admissions programs involving racial preferences. One faction, consisting mainly of white and some black conservatives, opposes affirmative action as reverse discrimination. The other, essentially multiracial and liberal in political outlook, defends such programs as needed measures to compensate for past discrimination and believes preferential programs have been the most effective means for bringing blacks and other minorities into the national mainstream.

Today, in the late 1990s, many blacks fear that the Supreme Court has forgotten the lessons of the nation's racist past and plans to end entirely affirmative action programs on grounds that special allowances for minority groups unfairly penalize members of the majority. They are especially troubled that the Court has struck down a remedial practice of drawing congressional district lines on the basis of race to expand black representation and let stand a lower-court ruling that invalidated the affirmative action program at the University of Texas Law School and could endanger all such plans at public education institutions. Critics argue that, in its emphasis on color-blind justice, the Court has ignored the basically racial justification for the Fourteenth and Fifteenth Amendments and the civil rights legislation of the 1960s by arguing that race cannot be used as a "factor" to correct the effects of three and a half centuries of racism.

Lawrence J. Hanks points out that the battle for black political equity has made tremendous strides since the late 1960s. The voting rights act of 1965 was a milestone in the modern African-American struggle for equality. It provided the catalyst for black voter registration and extensive black participation for the first time since Reconstruction, resulting in the election of a critical mass of black officials nationwide. By 1997 there were 8,658 black elected officials in the country, mostly at the local level. The state of Mississippi ranks first with 803, followed by Alabama (726), Louisiana (646), and Georgia (579).

Another important result has been the increased political prominence of black members of Congress. Black members of the House of Representatives grew from thirteen in 1970 to thirty-nine in 1999, a number that includes twelve women, a record high. One is Republican; the others are all Democrats and belong to the Congressional Black Caucus, which represents the interests of the thirty-eight black House Democrats. Because of members' high degree of solidarity, the caucus constitutes a significant voting bloc on Capitol Hill and gives African Americans a substantial voice in Washington politics.

Jesse Jackson's campaigns for the presidency as a Democratic candidate in 1984 and 1988 provide notable evidence of the fact that black political action has mainly shifted from the streets of America's cities where massive demonstrations had once been mobilized to promote civil rights to the halls of local, state, and national assemblies. The failure thus far, however, of black elected officials to muster sufficient power to markedly affect public policy toward minority issues remains a frustration for black communities and creates a source of vigorous dissent between liberal and conservative blacks over the agenda and tactics of black leadership.

A related area of concern for numerous American blacks, writes William R. Scott, is the role of blacks in the construction of the nation's foreign policy. Acutely appreciative for the first time of their identity as people of African descent, expanding numbers of African Americans have become concerned about the content of America's relations with African nations. Headed by lobbying organizations, such as TransAfrica in Washington, D.C., blacks have become increasingly engaged in efforts to affect U.S. policies toward the land of their ancestors. Scott surveys the history of black internationalism identifying milestones in the efforts of Americans of African ancestry to affect America's relations with the African continent.

Even though the racial tangle has yet to be set straight, the strength of color prejudice has subsided in the last part of the present century as a determinant of black social mobility. Preceding the findings of the president's commission on race, sociologist William J. Wilson contended that race relations in America had undergone fundamental changes, so much so that now the life chances of individual blacks have more to do with their economic class than with their day-to-day encounters with whites. The forces, he says, thwarting the upward mobility of the black underclass appear to be more related to the disappearance of factory work than to racial discrimination.

Debate over the causes of continued black deprivation raises hard questions about the future political course of African Americans. Charles Hamilton forecasts that the black agenda will be driven by the state of the black poor but notes that civil rights should not be ignored in a society that remains so race conscious. He also ponders the strategies leaders should chart in the coming century. His response envelops a range of options, such as coalition politics involving Hispanic and Asian Americans as well as massive public assistance programs and collective black action. The success, of course, of any plan cannot be predicted with any certainty. Perhaps the only thing that can be confidently said is that the nation's stability and prosperity in the new millennium depends considerably on its determination finally to make the American dream realizable for all its citizens; and actualizing that commitment depends on the development of a serious national dialogue on race directed toward racial healing across the color spectrum.

FOR FURTHER READING

Asante, Molefi K., and Mark T. Mattison. *The African American Atlas: Black History and Culture*. New York: Macmillan, 1998.

Bennett, Lerone, Jr. *Before the Mayflower: A History of Black America*. 6th rev. ed. New York: Penguin Books, 1993.

Franklin, John Hope. *The Color Line: Legacy for the Twentieth-First Century*. Columbia: University of Missouri Press, 1982.

———, and August Meier. *Black Leaders of the Twentieth Century*. Urbana: University of Illinois Press, 1982.

———, and Alfred A. Moss. *From Slavery to Freedom*. 2 vols. New York: McGraw-Hill, 1998.

Giddings, Paula. *When and Where I Enter: The Impact of Black Women on Race and Sex in America*. 2nd ed. New York: William Morrow & Company, 1996.

Harding, Vincent. *There Is a River: The Black Struggle for Freedom in America*. New York: Harcourt Brace, 1981.

Horton, James Oliver, and Lois E. Horton, eds. *A History of African American People: The History, Traditions and Culture of African Americans*. Detroit: Wayne State University Press, 1997.

18   ▼   William R. Scott and William G. Shade

Hughes, Langtson, ed. *A Pictorial History of African Americans*. 6th ed. New York: Crown Publishers, 1995.

Jenks, Christopher, and Paul E. Peterson, eds. *The Urban Underclass*. Washington, D.C.: Brookings Institution, 1991.

Jones, Jacqueline. *Labor of Love, Labor of Sorrow: Black Women, Work, and the Family from Slavery to the Present*. New York: Vintage Books, 1986.

Litwack, Leon, and August Meier, eds. *Black Leaders of the Nineteenth Century*. Urbana: University of Illinois Press, 1991.

Meier, August, and Elliot Rudwick. *From Plantation to Ghetto*. 3rd ed. New York: Hill & Wang, 1976.

Palmer, Colin A. *Passageways: An Interpretative History of Black America*. 2 vols. Orlando, Fla.: Harcourt College Publishers, 1998.

Quarles, Benjamin. *The Negro in the Making of America*. 3rd ed. New York: Touchstone Books, 1996.

Smallwood, Arwin D., with Jeffrey M. Elliot. *The Atlas of African American History and Politics: From the Slave Trade to Modern Times*. Boston: McGraw-Hill, 1998.

part 1.

Out of Africa

chapter 1

Africa, the Slave Trade, and the Diaspora

Joseph C. Miller

AFRICANS BROUGHT TO NORTH AMERICA as slaves were a small minority, probably fewer than 6 percent, of some twelve million men, women, and children shoved below the decks of ships lying at anchor off Africa's Atlantic shores between the fifteenth and the nineteenth centuries. Although they all shared the humiliation and brutality of enslavement in the New World, they came from diverse backgrounds in a continent as different from north to south, and from the coast to its vast interior, as were the Americas themselves. As African Americans they came to bear the common burdens of racial prejudice, burdens even heavier than the subjugation to masters and mistresses effectively unrestrained by law. However, they also created an infinite variety of new lives for themselves out of local circumstances— out of their work as miners, on sugar plantations, in tobacco fields, as domestic servants in town houses, in factories; out of their masters' cultural inclinations and economic fortunes; out of the backgrounds that their fellow slaves brought from Africa; and out of the personal resources—wits, skills, physical abilities— with which each of them had arrived. The experiences of the Africans taken to North America, disparate as they were, converged under the peculiar combination there of slavery and freedom in ways that distinguished their experiences from those of enslaved Africans in other parts of the New World.

AFRICAN BACKGROUNDS

Slaves were taken to the Americas from every inhabited part of Africa's Atlantic coast, from the Sahara Desert in the north to the Kalahari Desert in the south. In the fifteenth century, when the Portuguese bought their first captives in northwestern Africa, most Africans lived in highly localized agricultural communities, where they grew up learning farming and hunting techniques refined by their parents and grandparents who knew the delicate environment intimately and adapted to it over the years. Near the Sahara, in the desert-edge latitudes, long rainless months each year encouraged farmers to rely on drought-resistant millets that they planted in river valleys or other better-watered areas.

These farmers tried to maintain cordial relations with herders who devoted their mobile lives to cattle that they grazed in the drier lands. The herders passed through the farmlands during the dry season each year in search of winter pastures and eagerly exchanged livestock products for surpluses of grain that the farmers harvested. Soils there were too sandy, fragile, and shallow to sustain deep cultivation with the plow, and the hoe was the basic agricultural implement they used. But the herders had to move their animals constantly, across hundreds of miles, as they sought fresh, sweet grasses for them, and the farmers had to remain close by water and their fields. As a result, hoe cultivators and livestock raisers both specialized in separate ways of living and traded with each other.

Closer to the equator, in the Southern as well as the Northern Hemisphere, more plentiful and reliable rains created broad bands of wooded grasslands, known as savannas. These supported farmers who grew a wider variety of cultigens, of which sorghums were the most widespread. Just south of the Sahara, in the savannas known as the *sudan*, rice also figured prominently in the wetter zones. Farmers in these moist latitudes could disperse to live in scattered homesteads next to fields that they planted in the most fertile patches. The woods, however, harbored disease lethal to cattle, and so they had little direct contact with herders and purchased, from outside traders who had come to settle among them, leathers and other livestock products from the drier regions at the edge of the desert. The traders also bought slabs of rock salt cut from salty deposits deep in the Sahara, commodities so valuable in these salt-deficient latitudes that people sometimes used them as a currency facilitating other exchanges.

At the edge of the Sahara a series of towns had long since grown up as centers of the interregional trade between the farmers in the grasslands and the herders in the desert steppes. Since the eighth or ninth century, Saharan merchants had arrived at the heads of large caravans of camels bearing desert goods for sale and distribution throughout the grasslands and even into the forests beyond—also carrying imports that came all the way from the Mediterranean lands of North Africa. In these towns they met representatives of the diaspora of village traders. Some of these towns, like Timbuktu, on the northernmost reach of the Niger River where western Africa's largest river flowed into the desert before turning back to the south toward the Gulf of Guinea, had become famous throughout the Muslim world as sources of sub-Saharan gold, which Africans panned from the headwaters of the Niger and other rivers. They had also become centers of Islamic scholarship, as well as outposts of large African imperial powers that dominated large portions of the region at that time, such as Mali in the valley of the Upper Niger and Songhai, centered to the east along the middle course of the river. These Arabic-speaking merchants from North Africa called the desert edge *sahel* (literally "shore"), the name by which it is now often known, and characterized the savannas as the *sudan*, or "land of the blacks," from the dark appearance of their trading partners. In the wetter regions, the dispersed networks of sub-Saharan traders stimulated production of commodities that were in demand in the dry areas, just as they distributed products of the desert in the south.

From the latitude of the Gambia River all the way south to the mouth of the Zaire (or Congo) River, most of the coast was heavily forested, with islands, broad river mouths, and an extensive set of lagoons providing opportunities for people residing there to fish, produce marine salt from tidal evaporation pans, and transport numerous products in large dug-out canoes made from the huge hardwood trees of the tropical forests. The intricate waterways of the delta of the Niger River offered especially bountiful opportunities of this sort, and villages of specialized producers dotted the banks where traders came to buy local products for sale in markets in the interior. Farmers making their ways in the forests had opened clearings for towns and fields. Since the dimness of the light penetrating the dense canopy of trees was too little to sustain the grain cultigens of the savannas, they relied on yams and bananas as the staples of their diet. Peoples of the forest also harvested palm kernels (which they pressed to obtain cooking oil) and other fruits and nuts to sell to traders from the drier regions to the north. Along the vast network of waterways flowing into the Zaire River and draining the vast forests of central Africa, people fished and traded in villages linked by fleets of large canoes.

In the agricultural savannas, particularly those north of the West African forests but also those south of the mouth of the Zaire, farmers achieved the highest population densities found in any of the three principal types of environment. While numerous followers and compounds filled with well-fed wives and children signaled a chief's success, they also formed the demographic base from which those who later fell into slaving would draw.

Particularly in the grasslands where people depended heavily on their relatives, clients, and associates to prosper, communal loyalties were generally strong. Open pursuit of individual self-interest might appear to threaten the prized solidarity of the group, and personal ambition—and countervailing fears of witchcraft—inevitably strained relationships. Local environmental knowledge was so basic to agricultural success and herding that most people identified themselves—beyond the intimate, personal associations of kinship and alliance with other families through marriage—primarily by the regional cultures they and their neighbors developed to exploit the resources of the area in which they lived. Community identity thus emerged, at the most basic level, out of the distinctive habits of speech adopted by neighbors who lived and worked in close association reaching back over many generations, who married mostly among themselves, and who shared many concerns and historical experiences, all based on specializing in living in the same ecological niche. Especially in the forests, one of these ethnic communities might number only a few thousand people, all of whom shared, first of all, a common language, of which there were hundreds, or a local dialect of one language. There were thus many such groups, each intensely self-conscious but also dependent on its neighbors as buyers of its own specialized products and as suppliers of the necessities that it did not produce for itself; at the same time, each suspected its neighbors as strangers unintelligibly, and perhaps dangerously, different from themselves.

Nevertheless, all the communities living in the forests and savannas east of the Niger Delta shared a single cultural heritage through their assumed descent from the same ancestors; their languages, known collectively to modern linguists as "Bantu," all belonged to one closely related family as a result of that common history. Looser cultural and linguistic background commonalities also linked communities in West Africa, which displayed the distinguishing effects of many years of distinct historical experiences. Modern ethnographers have abstracted these limited common tendencies to define "culture areas" of broadly similar linguistic habits and shared institutions, such as the "Igbo" in the forests east of the lower Niger River or "Benin" and "Yoruba" in those to the west, and "Fon" in the southerly extension of savanna reaching the sea to the west of the "Yoruba," and "Akan" in the forests beyond the Volta River—all of these peoples living in the forests of what the Europeans later termed, in an even larger, and purely geographic imposition, "Lower Guinea." The people of "Upper Guinea," the heterogeneous area north and west of the "Akan" (beyond Cape Palmas), had entered the forests there in small groups from several neighboring savanna regions, and they had developed fewer comparably general cultural similarities. Fifteenth-century Africans would not have attributed much significance to common cultural heritages at this high level of abstraction, nor would they have recognized many of the ethnic names by which their descendants subsequently became known to the Europeans—who tended to label Africans according to the stereotypical, and often uncomplimentary, epithets bestowed by neighbors.

By the fifteenth century, trading and political accomplishments in many places had added overlays of broader identity beyond these local groups, based on shared commercial or industrial success. The residents of the Muslim trading towns of the *sahel* thought of themselves as members of broader mercantile or religious communities. Families specialized in complex and demanding technologies, like iron- and leather-working, or other skilled professions that drew people permanently out of farming, became dispersed in distinct guild-like communities, jealously marrying among themselves to protect their valuable technical knowledge, and often known by names analogous to the ethnic identities of the farmers among whom they lived. The marginality of these craft specialists to the landholding agricultural mainstream of life, as well as their humble status relative to the warrior and commercial elites of the era, has led some later observers to liken them to ranked "castes" on the Indian model, but the parallel is limited. The traders who dispersed southward from the towns of the *sahel* into the far western savannas and forest fringes spoke Soninke and Mande (the latter also known as Mandingo) languages, and they had carried these and other elements of their home cultures, including Islam, with them.

In fifteenth-century sub-Saharan Africa, only these merchants and the military aristocrats in control of the large empires and the desert trade adhered to the Muslim religion. Farmers in the villages retained older beliefs in spirits believed to confer fertility on the land and on women, in the powers of priests and kings to call the capricious rains on which they depended for plentiful harvests and for survival, and in the influence of ancestors in the affairs of their descendants. Islam, on the other hand, appealed to the political classes and merchants, who were less directly concerned with productivity and more engaged on broader social and economic scales, scales that the literacy and universalism of the Muslim religion helped them to manage. Thus Muslim Africans south of the Sahara found themselves suspended between the parochialism of the villages and the legal and theological refinement and cosmopolitanism of North African Islamic traders and clerics, with whom they had to collaborate economically and diplomatically. They therefore tended to combine elements of both worldviews.

Horse-riding warriors set the political tone of the era in the *sudanic* latitudes. From time to time they imposed tribute and a degree of enduring political unity over the populous regions along the Upper Niger through the mobility and power they gained from their mastery of cavalry warfare in the savannas. They had created a series of political systems: an "empire" under Soninke warriors known as Ghana long before the fifteenth century, and its successor, Mali, led since the thirteenth century by horsemen and aristocrats of Mande background. These militaristic aristocrats acquired their equine power by buying mounts from the desert merchants, paying for them mostly by selling gold. But the warrior aristocrats also used their mobility and military power to capture farmers, men, women, and children living in outlying regions. Some of these captives they kept as slaves for themselves, to feed and staff imperial courts where they had gained luxurious styles of living and surrounded themselves with personal followers. Other captives they sold to the merchants from the desert to buy more horses for their cavalry forces and thus to extend their political and military reach beyond what they might have managed from sales of gold alone. Literacy in Arabic added to the power they gained from their access to trading capital and to horses.

The towns, aristocratic compounds, and traders thus prospered from the coordination they achieved over great distances and brought a significant overlay of commercial and political integration to large parts of the farming villages of *sudanic* West Africa. Along the major trade routes linking the middle reaches of the Niger to the river's delta, Yoruba-speaking people at Ife and Bini-speaking people at Benin had consolidated extensive, but less intensely militarized, political systems, very likely by investing the wealth they amassed from taxing the trade goods moving through their lands. The landholding families influential in the Akan area derived their prosperity from commercial interests in sources of gold developed within their territories, but in the fifteenth century they had not yielded political authority to a single, central ruler.

Commercial and political success attracted people of many sorts to the ways of the wealthy and powerful. Slaves adopted the cultures and languages of their masters. Wives and children, in the large numbers assembled by lords and merchants through multiple marriages, spread the habits of their husbands and fathers back to their maternal homelands. So also did clients eager to share in patrons' prosperity, political subordinates seeking advancement, and others

Guinea in 1732

Those sold by the Blacks are for the most part prisoners of war, taken either in fight, or pursuit, or in the incursions they make into their enemies' territories; others stolen away by their own countrymen; and some there are, who will sell their own children, kindred, or neighbours. This has been often seen, and to compass it, they desire the person they intend to sell, to help them in carrying something to the factory by way of trade, and when there, the person so deluded, not understanding the language, is sold and deliver'd up as a slave, notwithstanding all his resistance, and exclaiming against the treachery. . . .

The kings are so absolute, that upon any slight pretense of offences committed by their subjects, they order them to be sold for slaves, without regard to rank, or possession. . . .

These slaves are severely and barbarously treated by their masters, who subsist them poorly, and beat them inhumanly, as may be seen by the scabs and wounds on the bodies of many of them when sold to us. They scarce allow them the least rag to cover their nakedness, which they also take off from them when sold to Europeans; and they always go bare-headed. The wives and children of slaves, are also slaves to the master under whom they are married; and when dead, they never bury them, but cast out the bodies into some by place, to be devoured by birds, or beasts of prey.

Many of those slaves we transport from Guinea to America are prepossessed with the opinion, that they are carried like sheep to the slaughter, and that the Europeans are fond of their flesh; which notion so far prevails with some, as to make them fall into a deep melancholy and despair, and to refuse all sustenance, tho' never so much compelled and even beaten to oblige them to take some nourishment: notwithstanding all which, they will starve to death; whereof I have had several instances in my own slaves both aboard and at Guadalupe.

Source: John Barbot, "A Description of the Coasts of North and South Guinea," in Thomas Astley and John Churchill, eds., *Collection of Voyages and Travels* (London, 1732).

pursuing power and wealth by association with those who had them. By the fifteenth century, these patterns had allowed Mande speakers to spread an overlay of cultural homogeneity throughout the valley of the Upper Niger and in the regions to the west. The strongly centralized kingdom at Benin united the region just west of the lower Niger and spread its political culture there. Political federation in the Yoruba and Akan parts of the forest had promoted looser sorts of economic and cultural integration.

The Bantu-speaking farming and fishing communities in the central African forests and in the savannas beyond toward the south had, by the fifteenth century, integrated their local economies on scales comparable to the degrees achieved in West Africa. Particularly where inexpensive transport by canoe was available, they too produced and distributed significant surpluses. However, they did so mostly without taking on the burdens associated with military conquest and integration: luxuriously appointed, slave-attended aristocratic compounds, and the feeding of large towns and families of merchants. Notables—heads of landowning communities, men wealthy from fishing or transporting goods along the rivers, owners of mineral resources like salt pans or outcrops of copper ores—formed flexible confederations on regional scales, but they lacked horses, or other military means, and incentives to concentrate power beyond a degree that might be termed conciliatory or "ceremonial." Individuals might achieve great personal authority on the basis of perceived abilities to respond to the circumstantial needs of communities—calling rains in times of drought, driving out disease or other evils that seemed to afflict them—but successors rarely could lay claim to the personal influence they had acquired. In the far south, along the margins of the Kalahari Desert, cattle were the basis of prosperity, and wealth and power derived from the possession of large herds.

Most of the Africans whom Europeans would buy as slaves thus had lived in small agricultural communities, cherished an intense loyalty to those with whom they had grown up, and as adults had become skilled in delicate techniques of exploiting the resources of the lands in which they lived. They offered respect, and usually wealth as well, to senior members of their families and to leaders of their villages. Some of them also recognized more distant, less personal forms of authority ranging from men of senior status, wealth, or spiritual authority in regional associations and confederacies to violent monarchs of exalted rank, incomparable wealth, and terrifying power, monarchs who lived hidden in sanctity, behind high walls amidst crowds of slaves and wives. The vague and general "ethnic" or cultural similarities apparent to later European observers, unable to appreciate the subtleties of Africans' lives, meant little to them. They produced surpluses—from home crafts or garden produce through staple crops and specialized and technologically refined rural industries—and exchanged their product for consumption and luxury goods, sometimes with neighbors, elsewhere in local public marketplaces, often through strangers, resident or itinerant, who traded for their

Leo Africanus Describes African Society

I have observed five degrees of men amongst the Negroes; the first of which are their kings or captains, for the word is here synonymous.

The second, their Caboceros, or chief men; which reducing to our manner of expression, we should be apt to call them Civil fathers; whose province is only to take care of the welfare of the city or village, and to appease any tumult.

The third sort are those who have acquired a great reputation by their riches, either devolved on them by inheritance or gotten by trade. And these are the persons which some authors have represented as noblemen; but whether they are in the right or not, shall hereafter plainly appear.

The fourth are the common people employed in the tillage of wines, agriculture, and fishing.

The fifth and last are the slaves, either sold by their relations, taken in war, or come so by poverty.

Source: Leo Africanus, *The History and Description of Africa*, trans. John Pory, ed. Robert Brown (New York: Burt Franklin, Publisher, n.d.), vol. 3, pp. 822–24.

livings. Although they strongly felt loyalty to their local community, they also sought personal advancement by moving among the many other, often broader social identities available to them. Small minorities of West Africans in touch with the Islamic lands, the world civilization of the eighth through the fifteenth centuries, had taken advantage of its commercial capital, universalistic religion, and literacy to gain enormous advantage, uncharacteristic of village life—with the achievements of Mali and Songhai most visible to outsiders. Elsewhere, Africans awaited access to comparable wealth and power to pursue similar paths to personal gain.

THE ATLANTIC ECONOMY AND THE SLAVE TRADE

Europeans created a vast new trading system between the fifteenth and the eighteenth centuries, bringing the continents around the Atlantic basin together in a dynamic economic network that stimulated economic growth in all of them, including Africa. Its three poles were the fast-developing mercantile economies of western Europe, the open lands and mineral resources of the Americas, north and south, and the populations of Africa. In combination, European financial capital, rich New World lands, and African workers generated rapid growth, centered on plantation-grown tropical agricultural commodities, and on precious metals, gold and silver, produced by Africans working in the Americas as slaves. From the point of view of the people in Africa, contact with the Atlantic economy brought previously unimagined quantities of imported goods—textiles, metalwares of several sorts vital to their own economies, alcoholic spirits, firearms, and currencies. From the point of view of the Europeans, Africans were willing to sell, first of all, gold, then ivory and various tropical gums and woods, and finally—and most enduringly—slaves.

Europe's interest in Africa originated not in tropical commodities or, particularly, in labor but rather in the *sudanic* gold that had been reaching the Muslim cities of the Mediterranean from Mali since long before the fifteenth century. The Renaissance Italians, the major southern European commercial and financial powers of the era, were the largest market for African gold from the Muslims. They were also the most active in the slave trade, which did not involve Africa but rather brought Slavic peoples from the shores of the Black Sea for sale in the Christian cities on the northern side of the western Mediterranean, from Venice to Seville. The Portuguese, who faced out away from the Mediterranean toward the Atlantic, simultaneously followed prevailing winds and currents down the barren coast of northwestern Africa in search of the gold they knew to come from beyond the Sahara. To return against the winds to Europe, they had to swing far out into the open sea to the west, where they found the uninhabited islands of the eastern Atlantic—Madeira, the Açores, the Cape Verde Islands—along the way.

By the 1440s, Portuguese mariners had reached the westernmost provinces of the Mali Empire, beyond Cape Verde between the Senegal and Gambia rivers, and by the 1460s they were sailing along the west-east-lying part of the West African coast, which they named Guinea. The 1480s found them at the mouth of the Zaire River, and by the 1490s their leading captains had turned the Cape of Good Hope at the very southern tip of the continent and were on their way out across the Indian Ocean toward Asia. Intending to pick up prevailing westerly winds of the higher latitudes of the Southern Hemisphere and then ride them eastward back toward the Cape, Africa, and India, Pedro Alvares Cabral, a Portuguese captain setting out for Asia followed the northeasterly trade winds far out across the Atlantic. Surprised to encounter the landmass of South America blocking his way in 1500, he claimed this massive territory for his king and named it Brazil for the red dyewood the Portuguese found in forests there.

Although the Portuguese sailing along the coasts of Africa were able to purchase modest quantities of gold from Malian merchants and found still more of the precious metal on the Guinea Coast, along a section of the shore that they called "Mina" (that is, "mine," in Portuguese, later dubbed the "Gold Coast" by the English), they competed only with difficulty against the dominant Muslim merchants of the *sahel* and *sudan* and their export routes across the Sahara. In the fragile desert-edge lands around the Senegal and the Gambia, droughts, which were frequent and sometimes devastating, periodically threw the farmers of the *sahel* into turmoil, forced them into violent struggles with one another, often led by militaristic kings, and created refugees and captives. Some of the people thus abandoned were bought by Portuguese as slaves, to compete with the Italian slave markets of the Mediterranean or to populate the islands of the eastern Atlantic. Others they sold in Spain, particularly in Seville, where they became slave companions and servants of the Spaniards, and in the newly claimed West Indian islands of the Caribbean, in the Americas. By shortly after 1500, the numbers of the people thus taken from Africa had become significant—perhaps two thousand or so in a typical year.

By the 1520s, the Portuguese had developed diplomatic and commercial interests in central Africa in the kingdom that controlled the south bank of the lower Zaire River. Known as Kongo, from the title of its monarch, the *mani* (or "lord") *kongo*. They had also started to develop the uninhabited equatorial island of São Tomé as a source of slave-worked cane sugar, a condiment then just starting to take its place as the principal sweetener in the European diet. There they began to bring larger numbers of Africans from the mainland as slaves to toil in fields laid out in large, specialized agricultural enterprises built around the crushing mills needed to press the sweet, sugar-yielding juices from the fresh cane. São Tomé planters needed so many enslaved Africans to cultivate and cut the cane on these plantations that their demands exceeded the ability of the Kongo kingdom to supply them. By the 1560s the Tomistas found more slaves farther south, among the Africans living in the valley of the Kwanza River, bought principally from their dominant warlord-ruler, from whose title, the *ngola*, they named the area Angola. Sailing short routes from the mainland to nearby islands like São Tomé, the Portuguese developed techniques of transporting larger and larger numbers of captive people on the open ocean and methods of stocking and carrying the substantial quantities of food and water necessary to keep them alive—although frequently in appalling conditions, and often at the cost of numerous deaths from malnutrition, neglect, and disease.

The Portuguese extended these early movements of enslaved Africans across the Atlantic to Brazil during the 1570s and multiplied, by a factor of four or five, the numbers they carried to more than 10,000 per year. In the same decade, a severe drought in Angola spread chaos through the African communities in the vicinity of the Kwanza, at the same time that the Portuguese had sent troops to occupy key posts along the river and at the nearby bay of Luanda in search of rumored mountains of silver somewhere in the interior. Failing to find instant riches comparable to those of Spain's "Indies"—Mexico and Peru—in the New World, these armies pillaged the valleys and hills along the Kwanza, while no-less-predatory bands of African marauders, who had joined together to survive the drought by plundering, escalated the numbers of people seized and sold. Markets for all these slaves now appeared in northeastern Brazil, where Dutch investors had enabled Portuguese planters to start to assemble larger sugar plantations that allowed the costly importation of slaves from Africa, mostly Angola. Portuguese merchants, entering Spain's New World domains under protection gained from the union of the Portuguese and Spanish monarchies under Philip II and Philip III (1580–1640), also began to deliver significant numbers of enslaved

Africans to the cities of the mainland American colonies of Spain under the terms of special royal contracts, termed—in Spanish—*asientos*. With the development of large-scale transatlantic transportation of African slaves at the end of the sixteenth century, these merchants both extended the familiar European style of urban slavery to the Spanish cities and amplified the newer rural agricultural slave labor system of the sugar plantations of São Tomé in the Americas. They also worked out techniques of financing, loading, feeding, and carrying large numbers of people in small spaces that became the basis on which later merchants built a massive transatlantic trade in slaves.

The Dutch, whose mercantile wealth and commercial interests in sugar refining underwrote the growth of the Brazilian plantations, then began a wide-ranging military assault on Portuguese interests on both sides of the Atlantic. The assault grew out of Protestant Dutch efforts to throw off Catholic Spanish rule in the Netherlands and was mounted under the leadership of the Dutch West India Company. Financed by mercantile interests, its ships interfered with Portuguese trading all along the African coast after 1621, and by the 1630s its armies took control of the sugar-producing portions of Brazil. Company commanders then turned to the African possessions of Portugal that supplied the slaves required to work the American plantations they had seized. Beyond capturing the Portuguese fort at Mina and its gold trade, during the 1640s they occupied Luanda, in Angola, and its sources of slaves. They soon lost both the sugar plantations of Portuguese America and the slaving colonies in Africa, however, to a determined counterattack by the Brazilians and so turned their attention in the 1650s to the Caribbean, where numerous islands held promise as plantations able to compete with Portuguese-controlled sugar from Brazil. There they helped English interests on the small leeward island of Barbados to convert the local economy from marginal smallholdings producing cotton, tobacco, and indigo, worked by European family labor and indentured servants, into plantations of substantial scale, producing sugar and holding Africans as slaves to cultivate the cane by the 1680s. When the English captured the much larger island of Jamaica from the Spaniards in 1671, they acquired the base from which they, followed by the French, who had taken control of the western end of the large Spanish island of Santo Domingo, would build the huge slave-worked West Indian sugar plantation complex of the eighteenth century.

Spain, with its huge territories in mainland central and northwestern South America, controlled a large enough population of Native-American peasants and workers—which had started to recover from the huge human losses, perhaps 90 percent of the precontact population, that had followed the introduction of European diseases in the sixteenth century—that its New World cities, plantations, and mines relied only secondarily on Africans as laborers. The silver and commodity produce of the mainland allowed it to leave its remaining island possessions in the Caribbean, principally Cuba but also Santo Domingo and Puerto Rico, outside the quickening race to grow sugar there.

Meanwhile the English in North America relied until the 1670s largely on settler families and the immigrant indentured. Nonetheless, a few Dutch slave ships headed for New Amsterdam (later New York City), and local shipping between the mainland and the Caribbean had brought a few Africans, some of them as slaves, to Virginia and Carolina in the early 1600s.

Sugar cultivation, rapidly becoming the commercial foundation of the colonial Caribbean and South American economies, was unsuited for the temperate climates of North America where during the 1620s tobacco emerged as the staple crop of the Chesapeake colonies of Virginia and Maryland and where a dwindling supply of white indentured servants led toward the end of the seventeenth century to a strong demand for African bound labor. By the early 1700s, more than half of all the laborers in the Chesapeake region were of African descent and enslaved. Elsewhere in British America, the numbers of enslaved Africans also increased markedly as settlers sought to satisfy rapidly expanding labor needs in the thirteen colonies at cheap prices and without substantial risk to local security. The Atlantic slave trade would provide the major source of slave labor there until the slave population could sustain itself through natural increase, but overall represented a small minority, probably less than 6 percent, of the African diaspora. Most—well over three-fourths—of the Africans who survived the ocean voyage, the so-called "Middle Passage," found themselves laboring as slaves in the sugar islands of the Caribbean or in Portuguese Brazil. A small number were herded ashore in the Spanish mainland colonies.

Sugar everywhere in the New World depended entirely on slave labor from Africa. The Portuguese, attempting to restore the prosperity of their Brazilian plantations and the English, French, and Dutch in the Caribbean, used trading companies, protected by the award of monopoly trading rights in Africa, to finance the early transition to the era of sugar and slaves in the New World in the 1670s. The Dutch West India Company, which had led the attack on the Portuguese possessions in Africa and Brazil, had earlier demonstrated the efficacy of pooling the assets of many merchants into a trading company, protected by government-chartered commercial privileges, to bear the costs and risks of transporting goods and people among three, or four, continents and over thousands of miles of ocean, under the hazardous conditions of piracy, naval conflict among the European powers, and the poor communications prevailing at the time.

The Lisbon-based Portuguese Companhia de Guiné was restricted to developing sources of slaves from Cacheu and Bissau, the old, and neglected, Portuguese trading posts on the Upper Guinea coast. The French Compagnie de Guinée, Compagnie du Sénégal, which concentrated its trading at the mouth of the Senegal River to the north, and the later Compagnie des Indes provided most of the enslaved Africans delivered to French Louisiana in the 1720s. The London-based Royal African Company established its principal bases at forts it added to those of the Portuguese and Dutch along the Gold

Coast and the area to the east. Prominent among the functions of these companies was use of their considerable capital resources to finance sales of the slaves they carried, on credit, to planters in the New World struggling through the initial, costly phases of investing in plantation-grown sugar. African slaves were, and long remained, among the largest of their investments.

Despite their size and the government protection these enterprises received to lure wealthy European investors to assume the considerable risks of the Africa trade, they all failed by the 1720s. They collapsed in part because planters often could not repay the loans given them to buy the large numbers of slaves that they needed and that the companies delivered. They failed also because smaller, independent merchants, with fewer attractive commercial alternatives in Europe, but also able to operate at lower cost, intruded on the royal monopolies awarded the large companies from the start. By the beginning of the eighteenth century, planting interests in Bahia, the major sugar-producing region in northeastern Brazil, developed a slave supply network of their own, largely independent of Lisbon, directly across the southern Atlantic to the eastern part of the "Mina" coast, which came to known as the Slave Coast (the Cote des esclaves) where English and French traders had begun to congregate. In France, the independent merchants from the port of Nantes made the Côte des esclaves the principal slave supply area on the lower Guinea coast, opened new sources of slaves farther along the coast in central Africa (the so-called Loango Coast north of the mouth of the Zaire) and accounted for the majority of the Africans landed as slaves in their main Caribbean island, Saint Domingue. The English "free traders" came from the smaller ports of the west of England, Bristol at first and then Liverpool, and followed the same commercial strategies as the French in supplanting the Royal African Company on the Slave Coast and moving on to central Africa.

Just after 1700 and the discovery of gold and diamonds in Minas Gerais in the Portuguese domains of south-central Brazil, two additional independent, but also relatively marginal, groups of merchants came to Angola in search of African laborers. Unable to compete with British-backed and often Portuguese government-favored traders with direct access to the precious metals of Brazil, Lisbon-based merchants entered the less protected market at Luanda to buy African captives, whom they sold for gold at Rio de Janeiro, the southern Brazilian port that developed to handle imports destined for the mines in Minas Gerais. To ensure their place in the valuable market for Brazilian gold, merchants based in Rio developed a strategy of using Angolan sources of slaves. Like the Bahians active on the Mina coast, the merchants in Rio reduced costs by adding to the mix of goods used to buy slaves a cane brandy distilled from the otherwise valueless molasses drained off sugar in preparation for shipment to Europe.

In North America, planters in Virginia and Carolina bought increasing numbers of slaves from the 1720s on. They acquired a few through their continuing regional commerce with the islands of the West Indies, but more arrived on English ships direct from Africa, seeking secondary destinations when their primary markets in the Caribbean were momentarily saturated, and on the small vessels of colonial merchants from Rhode Island. These merchants employed the same strategy as the Brazilians before them: they carried West Indian molasses home to New England, distilled it there to high-proof rum, and took it to the parts of the African coast less dominated by large merchants from Europe to buy slaves. Nonetheless, North American plantations represented only the smallest part of the huge demand for slaves being taken to the sugar plantations and mines of tropical America.

Thus, from the few thousand individuals taken each year in the early Old World trade, the number of Africans transported across the Atlantic first became significant at the end of the sixteenth century, reaching more than 10,000 in the 1570s. When slave-grown sugar expanded to the Caribbean in the 1640s, the volume of the slave trade doubled and then, by the end of the seventeenth century, tripled. Throughout the eighteenth century, with the entry of new groups of independent traders and the rush to extract the gold of Minas Gerais after 1700, the numbers of slaves rose irregularly to peaks of 80,000 or more per year in the 1780s and 1790s, with the pace being periodically broken by recurrent naval warfare among the competing European powers. The costs of the goods Europeans traded for slaves in Africa declined until about the 1650s but then rose consistently throughout the 1700s. So great was the demand for slaves, and so high the costs, that by about the 1750s, the French and then the Brazilians not long after 1800, began to sail around the Cape of Good Hope into the Indian Ocean in search of lower-cost slaves from eastern Africa.

By 1800, the trade had entered a significant decline. This was because of growing antislavery sentiments on either side of the Atlantic in the late eighteenth century. Generation during the American Revolution of the ideology of liberty, combined with strong religious and humanitarian ideas, moved framers of the new republic's constitution to ban the African slave trade, then widely seen as the most brutal aspect of black bondage. Pressed by a powerful antislavery lobby, the British Parliament in 1807 declared the slave trade illegal. Afterward, British-led efforts to abolish the slave trade reduced its volume from around 60,000 per year to below 50,000 by the 1840s, to around 20,000 in the 1850s, and to virtual insignificance after that. Distracted by revolution at home, the French lost their main sugar-producing island, Saint Domingue, to a revolt by the slaves there after 1791, and their merchants dropped out of the trade. Wars and other concerns on the continent, including pressure from the British, repeatedly interrupted French efforts to resume the slave trade after 1815, and France finally gave it up in 1845. When participation in slave trade was forbidden for English traders under the British flag, the Portuguese and Brazilians moved into the African markets abandoned by the northern European traders, greatly intensified their activity in eastern Africa, and rushed continuing large numbers of captives to Brazil, where plantations growing coffee and cotton supplemented the old sugar industry as markets. The Spaniards, with assistance from slavers from the United States left with no other markets, promoted sugar, and later coffee, plantations in Cuba, making it the principal Caribbean destination for slaves in the nineteenth century and the last branch of the trade to decline, finally in the 1860s.

Overall, historians have good evidence to fix the total numbers of Africans taken into the Atlantic at between eleven and thirteen million people, more than half of them in the eighteenth century. The British colonies in North America received only about 600,000, 5 percent of the total Atlantic trade, mostly between the 1720s and the 1770s.

AFRICA DURING THE ERA OF THE SLAVE TRADE

The slave trade had a deep impact on Africa as well as the Americas. The opportunity to acquire the commodities that European slavers offered allowed Africans to build new trading networks, to accumulate significant political power, to replace old structures of community based on birth and affinity with more deeply hierarchical aggregations of slave dependents, to create new configurations of ethnic identification, and—broadly—to integrate an increasing area inland from the coasts into the Atlantic economy. African buyers of these imported quantities of goods gained significantly from the exchanges and were attracted by the profits available to deliver the millions of men, women, and children sent to the coast to be embarked there as slaves.

As the trade increased, Europeans seldom went far inland and even less often participated actively in seizing the people enslaved. Their presence in Africa was mainly limited to small settlements on offshore islands or to brief visits to the beaches, where business was done at sites developed and maintained by their African trading partners, and fortified positions were built only along the Gold and Slave Coasts. The only arguable exception to the marginality of the European physical presence in Africa was the territory in Angola claimed by the Portuguese—a small area within the range of the guns of military fortresses at Luanda, along the lower Kwanza River, and at two or three isolated outposts in the interior, and at a small, secondary trading station to the south (Benguela). The inhabitants of the towns and trading posts in Angola, merchant families, a few owners of agricultural estates, militia officers, and the clergy, professed a certain limited loyalty to the crown in Portugal and to the limited complement of government officials posted there, but the dominant families in "Portuguese" Angola descended primarily from the African gentry and commercial interests in and around the colony, secondarily from immigrants from Brazil, and only in small part from immigrants from Europe; they were, in effect, locally born Africans, no more than nominally Portuguese in their political loyalties, entirely local in their economic strategies, and hardly distinguishable in appearance from neighbors recognized as "Africans."

Many Europeans who came to tropical Africa in the time of the slave trade fell victim to fevers, parasites, and other afflictions that thrived in the tropics: estimates are that no fewer than 40 percent of the European-born who arrived and attempted to stay in Africa survived the first year, and that about only about 10 percent would survive to normal life expectancies. Under these lethal circumstances, and given the ability and avidity of the Africans to deliver captive people efficiently to European merchants, they had no reason to involve themselves further. No doubt, had they tried, they would have been far too few in numbers to succeed; they certainly enjoyed no military advantage beyond the range of the cannon they carried on their ships. African traders and politicians, jealous of their own profitable trade routes, would have forcibly and promptly expelled them.

While the Europeans traded in the thoroughly commercialized economies of the Atlantic and calculated their gains in terms of currency prices prevailing in Europe, Africans functioned in economic systems that reckoned the value of things not in terms of their potential for exchange but for their usefulness, or utility. The Africans calculated equivalents directly as quantities: so many measures of grain equaled one chicken, so many guns given for an adult male slave. African buyers of goods and European sellers everywhere worked out a quantity, or barter, system in which goods were traded directly for other goods. The principal abstract units of exchange were physical quantities thought of as fixed: a specific number of iron "bars," "ounces" of gold, "bundles" of goods, and so on, depending on the area of the coast. Traders, though, could alter the size of the measure employed, so that the length of the "strings" of beads in a "bundle" grew longer when few slaves were available while the number of strings remained the same. European merchants thus effectively learned to trade in terms set by the Africans in utility-based value systems.

Africans bought primarily textiles in vast quantities, including elegant French brocades and velvets and Chinese silks for elite consumption, but mostly patterned English woolens and northern European linens and, increasingly throughout the eighteenth century, brightly colored cottons as well as strong indigo-dyed blue-black cotton cloth from India. By European currency prices, textiles accounted for more than half the value of Africans' imports. They also purchased spirits—American rums, French brandies, and English and Dutch gins—and Portuguese and French wines; alcohol in all forms probably amounted to another 20 percent. "Metalwares" of many sorts ranked next, with copper rods and bracelets, brass pans, actual bars of pig iron, and a great variety of knives, nails, and other finished metal hardware figuring prominently. Flintlock muskets, manufactured especially for the Africa trade, and gunpowder probably accounted for around 10 percent, by currency values, of African's imports. These firearms attracted a great deal of criticism from opponents of the trade, who alleged that they exacerbated violence in Africa; some of the proponents of the trade also objected because guns in the hands of Africans possibly endangered traders. The remainder of Africa's imports consisted of a great variety of other manufactured wares, prominently including Venetian glass beads and—particularly on the Slave Coast—billions of the distinctive small shells of a marine mollusk known as cowries, found only in the Indian Ocean.

Looking again at these imports in terms of their utilities in African systems of valuation suggests something of the reasons for giving up human beings— the basis of all wealth and power in Africa—for what, to the Europeans, seemed like cheap, even frivolous, trinkets. Africans may have used the muskets and powder that so alarmed Europeans to capture the people they sold, and while the weapons certainly contributed frightening noise, flames, and smoke to the violence, they may also have employed them as much, or more, for hunting and for protection. If control of a large and diverse following was a pervasive economic (and political) strategy, Africans would have prized guns because they frightened rather than because they killed. In some areas, iron bars replaced the products of the African iron-smelting industries that were running low on trees needed to maintain the high furnace temperatures. Iron imports thus protected agriculture and specialized the iron industry in the forging of finished tools; imported knives, particularly heavy machetes for chopping, axe heads, and other implements put metal tools in the hands of farmers and craftsmen who would not otherwise have had them to work with. Alcohol, while abused by some, served others as controlled means of entertaining dependents, of communicating with the spiritual forces in their lives, of firing the courage of soldiers about to enter battle, and of bringing collaborating groups together in somewhat inebriated unity.

Of great underlying significance to most Africans were the humble cowrie shells and copper goods, which Africans treated primarily as stores of wealth and as mediums of exchange, in short, as currencies. Although many of the less distinctive imported textiles were used immediately by ordinary people, Africans also hoarded the finer textiles they bought as additional stores of wealth, wore them as objects of ostentatious display, and exchanged them for people, not only the captives they sold to Europeans as slaves but also for women whom they kept as wives and for others retained as clients and other sorts of dependents; imported cloth, too, functioned as currency in the social economy of claiming rights in people as the continent's primary standard of wealth.

In African terms, then, the Atlantic trade offered certain gains that extended beyond the material productivity of iron, or direct consumption and investment of textiles they imported. Advantage consisted principally in exchanging the imports for the fundamental form of wealth in much of Africa: people, and the ability to control them. Or, to phrase the gains in more personal terms, imports allowed the people who got them first to distribute them to others in return for respect and authority. Some of these increases in power and numbers were gained by exchanging unwanted individuals—captives taken on a field of battle who could not otherwise have been kept alive, troublesome or unpopular youths already at the point of being driven out of their home communities, political rivals, criminals, or poor, despised, or dependent people too weak to resist outright victimization by others—for goods that the captor or seller could use to acquire the loyalty or services of more productive replacements, or new followers in greater numbers or with needed talents to contribute. A community elder might thus contrive to dispose of an overly assertive nephew in return for cloth, copper rods, and brandy in quantities that permitted him to buy a young slave woman as a third wife, to give one illustrative example; or, a blacksmith could expand his production by selling iron for the cast-off relatives of his customers, exchanging them for textiles that he sent off with traders who would bring him young men whom he would train to provide the unskilled labor for himself and his sons who practiced the secrets of his craft.

In other cases, the forced march toward the beach started with crop failures following a season of insufficient rainfall. Villagers facing starvation after inadequate harvests would disperse to find food, some seeking shelter with relatives but others foraging alone, where they were vulnerable to kidnapping. In extreme droughts, whole communities turned to raiding to support themselves and took captives among the plunder they seized to survive. Starving families might sell children to buyers who, whatever other fate might follow from the sale, at least might feed them; the alternatives were starvation at home, or infanticide. In the most extreme periods of drought, gangs of bandits preyed systematically on farmers living in the better-watered valleys, seizing their wives and children for sale. Other domestic violence, often linked to family indebtedness, similarly left relatives, again frequently children, abandoned as slaves.

The possible hazards that could turn a daughter, an unlucky soldier, or a failed trader alone and far from home—a women fetching water from the river, a youth tending his family's goats—into a captive helpless in the hands of strangers were endless and were multiplied many times over, because individual human greed and rationalization in the face of profound moral dilemmas were stimulated by the opportunities offered by the presence of European slavers at the coast. On the one hand, people committed such acts as these in defense of the solidarity of their communities; intense loyalties at home lessened the sense of moral obligation to strangers. On the other hand, betrayal within the group also eroded the very bonds meant, or professed, to be preserved. The tendency of the Europeans to offer their trade goods on credit, giving them to African buyers in anticipation of repayment in captives later on, brought men of no particular community standing, and therefore with relatively little to lose from engaging in disreputable tactics, into slaving and exacerbated the violations of conventional social and political morality.

Time after time, hoodlums systematically took advantage of opportunities like these, even organizing themselves as gangs that made their livings from kidnappings and outright attacks on villages, particularly in the *sudan*, where

An Eighteenth-Century Slave's Capture

The invaders pinioned the prisoners of all ages and sexes indiscriminately, took their flocks and all their effects, and moved on their way towards the sea. On the march the prisoners were treated with clemency, on account of their being submissive and humble. Having come to the next tribe, the enemy laid siege and immediately took men, women, children, flocks, and all their valuable effects. They then went on to the next district which was contiguous to the sea, called in Africa, Anamaboo. The enemies' provisions were then almost spent, as well as their strength. The inhabitants knowing what conduct they had pursued, and what were their present intentions, improved the favorable opportunity, attacked them, and took enemy, prisoners, flocks and all their effects. I was then taken a second time. All of us were then put into the castle [a European slave trading post], and kept for market. On a certain time I and other prisoners were put on board a canoe, under our master, and rowed away to a vessel belonging to Rhode Island, commanded by Captain Collingwood, and the mate Thomas Mumford. While we were going to the vessel, our master told us all to appear to the best possible advantage for sale. I was bought on board by one Robert Mumford, steward of said vessel, for four gallons of rum, and a piece of calico, and called Venture, on account of his having purchased me with his own private venture. Thus I came by my name. All the slaves that were bought for that vessel's cargo, were two hundred and sixty.

Source: A Narrative Life and Adventures of Venture, A Native of Africa (New London, Conn., 1798; expanded ed., Hamden, Conn., 1896).

domineering brigands surrounded themselves with gangs of slave mercenaries and used horses to gain overpowering advantage in such raiding. Elsewhere, as—for example—east of the lower Niger River, gangs of violence-prone con men made the rounds of farming villages to offer justice, probably of the variety that was difficult to refuse, by taking local disputants before a mysterious "oracle" that they presented as a kind of supreme judicial authority in the region. This practice in effect resolved such conflicts by deporting the parties adjudged guilty, often along with many of their relatives; the losers soon found themselves being marched toward the coast.

Elsewhere, warlords established themselves by sheer force and extorted people from every village within their reach. The armies of the great states occasionally met each other on the field of battle, where victors captured and sold, rather than killed, the vanquished. Some political regimes took slaving beyond such opportunistic strategies and survived by systematically raiding populations living beyond the areas they claimed as subject to their authority. The people subjected to such violence fled into defensible, but often less fertile or productive lairs, where they found themselves unable to support the large numbers of refugees clustered there. Hunger in turn compelled them to move out to raid farmers and other exposed populations. Such conflicts as these emerged from the ongoing tensions of African politics, but the goods from the Atlantic, and perhaps the firearms, prolonged them and added to their intensity, increased the numbers of their victims, saved some from assassination, and sent a portion of the survivors toward the coast. Even the droughts, although frequently stimulated by meteorological anomalies, had a more devastating impact on populations under stresses of the sort associated with slaving.

In the long run, the people who gained most from the slaving trade organized themselves as merchants specialized in the trade to and from the coast. In central Africa, hundreds of small traders, each accompanied by wives and younger relatives, ventured out in caravans of dozens and, eventually, hundreds of people, through the sparsely populated plains in search of captives to buy in remote centers of population. Specialized merchants organized their own caravans, manned by slaves, between the coast and major trading centers inland. The great waterways—the lower Niger and its delta, the Zaire in central Africa, the Senegal and the Gambia, as well as lagoons all along the coast of lower Guinea—were dotted with huge dugout canoes filled with paddlers, supplies, commodities, and slaves. Taking their profits in the form of people, often by buying and retaining slaves, these merchants assembled whole new trading communities and invented social institutions to control them. In the Niger Delta, for example, successful traders managed villages composed of populous wards termed "houses," largely inhabited by slaves and intended to man the large trading canoes used on the rivers. The ancestral farming communities organized around core groups of kinspeople began to add slaves, whom they put to work growing surplus for sale to neighbors, or even distant markets in towns, specialized in commerce.

In the aggregate, the "profits" of the Atlantic trade in Africa thus took the human form of people uprooted, often violently, and resettled as slaves around the large, powerful courts of new states or employed in new commercialized sectors of the region's economies and societies. In a less abstract sense, one of the major changes of the era was the reorientation of people's lives toward trading with the coast. This new commercial focus not only took the form of traders organizing whole new villages and transportation networks but also led the prosperous—and therefore increasingly numerous—merchant interests to assume positions of influence in the established political systems. In kingdom after kingdom, particularly near the coast, families from the commercial sector replaced factions who had derived their power from older sources in aristocratic lineage, in agricultural land, or in control of mineral resources and techniques of working them. In the extreme cases, the new commercial groups grew large enough and became sufficiently specialized to dominate whole territories, develop their own ways of living, and sometimes speak distinctive dialects; they acquired a sense of separate identity comparable to the older ethnic communities of the continent. These shifts toward more mercantilistic regimes gathered momentum particularly as the volume of the trade peaked in the last third of the eighteenth century.

The rise of African traders doing business with the Europeans, the outbreaks of violence that followed, political restructuring, and the concentrations of slaves and others in new commercial institutions tended to follow a single broad pattern over the centuries of exchanges with the Atlantic. Slaving gained momentum first, at the end of the sixteenth and in the seventeenth centuries, along coasts adjacent to the sites where the earliest, commodity phases of the Atlantic trade had appeared, and then failed. The principal early Atlantic commerce in lower Guinea was gold from the Gold Coast, until slaving gathered momentum in regions to the east that lacked similar mineral resources, along what became the Slave Coast.

From those roots, slaving spread simultaneously outward along the coasts and into the interior in the second half of the seventeenth century, particularly in lower Guinea and Angola. As the stimulus of the trade provoked domestic rivalries, raiders and traders created new states, which in turn became the frameworks around which their rulers and subjects built new ethnic identities. Typically, the trade allowed weak authorities in older kingdoms near the coast to consolidate their power internally at first, and frequently also to mount attacks on their neighbors. In every case, the peoples inland, at whose expense these first-generation states grew, armed and organized to defend themselves, and then created new polities from the heterogenous crowds of refugees they attracted; they consolidated their new states by integrating still more peoples whom they then went on to conquer. The famous large military states of eighteenth-century West Africa, Asante behind the Gold Coast and Dahomey inland from Ardra on the Slave Coast, took shape in this way at the end of the seventeenth century.

The merchants who sold the slaves on which the military aristocrats in each of these polities depended had to penetrate regions still farther from the coast to find captives, once the heirs of the violent founders of such states settled in and claimed political legitimacy. Bandits thus found themselves responsible for protecting—and not selling—the people they claimed to rule. In central Africa, traders' ventures into the interior stimulated new rounds of conflict off to the east and—eventually—political consolidation to bring order out of the chaos created. In western Africa, merchants working inland to the north of Asante and Dahomey reached the established commercial and slaving networks south of the Sahara Desert. Since towns and traders there already drew captives from existing sources, contact with the coast did not occasion immediate economic or political reorganization comparable to that south of the forest, but the added stimulus to raiding tended to discredit the political regimes involved and to drive them toward harsh forms of military domination. Afflicted peasant farmers from time to time sought protection beneath the banners of Muslim clerics, who drew on the religious law of Islam, which forbade Muslims from enslaving other believers, to declaim against the injustices. They occasionally roused their growing followings to revolt against existing regimes in religiously inspired "holy" wars, or *jihads*.

These sequences of local events, viewed on the largest geographical scales and over the entire three centuries of growing trade, formed moving waves of widespread and systematic, often state-sponsored, violence in both western and central Africa. The violence touched most of the western half of the continent at one time or another but in any single region lasted no more than a generation or two. It started near the Atlantic coast in the sixteenth and early seventeenth centuries, then moved inland as the volume of export rose at the end of the seventeenth century, and finally advanced toward the heart of central Africa and into the *sudanic* latitudes of western Africa as the trade reached its eighteenth-century climax. As raiders thrived and violence grew in any one neighborhood, most of its victims fled, forming refugee communities, and others were captured and sold; in only a few areas could populations bear the intensity of these disturbances for more than a generation or two. And so the violence died down, leaving abandoned fields and villages behind. As the wave passed, disturbances broke out anew farther from the coast, and farmers and merchants, with slaves acquired from the war zones inland, moved into the vacated territory, repopulating the land, forming new communities, and working out new ethnic identities. Where the wave had not yet reached, aristocrats of the old political order continued to rule. During the turbulence of its passing, warlords waxed powerful. In the relative calm after these storms, merchants built new states based on brokering the trade in slaves flowing from the violence then flaring farther inland and taking their profits in slaves retained from the caravans of captives moving through their domains.

All these forced movements of people had consequences that can be described in demographic terms, within Africa as well as beyond the continent. Outright depopulation—abandoned villages, human skeletons along the paths—was largely local and temporary. Overall population levels also rose and fell with climatic and epidemiological causes, and they varied as much from these causes, and sometimes inseparably from them, as from deaths attributable in direct ways to systematic slaving—in wars, among the captives being marched toward the coast, or from those finally sold and sent to the Americas. Africans responded creatively to the challenges of surviving in the midst of turmoil. They fled when times got bad, and they organized new states and created new communities in their own defense. They fed themselves by working harder, buying slaves to grow still more crops, and by adding New World cultigens—maize (Indian corn) in the grain-growing areas and manioc, or cassava, a hardy tuber adaptable to environments from the forest to the desert-edge—to their agricultural technology. In falling back on these high-calorie but less nutritious staples they sacrificed variety and balance in their diets, but eating them at least kept families alive.

The demographic pressures of the export trade, although quantitative evidence is lacking, were stronger in central Africa than in West Africa and may have exceeded the overall capability of populations there to reproduce themselves during the peak of slave exports at the end of the eighteenth century. Limiting the overall demographic effects on Africa, men outnumbered the women by a ratio of nearly two to one among the people herded onto the ships of the Europeans. The tendency to sell mostly men meant that Africans retained nearly twice as many females as males, and the reproductive capacities of these women in Africa would have raised overall birthrates there. The powerful African men in charge of the trade thus gained more women as wives or sexual partners, so that they contributed children to the families and followings that constituted wealth. In this way, and through populating new states and commercial networks with slave mercenaries, retainers, clients, and workers, Africans very likely kept more of the people taken captive, as slaves, than they sold. This observation restates in demographic terms the economic pattern, that Africans who gained from selling people into the Atlantic trade took their profits in the fundamental form of wealth in Africa, that is, in other people held in circumstances of greater dependency and subjugation.

Slavery thus increased markedly in Africa as a consequence of trade with the Europeans. Its expansion especially affected African women and children who came to constitute the enslaved African majority. Typically resettled near the coast, among mercantile-oriented communities that profited most from trade with the Atlantic, as isolated and impotent newcomers without kin to support them against older, powerful males, captive females and youth reenforced the patriarchal tendencies of African cultures. Some modern observers have attempted to contrast such slavery as "assimilative" and even benign, compared to the racial exclusivity and harshness of slavery in many parts of the Americas (including the American South). But the displacement, domination, and dishonor of lives devoid of the community support and participation basic to self-realization in Africa made enslavement there awfully burdensome as well.

With the underlying reproductive capacities of the population established, the patrons and masters of bondwomen could remove teenage males as they reached the age at which adolescent males everywhere rebel against authority at home. These "prime" youths were also the objects of greatest European demand for hard labor in the fields and mines of the Americas, and so they accounted for the majority of the slaves embarked. The girls grew up to become mothers of future slaves in Africa. Pressures on Africa's populations appeared in the growing proportions of women and, particularly in the nineteenth century, steadily increasing percentages of younger girls and boys among those sold into slavery.

Some historians have painted Africa during the era of the Atlantic trade in much more somber hues. It is tempting to translate the offensiveness of any form of slave trading or slavery that people feel today into exaggerations of the violence of the trade, of the numbers of people sold, or of long-term damage to Africa in the form of impoverishment or intensification of social and political hierarchies. Modern resentment at human suffering sometimes seeks outlets in interpreting the past, seeking to assign blame to one side or another. Uninformed images of the slave trade denies both the practice of slavery in Africa—or ignores its harshness—and the active part that Africans played in capturing and selling people. Even efforts to refute racial stereotypes can emphasize the hardships of the times in ways that inadvertently make Africans appear hardly more than passive victims, or as gullible people who traded their own folk for worthless trinkets. These attempts, however well-meaning, rest on the erroneous assumption that Africans then thought like Americans today, or Europeans. Instead an explanation for the Africans', and European's, behavior, cruel and even irrational as it may have been by modern standards on both sides, should be sought within the often tragic range of human rationality and irrationality, anywhere, or at any time.

THE "MIDDLE PASSAGE"

Although Europeans approached the Atlantic economy as a business proposition, and purchased and transported Africans in a self-interested, even inhumane spirit, the men, women, and children they carried experienced it in profoundly human terms of fear, suffering, and death. From the perspective of the Europeans, the profits of the voyage hinged on bringing enough of their suffering cargo across the ocean alive so that sale of the survivors would cover the considerable costs invested in the venture. For the Europeans, the "Middle Passage" across the Atlantic—so called, perhaps, because it was the second of the three long legs in the triangular voyage of a vessel out from Europe to Africa, west across the ocean to America with the slave aboard, and then back through the North Atlantic to Europe—but also, from the point of view of the captives, the passage between their march to the coast in Africa and their resettlement as slaves in the New World—was the most dangerous part of the enterprise, the part where survival of the slaves made or broke its investors.

At the eighteenth-century height of the trade, merchants in Liverpool, Nantes, or Lisbon prepared for the "Africa trade" by assembling partnerships that would distribute its considerable risks among several investors. Some contributed goods thought to be in demand on the African coast; others saw an opportunity of disposing of surpluses, spoiled goods, or inventories with no better market. Others might share the cost of the ship and its preparation for the voyage, or "outfit." Captains and supercargoes (the business agents in charge of the cargo, trading operations, and accounting records) sometimes specialized in slaving and would hire on in return for a share in the profits of the voyage. Similar combinations of interests lay behind the voyages that sailed from American ports, Newport, Rhode Island, or Bahia and Rio de Janeiro, though with a greater share held by planters interested in disposing of the by-products of their primary production of sugar meant for sale in Europe. In general, investors were hoping to realize their returns in Europe in cash and to put as little actual money—as opposed to goods, equipment, or personal services—into the voyage as possible; Africans, after all, paid in enslaved people, who would work without wages in the Americas, typically for planters who had ample lands and cattle and sugar and slaves but little money.

The slaving voyage was a highly indirect and uncertain way of making money, with greatly delayed returns at best.

Some of the sailing ships employed in the trade were specially built for carrying large numbers of people, with low-ceilinged decks constructed between the hold, the deep, often damp space at the bottom of the hull, and the open top deck from which the crew maneuvered the ship and its rigging. Most of the craft employed in the trade, however, were general merchantmen, two- or three-masted sailing vessels, often past their prime and sent off to the tropical waters off African shores as a way of ending their careers, as "guinea" worms encountered there burrowed into the wooden hulls and would render them unseaworthy usually after only a few voyages. Some were as small as 30 or 40 tons capacity, not large even by the standards of the time, which meant that they would be equipped to carry perhaps a hundred slaves; a few giants could board seven hundred or even eight hundred captives. The majority of ships were concentrated in the range of 150 to 200 tons and carried three hundred to four hundred slaves. Smaller vessels were uneconomical and dangerous on the open ocean; the largest ones took too long to wind up their huge cargoes and exposed crew and slaves to delays and thus to risks of disease while they lingered just offshore in Africa. Slavers carried crews larger than normal for merchant vessels of comparable size, since extra hands were needed to replace sailors who died and to control the slaves, or to defend against insurrection. Sailors knew of the deadly reputation of the African coast—the "white man's grave," as it was known—and might have to be impressed—kidnapped—for a voyage headed there, or their lives would have become so desperate that they found its hazards preferable to the alternatives open to them. The better-managed ships also carried "surgeons," that is, medical practitioners, sometimes trained in European scientific medicine and sometimes not, and also African assistants skilled in the healing techniques of Africa that the slaves understood.

The ships sailed out from Europe, or the Americas, with their holds filled with the wares in demand in Africa. Some, particularly if food was known to be in short supply on the portion of the coast to which they were destined, also carrried provisions for the slaves for the second leg of the voyage. They also brought the irons needed to chain their captives and other equipment specialized for restraining potentially rebellious passengers. Most vessels headed for well-known embarkation points—Luanda, Cabinda, or Molembo on the Loango Coast, Bonny or Brass or other towns in the creeks of the Niger Delta, Ouidah (Whydah) or one of the smaller ports on the Slave Coast, any of the several forts on the Gold Coast (Cape Coast, Axim, Elmina itself, etc.), the rivers of Upper Guinea, St. James fort on Bunce island at the mouth of the Gambia River, or St. Louis or Gorée near the mouth of the Senegal. Others aimed at no fixed destination but rather "coasted" from point to point, picking up a few slaves at each stop, following rumors of advantageous trade heard from other ships that they encountered as they went.

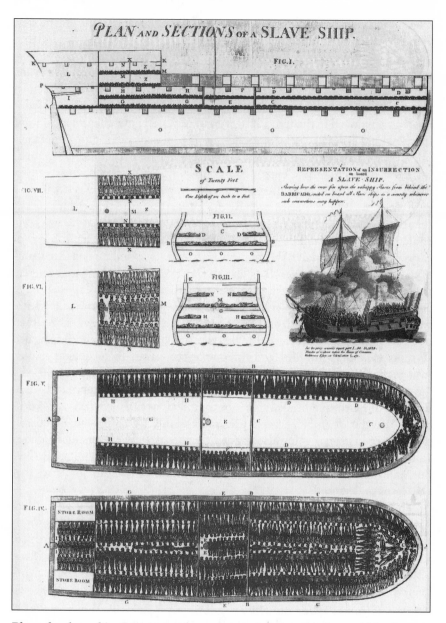

Plan of a slave ship. Large vessels were especially outfitted to enable them to carry as many individuals as possible within the smallest space, in conditions of extreme privation. From *An Essay on Colonization* by C. B. Wadstrom (London, 1744). Credit: The Library Company of Philadelphia.

Upon reaching the coast, the crew offloaded the bales and crates filled with merchandise, often employing skilled African canoemen to penetrate the dangerous surf that prevailed along the open coasts of lower Guinea, and set about converting the ship to carry its intended cargo of humans. These preparations involved buying and storing the food and—particularly—the water necessary to sustain several hundred people at sea for anywhere from four to twelve weeks; these supplies were critical, and their adequacy depended on assuming that the ship would complete its passage without serious delay. Several large ships attempting to buy provisions simultaneously at the same place could strain even a large port's ability to supply food. The crew also built in the low slave decks above the hold, mounted the chains, and strengthened the hatch to prevent escapes. Readying the ship in these ways might take weeks or months. While work proceeded on the vessel, the supercargo, captain, and other officers negotiated the purchase of their human cargo on shore, often buying slaves individually or in small groups, and made arrangements to have the people they purchased kept there in walled pens, called barracoons in English (from a Portuguese word for a temporary shelter set up to accommodate trade). Facilities of this sort were usually provided by African merchants and located where food and water were available, but European traders maintained slave pens of their own at the forts along the Gold and Slave Coasts and at Luanda.

The profitability of the voyage depended on the captain's or supercargo's skill in driving advantageous bargains, and success required great deftness and intimate knowledge of the distinctive commercial practices of the coast. Inexperienced traders found themselves badly taken by canny African customers, or stuck with colors or styles of merchandise unsalable in markets that were characterized by strong and volatile consumer preferences. Captains of competing ships sometimes exchanged portions of the goods they had brought with one another, in order to complete the exacting, diverse assortments of merchandise necessary to make up the "ounce," "bar," or "bundle" defined by the changing conditions of supply and demand that they encountered. Rhode Islanders, for example, supplied British slavers with the rum they lacked in return for textiles brought cheaply direct from England; in the same way, Bahians provided tobacco that Europe-based traders on the Mina (Slave) Coast needed, and Rio ships bought textiles from traders coming to Luanda from Portugal with the cane brandy they brought from Brazil. These lengthy preparations made it important to minimize the costs of managing pinned slaves while they waited, and so conditions in the barracoons were barely adequate to sustain the lives of the captives. However, since the fundamental commercial interest of the Europeans lay in keeping the slaves alive, excessive cruelty or neglect dangerous to their survival portended failure of the voyage.

When the ship finally lay in readiness and most of the slaves were purchased, boarding began. The captives were loaded in canoes or small boats and taken out to the large vessel lying at anchor well offshore. Along parts of the lower Guinea Coast, the dangerous surf made this operation another preserve of the skilled African boatmen, and a dangerous one for all concerned; in Upper Guinea and in central Africa, trade tended to be sheltered in bays, where the smooth surface of the water lessened the risks of a canoe capsizing, with loss of all or most of those aboard. On the ship, the crew awaited their prisoners in a state of tense alertness, since the degree of mobility allowed the slaves, as they were propelled over the high gunwales and then pushed down through the open hatch to the dark deck below, increased risks of accident or resistance. Boarding might take days, and sometimes weeks or months, in areas lacking developed onshore facilities for provisioning or for holding the slaves. Ships

Leaving Africa Enslaved

As the vessel drew nearer, we plainly saw the harbor and other ships of different kinds and sizes and we soon anchored amongst them off Bridgetown. Many merchants and planters came on board. . . . They put us in separate parcels and examined us attentively. They also made us jump, and pointed to the land, signifying we were to go there. We thought by this we should be eaten by these ugly men, as they appeared to us. When soon after we were all put down under the deck again, there was much dread and trembling among us and nothing but bitter cries to be heard all the night from the apprehensions. At last the white people got some old slaves from the land to pacify us. They told us we were not to be eaten, but to work, and were soon to go on land, where we should see many of our country people. This report eased us much, and sure enough, soon after we landed, there came to us Africans of all languages.

We were conducted immediately to the merchant's yard, where we were all pent up together, like so many sheep in a fold, without regard to sex or age. As every object was new to me, everything I saw filled me with surprise. What struck me first was that the houses were built with bricks and stones, and in every respect different from those I had seen in Africa, but I was still more astonished to see people on horseback. I did not know what this could mean, and indeed I thought these people were full of nothing but magical arts. While I was in this astonishment, one of my fellow prisoners spoke to a countryman of his about the horses who said they were the same kind they had in their country. I understood them, though they were from a distant part of Africa and I thought it odd I had not seen any horses there; but afterwards when I came to converse with different Africans, I found they had many horses amongst them, and much larger than those I then saw.

We were not many days in the merchant's custody, before we were sold after their usual manner. . . . On a signal given, (as the beat of a drum), buyers rush at once into the yard where the slaves are confined, and make a choice of that parcel they like best. The noise and clamor with which this is attended, and the eagerness visible in the countenances of the buyers, serve not a little to increase the apprehension of terrified Africans. . . . In this manner, without scruple, are relations and friends separated, most of them never to see each other again. I remember in the vessel in which I was brought over . . . there were several brothers who, in the sale, were sold in different lots; and it was very moving on this occasion, to see and hear their cries in parting.

Source: The Interesting Narrative of the Life of Olaudah Equiano or Gustavus Vassa the African (London, 1789).

taking on captives in this slow fashion, or those buying at several points along the coast, found themselves delayed for long periods with holds partially filled, their slaves sickening and starting to die, and provisions being steadily consumed by the survivors.

The accent then fell on speed, since the greater the delays in boarding or purchasing the slaves, and the longer the passage lasted, the more rapidly mortality increased. Food and water spoiled and ran short. Diseases incubating in the bodies of the slaves, particularly contagious maladies like tuberculosis, smallpox, or measles, could devastate a cargo. Members of the crew sickened

Horrors of the Middle Passage

On board some ships the common sailors are allowed to have intercourse with such of the black women whose consent they can procure. And some of them have been known to take the inconstancy of their paramours so much to heart as to leap overboard and drown themselves. The officers are permitted to indulge their passions among them at pleasure and sometimes are guilty of such excesses as disgrace human nature. . . .

The hardships and inconveniences suffered by the Negroes during the passage are scarcely to be enumerated or conceived. They are far more violently affected by seasickness than Europeans. It frequently terminates in death, especially among the women. But the exclusion of fresh air is among the most intolerable. For the purpose of admitting this needful refreshment, most of the ships in the slave trade are provided, between the decks, with five or sick air-ports on each side of the ship of about five inches in length and four in breadth. In addition, some ships, but not one in twenty, have what they denominate wind-sails. But whenever the sea is rough and the rain heavy it becomes necessary to shut these and every other conveyance by which the air is admitted. The fresh air being thus excluded, the Negroes' rooms soon grow intolerable hot. The confined air, rendered noxious by the effluvia exhaled from their bodies and being repeatedly breathed, soon produces fevers and fluxes which generally carries off great numbers of them.

During the voyages I made, I was frequently witness to the fatal effects of this exclusion of fresh air. I will give one instance, as it serves to convey some idea, though a very faint one, of their terrible sufferings. . . . Some wet and blowing weather having occasioned the port-holes to be shut and the grating to be covered, fluxes and fevers among the Negroes ensued. While they were in this situation, I frequently went down among them till at length their room became so extremely hot as to be only bearable for a very short time. But the excessive heat was not the only thing that rendered their situation intolerable. The deck, that is the floor of their rooms, was so covered with the blood and mucus which had proceeded from them in consequence of the flux, that it resembled a slaughter-house. It is not in the power of the human imagination to picture a situation more dreadful or disgusting. Numbers of the slaves having fainted, they were carried upon deck where several of them died and the rest with great difficulty were restored.

Source: Alexander Falconbridge, *An Account of the Slave Trade on the Coast of Africa* (London, 1788).

and died as well, leaving the remaining sailors shorthanded to manage the slaves and the ship. Ships becalmed in the low latitudes of the doldrums, which all voyages headed from tropical Africa to the Caribbean or North America had to cross, not only subjected their captives to prolonged hot, fetid, humid conditions on the slave deck but also became stinking time bombs of disease. Smallpox, often brought on board by slaves captured in times of drought and distress in their homelands, could sweep through the holds of the ships with devastating effect. Chronically, dysenteries acquired from contaminated water, and then communicated through the feces that accumulated in the slave deck, struck the slaves with such force that they impressed captains as the single greatest contributor to mortality. The slavers also believed that Africans died from an inexplicable lethargy, from which even forced feeding could not rescue them; despondency, even passively suicidal resignation, and shock from the horrors to which the slaves were exposed contributed to such despair, but starvation and dehydration surely played significant roles as well. Although some vessels completed the Middle Passage without a single reported death (if their records can be believed), losses to mortality typically ran in the vicinity of 10 to 15 percent by the eighteenth century, although a small proportion of voyages on which epidemics broke out, or that encountered abnormal delays, could lose 25 to 50 percent of their cargoes, and in exceptional cases, even more.

Upon making landfall in the Americas, captains, crews, and cargo faced still further delays, while the officers of the ports where they arrived quarantined slave ships out of not entirely unreasonable fears of the contagion they harbored. While waiting in the port for permission to land, they could at least take fresh water and supplies on board. Such delays provided time to clean up the surviving slaves and to restore them to whatever semblance of health and vitality could be achieved. Still, the haggard, emaciated, exhausted, ill, and frightened people, covered with oozing sores, prodded onto the deck when clearance finally was received struck observers as often little more than living skeletons. In a few places, such as the James and other deep rivers along the Chesapeake Bay in North America, captains sold their cargoes directly to planters with lands along the rivers' banks. Elsewhere, the slaves' point of entry was the towns of the Americas—Bridgetown in Barbados, Kingston in Jamaica, Charleston in South Carolina, Veracruz and Cartagena in the Spanish mainland territories and Havana in Cuba, Port-au-Prince in Saint Domingue, and San Juan in Puerto Rico, and in Brazil Bahia, Pernambuco, and Rio de Janeiro, not to mention dozens of other smaller ports and islands.

In these towns, merchants to whom the cargoes had been consigned took possession of the slaves and handled sale of them to their initial owners in the New World. Depending on the port of arrival in the Americas, these merchants, called "factors," employed a variety of selling strategies. In some places, they announced an offering price, accepted bids at that level for the slaves in the cargo who could bring it, then set another, lower price and sold the remaining slaves they could at it, and worked on down until all the least valued of the slaves had been disposed of; elsewhere, buyers initiated offers on individuals and small lots of the slaves in competition with one another, and the merchants sold to the highest bidders. On still other occasions, the whole group of slaves was confined in a walled yard, aspiring buyers were admitted, and at a given signal they were permitted to "scramble" for the individual slaves they preferred by laying their hands on them and marching them to the gate. Whatever the commercial arrangements, merchants uniformly tended to conceal the slaves' physical defects, exaggerated distinctive "tribal" characteristics and presented them naked for intimate physical examination in the most degrading circumstances imaginable.

These sales concluded the Middle Passage of the slaving voyage, but from the point of view of its investors in Europe they left unresolved the problems of realizing the proceeds from sale of the slaves back at home. Captains and merchants in the Americas often sold their cargoes of slaves on credit, taking payment in the form of commercial notes, or "bills of exchange," given by the planters promising payment in currency in London or Paris or Lisbon or Liverpool at some specified future point in time. The planters expected to make good on these promises by selling, in Europe, months later, the sugar or tobacco or cotton that they expected to employ the slaves they had bought to cultivate and harvest. These conventional business arrangements typically meant that the ships themselves were sold in the Americas or returned in ballast to Europe with the returns from the venture carried in the form of planters' bills. It was not an easy matter to rehabilitate a ship that had carried slaves for other cargoes.

The merchant sponsors of the venture in Europe could either sell the bills they received at once, at a discounted rate, or hold them in the hope that the coming harvest, often shipped on other vessels engaged in a shuttle trade between Europe and America, would sell at prices high enough to enable the planter to cover their full value. Only in the Spanish colonies and in Brazil during the mining boom, where slavers could hope for payment directly in silver or gold, could they aim to take their profits in more secure, prompt forms. By the time that a ship had been outfitted in its home port in Europe, had made its way to Africa, had lingered for months on the coast, and had completed the Middle Passage, and after the additional delays expectable in collecting from indebted planters, at least a year had elapsed under the best of circumstances; often two years passed, and less fortunate investors had to endure delays of three years. In the hundreds of total losses to piracy, naval war, shipwreck, disastrous mortality, or slave revolt, the returns never materialized.

Profits in a trade of this complexity, involving some 30,000 or so voyages, under greatly varying circumstances, over a span of four centuries, ranged from total loss to returns well above those prevailing in less risky forms of trade. Stories of the isolated instances of slavers who struck it rich in a single voyage surely circulated more widely than did word of the more common but humiliating voyages that ended in ruin. Traders valued goods on the African coasts at 100 percent above their costs of purchase, but, of course, such valuations were more an accounting convention than a realizable gain, since currency rarely circulated there. In any case, gains of this order only started to cover the considerable expenses of the voyage. Acquisition costs of slaves in Africa, stated in terms of what traders had paid for goods in Europe, sounded low in comparison to the currency values of the same slaves in the Americas. But optimistic expectations of gains were stated in terms of a very untypical male in prime physical condition, made no allowance for mortality, and did not anticipate losses and delays in collecting the returns in Europe. Rumored rich returns of this imaginary sort aside, the hazards were too many, Africa and the Americas too remote to influence advantageously, and captains and crews too unreliable for circumstances to turn out optimally on many occasions. But the rumors of easy riches attracted no shortage of naive beginners, traders down on their luck and desperate for a means to recover financially, and nervy speculators; large, experienced, cautious merchants had better odds of success and, by limiting their exposure to slaving amidst diverse other, safer investments, they could earn consistently respectable returns. Overall, profits from slaving would not have exceeded what economists call "economic rent," the general rate of interest and profit throughout the economy, perhaps 10 percent per annum in the European economy in these centuries. It would have required a fair number of very successful voyages to produce this average, balancing out the much greater number of failures and break-even ventures.

The eighteenth-century structures of the mature slave trade were the results of three centuries of earlier experimentation, hard lessons learned from the failures, and gradual improvements in the techniques of financing the trade and carrying its slaves. The sixteenth-century Portuguese, who had worked out the first ways of supporting modest numbers of captives at sea for extended periods of time, had barely managed to bring them back alive to nearby Europe; they had, fortuitously, found themselves with empty holds on the return from ventures out to Africa to sell bulky commodities for high-value but low-volume gold. Their intra-African trade before the 1570s involved even shorter distances. Mortality was nonetheless high. It had required the commercial wealth and sophistication of the Dutch to develop regular transatlantic transport of slaves to Brazil in that decade. Simultaneous reductions in the cost of slaves in Angola, during the chaos of the drought and warfare there, and opportunities to sell slaves for Spanish silver elsewhere in the Americas may have provided the extra margin of profit, on the return voyage to Europe, needed to recover from losses to mortality in the early years of the Middle Passage; those may have regularly reached 25 percent or more. The Dutch acquired a reputation for improved sailing technique, provisioning, and discipline in the first half of the seventeenth century, which the English and the French then adapted to their own transatlantic slaving, under the chartered companies, in the later decades of the 1600s. The free traders of the eighteenth century invested gains in further improvements, worked out more effi-cient strategies for feeding and disciplining their cargoes, and settled on the optimal size of the vessels they sent. They improved the organization of trade among themselves along the coasts of Africa, adding low-cost American cane brandies to the mix of goods sold, and supplementing gains from slaving with gold bought there from Brazilians and, later, silver from ships from the New World colonies of Spain. The English began to inoculate their slave cargoes against smallpox in the 1760s, and after the 1790s they employed Jennerian vaccines to reduce the ravages of that disease aboard the ships. Mortality accordingly declined throughout the eighteenth century, averaging around 10 percent by 1800 or so, and to half of that in the nineteenth-century trade. As the slaves survived, so the slavers prospered.

Individuals carried as slaves experienced little or none of this mercantilis-tic rationality, applied in the interest of their survival in the aggregate, although never in ways that respected their personal being. Captives set foot on the beaches after days or often weeks of forced marches in the interior with minimal rations. They waited there, often for weeks and months, in the crowded prisonlike conditions of the barracoons. They were terrified of the sea, which few of them had seen before, and which most feared—not unrea-sonably—as the abode of the dead. European ships, beneath their billowing white sails, they perceived as floating cloudlike on the horizon. They boarded the ships in dread, convinced that the Europeans were cannibals and meant to eat them; the huge copper cauldrons that sat on the ships' decks, meant for preparing the slaves' food, they perceived as intended to prepare the Euro-peans' meals from them, or to render their bodies directly into the imports that arrived in the holds of the ships. Stories recurrently circulated in Africa that centered on hellish images of boiling, baking, and rendering that, unknowingly, anticipated the fires that burnt the fields after the harvest and boiled the cane juice on the sugar plantations to which most slaves were des-tined. The red wines brought by the Europeans, it was said, were distilled from the blood of those who had been taken before; gunpowder, a particularly dan-gerous source of explosive smoke and flames, they saw as made from burning captives' bones. It was little wonder that some of those chained below decks lost their senses from fear, stopped eating or responding, and slipped in shock toward the terminal lethargy that so puzzled and enraged their captors.

Below decks, beneath securely bolted hatches, hundreds of bodies were chained in close, dark, airless proximity. Some ships had tiny bunks, really nothing more than shelves, on which slaves could recline; in others, the slaves lay side by side on the planking, rolling with the ship, bodies virtually touch-ing, for weeks on end. The crew attempted to obscure the stench that arose from the excreta of so many human beings trapped there together by white-washing the planking and bulkheads of the slave deck with lime or with strong solutions of vinegar, or fumigated by burning sulphur, gunpowder, tar, or other noxious chemicals. The unmistakable organic stink of most slave ships nonetheless trailed far downwind. The women were sometimes held in separate quarters above decks, but the crew intended this practice less to provide physical comfort than to give easy access to their bodies for sexual purposes. Discipline was thorough and rigid, partly to control the slaves and partly to keep careful accounts of the property of the venture, including taking daily rolls, or inventories, of the slaves and recording their illnesses and deaths for future reckoning to the backers of the voyage in Europe or America. The crew brought the male slaves above board regularly for exercise, and in some cases for feeding. At such times, with the slaves released from their chains, the captors watched their captives warily, whips and muskets in hand, for signs of unrest, and they dealt harshly with any who obstructed prescribed routines. It was then that they cleaned the areas below decks and removed the bodies of those who had died. Sharks, it was said, trailed the slave ships, in some cases all the way across the ocean.

Under the conditions of emotional shock, physical deprivation, and brutal treatment that slaves endured during the Middle Passage, mortality and sickness could hardly have been less. These occurred in spite of the slavers' earnest efforts to protect their property, although seldom—if ever—out of personal concern for the people they treated so harshly. The standards of food and water recommended by the end of the eighteenth century were comparable to those provided for soldiers and sailors in the armies and navies of the governments of Europe, and it is likely that the slaves ate better during their Middle Passage than they had during the previous weeks and months when they had been driven toward the coast in Africa. Medical science at that time had no remedies for most of the infestations from which the slaves suffered, and public sanitation—beyond quarantine of the afflicted—hardly existed. The Europeans, it was believed, died in Africa from miasmic poisons in the atmosphere, and the slaves under their care were thought to die from inherent weaknesses of their constitutions. In spite of the cruelties and hardships, most of the slaves survived to recover and work in the New World.

The extreme physical restraints imposed on them during the Middle Passage reduced the incidence of open revolt on the slave ships to scattered occasions. Cannon could be fired on threatening crowds of Africans, and a single misstep could mean a fatal fall into the sea. The crew never approached the slaves unarmed. Nonetheless, captives still mutinied from time to time, sometimes even gaining control of huge ships that they had no idea how to maneuver. The few dozen, perhaps a hundred, revolts recorded occurred often enough that the captors lived in constant fear and organized their ventures to prevent the slaves from breaking loose. Among the slaves, quiet conspiracy, biding one's time until arrival, and, surely, all manner of secret sorcery would have been the preferred strategies among those who retained the strength, presence of mind, and confidence to nurse their anger. Communication among the captives, who often spoke diverse and mutually unintelligible languages, was difficult, and coordination of their efforts suffered as a result. The slavers attempted to separate slaves who shared the same language, and revolts seem to have broken out particularly where groups from a single home region were able to collaborate. Captives confined together on a given ship formed bonds that they later called upon as former "shipmates" for the remainder of their lives as slaves in the Americas. Slaves survived the ordeal of the Middle Passage on the strength of courage, moral buoyancy, and sheer physical resilience.

ABOLITION OF THE TRADE
IN THE NINETEENTH CENTURY

Slaving continued to thrive in the Atlantic throughout the first half of the nineteenth century, in spite of growing British-led efforts to end a trade regarded by increasing numbers of reformers in Europe and the United States as a profound affront to human dignity. Impulses to abolish slaving in England arose from several sources. Evangelical Protestants in England, with Quakers and Methodists in the lead, agitated publicly from the middle of the century to recognize the humanity of the victims of the trade and urged the Parliament to prevent British subjects from participation in it. Other secular Enlightenment streams of thought fed into growing perception of the trade as not only immoral but also ultimately unprofitable. Economists saw opportunities for drawing profit in other ways from Africans, left in Africa as consumers of British exports and producers of raw materials for Britain. At the end of the century this largely intellectual and religious movement became a vehicle for broader political currents tending toward opening politics in Britain to mass participation. Religious fervor generated petitions signed by hundreds of thousands of ordinary people, who could not then vote for members of Parliament but who discovered principled protest as a means of making their voices heard. Those in power listened on an issue that did not directly challenge significant established interests uncomfortably close to home.

It was also recognized, and lamented, that British seamen on the Africa voyage died in large numbers. Some critics feared that the sugar islands of the West Indies had become unprofitable with the loss of the North American colonies after 1776 and were therefore no longer worth sustaining with continued infusions of slaves from Africa. The 1791 revolt of the slaves in French Saint Domingue—renamed Haiti by the victorious former slaves there—that all but removed France from the trade cast further doubt on the future of slavery itself in the British West Indies. War in Europe after 1793 disrupted the African trade further and brought additional, allegedly cheaper sources of sugar in the Indian Ocean under British rule. In Britain, Parliament itself remained deeply divided on the issue, but the domestic pressures, combined with changing assessments of Britain's national interest in the context of the war against Napoleon on the continent, produced a moment in 1807 when the abolitionists were able to advance their bill outlawing slaving on a favorable vote. From the first of January 1808, British subjects could no longer legally buy or carry slaves.

Abolition of the British trade, with the French temporarily driven out of slaving by the revolt in Saint Domingue and by naval blockade of France's continental ports, left the Portuguese and Brazilians temporarily as the principal slavers active in the Atlantic. England enjoyed substantial diplomatic influence over Portugal and her American colony and used it in the 1810s to conclude a series of treaties restricting slaving to the Atlantic south of the equator. The British navy dispatched a squadron to the coast of West Africa, once peace in Europe in 1815 had lessened its continental responsibilities there, and attempted to limit the activities of the dozens of slavers still buying captives there. The United States had abolished its trade in slaves also in 1807, partly as a result of moral and intellectual concerns like those fueling the movement in Britain and partly owing to a surplus of slaves then living in Virginia and elsewhere in the states of the Atlantic seaboard. But U.S. slavers nonetheless entered the Cuban trade of this era, under various legal subterfuges. The old English slaving interests in Liverpool found similarly indirect ways of supporting their slave-consuming customers in the Americas, particularly in Brazil. The Royal Navy established a West Africa Squadron to report on the movements of these ships, in violation of their nations' treaty commitments to Britain, and captured a few of them. The "recaptured" slaves on board the vessels seized were landed in Sierra Leone, the so-called "Province of Freedom" in Upper Guinea centered on the port of Freetown. There they were formally freed and entrusted to the care of the missionary interests that managed the colony.

The West Africa Squadron remained active and intrusive into the 1840s but barely inconvenienced the traders and certainly did not limit the overall volume of the trade. Meanwhile, the British government worked intermittently to pressure the slave-importing nations and colonies of the Americas to end their imports and, after British emancipation in 1834, to free their slaves as well. The French conceded the issue in 1848. The Brazilians, independent of Portugal since 1826 and much more dependent than the French on slavery, withdrew reluctantly after 1850. The United States, engaged with deep political concerns of its own with slavery in the 1840s and 1850s, cooperated only irregularly. The Spaniards in Cuba, with U.S. support, continued to import slaves until 1865. Thereafter, only a scattering of ships attempted to transport Africans to the Americas, under the pretense of signing them on under voluntary contracts of indenture. Free immigrants from Portugal, the Atlantic islands, and Italy replaced the slaves as low-paid, nominally free labor in Brazil. The British introduced Asians, as indentured laborers, to toil on the sugar plantations of the West Indies. In Angola, the Portuguese continued to buy people until the eve of World War I. The Atlantic slave trade thus ended where it had begun, moderate numbers of central Africans being taken to a tiny plantation island in the Gulf of Guinea.

Through abolition, the aggregate volume of the trade dropped only slightly, and irregularly, until the 1840s, when it entered a precipitous and effectively terminal decline that lasted through the 1850s and 1860s. The traders reorganized to elude the surveillance of the Royal Navy, improving their onshore facilities and working closely with the Africans who supplied the slaves to provision ships and assemble their cargoes in a matter of hours, rather than days or weeks. They were able to use larger, more efficient vessels as a result of the improved supplies of slaves in Africa. Their captives included more women and, particularly, more children and youths than during the height of the trade in the eighteenth century. They landed their captives in the Americas at small ports, or along abandoned beaches, in order to avoid detection by spies and British consuls positioned to report back to London on their activities. The slavers thus easily assumed the increased costs of illegality, or of the British pressure on their business.

As slaving declined irregularly during the nineteenth century, what remained of it was increasingly concentrated along Africa's Loango Coast, at Angolan ports south of the equator, and in the maze of waterways in the Niger Delta. Indian Ocean slaving in southeastern Africa became a significant contributor of captives, particularly for southern Brazil. The violence of the slaving in those regions was intense. Ivory hunters had led the turn to systematic slaving in southeastern Africa at the end of the eighteenth century, particularly when a severe drought subjected farmers and cattle raisers there to severe ecological pressures in the 1790s. Conflicts associated with the opening stages of slaving there, as throughout the history of slaving elsewhere in Africa, flared until the end of the nineteenth century. A particularly potent African form of military organization, employed to steal cattle and to capture women and children, emerged during the 1810s in Natal, the area south of the Limpopo River on the Indian Ocean coast. The people who took it up first thus became Zulu, famous for their military power. Many of their victims then imitated the Zulu to form other new, militarily dominant, highly mobile hordes of men, women, and their children and their herds of cattle. The wars of the 1820s and 1830s, exacerbated further by renewed drought, produced numerous captives, many of whom the Brazilians bought at the ports of Mozambique to carry across the Atlantic.

In West Africa exports of slaves ended, although very gradually, and left most kingdoms and trading networks of the region holding growing numbers of captives whom they could no longer sell for imports from abroad. Rulers of the large, and costly, slaving states there had lost the fundamental means by which they supported themselves. Supplies of slaves available increased at the same time, from Muslim-inspired holy wars that spread after 1800 through the *sudanic* latitudes along the fringes of the Sahara. Similar wars fought in the name of Islam generated captives all the way west to the headwaters of the Senegal River. The states and other communities in the forest region bought these captives and kept those they could no longer sell to Europeans to tend groves of palm trees, harvesting the red-orange nuts they bore, and pressing out the oil contained in them to sell to a new generation of "legitimate" traders, British and others, that appeared on the coast. British abolitionists touted the commerce in palm oil as "legitimate," in contrast—as they thought—to the condemned trade in slaves, and only gradually realized that Africans produced the new export commodities through intensified raiding and slaving of the very sort that they meant to eliminate. As the Atlantic trade declined, slavery and slave dealing spread even more widely in West Africa and underwrote the beginnings of a peasant economy there based on commercial agriculture.

IMAGES OF AFRICA, FROM AMERICA

Slaveholders in the Americas realized little of the history of Africa, slaving, and the diaspora now recovered in an age of reduced racial pretension and vastly increased knowledge. At the time, masters saw only strange dark faces and imagined the thoughts in the slaves' heads through their own stereotyped fantasies of a savage continent. They substituted invented "tribal," almost racial, identities and characters, based on the ethnic and cultural differences that Africans brought with them from their communities as substitutes for true understanding. These tribal notions—about the "Coromantees," "Eboes," "Angolans," or "Mandingo"—only crudely approximated the subtle and complex realities of Africans' lives, at best. Some names, like "Mina," really reflected only the port where the Europeans had purchased the slaves. Others referred generally to the region from which slaves came, and even then not always in terms on which even the Europeans could agree; for the Portuguese, "Angola" meant the coast south of the Zaire River, while for the English it meant the Loango Coast to the north. Other labels, like "Eboe" (Igbo) or "Mandingo" (Mande), referred only to linguistic and cultural backgrounds much broader and vaguer than the actual communities in which the people designated by them had in fact been raised. Attributed "ethnic" identities of this sort reflected the evolving history of Africa at the time, including the new communities forming around the currents of trade, rather than a permanent, inherent character of the people to whom they were applied. They were also products of European and American needs to categorize, although incomprehendingly, the African strangers in their midst, and thus to calm the fears they aroused.

Most of the Africans landed in the Americas had been forcibly removed from home and community and experienced enslavement as profoundly lonely and isolating. But by the time they set foot on shore in the New World they had already started to draw on these same general similarities of origin as the only means available of finding common ground with their fellow slaves, at the start no less strangers to them than to their captors, through sharing ships' holds during the Middle Passage, time spent together in merchants' barra-coons, and then common experiences in mining camps and plantation bar-racks. From beyond the trauma of capture, the march to the coast, the Middle Passage, and sale, they drew on various recollections of home, along with the intensely shared experience of slavery, to start to build new lives together, in the New World.

Where the trade continued to provide a stream of new arrivals from Africa, they must have heard news from home and found it easier to replen-ish traditions from the past. Large concentrations of slaves, in towns or on plantations of substantial size, enabled them to live more in worlds they cre-ated for themselves than did isolation among Europeans on small farms or in the big houses of the plantations. Where European slavers concentrated heavily on one or two ports in Africa, the slaves came from similar back-grounds and they added identifiably specific ethnic flavors to their lives. Conditions favored preservation of such identifiably African practices more in the islands of the Caribbean, particularly those of the French, and in northeastern Brazil than in North America. The English brought slaves from many parts of Africa, and so Africans in their colonies tended to develop cul-tures of vaguer ethnic quality. They also terminated their trade earlier than the continental European nations, thus cutting off the sources of cultural renewal from Africa. In the British North American colonies, later the United States, slaves managed to establish families of their own early in the eighteenth century, lessening the need for further imports, and eventually—certainly by the nineteenth century—raising their children more and more as Americans. They thus lost touch with their roots in Africa more than did their counterparts in the Caribbean or Brazil.

American images of Africa, particularly in the United States, divided into white racist stereotypes of a primitive land, largely unchanging until the impo-sition of European colonial authority at the end of the nineteenth century, and African-American dreams of lives less beleaguered than their own. Both sides of the racially defined societies of America thus created memories that became unmoored from the realities of the Africa their ancestors had known, during the era of the continent's integration into the merchant capitalist economy of the Atlantic. There, in fact, ordinary people, often trapped in the insoluble dilemmas of human life everywhere, made what they could of tragic circum-stances they could not control. They thought in terms very unlike those pre-vailing later in the modern "West," and decisions that made sense to them are not always immediately intelligible today. To a lesser degree, the Europeans who bought captives there also lived in a world unlike our own and commit-ted deeds that, today, would bring universal condemnation. Beyond the feel-ings of outrage that the sufferings of that era can evoke in the present age, there lived human beings whose contributions to them we can seek to under-stand, even if we do not approve.

FOR FURTHER READING

Blackburn, Robin. *The Making of New World Slavery: From the Baroque to the Modern 1492-1800*. London: Verso, 1998.

Conniff, Michael L., and Thomas J. Davis. *Africans in the Americas: A History of the Black Diaspora*. New York: St. Martin's, 1994.

Curtin, Philip D. *The Atlantic Slave Trade: A Census*. Madison: University of Wisconsin Press, 1972.

———. *Economic Change in Pre-Colonial Africa: Senegambia in the Era of the Slave Trade*. Madison: University of Wisconsin Press, 1975.

———. *The Rise and Fall of the Plantation Complex: Essays in Atlantic History*. 2nd ed. New York: Cambridge University Press, 1998.

Eltis, David. *Economic Growth and the Ending of the Transatlantic Slave Trade*. New York: Oxford University Press, 1989.

Inikori, Joseph E., and Stanley Engerman, eds. *The Atlantic Slave Trade: Effects on Economies, Societies, and Peoples in Africa, the Americas, and Europe*. Durham, N.C.: Duke University Press, 1992.

Klein, Herbert S. *African Slavery in Latin America and the Caribbean*. New York: Oxford University Press, 1988.

Law, Robin C.C. *The Slave Coast of West Africa 1550-1750: The Impact of the Atlantic Slave Trades on an African Society*. New York: Oxford University Press, 1991.

Lovejoy, Paul E. *Transformations in Slavery: A History of Slavery in Africa*. New York: Cambridge University Press, 1983.

Manning, Patrick. *Slavery and African Life: Occidental, Oriental, and African Slave Trades*. New York: Cambridge University Press, 1990.

Meillassoux, Claude. *The Anthropology of Slavery: The Womb of Iron and Gold*. Chicago: University of Chicago Press, 1992.

Miers, Suzanne, and Igor Kopytoff, eds. *Slavery in Africa: Historical and Anthropological Perspectives*. Madison: University of Wisconsin Press, 1977.

Miller, Joseph C. *Way of Death: Merchant Capitalism and the Angolan Slave Trade, 1730-1830*. Madison: University of Wisconsin Press, 1996.

Solow, Barbara L., ed. *Slavery and the Rise of the Atlantic System*. New York: Cambridge University Press, 1991.

Thomas, Hugh. *The Slave Trade: The Story of the Atlantic Slave Trade, 1440-1870*. New York: Simon & Schuster, 1997.

Thornton, John K. *Africa and Africans in the Making of the Atlantic World, 1400-1800*. 2nd ed. New York: Cambridge University Press, 1998.

part 2.

This "Peculiar Institution"

chapter 2

Creating a Biracial Society, 1619-1720

Jean R. Soderlund

F ROM THE TIME THE FIRST AFRICANS stepped onto Virginia's shore, the English mainland colonies moved toward a biracial society, one in which people from Africa and their descendants—including those of mixed African and European heritage—held a subordinate legal, social, and economic status. This caste system originated in three distinct circumstances: the demand for workers (especially on southern plantations); the availability of human beings for sale by means of the Atlantic slave trade; and the cultural predisposition of the English to regard darker-skinned people as inferior, and hence, suitable for enslavement. In the English colonies, this racial hierarchy was first articulated to its fullest in the West Indies, particularly in Barbados, which served as a model for the mainland plantation colonies in the Chesapeake Bay region and South Carolina. New England and the Middle Atlantic region, although less entrenched in slave ownership than the southern provinces, also profited from the labor of enslaved Africans and erected a hierarchical social framework based on notions of race.

The origins of black bondage in English America can be found primarily in the need for laborers to plant, cultivate, harvest, and process highly profitable staple crops. Without this demand for labor and the capital to purchase Africans, slavery would have remained a marginal institution. But also important were the power English colonists had to keep other humans enslaved and their willingness to use that power. Africans arrived in chains, far from their homelands and usually isolated from people they had known. They were sold quickly, becoming subject to the owner's authority and restrictive colonial laws. The fact that slaves were defined as property gave masters wide powers under the English common law, even without specific statutes establishing and governing the institution. The inclination of English men and women to exploit Africans as slaves came from ethnocentrism, hierarchical beliefs, and prejudice against blackness, all leading to the idea that Africans were an inferior, pagan people who could be held as property. To justify keeping Africans as slaves, English colonists used color of skin more than any other attribute such as religion or customs.

The English used the same rationale for enslaving Native Americans, whom they also considered a debased, heathen race. Some colonizers expected to exploit the indigenous people of America as had the Spanish, but high mortality among Indians, the opportunity to escape when held as slaves in the vicinity of their homes, and the colonists' military weakness prevented large-scale enslavement of Native Americans. When the English had the opportunity to enslave Indians, they displayed few qualms about the practice. New Englanders sold prisoners of war to the West Indies and elsewhere after the Pequot massacre of 1637 and Metacom's War forty years later. South Carolinians stimulated a brisk slave trade with southern Indians who captured members of competing tribes. The Carolina merchants found a market for the enslaved Indians in the Caribbean.

During the period before 1660, the English founded colonies successfully in three regions of the New World: the West Indies, the Chesapeake, and New England. Slavery existed in each of these areas but with differences that underscored the importance of economic factors in fostering its growth. In Barbados, planters moved rapidly into the business of making sugar in the 1640s. Two decades later, enslaved Africans constituted 90 percent of the island's labor force. The Chesapeake colonies of Virginia and Maryland created a plantation society based on tobacco, but until after 1680 white indentured servants remained the principal source of labor. In New England, where family farms, fishing, and shipping constituted the basis of the economy, slavery never became dominant, despite the fact that Massachusetts was the first English colony to provide a written rationalization for human bondage.

SLAVERY IN BARBADOS

Though not the first permanent English colony in the New World, Barbados predated others in adopting slavery as its primary source of labor. The island's development influenced other English colonies in the Caribbean—the Leewards and Jamaica—and in British North America as well. In 1627, the English settled the lush island 21 miles long by 14 miles wide; for about a decade it drew young male indentured servants with the promise of 10 acres of land as freedom dues. When all of the arable land on the tiny island had been distributed by 1638, Barbados became a much less attractive destination for English people. During these early years, settlers lacked a highly marketable crop. They tried tobacco and cotton, but produced only a poor grade. Some planters also grew and refined sugar during the 1630s, but it was not until after 1640 that the sugar economy moved into full swing. The Dutch assisted the conversion by offering to market the sugar in Amsterdam at high prices. The Dutch could interlope in the English colonies at this time because the English government was disrupted by civil war. Crucially, Dutch slave traders promised to sell enslaved Africans to the Barbados planters, who needed large numbers of workers to produce sugar and expected few voluntary bondsmen from England. Sugar was highly labor intensive, requiring about one worker per acre of cane. It also required significant capital. Once the success of sugar became known, wealthy English investors bought up land from ordinary Barbados farmers, acquired expensive machinery for processing the cane, and purchased hundreds of Africans. Barbados developed on a capitalist model, as a place to make money, rather than as a home in which to raise a family. Africans faced severe exploitation by planters who thought it cheaper to replace laborers who died from overwork and inadequate food than to provide reasonable living and working conditions. Almost overnight, Barbados was transformed into a society dominated by rich planters, with an economy so focused on sugar cultivation that it was dependent upon England, Ireland, and North America for food and lumber.

The English planters in Barbados experienced little, if any, hesitation before purchasing human beings as slaves. Twenty-seven thousand Africans toiled in the island's sugar fields in 1660, surpassing the number of whites. After that date, the black population continued to grow while the number of whites declined. The planters eagerly participated in the Atlantic slave system that the Portuguese, Spanish, and Dutch had expanded over the previous two centuries. Because mortality under the sugar regime ran so high that Africans could not naturally reproduce their numbers, the planters found it necessary to import slaves. Between 1640 and 1700, an estimated 135,000 Africans were imported into Barbados, yet in the latter year about 42,000 survived.

The Barbadians, like other English and Europeans, justified enslaving Africans for life—and for the lives of their progeny—on the grounds that these dark-skinned people were pagan, uncivilized, and inferior human beings. Europeans believed that hierarchies existed in human society, with Christians, for example, superior to heathens. Europeans found serious deficiencies in African religion, social customs, dress, and political organization; they considered the people of sub-Saharan Africa lower on the scale of humanity and justifiably enslaved. Most crucial for the English was skin color. English language and culture differentiated sharply between white and black, with whiteness denoting what was good and pure, and blackness suggesting sin and filth. Some in Tudor and Stuart England suggested that the Africans' dark brown color resulted from God's biblical curse on the descendants of Ham, who had viewed the nakedness of his father, Noah.

The English, like other Europeans, focused on differences rather than on traits they held in common with Africans, traits such as belief in a single Creator, overwhelming physical similarities, and comparable livelihoods as agriculturalists and livestock raisers. In encounters with Africans, the English compared favorably their own light skin to the Africans' darker color. They exaggerated the variation in skin shade by calling Africans "blacks," or using the Spanish and Portuguese term *Negroes*. While the demand for labor was the fundamental reason for slavery's development in Barbados, these English cultural attitudes, the example of the Portuguese, Spanish, and Dutch, and the existence of the Atlantic slave trade made the decision to purchase Africans seem natural. Because Africans seemed so different, they could be held as property. As troubling as it is to contemplate, many English masters considered their slaves much like livestock.

In 1661, the Barbados ruling class legislated an intricate slave code. It was of prime influence on lawmakers in other English colonies as they became concerned about keeping control over growing populations of forced laborers. In writing the law, Barbados assemblymen had economic motives in wanting to legalize permanent, hereditary bondage and retain power over recalcitrant workers. But the legislators also betrayed their belief that the physical and cultural inferiority of Africans meant that they should not be subject to the same protections and laws as whites. The code's preamble labeled blacks "an heathenish, brutish and an uncertaine, dangerous kinde of people." The Barbados code defined slaves as both property and human beings, with more emphasis on the former. As chattel whose bondage was lifelong and heritable, they held a status that had been eliminated from practice among the English for centuries. Slaves lacked most of the rights of free whites and indentured servants. Only to a minimal extent did the Barbados code give Africans protection. A master could without penalty injure or kill a slave during punishment; if the owner murdered an African for no reason, and this could be proven, the maximum penalty was a fine of about £25. The code distinguished in a number of ways between indentured servants and slaves. Even minimum living standards differed, for the code specified food and clothing allowances for servants but only clothing allotments for slaves. Servants had the right to a jury trial and could sue their masters in court if not treated decently. Masters could be charged with murder if they killed a servant and fined for failure to provide medical care. Servants had their terms extended by several years for theft, physically attacking their master, or running away, while an enslaved African would be whipped, branded, or even put to death for these same misdeeds.

Planters in Barbados and other colonies reserved the most barbaric sentences for slaves accused of rebellion. When a plot was uncovered in Barbados in 1675, the magistrates executed thirty-five Africans by burning them alive or beheading them and dragging their bodies through the streets. The intent, of course, was to make an example of them to other slaves. In Jamaica, where mountains and its larger size increased the possibility of successful uprisings, the authorities tried to deter plotters with even more extreme measures. After a 1678 insurrection, a white overseer described the torturing of

The great majority of African captives were destined for Latin America and the Caribbean, where they were employed on large plantations harvesting crops like sugar and indigo. From *Pomet's Compleat History of Druggs* (London, 1737). Credit: The Library Company of Philadelphia.

one participant: "His leggs and armes was first brocken in peeces with stakes, after which he was fasten'd upon his back to the Ground—a fire was made first to his feete and burn'd uppe by degrees; I heard him speake severall words when the fire consum'd all his lower parts as far as his Navill. The fire was upon his breast (he was burning neere 3 houres) before he dy'd."

The Barbados code of 1661 contained provisions that would become common in slave codes in other English colonies. Their purpose was to control the behavior of blacks and thereby prevent opportunities for rebellion. Planters were expected to police their slaves and keep them from acquiring weapons. Blacks were forbidden to travel without a pass and could be whipped by any white who discovered them abroad without written permission. The Barbados lawmakers omitted from their slave code any injunction against interracial sex, probably because they wanted to retain legal access to slave women. Mulatto children sometimes received higher status than Africans, with such job assignments as house servant or craftsman, but if their mother was a slave, then so were they. Occasionally an owner/father freed his mulatto children and their mother, but manumission was rare in seventeenth-century Barbados. Freed people remained subject to the slave code and could not vote, own any considerable amount of land, or hold well-paying jobs. Thus Barbados, like other English colonies subsequently, created a caste system based on skin color and perceptions of race. All Africans and their children, even those who were half English, were classified as blacks and retained a subordinate legal and social status.

While the founding of Virginia predated Barbados by twenty years, the transition from a labor force dominated by indentured servants to one comprised largely of slaves proceeded much more slowly there and in neighboring Maryland than in the sugar islands. The Jamestown settlement faltered badly for a decade after initial landfall in 1607. Many of the colonists were ill-suited for agriculture and refused to work. They stirred up trouble with the Native Americans by stealing their corn and attacking them without provocation. Mortality was devastatingly high as a result of disease and lack of food. Virginia gained a more secure footing after 1617 with the adoption of tobacco as its cash crop. Just as Barbadians would later find a market in Europeans' craving for sugar, Virginians tapped a new, quickly expanding market for American "smoke." At the same time, the Virginia Company revised its policies so that individual planters could own land. Indentured servants were attracted to the colony with the promise of acreage at the end of their service.

SLAVERY IN VIRGINIA AND MARYLAND

The first record of Africans in Virginia dates from 1619, though at least one woman may have come earlier. While some historians have conjectured that these blacks became indentured servants, little is known of their status. According to colonist John Rolfe, a Dutch ship left "twenty and odd Negroes" at the plantation of Abraham Piersey, a representative of the Virginia Company and the wealthiest man in the colony. While slave traders brought more Africans in subsequent years, no great shift to slave labor occurred soon. In 1625, Africans numbered twenty-three of a total Virginia population of more than twelve hundred. Fifteen were the property of two men: Abraham Piersey and George Yeardley, who had served as governor. After the founding of Maryland in 1634, the percentage of Africans in the Chesapeake population remained low. In 1660, about nine hundred blacks and twenty-four thousand Europeans lived in Virginia and Maryland. The contrast by that year with Barbados, where Africans outnumbered whites, can be explained by the continuing immigration of European servants. Unlike the situation on the small sugar island, good tobacco land remained available in the Chesapeake until at least 1660. Only after that date, as accessible land became scarcer and more tempting opportunities emerged in Carolina and the Middle Colonies, did the supply of white labor decline. When the number of white immigrants decreased, but the demand for labor continued to grow, Chesapeake tobacco planters turned to African slaves. The percentage of blacks in the total population expanded from 3.6 percent in 1660, to 7 percent in 1680, 13 percent in 1700, and 19 percent in 1720. In the late seventeenth century, the monopoly of the Royal African Company to import enslaved Africans into English colonies limited the development of slavery in the Chesapeake. When the monopoly ended in 1698, the supply of black laborers increased greatly.

Much debate has surrounded the status of the blacks in Virginia prior to the 1660s, when the assembly passed a series of statutes formally establishing slavery. Some historians have argued that Africans were treated much like white indentured servants in these early years, while others point to distinctions made between Africans and Europeans. During these decades, some blacks achieved freedom and even acquired land. But others remained servants

The First Africans Arrive in Jamestown

John Rolfe to Sir Edwin Sandys, January? 1619/20.

About the latter end of August, a Dutch man of Warr of the burden of a 160 tunes arriued at Point-Comfort, the Commador[s] name Capt Jope, his Pilott for the West Indies one M[r] Marmaduke an Englishman. They mett wth the Trer in the West Indyes, and determyned to hold consort shipp hetherward, but in their passage lost one the other. He brought not any thing but 20. and odd Negroes, w[ch] the Governo[r] and Cape Marchant bought for victualle (whereof he was in greate need as he p/re/tended) at the best and easyest rate they could. He hadd a lardge and ample Comyssion from his Excellency to range and to take purchase in the West Indyes.

Source: Susan Myra Kingsbury, ed., *The Records of the Virginia Company of London*, 4 vols. (Washington, D.C.: U.S. Government Printing Office, 1933), 3:243.

for life, despite the lack of a law condoning perpetual bondage. Virginians, like colonists elsewhere, adopted slavery by custom, codifying its existence only after its significance became clear.

Evidence concerning slavery in Virginia before 1640 is spotty. Traders sold Africans to white Virginians much as they would have marketed them in other colonies, as part of the Atlantic slave system that took people from Africa to serve as slaves in the New World. Early Virginia documents distinguished consistently between white servants and blacks, always with the suggestion that Africans were subordinate. In a 1627 will, Governor George Yeardley bequeathed his "goode debts, chattels, servants, negars, cattle or any other thing" to his heirs. Censuses of the 1620s point to a lower regard for Africans: English settlers were listed with full names while most Africans were enumerated simply with a first name or designated as "negar" or "Negro." For example, Anthony and Mary Johnson, who by the 1650s acquired a plantation of 250 acres and owned a slave, were referred to as "Antonio a Negro" and "Mary a Negro Woman" in earlier records. On the other hand, the fact that

Virginia Law, 1661/62

ACT CII, Run-aways.

WHEREAS there are diverse loytering runaways in this country who very often absent themselves from their masters service and sometimes in a long time cannot be found, that losse of the time and the charge in the seeking them often exceeding the value of their labor: *Bee it therefore enacted* that all runaways that shall absent themselves from their said masters service, shalbe lyable to make satisfaction by service after the times by custome or indenture is expired (vizt.) double their times of service soe neglected, and if the time of their running away was in the crop or the charge of recovering them extraordinary the court shall lymitt a longer time of service proportionable to the damage the master shall make appeare he hath susteyned, and because the adjudging the time they should serve is often referred untill the time by indenture is expired, when the proofe of what is due is very uncertaine, *it is enacted* that the master of any runaway that intends to take the benefit of this act, shall as soone as he hath recovered him carry him to the next commissioner and there declare and prove the time of his absence, and the charge he hath bin at in his recovery, which commissioner thereupon shall grant his certificate, and the court on that certificate passe judgment for the time he shall serve for his absence; and in case any English servant shall run away in company of any negroes who are incapable of making satisfaction by addition of a time, *it is enacted* that the English soe running away in the company with them shall at the time of service to their owne masters expired, serve the masters of the said negroes for their absence soe long as they should have done by this act if they had not beene slaves, every christian in company with them shall by proportion among them, either pay lower thousand five hundred pounds of tobacco and caske or fower yeares service for every negroe soe lost or dead.

Source: William H. Hening, ed., *Statutes at Large* (Richmond: State of Virginia, 1809–23), vol. 2, pp. 116–17.

blacks like the Johnsons obtained freedom and land demonstrates that a rigid system of perpetual servitude was not yet in place in Virginia before 1640. While some Africans who came during the early years remained enslaved throughout their lives, others like the Johnsons and Anthony Longoe, who obtained his freedom in 1635, held a status closer to indentured servitude.

After 1639, evidence that slavery existed in Maryland and Virginia—and that lifetime hereditary bondage was judged appropriate for Africans but not for Europeans—is more plentiful. Maryland moved much more quickly than Virginia, for just five years after settlement the assembly noted the legality of slavery, parenthetically, in two separate laws. One act placed limits on the terms of service of "all persons being Christians (Slaves excepted)" who arrived in the colony as servants without indentures; the other law provided that "all the Inhabitants of this Province being Christians (Slaves excepted) Shall have and enjoy all such rights liberties immunities priviledges and free customs within this Province as any naturall born subject of England." In Virginia in 1640, the court distinguished between two white servants and an African who ran away by requiring the whites to serve four additional years while the black man received a term for life. From the 1640s on, colonial records made more frequent reference to lifetime bondage for Africans and their children. The tax laws of both Virginia and Maryland, passed in 1643 and 1654 respectively, further demonstrated that the colonists viewed Africans as different from

Maryland Act Concerning Negroes and Other Slaves, 1664

An Act Concerning Negroes & Other Slaves

Bee itt Enacted by the Right Hon[ble] the Lord Proprietary by the advice and Consent of the upper and lower house of this present Generall Assembly That all Negroes or other slaves already within the Province And all Negroes and other slaves to bee hereafter imported into the Province shall serve Durante Vita And all Children born of any Negro or other slave shall be Slaves as their fathers were for the terme of their lives And forasmuch as divers freeborne English women forgettfull of their free Condicõn and to the disgrace of our Nation doe intermarry with Negro Slaves by which alsoe divers suites may arise touching the Issue of such woemen and a great damage doth befall the Masters of such Negros for prevention whereof for deterring such freeborne women from such shamefull Matches Bee itt further Enacted by the Authority advice and Consent aforesaid That whatsoever free borne woman shall inter marry with any slave from and after the Last day of this present Assembly shall Serve the master of such slave dureing the life of her husband And that all the Issue of such freeborne woemen soe marryed shall be Slaves as their fathers were And Bee itt further Enacted that all the Issues of English or other freeborne woemen that have alreaoy marryed Negroes shall serve the Masters of their Parents till they be Thirty yeares of age and noe longer.

Source: William H. Browne et al., ed., *Archives of Maryland*, 65 vols. (Baltimore, Maryland Historical Society, 1883–1952), I, pp. 533–34.

themselves. Everyone who worked in the field was to be taxed—all men and black women. White women apparently were not expected to tend tobacco. Both colonies also excepted blacks, but not white servants, from the obligation to bear arms.

As more and more Africans arrived in the Chesapeake colonies after 1660, the assemblies responded by passing laws to define and justify slavery. And as in Barbados, they devised statutes to control blacks as well. The result was legal entrenchment of the institution and the narrowing of opportunities for Africans to become free. In the early 1660s, Virginia joined Maryland in enacting laws that recognized differences in the terms of white servants and African slaves. Statutes passed by both colonies defined slavery as lasting a person's lifetime and descending from mother to child. Colonists conceived slavery to be the normal status for Africans but not for Europeans.

In the last third of the seventeenth century, both Chesapeake colonies created in statute a clearly articulated caste system based on race. A person's racial classification denoted status: all Africans and their descendants experienced severe discrimination, whether enslaved or free. Chesapeake lawmakers also made emancipation as difficult as possible. In 1667, Virginia ruled that conversion to Christianity would not result in freedom. Two years later, the assembly held that any master who killed a slave during punishment would not be guilty of a felony. The evolving Black Codes banned interracial marriage,

Virginia Act for Preventing Negroes Insurrections, 1680

ACT X, An act for preventing Negroes Insurrections.

WHEREAS the frequent meeting of considerable numbers of negroe slaves under pretence of feasts and burialls is judged of dangerous consequence; for prevention whereof for the future, *Bee it enacted by the kings most excellent majestie by and with the consent of the generall assembly, and it is hereby enacted by the authority aforesaid,* that from and after the publication of this law, it shall not be lawfull for any negroe or other slave to carry or arme himselfe with any club, staffe, gunn, sword or any other weapon of defence or offence, nor to goe or depart from of his masters ground without a certificate from his master, mistris or overseer, and such permission not to be granted but upon perticuler and necessary occasions; and every negroe or slave soe offending not haveing a certificate as aforesaid shalbe sent to the next constable, who is hereby enjoyned and required to give the said negroe twenty lashes on his bare back well layd on, and soe sent home to his said master, mistris or overseer. *And it is further enacted by the authority aforesaid* that if any negroe or other slave shall presume to lift up his hand in opposition against any christian, shall for every such offence, upon due proofe made thereof by the oath of the party before a magistrate, have and receive thirty lashes on his bare back well laid on.

Source: William H. Hening, ed., *Statutes at Large* (Richmond: State of Virginia, 1809–23), vol. 2, pp. 481–82.

forbade owners from freeing their slaves except under extraordinary circumstances, and restricted slaves from traveling without permission, marrying legally, holding property, testifying against whites, or congregating in groups. In 1705, the Virginia assembly declared all slaves to be real estate rather than personal property, a change Barbados had made in 1668. Virginia also gathered its various laws governing slavery into the slave code of 1705, an action Maryland took in 1715.

As in Barbados, these statutes limited the liberties of free blacks, for legislators generally failed to distinguish between enslaved and free Africans when proscribing behavior. In 1705, for example, the Virginia assembly made it illegal for any black person to strike any white, even an indentured servant. This included self-defense. Free blacks were barred from owning white servants, holding office, and testifying in court. They constantly faced the threat of reenslavement. Thus, during the years from 1660 to 1720, as the population of Africans and African Americans grew in the Chesapeake, colonial elites developed increasingly rigid legal codes that restricted the rights of slaves and free blacks. These laws, including ones against miscegenation, raised the wall between blacks and whites and bonded the loyalties of lower-class whites to the elites, thus reinforcing social hierarchy based on skin color rather than economic condition.

SLAVERY IN NEW ENGLAND

In New England, slavery developed in yet another variation. While the Puritan magistrates of Massachusetts Bay Colony established the institution by statute as early as 1641, the employment of enslaved Africans remained marginal throughout the region. In 1660, blacks numbered six hundred of a total New England population of thirty-three thousand; until 1720 they were about 2 percent of the region's inhabitants. The foundations of New England's economy were farming, fishing, and trade. Families supplied most of the labor needed to raise grains and livestock. Those who required additional help employed day laborers for busy times such as planting and harvest or, if they had the capital, purchased a few indentured servants or slaves. Only in Rhode Island's fertile Narragansett country where large dairy and cattle estates had been formed did planters own considerable numbers of Africans.

In the words of historian Winthrop Jordan, "The question with New England slavery is not why it was weakly rooted, but why it existed at all." His conclusion was that New Englanders, like other English people, were prepared by their ethnocentric attitudes to regard Africans as "strangers" who could be justifiably enslaved. Focusing on differences in skin color, customs, and religion, the Puritans regarded Africans as "other." Nevertheless, Jordan also demonstrated that economic interest was important, for New England merchants quickly saw promise in a lucrative trade with the burgeoning sugar islands. While exploiting the labor of Africans in wheat and rye fields proved unnecessary, sending provisions to Caribbean sugar plantations became the backbone of New England trade.

For both cultural and economic reasons, New Englanders had little inclination to question the enslavement of blacks. The Massachusetts Bay Colony, in its Body of Liberties of 1641, limited slavery to "lawfull Captives taken in just warres, and such strangers as willingly sell themselves or are sold to us." Connecticut and Plymouth adopted the same policy, which justified both the sale of Native Americans whom they took as prisoners of war and the purchase of Africans who were captured by someone else. Even in Rhode Island, where the government tolerated Europeans of various religions and attempted to

The Slave Trade in Early Rhode Island

Governor Samuel Cranston to the Board of Trade, 1708

I. That from 24th of June, 1698, to the 25th of December, 1707, we have not had any negroes imported into this colony from the coast of Africa, neither on the account of the Royal African Company, or by any of the separate traders.

2 That on the 30th day of May, 1696, arrived at this port from the coast of Africa, the brigantine *Seaflower*, Thomas Windsor, master, having on board her forty-seven negroes, fourteen of which he disposed of in this colony, for betwixt £30 and £35 per head; the rest he transported by land for Boston, where his owners lived.

3 That on the 10th of August, the 19th and 28th of October, in the year of 1700, sailed from this port three vessels, directly for the coast of Africa; the two former were sloops, the one commanded by Nicho's Hillgrove, the other by Jacob Bill: the last a ship, commanded by Edwin Carter, who was part owner of the said three vessels, in company with Thomas Bruster, and John Bates, merchants of Barbadoes, and separate vessels arriving safe to Barbadoes from the coast of Africa, where they made the disposition of their negroes.

4. That we have never had any vessels from the coast of Africa to this colony, nor any trade there, the brigantine above mentioned excepted.

5. That the whole and only supply of negroes to this colony, is from the island of Barbadoes; from whence is imported one year with another, betwixt twenty and thirty, and if those arrive well and sound, the general price is from £30 to £40 per head.

According to your Lordships' desire, we have advised with the chiefest of our planters, and find but small encouragement for that trade to this colony; since by the best computation we can make, there would not be disposed in this colony above twenty or thirty at the most, annually; the reasons of which are chiefly to be attributed to the general dislike of our planters have for them, by reason of their turbulent and unruly tempers.

And that most of our planters that are able and willing to purchase any of them, are supplied by the offspring of those they have already, which increase daily; and that the inclination of our people in general, is to employ white servants before negroes.

Source: Elizabeth Donnan, ed., *Documents Illustrative of the Slave Trade to America* (Washington, D.C., 1930–35), pp. 107–110.

deal fairly with Indians, slavery and the slave trade flourished. A law passed in 1652 by representatives of two of the four Rhode Island towns limited bondage to ten years. The statute had little or no effect, in part because the two towns most involved in purchasing slaves had not given their consent.

Although slavery was milder in New England than in the West Indies or southern mainland colonies, primarily because relatively few Africans lived in the region, legal codes nevertheless defined both enslaved and free blacks as a separate and subordinate caste. The penalty suffered by New England slaves for striking whites was less severe than in the plantation colonies, but still the law privileged Europeans of every status. Emancipation remained a possibility in New England, although masters were required to post bond to provide support in case the freed person should lack employment or become disabled in later years. Masters were subject to a charge of murder if they killed a slave, including their own. And while Massachusetts banned sexual relationships and marriages between whites and blacks, none of the other New England colonies followed suit. The marriages of slaves had legal standing and could not be disrupted legally, for blacks were allowed, in fact required, to marry under the same rules as whites.

Despite this relatively moderate regime for slaves, New England's laws concerning the status of free blacks underscored the Puritans' commitment to marking all dark-skinned people as a caste separate from whites. Like the English of the West Indies and the Chesapeake, New Englanders created a rigidly biracial society. Slave codes banned *all* blacks and Native Americans from bearing arms, required them to carry passes when traveling, and prohibited them from being on the streets at night after nine. None of the New England colonies allowed freed people to serve on juries or vote, nor admitted more than a few black children to the public schools. Free blacks were subject to special laws and discrimination that limited their economic opportunities. Most did the same kinds of jobs they had performed as slaves. In Boston, freed people could not own pigs; in South Kingston, Rhode Island, they could own no livestock at all. In 1717, Connecticut went so far as to pass a law forbidding free blacks from residing, purchasing land, or setting up a business in a town without obtaining permission. Although probably not enforced, the law pertained to people already living in towns, thus making their residence and livelihood cruelly tenuous.

While New England developed an extensive legal framework for its caste society, slaves remained a small proportion of the labor pool. Their employment in the cities and on farms must be considered a by-product of the West Indies trade. When sea captains returned home with molasses to distill into rum, they also brought "parcels" of Africans for sale. Massachusetts and Rhode Island merchants participated in the transatlantic slave trade, carrying Africans to the West Indies and mainland colonies. New England's export of fish, livestock, foodstuffs, and lumber to the sugar islands provided much of the credit the region needed to pay for English manufactures; the distilling and sale of rum to Africa and the mainland American colonies supplemented this trade. The Caribbean connection rescued an economy that lacked staple crops like sugar and tobacco that the British Isles and Europe wanted. When the West Indies market emerged after 1640, John Winthrop appreciated its importance. He wrote that the Massachusetts economy was saved when "it pleased the Lord to open to us a trade with Barbados and other Islands in the West Indies." Although a relatively small number of New Englanders owned black slaves, the region was equally implicated in the Atlantic slave system with Barbados and Virginia. New Englanders failed to question African servitude because the slave trade often formed the basis of their livelihood.

By the time South Carolina and the Middle Colonies became part of England's American empire in the 1670s and 1680s, Anglo-American slavery was well defined. Their founders knew the institution and few questioned it. The adoption of slavery in South Carolina and Pennsylvania, settled by very different groups of English people, demonstrates how deeply ingrained was the assumption that blacks were an inferior race. Africans were inextricably linked with slavery and subordinate status in English minds.

SLAVERY IN SOUTH CAROLINA

South Carolina was "the colony of a colony"; it was established in 1670 to furnish provisions to Barbados. Many early white settlers migrated because they had capital to develop plantations and owned Africans to do the work, but could obtain insufficient land on Barbados. The Carolina proprietors offered generous acreages; planters with a family and just a few slaves could gain hundreds of acres. From the colony's outset, blacks constituted one-fourth to one-third of the population. They produced livestock, food, firewood, and barrel staves for Barbados and other Caribbean islands. The institution of slavery did not develop in South Carolina: it was imported from Barbados.

The West Indies provisions trade had limited potential, primarily because merchants in New England and the Middle Colonies made excellent connections there, so Carolinians looked for alternative ways to get rich. Like other American colonists, they needed credits to pay for manufactured goods from England. The settlers established trade with Native Americans for deerskins, which found a ready market in England. They also encouraged enslavement of Indians by purchasing thousands of people for sale in the West Indies. The volume of this trade in humans is suggested by the fact that, although most of the enslaved Indians were exported, in 1708 they constituted 15 percent of the colony's population.

The commodity that proved most successful was rice. It helped white South Carolinians become the wealthiest of mainland British colonists. But for blacks the consequences of rice monoculture in the Carolina coastal lowlands were far less positive. Before planters adopted full-scale rice production, slaves had performed a variety of jobs in crafts, timber, livestock, and agriculture. Their workloads were moderate, especially in comparison with those who suffered under the severe sugar regime of Barbados. With the conversion to rice, planters imported thousands of enslaved Africans, to the extent that blacks reached 70 percent of the coastal population. By 1708, they outnumbered whites in the colony as a whole.

"Injured Humanity." This broadside, published by Samuel Wood in New York in 1805, illustrates the brutal methods slaveholders employed to coerce slave labor, including the use of collars, whips, and masks. Credit: The Library Company of Philadelphia.

The South Carolina legislature responded to the rising number of blacks by adopting a harsh slave code modeled on that of Barbados. The 1696 South Carolina law was the first comprehensive code issued by an English mainland colony. The collective frame of mind of the assemblymen can be identified in its language, which alleged that slaves were "of barbarous, wild, savage natures, and such as renders them wholly unqualified to be governed by the laws, customs, and practices of this Province." Among its provisions, the law's barbarity is demonstrated by the punishments it set for running away, a special concern of Carolina masters whose slaves could escape to Spanish Florida, the towns of sympathetic Native Americans, or autonomous Maroon communities in remote areas. The 1696 code provided that slaves who attempted to flee the colony should be executed. If blacks did not try to leave South Carolina when they absconded, then they received punishments of increasing severity with each offense: whipping, branding with an R, whipping and an ear cut off, castration for men and removal of the other ear for women, and death or laming. In subsequent years, the assembly refined the 1696 code, adding a requirement for passes and establishing a patrol system that incorporated the militia. Like West Indian planters, whites in South Carolina believed that harsh measures were needed to overpower the black majority—in the words of the 1696 code, to "restrain the disorders, rapines and inhumanity, to which [slaves] are naturally prone and inclined."

As the rice regime became more entrenched, much of the flexibility in job assignments and living conditions that had existed during the colony's early years was lost. In 1717, the colony prohibited sexual relations between whites and blacks, whether enslaved or free. In 1721, free blacks lost the franchise (some had voted before that year), and after 1722, emancipated slaves had to leave the colony within a year or be reenslaved. The South Carolina legislature expected to avoid the question of freed people's status by eliminating their presence.

SLAVERY IN THE MID-ATLANTIC COLONIES: PENNSYLVANIA

The adoption of slavery in the Mid-Atlantic colonies, particularly Pennsylvania, provides an instructive comparison with South Carolina. The Dutch had imported Africans into New Netherland as early as 1626; by the English takeover in 1664, slavery was firmly rooted in the region. Of the Middle Colonies, New York had the highest proportion of blacks in the population: 11.5 percent in 1703 and 15 percent in 1723. The comparable proportions in the Chesapeake were 13 percent and 19 percent, respectively. The ubiquity of racism in English America, however, is best exemplified by Pennsylvania. Established in 1681 by William Penn, a leading Quaker, the colony was to be a "holy experiment" in cooperation among people of different religions and backgrounds, with particular attention to relations between Indians and whites. Despite warnings against perpetual bondage by a few Friends, including George Fox, the founder of Quakerism, slavery quickly became woven into the social fabric of the young settlement. A majority of the early Quaker elite owned slaves. Until 1720, blacks made up approximately 12 percent of Philadelphia's population and were a sizable proportion of the rural workforce. Penn himself purchased enslaved Africans, arguing that they were preferable to indentured servants because they could be held for life. His concern about fair treatment included Native Americans but not the people of Africa. A number of wealthy immigrants to the new colony came from the West Indies. They brought both their slaves and their connections to establish trade between the islands and the Quaker colony, a trade that included importation of blacks. Like New England, Pennsylvania found a market for its livestock, lumber, and foodstuffs in the sugar islands. This trade proved essential to the colony's growth. A few Pennsylvania Quakers questioned the morality of slaveholding during the first decades. Among them were four Germantown Friends who in 1688 issued the first American antislavery protest; they warned that people in Europe would be shocked to learn "that the Quackers doe here handel men, Licke they handel there the Cattle." After 1720, the number of manumissions slowly grew, and slave ownership came under increasing attack as a sinful and unjust practice. The influx of Germans and Scots-Irish from the 1720s to the 1750s provided employers with the option of purchasing indentured servants rather than enslaved African women and men.

In the early years, however, most Pennsylvanians simply accepted the practice of slaveholding as worked out in other English colonies. The *Frame of Government*, the *Laws Agreed Upon in England*, and the assembly's initial legislation neither legalized nor banned slavery. Slaveholders relied on custom to protect their property rights. At first, blacks were subject to the same courts and laws as whites, but gradually the colony established the racial line. In 1700, the assembly, dominated by Quakers, recognized differences in the terms of servants and slaves; at about the same time it established separate courts without juries for all blacks, slave and free. Provincial law also held that the rape of a white woman, buggery, and burglary were capital offenses for blacks but not for whites, and ordered black men who attempted rape of a white woman to be castrated. Then in 1706 the assembly revised this law by prescribing for attempted rape or theft thirty-nine lashes, branding on the forehead with the letter R or T, and exportation from the province. In 1726 Pennsylvania established a comprehensive slave code. While more lenient toward slaves than the codes of South Carolina and Virginia, it seriously restricted the activities of free blacks, who could be returned to bondage for vagrancy or marrying a white. Justices of the peace could bind out free black children as apprentices without the parents' consent. Pennsylvania did not force freed people to leave its borders, nor did the colony restrict in-migration from other regions. Nevertheless, it established a caste system based on skin color as clearly and as certainly as any other English province.

The Germantown Protest, 1688

This is to ye Monthly Meeting held at Rigert Worrells.

These are the reasons why we are against the traffick of mensbody as followeth: Is there any that would be done or handled at this manner? viz. to be sold or made a slave for all the time of his life? How fearfull and fainthearted are many on sea when they see a strange vassel being afraid it should be a Turek, and they should be tacken and sold for Slaves in Turckey. Now what is this better done as Turcks doe? yea rather is it worse for them, weh say they are Christians for we hear, that ye most part of such Negers are brought hither against their will & consent, and that many of them are stolen. Now tho' they are black, we cannot conceive there is more liberty to have them slaves, as it is to have other white ones. There is a saying, that we shall doe to all men, licke as we will be done our selves : macking no difference of what generation, descent, or Colour they are. And those who steal or robb men, and those who buy or purchase them, are they not all alicke? Here is liberty of Conscience, weh is right & reasonable, here ought to be lickewise liberty of ye body, except of evildoers, weh is an other case. But to bring men hither, or to robb and sell them against their will, we stand against. In Europe there are many oppressed for Conscience sacke; and here there are those oppressed weh are of a black Colour. And we, who know that men must not comitt adultery, some doe conmitt adultery in others, separating wifes from their housbands, and giving them to others and some sell the children of those poor Creatures to other men. Oh! doe consider well this things, you who doe it, if you would be done at this manner? and if it is done according Christianity? you surpass Holland & Germany in this thing. This mackes an ill report in all those Countries of Europe, where they hear off, that ye Quackers doe here handel men, Licke they handel there ye Cattle ; and for that reason some have no mind or inclination to come hither. And who shall maintaine this your cause or plaid for it ? Truely we can not do so except you shall inform us better hereoff, viz. that christians have liberty to practise this things. Pray ! What thing in the world can be done worse towarts us then if men should robb or steal us away & sell us for slaves to strange Countries, separating housband from their wife & children. Being now this is not done at that manner we will be done at, therefore we contradict & are against this traffick of men body. And we who profess that it is not lawfull to steal, must lickewise avoid to purchase such things as are stolen, but rather help to stop this robbing and stealing if possibel and such men ought to be delivred out of ye hands of ye Robbers and set free as well as in Europe. Then is Pennsilvania to have a good report, in stead it hath now a bad one for this sacke in other Countries. Especially whereas ye Europeans are desirous to know in what manner ye Quackers doe rule in their Province & most of them doe loock upon us with envious eye. But if this is done well, what shall we say, is don evil?

If once these slaves (weh they say are so wicked and stubbern men) should joint themselves, fight for their freedom and handel their masters & mastrisses, as they did handel them before; will these masters & mastrisses, tacke the sword at hand & warr against these poor slaves, licke we are able to believe, some will not refuse to doe? Or have these negers not as much right to fight for their freedom, as you have to keep them slaves?

Now consider well this thing, if its good or bad ? and in case you find it to be good to handel these blacks at that manner, we desire & require you hereby lovingly that you may informe us herein, which at this time never was done, viz.

The Germantown Protest, 1688 (cont.)

that Christians have Liberty to do so, to the end we shall be satisfied in this point, & satisfie lickewise our good friends & acquaintances in our natiff Country, to whose it is a terrour or fairfull thing that men should be handled so in Pensilvania.

This was is from our meeting at Gemantown hold ye 18 of the 2 month 1688 to be delivred to the monthly meeting at Richard Warrels.

gerret hendricks
derick op de graeff
Francis daniell Pastorius
Abraham op den graef

Source: "The Germantown Protest" in Albert P. Blaustein and Robert L. Zangrando, eds., *Civil Rights and the American Negro* (New York: Washington Square Press, 1968), pp. 10–12.

CONCLUSION

By 1720, the practice of slavery ranged widely in the British colonies, from the West Indies where unremitting toil in the sugar fields and early death awaited newly arrived Africans, to New England and Pennsylvania, where tasks were varied and emancipation remained possible. Everywhere, however, blacks held a subordinate position whether they were enslaved or free. This caste system based on notions of race had its origins in both the English dependence on slave labor and their cultural prejudice against dark-skinned people. The plantation colonies relied on blacks to produce sugar, tobacco, and rice, while New England and the Mid-Atlantic region benefited from the trade that profitable staple crops occasioned. Colonial British America developed economically from the labor of Africans and their American-born children. English colonists participated in the Atlantic slave system because it was already in place and because it profited them richly. They justified the adoption of slavery and their barbaric laws by arguing that Africans were an inferior race. The entrenchment of slavery reinforced that belief.

FOR FURTHER READING

Berlin, Ira. *Many Thousands Gone: The First Two Centuries of Slavery in North America.* Cambridge: Belknap Press of Harvard University Press, 1998.

Blackburn, Robin. *The Making of New World Slavery: From the Baroque to the Modern 1492–1800.* New York: Verso, 1998.

Breen, T. H., and Stephen Innes. *"Myne Owne Ground": Race and Freedom on Virginia's Eastern Shore, 1640–1676.* New York: Oxford University Press, 1982.

Carr, Lois Green, Philip D. Morgan, and Jean B. Russo. *Colonial Chesapeake Society.* Chapel Hill: University of North Carolina Press, 1988.

Dunn, Richard S. *Sugar and Slaves: The Rise of the Planter Class in the English West Indies, 1624–1713*. New York: W. W. Norton & Co., 1973.

Greene, Lorenzo Johnston. *The Negro in Colonial New England*. New York: Columbia University Press, 1942.

Jordan, Winthrop D. *White over Black: American Attitudes Toward the Negro, 1550–1812*. Chapel Hill: University of North Carolina Press, 1995.

Kolchin, Peter. *American Slavery: 1619–1877*. New York: Hill & Wang, 1994.

McCusker, John J., and Russell R. Menard. *The Economy of British America, 1607–1789*. Chapel Hill: University of North Carolina Press, 1991.

Morgan, Edmund S. *American Slavery American Freedom: The Ordeal of Colonial Virginia*. New York: W. W. Norton & Co., 1995.

Nash, Gary B. *Red, White, and Black: The Peoples of Early North America*. 3rd ed. Englewood Cliffs, N.J.: Prentice Hall College Division, 1991.

———, and Jean R. Soderlund. *Freedom by Degrees: Emancipation in Pennsylvania and Its Aftermath*. New York: Oxford University Press, 1991.

Thornton, John K. *Africa and Africans in the Making of the Atlantic World. 1400–1800*. New York: Cambridge University Press, 1998.

Walvin, James. *Questioning Slavery*. New York: Routledge, 1997.

Wood, Peter H. *Black Majority: Negroes in Colonial South Carolina from 1670 through the Stono Rebellion*. New York: W. W. Norton & Co., 1996.

chapter 3

Africans in Eighteenth-Century North America

Peter H. Wood

ELL BEFORE THE ARRIVAL OF COLUMBUS IN 1492, the diverse Indian peoples who had inhabited the Americas for at least 15,000 years encountered occasional newcomers. We know, for example, that Vikings from Norway and Greenland settled for several years in Newfoundland around 1000 A.D. There are interesting indications that other ocean voyagers may also have appeared once or twice from Europe, Africa, and Asia at earlier times. Did these visitors arrive voluntarily, or were they simply swept to America by powerful winds and currents? We do not know for sure, but there is little evidence as yet that they stayed long, traveled widely, or had any significant genetic or cultural impact. These hazy pre-Columbian contacts make rich subjects for speculation, but they appear to have been brief and limited encounters at best. It was not until Columbus that transatlantic voyages could at last be regularly repeated, and then endlessly continued, building ever-increasing links between continents and human populations that had known virtual isolation. The enormous forced diaspora of African peoples to the Western Hemisphere is part of this larger pattern.

Within a generation of Columbus's arrival, strange diseases, destructive warfare, and harsh labor policies decimated the local population of the West Indies, and, eager to exploit the bounty of these semitropical landscapes at all costs, Spanish traders began to import workers from Africa. During the next three centuries other European powers—Portugal, France, Holland, and England—competed in this brutal and highly profitable traffic, selling captive workers to the labor-hungry European colonies in America. All told, well over twelve million persons from diverse African cultures endured this exodus, and several million others perished in the so-called Middle Passage. No larger forced migration had occurred in all of human history. Most of these newcomers were put to work clearing land and harvesting crops on large plantations in the Caribbean and in Central and South America.

In relation to the entire transatlantic slave trade, relatively few Africans, perhaps no more than 600,000, were brought to North America. (Brazil, in comparison, absorbed 2.5 million.) Most of the new arrivals reached the mainland English colonies on the Atlantic seaboard after 1700. Although the Spanish had established a settlement at St. Augustine in Florida in 1565, it remained a small outpost intended primarily to protect Spanish shipping lanes. The French colonized Canada in the seventeenth century and Louisiana in the eighteenth century, importing to the latter colony several thousand Africans who, although their numbers were small, would eventually make dramatic contributions to the culture of the deep South and of America more broadly. But the English eventually orchestrated the largest flow of unfree African workers to the North American continent.

As white landowners shifted from a labor system of indentured servitude to one of chattel slavery near the end of the seventeenth century, the African population in certain English mainland colonies swept upward. In the forty years between 1680 and 1720, the proportion of blacks in Virginia's population jumped from 7 percent to 30 percent. "They import so many Negros hither," observed planter William Byrd II, "that I fear this Colony will some time or other be confirmed by the Name of New Guinea." In South Carolina during the same four decades the African increase was even more pronounced: from 17 percent to 70 percent. "Carolina," commented Swiss newcomer Samuel Dyssli in 1737, "looks more like a negro country than like a country settled by white people." By the 1740s and 1750s an average of five thousand persons per year, arriving directly from Africa or via the West Indies, were being sold into bondage on American docks. Between 1770 and 1775, Charleston, South Carolina, alone received four thousand slaves per year through the quarantine station at Sullivan's Island, "the Ellis Island of Black America."

Most blacks reached North America relatively late in the whole transatlantic deportation, and they made up a surprisingly small proportion of the entire forced diaspora—probably as little as 5 percent. The passage from West Africa to North America was even longer and more arduous than to countries farther south, but the climate and the work regime in North America proved slightly less devastating on balance. So survival rates were higher, life expectancy extended further, and natural increase made itself felt more rapidly than in most New World plantation cultures. U.S. planter-capitalists were not blind to these demographic patterns. Since they possessed an expanding labor force, subjected to hereditary servitude, they were eventually willing to tolerate an end to the American slave trade, even while arguing fiercely for the preservation and extension of race slavery itself.

By 1807, therefore, the legal importation of Africans had finally been abolished by the government of the young United States. As a result, the majority of black Americans living in the United States today are the descendants of African men and women hauled to North America by aggressive English and American traders in the course of the eighteenth century. It is worth remembering, for comparison, that the largest migrations to the United States from Europe did not take place until the late nineteenth and early twentieth centuries. So the average white resident in the United States has a shorter American ancestry than the average African-American citizen. The fact that African Americans arrived in large numbers at an early stage means that, despite the enormous constraints of slavery, they had an immediate, varied, and lasting influence on the evolution of American culture that is only now beginning to be understood more fully.

THE FIRST AFRICANS IN THE NEW WORLD

During the sixteenth century a few Africans had penetrated the North American interior in the company of Spanish explorers, as they moved out of the West Indies in search of Indian slaves, precious metals, and possible routes to the Pacific. In 1528, for example, Panfilo de Narvaez led a huge contingent of four hundred persons, white and black, to the Gulf Coast of Florida, but poor planning, harsh conditions, and fierce Indian resistance soon devastated the entire force. Only four survivors—three Spaniards and an African named Estaban—managed to return to Mexico City in 1536 after spending years among the diverse peoples of the South and Southwest. (Their experiences are recorded in the fascinating narrative of one survivor, Cabeza de Vaca.) Authorities in New Spain quickly retained Estaban as a guide for further exploration of the Southwest, where he met his death among the Pueblos in 1539. Estaban's unusual life provides a glimpse of the experiences that faced other African soldiers who accompanied early Spanish invaders throughout the Americas.

By the seventeenth century, black persons were again present among the sailors, traders, and colonists who probed the Atlantic seaboard. Frequently they had spent time in the West Indies and spoke one or more European languages; often they were of mixed European and African ancestry. The Dutch colony of New Netherland provides a case in point. In 1612, only three years after Henry Hudson had claimed the area for Holland, a mulatto crewman named Juan Rodriguez from the West Indies deserted a Dutch ship in the Hudson River and spent a year among the Indians trading for pelts. By 1628 the Dutch had constructed a crude fort at the tip of Manhattan Island and planned to import enslaved Africans to augment the supply of farm laborers in the village of New Amsterdam. Several years later the Dutch West India Company imported additional slaves from the Caribbean to rebuild the fort, and by 1639 a company map showed a slave camp 5 miles north of the town containing newcomers from the West Indies.

Although most black settlers were legally enslaved and some apparently lived in a separate settlement, these few initial African residents did not lead a life totally apart from other colonists in New Amsterdam. Some were armed and took part in raids against the local Indians; others were granted "half freedom" (where they lived independently but continued to pay an annual tax); still others were manumitted completely by their owners. A few who professed Christianity were permitted to marry within the Dutch Reformed Church. Among fifty marriages recorded by the New Amsterdam Church from 1639 to 1652, thirteen involved unions between black men and black women. In another, a European settler married a woman from Angola. The same Dutch ships that provided a few Africans to New Amsterdam occasionally traded with the infant English colonies as well. In 1619, for example, a Dutch vessel unloaded a score of Africans at Jamestown in Virginia, in exchange for much-needed provisions. But for the most part, the powerful Dutch slave traders confined their major traffic to the burgeoning plantation economies of the South Atlantic.

By the mid-1650s, however, stark changes were under way, influenced in large part by the struggles for power between rival seaborne European empires. In 1654 the Dutch lost control of Brazil, where they had been shipping thousands of Africans, so distant New Netherland suddenly became a more attractive destination for Dutch slavers from the South Atlantic. The first shipload of several hundred persons brought directly from Africa arrived at the mouth of the Hudson in 1655. More shipments followed, and many of the enslaved passengers were promptly resold to English planters in the Chesapeake colonies seeking additional workers. When the English seized New Amsterdam in 1664 and renamed it New York, hundreds of Dutch-speaking black residents found that their situation took a turn for the worse.

A similar broad pattern of change for black newcomers also appeared in the English mainland colonies. Numbers increased gradually; racial designations took on new significance; legal codes imposed hereditary enslavement; and profit-conscious traders eventually undertook the importation of slaves directly from Africa. Records from the Plymouth colony (founded by the so-called "Pilgrims" in 1620) show that at least one "blackamoor" was present in the community by the early 1630s. The journal of John Winthrop, governor of the larger Massachusetts Bay colony (founded in 1630), makes clear that in 1638, not long after the English defeat of the neighboring Pequots, a Boston sea captain carried Indian captives to the West Indies and brought back "salt, cotton, tobacco, and Negroes." Six years later, in 1644, Boston merchants sent several ships directly to the West African coast, a small beginning to a pattern of New England slave trading that would continue for a century and a half.

INSTITUTIONALIZATION OF SLAVERY AND RACE

At the start of the seventeenth century Christian Europeans still tended to see political and religious, not physical, differences as the key divisions among mankind. Enemies in foreign wars and adherents to different faiths could be captured and enslaved. Hence, John Smith, a leader of the English colony at Jamestown, had been forced briefly into slavery by the Muslims when fighting in eastern Europe as a young man; "infidel" Pequots who opposed Winthrop's men in New England were sold into bondage in the Caribbean. Such enslavement was not always for life; conversion to the religion of the captor and other forms of good behavior could result in freedom. A law passed in the colony of Rhode Island in 1652 even attempted to limit the term of involuntary servitude to ten years.

But within half a century this somewhat ambiguous situation had changed dramatically in numerous ways. The population pressure at home that had provided the labor pool for England's initial colonies decreased in the wake of the Great Plague of 1665. Efforts to substitute Native American labor proved counterproductive, for colonists needed Indians as allies and trading partners. Moreover, Indian numbers continued to decline sharply due to devastating epidemics of novel diseases. With the establishment of tobacco as a profitable staple in the Chesapeake, the demand for fresh labor increased steadily, as did the wealth needed to obtain it. As Virginia's expanding economy reached the threshold where it could absorb whole shiploads of new workers imported directly from Africa, England's aggressive mercantilists proved ready to supply them. The new Royal African Company, which inherited the monopoly on English slave trading in 1672, began its direct shipment of Africans to the North American mainland in 1674.

Three other changes consolidated this grim transition. In a surprising exception to the English legal tradition that children inherited the status of their father, it was agreed that in the case of African Americans, the offspring would inherit the status of their mother. Hence, the children of an enslaved female would also be enslaved for life—a switch which dramatically increased the long-term profitability of owning a black woman. Secondly, the "headright" system, by which planters received new land for every family member or European servant they brought to the colony, was expanded to encourage the importation of Africans. Self-interested planter-magistrates, who were rich enough to make the expensive initial investment in enslaved workers brought from Africa, allowed themselves to obtain free land, as well as valuable labor, through every purchase. Finally, English colonists gradually agreed, first informally and then through legislation, that physical appearance—"race"—rather than religion would be the primary key to enslavement. While non-Christians could accept Christianity and demand freedom, blacks could not change their appearance in order to improve their status and regain control of their own labor.

A GROWING BLACK PRESENCE

All of these interrelated changes took place during the second half of the seventeenth century, but the African population in North America remained extremely small compared to both the overall population of the colonies and the New World black population as a whole. By 1700 there were perhaps one thousand black New Englanders in a population of roughly ninety thousand. Neighboring New York contained more than two thousand African Americans in a total population of fewer than twenty thousand, but in the younger colonies of New Jersey, Pennsylvania, and Delaware, the number of blacks was smaller. In Maryland, a population exceeding thirty thousand people included approximately three thousand Africans; Virginia, with more than sixty thousand inhabitants was twice as large, but the proportion of Africans, numbering nearly six thousand by 1700, was roughly the same. In the Carolinas there were fewer than seventeen thousand Europeans and four thousand Africans as yet. The entire black population of the English mainland colonies, therefore, was still well below twenty thousand persons in 1700, a small speck in relation to the 1.6 million people who had already been deported from Africa to the Caribbean and Central and South America in the previous two centuries.

All this changed significantly after 1700. In the larger Atlantic context, the number of Africans deported to North America still remained small, probably totaling no more than 5 percent of the entire African diaspora by the time the international slave trade ended in the nineteenth century. But within the colonies of British North America, the transformation was dramatic. Rising immigration from Europe prompted unprecedented growth throughout the colonies, but the flow of workers from Africa grew at an even faster rate. Recent research shows that between 1760 and 1775, when both these streams of fresh arrivals reached new heights, the sum of all Scottish, English, and German newcomers totaled 82,000, while Africans numbered 84,500, mostly concentrated in the southern colonies. During these fifteen years before the American Revolution, out of 221,500 newcomers known to have crossed the Atlantic to British North America, nearly 40 percent of them were brought from Africa.

AFRICAN LIFE IN EIGHTEENTH-CENTURY NORTH AMERICA

In contrast to the largely English migrations of the seventeenth century, many of the eighteenth-century European newcomers did not speak English as their native tongue. Others did not share a belief in Protestant Christianity. In addition, some had little knowledge or respect concerning the English Crown, and a great many came as indentured servants whose labor had been sold to others for a span of years. But what applies to many of these European arrivals applies far more dramatically to virtually all the Africans. The small proportion who had worked in the West Indies before coming to North America had heard limited English and perhaps glimpsed a version of Protestantism from afar, but all were only beginning to discover the harsh workings of the powerful British empire, and all were consigned to hereditary bondage by the mere fact of their racial origin. Year after year, shipload after shipload, they entered American harbors. Week after week, decade after decade, the local gazettes ran prosaic notices to advertise their arrival:

> Just Imported in the Ship Emperor, Charles Gwin Commander, about Two Hundred and Fifty fine healthy Slaves directly from Africa; to be sold on Wednesday the 29th... (*South Carolina Gazette*, April 20, 1752.)

Men and women described as "healthy" in promotional advertisements often proved emaciated, despondent, and sick in body and spirit after the debilitating Middle Passage. Some died before they could be sold; others opted for suicide over forced bondage. A few were sold to northern farmers needing an additional hand or to urban artisans who planned to teach them a trade. But the vast majority were sold directly to colonial plantations along the southeastern seaboard from the Chesapeake Bay to South Carolina—and, after mid-century, to Georgia. There they were put to work with other Africans clearing land, planting crops, and taking in the annual harvest. The daily labor routine, while always arduous, varied significantly depending upon the size and location of the plantation, the time of year, and the nature of the crop. Wheat

Slavery in Eighteenth-Century Virginia

§ 50. Their servants they distinguish by the names of slaves for life, and servants for a time.

Slaves are the negroes and their posterity, following the condition of the mother, according to the maxim, *partus frequitur ventrem*. They are called slaves, in respect of the time of their servitude, because it is for life.

Servants, are those which serve only for a few years, according to the time of their indenture, or the custom of the country. The custom of the country takes place upon such as have no indentures. The law in this case is, that if such servants be under nineteen years of age, they must be brought into court to have their age adjudged; and from the age they are judged to be of, they must serve until they reach four and twenty; but if they be adjudged upwards of nineteen, they are then only to be servants for the term of five years.

§ 51. The male servants, and slaves of both sexes, are employed together in tilling and manuring the ground, in sowing and planting tobacco, corn, &c. Some distinction indeed is made between them in their clothes, and food; but the work of both is no other than what the overseers, the freemen, and the planters themselves do.

Sufficient distinction is also made between the female servants, and slaves; for a white woman is rarely or never put to work in the ground, if she be good for anything else; and to discourage all planters from using any women so, their law makes female servants working in the ground tithables, while it suffers all other white women to be absolutely exempted; whereas, on the other hand, it is a common thing to work a woman slave out of doors, nor does the law make any distinction in her taxes, whether her work be abroad or at home.

Source: Robert Beverley, *The History of Virginia, in Four Parts.* Reprinted from the Author's Second Revised Edition, London 1722 (Richmond: J.W. Randolph, 1855), pp. 219–22.

and tobacco in the Chesapeake region, along with rice and indigo farther south, each created their own calendar of demands.

Individuals, regardless of their age or background, quickly realized that survival would depend in part upon adopting foreign behavior and setting aside many old and familiar ways. This realization was strengthened by a "seasoning" period in which new slaves adjusted to their alien surroundings and learned, often brutally, that they were no longer their own masters. They would be obliged instead to submit to an external, unremitting, and arbitrary system of discipline and control in virtually every aspect of life. Reluctantly but inevitably, these Africans adopted at least the appearance of compliance, absorbing a series of new skills and lifeways, both from their masters and from other African Americans who had lived in the area for several years or several generations. Paradoxically, these newcomers confronted two continents at once. On one hand, they experienced a stark introduction to contradictory elements of European culture in the age of merchant capitalism. On the other hand, they confronted the strange new environment of colonial North America.

By necessity, therefore, there was much to learn: new words, new foods, new tools, new stars, new clothes, new beliefs. But there was also much that could be remembered and adapted to the alien world of the American plantation. The same masters who demanded obedience also welcomed signs of money-saving self-sufficiency and of Old World skills that could be beneficial to the plantation economy. They frequently encouraged individual Africans who already knew how to fashion and bake clay pottery, how to cook okra and sweet potatoes, how to shape metal tools and carve canoes, how to herd cattle and kill alligators, how to cast nets for shrimp and fish, how to weave baskets from palmetto leaves and sweet grass, how to grow gourds and fashion them into containers and instruments. They were particularly attentive to persons and groups who had prior experience with semitropical West African crops such as rice, indigo, and cotton that would gradually transform the economy and landscape of the South.

While American planters encouraged and drew upon various advantageous skills among their African workers, they tolerated or overlooked a great many other cultural traits that were kept alive in the slave quarters through resourcefulness. Vital everyday matters such as house construction, hairstyles, and modes of dress were subjects of constant negotiation. Slaves given an English name by their master might also retain a separate name from Africa, just as a black musician who learned to play the European fiddle to satisfy an English master might also build and play an African stringed instrument, using a traditional scale and rhythm, when entertaining fellow African Americans at the end of a long workday. Where African skills seemed dangerous to white overlords, skills such as the ability to communicate through drumming or to practice herbal medicine, efforts were made—with little success—to legislate such practices out of existence.

Price-Curant in Philadelphia. *May* 15.
Wheat, 3/6. *Indian Corn,* 2 ſ 3. *Flour,* 10s. *White
Bisket,* 17 s. *Midling do.* 13 ſ 6. *Ship do.* 10 ſ 5. *Brown
do.* 9 ſ 6. *Rum,* 2 ſ 4. *Molaſſes,* 18 d. *Pork,* 42 ſ 6 to 50s.
Beef 30 s. *Muſcov. Sugar,* 20 to 30 s. *Pitch,* 15 s. *Tar*
20 s. *Turpentine* 8 ſ 6. *Cotton* 12 d. *per lb. Ginger* 30s.
Loaf-Sugar 14 to 20 d. *Piemento* 15 d.

To be S O L D,

BY *William Spafford* in *Front-
ſtreet,* one young Negro Man, and a very likely Negro Boy, at very reaſonable
Rates, for ready Money.

To be S O L D,

BY *Robert Edgill,* at his Store next Door
to *Robert Ellis's* in *Water-*ſtreet, ſeveral likely Negro
Men and Boys, Choice Rum, Muſcovado and Clay'd Sug-
gar, and ſundry ſorts of dry Goods, at reaſonable Rates.

For *B A R B A D O S* directly,

THE Sloop *Advantage, Chriſto-
pher Luſher* Maſter, will ſail in 12 Days,
having two thirds of her Lading ingaged.
For Freight or Paſſage agree with the ſaid
Maſter at Mr. *Clymer's* Wharff.

To be S O L D,

BY *Thomas Hatton* or *David Falconar,* a
Parcel of Servants of both Sexes, newly arrived in
the *Penn-*Galley, *Edward Kirk* Maſter, from *Dublin,* ſundry
of the Men brought up to valuable Trades, and the reſt, with
the Women and Girls, fit for any Buſineſs in City or Country, being Young and Healthy. Alſo a good Choice of
Iriſh Linnen Cloth of ſundry Sorts and Prices. All which
are to be diſpoſed of at reaſonable Rates.

For *South-Carolina,* directly,

THe Schooner *Mary, Richard
Berwick* Maker, intends to ſail in 10
Days at fartheſt, half of her Lading being
ready. For Freight or Paſſage agree with
the ſaid Maſter, or *Thomas Leech,* or *John
Hyatt,* in *Philadelphia.*

To be S O L D,

BY *Titan Leeds,* a Plantation containing
300 Acres or thereabouts, with a large Stone and Brick
Houſe, a Barn and other Out-Houſes, 100 Acres whereof
is clear'd, three bearing Orchards containing 14 Acres, 20
Acres of good Meadow, ſcituate and being in the Town-
ſhip of *Springfield* and County of *Burlington,* in *Weſt-New-
Jerſey,* about 4 Miles from the Town of *Burlington.* Whoever inclines to purchaſe the ſame may apply to *Titan Leeds*
aforeſaid, at the Houſe of *Thomas Hunlock,* Eſq; in *Burlington,* and know the Terms of Sale.

RUN away, the 26th of *May* Inſt. from
John Leacock, at *Pool-*Forge, two Servant Lads, one
named *Anthony Lee,* a tall Fellow, bandy Leg'd, he is tal-
kative and can tell his Story very plauſibly, born in *Lanca-
ſhire* in *England,* had on when he went away a blue great
Coat, Ozenbriggs Jacket and Trowſers, blue Worſted
Stockings, a good Felt Hat, a blue Shirt and good Shoes.
The other a ſmall Boy, about 14 or 15 Years old, named
James Eſington, he has a caſt with his Eye, he Reads and
Writes pretty well, and was born in *London,* had on a blue
great Coat, Ozenbriggs Jacket, Leather Breeches and a
ſtriped Cap. They went away in Company with a Servant
of *Samuel Brown,* a full Faced chunkey Fellow, of a red
Complexion. Whoever takes up the ſaid Servants and

Advertisement of a slave sale, from *America Weekly Mercury* (May, 1734). Credit:
The Library Company of Philadelphia.

RELIGION

If it was hard for members of the planter class, despite all the sanctions available to them, to legislate successfully against such activities as playing drums and collecting herbs, then it was far harder for them to control effectively the personal belief systems of their enslaved workers. When an Anglican missionary in colonial South Carolina asked an African-born slave why he resisted accepting Christianity, the man replied simply, "I prefer to live by that which I remember." During the late seventeenth and early eighteenth centuries, Englishmen who may earlier have converted an occasional bond servant now had difficulty fathoming, or altering, the enduring beliefs of workers brought directly from Africa. In part, the shifting demographic proportions meant that in any given slave community there were likely to be more persons, representing more African cultures, who had arrived more recently. Newcomers were less likely to have lived in the West Indies—separated from Africa and exposed to European colonization.

Nevertheless, for a variety of reasons the basic tenets of Protestant Christianity gradually took hold among an increasing proportion of black Americans during the course of the eighteenth century. While some slaves undoubtedly viewed acceptance of their master's faith as a betrayal, others may have seen conversion as a means for ingratiating themselves, or for informing themselves about the hidden sources of obvious European power. If some sought to identify with their oppressors and accepted a version of Christianity which taught compliance, then others sensed quickly the subversive potential of a faith which affirmed that "the meek shall inherit the earth." On the eve of the American Revolution, a black preacher in Georgia expounded the belief that the Christian "God would send Deliverance to the Negroes, from the power of their Masters, as He freed the Children of Israel from Egyptian Bondage."

Moreover, Protestantism itself changed in the course of the century. Having discarded the notion of saints during the Reformation, Protestants could never offer the array of sacred figures that appealed to many Africans when they encountered Catholicism in the Caribbean and Latin America. But the midcentury revival known as the First Great Awakening, with its emphasis on individual salvation, fostered egalitarian thinking, lay preaching, and stress on baptism. It also brought more participatory music, bodily animation, and personal testimony into Protestant services. All these trends held attraction for potential African converts and helped win pockets of followers. They in turn converted others to an emerging and varied "black church" that incorporated Protestant beliefs while still retaining distinctive non-European elements of style and content. The process took many generations and must have involved deep controversy and debate. Unfortunately, we have almost no documentary record for this spiritual odyssey, which represents one of the most intriguing and little-known chapters in American intellectual and religious history.

FAMILY AND COMMUNITY

If any one aspect of enslavement shook the belief systems of Africans and tested their capacity to survive, it was the overwhelming destruction of family and community bonds. Just as historians have debated the awesome impact of the slave trade on those who stayed behind—the removal of parents or loved ones, the exaggeration of local rivalries and jealousies, the escalation of warfare, the decimation of villages, the disruption of peaceful trade—they have also argued over the consequences of removal for those deported to America. It is possible, on one hand, to overemphasize the destructiveness of the Middle Passage and underestimate the resilience of the captives themselves, stressing that they lost not only their stable families but also their capacity to re-create similar family structures in the New World. But it is equally possible, on the other hand, to de-emphasize the horrors of enslavement or to romanticize the phoenix-like capacities of African peoples in such a way that family and community structures seem to revive and flourish miraculously amid the chaos of slavery.

The complex truth lies somewhere between these two extreme representations. Masters proved reluctant to sanction marriage in ways that might foster dignity and self-esteem, traits that slaveholders often worked to destroy. At the same time, however, they grew increasingly aware that the bonds of family could make workers more reliable and interdependent, less willing to run away or rebel for fear of retribution against loved ones. For their part, enslaved Africans found themselves in an alien universe, populated by domineering Europeans and dark-skinned people from separate cultures who all looked, spoke, and behaved in different ways. The extreme isolation created by these surroundings also generated the will to overcome such loneliness. New personal ties were forged, one link at a time, reducing the social and cultural distance between once-separate African groups. The children and grandchildren of these unions, increasingly similar in appearance and behavior over time, emerged as a new and distinctive variety of colonist: the African American.

These "country-born" individuals harbored no personal knowledge of Africa. They frequently distinguished themselves from the "saltwater Negroes" who arrived annually by ship, unable to speak English and unfamiliar with the habits of the country and the grinding work routine of the American gulag. But they grew up in a diverse community, hearing various languages and learning a variety of folkways. Occasionally, although not always, viable families could emerge and endure under even the harshest physical conditions, but their long-term sanctity and stability remained tenuous at best. A kind master could die; a lazy overseer could be replaced; an outspoken spouse could be sold; an overburdened parent could fall ill. Personal relationships, however strong and supportive, inevitably remained tenuous and fragile among the enslaved. For many of the people, much of the time, accepting this drastically diminished world became a necessity of bodily survival. Yet there were always those who resisted complete accommodation and who helped others to resist through their example.

RESISTANCE, REVOLT, AND THE REVOLUTION

Persons who live in relative freedom have great trouble imagining life in perpetual bondage. Confronted with the horrors of enslavement, we often ask why resistance was not more common, more aggressive, and more successful. Even in framing such questions, we demonstrate that we still have not fathomed the full magnitude of the domination or the enormous odds against rebellion. Nor have we registered sufficiently the myriad small ways in which individuals opposed and undermined the system as part of their continued struggle for survival. Like any oppressed work force denied the fruits of its labor, enslaved Americans often broke or "misplaced" or appropriated their tools. They frequently damaged the crops they were compelled to produce by refusing to plant and harvest on time, neglecting to weed or water the fields properly, or failing to process and transport the annual yield swiftly and efficiently.

Planters throughout the colonies came to know that numerous workers would be "sick" when work in the fields was heaviest. They also learned that imposing harsh conditions and severe punishments could result in the clandestine destruction of valuable crops. Burning down a barn full of tobacco or rice at harvest time, for example, offered one means of swift retaliation. Such acts of arson occurred frequently, for they provided immediate respite from intensive labor; they cost the master significant profits; and they proved notoriously difficult crimes to prove. Another clandestine act—poisoning—went beyond property damage in inflicting retribution. Slaves were intimately involved with every aspect of food preparation, and many had access to knowledge, from both sides of the ocean, regarding lethal plants. Since suspicion quickly focused upon house servants in the kitchen, the risks were high, but it only took occasional incidents, real or suspected, to keep a constant undercurrent of fear alive in the planter community.

Of far greater risk were acts of overt aggression. Statutes made it legal for free persons to kill slaves who struck them, whether in anger or self-defense. Nevertheless, acts of homicide against overseers or masters and their families occurred on a regular basis, and even the swift, and near certain, public execution of accused persons did not serve to prevent such desperate acts. Slave violence ranged from these sudden individual acts, usually unpremeditated and aimed at a single vulnerable tormentor, to more elaborate conspiracies, involving numerous persons and aimed at a whole community, or even at the entire slave system itself. As in any prison or gulag, thought of open rebellion was virtually universal; talk of such matters was far more guarded, and the undertaking itself was the bold and rare exception, for a number of obvious reasons.

A Cruel Scene Witnessed
by Hector St. John Crévecour

I was not long since invited to dine with a planter who lived three miles from
——, where he then resided. In order to avoid the heat of the sun, I resolved to
go on foot, sheltered in a small path, leading through a pleasant wood. I was
leisurely travelling along, attentively examining some peculiar plants which I
had collected, when all at once I felt the air strongly agitated, though the day
was perfectly calm and sultry. I immediately cast my eyes toward the cleared
ground. from which I was but at a small distance, in order to see whether it was
not occasioned by a sudden shower; when at that instant a sound resembling a
deep rough voice, uttered, as I thought, a few inarticulate monosyllables.
Alarmed and surprised, I precipitately looked all round, when I perceived at
about six rods distance something resembling a cage, suspended to the limbs of
a tree; all the branches of which appeared covered with large birds of prey, flut-
tering about, and anxiously endeavouring to perch on the cage. Actuated by an
involuntary motion of my hands, more than by any design of my mind, I fired
at them; they all flew to a short distance, with a most hideous noise: when, hor-
rid to think and painful to repeat, I perceived a negro, suspended in the cage,
and left there to expire! I shudder when I recollect that the birds had already
picked out his eyes, his cheek bones were bare; his arms had been attacked in
several places, and his body seemed covered with a multitude of wounds. From
the edges of the hollow sockets and from the lacerations with which he was dis-
figured, the blood slowly dropped, and tinged the ground beneath. No sooner
were the birds flown, than swarms of insects covered the whole body of this
unfortunate wretch, eager to feed on his mangled flesh and to drink his blood.
I found myself suddenly arrested by the power of affright and terror; my nerves
were convulsed; I trembled, I stood motionless, involuntarily contemplating the
fate of this negro, in all its dismal latitude. The living spectre, though deprived
of his eyes, could still distinctly hear, and in his uncouth dialect begged me to
give him some water to allay his thirst. Humanity herself would have recoiled
back with horror; she would have balanced whether to lessen such reliefless distress, or mercifully with one blow to end this dreadful scene of agonising torture! Had I had a ball in my gun, I certainly should have despatched him; but
finding myself unable to perform so kind an office, I sought, though trembling,
to relieve him as well as I could. A shell ready fixed to a pole, which had been
used by some negroes, presented itself to me; I filled it with water, and with
trembling hands I guided it to the quivering lips of the wretched sufferer. Urged
by the irresistible power of thirst, he endeavoured to meet it, as he instinctively
guessed its approach by the noise it made in passing through the bars of the
cage. "Tankè, you whitè man, tankè you, putè somè poison and givè me." "How
long have you been hanging there?" I asked him. "Two days, and me no die; the
birds, the birds; aaah me!" Oppressed with the reflections which this shocking
spectacle afforded me, I mustered strength enough to walk away, and soon
reached the house at which I intended to dine. There I heard that the reason
for this slave being thus punished, was on account of his having killed the overseer of the plantation. They told me that the laws of self-preservation rendered
such executions necessary; and supported the doctrine of slavery with the arguments generally made use of to justify the practice; with the repetition of which
I shall not trouble you at present.—

Source: Letters from an American Farmer . . . (London, 1783), pp. 163–64.

Urban slaves were closely watched, and rural slaves were widely dispersed; formal patrols were commonplace, and informants were everywhere. Long working hours and wide distances made communication difficult, as did forced illiteracy and diverse ethnic backgrounds.

Despite such huge obstacles, brave individuals joined in risky coalitions to attempt mass escape or armed insurrection. The leaders, like any guerrilla commanders, always had to consider the same configuration of issues. Could they build a wide coalition without fostering discord or betrayal? Could they take advantage of dissent among whites, or natural disasters such as storms or epidemics, without sacrificing control over timing? Could they make, sequester, or capture sufficient weapons to win initial victories that would bring additional people and resources to their cause? Could they generate the ruthless violence needed for such an undertaking while still enforcing the level of order, restraint, and cooperation needed to make it a success? Could they learn from past experiences without becoming too discouraged by the woeful outcome of past conspiracies? More often than not, the answer to several of these questions was "No," and the plotters reluctantly dropped their scheme before crossing the dangerous Rubicon.

Occasionally, however, events took on a life of their own, as rumors of revolt fueled fears among whites and raised hopes among blacks. Word of a foreign war, a heavenly sign, or a servile rebellion in some other colony could quickly bring matters to a head, increasing the sense of urgency among slaves and the feelings of paranoia among those who exploited them. In New York City, in 1712, enslaved workers set fire to a building and attacked those summoned to put out the blaze. They managed to kill nine persons and wound seven others, but they failed to spark a larger revolt. Half a dozen accused conspirators committed suicide after their capture, and more than twenty were put to death, some by burning alive. According to New York's governor, "There has been the most exemplary punishment that could possibly be thought of."

In 1729 in Louisiana, war with the Natchez Indians allowed Africans to plan an uprising against their French masters. But the plot was uncovered, and eight of the leaders, including a trusted African-born overseer named Samba Bambasa, were broken on the wheel. Ten years later in South Carolina, word of the outbreak of war between England and Spain helped prompt the Stono Rebellion, in which scores of slaves killed their English masters and began marching toward Spanish St. Augustine, only to be intercepted before their numbers could swell. Fearful of the colony's expanding black majority, officials displayed the heads of executed rebels on poles to discourage future revolts. In addition, they placed a prohibitive duty on slaves imported from abroad for several years, and they passed a new Negro Act further restricting the movement and assembly of black South Carolinians. A suspected slave plot on New York in 1741 led to even more fearsome reprisals fueled by suggestions of clandestine support and encouragement from Spanish Jesuits and local poor whites.

The Stono Revolt in South Carolina, 1741

On the 9th day of September last being Sunday which is the day the Planters allow them to work for themselves, Some Angola Negroes assembled, to the number of Twenty; and one who was called Jemmy was their Captain, they suprized a Warehouse belonging to Mr. Hutchenson at a place called Stonehow [sic—]; they there killed Mr. Robert Bathurst, and Mr. Gibbs, plundered the House and took a pretty many small Arms and Powder, which were there for Sale. Next they plundered and burnt Mr. Godfrey's house, and killed him, his Daughter and Son. They then turned back and marched Southward along Pons Pons, which is the Road through Georgia to Augustine, they passed Mr. Wallace's Tavern towards day break, and said they would not hurt him, for he was a good Man and kind to his Slaves, but they broke open and plundered Mr. Lemy's House, and killed him, his wife and Child. They marched on towards Mr. Rose's resolving to kill him; but he was saved by a Negroe, who having hid him went out and pacified the others. Several Negroes joyned them, they calling out Liberty, marched on with Colours displayed, and two Drums beating, pursuing all the white people they met with, and killing Man Woman and Child when they could come up to them. Collonel Bull Lieutenant Governor of South Carolina, who was then riding along the Road, discovered them, was pursued, and with much difficulty escaped & raised the Countrey. They burnt Colonel Hext's house and killed his Overseer and his Wife. They then burnt Mr. Sprye's house, then Mr. Sacheverell's, and then Mr. Nash's house, all lying upon the Pons Pons Road, and killed all the white People they found in them. Mr. Bullock got off, but they burnt his House, by this time many of them were drunk with the Rum they had taken in the Houses. They increased every minute by new Negroes coming to them, so that they were above Sixty, some say a hundred, on which they halted in a field, and set to dancing, Singing and beating Drums, to draw more Negroes to them, thinking they were now victorious over the whole Province, having marched ten miles & burnt all before them without Opposition, but the Militia being raised, the Planters with great briskness pursued them and when they came up, dismounting; charged them on foot. The Negroes were soon routed, though they behaved boldly several being killed on the Spot, many ran back to their Plantations thinking they had not been missed, but they were there taken and [sic] Shot, Such as were taken in the field also, were after being examined, shot on the Spot, And this is to be said to the honour of the Carolina Planters, that notwithstanding the Provocation they had received from so many Murders, they did not torture one Negroe, but only put them to an easy death. All that proved to be forced & were not concerned in the Murders & Burnings were pardoned, And this sudden Courage in the field, & the Humanity afterwards hath had so good an Effect that there hath been no farther Attempt, and the very Spirit of Revolt seems over. About 30 escaped from the fight, of which ten marched about 30 miles Southward, and being overtaken by the Planters on horseback, fought stoutly for some time and were all killed on the Spot. The rest are yet untaken. In the whole action about 40 Negroes and 20 whites were killed. The Lieutenant Governour sent an account of this to General Oglethorpe, who met the advices on his return from the Indian Nation He immediately ordered a Troop of Rangers to be ranged, to patrole through Georgia, placed some Men in the Garrison at Palichocolas, which was before abandoned, and near which the Negroes formerly passed, being the only place where Horses can come to swim over the River Savannah for near 100 miles, ordered out the Indians in pursuit, and a Detachment of the Garrison at Port Royal to assist the Planters on any Occasion, and published a Proclamation ordering all the Constables &c. of Georgia to pursue and seize all Negroes, with a Reward for any that should be taken. It is hoped these measures will prevent any Negroes from getting down to the Spaniards.—

Source: Allen D. Candler, ed., *The Colonial Records of the State of Georgia* (Atlanta, Charles P. Byrd, 1913), vol. 22, pp. 233-35.

By far the largest rift in the American ruling class occurred during the decades of the American Revolution, and enslaved African Americans were not slow to exploit this division to their best advantage. When free colonists took to the streets in 1765 to demand repeal of the Stamp Act imposed by British Parliament, slaves in Charleston began to chant "Liberty! Liberty!" in ways that frightened local officials. As the push for independence from English rule gained support in the North American colonies, leaders of the movement such as Patrick Henry and George Washington expressed well-founded fears that the British command might resort to arming the slaves in order to intimidate white planters into submission. In the spring of 1775 a free black pilot in the port of Charleston predicted to less informed workers on the docks, "There is a great war coming" that will "help the poor Negroes." Several months later, accused of helping the British smuggle guns to the blacks and Indians, the pilot was condemned and burned alive by the town's provisional revolutionary government.

In the fall of 1775, Virginia's Governor Dunmore issued a proclamation offering freedom to black men who took up arms with the British forces against the rebels. Many hundreds soon risked their lives to flock to his standard, only to die of smallpox in the crowded refugee camps. But with more than 500,000 blacks living in the rebellious colonies amid fewer than two

Philip Fithian's Diary on Negroes in Virginia

[April 4, 1774]—... After Supper I had a long conversation with M^rs. Carter concerning Negroes in Virginia, & find that She esteems their value at no higher rate than I do. We both concluded, (I am pretty certain that the condusion is just) that if in M^r. Carters, or in any Gentlemans Estate, all the Negroes should be sold, & the Money put to Interest in safe hands, & let the Lands which these Negroes now work lie wholly uncultivated, the bare Interest of the price of the Negroes would be a much greater yearly income than what is now received from their working the Lands, making no allowance at all for the trouble & Risk of the Masters as to the Crops, & Negroes.—How much greater then must be the value of an Estate here if these poor enslaved Africans were all in their native desired Country, & in their Room industrious Tenants, who being born in freedom, by a laudable care, would not only enrich their Landlords, but would raise a hardy Offspring to be the Strength and the honour of the Colony.

[September 8, 1774]—.... Something alarming happened a few nights ago in the Neighbourhood at M^r. *Sorrels* a House in Sight—It is supposed that his Negres had appointed to murder him, several were found in his bed chamber in the middle of the night—his Wife waked—She heard a whispering, one perswading the other to go—On this She waked her Husband, who ran to his Gun; but they escaped in the dark—Presumption is so strong together with a small confession of the fellows, that three are now in Prison—

Source: John Roger Williams, ed., *Journal and Letters, 1767–1774* (Princeton, N.J.: Princeton University Press), 1:145, 190.

million whites, both sides paid close attention to this widespread population. Those charging England's George III with "enslaving" them through unfair taxation now had to face the contradiction of their own slaveholding. Mocked by Tories for refusing to include African Americans in their revolution, the Patriots moved quickly to allow free blacks to take part in the armed struggle. Some 5,000 blacks served with the Revolutionary Army during the course of the War of Independence, but the move to enlist slaves into service with promises of freedom was postponed throughout the entire conflict.

Following the defeat of the British and the surrender of General Cornwallis at Yorktown in 1781, thousands of African Americans who had cast their lot with the losing side were obliged to withdraw. Several thousand went by boat from New York City to Nova Scotia, for example, and some of these persons eventually made their way back to the West Coast of Africa. Others, the property of loyalist slaveholders or the victims of unscrupulous dealings by British officers, found themselves deported to the sugar plantations of the West Indies. A few, but not many, of the black workers who had endured the war behind rebel lines received their freedom as part of an upswing in egalitarian thinking brought on by the rhetoric of the Revolution and the spread of evangelical Christian beliefs. George Washington and Robert Carter each manumitted several hundred persons from bondage in the decades after Yorktown, but they proved exceptions among southern planters in this regard.

At Philadelphia in 1787, when the issue of apportioning state representatives for a new national government arose in the Constitutional Convention, southern delegates argued that slaves should be fully counted, since that would expand the congressional representation given to slaveholding states. For varied reasons, northern delegates took the position that enslaved blacks were property and should not be given any weight whatsoever in apportionment. Those northerners with a more racist bent found it demeaning to equate free whites with Africans in bondage; those favoring abolition felt it risky to affirm the institution of slavery in the new Constitution. The eventual "three-fifths compromise" pleased none of these parties, but by allowing each state to count every slave as three-fifths of a free person for the determination of representation and direct taxes, it enshrined the institution of slavery in the founding document of the United States in a way that would haunt and embarrass future generations.

Bowing to the power of proslavery delegates, the framers went on to affirm the right of slaveholders to demand the return of fugitive slaves escaping into another state, and they banned the Congress in advance from taking any action to prohibit the African slave trade to the new republic for at least two decades. The new Constitution, ratified in 1789, represented a dream come true for a generation of relatively prosperous white men who opposed hereditary monarchy and defended the sanctity of private property, human or otherwise. But it was a crushing setback for most of the new nation's 750,000 African Americans, for most resided in the South and remained in bondage. Indeed, of more than 640,000 residing in the states below Pennsylvania, fewer than one in twenty possessed freedom. In contrast, scarcely one-tenth as many blacks lived in the states from Pennsylvania northward through New England. Of these, almost one-third (nearly 18,000 persons) were already free, and others, as abolitionist forces influenced state constitutions, could look forward to legal freedom—although not to social equality.

CONCLUSION

Enslaved or free, North or South, African Americans in the new United States faced trying circumstances during the 1790s. If the success of the Haitian Revolution sparked hope that the Enlightenment ideals of liberty and equality could cross racial boundaries, it also prompted a backlash of fear and repression among the white majority. In one congregation after another, from one Protestant denomination to the next, aspirations for integrated Christian worship gave way first to increased discrimination and then to outright separation. In a process that two hundred years later might be characterized as "ethnic cleansing," momentum swung in favor of those willing to strengthen social and political barriers along racial lines. Idealistic signs of potential harmony and amelioration gave way to hardened racism and sanctioned exploitation in ways that forced separation and invited bitter reaction.

The pathos of this tragic era is well illustrated by what occurred in Richmond, Virginia, capital of the largest slave state, in late August 1800. A slave blacksmith named Gabriel organized hundreds of rebels in a well-planned conspiracy that was foiled only by a last-minute disclosure and hurricane-force summer storm. Faced with death, one of the captured leaders invoked the name of another revolutionary Virginian. "I have nothing more to offer than what General Washington would have had to offer, had he been taken by the British officers and put to trial by them," the accused conspirator told the court. "I know that you have predetermined to shed my blood," the political prisoner continued. "Why then all this mockery of a trial?" Influenced by the rhetoric of the previous forty years, and unafraid to employ it against the hypocrisy of his captors one final time, he concluded eloquently: "I have ventured my life in endeavouring to obtain the liberty of my countrymen, and am a willing sacrifice to their cause; and I beg, as a favour, that I may be immediately led to execution."

FOR FURTHER READING

Berlin, Ira. *Many Thousands Gone: The First Two Centuries of Slavery in North America.* Cambridge: Belknap Press of Harvard University Press, 1998.

Davis, David Brion. *The Problem of Slavery in the Age of Revolution, 1770–1823.* 2nd ed. Ithaca, N.Y.: Cornell University Press, 1999.

Frey, Sylvia R. *Water from the Rock: Black Resistance in a Revolutionary Age.* Princeton, N.J.: Princeton University Press, 1991.

Gates, Henry Louis, and William Andrews, eds. *Pioneers of the Black Atlantic: Five Slave Narratives from the Enlightenment, 1772–1815.* Washington, D.C.: Counterpoint Press, 1998.

Genovese, Eugene. *Rebellion to Revolution: Afro-American Slave Revolts in the Making of the New World.* Baton Rouge: Louisiana State University Press, 1992.

Hall, Gwendolyn M. *Africans in Colonial Louisiana: The Development of Afro-Creole Culture in the Eighteenth Century.* Baton Rouge: Louisiana State University Press, 1995.

Higginbotham, A. Leon, Jr. *In the Matter of Color: Race and the American Legal Process: The Colonial Period.* New York: Oxford University Press, 1980.

Huggins, Nathan I. *Black Odyssey: The African-American Ordeal in Slavery.* New York: Vintage, 1990.

Jordan, Winthrop D. *White Over Black: American Attitudes Toward the Negro, 1550–1812.* Chapel Hill: University of North Carolina Press, 1995.

Kolchin, Peter. *American Slavery: 1619–1877.* New York: Hill & Wang, 1994.

Kulikoff, Allan. *Tobacco and Slaves: The Development of Southern Cultures in the Chesapeake, 1680–1800.* Chapel Hill: University of North Carolina Press, 1988.

Littlefield, Daniel C. *Rice and Slaves: Ethnicity and the Slave Trade in Colonial South Carolina.* Baton Rouge: Louisiana State University Press, 1991.

Morgan, Edmund S. *American Slavery, American Freedom: The Ordeal of Colonial Virginia.* New York: W. W. Norton & Company, 1995.

Morgan, Philip D. *Slave Counterpoint: Black Culture in the Eighteenth-Century Chesapeake and Lowcountry.* Chapel Hill: University of North Carolina Press, 1998.

Mullin, Michael. *Africa in America: Slave Acculturation and Resistance in the American South and the British Caribbean, 1736–1831.* Urbana: University of Illinois Press, 1995.

Pierson, William D. *Black Yankees: The Development of an Afro-American Subculture in Eighteenth-Century New England.* Amherst: University of Massachusetts Press, 1988.

Quarles, Benjamin. *The Negro in the American Revolution.* Chapel Hill: University of North Carolina Press, 1996.

Sobel, Mechal. *The World They Made Together: Black and White Values in Eighteenth-Century Virginia.* Princeton, N.J.: Princeton University Press, 1989.

Wood, Peter H. *Black Majority: Negroes in Colonial South Carolina from 1670 through the Stono Rebellion.* New York: W. W. Norton & Co., 1996.

Wright, Donald R. *African Americans in the Colonial Era: From African Origins through the American Revolution.* Arlington Heights, Ill.: Harlan Davidson, 1990.

chapter 4

In Search of Freedom

Slave Life in the Antebellum South

Norrece T. Jones Jr.

 FEW SYSTEMS OF HUMAN EXPLOITATION have been as devastating or as decisive in producing lasting hostilities as the transatlantic slave trade and the institution of black enslavement that fueled its existence. Beginning in the fifteenth century, between ten million and twelve million Africans were captured and then shipped to various points of bondage in the Americas. The full impact of this unprecedented forced migration cannot be appreciated until one considers that probably another ten million to twelve million captives died in the treacherous march to the African coast and the harrowing ocean voyage. Although fewer than five hundred thousand of those who survived the ordeal of savage disruption and displacement found themselves enslaved in North America, this segment of the African diaspora grew to a population of four million by the time of the Civil War. The way of life these bondpeople experienced in the antebellum era, the last sixty-five years of black American captivity, is the focus of this essay.

By 1800 the overwhelming majority of North American bondpeople were concentrated in the southern United States. There, brute force, unrewarded toil, sordid punishment, and draconian codes severely circumscribed their world. Rarely were these boundaries broken. The testimony of the women, men, and children subjected to the ubiquitous restrictions of racial servitude mostly reveals, however, a burning desire to be free and continuing conflict with those who denied them their liberty. The overarching relationship with the ruling race was one of obdurate conflict.

The odds against successful revolt in the antebellum South were more formidable than what generally has been acknowledged. The enslaved were confronted not only by geographic, demographic, and militaristic factors that

"Selling a Mother from Her Child." *American Anti-Slavery Almanac for 1840* (New York: American Anti-Slavery Society, 1839). Credit: The Library Company of Philadelphia.

undermined rebellion but by a stolidly racist society at large, both in the South and North. Political events during the nation's birth illustrate the prevalence of racial prejudice in the new republic and devotion to its preservation as a white man's country. Despite the sacrifices of five thousand blacks to the revolution to end British colonial rule and despite the rhetoric of human equality and inalienable rights, after the war most of the states in postrevolutionary America denied free blacks the right to vote. Instead, slaveholding and non-slaveholding northern and southern whites, intent on hammering out an acceptable national Constitution, discussed not whether freedmen should vote but how enslaved blacks should be counted in apportioning population-based congressional representation among whites.

The era's spirit of liberty, conjoined with black freedom suits and the appeals of white humanitarians, inspired, however, the passage of gradual emancipation acts throughout the North just after the Revolution. By 1830 there were fewer than three thousand slaves in the North where some bondsmen had been freed for service in the Continental Army and where many of the region's slaveholders had liquidated their human property by selling their slaves south. In fact, during the early national period, there was a precipitous drop in the black populations of almost every northern state. In New York alone, blacks were reduced from 7.6 percent of the inhabitants in 1790 to only 2.3 percent in 1830. In 1800 the United States had a population of 5.3 million; 18.9 percent of it, or 1 million individuals, were African American or African. Any hope among slaves that they might find allies in their struggle against bondage from anyone other than blacks was tempered by a worsening in white attitudes toward people of color. In their evolving consciousness as a class, white workers distanced themselves from blacks by defining not only their labor but also their very identity as the exact opposite of all they imagined about enslaved and free blacks. In fact, white laborers formed the vanguard of a new vogue in the 1830s that was to become a national obsession: minstrelsy. This new form of entertainment demonstrated the powerful lure black song and dance had for white audiences and performers as well as the prevalence of white racism. Minstrelsy involved white men painting their faces black with burnt cork and grossly imitating black behavior; their interpretations were as ugly as the tattered clothing, elephantine gestures, and malapropisms that became the staples of their stage acts.

Denigration of blacks occurred in the visual arts as well. Although almost always depicted as servants, the blacks on the canvases of eighteenth-century artists such as Charles Wilson Peale were normally given a certain dignity and respect. Such sympathetic portraitures nearly vanished in the antebellum period as notions of black inferiority dominated artistic representations of the Negro. By the 1850s the American public was being bombarded with caricatures of blacks, ugly depictions that amplified white visions of African incipience. Lithographers and publishers Currier & Ives printed such images by the thousands. But these hateful images were not the only signs of a hardening racism. Northern blacks were often subjected to racial pogroms in which white mobs assaulted blacks and stole or destroyed their property. Violent Negrophobic action sharply reduced whatever comfort non-southern blacks derived from the legal status of "free people of color."

The status and treatment of northern and southern free blacks places in context the social position and perception of antebellum slaves. White racism was a critical dimension circumscribing black life, free and slave, everywhere in antebellum America. From the vast complex of odious attitudes and actions that proscribed their liberties, blacks of different classes discerned that the hostility toward them only varied in degree. It awakened some to recognize and esteem points of similarity that they had failed to see before. The study of free blacks also shows an ideological and cultural connection between emancipated and enslaved African Americans manifested in some common worldviews. Extensive free black migration throughout the United States, a vigorous domestic slave trade, and the illegal importation of Africans that lasted through the Civil War facilitated contact among all classes of blacks and kept the intellectual and cultural tenets of black life related.

RELATIONS BETWEEN SLAVES AND THEIR ENSLAVERS

In the contest between enslavers and slaves, blacks had neither the arms nor the numbers to end slavery. But this conflict was about mental as well as physical captivity. The enslaved were subjected to propaganda that sought to channel all thinking about freedom into master-controlled venues such as manumissions for good behavior or opportunities for self-purchase. The words and actions of the ruling race taught that any revolutionary pursuit of freedom was more than foolish: it was mad. After the discovery and suppression of perhaps the best-conceived conspiracy against slavery during the antebellum period, the

Reverend Dr. Richard Furman advised South Carolinian blacks to keep the mad from inspiring the sane, and thus remain safe. Acknowledging that there were pockets of black sedition in the South, like the South Carolina Low Country, Furman cautioned that in the entire United States, Negroes, "including all descriptions, bond and free," continued to be "but little more than one sixth part of the whole number of inhabitants." He explained that a federal defense, national racism, would work against them. As for fellow whites who "favour[ed] the idea of general emancipation," Furman predicted they would change their position if ever faced with black insurrection: "Were they to see slaves in our Country, in arms, wading through blood and carnage to effect their purpose, they would do what both their duty and interest would require; unite under the government with their fellow-citizens at large to suppress the rebellion, and bring the authors of it to condign punishment."

Advice to Masters, 1837

Order

Preserve order in all your actions, and your negroes will imitate you. For instance, if you ride by a fence that has been broken down, and you have a boy with you, make him stop and repair it; if you have no boy, get down, and do it yourself. Let every negro about you, and on your plantation, be made to observe this. I make it an offence, severely punishable, for any of my slaves to pass by any thing out of repair, without either stopping to put it to rights, or informing the proper person whose business it is to do so . . .

I have seen negroes pass over bridges which had great holes in them, fifty times, and never take the trouble to mend them, when one log of wood could easily have done so. If negroes of mine did the like, be they male or female, if they were old enough to have discretion, I would punish them for the negligence.

The master should make it his business to show his slaves, that the advancement of his individual interest, is at the same time an advancement of theirs. Once they feel this, it will require but little compulsion to make them act as becomes them.

Morals

. . . I particularly enjoin upon my slaves, the observance of their marriage contracts. In no instance do I suffer any of them to violate these ties—except where I would consider myself justified in doing so. Independently of the excellence of such an institution itself, it has the additional advantage of keeping your negroes at home.

If there be a church in the vicinity of the planter's residence, he should oblige all of his negroes to attend it, at least once a day. This has an excellent effect. Most negroes take Sunday as their day of visiting; and it not unfrequently happens, that they do more mischief on that day, by colleagueing themselves, than on any other. Now, the attendance upon church permits them to meet their relatives and friends there, and, at the same time, keeps them out of all mischief. It is rarely that any one can attend a house of religious worship without gaining some wholesome information. And the slave will generally learn, at such places, the reasons which sanction the master to exact of him his respective duties.

Source: The Farmers Register, Jan. 1, 1837.

Beneath this confident assertion of white impregnability lay an anxious fear. To keep it at bay, slaveowners pursued a number of stratagems. While most whites, North and South, saw blacks as inferior, their confidence in that opinion depended significantly on the control they believed they held over the black masses. The beliefs of absolute dominance they developed to assure themselves of security in the midst of millions of repressed blacks were reflected not only in their posture and practices toward slaves but in their imaginations. Fantasies about a vast mass of subordinated blacks were acted out in theaters everywhere where African Americans were symbolically debased and dehumanized and where white superiority and security were systematically affirmed.

The psychological assault on slaves was persistent but was given profound physical meaning whenever they found themselves on the auction block. Treated like brute animals for sale, the experience indelibly burned subordination into their consciousness. Men and women were often stripped to the waist so their sturdiness could be appraised; sometimes, slave traders would knead female stomachs to prove their capacity for producing offspring. And, sometimes, male and female chattels had their unetched backs displayed as evidence of obedient rather than unruly behavior which would have been evidenced in an embossed canvas of flesh etched with scars from whippings.

Surveillance of slaves was part of the system of control. Former slaves recalled the "paddyrollers," whites who were hired to watch over the movement of slaves, to ensure that slaves encountered off their owners' property had proper permission and to apprehend those who did not. They remarked that overseers, another agent of slave control, often delighted in administering beatings of recalcitrant slaves, especially in the whipping of females. In his 1849 autobiography, Kentucky-born former slave Henry Bibb lamented that he had not been able to protect his wife when Madison Garrison took her and declared that he would beat her. Bibb, his wife, and their child were being held by Garrison in a Louisiana prison while he sought buyers for them. With a hickory timber paddle in hand, "about one inch thick, three inches in width, and about eighteen inches in length," Garrison took Mrs. Bibb into a prison room. As her husband recorded, he had "often heard Garrison say, that he had rather paddle a female, than eat when he was hungry, that it was music for him to hear them scream, and to see their blood run." Those designated for this sort of punishment were always "stripped naked" first.

Disregard for the gender, age, and marital status of slaves was part of whites' disdain. When the father of Virginia slave Elizabeth Keckley was sold to owners in Tennessee, the family was devastated. Writing as a free woman in 1868, Keckley, who had purchased herself and eventually became the White House dressmaker for Mary Todd Lincoln, remembered vividly the separation, her parent's grief, and the chilling response of her mother's owner. After being told to stop her "nonsense" and "putting on airs," the mother of Keckley was rebuked for acting as if her husband was the only slave "sold from his family,"

Abolitionists Describe "Slavery As It Is"

The slaves are often tortured by iron collars, with long prongs or "horns," and sometimes bells attached to them—they are made to wear chains, handcuffs, fetters, iron clogs, bars, rings, and bands of iron upon their limbs, iron marks upon their faces, iron gags in their mouths, &c.

In proof of this, we give the testimony of slaveholders themselves. under their own names; it will be mostly in the form of extracts from their own advertisements, in southern newspapers, in which, describing their runaway slaves, they specify the iron collars, handcuffs, chains, fetters, &c., which they wore upon their necks, wrists, ankles, and other parts of their bodies. . . .

WITNESSES	TESTIMONY
Mr. Hazlet Loflano, in the *Spectator,* Staunton, Virginia, Sept. 27, 1838.	"Ranaway, a Negro named David—with some *iron hobbles around each ankle.*"
Mr. T. Enggy, New Orleans, Gallatin street, between Hospital and Barracks, *N.O. Bee,* Oct. 27, 1837.	"Ranaway. Negress Caroline—had on *a collar with one prong turned down.*"
Mr. Francis Durett, Lexington, Lauderdale county, Ala., in the *Huntsville Democrat,* August 29, 1837.	"Ranaway, a Negro man named Charles—had on a *drawing chain,* fastened around his ankle with a house lock."
H. Gridly, sheriff of Adams county, Miss., in the *Memphis* (Tenn.) *Times,* September, 1834.	"Was committed to jail, a Negro boy—had on a *large neck iron* with a *huge pair of horns and a large bar or band or iron* on his left leg.
Mr. T. J. De Yampert, merchant, Mobile, Alabama, of the firm of De Yampert, King & Co., in the *Mobile Chronicle,* June 15. 1838.	"Ranaway, a Negro boy about *twelve* years old—had round his neck a *chain dog-collar,* with 'De Yampert' engraved on it."
Mr. Charles Curcner, New Orleans, in the *Bee,* July 2, 1838.	"Ranaway, the Negro, Hown—has a *ring of iron on his left foot.* Also, Grisee, his *wife,* having a *ring and chain on the left leg.*"
Mr. Francis Durett, Lexington, Alabama, in the *Huntsville Democrat,* March 8, 1838.	"Ranaway ———, a mulatto—had on when he left, a *pair of handcuffs* and a *pair of drawing chains.*"
B. W. Hodges, jailor, Pike county, Alabama, in the *Montgomery Advertiser,* Sept. 29, 1837.	"Committed to jail, a man who calls his name John—he has a *clog of iron on his right foot which will weigh four or five pounds.*"
P. Bayhi, captain of the police, in the *N. O. Bee,* June 9, 1838.	"Detained at the police jail, the Negro wench Myra—has several marks of *lashing,* and has *irons on her feet.*"

The foregoing advertisements are sufficient for our purpose, scores of similar ones may be gathered from the newspapers of the slave states every month.

Source: Theodore Dwight Weld, *American Slavery As It Is . . .* (New York, American Anti-Slavery Society, 1839), pp. 79–81.

and as though she were the "only [slave who] had to part." What next was said suggests that countless white women viewed female slaves as unlike themselves. Herself a mother and a wife, the plantation mistress declared: "There are plenty more men about here, and if you want a husband so badly, stop your crying, and go find another."

THE TREATMENT OF SLAVE WOMEN

Southern white men articulated a sense of honor that demanded violent retaliation against any disrespect, especially toward one's family, and white women were held up as paragons of feminity and morality to be protected at all costs. But black women and men were accorded treatment diametrically opposed to such values. Slave women were forced to perform work that the ruling race considered unthinkable for white women, and black men who dared to defend black women invariably suffered swift punishment, sometimes death.

According to scholar Angela Davis, the widespread sexual violence that slave women were subjected to was aimed at black men as well. Citing the worldwide history of conquering forces' rape of women, the just fruits of war, she argues that such attacks functioned not only as a source of sexual gratification but as a way to impress upon vanquished men the totality of their subjugation. Perhaps to deflect attention from white rapists and the mulatto children, whom they either kept as slaves for themselves and their white children, or, just as often, sold, some of the South's most respected and enterprising minds created and perpetuated negative myths about black sexuality.

Opportunities abounded in the South to inflame white passions. The paucity of clothing provided slave laborers and the nature of much of their work gave onlookers frequent exposure to black bodies. Travelers to the South often commented on bondsmen "stripped to the waist" as they toiled in urban industries. It is not too much to assume that long hours of hauling and pressing tobacco as well as other strenuous work developed ample muscles that must have glistened with sweat under the hot southern sun. Slave women, to prevent the bottoms of their dresses from getting wet, commonly drew them up with a string, popularly known as a "second-belt," whenever they mopped floors or engaged in outdoor tasks. Glimpses of dark flesh probably confirmed for many the primordial sexuality of physically mature but supposedly mentally infantile blacks. The product of these perceptions, combined with the power to act on them, was detailed graphically by Harriet Jacobs after she escaped to the North. Writing in 1861 as alias fugitive Linda Brent, Jacobs recounted how she had been sexually stalked for years, beginning while still an adolescent, by her owner, a prominent North Carolina physician and father of eleven slave children. After describing her life with these enslavers, she sternly admonished northerners who, despite their knowledge of "this wild beast of Slavery," acted "the part of bloodhounds" by tracking and returning slave self-emancipators to lifelong bondage.

"How Slavery Improves the Condition of Women." *American Anti-Slavery Almanac for 1840* (New York: American Anti-Slavery Society, 1839). Credit: The Library Company of Philadelphia.

SLAVE LABOR AND COERCION

While certainly most slave men and probably a significant number of bond-women were spared the sexual exploitation of ruling whites, none except those too young or too old would have escaped the grueling and tedious rigors of slave labor. On average, from sunup to sundown, enslaved blacks did everything from hoeing to cooking and carpentry to weaving. During harvest time, all slaves, whether house or field workers, usually were put to work gathering and preparing a variety of cash crops for market. A day's labor could easily stretch to fourteen hours. Those slaves assigned to labor in the urban dwellings or plantation "Big House" of wealthy slaveholders are traditionally described as "privileged." Their duties could entail crack-of-dawn marketing, ironing, cleaning, and a host of other tasks that sometimes ended with their serving late-night parties. Rarely were these servants not "on call." But the vast majority of slaves worked outside, locked in a perennial cycle of planting, weeding, and harvesting.

Roughly three-quarters of the slave population toiled in the fields, and most of them labored in gangs that produced cotton, the prominence of which ascended steadily following the 1790 invention of the cotton gin. The amount of work done by a healthy adult bondsman, or "full hand," was used to establish a standard for other slaves. Female slaves, especially those pregnant or nursing, sometimes were put in all-women gangs and designated "three-quarter" or half hands. Both women and men were expected to pick anywhere from 90 to 150 pounds of cotton a day. The cotton boom of the late antebellum period, and the added burden that it put on workers, probably explains the marked increase in the number of miscarriages among slave women.

With a season that began in late July or early August and lasted almost until the new year, in an area expanding from North Carolina through Arkansas and, later, Alabama and Mississippi, enslaved blacks made cotton an extraordinarily profitable crop. Their crowning glory, however, was the contribution they made to the economy of the South and to the country as a whole. By the end of the antebellum period, the South was marketing all but one-quarter of the nation's exports. It is no wonder that before the Civil War, the South was home to the twelve richest counties in the country. Whether producing sugar in Louisiana; rice in South Carolina and Georgia; tobacco in Virginia, North Carolina, Kentucky, and Tennessee; or toiling in mines, foundries, and other industries, the backbreaking labor of Africans and African-American slaves bestowed upon this land tremendous wealth that they never shared.

When interviewed years later, former slaves remembered bitterly their unpaid toil and how they had protested against their plight. So common was their destruction of tools that southern whites invented an almost indestructible multipurpose implement they called a "nigger hoe." In response to slave work slowdowns and other acts of resistance, slaveowners hired a corps of assistants to help them monitor closely slave movements and actions—particularly in the field. Even children, who were set by their owners to doing light and not-so-light tasks between the ages of eight and twelve, felt the gaze and the wrath of their overseers. A mother who had escaped to Canada reported making pads for her children's heads after they had developed sore spots and lost hair from the constant carrying of water buckets to workers in the field. Nancy Williams, an ex-slave from Virginia, never forgot what happened to her as a little girl when she and other children were directed to pick worms from tobacco leaves. Many decades later, Williams recalled that her master, discovering that she had missed some, "Picked up a hand full of worms, . . . an' stuffed 'em inter my mouth; Lordy knows how many of dem shiny things I done swallered, but I sho' picked em off careful arter dat."

Beatings were a constant reminder of any unfinished or poorly done task; avoiding them was a primary motivation for adult slaves. Charles Ball, a Maryland bondsman who early in the nineteenth century was separated from his wife and children when his owner sold and shipped him to South Carolina, described intimately each detail of commonly used beating implements

> The staff is about twenty-two inches in length, with a large and heavy head, which is often loaded with a quarter or half a pound of lead wrapped in cat gut, and securely fastened on, so that nothing but the greatest violence can separate it from the staff. The lash is ten feet long, made of small strips of buckskin, tanned so as to be dry and hard, and plaited carefully and closely together, of the thickness, in the largest part, of a man's little finger, but quite small at each extremity. At the farthest end of this throng is attached a cracker, nine inches in length, made of strong sewing silk, twisted and knotted, until it feels as firm as the hardest twine.

Historian Jacqueline Jones has summarized the place of violence in American slavery by calling it "an economic and political system by which a group of whites extracted as much labor as possible from blacks (defined as the off-spring of black or mulatto mothers) through the use or threat of force."

SLAVE SOCIETY AND THE CREATION
OF AFRICAN-AMERICAN IDENTITY

According to the 1850 census, almost half of all slaves during the decade before emancipation were fourteen years old or younger. They, like slave youth before them, learned their most lasting and important lessons from a network of blood-related and fictive kin. These youths were taught whenever and wherever elders could find some time and space, usually in the slave quarters after the day's work. The culture, ideas, values, and worldview they learned were grounded securely in a framework of African and American concepts.

Whether part of the majority that lived on plantations with twenty or more slaves or the smaller group bound to farms where it was far harder to create autonomous space, both African-born and New World Africans grasped firmly the link between autonomy and freedom. No matter what the proximity of slaves was to those who enslaved them, a black group consciousness convinced most to distance themselves as far away from the dominant population as possible. This conviction would never have taken root had the multitude of different African ethnic groups, many harboring ancient hostilities toward the other, not been able to coalesce as a single people. The process was complex and no one has offered more powerful or perceptive insights about it than historian Sterling Stuckey. He argues that through common threads of religion, art, music, and dance, all symbolized in the "ring shout," a tradition derived from African ceremonies, formerly distinct ethnicities re-created themselves and merged together by simultaneously unraveling and reweaving both old and new patterns.

What African captives retained from their homeland was shaped by its utility for them collectively. Those African words that the widest number of people would have recognized, for example, stood a far stronger chance of surviving than those known only to a small group. For generations, parents kept memories of Africa alive partly by giving their children African day names. Because fathers were more likely to be separated from their wives and offspring through sale than mothers from their husbands and children, sons often were named after their fathers or grandfathers to remember those vital connections. Both parents confronted the harsh reality that one day they might not be there to guide their loved ones; this truth may explain why they so doggedly held on to African familial traditions and beliefs that provided support through an extensive kinship system.

GENDER AND FAMILY IN SLAVE SOCIETY

In the complicated syncretizing of African and North American realities, a critical component of black survival was the reconstruction of African concepts about gender. Despite the vastly different cultures of Africa, certain generalizations can be made about views of women and men and the roles that each sex should play. No matter from which ethnic group these Africans came, their beliefs about maleness and femaleness are broadly discernible. Men were responsible not only for any hunting that was done, but for the military protection of the entire community. African women helped to feed everyone through their extensive agricultural production and provided almost all the child care, cleaning, cooking, and washing needs for the group as a whole. But African concepts about the place of both men and women would never again be the same.

Just how dramatically the roles and expectations of New World Africans shifted is revealed in one of the most famous accounts of a confrontation between a slave and the man employed to break his spirit. Recorded by Frederick Douglass, who became the most famous African-American abolitionist and nineteenth-century black leader, the account is rarely recited completely. When he was about sixteen years old, Douglass fought a two-hour battle with Edward Covey, an older white male who "enjoyed the most unbounded reputation for being a first-rate overseer and negro-breaker." Douglass considered this particular struggle to be the "turning point" in his life. He wrote, "It rekindled the few expiring embers of freedom, and revived within me a sense of my own manhood." His fate could have been very different. During the fight, Covey ordered two slaves to restrain the young Douglass; both refused. One was a large and "powerful" woman named Caroline whom Douglass declared "could have mastered me easily, exhausted as I was." Because of her aid to Douglass, she received "several sharp blows" from Covey. While men sometimes intervened on behalf of women, so too did women for men, but both knew that, such assistance could not be depended upon.

It is striking that in the testimony of slaves, there is almost no criticism of black men who stood by without acting or failed to retaliate upon discovering that their mothers, sisters, aunts, wives, or lovers had been sexually violated by white men. Similarly, there is very little evidence that the women who succumbed to sexual violence and then carried and bore the product of that violence were ostracized by other slaves. Generations of black adults molded black girls and boys to believe and to pass on to their progeny a determination to do whatever they individually and collectively needed to survive and subvert the institution of slavery. By instilling a strong spirit in each sex, slave families assured that the struggle against bondage would not be gendered. One slave mother conveyed these lessons in a way that her daughter never forgot. She warned: "I'll kill you, gal, if you don't stand up for yourself. Fight, and if you can't fight, kick; if you can't kick, then bite."

Slave women progressed further in their thinking about gender than men. Enslaved males, consistent with patriarchal patterns in Africa, typically viewed women as responsible for child care and most domestic tasks. This outlook was reinforced by slaveholders whose views of women's place and duties resembled those in African societies. By assigning slave women all of the clothes washing and housecleaning, white males explicitly recognized slave men's right to be relieved, except as a form of punishment, from "women's work."

Although male slaves held fast to certain traditional beliefs about gender, they cooperated with their women to create viable family structures and styles under slavery's heavy stress. How best to preserve the family unit and the ideas shaping its distinctive character was one of the great challenges that enslaved men and women faced. In meeting this task, slaves created discrete rules to govern marriage, courtship, and premarital sex. Unlike the white elite, who typically entered endogamous relations by marrying first cousins, slaves maintained a rigid exogamy. There were also strict rules about courting: boys seem to have been granted permission at an earlier age than girls. Young women adorned themselves with ribbons and perfumed their dresses with certain flowers; special songs from boys confirmed their interest. Evidence exists that young men would also demonstrate their seriousness as well as prove their manliness by defying the rules against unsanctioned absences by visiting sweethearts without the requisite "passes" from masters.

In light of slave rules against what they saw as incestuous bonds and the near impossibility of finding suitable mates on small farms with just one or two slaves, a good deal of after-hour and nightly travels, customarily done by the males rather than the females, was widespread. Both sexes, however, ventured out to social affairs that were far more common than thought. Fiddling, dancing, eating, and, not infrequently, drinking spirituous refreshments characterized many of these gay and festive gatherings. Devout Christians and pretenders alike took advantage of religious meetings to commune with prospective mates. Wherever they met, however, permission to court usually had to be obtained first from the girl's parents. As for premarital sex, slaves seemed to have followed African patterns. In most African societies, women did not have children before marriage, but there were exceptions. Some groups in West Africa imposed no social sanctions against a young woman who had given birth outside of wedlock. Remnants of each cultural norm were found among Africans and their descendants in North America.

The great emphasis on family ties kept alive a special adoration of motherhood among slaves. This positive trait provided added means, however, for slaveowners to control slave behavior with threats to sell rebellious family members. The threats of slave masters and mistresses to disrupt family life, which slaves collectively cherished, were not idle talk. For punitive and economic reasons, between 1810 and 1820, more than 130,000 slave chattels were sold and driven across the Appalachian Mountains to work in the Southwest. On average, from 1820 to the Civil War, more than 200,000 slaves were forcefully removed each decade to newer fields of slavery primarily in Georgia, Alabama, Mississippi, Louisiana, and Texas. As a consequence, it is estimated that one out of every three first marriages among Upper South slaves was aborted.

Decisions to enter motherhood and fatherhood were especially complex under slavery. The high mortality of slave babies, about twice that of white infants, may have influenced slaves to have large families. The pervasive threat of sexual violence and coercion may also have had an impact on prospective enslaved parents. What could await any black captive, man or woman, single, married, or engaged, was given rare exposure in a 1937 interview. Working with the "Negro Writers' Unit" of the Federal Writers' Project in Florida, African-American Pearl Randolph spoke with two "pitifully infirm" ex-Virginia slaves.

Mr. and Mrs. Sam Everett, eighty-six and ninety, respectively, met as slave children on the plantation of "Big Jim" McClain near Norfolk, Virginia. McClain, who owned more than one hundred slaves, "mated indiscriminately" those whom be thought would produce "strong, healthy offspring"; no regard was given to their marital status. If any resisted, he made them fornicate in front of him. The same was demanded of slave couples whom McClain felt were "not producing children fast enough." Not only did McClain invite friends to watch and participate by allowing them to take and to have whatever slaves they desired, but he and his party sometimes "forced the unhappy husbands and lovers of their victims to look on."

The Everetts were not speaking from hearsay. Louisa Everett, whose childhood name was "Nor," confided:

> Marse Jim called me and Sam ter him and ordered Sam to pull off his shirt—that was all the McClain niggers wore—and he said to me, "Nor, do you think you can stand this big nigger?" He had that old bull whip flung acrost his shoulder, and Lawd, that man could hit so hard! So I jes said "yassur, I guess so," and tried to hide my face so I couldn't see Sam's nakedness, but he made me look at him anyhow.
>
> Well he told us what we must get busy and do in his presence, and we had to do it. After that we were considered man and wife. Me and Sam was a healthy pair and had fine, big babies, so I never had another man forced on me, thank God. Sam was kind to me and I learnt to love him.

When black women and men decided to have a child, whether in or out of wedlock, they were exercising a rare opportunity to make a choice in a world with few choices. That many women became mothers before entering into long-term relations or marriages with men who were not always the fathers suggests communitywide approval. It is inconceivable that such a pattern could have evolved had black men collectively shunned women who had children by men other than themselves, black or white. Just as bondpeople of both sexes enforced rules of exogamy, slave men and women tried to abide as closely as they could to their traditions, both old and new, of courting, parenting, and sexuality.

From birth to death, a community of blood-related and biologically unrelated black adults guided slave youth. Through honorific titles such as "Uncle," "Aunt," "Mother," "Father," "Sister," or "Cousin," slave children learned of a black world that enveloped far more than the confines legally prescribing them. If liberty was to be theirs, as each unfree generation insisted it would, unity among enslaved and free blacks was key. Tales of success and failure filtered through slave quarters; reports of black northerners and southerners who aided escapees by providing food and housing, as well as individual and group betrayals that divulged fugitive routes, hammered in a similar message of the urgent need for racial cooperation.

Besides preserving their history in voluminous oral texts, black elders perfected, taught, and promoted every stratagem that they believed would help their people to survive. Perhaps none was more effective than the broad mask of servility that they coached all to wear in order to disguise their desire for freedom. So effective were slave performances in satisfying the innermost desires of white audiences generally and slaveholding whites in particular that when thousands of ostensibly happy slaves vanished, only to reappear armed and unsmiling in U.S. military attire, southern whites suffered a collective shock. Few nightmares were as terrifying to whites as blacks in arms. Their final solution to this recurring horror was a decision to take no black prisoners from among captured Union troops. The 1864 massacre of three hundred black soldiers after their surrender at Fort Pillow in Tennessee proved the seriousness of Confederate intentions.

CONCLUSION

Despite the initial rejection of black soldiers by the northern government and civilian authorities, almost two hundred thousand African-American men, mostly southerners, eventually served in the Union forces. In the War of Secession, countless black women, working as spies, nurses, scouts, and cooks, sacrificed their service and sometimes their lives for the Union cause. The valor and determination of both sexes were simply the culmination and congealing of behaviors established in a much older war. To them, the aim of each was the same: freedom. One among the liberated and, hence, victorious was Hawkins Wilson. What had helped him and millions of others to survive and to wage their seemingly endless battles before Emancipation still exerted enormous power after 1865.

In an 1867 letter that the recently married Texas freedman forwarded through a relief agency, Wilson tried desperately to reconstruct a Caroline County, Virginia, family that white slaveowners and their agents had separated twenty-four years earlier. After providing a lengthy list of his "dearest relatives," where they had lived more than two decades past, and the names of their former owners, Hawkins enclosed the following inquiry:

Dear Sister Jane, Your little brother Hawkins is trying to find out where you are and where his poor old mother is. Let me know and I will come to see you. I shall never forget the bag of biscuits you made for me the last night I spent with you. Your advice to me to meet you in Heaven has never passed from my mind and I have endeavored to live as near to my God, that if He saw fit not to suffer us to meet on earth, we might indeed meet in Heaven. Please send me some of Julia's hair whom I left a baby in the cradle when I was torn away from you. I know that she is a young lady now, but I hope she will not deny her affectionate uncle this request. Thank God that now we are not sold and torn away from each other as we used to be.

Hawkins Wilson's dream of family reunion was shared by the masses of other freedmen. After Emancipation the search for separated kinfolk, as well as loved ones, constituted a primary preoccupation of black southerners. Reunion, in their minds, was connected with the very essence of freedom.

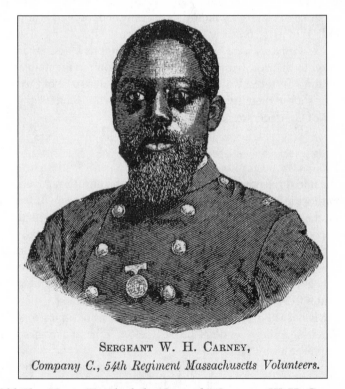

SERGEANT W. H. CARNEY,
Company C., 54th Regiment Massachusetts Volunteers.

"The Old Flag Never Touched the Ground." Sergeant W. H. Carney of the 54th Massachusetts Volunteers was among the hundreds of African-American soldiers in the Civil War. From James M. Guthrie's *Campaigns of the Afro-American* (Philadelphia, 1899). Credit: The Library Company of Philadelphia.

FOR FURTHER READING

Aptheker, Herbert. *American Negro Slave Revolts*. New York: International Publishers Co., 1983.

Blassingame, John W. The *Slave Community: Plantation Life in the Antebellum South*. New York: Oxford University Press, 1979.

Degler, Carl N. *Neither Black Nor White: Slavery and Race Relations in Brazil and the United States*. Madison: University of Wisconsin Press, 1986.

Elkins, Stanley M. *Slavery: A Problem in American Institutional and Intellectual Life*. 3rd rev. ed. Chicago: University of Chicago Press, 1976.

Fogel, Robert W., and Stanley L. Engerman. *Time on the Cross: The Economics of American Negro Slavery*. New York: W. W. Norton & Co., 1995.

Fox-Genovese, Elizabeth. *Within the Plantation Household: Black and White Women of the Old South*. Chapel Hill: University of North Carolina Press, 1988

Franklin, John Hope, and Loren Schweninger. *Runaway Slaves: Rebels on the Plantation*. New York: Oxford University Press, 1999.

Gates, Henry Louis, ed. *The Classic Slave Narratives*. New York: New American Library, 1987.

Genovese, Eugene D. *Roll, Jordan, Roll: The World the Slaves Made*. New York: Random House, 1976.

Gomez, Michael A. *Exchanging Our Country Marks: The Transformation of African Identities in the Colonial and Antebellum South*. Chapel Hill: University of North Carolina Press, 1998.

Gutman, Herbert. *The Black Family in Slavery and Freedom, 1750–1925*. New York: Random House, 1977.

Jones, Norrece T., Jr. *Born a Child of Freedom, Yet a Slave: Mechanisms of Control and Strategies of Resistance in Antebellum South Carolina*. Hanover, N.H.: University Press of New England, 1990

Joyner, Charles. *Down By the Riverside: South Carolina Slave Community*. Urbana: University of Illinois Press, 1986.

King, Wilma. *Stolen Childhood: Slave Youth in Nineteenth-Century America*. Bloomington : Indiana University Press, 1995.

Kolchin, Peter. *American Slavery: 1619–1877*. New York: Hill & Wang, 1994.

Levine, Lawrence W. *Black Culture and Black Consciousness: Afro-American Folk Thought from Slavery to Freedom*. New York: Oxford University Press, 1978.

Owens, Leslie H. *This Species of Property: Slave Life and Culture in the Old South*. New York: Oxford University Press, 1976.

Raboteau, Albert J. *Slave Religion: The "Invisible Institution" in the Antebellum South*. New York: Oxford University Press, 1980.

Stampp, Kenneth. The *Peculiar Institution: Slavery in the Antebellum South*. New York: Vintage, 1989.

Stevenson, Brenda E. *Life in Black and White: Family and Community in the Slave South*. New York: Oxford University Press, 1996.

Stuckey, Sterling. *Slave Culture: Nationalist Theory and the Foundations of Black America*. New York: Oxford University Press, 1987.

White, Deborah G. *Ar'n't I a Woman?: Female Slaves in the Plantation South*. Rev. ed. New York: W. W. Norton & Co., 1999.

chapter 5

"Though We Are Not Slaves, We Are Not Free"

Quasi-Free Blacks in Antebellum America

William G. Shade

HEN THE FIRST "TWENTY NEGARS" were dragged by John Rolfe from a "dutch man of warre" onto the Virginia shore in 1619, they no doubt had been slaves, but under English law they were simply servants like the vast majority of seventeenth-century migrants to the colony. When it became economically more feasible to purchase Africans than white indentured servants, the colonists codified their law, at first limiting the behavior of the African Americans and then eventually creating a status, previously unknown to the Common Law, of chattel slave for life. Briefly there had been a handful of white slaves in Maryland—free-born women who had married slaves—but in time the new status became associated solely with African Americans. As a result, the worldview of British North Americans moved toward a bipolar racial optic in which people were seen as either black or white.

By the time of the American Revolution slavery was entrenched in all of the colonies of British North America, and practically all the people there of African ancestry were enslaved. In 1776 when Thomas Jefferson wrote that "all men are created equal" in justification of the rebellion of the thirteen colonies, free blacks numbered only a few thousand. Few of the revolutionaries were willing to face up to the contradiction between the existence of African-American slavery and their rhetoric concerning the rights of man. Jefferson had included a condemnation of slavery and the slave trade in his draft Declaration, but the Continental Congress quickly removed it. The position of most of the revolutionary generation was one of ambivalence and, consequently, the patriots' attempts to include African Americans in their revolution were hesitant and had mixed results.

Upon taking command of the Continental Army, George Washington ordered recruiters to avoid "any stroller, negro, or vagabond, or person suspected of being an enemy to the liberty of America." Debates about accepting the services of African Americans were complicated by the decision of Lord Dunmore—the loyalist Governor of Virginia—to offer freedom to slaves who would sustain the cause of the Crown. Literally thousands of blacks fled to the English and freedom in the course of the war. Jefferson estimated thirty thousand fugitives from Virginia alone. South Carolina's contemporary historian of the Revolution thought his state lost twenty-five thousand, while three-quarters of Georgia's slaves emancipated themselves when the opportunity presented itself. As the fortunes of war shifted in favor of the rebels, black recruits to the patriot cause mounted and eventually five thousand African Americans—mostly from northern colonies—served the cause of independence as soldiers.

The participation of African Americans combined with the ideology of the Revolution to unleash a wave of public and private emancipation. Considering that before 1774 there had been few signs of abolitionist sentiment anywhere in the colonies, the Revolution ushered in unprecedented change in the legal status of black Americans, creating what Ira Berlin termed "the Free Negro Caste."

FREE BLACKS IN THE NEW REPUBLIC

Within a quarter-century all of the states north of the Mason-Dixon line had provided for the elimination of slavery and the Northwest Ordinance extended the prohibition on the "peculiar institution" west to the Mississippi in the area north of the Ohio River. Vermont's constitution of 1777 specifically banned slavery. While it was not until 1857 that New Hampshire actually outlawed slavery and declared blacks citizens, most whites took the position that the Declaration of Rights in the new state constitution had freed the handful of slaves in that state. Massachusetts was more direct. In the 1783 case of Quok Walker, the state supreme court declared that slavery violated the constitution of 1780. Pennsylvania's 1780 law that all blacks born after that year would be free when they reached adulthood became a model for other states. Connecticut and Rhode Island quickly followed suit passing similar acts, but it was not until 1799 and 1804 that gradual emancipation became a reality in New York and New Jersey.

Ninety percent of all African Americans, however, lived below the Mason-Dixon line. While there was some agitation to end slavery in the Upper South, the main effect of the Revolution was to encourage private manumission. As the northern states enacted gradual universal abolition, the southern states made it easier for masters to individually free their slaves and also moved against the traffic in slaves. The two fastest growing evangelical denominations, whose influence extended across the slave states and whose message attracted blacks as well as whites, spoke out. In 1784 the Methodists declared that slavery was "contrary to the golden laws of God." Five years later the Baptists came out against slavery as a violation of the rights of nature and "inconsistent with republican government."

Yet the new Constitution of the United States reflected the same ambiguity that haunted the Declaration of Independence. The portions of the Constitution referring to slavery were so carefully worded that they failed to directly confront the issue of human bondage. The "three-fifths clause" in Article I, Section 3, that allowed southern states to claim representatives and presidential electors based on this odd formula, referred to slaves as "other persons." In Article IV, Section 2, the provision for the return of fugitive slaves considered them along with other fugitives from the law and termed them persons "Held in Service or Labor." The third part of the Constitution that made direct reference to slaves was Article II, Section 9, which involved the international slave trade and the prohibition on congressional interference with this trade for twenty years—until 1807. In this clause slaves were called "Persons as any state shall think proper to admit." These provisions, however, when combined with the comity clause, a willingness to accept the "due rights of the states," and the extraterritorial reach of state laws on property made it possible for the "peculiar institution" not only to exist, but also to prosper.

Because the largest slaveholding states in the North introduced gradual emancipation that freed only those born after a certain date when they reached adulthood, the "free" North contained a sizable number of slaves well into the nineteenth century. While three-quarters of the northern blacks were free by 1810, there were still 20,000 slaves north of the Mason-Dixon line. Slavery was disappearing from the border state of Delaware at about the same rate through private manumission. By 1840 nearly two-thirds of the African Americans living in the District of Columbia were free, while there were still more than one thousand slaves in the North.

Gradual emancipation, private manumission, and flight boosted the number of free blacks in the border states and the North. After revolution broke out on Santo Domingo in the Caribbean, free mulatto refugees fled to the southern cities of Charleston, Savannah, and New Orleans. Between the end of the American Revolution and the War of 1812, the quasi-free black population grew at a staggering rate. From 1790 to 1810 it increased by more than 300 percent; one in every seven African Americans was legally free. In the Upper South the number tripled and 10 percent of the black population was free. In the lower South the only sizable concentrations of free blacks were in the Atlantic port cities and along the Gulf Coast. When Louisiana became a state in 1812, 18 percent of its black population was free.

The proportion of free blacks in the African-American population of both the North and Upper South grew during the antebellum years, but in the lower South, where it was at its height in 1810, it declined. By 1850 there were approximately the same number of free blacks in the United States as there had

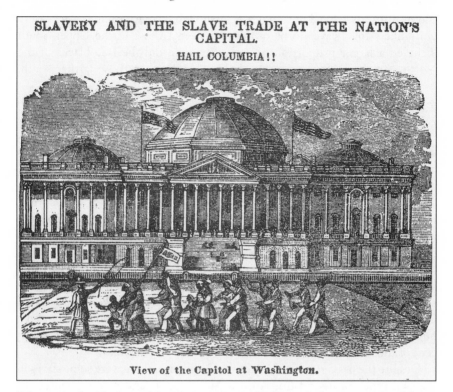

SLAVERY AND THE SLAVE TRADE AT THE NATION'S CAPITAL.

HAIL COLUMBIA!!

View of the Capitol at Washington.

"Slavery in the Shadow of the Nation's Capitol." Though the importing of slaves to the United States was halted by 1807, abolitionists continued to fight for the dissolution of the institution itself. From *Slavery and Slave Trade in Nation's Capital* (New York, 1846). Credit: The Library Company of Philadelphia.

been slaves at the time of the Revolution. A majority of these African Americans lived in the South, and 85 percent of those lived in the Upper South.

The status and character of the free black population differed greatly by region. Northern blacks were freed indiscriminately as a group and reflected the conditions of slavery in the region. They tended to be dark skinned, relatively urban, and generally unskilled. While the free blacks of the lower South were similarly urban, they included a much larger number of mulattoes. In the North less than one-third of the free African-American population was of mixed ancestry, but in the lower South three-quarters were. These "people of color" set themselves apart from the mass of African-American slaves in the region, calling themselves "creoles," or *gens de coulour.* This light-skinned elite that was the product of selective manumission of planters' own descendants included a few families that were exceedingly wealthy, well educated, and sometimes also substantial slaveholders.

Most free blacks in the South were less concentrated in urban areas than were either those in the lower South or those in the North. Seventy-two percent of all free blacks in the South lived in Virginia, Maryland, and Delaware, and most of these lived in rural areas. Although everywhere free blacks were more likely than slaves to be of mixed ancestry, those in the Upper South included a larger proportion of mulattoes than did the free blacks of the North, but they were as a group darker skinned than those farther south.

THE DECLINING ECONOMIC AND LEGAL STATUS OF FREE BLACKS

In the antebellum period the economic condition and legal status of free blacks deteriorated everywhere. The slave states grew more restrictive, limiting private manumission, encouraging colonization, and circumscribing the day-to-day lives of free blacks with a system of curfews and passes. In Georgia, Florida, and Alabama the legislatures even mandated white guardianship. Migration was prohibited or limited, as was public assembly and black preaching. Vagrancy laws weighed on those in the South who could be sold into servitude. Laws also limited ownership of dogs and guns—the symbols of white southern manhood and independence. The extension of suffrage to all white adult males was accompanied by the disfranchisement of blacks not only in the Upper South, where a few had voted, but also in the North. By 1840 when a huge proportion of whites turned out for the presidential election only 8 percent of the free blacks lived in states where they could vote.

Despite the passage of the Northwest Ordinance, there were some slaves in the Old Northwest, and free African Americans in the region lived under restrictive "Black Codes" modeled on the laws of the southern states. Only in Illinois was there a serious movement to introduce slavery after statehood, but the midwestern states never allowed blacks to vote and denied African Americans most of the legal rights of citizens. They also had constitutional prohibitions against black immigration although by 1840 nearly one-fifth of the northern free black population lived in the new western states. Most had fled from the South, and a majority were light skinned. By the time of the Civil War there were almost as many free blacks in Ohio, Indiana, and Illinois as in Virginia.

Prejudice led to antiblack violence throughout the North. The most famous "race riot"—the euphemism for white attacks on free blacks and their property—occurred in Cincinnati in 1829, but there were others elsewhere—in Philadelphia, New York, Pittsburgh, and then again in Cincinnati in 1841. A few cases, such as that in Providence in 1831, produced retaliatory violence from the blacks, but the almost festive spirit of racist white mobs was caught by the Philadelphia rioter who explained that he and his friends were just out "hunting the nigs."

The general climate of prejudice created a pattern de facto as well as de jure segregation that separated the races socially. Intermarriage was generally barred. Schools were segregated, but so too were theaters, hotels, restaurants, hospitals, and cemeteries. Streetcars, stages, railroads, and steamboats developed a pattern of segregated accommodations that were separate and distinctly not equal. Residential segregation and something resembling modern urban ghettos were rather slow to develop in the "walking city." W. E. B. DuBois showed in his classic study of Philadelphia that blacks often lived on the cross streets and alleyways, between streets lined with homes, often the homes of prosperous whites. As the economic situation of free blacks deteriorated, however, areas with names like "Nigger Hill" and "New Guinea" appeared, and housing segregation began to force respectable blacks into undesirable areas often associated with crime, prostitution, gambling, alcohol, and drugs.

EDUCATION, LITERACY, AND EMPLOYMENT

As with other aspects of free black life, education defies generalization and illustrates the ambiguous and conflicting position of the quasi-free people. In the eighteenth century, Protestant groups promoted education to enable the masses to read the Bible. White groups such as the New York Manumission Society opened African schools in the eighteenth century. In Newport, Boston, Philadelphia, and New York City, schools educated various classes of black children. The struggle for education was made arduous by white prejudice that deprived blacks of public support in these efforts or segregated and degraded them. Although some African Americans were admitted to public schools before 1820, generally they were assigned to separate and unequal institutions even in New England. New York, Pennsylvania, and Ohio provided (segregated) education, but even that was denied in most midwestern states until the 1850s.

In the South, wealthy urban mulattoes established their own schools, and in New Orleans the Catholic Church provided for the education of some black children, but generally throughout the region quasi-free blacks were barred from those schools that existed. Baltimore and Washington stood out as exceptions in which a few black schools connected to churches were established. African-American education relied primarily on private sources and consequently reflected the differences between the Upper South and lower South. Nearly all the free blacks of Charleston and Mobile were literate, as were three-fourths of those in New Orleans and Savannah. In the Upper South, however, literacy was less prevalent; in Richmond, for instance, two-thirds of the free blacks could not read or write.

The situation in the North was worse than that in Charleston and Mobile, but better than in the remainder of the southern cities. The census of 1850 reveals that four-fifths of the urban free black adults were literate. In Boston that figure reached 90 percent, and in Providence, 96 percent. Yet the example of Boston reveals the ambiguous nature of the achievement. After a good deal of organized effort to gain access to the white public school system of Massachusetts, blacks were successful in most of the smaller towns but still shut out in Boston. In 1849 Benjamin Roberts brought suit to have his daughter admitted to the nearest school. The state supreme court ruled that separate-but-equal facilities did not violate the commonwealth's constitution. Fortunately, the reform-minded "Know-Nothing" (anti-Catholic) dominated legislature passed a bill in 1855 prohibiting segregation.

Illiteracy and racial prejudice combined to restrict economic opportunity for free blacks, but the different nature of the free African-American communities in the lower South, the Upper South, and the North meant that the caste endured a variety of economic conditions. In Charleston three-fourths of the free blacks were in skilled trades—carpenters, tailors, millwrights, and barbers. Much the same was true in New Orleans where the 1850 census reported 1 architect, 4 doctors, and 64 merchants; in all 165 men—that is, 9 percent of the city's free black population—engaged in "pursuits which may be considered as requiring an education." The most frequently listed occupation was "artisan," a category including 355 carpenters and 278 masons. Only 10 percent were listed as laborers. In rural Louisiana there were 158 farmers and 244 planters, nearly all of whom were mulattoes.

The situation in the Upper South was quite different. The proportion of skilled and unskilled in Richmond was inverse to that in Charleston. Also, because Richmond was much more deeply involved in manufacturing, half of the black men worked in the factories, mills, and foundries. One-third had skilled jobs, and the remainder were marginal laborers plagued by irregular employment. Two-thirds of those in the Upper South lived in rural areas. In North Carolina 75 percent were farmers or farm laborers, and the others worked in tanneries, in turpentine stills, or as woodcutters. These were the poorest of the free blacks, and some were living in situations with long-term indentures.

The situation in the lower South deteriorated in the final decade before the Civil War. While the light-skinned elite continued to do fairly well, the rest of the blacks were being forced closer to slavery. Almost everywhere in the cities of the South, free blacks faced increasing competition from the wave of Irish and German immigrants entering the country in the 1840s and 1850s. As many more immigrants entered the northern cities, this pressure was more acutely felt by free blacks there. A detailed study of Philadelphia has charted the sharp deterioration of the economic conditions of free blacks in that city, especially after 1840 as the Irish took over jobs traditionally considered suitable only for black workers.

Northern free blacks were even more concentrated in urban areas than were those of the lower South. Philadelphia, New York, Boston, and Cincinnati all had large free black populations. But, because of the large number of middle-sized towns in the North, only one-third of New York state's free blacks lived in New York City and Brooklyn, and only one-fifth of those in Pennsylvania lived in Philadelphia. In northern cities between two-thirds and four-fifths of the free black males were unskilled.

The general employment situation of free blacks in the North can be seen in the comparison put forward in the 1850 census between Louisiana and New

Orleans, on the one hand, and Connecticut and New York City, on the other. In Connecticut only 7 percent were farmers; most free blacks lived in towns. More than half of all employed men were laborers. Barbers, shoemakers, and other artisans made up only 7 percent of the employed male free blacks. The largest single profession was seamen, which accounted for 16 percent of the workers. The census counted "only twenty individuals in occupations requiring education" comparing the situation unfavorably to that in Louisiana.

The census also compared New York City unfavorably to New Orleans. Only one-fifth of New York's employed free blacks were mulattoes, and "sixty were clerks, doctors, druggists, lawyers, merchants, ministers, printers, students or teachers"—2 percent of those employed. In fact, New York had twenty-one ministers and nine doctors, and New Orleans had one minister and four doctors. New York had four printers and four lawyers, while New Orleans had none of either profession. New Orleans had twelve teachers and New York only eight. The real difference was in clerks and merchants, who together provide 125 of New Orleans's 165 educated professionals, and almost all of whom were mulattoes dependent entirely on the patronage of whites. In New York about one-third of the free black men were day laborers and an equal proportion were domestics—coachmen, servants, and butlers. Thirteen percent of the African-American men employed in New York City in 1850 were seamen, but only 12.5 percent were in skilled trades. In this proportion of skilled laborers, New York was typical of northern cities where free blacks were less likely to have skills than in Charleston and New Orleans.

FREE BLACK FAMILIES AND COMMUNITIES

Free blacks tended to be predominantly female, a demographic condition that affected the economic role of women and their position in the family throughout the country. Although it took many forms, the family was the basic institution of the free black communities, providing the economic, psychological, and social support necessary for community's survival. Its strengths and weaknesses reflected the strengths and weaknesses of the free African-American communities, and its distinctive structure reflected the conditions of these communities.

The mulatto elite of the lower South was the product of miscegenation primarily between white men and female slaves and the subsequent manumission of the children and sometimes of the mothers themselves. As a consequence the group tended to have skills, education, and white patronage enabling them to replicate the cultural mores of the whites and create a degree of marital stability. Family became a crucial defining element of this elite, and marital alliances between prominent families helped sustain their privileged economic position.

While this group followed the white middle-class model, and rural free black families resembled in their structure that of the poor whites, in the southern cities, including New Orleans and Charleston, where women made up nearly three-fifths of the free black population, a disproportionate number of female-headed households and a high proportion of free black women worked outside the home as maids, cooks, washerwomen, and peddlers. In the countryside, free black women worked in similar capacities for local whites and sometimes labored in the fields as well.

The situation for free black families in the North resembled that in southern cities. There were a large number of single adult women in these communities and a relatively large number of female-headed households—in Philadelphia and Boston slightly more than one-fifth of all households. Paradoxically the private role of free black women resembled that of whites of similar economic condition in that they were essential to the family economy, while their public role was more pervasive than that of all but a small segment of white middle-class women. A detailed study of free black families in Boston has shown that their importance in "the family economy facilitated an expansion of their social and political influence in community affairs."

In Boston one found a variety of family situations among free blacks. The majority lived in black households either as members of a nuclear family or as boarders. The average African-American household in Boston in 1850 contained a married couple and two children; three-quarters of the city's black children lived in two-parent households. Since white institutions refused to accept them, homeless African-American children had to depend upon the kindness of strangers, and consequently 9 percent of Boston's black children lived with people who probably were not their biological parents. Many were kin or church members, and in general the Boston situation was better than that in cities like Providence where such children were often bound out as servants to white families.

There were almost twice as many single adult females as there were single adult males, and fewer than half of Boston's adult African-American women were married. Free blacks married generally in their twenties with the grooms being usually two years older than the brides. As the age of the groom rose, however, the differential increased so that if a free black woman reached her thirties without marrying she probably never would. Marriage was also affected by skin color. Basically blacks married blacks and mulattoes married mulattoes, but in mixed marriages men were generally the darker partner. In those involving whites only two white men were married to black women, but eleven white women were married to black men.

Married free black women generally held two "jobs," working as domestics outside the home while running their own households. A large number of African-American women took in boarders. In 1850 one-third of Boston's black households contained boarders and as economic conditions deteriorated during the 1850s the proportion grew to 40 percent as more free blacks were forced to move in with kin. The "hidden depression" of the 1850s hit the blacks particularly hard and it had destructive effects on the African-American family. Not only were more people forced to move in with relatives, but the proportion of black children living in two-parent households declined and the number of women working outside the home soared. In Boston well over half of the married women and maybe as many as three-quarters of the unmarried women and teenage girls were employed workers.

A large number of single black men lived in boarding houses clustered in a neighborhood separate from "the hill" where the more respectable married families lived. For these young men—many of whom were seamen—their boarding houses functioned as social organizations of an often rough sort, supporting their drinking, small-time gambling, and casual sex. The connection between these black neighborhoods remained, and men who in their teens and early twenties were fancy dressers, womanizers, gamblers, and drinkers often "got married, got religion and moved to the hill."

AFRICAN-AMERICAN CHURCHES
AND BENEVOLENT SOCIETIES

In 1849 Martin R. Delaney wrote to Frederick Douglass, "As among our people generally the Church is the Alpha and Omega of all things." African Americans underwent a "spiritual holocaust" in the process of enslavement, but since the late eighteenth century, they have been characterized by their commitment to their churches. Essentially the congregation provided day-to-day support of both a spiritual and material nature to their believers and functioned as the hub of small communities, providing a context for their social life as well. The black ministers were both spiritual advisors and community leaders, condemning segregation and slavery, but also warning against the usual variety of personal sins.

Even though white Baptists and Methodists proselytized among the slaves and free blacks and gained thousands of converts, separate black churches quickly appeared. In Philadelphia Richard Allen and Absolom Jones took the first step toward creating a national African-American sect when they were expelled from St. George's Methodist Church, which they had attended and where Allen had preached. Personal and theological differences between them led Jones and his followers to establish St. Thomas African Episcopal Church, which retained its relation to the white parent body, and Allen to found the independent Bethel African Methodist Episcopal Church (AME).

In 1816 representatives of the various African Methodist churches that had grown up in the region met in Philadelphia to form a national AME body, choosing Allen as its first bishop. At the beginning of the nineteenth century black Baptist churches appeared in Boston, New York, Philadelphia, and other northern cities. Reverend Thomas Paul, who first organized a black church in Boston, became famous as the pastor of the Abyssinian Baptist Church in New York. There were also separate black Presbyterian and Episcopal congregations in the North, although they generally retained some affiliation with the parent bodies.

In the South, Morris Brown led an AME congregation in Charleston, South Carolina, but he was driven from the city in the wake of the Denmark Vesey slave conspiracy of 1822. In Virginia black Baptist churches grew up in Richmond, Norfolk, and Petersburg, but eventually these were undermined by the repressive laws passed in response to the Nat Turner revolt in 1831. Not only in Virginia but also in North Carolina, Alabama, and Georgia, tight restrictions were imposed on independent black congregations. Only in parts of the Upper South did African-American Baptist churches survive white persecution.

Aside from the churches, the free black communities contained benevolent societies and fraternal organizations that greatly enhanced the quality of African-American life. Mutual benefit societies originated to provide a decent burial of members and to collectively respond to natural disasters that could ruin an individual artisan, but their scope extended to helping fellow blacks improve their position in life by encouraging thrift, hard work, moral life, and

An Experience in the Life of Richard Allen

A number of us usually attended St. George's church in Fourth street; and when the colored people began to get numerous in attending the church, they moved us from the seats we usually sat on, and placed us around the wall, and on Sabbath morning we went to church and the sexton stood at the door, and told us to go in the gallery. He told us to go, and we would see where to sit. We expected to take the seats over the ones we formerly occupied below, not knowing any better. We took those seats. Meeting had begun, and they were nearly done singing, and just as we got to the seats, the elder said, "Let us pray." We had not been long upon our knees before I heard considerable scuffling and low talking. I raised my head up and saw one of the trustees, H—— M—— , having hold of the Rev. Absolom Jones, pulling him up off of his knees, and saying, "You must get up— you must not kneel here." Mr. Jones replied, "Wait until prayer is over." Mr. H— — M—— said "No, you must get up now, or I will call for aid and force you away." Mr. Jones said, "Wait until prayer is over, and I will get up and trouble you no more." With that he beckoned to one of the other trustees, Mr. L—— S—— to come to his assistance. He came, and went to William White to pull him up. By this time prayer was over, and we all went out of the church in a body, and they were no more plagued with us in the church. This raised a great excitement and inquiry among the citizens, in so much that I believe they were ashamed of their conduct. But my dear Lord was with us, and we were filled with fresh vigor to get a house erected to worship God in. Seeing our forlorn and distressed situation, many of the hearts of our citizens were moved to urge us forward; notwithstanding we had subscribed largely towards finishing St. George's church, in building the gallery and laying new floors, and just as the house was made comfortable, we were turned out from enjoying the comforts of worshipping therein. We then hired a store-room and held worship by ourselves ... Here was the beginning and rise of the African church in America.

Source: George A. Singleton, ed., *The Life Experience and Gospel Labors of the Rt. Rev. Richard Allen* (New York: Abingdon Press, 1960), pp. 25–26.

Richard Allen and Daniel Coker were among the founders of the African Methodist Episcopal church in Philadelphia in 1816, one of the most significant of the early African-American institutions. From *Daniel Payne's History of the AME Church*, Philadelphia. Credit: The Library Company of Philadelphia.

self-respect. Jones and Allen's Free African Society formed in 1787 was both spiritual and social in its purpose, establishing a cemetery, supporting informal education, and finding apprenticeships for orphans. By the 1830s such self-culture collectives had spread across the North; in Philadelphia alone there were more than one hundred such groups. The Philadelphia Library Company for Colored Persons provided a reading room and supported lyceum lectures. The Phoenix Society in New York City similarly supported a library, a school, and lectures on subjects ranging from literature to the mechanical arts.

Of a more social nature were the African-American secret societies, the most famous being the Masons founded by Prince Hall in 1787. A part-time Methodist preacher and leader of the Free African Society of Boston, Hall had been a Mason since before the Revolution. Eventually lodges were established in Providence, Baltimore, Washington, even Louisville and New Orleans. The degree to which these groups, the mutual aid societies, and the churches formed an interlocking network within the free black community can be seen in the fact that Philadelphia's black Masons were organized by Reverend Jones, Bishop Allen, and the abolitionist businessman James Forten.

The churches and benevolent societies of the northern free black communities provided the basis for the various political movements of the antebellum era. These groups advocated strategies ranging in a spectrum from complete biological and cultural assimilation through cultural pluralism and communal action to separatism and black nationalism. Generally these seemingly separate racial ideologies were woven together, the emphasis depending upon the context. All elements of the spectrum emphasized both race pride and the Puritan ethics of thrift, industry, and economic accumulation. Much of the debate among African Americans concerned how, as W. E. B. DuBois would later write, "to make it possible for a man to be both a Negro and an American, without being cursed and spat upon by his fellows, without having doors of Opportunity closed roughly in his face."

THE COLONIZATION AND ABOLITION DEBATES

From the end of the eighteenth century, some African Americans advocated the return of American blacks to an African homeland. The Free African Society of Newport made such a proposal in 1789, but the first attempt to implement the idea grew out of the activities of Paul Cuffe, a New England shipowner who carried thirty-eight American blacks to Sierra Leone in 1815. Whites, primarily from the Upper South, joined the following year to establish the American Colonization Society (ACS), which encouraged the establishment of Liberia in West Africa to which the organization transported four thousand free blacks during the next two decades. From its founding, most free blacks were hostile to the organization's goal of deportation. When in 1828 Samuel Cornish and John Russwurm founded the nation's first African-American newspaper, *Freedom's Journal*, one of their main targets was the colonization movement. As a result of their efforts blacks were influential in moving white abolitionists like William Lloyd Garrison to turn against colonization and toward immediatism.

Before Garrison spoke out, however, a Boston secondhand clothing dealer, whose father was a slave in North Carolina, produced one of the most militant and widely circulated calls for abolition. *David Walker's Appeal . . . to the Coloured Citizens of the World . . .* denounced colonization and called upon slaves to rise up in rebellion and cast off their "infernal chains."

Walker had been an agent for *Freedom's Journal*, and its editor Cornish had proposed calling a national African-American convention. These conventions that met yearly throughout the antebellum era and essentially formed a national organization advocating for free blacks those interests that appeared

The First African-American Newspaper, 1827

We wish to plead our own cause. Too long have others spoken for us. Too long has the publick been deceived by misrepresentations, in things which concern us dearly, though in the estimation of some mere trifles; for though there are many in society who exercise towards us benevolent feelings; still (with sorrow we confess it) there are others who make it their business to enlarge upon the least trifle, which tends to the discredit of any person of colour; and pronounce anathemas and denounce our whole body for the misconduct of this guilty one. We are aware that there are many instances of vice among us, but we avow that it is because no one has taught its subjects to be virtuous; many instances of poverty, because no sufficient efforts accommodated to minds contracted by slavery, and deprived of early education have been made, to teach them how to husband their hard earnings, and to secure to themselves comfort.

Education being an object of the highest importance to the welfare of society, we shall endeavour to present just and adequate views of it, and to urge upon our brethren the necessity and expediency of training their children, while young, to habits of industry, and thus forming them for becoming useful members of society. It is surely time that we should awake from this lethargy of years, and make a concentrated effort for the education of our youth. We form a spoke in the human wheel, and it is necessary that we should understand our pendence on the different parts, and theirs on us, in order to perform our part with propriety.

Though not desiring of dictating, we shall feel it our incumbent duty to dwell occasionally upon the general principles and rules of economy. The world has grown too enlightened, to estimate any man's character by his personal appearance. Though all men acknowledge the excellency of Franklin's maxims, yet comparatively few practise upon them. We may deplore when it is too late, the neglect of these self-evident truths, but it avails little to mourn. Ours will be the task of admonishing our brethren on these points.

The civil rights of a people being of the greatest value, it shall ever be our duty to vindicate our brethren, when oppressed; and to lay the case before the publick. We shall also urge upon our brethren, (who are qualified by the laws of the different states) the expediency of using their elective franchise; and of making an independent use of the same. We wish them not to become the tools of party.

Source: Freedom's Journal, March 16, 1827.

at the time. The first such convention met in Philadelphia in 1830 to establish the American Society of Free Persons of Colour under the leadership of Bishop Allen. In the 1830s the convention movement provided the focus for reform activity, emphasizing moral uplift—temperance, education, hard work, and homeownership. The conventions appealed to black churches, petitioned Congress, and urged African Americans to learn trades and create a sense of individual and group self-respect. Essentially their main goal was assimilation, and they denounced colonization. Most of these black leaders were also involved in the movement to abolish slavery.

When the American Anti-Slavery Society (AAS) was organized in Philadelphia in December 1833, James Babadoes of Boston, Forten's son-in-law Robert Purvis, and James McCrummill, a Philadelphia dentist, signed the declaration of sentiments which Garrison had written in McCrummill's home. Eventually they and four other African Americans including New York Episcopal minister Peter Williams were appointed to the board of managers. In 1839–40, when the abolition movement split and the American and Foreign Anti-Slavery Society was formed, most black leaders aligned with the new group while a small group of loyal Garrisonians in Boston and Philadelphia remained in the AAS, in which reform interests remained eclectic.

The majority of white abolitionists in America were women, and black women also played a major role in the movement. The Female Anti-Slavery Society of Salem, Massachusetts, was founded in 1832 by African-American women who had participated in the Boston Female Antislavery Society and in the Philadelphia Female Antislavery Society. When the First Anti-Slavery Convention of American Women was held in 1837, African Americans Susan Paul and Sarah M. Douglas were chosen as officers.

In addition to filling key leadership positions, blacks served the abolition movement in a variety of ways. Most important was the publication of slave narratives written by fugitives who had escaped the "peculiar institution." Frederick Douglass, who penned the most famous narrative, also became one of the best-known black abolitionist lecturers and the leading black editor of his day. But Douglass was not alone. Free black men and women published narratives, lectured, and edited newspapers such as the *Mirror of Liberty*, the *Weekly Advocate*, and the *Colored American* in the cause of abolition. These papers, like the convention movement, included a broad agenda informing free blacks about matters concerning African Americans throughout the country, fighting discrimination, and encouraging moral uplift.

Free blacks took an immediate role in combating the "peculiar institution" through their work in what was popularly known as the "Underground Railroad." An informal network of black resistance that aided fugitive slaves, it was never organized as systematically as the post–Civil War myth implied. Individuals like Harriet Tubman made many forays into the South to lead small bands of slaves to freedom. Vigilance committees were organized in the major cities to collect money and clothes for fugitives and, most importantly, to provide shelter. Eventually in the 1850s following the passage of the Fugitive Slave Law of 1850, these vigilance committees were involved in a series of cases involving fugitives that served to heighten tension between the North and the South.

In the 1840s the convention movement brought to the fore a new militant generation of leaders who shifted toward more direct political action. Men like Douglass and Henry Highland Garnet were critical of white reformers and willing to emphasize black independent action. The free black convention at Hartford in 1840 focused on the problem of the political impotence of African Americans. Putting on a national agenda efforts that had started at the local level and were symbolized by the *Appeal of Forty Thousand Citizens* (1838) opposing disenfranchisement in Pennsylvania, they launched a campaign to reduce the New York restrictions on black voters.

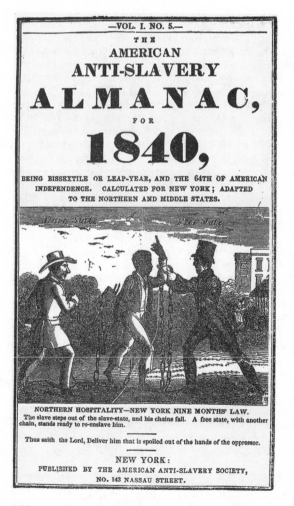

American Anti-Slavery Almanac for 1840 (New York: American Anti-Slavery Society, 1839). Credit: The Library Company of Philadelphia.

Reverend Garnet startled the 1843 convention with his "Address to the Slaves," calling upon them to rise against their masters: "You had better all die—*die* immediately, than live slaves and entail wretchedness upon your posterity." After a long debate between Garnet and Douglass, it was rejected as part of the convention record by a single vote. Four years later in Troy, New York, when Garnet again delivered the same message, it was accepted by the convention.

Address of Black Abolitionist James Forten Jr., 1836

My friends, do you ask why I thus speak? It is because I love America; it is my native land; because I feel as one should feel who sees destruction, like a corroding cancer, eating into the very heart of his country, and would make one struggle to save her;—because I love the stars and stripes, emblems of our National Flag—and long to see the day when not a slave shall be found resting under its shadow; when it shall play with the winds pure and unstained by the blood of "captive millions."

Again, the South most earnestly and respectfully solicits the North to let the question Slavery alone, and leave it to their bountiful honesty and humanity to settle. Why, honesty, I fear has fled from the South, long ago; sincerity has fallen asleep there; pity has hidden herself; justice cannot find the way; helper is not at home; charity lies dangerously ill; benevolence is under arrest; faith is nearly extinguished; truth has long since been buried, and conscience is nailed on the wall. Now, do you think it would be better to leave it to the bountiful honesty and humanity of the South to settle? No, no. Only yield to them in this one particular and they will find you vulnerable in every other. I can tell you, my hearers, if the North once sinks into profound silence on this momentous subject, you may then bid farewell to peace, order and reform; then the condition of your fellow creatures in the southern section of our country will never be ameliorated; then may the poor slave look upon his weighty chains, and exclaim, in the agony of his heart, "To these am I immutably doomed; the glimmering rays of hope are lost to me for ever; robbed of all that is dear to man, I stand a monument of my country's ingratitude. A *husband*, yet separated from the dearest tie which binds me to this earth. A father, yet compelled to stifle the feelings of a father, and witness a helpless offspring torn by a savage hand from its mother's fond embrace, no longer to call her by that endearing title. A wretched slave, I look upon the departing brightness of the setting sun, and when her glorious light revisits the morn, these clanking irons tell me I am that slave still; still am I to linger out a life of ignominious servitude, till death shall unloose these heavy bars—unfetter my body and soul."

You are called fanatics. Well, what if you are? Ought you to shrink from this name? God forbid. There is an eloquence in such fanaticism, for it whispers hope to the slave; there is sanctity in it, for it contains the consecrated spirit of religion; it is the fanaticism of a Benezet, a Rush, a Franklin, a Jay; the same that animated and inspired the heart of the writer of the Declaration of Independence. Then flinch not from your high duty; continue to warn the South of the awful volcano they are recklessly sleeping over; and bid them remember, too, that the drops of blood which trickle down the lacerated back of the slave, will not sink into the barren soil. No, they will rise to the common God of nature and humanity, and cry aloud for vengeance on his destroyer's head.

Source: James Forten Jr., *An Address Delivered before the Ladies Anti-Slavery Society of Philadelphia, April 14, 1836* (Philadelphia, 1836), pp. 10–13.

Aside from this growing militancy, the conventions talked increasingly of racial solidarity and collective support for economic advancement. They debated the value of segregated education and the necessity of independent institutions. The convention in 1853 pushed the idea of separate black institutions to serve black needs, but also to make blacks more effective members of American society. This position placed a greater emphasis on racial solidarity, the support of black businesses, and race pride. The convention advocated not only manual labor schools for blacks but also a national African-American museum and library.

Others, however, carried separatism and black nationalism further. Following the passage of the Fugitive Slave Law of 1850 between three thousand and five thousand blacks fled the United States to Canada. One of them was the physician Martin R. Delany, who had denounced the ACS as "arrant hypocrites" and proclaimed that blacks were "Americans having a birthright citizenship." But by the end of the 1850s, he turned against assimilation and traveled to the Niger Valley in Africa, perhaps to prepare the way for a mass exodus.

On the eve of the Civil War, most black leaders were disillusioned and at least considered the idea of colonization. Even Douglass, who had emerged as the foremost spokesman of African Americans and who had consistently insisted upon integration, was discouraged by the Republicans' stand on slavery. However, once the war commenced, he and most of the leaders of the free black community rallied to the cause of Union. Delany became an officer in the Union Army. Eventually nearly 200,000 African Americans would fight for freedom in the Civil War.

CONCLUSION

The antebellum experience of quasi-free African Americans cautions against the easy analogy incorporated in the idea that today's urban blacks are simply "the last of the immigrants." Their arrival in British North America actually predates that of those usually termed immigrants by a century and their experience with slavery was shared by no other group. Those who were free during the era of slavery were primarily an urban population in a predominantly rural nation. Like most European immigrants of the nineteenth century, African Americans faced prejudice and social stigma, but in ways that no European ethnic or religious group was forced to endure. African Americans were deprived of their rights as citizens and subjected to legally enforced discrimination and segregation in nearly all walks of life. As Alexis de Tocqueville wrote in *Democracy in America*:

> When the Negro dies, his bones are cast aside, and the distinction of conditions prevail even in the equality of death. Thus the Negro is free, but he can share neither the rights nor the pleasures, not the labor, nor the afflictions, nor the tomb of him whose equal he has been declared to be; and he cannot meet him upon fair terms in life or in death.

Rev. Henry Highland Garnet on Self-Defense, 1843

Brethren, the time has come when you must act for yourselves. It is an old and true saying that, "if hereditary bondmen would be free, they must themselves strike the blow." You can plead your own cause, and do the work of emancipation better than any others. The nations of the world are moving in the great cause of universal freedom, and some of them at least will, ere long, do you justice. The combined powers of Europe have placed their broad seal of disapprobation upon the African slave-trade. But in the slave-holding parts of the United States, the trade is as brisk as ever. They buy and sell you as though you were brute beasts. The North has done much—her opinion of slavery in the abstract is known. But in regard to the South, we adopt the opinion of the *New York Evangelist*—We have advanced so far, that the cause apparently waits for a more effectual door to be thrown open than has been yet. We are about to point out that more effectual door. Look around you, and behold the bosoms of your loving wives heaving with untold agonies! Hear the cries of your poor children! Remember the stripes your fathers bore. Think of the torture and disgrace of your noble mothers. Think of your wretched sisters, loving virtue and purity, as they are driven into concubinage and are exposed to the unbridled lusts of incarnate devils. Think of the undying glory that hangs around the ancient name of Africa—and forget not that you are native born American citizens, and as such, you are justly entitled to all the rights that are granted to the freest. Think how many tears you have poured out upon the soil which you have cultivated with unrequited toil and enriched with your blood; and then go to your lordly enslavers and tell them plainly, that you *are determined to be free*. Appeal to their sense of justice, and tell them that they have no more right to oppress you, than you have to enslave them. Entreat them to remove the grievous burdens which they have imposed upon you, and to remunerate you for your labor. Promise them renewed diligence in the cultivation of the soil, if they will render to you an equivalent for your services. Point them to the increase of happiness and prosperity in the British West Indies since the Act of Emancipation.

Tell them in language which they cannot misunderstand, of the exceeding sinfulness of slavery, and of a future judgment, and of the righteous retributions of an indignant God. Inform them that all you desire is FREEDOM, and that nothing else will suffice. Do this, and for ever after cease to toil for the heartless tyrants, who give you no other reward but stripes and abuse. If they then commence the work of death, they, and not you, will be responsible for the consequences. You had better all die—*die immediately*, than live slaves and entail your wretchedness upon your posterity. If you would be free in this generation, here is your only hope. However much you and all of us may desire it, there is not much hope of redemption without the shedding of blood. If you must bleed, let it all come at once—rather *die freemen, than live to be slaves*. . .

From the first moment that you breathed the air of heaven, you have been accustomed to nothing else but hardships. The heroes of the American Revolution were never put upon harder fare than a peck of corn and a few herrings per week. You have not become enervated by the luxuries of life. Your sternest energies have been beaten out upon the anvil of severe trial. Slavery has done this, to make you subservient, to its own purposes; but it has done more than this, it has prepared you for any emergency. If you receive good treatment, it is what you could hardly expect; if you meet with pain, sorrow, and even death, these are the common lot of slaves.

Fellow men! Patient sufferers! behold your dearest rights crushed to the earth! See your sons murdered, and your wives, mothers and sisters doomed to prostitution. In the name of the merciful God, and by all that life is worth, let it no longer be a debatable question whether it is better to choose *Liberty or death*.

Source: A Memorial Discourse; by Rev. Henry Garnet, delivered in the Hall of the House of Representatives, Washington . . . February 12, 1865, with an introduction by James McCune Smith (Philadelphia, 1865), pp. 44–51.

During the three decades before the Civil War as waves of Irish and German immigrants swept across the Atlantic, the Jim Crow system of segregation in the North and the Black Codes that governed free blacks in the South became increasingly restrictive. When emancipated, the African-American population possessed far fewer skills, a lower level of education, and much less capital than those immigrants upon arrival. Because of prejudice and legal restrictions—restrictions supported by the new immigrants who often found that adopting the racial ideology that justified such discrimination represented an essential aspect of their own successful assimilation, even those African Americans who had skills found themselves unable to employ them.

The Racial Situation in America, 1857

I repeat, it is difficult to understand what is the genuine public feeling on this entangled question; for with all the demonstrations in favor of freedom in the north, there does not appear in that quarter to be any practical relaxation of the usages which condemn persons of a African descent to an inferior social status. There seems, in short, to be a fixed notion throughout the whole of the states, whether slave or free, that the colored is by nature a subordinate race; and that, in no circumstances, can it be considered equal to the white. Apart from commercial views, this opinion lies at the root of American slavery; and the question would need to be argued less on political and philanthropic than on physiological grounds. . . .

It may have been merely a coincidence, but it is remarkable, that all with whom I conversed in the States on the distinction of race, tended to the opinion that the negro was in many respects an inferior being, and his existence in American an anomaly. The want of mental energy and forethought, the love of finery and of trifling amusements, distaste of persevering industry and bodily labor, as well as overpowering animal propensities, were urged as general characteristics of the colored population; and it was alleged, that when consigned to their own resources, they do not successfully compete with the white Anglo-Americans; the fact being added, that in slavery they increase at the same ratio as the whites, while in freedom, and affected with the vices of society, the ratio of increase falls short by one-third. From all that I have since heard of the free people of color, I believe these remarks to have been largely a result of prejudice. . .

Throughout the greater part of New England States, likewise in the states of New York, Pennsylvania, etc., there is a rigorous separation of the white and black races. In every city, there are white and black schools, and white and black churches. No dark-skinned child is suffered to attend a school for white children. . . .

As an explanation of these distinctions, I was informed that white would not sit beside colored children; and further, that colored children, after a certain age, did not correspondingly advance in learning—their intellect being apparently incapable of being cultured beyond a certain point. From whatever cause, it was clear that a reluctance to associate with persons of negro descent was universally inculcated in infancy, and strengthened with age. The result is a singular social phenomenon. We see, in effect, two nations—one white and another black—growing up together within the same political circle, but never mingling on a principle of equality.

Source: William Chambers, *Things As They Are in America* (London: William and Robert Chambers, 1857), pp. 354–63.

Faced with racist prejudice, legal discrimination, and the competition from the European immigrants for the least attractive and most menial jobs, the economic situation of African Americans deteriorated badly. The proportion of free blacks holding skilled jobs—always low outside the elite mulatto communities of the lower South—declined. This economic crisis weakened the free black family and further strained the meager resources of black churches, beneficial societies, and social protest organizations. In 1857, on the eve of the Civil War, William Chambers, a prescient Scottish visitor wrote, "We see, in effect, two nations—one white and another black—growing up together within the same political circle, but never mingling on a principle of equality," an eerie anticipation of the 1968 Kerner Commission report on urban violence.

FOR FURTHER READING

Berlin, Ira. *Slaves without Masters: The Free Negro in the Antebellum South.* New York: The New Press, 1992.

Curry, Leonard P. *The Free Black in Urban America, 1800–1850: The Shadow of the Dream.* Chicago: University of Chicago Press, 1981.

Franklin, John Hope. *The Free Negro in North Carolina, 1790–1860.* Chapel Hill: University of North Carolina Press, 1995.

Hanger, Kimberly S. *Bounded Lives, Bounded Places: Free Black Society in Colonial New Orleans, 1769–1803.* Durham, N.C.: Duke University Press, 1997.

Horton, James Oliver, and Lois E. Horton. *Black Bostonians: Family Life and Community Struggle in the Antebellum North.* Rev. ed. New York: Holmes & Meier Publishing, 1999.

———. *In Hope of Liberty: Culture, Community, and Protest among Free Northern Blacks, 1700–1860.* New York: Oxford University Press, 1998.

Johnson, Michael P., and James Roark. *Black Masters: A Free Family of Color in the Old South.* New York: W. W. Norton & Co., 1986.

Litwack, Leon. *North of Slavery: The Negro in the Free States, 1790–1860.* Chicago: University of Chicago Press, 1965.

Melish, Joanne Pope. *Disowning Slavery: Gradual Emancipation and "Race" in New England, 1780–1860.* Ithaca, N.Y.: Cornell University Press, 1998.

Nash, Gary B. *Forging Freedom: The Formation of Philadelphia's Black Community, 1720–1840.* Cambridge: Harvard University Press, 1991.

Pease, Jane H., and William H. Pease. *They Who Would Be Free: Blacks' Search for Freedom, 1830–1861.* Urbana: University of Illinois Press, 1990.

Quarles, Benjamin. *Black Abolitionists.* New York: De Capo Press, 1991.

Swift, David. *Black Prophets of Justice: Activist Clergy Before the Civil War.* Baton Rouge: Louisiana State University Press, 1989.

White, Shane. *Somewhat More Independent: The End of Slavery in New York City, 1770–1810.* Athens: University of Georgia Press, 1995.

Winch, Julie. *Philadelphia's Black Elite: Activism, Accommodation, and the Struggle for Autonomy, 1787–1848.* Philadelphia: Temple University Press, 1988.

Zilversmit, Arthur. *The First Emancipation: The Aftermath of Slavery in the North.* Chicago: University of Chicago Press, 1967.

part 3.

The Reconstruction
and Beyond

chapter 6

Full of Faith, Full of Hope

The African-American Experience
from Emancipation to Segregation

Armstead L. Robinson

MERICAN SLAVERY DISINTEGRATED during the Civil War, and its demise precipitated the collapse of the Confederate quest for national independence. During the decades immediately following the destruction of the South's peculiar institution, conflict inevitably erupted as members of the "Freedom Generation" (former slaves and their immediate descendants) struggled to realize their hopes for economic, political, and social equality. Intense debate over the meaning of freedom occurred both within the states of the former Confederacy and across the nation. During the Reconstruction period, which is generally dated from 1865 when the war ended to 1877 when President Rutherford B. Hayes withdrew the last federal troops from the South, two questions dominated national politics: How could the shattered Union be restored? and How could American society be restructured to accommodate the aspirations of the freed slaves?

In Washington there was deep division over the answers to these two questions between the new President Andrew Johnson and the Republican majority in Congress. An ex-Democrat from Tennessee who had become president when Lincoln was assassinated only five days after Lee surrendered to Grant at Appomattox, Johnson proposed rapid restoration of the southern states. To this end he issued wholesale pardons of Confederates and encouraged the white leaders of the antebellum states to reestablish civil governments of their own providing only that they profess their loyalty to the United States and accept the new Thirteenth Amendment to the Constitution abolishing slavery.

When Congress finally met in December 1865, the Republicans rejected the legitimacy of these "presidential governments" and denied the admission of their newly elected representatives to seats in the House and Senate. They believed that the process initiated by the president had neither sufficiently punished the former rebels nor provided for the protection and representation of the former slaves. The presidential governments were in the hands of the old white elite, who sent such notorious traitors as Alexander Stephens, the former vice president of the Confederacy, to Washington as congressmen. At the same time these revived governments in the southern states had established wide-ranging "Black Codes," which segregated the former slaves and circumscribed their rights in the interest of their former owners. After a year of controversy between the president and Congress and the 1866 congressional elections in which the northern voters endorsed the Republican's approach to Reconstruction, Congress initiated its policy in 1867. This consisted of four acts establishing procedures for the readmission to the Union of the former Confederate states and two amendments to the Constitution—the Fourteenth, which made the former slaves "citizens of the United States" entitled to "equal protection of the laws," and the Fifteenth, which ensured the rights of citizens to vote would not be "denied or abridged by the United States or by any State on account of race, color, or previous condition of servitude."

Under the watchful eye of the U.S. Army, voters were registered, state conventions wrote more democratic constitutions providing for universal manhood suffrage, and governments were established in the southern states with the participation of the former slaves as both voters and officeholders. But their reign was short-lived. Angry southern whites using both paramilitary violence and the terrorism practiced by organizations like the Ku Klux Klan and legitimate political activity organized by the revitalized Democratic Party in both the North and the South to reverse the Republican policies and the southern states by reestablishing white rule. In slow but decisive steps during the 1880s the Radical policies of integration were replaced by racial segregation, which was eventually written into southern constitutions and civil law during the 1890s.

Amid this fierce struggle, the Freedom Generation managed to fashion a postslavery culture which rested on family, self-reliance, and the church. They reknit family units scattered by slavery, closed the literacy gap, acquired more than 18 million acres of farmland, and along the way, erected a full panoply of religious, educational, cultural, and social institutions. These successes at community building, however, could not prevent the descendants of the slaves and even those blacks who had been free before the Civil War from falling victim to the vicious system of racial segregation. In 1896, the Supreme Court ruled, in *Plessy* v. *Ferguson*, that Jim Crow laws conformed to the Constitution so long as the states promised to provide what they quickly failed to deliver: "separate but equal" services in racially segregated facilities.

THE FREEDMEN AND AMERICAN SOCIETY

In the midst of the war, Abraham Lincoln issued the Emancipation Proclamation on January 1, 1863. In its aftermath, Americans, black as well as white, North as well as South, began to grapple with an issue that had been deferred by chattel slavery: What place should freed blacks occupy in American society? Bishop Daniel Payne of the African Methodist Episcopal Church took up this issue during the Civil War in a sermon, "Welcome to the Ransomed," which he delivered in Washington, D.C. Payne looked beyond the military struggle between North and South as he urged newly freed blacks to adopt the Protestant religious values of the AME Church. "Enter the great family of Holy Freedom," he exhorted, "not to lounge in sinful indolence, not to degrade yourselves by vice, nor to corrupt society by licentiousness ... but to the enjoyment of a well-regulated liberty."

In its missionary activities in the South during and after the Civil War, the AME church urged the freedpeople toward self-reliance to be achieved through religion, education, hard work, and the acquisition of property.

The Emancipation Proclamation, 1863

President Lincoln issued a preliminary proclamation after the Union victory at the Battle of Antietam in September 1862 and urged the Border States to adopt compensated emancipation plans. On January 1, 1863, he issued the Emancipation Proclamation which in the context of the war and the Constitution used the war powers to free the slaves in the areas in rebellion. It signaled a shift in policy, making emancipation a Union war aim and was an important step toward the freeing of all the slaves by adoption of the Thirteenth Amendment to the Constitution in 1865.

That on the first day of January, in the year of our Lord one thousand eight hundred and sixty-three, all persons held as slaves within any state or designated part of a state, the people whereof shall then be in rebellion against the United States, shall be then, thenceforward, and forever, free; and the Executive Government of the United States, including the military and naval authority thereof, will recognize and maintain the freedom of such persons, and will do no act or acts to repress such persons, or any of them, in any efforts they may make for their actual freedom.

That the Executive will, on the first day of January aforesaid, by proclamation, designate the states and parts of states, if any, in which the people thereof, respectively, shall then be in rebellion against the United States; and the fact that any state, or the people thereof, shall on that day be in good faith represented in the Congress of the United States, by members chosen thereto at elections wherein a majority of the qualified voters of such states shall have participated, shall, in the absence of strong countervailing testimony, be deemed conclusive evidence that such state, and the people thereof, are not then in rebellion against the United States.

Source: "The Emancipation Proclamation" in Albert P. Blaustein and Robert L. Zangrando, eds., Civil Rights and the American Negro (New York: Washington Square Press, 1968), pp. 200–201.

Black missionaries and black churches reiterated Bishop Payne's message to the freedpeople to turn their energies toward the work of community building essential to "the enjoyment of a well-regulated liberty." The contest between white and black southerners for control over the contours of post-slavery race relations became the framing issue for the next half century of African-American experience.

So crucial were these issues for defining the economy, society, and polity of the postwar South that even before the Civil War ended some southern whites expressed concern about the implications of black freedom. About three months prior to surrendering, Confederate General-in-Chief Robert E. Lee had endorsed a proposal to arm Confederate slaves as a last-ditch measure to avert defeat and gave his full blessing to the revolutionary idea that freedom should granted to those slaves who served loyally. Explaining his rationale for departing so radically from antebellum racist ideology, Lee articulated clearly the central concern motivating white southerners confronting the aftermath of slavery. "If it end in subverting slavery it will be accomplished by ourselves," he urged, "and we can devise the means of alleviating the evil consequences to both races. I think, therefore, we must decide whether slavery shall be extinguished by our enemies and the slaves be used against us, or [we] use them ourselves at the risk of the effects which may be produced upon our social institutions."

The North also found cause to debate the future of race relations in post–Civil War America. Although Lincoln eventually abandoned the goal of colonization of the freedmen, he did so only after experiments in Haiti and in Central America ended in total failure. Lincoln could not find sufficient numbers of blacks willing to participate in these experiments, and those who did go experienced hardships, which persuaded them that their destiny lay in the United States.

The debate over the means of providing for the welfare of former slaves continued throughout the Civil War. After many false starts, Congress and Lincoln agreed, in February 1865, to establish a federal welfare agency, the Bureau of Refugees, Freedmen, and Abandoned Lands, to supervise social reconstruction in former slaveholding states. Congress gave the Freedmen's Bureau responsibility for both refugees (white southern unionists) and freedmen (black former slaves) and consigned to the bureau some 10 million acres of abandoned southern farmland to be seized for nonpayment of Union war taxes. The bureau was charged to devise an equitable method for redistribution of this land in 40-acre plots to whites and blacks whose loyalty made them eligible for postwar federal aid.

We cannot know how the implementation of this plan might have altered the contours of post–Civil War American society, but we do know that the assassination of Lincoln on April 14, 1865, brought the southern-born former slaveholding Democrat Andrew Johnson to the presidency. Once in office, Johnson blocked implementation of the bureau plan by granting thousands of presidential pardons to the former slaveholders about to lose land due to tax defaults. Because the American Constitution gives the president irreversible pardoning power, Congress could do nothing to preserve the plan that would have provided access to land for one-third of former slave families. By 1910, self-reliance had enabled freedpeople to acquire almost twice as much land as the bureau plan would have made available, but in the immediate postwar period, the absence of ready access to "free" land meant that most former slaves had few economic choices open to them. Circumstance compelled them to seek waged labor positions on land owned by whites, many of whom were bitter former slaveholders still enraged over the defeat of the Confederacy and impoverished by the failure of their crusade for national independence.

The stillbirth of postwar land reform did not occur without strong protest from those most directly affected. The awkward task of explaining the disappearance of land set aside by Congress for redistribution fell to officials of the bureau who chose not to implicate president Johnson. Bureau officers instead tried to persuade crowds of enraged and frustrated freedpeople that it was they who had misunderstood congressional intent. In the Georgia and South Carolina Sea Islands, blacks who had received land earlier during Sherman's 1864–1865 march to the sea put up such stout resistance that bureau officers called on the Union army to assist in returning possession of the land to former slaveholders.

An angry speech delivered by a freedman, Bayley Wyatt, at Yorktown, Virginia, in the autumn of 1866 suggests how vigorously many former slaves reacted to news that they would not receive promised land. When informed that not only would there to be no general redistribution of land to freedpeople, but even the small parcels on which a few thousand lucky blacks had lived provisionally were to be turned back to their former masters, Wyatt invoked the hard days in slavery when "we made bricks without straw under old Pharo." When war came, slaves "sacrificed all we had to come to the Yankees." Responding to listeners who might question whether the freedpeople owned any property before the war, Wyatt pointed out, "Some of us had some money to buy our freedom, and some of us had a house, and some of us had cattle with which we hoped sometimes to buy our freedom." Far from pleading for unearned gifts from the Yankees, Wyatt grounded the claim to land in the sweated equity blacks had amassed through ten generations of uncompensated toil in slavery. "I may state to all our friends," he argued, "and to all our enemies, that we has a right to the land where we are located. For why? I tell you. Our wives, our children, our husbands, has been sold over and over again to purchase the lands we now locate upon; for that reason we has a divine right to the land."

Bayley Wyatt recognized that Yankees did not feel responsible for the sins of the slaveholders. Thus he did not stop at this very direct claim for title to land in the southern states, but rather proceeded to remind northerners in his audience of the sufficient contribution enslaved blacks had made to the much vaunted prosperity of the urbanizing-industrializing North. "And then didn't we clear the lands and raise crops of corn, of cotton, of tobacco, of rice, of sugar, of everything?" he reminded them. " And then didn't the large cities in the North grow on the cotton and the sugars and the rice that we made? Yes! I appeal to the South and to the North if I hasn't spoken the words of truth. I say they have grown rich and my people is poor." Such arguments availed nothing in the face of the subversive use of presidential pardoning power by Andrew Johnson. Yet Wyatt's rhetoric suggests the sharply conflicting interests evident as whites and blacks inside and outside the defeated South contested for power amid their common struggle to adjust to the demise of slavery.

THE FAILURE OF RADICAL RECONSTRUCTION

Not even Lincoln's legendary political skills could have averted bitter conflict between the president and Congress for control over the process. The enlistment of nearly two hundred thousand blacks into federal forces left the former slaves with a compelling claim to full citizenship. Both the Democrats (out of power during the Civil War) and the Republicans (anxious to prolong their new power) saw resolution of the core issues of Reconstruction as of vital importance to the postwar balance of political power. Republican efforts to grant full civil rights to the former slaves inevitably became a contested issue.

The maladroit policies of President Johnson transformed this unavoidably difficult situation into a prolonged, bitter, and highly partisan political stalemate. Having assumed the presidency after Lincoln's assassination, Johnson sought to be elected president in his own right. Doing so required revival of the southern wing of the Democratic Party, and Johnson did everything he could to facilitate the speedy return to power of friendly conservatives in the states of the former Confederacy. New state and local governments then turned quickly to the matter of racial domination, enacting the Black Codes that made mockery of emancipation by depriving freedpeople of civil privileges in areas such as voting, jury service, office holding, the right to bear arms, and, most important, landownership. The Johnson state governments restored as much of the old order as they dared.

Remarkably, less than eight months after Lee signed the final surrender, the southern political elite stood poised to resume its former position in the national government. Had Congress admitted the delegations sent forward in 1865, direct federal involvement in the affairs of the formerly seceded states would have come to an end, but the severity of the Black Codes helped turn the tide. Public opinion in the North saw these laws as well as the appearance of rebel leaders in Washington as a defiant attempt by intransigent southern aristocrats to deny the hard-won results of Union victory and revive the slave power in a new form. As a result, the Republicans rejected the electoral credentials of every member of Congress from a formerly seceded state. While the Johnson regimes remained in power inside the South, the congressional

Republicans worked to both guarantee minimum civil rights to the former slaves and to prolong their own control of national government, which they had gained when secession reduced the number of Democrats in Congress by 50 percent.

Postwar Republicans had much to defend. Operating under cover of appeals to "national emergency," the party had enacted, in rapid-fire succession, a series of laws that permanently transformed the hitherto conservative position of the federal government on economic development issues. Wartime Republican majorities established a national banking system, national paper currency, direct excise and income taxation, indirect subsidies for railroad construction, aid to higher education, and high protective tariffs for American "home" industries. Before and during the war, Democrats heatedly contested each of these issues. Thus they anxiously awaited, in the immediate postwar years, the return of their southern colleagues, so they could jointly attempt to rescind as much of the Republicans' wartime legislative revolution as possible.

Led by Thaddeus Stevens and Charles Sumner, a nationalist faction within the Republican party that came to be known as the Radicals dominated the Joint Committee on Reconstruction appointed in December 1865 to craft a policy that would protect the freedmen and preserve Republican control over the national government. In the ensuing thirty months, the joint committee submitted a series of measures intended to refashion southern political culture so dramatically as to forever bar a return to power of the "white only" Democratic political leadership that had carried eleven southern states out of the Union. The committee proposed renewal of the Freedmen's Bureau, passage of a federal civil rights law, submission of a constitutional amendment to make citizens out of former slaves, the enfranchisement of freedmen and the disfranchisement of former Confederates, and the subjection of all the seceded states to strict congressional scrutiny as part of the process of gaining readmission to the federal Union. While Johnson fought each measure, the Radicals systematically gained passage of their program over the next two years by using two-thirds majorities to override repeated presidential vetoes.

Enactment of the Reconstruction Acts in 1867 shifted the focus of attention to the struggle in the states over implementation of the congressional plan for facilitating readmission and postslavery adjustment. At its core, this plan envisioned the creation of new biracial Republican alliances in the former seceded states. Using the black 40 percent of the southern population as a base, Radicals reckoned that they could quickly forge a "natural majority" by persuading as few as 25 percent of native whites to become Republicans. This majority would then have the power to dominate southern state and local government for many decades to come. In a number of states, the initial results seemed encouraging; black and white voters sent heavy Republican majorities to state constitutional conventions and to state legislatures in 1867 and 1868.

Because of constitutional provisions that gave the president control over the armed forces, the Radicals in Congress could provide almost no direct assistance to the newly created biracial state governments in the South. When Johnson remained adamantly opposed to the congressional Republican program, the Radicals pushed through acts curtailing executive powers and attempted to remove Johnson the following year. Although Congress did impeach the president, the Senate failed to convict him by a single vote when seven self-described "Stalwarts" refused to join the Republican majority. The weakened president thus completed his term in 1869, handing the presidency over to the Civil War hero Ulysses S. Grant. Support for Republican economic liberalism did not alter Grant's conservative social philosophy; he steadfastly refused to employ federal military power to intervene in southern civil affairs, even in the face of premeditated political violence.

This narrowing of the scope of federal activism in the area of civil rights produced controversy of its own. Women objected with special intensity to the plan to draft a constitutional amendment to guarantee voting rights only for black males. Because the Fourteenth Amendment had granted American citizenship to "all persons born or naturalized" in the United States, the way seemed clear for a Fifteenth Amendment, which simply guaranteed the right to vote for *all* "citizens" of appropriate age, this without reference to gender. The congressional Republicans who balked at this "strong" version of the amendment angered militant advocates of immediate female suffrage.

The former slave orator Frederick Douglass found himself in a difficult predicament over the issue of woman suffrage. Consistent support for women's rights had made him a hero after the 1848 Seneca Falls Convention, yet in the postwar era Douglass discovered that he could not retain influence simultaneously within radical suffragist and conservative Republican circles. Douglass, who believed that black men needed the ballot to protect the new rights of all African Americans, urged women to postpone their own demands and accept suffrage for black men as the best deal they could get. He was aware that the Democrats were manipulating the women's suffrage issue to defeat any form of black suffrage. But the female former slave abolitionist Sojourner Truth took Douglass severely to task in a pointed and bitterly ironic address to the 1868 annual meeting of the National Equal Rights Association. She argued, "There is a great stir about colored men getting their rights, but not a word about the colored woman. . . . I want women to have their rights. In the courts women have no rights, no voice; nobody speaks for them. . . . Men have got their rights, and women has got no rights." In the end, Congress enacted a narrow version of the Fifteenth Amendment, protecting voting rights for black men without explicitly mentioning women.

Nonetheless, the grant of suffrage during Reconstruction allowed freedmen to make significant advances. Blacks participated enthusiastically in the rituals of political culture, and a very high proportion of those eligible registered and cast ballots. Hundreds of blacks won elective office at every level of American politics. The state of Mississippi sent two blacks to the United States Senate and more than a score other African-American men served in the House of Representatives. But southern conservatives refused so easily to surrender control over local and state government. The avidity with which blacks participated in the political process and the independence with which they cast their ballots helps to explain why political violence formed an essential component of southern conservative strategy.

The Reconstruction Amendments to the Constitution

The Reconstruction Era after the Civil War produced one of the major constitutional revolutions in American history as the Republicans forced through three amendments to the U.S. Constitution which freed the slaves, provided the freedmen with citizenship and protected their civil rights, and extended to them the right to vote. The majority of congressional Democrats, who cast themselves as protectors of the white South, opposed each of these changes.

AMENDMENT XIII
Passed by Congress February 1, 1865.
Ratified December 18, 1865.

Section 1. Neither slavery nor involuntary servitude except as a punishment for crime whereof the party shall have been duly convicted, shall exist within the United States, or any place subject to their jurisdiction.

AMENDMENT XIV
Passed by Congress June 16, 1866.
Ratified July 28, 1868.

Section 1. All persons born or naturalized in the United States, and subject to the jurisdiction thereof, are citizens of the United States and of the State wherein they reside. No State shall make or enforce any law which shall abridge the privileges or immunities of citizens of the United States; nor shall any State deprive any person of life, liberty, or property, without due process of law; nor deny to any person within its jurisdiction the equal protection of the laws.

Section 2. Representatives shall be apportioned among the several States according to their respective numbers, counting the whole number of persons in each State, excluding Indians not taxed. But when the right to vote at any election for the choice of electors for President and Vice President of the United States, representatives in Congress, the executive and judicial officers of a State, or the members of the legislature thereof, is denied to any of the male inhabitants of such State, being twenty-one years of age, and citizens of the United States, or in any way abridged, except for participating in rebellion, or other crime, the basis of representation therein shall be reduced in the proportion which the number of such male citizens shall bear to the whole number of male citizens twenty-one years of age in such State.

AMENDMENT XV
Passed By Congress February 27, 1869
Ratified March 30, 1870.

Section 1. The right of citizens of the United States to vote shall not be denied or abridged by the United States or by any State on account of race, color, or previous condition of servitude.

White Democrats employed a carefully devised and deviously implemented program first to frustrate the new biracial coalitions, then to divide the voters along racial lines, and, finally, to inflame racial tensions between poorer black and white southerners. Once it became clear that black voters could not be cajoled, bribed, or bullied into casting their precious ballots for racist conservatives, vigilante-style groups sprang into existence throughout the southern states. These groups directed their activities at the white and black leadership of the biracial southern Republican parties. Where intimidation failed to work, vigilante-style violence practiced by paramilitary groups such as the Ku Klux Klan led to the politically motivated murders of thousands of black and white Republicans. As the federal government failed to actively intervene to protect Republicans' right to vote freely, the number of Republican voters decreased in concert with escalating violence. Eventually, southern conservatives "redeemed" their states by replacing biracial governments friendly to the Radical Republicans with white-line racialist regimes loyal to the Democratic Party.

While contests for elective office occurred only periodically, daily struggles for the necessities of life dominated the agendas of the millions of former slaves. Freed people emancipated with neither land nor money had, in most instances, to rely upon their own efforts to care for themselves. The question of whether enslavement had left enduring psycho-social scars on the former slaves was hotly contested in the postslavery years, and is even today. The question of the effect life in slavery had on freed people and how long these effects would persist became central to the challenge confronting the Freedom Generation.

Few southern whites believed that the former slaves could cope well with the challenges of freedom. William G. Brownlow, the Republican governor of Tennessee, openly expressed pessimism about whether former slaves could keep body and soul together amidst the difficult conditions present in 1865.

Speech by Black Congressman John R. Lynch, 1882

The impartial historian will record the fact that the colored people of the South have contended for their rights with a bravery and a gallantry that is worthy of the highest commendation. Being, unfortunately, in dependent circumstances, with the preponderance of the wealth and intelligence against them in some localities, yet they have bravely refused to surrender their honest convictions, even upon the altar of their personal necessities. They have said to those upon whom they depended: You may deprive me for the time being of the opportunity of making an honest living; you may take the bread out of the mouths of my hungry and dependent family; you may close the school-house door in the face of my children; yea, more, you may take that which no man can give, my life, but my manhood, my principles you cannot have!

Source: *Congressional Record*, April 27, 1882, 47th Cong., 1st Sess. XIII, pp. 3384–87.

"The negroes, like the Indian tribes," Brownlow predicted, "will gradually become extinct, having no owners to care for them, and not owning property in them, they will cease to increase in number—cease to be looked after and cultivated—while *educated* labor will take the place of slave labor. Idleness, starvation and disease will remove the majority of this generation. The better class of them will go to work to sustain themselves." Census reports, however, demonstrate the error of Brownlow's prediction; the numbers of blacks steadily increased in the decades after emancipation, along with their economic and social independence.

The economic base for the successful transition from slavery to freedom came primarily from continued southern reliance on commercial production of the same staple crops (cotton, tobacco, sugar, hemp, and rice) that slaves had cultivated prior to the war. So long as the South remained primarily agrarian, its economy would contain sectors in which the freed people could find employment, although most such jobs paid little beyond bare subsistence. While hardly the comfortable life in freedom the slaves had hoped to find, subsistence employment gave the freed people the means to survive and then move toward independence. The former slaves tried virtually every strategy possible to better conditions for themselves and their families. As one freed-

THE RESULT OF THE FIFTEENTH AMENDMENT,
Rise and Progress of the African Race in America and its final accomplishment, and celebration on May 19th A.D. 1870.

The Civil War amendments, and especially the Fifteenth Amendment granting the right to vote to black males, were widely celebrated and represented the belated guarantee of constitutional rights to black Americans that would form the basis for the civil rights gains of the twentieth century. Credit: The Library Company of Philadelphia.

man put the matter, "What's de use of being free if you don't own land enough to be buried in? Might juss as well stay slave all yo' days."

Black ambitions to own land encountered a major obstacle, the adamant refusal by white landowners for years after the Civil War to sell land to them. "In many portions of the Mississippi Valley," wrote one observer, "the feeling against any ownership of the soil by negroes is so strong, that the man who would sell small tracts to them would be in actual personal danger. Every effort will be made to prevent negroes from acquiring lands; even the renting of small tracts to them is held to be unpatriotic and unworthy of a good citizen." Small wonder then that a large majority of freedpeople experienced systematic frustration in their determined crusade to move beyond subsistence wages and toward the self-sufficiency of landownership.

Agriculture in the postwar South underwent a prolonged decline in the decades after the Civil War. The shortage of capital to fund repairs of war damage acted as a drag on economic recovery. But war damage merely exacerbated the economic sluggishness produced by the poorly developed state of southern credit, marketing, transportation, and communication facilities: all impediments inherited from slavery. However, the most important factor retarding the postwar economy was the weakness in market demand for southern agrarian staples. Demand for cotton, sugar, rice, and tobacco remained stagnant for decades. In turn, this left little room in the market for new producers, like the millions of former slaves, anxious to acquire property as a means to economic and social independence.

Although most of the Freedom Generation remained landless, adverse conditions did not prevent a substantial number from becoming small landowners. Freed blacks acquired property most readily in areas outside the centers of commercial agriculture. Thus the greatest concentration of black landowners appeared in the regions with depleted soil along the Atlantic and Gulf coastlines and in the southern "backcountry." Blacks who acquired land did so in painfully small increments; they moved from sharecropping to share tenancy, from tenancy to partial ownership, and finally to full landownership. Of the 900,000 black farming families recorded by the U.S. Census in 1910, 20 percent claimed full ownership, 5 percent claimed partial ownership, and 75 percent remained sharecroppers and tenants. This remarkable rate of acquisition shows that racial discrimination impeded but did not prevent property accumulation among the freedpeople in the five decades after emancipation.

Freedpeople in urban areas also experienced mobility into the middle and upper classes. In 1860, slaves made up 80 percent of southern artisans. Long after the war, freedmen became barbers, butchers, and blacksmiths, dominating trades that provided an important source of economic independence. In addition, a small group of hardy freed entrepreneurs embarked upon independent business ventures. Poorly developed transportation made drayage (conveying freight) a lucrative occupation for freed entrepreneurs who acquired wagons and teams. Robert Reed Church, a Memphis freedman, parlayed a small initial capital stake into a substantial fortune by focusing on leisure and real estate; Church busied himself acquiring saloons, "fancy houses," and rental property in areas populated by blacks. By 1890, this entrepreneurial acumen had enabled Church to amass a fortune, which made him the first millionaire in Afrrican-American history.

Geographic mobility offered landless blacks some alternative avenues of opportunity, and migration assumed many forms. Large numbers of freedpeople abandoned agrarian life and moved to urban areas; the destinations tended to be inside the South until the 1890s when urban areas in the mid-Atlantic and midwestern states began receiving large black migrations. Agriculture remained the primary occupation, and it appears that the bulk of black migrants moved in search either of higher wages or of opportunities for landownership. The quest for higher wages prompted movement out of the Atlantic coastal states and into the new cotton regions in the Georgia, Alabama, and Mississippi "black belts"; in the Southwest, black migrants emerged in Arkansas, Texas, and Louisiana. A series of concerns (anger over political violence, frustration over lack of opportunity, and land hunger) prompted three large organized migrations: the back-to-Africa Liberian exodus of 1877–1879; the Kansas "Exodusters" of 1879–1881; and the utopian black township movement to Oklahoma in the 1890s. Although at the turn of the century most of the Freedom Generation remained in the former slaveholding states, post–Civil War migrations set the stage for the rural-to-urban movements that reshaped the contours of life among African Americans in the twentieth century.

THE DEVELOPMENT OF AFRICAN-AMERICAN INSTITUTIONS

Although political participation and economic autonomy played a crucial role in the postwar life, it was in the realm of community building that blacks achieved their most significant long-term gains. Family reunification became the first task undertaken by most former slaves. During the Civil War and continuing for years thereafter, freedpeople did what they could to reknit the fabric of family life frayed during slavery. For many freedpeople, reunification involved solemnizing marriages begun during slavery. The Freedom Generation used the Freedmen's Bureau as well as local courts to solemnize scores of thousands of existing unions, a surprising number of which had endured for many decades. In other instances, reunification involved extensive travel in search of kin forcibly separated from their families. The former slave William Curtin, for example, rejoiced over the return, at war's end, of his father, who had been sold to Virginia from Georgia: "Dat was de best thing about de war setting us free, he could come back to us." Not all quests ended happily. Indeed, the often-futile attempt to reconstitute black family units disrupted during slavery was a frequent preoccupation. Lucinda Lowery posted this notice:

Information Wanted, of Caroline Dodson, who was sold from Nashville [Tennessee], Nov. 1st, 1862, by James Lumsden to Warwick, (a trader then in human beings), who carried her to Atlanta, Georgia, and she was last heard of in the sale pen of Robert Clark, (a human trader in that place,) from which she was sold. Any information of her whereabouts will be thankfully received and rewarded by her mother.

Until late in the 1880s, such notices appeared in black newspapers, offering powerful testimony to the strength of family ties fashioned in bondage and then disrupted by chattel slavery.

Enumerations of the American population taken between 1870 and 1910 reveal the overwhelming preponderance of two-parent families among rural and urban blacks, North and South. More than 90 percent of rural blacks lived in kin-based extended family units; 80 percent of urban blacks were similarly situated. Thus did an "invisible" institution of the slave community (the extended family) emerge in the wake of emancipation. The emphasis upon family imposed heavy responsibilities on postwar blacks who took on the burden of procuring the necessities of life both for themselves and for their dependents.

THE BLACK CHURCH

This quest for independence arose principally from the black churches, which served as the primary pillar in the indigenous process of community development that enabled freedpeople to avoid wallowing in a postslavery trough of "idleness, starvation, and disease." From this base arose a full array of benevolent, social, and educational institutions, in rural as well as in urban areas. And, it was these independent institutions controlled by black people that facilitated the successful adaptation to freedom.

Because most of the southern states did not provide publicly supported social services, black communities were compelled to turn inward, to find spiritual resources for survival, and to erect an institutional infrastructure to provide essential services for the sick, elderly, dead, and dying. By pooling scarce resources in church-sponsored social and benevolent agencies, the freedpeople employed a sturdy self-reliance that enabled them to meet successfully the challenge of caring for themselves and for their dependents. Locally governed churches provided the sites from which the freedpeople launched most of the independent social, benevolent, and educational institutions that ensured the survival of the Freedom Generation.

Even within the same denomination, urban/rural differences exerted strong influences. In the city of Memphis, Tennessee, for example, a former slave preacher named Morris Henderson assumed the leading role in erecting an independent black social infrastructure. Early in 1865, the Reverend Henderson left comfortable quarters in the basement of the white-controlled First

Baptist Church in favor of an outdoor "brush arbor." This move symbolized the determination of the recently freed to seek places where they could worship without supervision or interference. By 1869, Henderson's church claimed a membership of more than 2,500 adults: the largest among the black churches in Memphis. In 1870, Henderson moved into a new building on Beale Street, the location where the Beale Street Baptist Church stands to this day, and First Baptist Beale became the "Mother Church" for many satellite churches, which embarked on community building in other parts of Memphis. Reverend Henderson and his wife, Mary, assumed responsibility for social and benevolent activity in their church, out of which would emerge such groups as the Daughters of Zion, the Sisters of Zion, and the Sons and Daughters of Zion, who pooled the meager resources of impoverished urban blacks for mutual aid.

In rural Iberia Parish, Louisiana, 200 miles west of New Orleans, similar institutions arose appropriate to the agrarian circumstances. Beginning in 1868, a group of families related by marriage and kin ties that had survived during slavery took advantage of the 1866 federal Homestead Act to purchase a series of adjoining parcels of land. In 1873, this group of extended families established the independent settlement of Free Town and set aside land for Mt. Olive Baptist Church, named to symbolize arrival in a place of independent refuge. An equal number of men and women signed the church charter, and under the leadership of Reverend Robert Dyas and his wife, Sarah, the settlement moved quickly to establish its own church, cemetery, and school. Mt. Olive functioned as the center of community life, with a small store for supplies and a gristmill to grind cereal grain into meal and flour. The church also spawned a Young Men's Mutual Society which then organized an agricultural co-op to supply credit that independent black landowners often found extremely difficult to acquire. Mt. Olive stands today as substance and symbol of the efficacy and staying power of the family-based self-help infrastructure devised by the Freedom Generation.

Church-based community development left a quite varied legacy. The churches where most former slaves worshiped emphasized direct religious experience over liturgical piety. Color-caste and social class factors also influenced preferences among numerous Christian denominations. The Baptist Church became the favored denomination among the poor, darker-skinned working-class majority of freedpeople, while the AME church drew its adherents principally from a somewhat more affluent and lighter-skinned minority. In 1906, the National Baptist Convention, largest of the black-dominated religious groups, claimed more than 2.2 million members; the second largest group, the AME, claimed about 500,000 members. Other Protestant denominations, the Presbyterians and the Episcopalians, attracted markedly smaller number of literate, light-skinned professionals and entrepreneurs. And only in the state of Louisiana did Catholicism claim substantial numbers of black adherents.

EDUCATION

Nothing better illustrates the significance of community-based institution building than progress achieved by the freedpeople in the struggle to throw off the blanket of illiteracy with which slavery had shrouded them. Southern states displayed such penury toward the education of blacks that religious groups bore the principal burden of primary education until late in the nineteenth century. Attempts undertaken during the Civil War to educate freedpeople supplied the foundation, in postwar years, for a church-based network of privately funded primary schools throughout the South. Black churches organized thousands of Sabbath Schools, designed to provide freedpeople with the rudimentary skills necessary for independent biblical study. This Protestant emphasis on personal engagement with the Scriptures led to a more general demand for formal schooling for younger blacks.

Commenting on the alacrity with which freed children in Memphis responded to new opportunities for education, a skeptic wrote: "The Negroes, particularly the children, show an insatiable desire to learn—a greedy fondness for books." The intensity of educational interest displayed in Memphis attracted the attention of a philanthropist from the state of Pennsylvania, Dr. Francis LeMoyne, who donated $20,000 in 1869 to help to build a college "To fit Men and Women for entering early into the practical business of life." LeMoyne Normal and Commercial School opened its doors in the fall of 1871; and LeMoyne-Owen College continues today to discharge its educational mission as an historically black liberal arts college.

This pattern recurred throughout the southern states. Opened during the Civil War/Reconstruction era in response to demands among freedpeople for education, these black schools rapidly evolved into normal schools, colleges, and universities. Fisk University grew out of a school opened at Nashville, Tennessee, in 1866. Lincoln University in Jefferson City, Missouri, Howard University in the national capital, and Morehouse College in Atlanta, Georgia, all opened their doors in 1867. In fact, practically every one of the historically black colleges and universities now in operation dates its founding to the period 1865 to 1915.

An assessment of progress in black literacy reveals the impact of access to education. The 1870 U.S. Census reported an 85 percent adult literacy rate for southern whites compared to less than 10 percent for black adults; only 8 percent of freed children of school age attended school while 33 percent of southern white children did. By 1910, the emphasis among members of the Freedom Generation on educating the young had significantly altered these figures. The 1910 U.S. Census reported that white school attendance had doubled to 60 percent, while the rate for blacks was 43 percent: an increase of more than 400 percent. Access to formal education led to enhanced literacy. For while former slaves (blacks over age sixty-five) reported literacy of 20 percent (compared to 85 percent for whites over sixty-five), blacks ages ten to fourteen recorded an 80 percent literacy rate in comparison to a 95 percent literacy rate for southern whites of the same age. The rapid closure of the literacy gap between white and black adolescents suggests that forty years of emphasis on schooling had brought younger members of the Freedom Generation to a literacy rate within striking distance of their generational peers.

No person better exemplified the positive impact of access to education on black upward mobility than Booker T. Washington. Born into slavery in 1856 in Franklin County, Virginia, Washington would gain fame as the head of Tuskeegee Institute, an agricultural and technical school created by blacks in central Alabama as a "college" to educate local youths. Washington's formal education came at Hampton Institute, an agricultural and technical school founded in 1868 by Union General Samuel Chapman Armstrong to educate "contrabands" at Fortress Monroe. When black leaders from Tuskeegee asked Armstong to suggest someone to oversee creation of their school, Armstrong named his prize pupil, Booker T. Washington, as the freedman best qualified to duplicate in Alabama what had been achieved in Virginia. From humble beginnings in 1881, Washington succeeded not only in creating at Tuskeegee an institution devoted to practical education but in making himself the most powerful African-American of his day. Ties to captains of industry, to philanthropists, and to leading Republicans like the future president Theodore Roosevelt would transform Booker T. Washington into a major figure in American life.

As significant as were Washington's later achievements, his early life sheds light on the grim circumstances in which most members of the Freedom Generation lived. Shortly after emancipation, Washington's stepfather moved the family from the plantation on which they had lived to a new residence in West Virginia where he had served his duty tour as a Union soldier. While Washington proved to be an exceptionally bright ten-year-old, the pressure of economic necessity compelled a division of time between rudimentary education and labor in the salt and coal mines. Encouragement from his mother, who secured work in domestic service, allowed him to leave the mines and continue his journey to higher education at Hampton Institute.

BLACK WOMEN ORGANIZE

Although talent and good fortune separated Washington from the mass of freedpeople, the ambition for improvement that motivated him was widespread. A remarkable group of black women led the way in refashioning the institutional infrastructure improvised during the first decades after emancipation. Maggie Lena Walker became the first woman bank president in the United States when she founded the Saint Luke Penny Savings Bank in Richmond, Virginia, in 1903. Born in 1867, Walker, in 1883, graduated from Richmond's Colored Normal School; she taught school, helped found Woman's Union (an insurance company), and was selected, in 1899, to serve as Right

Worthy Grand Secretary of the Independent Order of St. Luke, a black mutual benefit society. Mary McLeod Bethune founded the Daytona (Florida) Normal and Industrial School for Training Negro Girls in 1904, using "$1.50 and a prayer." Born to freed parents in South Carolina in 1875, Bethune received her primary education at a school operated by the Presbyterian Board of Missions for Freedmen. After a 1922 merger with an all-boys school, Bethune changed the name of the institution she founded to that which it bears today, Bethune-Cookman College.

The impetus for institution building in northern cities often came from southern migrants. Jane Edna Hunter, born in 1882 to freed parents in South Carolina and educated at an AME normal school, went to Cleveland, Ohio, in 1905 to pursue a nursing career for which she had trained at Hampton Institute. Personal experience with the harsh conditions in which single southern female migrants generally lived pushed Hunter into organizing a group of black women pledged to give a nickel per week to support the Working Girls' Home Association, which they founded in 1911. When migration from the South increased Cleveland's black population 300 percent between 1910 and 1920, the city's association was forced to make radical changes to meet new demands for social services. Renaming her group after the eighteenth-century black poet Phillis Wheatley, Hunter devised a plan of expansion which led to the opening of an eleven-story facility in 1927, making the Phillis Wheatley Association the largest independent black settlement house in the United States.

Such examples of female social activism were repeated throughout the nation. Nothing better captures the motives for this activism than a speech delivered by Nannie Burroughs in 1900 to the National Baptist Convention's annual meeting. Burroughs, born in Richmond in 1878, titled her speech "How the Sisters are Hindered from Helping"; her appeal won approval for the creation of a Woman's Convention to serve as an outlet for women's "burning zeal" to serve the interests of the race. The assumption by black

The Convention of The National Association of Colored Women, 1904

The National Association of Colored Women's Clubs in the fourth convention assembled, with gratitude acknowledge the Divine guidance of the Supreme Ruler of the Universe and thank Him for the preservation of our President, executive officers and other members.

We pledge renewed efforts and loyalty along all lines in this, our national organization, continuing to stand for adherence to our motto "Lifting as We Climb," for we believe that in it lies the future hope of the race.

Source: Minutes of the Fourth Convention of the National Association of Colored Women, held at St. Paul's Church, St. Louis, Missouri, July 11 to 16, 1904.

women of primary responsibility for social and benevolent activity continued unabated, leading to the founding in 1896 of the National Association of Colored Women (NACW), dedicated to promoting "the welfare of our race." On NACW's Founding Board were many prominent black women, including Olivia Davidson Washington, wife of Booker T. Washington. Mary Church Terrell, first NACW president, daughter of the Memphis millionaire Robert Reed Church and a graduate of LeMoyne College, captured the essence of black female benevolent activism in a speech delivered to the New York Charity Organization Society in 1910. "If anyone should ask me what special phase of the colored American's development makes me the most hopeful of his ultimate triumph over present obstacles," Terrell wrote, "I should answer unhesitatingly, it is the magnificent work the women are doing to regenerate and elevate the race."

Female benevolent activity relied on small donations and volunteer activity to support relief work. Similar methods generated the many millions of dollars raised to pay for construction, in the years 1885 to 1915, of the monumental church edifices that now stand in cities North and South, edifices which give elegant and eloquent testimony to the success of community building initiated by members of the Freedom Generation.

THE RISE OF JIM CROW

When Mary Church Terrell expressed optimism about "ultimate triumph over present obstacles," she referred, obliquely, to the period of intense racial crisis that confronted African-Americans at the turn of the century. Contestation over racial issues occurred both among African Americans and between blacks and whites. Regionwide passage of Jim Crow segregation laws focused interracial strife on issues of equal access to public activities and facilities. And friction between blacks reflected principled disagreement over the best strategy for ameliorating the problems besetting African Americans. These multiple dimensions of the movements protesting racialism and segregation would remain at the forefront of concern for the balance of the twentieth century.

Statutory racial segregation emerged in the 1880s as southern states enacted laws mandating separation of blacks and whites. Jim Crow began in Tennessee in 1881 with the enactment of a law allowing railroads to offer separate first-class accommodations for black and white passengers. Soon thereafter, the long-simmering friction over black claims for equality erupted in the wake of a second period of failed interracial political alliance. In the same way that Radical Reconstruction collapsed amid organized political violence, so did the Populist Movement. The failure of the farmers' crusade, which had initially supported biracial activity, to achieve agrarian reform left a residue of embittered racialism that found expression both in political violence and in discriminatory laws. And while individual southern states worked to enact Jim Crow statutes, the ideology of social Darwinism accorded the sanction of "science" to Eurocentric racism. By 1910, Jim Crow had spread throughout the South, mandating cradle-to-grave segregation of whites and blacks in the public sphere.

Questions about how best to counter racialist violence, Jim Crow laws, and scientific racialism sparked intense debate among African Americans. Far from achieving a consensus, black educators, politicians, intellectuals, and social activists articulated sharply conflicting strategies that reflected the broadened spectrum of social conditions among blacks in the late nineteenth century. The core issue was this: Should blacks fight against Jim Crow or acquiesce in that which they could not control while building strength for a counterattack when conditions improved? Mobility and class differentiation had created bases for diversity and dissent unimaginable amid the generalized poverty characteristic of the immediate postslavery years.

Late in his life, Frederick Douglass attempted to formulate a platform for unified action and watched in shocked horror as the number of lynchings rose dramatically amid the tumult of the 1880s. Averaging 100 each year for thirty years, lynchings took place throughout the South. They were especially prevalent in thinly populated rural areas recently experiencing significant black in-migration. The ritual public murders generally involved black male "strangers" who were falsely accused of sexual assault on local white women. The fateful coincidence of lynchings, Jim Crow laws, and social Darwinism prompted a deeply concerned Douglass to ask, in 1889, whether "American justice, American liberty, American civilization, American law, and American Christianity could be made to include and protect alike all American citizens in the rights which have been guaranteed to them by the organic and fundamental laws of the land."

"Lawless Burning of Men 'By the Many.'" The practice of violence against slaves common before abolition endured after emancipation with the mob lynching of free blacks, which reached epidemic proportions in the 1890s. From *American Anti-Slavery Almanac for 1840*. Credit: The Library Company of Philadelphia.

CONFRONTING LYNCH LAW

Douglass was joined in his attack on lynching and racialism in 1892 by the black journalist Ida B. Wells. Born a slave in 1862, Wells received her primary and collegiate education in Mississippi. After working as a teacher for several years, Wells purchased, in 1889, part ownership in a newspaper, the *Memphis Free Speech and Headlight*, published by the Beale Street Baptist Church, from which she launched a vigorous assault against lynching. Frustration over the complicity of city leaders prompted Wells to urge Memphis blacks to join the migration to Oklahoma. The departure of several thousand workers angered local businessmen who found in a May 1892 editorial a pretext for silencing Ida B. Wells. For not only did Wells dispute ritual charges of sexual assault against victims of lynching but also she questioned whether repeated reliance on false charges might not be "very damaging to the moral reputation of [white] women." Within days, irate civic leaders forced closure of the *Free Speech* and exiled Ida B. Wells to Chicago.

Once in Chicago, Wells maintained her activism. She soon launched a vigorous protest against the decision by organizers of the 1892–1893 Columbian Exposition to deny the inclusion of an exhibit by American blacks, revealing

Ida B. Wells-Barnett on Lynching

.... If the Southern citizens lynch Negroes because "that is the only successful method of dealing with a certain class of crimes," then that class of crimes should be shown unmistakably by this record. Now consider the record.

It would be supposed that the record would show that all, or nearly all, lynchings were caused by outrageous assaults upon women; certainly that this particular offense would outnumber all other causes for putting human beings to death without a trial by jury and the other safeguards of our Constitution and laws.

But the record makes no such disclosure. Instead, it shows that five women have been lynched, put to death with unspeakable savagery during the past five years. They certainly were not under the ban of the outlawing crime. It shows that men, not a few, but hundreds, have been lynched for misdemeanors, while others have suffered death for no offense known to the law, the causes assigned being "mistaken identity," "insult," "bad reputation," "unpopularity," "violating contract," "running quarantine," "giving evidence," "frightening children by shooting at rabbits," etc. Then, strangest of all, the record shows that the sum total of lynchings for these offenses—not crimes—and for the alleged offenses which are only misdemeanors, greatly exceeds the lynchings for the very crime universally declared to be the cause of lynching ... Instead of being the sole cause of lynching, the crime upon which lynchers build their defense furnishes the least victims for the mob. In 1896 less than thirty-nine per cent of the Negroes lynched were charged with this crime; in 1897, less than eighteen per cent; in 1898, less than sixteen per cent; in 1899, less than fourteen per cent; and in 1900, less than fifteen per cent, were so charged.

Source: The Independent (N.Y.), May 16, 1901.

the influence of scientific racialist dogma that blacks had never accomplished anything worthy of representation on the "Great White Way," the name given to the exposition's brightly lighted main promenade. Wells sought out Frederick Douglass and persuaded him to join, both in publishing an antilynching pamphlet, "The Reason Why: The Colored American Is Not In The World's Columbian Exposition." Douglass bemoaned the decision as a lost opportunity "to show some results of our first thirty years of acknowledged manhood and womanhood." Ridiculing the denial of black achievement by exposition organizers, Douglass argued instead that they excluded blacks because of their unwillingness to acknowledge that slavery had existed and their reluctance to broach the subject of black achievement lest such an exhibit implicitly condemn widespread lynching. Douglass saw the epidemic of lynching as "proof that the Negro is not standing still . . . he is alive and fighting his way to better conditions than those of the past." Precisely because "the enemies of the Negro see that he is making progress," insisted Douglass, "they naturally wish to stop him and keep him in just what they consider his proper place."

Concerns about the "proper place" for African Americans and the best strategy for coping with violent racial conflict remained at the forefront, particularly among those charged with responsibility for symbolic evocations of "progress." Organizers of the Cotton States Exposition planned for Atlanta in 1895 adopted a radically different tact than had the organizers of the Columbian Exposition. Rather than exclusion, they authorized the construction of a "Negro Building" and invited Booker T. Washington to give the opening address. A champion of the interests of black landowners who generally approved of an emphasis on education to improve farm productivity, Washington viewed his Atlanta speech as an opportunity to bring about racial peace through a carefully crafted appeal to the self-interests of the growth-oriented political and business boosters of the "New South." Without hope of effective enforcement of civil rights from the national government, Washington saw little value in Frederick Douglass's appeals to American constitutional idealism. "Our greatest danger," Washington argued in his famous Atlanta address, "is that in the great leap from slavery to freedom we may overlook the fact that the masses of us are to live by the production of our hands, and fail to keep in mind that we shall prosper in proportion as we learn to dignify and glorify common labor, and put brains and skills into the common occupations of life. . . . It is at the bottom of life that we must begin, not at the top. . . . Nor should we permit our grievances to overshadow our opportunities," Washington submitted in disapproval of Ida Wells's strident protest. He also insisted that "the wisest among my race" deemed "agitation of questions of social equality [as] the extremest folly." These views prompted Washington to offer a compromise to the South's best men: he would acquiesce in segregation, which he felt powerless to overturn in the short run, in return for the end of lynching. As Washington put it, "In all things that are purely social we can be as separate as the fingers, yet one as the hand in all things essential to mutual progress." Delivered seven months after Frederick Douglass's death, the speech prompted the *New York World* to describe Washington as "a negro Moses."

Dissonant responses to the hallmark speech of Washington's career reflected the importance of this symbolic passing of the torch of African-American leadership. Considerably less complimentary reviews came from a number of black intellectuals, most prominent of whom was the Harvard-trained sociologist W. E. B. DuBois. This cofounder of the NAACP sharply criticized Washington's effort to fashion an accommodation with segregation laws as well as his emphasis on industrial education. Instead, DuBois advocated bold action in behalf of civil rights and argued for the use of liberal arts education to create a "Talented Tenth"; DuBois saw educating elite blacks as the best method of proving to a doubting world the civilizing capacity of African Americans.

Washington also met similar harsh criticism even from those more familiar with the realities of the agrarian South. Ida B. Wells, herself a former slave and product of Hampton, acknowledged the salience of industrial education for improving the lives of rural-agrarian blacks, but chastised Washington for his emphasis on Tuskeegee to the detriment of other black colleges and universities. Above all, however, Wells found fault with Washington's stand on the central issue of the day, whether blacks should acquiesce in segregation or fight openly against it. "It is indeed a bitter pill," she wrote, "to feel that much of the unanimity with which the nation today agrees to Negro disfranchisement comes from the general acceptance of Mr. Washington's theories."

Booker T. Washington remains an enigma. Was the "Wizard of Tuskeegee" unaware of the uses white supremacists made of his compromise, or did he believe that elite southerners could control former Populists who eventually supported Jim Crow so enthusiastically? It may well be that Washington's personal relations with the power elite led him to err badly in estimating the virulence of racialism and the efficacy of heavy reliance on the influence his elite patrons could exert upon turn-of-the-century southern politics.

Booker T. Washington died in 1915, shortly before World War I opened the way for more than a million southern blacks to head north in search of opportunity. Left unresolved in debates between Washington and his critics was the strategic question: Should blacks attempt to "use segregation as a weapon to remove segregation?" How far to rely on self-reliance? When to form alliances with whites? With which ideological factions should such alliances be forged? When to rely on constitutional litigation as opposed to direct protest? These issues continued to remain matters of contention well into the twentieth century.

CONCLUSION

Despite the obstacles set in their path, the members of the Freedom Generation imparted a legacy of achievement to its progeny. And their earnest desire for recognition of their achievements found powerful symbolic expression in the successful agitation launched by black Virginia attorney Giles B. Jackson concerning the 1907 celebration of the tercentennial of English settlement at Jamestown. Much as had Ida B. Wells, Jackson sought recognition of black achievements in this celebration of American nationality. Like Wells, Jackson believed any such exhibit was woefully incomplete if it lacked evidence of the material advances made by African Americans after slavery.

Centennial organizers initially responded ambivalently, but a persistent Giles G. Jackson eventually won out. When he received the go-ahead in 1903, Jackson incorporated "The Negro Development and Exposition Company of the United States." He then set out to procure and exhibit examples of "everything" blacks had done so that "the world may form a correct opinion of the Negro race in this country." Jackson solicited financial support from every former slaveholding state and from Congress. North Carolina appropriated $5,000, and was the only state to give financial support. Congress appropriated $100,000 to assist the project. President Theodore Roosevelt visited the Negro Exhibit in June 1908, as subsequently did Booker T. Washington, both of whom expressed amazement at the range of displays it contained. In this large three-story building designed and constructed by blacks were displayed some ten thousand individual exhibits; they covered the gamut of artistic, literary, industrial, and handicraft work submitted by black religious, educational, and social groups throughout America.

Giles B. Jackson took special pride in statistics that showed the scope and scale of organizational activity undertaken by the Freedom Generation. Jackson pointed out that the 1900 U.S. Census counted twenty-four thousand black church buildings "with a seating capacity of six millions, eight hundred thousands"; property owned by these churches was valued at $26,662,448. The commitment to education remained so strong that blacks contributed more money in 1900 to support black primary schools ($1,469,000) than the $1,346,000 that was appropriated by southern state governments. Higher education remained an object of interest as well, enabling Jackson to report, "There are now in the country 136 colleges and 'Industrial Schools' exclusively for the education of negroes." The proliferation of urban social service agencies evidenced continued self-reliance. "The results were simply marvelous," Jackson concluded, "and we think it not too much to say that the Negro Exhibit was the central figure of the Exposition." The expansive pleasure Giles B. Jackson expressed concerning the Negro Exhibit reflected the understandable pride former slaves and their children took in the construction of a self-sustaining black community. Their achievements had proven skeptics like the Tennessee Reconstruction Governor Brownlow to be unequivocally wrong.

Nonetheless, the subjugation of the Freedom Generation to domination by *de jure* segregation shows that post–Civil War America did not achieve the hoped-for transition to racial democracy. This failure led, in the twentieth century, to the massive out-migration of African Americans from the former slaveholding states to urban regions throughout the United States. The legacy of failed racial democracy evident in the Jim Crow laws would help precipitate the Civil Rights movement a half-century later, and the seeds of the contemporary "urban crisis" were sown in the racial discrimination experienced by so many African-American urban emigrants. The lost opportunities of the emancipation era reveal that America had yet to honor fully the compact the Great Emancipator, Abraham Lincoln, made solemnly at Gettysburg: the sacred pledge that saving the Union by the destruction of chattel slavery would promote "A New Birth of Freedom" in a unified America.

FOR FURTHER READING

Anderson, James D. *The Education of Blacks in the South, 1860–1935*. Chapel Hill: University of North Carolina Press, 1988.

Ayers, Edward L. *The Promise of the New South: Life After Reconstruction*. New York: Oxford University Press, 1993.

Carby, Hazel. *Reconstructing Womanhood: The Emergence of the Afro-American Woman Novelist*. New York: Oxford University Press, 1990.

Foner, Eric. *Reconstruction: America's Unfinished Revolution, 1863–1877*. New York: Harper & Row, 1988.

Gatewood, Willard B. *Aristocrats of Color: The Black Elite, 1880–1920*. Bloomington: Indiana University Press, 1990.

Gilmore, Glenda E. *Gender and Jim Crow: Women and the Politics of White Supremacy in North Carolina, 1896–1920*. Chapel Hill: University of North Carolina Press, 1996.

Gutman, Herbert G. *The Black Family in Slavery and Freedom, 1750–1925*. New York: Vintage, 1977.

Higginbotham, Evelyn Brooks. *Righteous Discontent: The Women's Movement in the Black Baptist Church, 1880–1920*. Cambridge: Harvard University Press, 1994.

Hunter, Tera W. *To 'Joy My Freedom: Southern Black Women's Lives and Labors after the Civil War*. Cambridge: Harvard University Press, 1997.

Jaynes, Gerald D. *Branches Without Roots: Genesis of the Black Working Class in the American South, 1862–1882*. New York: Oxford University Press, 1990.

Johnson, Daniel M., and Rex M. Campbell. *Black Migration in America: A Social Demographic History*. Durham, N.C.: Duke University Press, 1981.

Jones, Beverly Washington. *Quest for Equality: The Life and Writings of Mary Eliza Church Terrell, 1863–1954*. Brooklyn, N.Y.: Carlson, 1990.

Levine, Lawrence W. *Black Culture and Black Consciousness: Afro-American Folk Thought from Slavery to Freedom*. New York: Oxford University Press, 1978.

Litwack, Leon F. *Been in the Storm So Long: The Aftermath of Slavery*. New York: Knopf, 1980.

———. *Trouble in Mind: Black Southerners in the Age of Jim Crow*. New York: Knopf, 1998.

Meier, August. *Negro Thought in America, 1880–1915*. Ann Arbor: University of Michigan Press, 1963.

Neverdon-Morton, Cynthia. *Afro-American Women of the South and the Advancement of the Race, 1895–1925*. Knoxville: University of Tennessee Press, 1991.

Ransom, Roger, and Richard Sutch. *One Kind of Freedom: Economic Reconstruction in the South.* New York: Cambridge University Press, 1977.

Thompson, Mildred I. *Ida B. Wells-Barnett, An Exploratory Study of an American Black Woman, 1893–1930.* Brooklyn, N.Y.: Carlson, 1990.

Walker, Clarence E. *A Rock in a Weary Land: The African Methodist Episcopal Church during the Civil War and Reconstruction.* Baton Rouge: Louisana State University Press, 1982.

Woodward, C. Vann. *The Strange Career of Jim Crow.* 3rd rev. ed. New York: Oxford University Press, 1989.

chapter 7

Blacks in the Economy from Reconstruction to World War I

Gerald D. Jaynes

A T THE CLOSE OF THE CIVIL WAR, four million newly emancipated slaves entered a second-class status situated somewhere between actual liberty and slavery. They joined the ambiguous social and legal space occupied by one-half million blacks who had been nominally free before the war. African Americans as a group and their white allies in the North understood that without black property and voting rights, the Emancipation Proclamation had no functional meaning either for black Americans or for American democracy. Political citizenship for African-American men was theoretically achieved, of course, when Congress passed the Thirteenth, Fourteenth, and Fifteenth Amendments to the Constitution and the Civil Rights Act of 1866. But within the next quarter-century those victories were rescinded as, state by state, the South disenfranchised black voters near the end of the nineteenth century. Moreover, with respect to economic security, the freedpeople received no financial reparations for two and one third centuries of bondage. In particular, Congress refused to confiscate farmlands from supporters of the former Confederacy, who were perceived as a competent managerial elite, for distribution to the freedmen, who were viewed as uneducated laborers without any experience as independent farmers. Simultaneously, the federal government refused to make financial loans to plantation owners so that the war-ravaged South could reconstitute its economy on a sound basis.

Overwhelmingly, former slaves entered freedom with nothing to sell but their labor. Their employers were primarily former slave owners who were bereft of capital, low on credit, and accustomed to having absolute power over black labor. Between the former slaves and slave owners stood the freedpeople's newfound right to move freely and the Bureau of Refugees, Freedmen, and Abandoned Lands, commonly called the Freedmen's Bureau. Created in March 1865 as a compromise between congressional members aligned for and against land confiscation, the bureau was intended to protect the rights of former slaves and to ensure a smooth and timely return to the production of cotton, sugar, tobacco, and rice, which had been severely reduced during four years of war.

Black reconstruction had in fact already begun during the Civil War as thousands of runaway slaves wreaked havoc on the Confederacy's war effort. Many of them maintained that they held a right to the lands abandoned by slave owners in the wake of advancing Union Armies and had to be removed by military force from their new homesteads. After the war, blacks possessed the freedom of continued migration; many former slaves from the Upper South and Southeast moved to the Southwest where the fertile cotton lands of Arkansas, Mississippi, and Louisiana allowed planters to offer higher wages than elsewhere. Between 1860 and 1910, the South Atlantic states' share of the African-American population declined from 46 percent to 42 percent while the share of the western and south-central states rose from 15 percent to 20 percent.

FROM SLAVERY TO SHARECROPPING

The system of sharecropping evolved as a choice neither freedpeople nor planters considered ideal. Planters preferred to organize plantation labor into work gangs similar to the slavery system, and freedpeople wanted to own and work their own farms. During the initial years of Reconstruction, former slaves and slaveowners faced off in a struggle to determine the specifics of the labor-management relations. The former slaves rebelled against the attempt by owners of large plantations to simulate the labor relations of the slave regime.

During the immediate postbellum period, as had been typical during slavery, on large cotton plantations, several work gangs were employed under the supervision of a headman or overseer, and decision-making authority funneled down the hierarchy. Freedmen, women, and adolescents were organized into these labor crews, but many freedpeople refused to work under gang foremen who often were the same men who as plantation "drivers" had disciplined them with the threat of the lash. Black workers now demanded and won more freedom in the performance of their daily tasks especially in the conduct of their off-duty personal affairs.

On the heavily capitalized sugar plantations of Louisiana, and, to a lesser extent, on the larger rice plantations of South Carolina and Georgia, the plantations that survived Reconstruction intact were generally able to maintain closely supervised work crews who were paid money wages. However, the majority of laborers on tobacco and cotton plantations worked in gangs for a sharewage, usually one-third to one-half of the net proceeds of the crop that was divided between anywhere from ten to fifty workers after the crop was harvested and sold by the planter. Moreover, for most sharecroppers the contracted payments were due in a lump sum at the end of the crop year. In either case, during the year, laborers obtained their subsistence food and clothing, usually on credit, from either plantation stores or independent merchants.

Under this system, the Freedmen's Bureau adjudicated thousands of labor disputes between planters and laborers, most involving labor turnover as African Americans attempted to change jobs when it suited them. Labor turnover was most frequently due to harsh means of supervision by plantation owners, such as whippings, and to the inability of a huge percentage of financially embarrassed planters to pay laborers their wages at the end of the year. But the bureau was also involved in settling many arguments over work rules and payment arrangements.

In 1866 and 1868, disastrous weather conditions that caused large-scale crop failures left many planters unable to pay their debts to creditors and

"The Heritage." After emancipation, many newly freed blacks faced difficult economic circumstances as they competed for jobs and land in the postwar South. From Mary Helm's *The Upward Path* (Atlanta, 1904). Credit: The Library Company of Philadelphia.

laborers. As a result, large numbers of laborers received only partial wages or no wages for a full year's work. This experience led to wholesale abandonment of plantations as laborers searched for employers able to pay them wages during the harvest season. Furthermore, it created extreme distrust among black workers toward their employers. Problems regarding no pay and low pay led to a large reduction in the labor force for two years, when workers reallocated their time and activities toward household chores and school.

The Freedmen's Bureau stepped into the dispute and ruled that while workers who were promised money wages were employees and could be paid after the employer had sold the crop, sharelaborers were part owners of the crop. And, as part owners, they had the right to demand division of the crop in the

Tenant Farming in Alabama, 1889

Of course when the war ended the colored people had nothing on which to live while the first crop was being made. Thus, in addition to renting the land on which to make the first crop they had to get the local merchant or someone else to supply the food for the family to eat while the first crop was being made. For every dollar's worth of provisions so advanced the local merchant charged from 12 to 30 per cent interest. In order to be sure that he secured his principal and interest a mortgage or lien was taken on the crop, in most cases not then planted. Of course the farmers could pay no such interest and the end of the first year found them in debt—the 2nd year they tried again, but there was the old debt and the new interest to pay, and in this way the "mortgage system" has gotten a hold on everything that it seems impossible to shake off. Its evils have grown instead of decreasing, until it is safe to say that 5/6 of the colored farmers mortgage their crops every year. Not only their crops before, in many cases, they are actually planted, but their wives sign a release from the homestead law and in most every case mules, cows, wagons, plows and often all household furniture is covered by the lien.

At a glance one is not likely to get the full force of the figures representing the amount of interest charged. Example, if a man makes a mortgage with a merchant for $200 on which to run during the year the farmer is likely to get about $50 of this amount in February or March, $50 May, $50 in June or July and the remainder in Aug. or Sept. By the middle of Sept. the farmer begins returning the money in cotton and by the last of Oct. whatever he can pay the farmer has paid, but the merchant charges as much for the money gotten in July or Aug. as for that gotten in Feb. The farmer is charged interest on all for the one year of 12 months. And as the "advance" is made in most cases in provisions rather than cash, the farmer, in addition to paying the interest mentioned, is charged more for the same goods than one buying for cash. If a farmer has 6 in a family say wife and 4 children, the merchant has it in his power to feed only those who work and sometimes he says to the farmer if he sends his children to school no rations can be drawn for them while they are attending school.

After a merchant has "run" a farmer for 5 or 6 years and he does not "pay out" or decides to try mortgaging with another merchant the first merchant in such cases usually "cleans up" the farmer, that is takes everything, mules, cows, plows, chicken's fodder—everything except wife and children.

Source: The Journal of Negro Education (1948) XVII, p. 46.

field after which they could dispose of their share as they wished. Because of the huge number of landlords who were defaulting on their payments to laborers, the ruling, backed by the bureau's use of the military, led more laborers to demand shares; it was clear that form of payment provided greater worker security than postharvest wages. By 1867 only those planters with solid reputations of solvency and access to cash or credit could hire labor for wages, since African Americans were increasingly demanding to work for a share of the crop, which in their words, made them "part owners of the crop."

The system of paying laborers in crops while still working them in large gangs frequently resulted in severe labor-incentive problems and inefficient work. Because all workers received a portion of the entire gang's share, some workers recognized that their share of the crop would not be substantially reduced if they lagged on the job. Better workers felt that they were being cheated and refused to work with those they considered inefficient. These factors increased absenteeism and other poor work habits that undermined productivity. To solve the problem of the free rider, planters reduced the size of work gangs and permitted workers to choose their coworkers.

During approximately a ten-year period, from 1865 to 1875, planters and laborers experimented with many types of labor systems. By the late 1860s, many aspects of managerial authority had flowed from planters to laborers as small groups of men and women formed work groups that collectively contracted with planters for a group share of the crop. These work groups called variously "squads," "associations," and "clubs," frequently functioned as democratic majority-rule worker collectives that seriously threatened the managerial authority of planters.

During the 1870s, throughout the cotton- and tobacco-producing areas of the South, the scaling down of workgroup size to better meet demands for efficiency and equity among workers, the practice of allowing self-selection of coworkers, and blacks' demand for family autonomy led to the proliferation of share tenancy for one-half the crop among families working a small farm to themselves. Whether the planters anticipated it or not, the individualism inherent in family share tenancy destroyed the collective esprit of the cotton and tobacco laborers, and unlike the wage hands on sugar plantations who continued to agitate and sometimes to lead insurrections against employers and the state for better working conditions, share tenants became a conservative workforce whose deep but unvoiced animosity for their plight only occasionally led to organized activism.

REINSTITUTION OF WHITE SUPREMACY

Despite the conservatism that came to characterize black share tenants, the planter class early recognized radical impulses within African-American agrarianism that advocated they transfer economic and political power from the landowning and former slaveholder class to the working classes of the South.

Such aspirations to institute southern economic and political democracy posed a serious threat to established property interests, which planters determined should be swiftly suppressed. By defining the political and economic contest as determining which race would control the South, as opposed to the real issue of which classes would control its political and economic institutions, the planters and their supporters managed to focus all questions on the issue of race. To exclude African Americans from the political process and to prevent them from using collective efforts to improve their economic status, the Ku Klux Klan and other terrorist organizations employed extreme violence and terrorism such as the practice of lynching.

The planters' campaign began at the end of the Civil War during the state constitutional conventions of 1865 and early 1866, held under the lenient provisions of President Andrew Johnson's program for reunion. Many of the delegates were former slave owners and had been officers in the military and civil branches of the Confederate government. Emboldened by the former slaveholding president's conciliatory posture, the conventions drafted and passed constitutions that defined in no uncertain legal terms the inferior civil status of blacks in their states. These statutes came to be known as the Black Codes.

The Black Codes made it clear that in the postwar South black men and women would be second-class citizens with few rights. Blacks were explicitly denied the right to vote, to serve on juries, and to testify in cases involving white defendants. However, the major thrust of the codes was to curtail the ability of former slaves to improve their economic circumstances through better employment. The state of Mississippi passed one of the earliest and most repressive Black Codes. All resident blacks were required to possess written evidence, by January of each year, that they were employed for the ensuing year. To further immobilize blacks the code contained an anti-enticement law that made it a crime for any employer to attempt to hire a freedperson who was working for another employer, and backed it with a fine of $500 or a prison sentence. Workers who left their employment before the end of a contract forfeited their entire wages, and the code authorized any white person to arrest any black who had quit a job before expiration of a contract. To further guarantee a docile black force, freedmen were prohibited from renting land.

Just in case freedpeople found any loopholes in Black Codes, southern states passed a vagrancy law aimed at restricting occupational mobility and general free movement. The vagrancy laws imposed fines or involuntary labor on broad categories of blacks who were considered engaged in antisocial or nonproductive activities, identified as "rogues," "jugglers or persons practicing unlawful games or plays," and "persons who neglect their calling or employment." South Carolina's vagrancy law was just as draconian, singling out "common gamblers, persons who lead disorderly lives or keep or frequent disorderly or disreputable houses; . . . those who are engaged in representing . . . without license, any tragedy, interlude, comedy, farce, play; . . . exhibition of the circus, sleight of hand, wax-works; . . . fortune-tellers, sturdy beggars, common drunkards."

After wresting control of Reconstruction from the president whose polices were undermining Republican objectives, Congress voided the Black Codes through the Civil Rights Act of 1866, which outlawed discrimination. But the codes had become a precedent for state legislation after Reconstruction ended, and whites moved to institute a legal system of discrimination and segregation throughout former states of the Confederacy.

By the 1880s, after the overthrow of Reconstruction, the southern states reinstituted the spirit of the Black Codes by passing regulatory legislation that made no mention of race, and, therefore, presumably bypassed constitutional objections, but was directed against black people. Antienticement and vagrancy laws were passed; rural blacks' ability to supplement their diets through hunting and fishing was proscribed; and various petty crimes, such as damage of private property and theft of objects of small value, were made felonies punishable by forced servitude as convict labor. Sharecroppers were legally defined as wage laborers, and were deprived of their rights to the crop and a first lien on that crop to protect their wages. Perhaps the most detrimental legislation was the so-called "embezzlement" or "false pretense" laws such as one in Alabama, which made it a crime for a laborer indebted to an employer to end his job without permission. Such laws could keep sharecroppers, who had to accept loans from their landlords in order to subsist during the year, tied for several years to one employer.

In the South, by the end of the nineteenth century, the force of the new state laws and the nonenforcement of civil protections embodied in federal laws had effectively repealed the legislative triumphs of the Reconstruction period: the Civil Rights Act of 1866, and the Thirteenth, Fourteenth, and Fifteenth Amendments to the United States Constitution. With blacks lacking protections in a white-controlled legal system, any white was virtually free to discriminate against any black, the Fourteenth Amendment's equal protection of citizens' rights was nullified, and black male suffrage granted by the Fifteenth Amendment had been essentially eliminated by new state voting and registration laws. Overall, the civil status of blacks—stripped of the vote, segregated in separate schools and public conveyances, and deprived of standing in court against whites—demonstrated that while the Thirteenth Amendment's ban of slavery still held, its effects had been restricted about as far as was practically possible.

A major cost of race discrimination and segregation was the absence of any political bonds between black and white workers. Devastated by the Civil War and the credit famine and crop failure in the war's immediate aftermath, small white farmers in the upland regions of the cotton South also became impoverished. From the last quarter of the nineteenth century onward, while labor on large cotton plantations in the lower South was overwhelmingly black, relatively small farms owned and worked by white families produced increasing quantities of cotton in the piedmont regions of the Upper South. White and black cotton producers became victims of a brutal economic system wherein low cotton prices throughout the latter nineteenth century and most of the first half of the twentieth tied them to a cycle of credit advances, poverty, and debt to landowners and merchants that for many often became a cruel form of debt peonage.

INDUSTRIAL LABOR

According to the United States census of 1890, approximately 90 percent of the black population of roughly 7.5 million Americans lived in the South, and a huge majority of African Americans were employed as laborers in agriculture and in personal service.

By 1900, employment in the South was dominated by a pattern of segregation wherein one race, through economic competition, politics, or violence, essentially drove the other race from many occupations. The textile industry, which hardly existed in the South before the Civil War, was now nearly completely staffed by white men, women, and children. Economic segregation exhibited a perverse symmetry, with black and white families involved in cotton production largely separated by geography whereas black and white families involved in manufacturing were separated only by the refusal of textile employers to hire African Americans.

Many blacks worked outside the plantations, where they found employment with railroads, in coal mines, in the growing lumber mills, and turpentine industries that became important to the southern economy, and in the tobacco factories centered in the Upper South. Moreover, black labor, because it could be obtained cheaply from plantations, was a major factor in the rise of the southern iron and steel industries. Many of these industries managed to keep wages low and working conditions harsh by using convict labor hired from the state alongside free wage earners.

Before the Civil War, skilled slaves, hired out by their masters, often competed with white craftsmen for work. Competition from slaves lowered wages and impeded unionization. Instead of opposing the institution of slavery that was responsible for the conditions, southern white workers generally became antagonistic toward the slaves themselves, and, in the North, blacks were similarly despised by the white working classes. This tradition of antagonism between black and white workers was affirmed during the draft riots of 1863 in New York, when thousands of rioting working-class members attacked African-American men, women, and children to protest class-biased draft laws and the Republican Party. In 1865, white workers in the Baltimore shipyards and docks waged a long and victorious strike to drive blacks from the better-skilled jobs. In Washington, D.C., the white bricklayers' union expelled four members found working with blacks on a government job in 1869.

Only in industries where large numbers of African Americans had acquired

Black Workers in Southern Industries, 1890-1920

Industry	White Male	White Female	Black Male	Black Female	Percent Black Male	Percent Black Female
Cotton Textiles						
1890 Operatives	15,966	17,882	2,648	545	14.2	2.96
1900 Operatives	47,654	38,653	958	317	1.97	0.81
1910 Laborers	11,454	2,459	3,900	342	25.7	12.2
Operatives	55,323	43,849	749	335	1.33	0.76
Loom fixers	2,217	0	4	0	0.18	0
1920 Laborers	26,147	8,326	9,201	2,385	26.0	22.3
Operatives	68,119	51,725	1,124	638	1.62	1.22
Loom fixers c	2,043	0	6	0	0.29	0
Furniture						
1900 Employees	627		77		10.9	
1910 Laborers	2,691		575		17.6	
Semiskilled	1,815		160		8.1	
1920 Laborers	3,750		974		20.6	
Semiskilled	2,348		212		8.3	
Saw and Planing Mills						
1890 Employees	12,977		12.852		49.8	
1900 Employees	21,836		25,171		53.5	
1910 Laborers	43,573		73,612		62.8	
Semiskilled	11,377		7,562		39.9	
Sawyers	7,642		2,361		23.6	
1920 Laborers	45,533		77,515		63.0	
Semiskilled	10,206		5,242		33.9	
Sawyers	7,327		2,041		21.8	
Tobacco						
1890 Operatives	4,622	1,795	8,055	4,320	63.5	70.6
1900 Operatives	4,987	3,200	7,858	4,698	61.2	59.5
1910 Laborers	1,796	719	5,343	2,279	74.8	76.0
Operatives	3,692	4,938	5,621	6,892	60.4	58.3
1920 Laborers	4,478	2,519	12,242	7,549	73.2	75.0
Operatives	6,013	6,693	8,012	10,232	77.8	78.7
Iron and Steel						
1890 Employees	2,476		2,731		52.4	
1900 Employees	3,748		5,681		60.3	
1910 Laborers	2,959		8,412		74.0	
Semiskilled						
Blast furnace	768		635		45.3	
Car and	1,417		177		11.1	
railroad shops						
Furnacemen, etc.	255		1,045		80.4	
Molders, etc.	2,429		774		24.2	
1920 Laborers	6,061		18,475		75.3	
Semiskilled	5,695		3,112		35.3	
Furnacemen, etc.	169		666		79.8	
Molders, etc.	2,745		1,105		28.7	

Sources: U.S. Bureau of the Census, *Report on Population*, 11th Census (1890), part 2 (Washington, D.C.: Government Printing Office, 1900), table 116; *Special Reports: Occupations*, 12th Census (1900), (Washington, D.C.: GPO, 1904), table 41; *Population: Occupational Statistics*, 13th Census (1910), vol. 4 (Washington, D.C.: GPO, 1914), table VII; *Population: Occupations*, 14th Census (1920), vol. 4 (Washington, D.C.: GPO, 1923), chap. 7, table 1.

experience as slaves, where difficult-to-obtain technical training was not needed, and where unionization among whites was not strong were blacks able to maintain a presence. Indeed, blacks were often used to break emerging or weak unions. For example, during the decades after 1870, blacks pushed many whites from the iron and coal industries as iron and coal producers in Georgia, Alabama, and Tennessee recruited black labor for semiskilled jobs in order to break the strength of incipient labor organization among whites.

On the other side of the ledger was the contract construction industry where, throughout the South, thousands of freed slave craftsmen were a strong economic force into the twentieth century. From among their ranks arose many black contractors who, unfortunately, along with black skilled workers, were gradually squeezed out of the mainstream of the industry by white contractors and craftsmen who generally refused to work with or for blacks. Moreover, the discrimination in granting training, and providing educational opportunities in the private and public sectors prevented African Americans from adapting skills to technologically changing crafts. This was especially true in the newer electrical, plumbing, and mechanical trades which developed in the late nineteenth and early twentieth centuries.

Such disabilities meant that African Americans typically were forced to compete against white unions or had to accommodate themselves to racially based union privileges. In Baltimore, black craftsmen driven from the shipyards organized a cooperative shipbuilding company and operated it successfully for two decades until changing conditions in the industry caused it to fail. The leader of the Baltimore shipyard workers, Samuel L. Meyers, became president of the Colored National Labor Union, which sought to organize African-American laborers and was a major national force in black union activity during the latter part of the nineteenth century. But the Colored National Labor Union, tied to the Republican Party's philosophy that employers and workmen should cooperate and that laborers' greatest achievements would be to become business proprietors themselves, largely became a middle-class organization that provided no sound basis for development of a trade union movement among African Americans.

Throughout America, unionization benefited only white workers, who did their best to exclude blacks from occupations over which unions had control. Whereas at the end of the nineteenth century African Americans could be found in various occupations in the South, by the late 1920s growing union control over these positions would result in losses of jobs for blacks. In the late nineteenth and early twentieth centuries, for example, blacks were employed by railroads as firemen, brakemen, and even as engineers, but unionization led to their ouster as white unionists launched a vicious campaign to make the occupations all white. In some cases, the desire to rid an occupation of black competition led to extreme violence. When the Brotherhood of Railroad Workers in Memphis, Tennessee, placed a bounty of $300 on the heads of black firemen, three African-Americans were kidnapped and murdered for the reward.

Throughout most of the first two-thirds of the twentieth century, the only railroad employment open to blacks would be the demanding physical labor of building and repairing the rails and of being porters, cooks, and waiters.

During the late nineteenth century, two disparate philosophies of trade unionism competed to determine the character of the labor movement in the United States. The more conservative philosophy was represented by the independent, and largely self-interested, craft unions that basically sought to improve the working conditions of their memberships by erecting barriers to prevent outsiders from competing with them. The alternative was to organize workers by industry so that the interests of an industrial union would be tied to every craft practiced in the industry. This philosophy was represented by the Knights of Labor, organized in Philadelphia in 1869, who in their own words sought to "promote [the] welfare of the masses." At its 1893 national convention, the recently formed American Federation of Labor unanimously resolved that working people must unite regardless of "creed, color, sex, nationality, or politics": but its organizational structure and philosophy, which gave so much power to locally organized crafts, allowed rabid racism and exclusion of blacks to persist in most locals, and few African Americans gained entry to the union. By contrast the Knights of Labor organized independent of race, but they too could not overcome the specter of racial animosity. Many chapters of the Knights of Labor had separate black and white locals.

Nonetheless, a few biracial unions arose that reached an accommodation between the races. Numerous dockworkers along the southeastern seaboard in places such as Charleston in South Carolina, New Orleans in Louisiana, and Mobile in Alabama formed biracial unions that shared employment and union offices through a kind of racial quota system. Frequently whites received more

A Black Worker on the Knights of Labor, 1886

I am a colored man. I had a letter sent me from Georgia by a colored man asking if colored men would be recognized in the Knights of Labor, and I have had similar questions from others of my race, both in New York and Brooklyn. My answer is yes and I especially refer to the case of the colored delegate to Richmond from D.A. 49. I myself belong to a local that is wholly composed of white men, with two exceptions, and I hold a very high position of trust in it. I was elected junior delegate to the D.A. and there is no office in the organization that I could not be elected to.

I will say to my people, Help the cause of labor. I would furthermore say to colored men, Organize. I also appeal to you to support Henry George and the K[nights] of L[abor] You will never gain anything from the Republican Party . . . You are a man. Let us break this race prejudice which capital likes. Let us put our shoulders to the wheel as men and victory is ours.

Source: *John Swinton's Paper* (N.Y.), October 10, 1886.

178 ▼   Gerald D. Jaynes

than the share warranted by their numbers. And in the coal fields of southern Ohio, western Pennsylvania, and West Virginia, the United Mine Workers achieved a similar biracial accommodation. Among the United Mine Workers, blacks were influential in union activities, and some, such as Richard L. Davis, would rise to national office in the union hierarchy during the twentieth century. Even so, at the turn of the twentieth century, the relationship between the labor movement and African Americans was primarily a contentious and competitive affair that weakened the economic goals of both.

WOMEN'S EMPLOYMENT

African Americans' strongest asset in a discriminatory environment was their willingness to work harder, longer, and for less pay—simply because they had to if work was to be had at all. The labor market condition of African-American women typified this status. According to the censuses of 1890 and 1900, black women were overwhelmingly employed in domestic service and on farms. For example, according to the census of 1900, an astonishing 96 percent of African-American women working for wages were employed as either field-workers, house servants, waitresses, or laundry workers. Throughout the nation, the discrimination against blacks in general kept African Americans in such poverty that even lower-middle-class whites could afford to hire black women as cooks and housecleaners. These positions involved long hours under close supervision and offered the lowest of wages. Many African-American women set up their own laundry businesses, contracting to wash the clothes of a number of white families each week. This backbreaking labor was the main support of many African-American households.

In the few instances where African-American women could obtain alternative sources of employment they chose to abandon domestic work, sometimes for factory labor. Along the southeastern seaboard, they found seasonal employment in the dirty and difficult working conditions in the seafood processing industry. In many seaport towns, African-American women (and men) engaged in the excruciatingly dirty, smelly, and physically demanding task of shucking oysters. During the oyster industry's busy season, September through April, domestic workers in such towns were difficult to hire, but the seasonality of the work meant that ultimately some of the women would have to return to domestic labor.

Slaves had provided the primary labor source in antebellum Virginia tobacco plants and, after the Civil War, African Americans remained a significant factor in the tobacco factories of the Upper South. By 1910, the eleven former Confederate states employed more than eight thousand African-American women in the least desirable and lowest-paying occupations in tobacco factories, primarily restricted to the cigar and chewing tobacco sectors of the industry. The newer, more mechanized, and higher-paying cigarette industry came to be dominated by white women's labor. This practice was replicated in the cotton textile industry where black women were virtually shut out of an industry that became the major employer of women.

THE FIRST MASS URBANIZATION

Between 1880 and 1910, nearly seventeen million Europeans emigrated to the United States. These immigrants overwhelmingly entered the country though the ports of New York and New Jersey and spread throughout the northeastern and midwestern United States where they swelled the size of the labor force and precipitated a great competition for jobs, housing, and other resources. There was little demand for African-American labor outside the South, and migration of blacks out of the South during this period was relatively low.

In the northern states, the discriminatory conditions that had existed before the Civil War continued throughout the nineteenth century and well into the twentieth. Furthermore, the continuing arrival of millions of immigrants from Europe crowded African Americans out of jobs they had held and made it all but impossible for them to secure employment in newer occupations. The combination of discrimination, employers' preferences for white immigrants, and crowded urban labor markets restricted black men's and women's employment to only a few areas.

In cities like Atlanta, Chicago, New Orleans, New York, Philadelphia, Baltimore, San Francisco, and hundreds of smaller towns, with few exceptions, blacks were proscribed from employment in all but menial laboring and personal service positions. Blacks with higher levels of education and skills had to accept employment well below their abilities or they had to find some way to operate a business within the segregated African-American community. For example, in his 1899 study *The Philadelphia Negro*, W. E. B. DuBois wrote of a young African American who had graduated from the University of Pennsylvania with a degree in engineering but could only find employment as a waiter. He wrote also of well-educated young black women who, seeking employment as clerical workers and secretaries, were constantly turned away because no office would hire a nonwhite person. Alexander Bouchet, a brilliant honors graduate of Yale and only the fourth American to earn a doctorate in physics, spent his life teaching in a segregated boys high school in Philadelphia.

But the eruption of World War I in 1914 would halt the European migration and also create a boon for industry in the United States. Northern employers, starved for workers, turned to the South, and a great competition for labor developed. Hundreds of agents from northern and southern factories scoured the rural South searching for laborers while evading the landlords and local authorities who fought, sometimes with violent extralegal methods, to retain black labor in the rural South.

Approximately 525,000 African Americans migrated to the urban North between 1910 and 1920 in search of the promised land depicted by urban labor agents. Prior to the war, African-American migrants in the urban North had been primarily restricted to employment as janitors, porters, and servants, but during the war, blacks, newcomers, and old urban dwellers alike were hired for jobs that had previously been restricted to whites. For the most part, however, African-American men were still employers' second choice to white labor. African-American men were typically preferred for heavy and exacting labor or in areas "designated" for blacks because they required work in extreme heat, moisture, dust, or some other undesirable condition, such as jobs performed by asphalt workers during the heat of summer and by workers in the acid baths in the iron and steel industry.

Nonetheless, the move northward and into the factories had begun. In Chicago, in 1910, more than 51 percent of African-American men were in domestic and personal service; in 1920 this percentage had fallen to 28 percent even though the black population had increased significantly. By 1920, factory work would become the most important source of employment for black men, and they would even manage to increase their representation in semiskilled jobs.

CONCLUSION

Opportunities for African-American women were less available. While more jobs opened for them in manufacturing and trade, black women were still overwhelmingly restricted to domestic service, where 64 percent of employed African-American women labored. These restrictions applied regardless of skill and qualifications. Their high school and college educations earning them no greater employment opportunity than those found by illiterates from tobacco plantations, urban-born and educated black women were unable to obtain work anywhere but in domestic service.

At the beginning of the twentieth century, the position of African Americans in the labor market, as badly limited as it was, could nonetheless only compare favorably to a slavery that had been escaped a mere 35 years earlier. The initial three decades of the new century would bring even greater improvements in many African Americans' economic positions. As a group, black Americans would become much less concentrated in the rural South and would be better represented in manufacturing and trade industries. But they would remain severely underrepresented as artisans in clerical, business, and professional positions. Overwhelmingly, African-American women would continue to have few opportunities outside domestic and personal service occupations, and black men would find themselves chiefly relegated to positions as common laborers. A majority were still tied to occupations connected to agriculture in the rural South. There the everyday task of making a living proved difficult even in the best of years.

FOR FURTHER READING:

Daniel, Pete. The *Shadow of Slavery: Peonage in the South, 1901–1969*. Urbana: University of Illinois Press, 1990.

DeCanio, Stephen J. *Agriculture in the Postbellum South: The Economics of Production and Supply*. Cambridge: MIT Press, 1974.

Foner, Eric. *Reconstruction 1863–1877: America's Unfinished Revolution*. New York: Harper & Row, 1989.

Higgs, Robert. *Competition and Coercion: Blacks in the American Economy*. Chicago: University of Chicago Press, 1977.

Jaynes, Gerald D. *Branches without Roots: Genesis of the Black Working Class in the American South, 1862–1882*. New York: Oxford University Press, 1990.

Jones, Jacqueline. *Labor of Love, Labor of Sorrow: Black Women, Work, and the Family from Slavery to the Present*. New York: Vintage, 1988.

Litwack, Leon F. *Been in the Storm So Long: The Aftermath of Slavery*. New York: Vintage, 1989.

————. *Trouble in Mind: Black Southerners in the Age of Jim Crow*. New York: Alfred A. Knopf, 1998.

Mandle, Jay R. *Not Slave, Not Free: The African Economic Experience since the Civil War*. Durham, N.C.: Duke University Press, 1994.

Ransom, Roger L., and Richard Sutch. *One Kind of Freedom: The Economic Consequences of Emancipation*. New York: Cambridge University Press, 1977.

Rosengarten, Theodore. *All God's Dangers: The Life of Nate Shaw*. New York: Vintage, 1984.

Saville, Julie. *The Work of Reconstruction: From Slave to Wage Laborer in South Carolina, 1862–1882*. New York: Cambridge University Press, 1994.

Woodman, Harold. *New South, New Law: The Legal Foundations of Credit and Labor Relations in the Postbellum South*. Baton Rouge: Louisiana State University Press, 1995.

Wright, Gavin. *Old South, New South: Revolutions in the Southern Economy since the Civil War*. Baton Rouge: Louisiana State University Press, 1996.

chapter 8

In Search of the Promised Land

Black Migration and Urbanization, 1900–1940

Carole C. Marks

THE DUAL PROCESSES OF URBANIZATION AND MIGRATION dramatically increased the proportion of blacks living in northern cities between 1916 and 1940. Before the twentieth century, black migration from rural to urban areas occurred within the South, but after the turn of the century, migration to the North grew considerably. In the summer of 1916, a steady stream of descendants of slaves flowed northward to the booming war economies of cities such as Pittsburgh, Chicago, and Detroit. The flow quickly reached flood stage. In two years, more than 300,000 migrants made their way north. By 1930, nearly two million blacks had left the South. This dramatic demographic shift—called the Great Migration— involved the uneasy mingling of the cultures of southern and northern blacks and the eventual evolution of a new urban African-American culture.

CAUSES OF THE GREAT MIGRATION

Two major forces sparked the exodus: agricultural devastation in the South, and the Great War in Europe. The boll weevil invasion from Mexico, which began in the 1890s and destroyed cotton crops throughout the South, elimi- nated a major source of regional employment. Coupled with nascent indus- trialization, the crisis transformed traditional employment patterns; jobs once set aside for blacks—working on the railroads, working as barbers, working as street cleaners—became coveted by whites. Blacks increasingly went unem- ployed.

At the same time, the war in Europe created a shortage of unskilled labor and hundreds of thousands of jobs in the North. The recruitment of black workers from the South began cautiously but gained momentum as fears of an unqualified black labor force were replaced by experience with able and willing workers. After a visit to Cleveland in 1917, a federal investigator reported, "A big manufacturing concern has followed the practice for a number of years of sending a recruiting agent into the South among negro schools that have trades departments and picking out good material, and using these young men during the summer vacation. In this way, they have built up a very strong force of colored workers."

While individuals cited myriad reasons for migrating, a faltering southern economy and a booming northern one represented the backdrop against which the migration forces mainly played out. Historian Louise Kennedy has highlighted the "general predominance of the economic motive" in this process and points out that black migration has historically occurred when there were floods and crop failures in the South (1878–1879, 1916–1918, and 1923) and there were increased demands for workers in other parts of the country. The sheer volume of the movement would not have been sustained without the bust of the South and boom of the North.

In the period 1900 to 1910, black migration from the South was significant, but not as dramatic as it was in the period 1910 to 1920. As economic historian Gavin Wright explains, "What happened during the high-pressure years of 1916–19 was not simply a change in racial employment policies but a redirection of the geographic scope of unskilled labor markets."

The extent to which the migrants were motivated by economic concerns is a matter of debate. "As indisputably important as the economic motive was," historian Lawrence Levine observes, "it is possible to overstress it so that the black migration is converted into an inexorable force and Negroes are seen once again not as actors capable of affecting at least some part of their destinies, but primarily as beings who are acted upon—southern leaves blown north by the winds of destitution." James Grossman argues further that economic changes do not provide sufficient insight into the migrants, their values, or their experiences.

Labor migrants were active participants in the migration process. They decided the timing of their moves, making decisions about location, specific employment, and even the nature of that employment. They constantly attempted to control the world around them through negotiation, bargaining, and compromise. As Joseph Trotter states, in fundamental ways, migrants

Net Migration from the South, 1900 to 1930

Decade	Native White	Black
1900–1910	69,000	194,000
1910–1920	663,000	555,000
1920–1930	704,000	903,000

Source: Hope T. Eldridge and Dorothy S. Thomas, *Population Redistribution and Economic Growth*, vol. 3 (Philadelphia: American Philosophical Society, 1964).

actively shaped and directed their own existence. When asked why she left the South, one migrant replied, "I left Georgia because I wanted better privileges." When asked if that meant "mixed schools, white churches, and association with white people in their homes generally," she responded, "No, I don't care nothing about that, but I just want to be somewhere where I won't be scared all the time that something is going to break loose."

The South in 1916 was not so much a backward region as an isolated one. Industrialization had begun there as early as the 1880s, when campaigns for economic development brought investment and mechanization to a variety of enterprises. But development in the New South did not mean upward mobility for its workforce. In comparison to those in the Northeast and Midwest, southern workers were grossly underpaid. Wages in the South were only about two-thirds of those paid elsewhere. These disparities were due to several factors: the legacy of slavery, which had depressed wages; the South's slow recovery from the devastating Civil War; and its overreliance on cotton.

Mechanisms that would have facilitated the normal movement of labor from low-wage to high-wage settings were all but absent. Indeed the South, in its relationship to the economically advanced North, represented more of a colony of raw material export than an equal trading partner. Less developed in every aspect of production, it was dependent on the North for much of its financing and manufacture. Indigenous industries like tobacco manufacture, furniture making, and mining failed to generate surplus capital. In the absence of a reciprocal exchange of workers and products, the information channels crucial for employment were missing. Before the migration, skilled white and black workers, traditionally the first labor sector to take advantage of migration inducements, remained in the South. Given the wage disparity, the failure to relocate would seem irrational, but inadequate sources of information about employment opportunities elsewhere would explain their immobility.

With the beginning of the First World War in Europe in 1914, the supply of northern labor began to dwindle. European migrants who had been entering the United States at a rate of more than a million a year since 1900 were cut off almost entirely. Coupled with a labor shortage, the increase in orders for war materials and supplies kindled a heightened search for alternative sources.

WHO CAME NORTH?

Labor recruitment from the South involved both white and black workers. In fact, as Nell Irvin Painter points out, white southerners migrated north in far greater numbers than blacks, but their migration did not attract the same attention or violence. A federal investigator observed, "Other races have come to the city bringing all their foreign customs, superstitions, and varying modes of living, and although they have come to this industrial center in large numbers, their coming has not been attended by outbursts of hatred and demonstrations in public places. They have been accepted—not always as a desirable element—but at least as something to be tolerated."

Not every able-bodied worker went north. Labor recruitment from the South was highly selective. Perhaps half or more came from the region's towns and cities, and had long since left agricultural work. For instance, the great majority of departures from the Alabama steel towns of Birmingham and Bessemer were experienced miners who were headed for the coal fields of Kentucky, West Virginia, and Pennsylvania.

Moreover, the "typical migrant," often characterized as an illiterate "share-cropper" desperate for work, was actually a distinct minority of the migrating population. As Florette Henri points out, since so much of the South was rural, the number of different occupations represented by the migrants was quite large, and may be mostly explained by the simple diversity of rural employment. The area's countryside, says Peter Gottlieb, was sprinkled with sawmills, logging camps, railroad construction and tie-cutting camps, turpen-tine camps, brickyards, coal mines, steel mills, and river or ocean docks. The repeated shifts from farm to nonfarm work, he adds, and the attainment of an independent status allowed rural blacks to link their routine lives to the urban-izing world of the South and the nation. "Consequently, rural blacks were already partially inducted into industrial and urban modes of labor by 1916, well prepared to seek the best-paying line of work they could find." Moreover, established tenants did not leave the South in any great numbers.

The "induction" of migrants into industrial and urban modes involved more than just their labor. The desire to obtain autonomy and operate inde-pendently was often evident. Commitment to education for themselves and their children, to community uplift, and to the emergence of voluntary self-help organizations, benevolent and mutual aid societies, lodges and literary associations head the list of strategies used by black southerners to shape their world. By the time of the migration, a second generation had erected, sup-ported, and controlled a host of these religious, educational, and social insti-tutions in the South. As is evident from their testimony, migrants took these skills, and at times the institutions themselves, with them to the North.

The decision to leave varied greatly. Some talked of "freedom and indepen-dence" as their primary motives. Others intended to stay only long enough to collect a little savings. As one migrant said of her husband, "He first planned to work and go back, like so many others. So many of the people that came here back in those days didn't come here to stay. They didn't like it here. They did-n't like the weather. It was so different to their way of life at home." Another migrant who had begun working as a farmer and had "drifted to public works in Anniston" had gone into foundry work. He transferred to the North for a higher wage, but stated he was "going home for the winter" as the weather got colder and he wanted to protect his health. Having saved enough money to sur-vive down South comfortably until the spring, he planned to go back to work up North after the weather broke.

For many others, transportation costs precluded the journey to the promised land. Train fares for those who worked outside the wage economy were obviously prohibitive. Many who did work for a wage found that they had to make the journey north in stages, stopping off and working at several intermediate points in the South. This "step migration," as it is called, could take years. One woman, Sara Brooks, took almost fifteen years to retrieve three sons left behind in Orchard, Alabama, and reunite her family.

Migrants' Letters

Mobile, Ala., Jan. 8, 1917

Dear Sir: I am writing you to see if you can furnish me with any information in regards to colored men securing employment. I would like to know if you could put me in touch with some manufacturing company either some corporation that is employing or in need of colored men. My reason is there are a number of young men in this city of good moral and can furnish good reference—that is anxious to leave this section of the country and go where conditions are better. I taken this matter up with Mr. —— of Boston and he referred me to you. I myself is anxious to leave this part of the country and be where a negro man can appreshate beaing a man at the present time I am working as office man for a large corporation which position I have had for the past 11 years, having a very smart boy in his studies I wish to locate where he could recive a good education. I could at a few days notice place 200 good able bodied young men that is anxious to leave this city. these men I refer to is men of good morals and would prove a credit to the community. If you can furnish me with the desired information it will be gladly received. it makes little or no difference as to what state they can go to just so they cross the Mason and Dixie line. trusting you will furnish me with any information you have at hand at an early date, I await your reply.

Dapne, Ala., 4/20/17

Sir: I am writing you to let you know that there is 15 or 20 familys wants to come up there at once but cant come on account of money to come with and we cant phone you here we will be killed they dont want us to leave here & say if we dont go to war and fight for our country they are going to kill us and wants to get away if we can if you send 20 passes there is no doubt that every one of us will com at once. we are not doing any thing here we cant get a living out of what we do now some of these people are farmers and som are cooks barbers and black smiths but the greater part are farmers & good worker & honest people & up to date the trash pile dont want to go no where These are nice people and respectable find a place like that & send passes & we all will come at once we all wants to leave here out of this hard luck place

Cleveland, Ohio, Aug. 28, 1917

hollow Dr. my old friend how are you to day i am well and is doing fine plenty to eat and drink and is making good money in fact i am not in the best of health i have not had good health sence i ben here. i thought once i would hefter be operrated on But i dont no. i were indeed glad to recieve that paper from Union Springs.

Migrant selectivity involved not only experience but also age and gender. Young healthy males were the most sought-after population, induced mostly to do the dirty work of northern industry. Although there is much emphasis in the literature that changes in attitudes caused the migrants' willingness to leave, disruptions within southern rural economies that reversed the position of sons from unpaid helpers to "wage contributors to annual family income" played their part. This shift created a desire for "freedom and independence"

Migrants' Letters (cont.)

* * *

i have seval nochants of coming back, yet i am doing well no trouble what ever except i can not raise my children here like they should be this is one of the worst places in principle you ever look on in your life but it is a fine place to make money all nattions is here, and let me tell you this place is crowded with the lowest negroes you ever meet. when i first come here i cold hardly ever see a Negro but no this is as meny here is they is thir all kinds of lollers. gamblers pockit pickers you are not safe here to walk on the streets at night you are libble to get kill at eny time thir have ben men kill her jest because he want allow stragglers in his family. yet i have not had no trouble no way. and we are making good money here. i have made as hight at 7.50 per day and my wife $4 Sundays my sun 7.50 and my 2 oldes girls 1.25 but my regler wegers is 3.60 fore 8 hours work. me and my family makes one hundred three darlers and 60 cents every ten days. it don cost no more to live here than it do thir, except house rent i pay 12 a month fore rent sence i have rote you everything look closely and tell me what you think is best. i am able to farm without asking any man fore enythin on a credit

Philadelphia, Pa., Oct. 7, 1917

Dear Sir: I take this method of thanking you for yours early responding and the glorious effect of the treatment. Oh. I do feel so fine. Dr. the treatment reach me almost ready to move I am now housekeeping again I like it so much better than rooming. Well Dr. with the aid of God I am making very good I make $75 per month. I am carrying enough insurance to pay me $20 per week if I am not able to be on duty. I don't have to work hard. dont have to mister every little white boy comes along I havent heard a white man call a colored a nigger you no now—since I been in the state of Pa. I can ride in the electric street and steam cars any where I get a seat. I dont care to mix with white what I mean I am not crazy about being with white folks, but if I have to pay the same fare I have learn to want the same acomidation. and if you are first in a place here shoping you dont have to wait until the white folks get thro tradeing yet amid all this I shall ever love the good old South and I am praying that God may give every well wisher a chance to be a man regardless of his color, and if my going to the front would bring about such conditions I am ready any day—well Dr. I dont want to worry you but read between lines; and maybe you can see a little sense in my weak statement the kids are in school every day I have only two and I guess that all. Dr. when you find time I would be delighted to have a word from the good old home state. Wife join me in sending love you and yours.

Source: Emmett J. Scott, ed., "Letters of Negro Migrants of 1916–1918," *Journal of Negro History,* IV (July 1, 1919), pp. 290–340.

from family patterns of subsistence farming. For both young men and wives, the decision was made to migrate in the hope of greater personal autonomy.

One farmer gave the following account of his journey north: "I had some boys working in Birmingham, so I went there first, Everything looked pretty good and I decided to bring the old lady to Birmingham, which I did. We got along pretty good there, but I heard about work up here, so me and my sons came up here, and after we got all settled, sent back for my wife and daughter." In many cases, sons were sponsored by families, who would later follow them if they prospered.

In one Pittsburgh iron mill, during the years 1916 to 1930, 45 percent of the African-American migrants hired were between the ages of fifteen and twenty-four (who made up only 21 percent in this age group for the population as a whole). The ease with which single men could "quickly respond to sudden economic opportunities" in part explains this preponderance. It has also been argued that young blacks in the South had a lower tolerance of Jim Crow than their elders and were therefore more disposed to migration.

Unlike previous labor migrations, however, a significant proportion of the migrating population was married and had to make special arrangements for families. Afraid to abandon their families for too long while they searched for work, fathers needed prior knowledge about which companies were employing migrants, how much they were paying, and how much of his wages could be saved. One migrant detailed his bargaining strategy: "I have a wife and she is a very good cook. She has lots of references from the north and south. Now dear sir if you can send me a ticket so I can come up there and after I get straightened out I will send for my wife." Another tried to bargain for her son, stating he was a very good boy and would not cause trouble.

Wives were often left behind and, became responsible for keeping the family together. Women would sell household items, move in with other family members, and take on employment outside the home to support themselves and their children. Sara Brooks, encouraged by her brother to move to Cleveland, saved for the trip. "My brother wanted me to come up here to Cleveland with him, so I started to try to save up what little money I had. . . . But I saved what I could, and when my sister-in-law came down for me, I had only eighteen dollars to my name, and that was maybe a few dollars over enough to come up here. If I'm not mistaken it was about a dollar and fifteen cent over."

Family resources were also bolstered by remittances sent home by labor migrants. These monies were used both to sustain the family and, as was often noted, "to save the fare." In her research on black women, work, and family life, Jacqueline Jones has discovered that a constant flow of letters containing cash and advice between the North and South facilitated the gradual migration of whole clans and even villages. Women also negotiated labor contracts through domestic agencies, where northern employers agreed to pay transportation north in exchange for their labor, a system also used to bring women from other parts of the world to the United States.

Migrants were directed to specific industrial centers, industries, even jobs. Between 1910 and 1920, for example, New York experienced a 66 percent increase in its African-American population, Chicago a 148 percent increase, Detroit a 611 percent increase, and Philadelphia a 500 percent increase. By 1920, almost 40 percent of the black population in the North was concentrated in these four cities.

Other demographic shifts accompanied the migration. In 1910, only 10 percent of the African-American population lived in the North. By 1940, it had risen to 22 percent. In 1890, nearly two-thirds of all black male laborers worked in agriculture. By 1930, less than half did so. At the same time the number of black schoolteachers more than doubled, and the number of black-owned businesses tripled, while black illiteracy declined from 61 to 15 percent because of the growth of (segregated) public schools.

LIFE IN THE NEW BLACK CENTERS

The great bulk of migrants found their way into manufacturing industries. Gains were most dramatic in the packing houses and steel industries in Chicago. In packing houses, there were sixty-seven blacks employed in 1910 and nearly three thousand in 1920. In steel, black representation increased from 6 percent in 1910 to 17 percent in 1920. As migrants poured into northern cities, Henry Ford started a small experiment to see if black workers could be used on the assembly line. The result was that the name of Ford became synonymous with northern opportunity which was reflected in a great many blues songs written about the Ford company and Ford products. But opportunity in the North had its price. Many of those who followed skilled crafts in the South were barred from them in the North by company policy, union regulations, or craft tradition where there was no union.

Migrants cited a number of reasons for choosing their places of destination revealing a combination of economic and noneconomic motives. When one migrant woman's husband moved to Cincinnati, she wrote him a letter back. "My older sister had come to Pittsburgh, and I took her as a mother because I had lost my mother. And I wrote him back and said, 'I don't want to stay in Cincinnati. I want to go to Pittsburgh.' Next letter I got, he got a job in Pittsburgh and sent for me."

Once settled, migrants worked hard to achieve their version of the American dream. One migrant told the Chicago Race Commission, established to ease tensions after the 1919 race riot, that after coming to Chicago, he worked in a foundry as a moulder's helper until he learned the trade. The migrant explained: "'I can quit any time I want to, but the longer I work the more money it is for me, so I usually work eight or nine hours a day. I am planning to educate my girl with the best of them, buy a home before I'm too old, and make life comfortable for my family.'"

The creation of the largely African-American ghettoes in the northern

cities of the United States began in the 1920s. Generally, before the migration, blacks were dispersed in several areas of the cities in sections small in
number. Often they lived in relative obscurity and invisibility. The 1920s witnessed a much greater concentration, in Chicago on the South Side, in New
York in Harlem, and in both North and South Philadelphia neighborhoods.

The concentration was related, according to the commission's report, to
tangible issues such as competition for better-paying jobs, scarce housing
resources, and the struggle for control over city government and other institutions. Whites would flee areas when blacks moved in or would try,
conversely, to keep blacks out. The whole apparatus of government participated in creating de facto segregation—under a general assumption that separation was best.

In some cities, migrants were also separated from other elements of the
black community. Pittsburgh's black elite enjoyed a social and organizational
life largely separate from that of other blacks in the community. Earlier
migrants to the city from the Upper South who had risen out of the black

"Negro Jobs"

There were plants employing Negroes for certain grades of work and others refusing to employ them on the similar processes for reasons adequate and sufficient
to each respectively. Some of the plants have what they call "labor policies" which
summarily exclude all Negroes as below the standard for workers; others with the
identical processes regard them as best fitted for their work. No standard appears
to be observed; no objective basis for selecting a labor supply seems to exist. Generally speaking the following factors are important in influencing the use of
Negroes:

1. Tradition, or the fixed custom of using Negroes in certain portions
    because they are supposed to be by nature better equipped for it; or
    because they are popularly regarded as "Negro jobs."
2. The unavailability of white labor.
3. The relatively cheaper cost of Negro labor.
4. The nature of the work which because of its general disagreeableness
    atracts only the worst class of white labor, and those only temporarily.
5. The nature of the industry making necessary a large proportion of
    unskilled labor capable of sustained physical exertion.
6. The seasonal character of the industry requiring a ready, fluid labor sup-
    ply available in need.

Throughout the city the plants that employ Negroes, with a very few exceptions,
may readily be pointed out by holding in mind one or more of the considerations
listed above. The Baltimore industries, it will be recalled, are highly diversified.
This fact militates strongly against any uniformity in proportions of persons, especially Negroes, employed. Again, its industries in many instances are developed
and frequently controlled by outsiders who seek this locality for certain outstanding advantages. This fact further militates against uniformity of policy.

Source: Opportunity, 1 (June 1923), pp. 12–19.

lower class also sought to distance themselves from the newcomers. Southern blacks' recent arrival in the city, lack of education, and rural background set them apart from skilled and unskilled wage earners as well as from the elite. Although some southerners came from cultured urban or landowning rural families, the shortage of housing forced them to live among the unstable lower class. Perhaps because of this, African-American migrants in northern cities formed communities that consisted of many of the same people from the southern communities left behind. And, in fact, researchers commented that one would often find blocks of people from the same general area of Georgia, Alabama, or North Carolina.

The reactions of migrants to their new surroundings varied greatly. In *Maggie's American Dream*, James Comer describes his mother's reaction to Chicago in the 1920s: "To hear people talk about Chicago, as I had heard my sister talk when I was still in Memphis, you'd think that money was dropping off trees. They would say that you just didn't have to want for anything; you could have whatever you want. While still down South, I thought to myself, I'll wait and see what it's like. And, sure enough, East Chicago wasn't what I had been told. It was quite a letdown." By contrast, a migrant from Mississippi explained her preference for Chicago: "Up here, you see, when I come out on the street I walk on nice smooth pavements. Down home I got to walk home through the mud."

What did not vary was substandard housing and segregation. In Chicago, white hostility virtually closed the housing market to blacks and created a physical ghetto on the city's south side. Likewise, in Milwaukee, as blacks lost out in the competitive bid for better jobs, they were forced deeper and deeper into the most dilapidated sections of the city.

Yet even in the face of discrimination and exclusion, migrants determined to move forward. Black building and loan associations flourished, and there was a steep rise in the number of black clerks and professionals between 1920 and 1930. One migrant bought an undeveloped lot in Chicago for little money, waited for the city to put in streets and then he built a house. His wife explained, "We got a contractor from Chicago. He borrowed so much money from us that by the time he got the house up we didn't owe him a dime. But with the help of my husband, when he come home from work, and his brothers and friends, we got this house up." By the time of the Depression, they had built two duplexes with two rental properties in addition to their own and lived well through the Depression, compared to others.

One of the most troubling areas of concern was public schools. Because there were fewer classes available and students often came north with less education, blacks were forced to attend classes with much younger students, adding to the assessment that they were of lower intelligence than whites. Yet Maggie Comer was able to exploit the negative aspects of her educational experience. "They got interested in me when they see I was a great big girl and I didn't know how to read and write. I got quite a bit of help from them. Soon I was able to read and write my name and count to one hundred and so forth." But Maggie's school experiences cannot be separated from her other work. After school, she would "have to rush home to cook for the whole family—for her husband, my two brothers, her, and a couple of roomers she had. Then I had to wash clothes until twelve or one o'clock at night."

Industrial jobs were for men only. But married men quickly discovered that the fabulous wages promised by the labor agents were not sufficient to house

The Chicago Riot, 1919

In July, 1919, a race riot involving whites and Negroes occurred in Chicago. For some time thoughtful citizens, white and Negro, had sensed increasing tension, but, having no local precedent of riot and wholesale bloodshed, had neither prepared themselves for it nor taken steps to prevent it. The collecting of arms by members of both races was known to the authorities, and it was evident that this was in preparation for aggression as well as for self-defense.

Several minor clashes preceded the riot. On July 3, 1917, a white saloon-keeper who, according to the coroner's physician, died of heart trouble, was incorrectly reported in the press to have been killed by a Negro. That evening a party of young white men riding in an automobile fired upon a group of Negroes at Fifty-third and Federal Streets. In July and August of the same year recruits from the Great Lakes Naval Training Station clashed frequently with Negroes, each side accusing the other of being the aggressor.

Gangs of white "toughs," made up largely of the membership of so-called "athletic clubs" from the neighborhood between Roosevelt Road and Sixty-third Street, Wentworth Avenue and the city limits—a district contiguous to the neighborhood of the largest Negro settlement—were a constant menace to Negroes who traversed sections of the territory going to and returning from work. The activities of these gangs and "athletic clubs" became bolder in the spring of 1919, and on the night of June 21, five weeks before the riot, two wanton murders of Negroes occurred, those of Sanford Harris and Joseph Robinson. Harris, returning to his home on Dearborn Street about 11:30 at night, passed a group of young white men. They threatened him and he ran. He had gone but a short distance when one of the group shot him. He died soon afterward. Policemen who came on the scene made no arrests, even when the assailant was pointed out by a white woman witness of the murder. On the same evening Robinson, a Negro laborer, forty-seven years of age, was attacked while returning from work by a gang of white "roughs" at Fifty-fifth Street and Princeton Avenue, apparently without provocation, and stabbed to death.

Negroes were greatly incensed over these murders, but their leaders, joined by many friendly whites, tried to allay their fears and counseled patience....

Aside from general lawlessness and disastrous riots that preceded the riot here discussed, there were other factors which may be mentioned briefly here. In Chicago considerable unrest had been occasioned in industry by increasing competition between white and Negro laborers following a sudden increase in the Negro population due to the migration of Negroes from the South. This increase developed a housing crisis. The Negroes overran the hitherto recognized area of Negro residence, and when they took houses in adjoining neighborhoods friction ensued. In the two years, just preceding the riot, twenty-seven Negro dwellings were wrecked by bombs thrown by unidentified persons.

Source: Chicago Commission on Race Relations, *The Negro in Chicago; A Study of Race Relations and a Race Riot* (Chicago, 1922), pp. 595–601.

and clothe their families. Black women were forced into the labor market so that families could survive. Their incomes, meager as they were, not only saved families from destruction but sometimes provided capital for business ventures. There were few industrial opportunities for women. Once found, they were seized with tenacity. "I'll never work in nobody's kitchen but my own any more," Miss T. S. told the Chicago Race Commission in 1920. "No indeed! That's the one thing that makes me stick to this job." Many others were not as fortunate and were forced into domestic service—what W. E. B. DuBois called "despised labor for a despised population."

Black women transformed domestic service from live-in work to day's work because it fit better with the lifestyles adopted in the North. "The living-in jobs just kept you running, never stopped," stated one woman. "Day or night you'd be getting something for somebody. You'd serve them. It was never a minute's peace. . . . But when I went out days on my jobs, I'd get my work done and be gone, I guess that's it. This work had an end."

BLACK SOLUTIONS TO BLACK PROBLEMS

Often the institutions formed during the migration are seen as having their origins in the segregation migrants found. It has been suggested that in Chicago blacks responded to white hostility by trying to build a self-contained community that would provide all of the advantages of white Chicago. But their institutions were not only created out of reaction to discrimination but also as a proactive force to build a base of economic power. In many cities, these communities were constructed by a new elite of black leaders, products of the migration, who prospered in the segregated, urban world of the North. In Chicago, these new elites established black businesses, formed political alliances, and participated in the organization of social agencies.

Oscar De Priest represents a typical example of the community-based African-American politician. Born in Alabama in 1889, he came to Chicago to work as a house painter. Over the years, he shifted into a successful real estate business and, in 1904, was elected to the Cook County Commission. During the migration years, De Priest became the first black alderman and later the first black elected to Congress from the North. In a less dramatic instance, George Bailey Sr., who had been raised in Greenwood, Mississippi, came to Philadelphia to work at the Campbell Soup Company. He had opened two community markets by 1922 which became vital centers of black enterprise. "If you were looking for a place to stay, a job, or news of relatives," wrote one observer, "or if you wanted to send a package home, you went to the store."

The institutional forms that accompanied migration were also unique to their new circumstances. A combination of need born of white racism, black self-help initiatives, and white philanthropy at the turn of the century helped to produce a black hospital movement, improving health care for blacks. By the mid-1920s, there were more than two hundred black hospitals and more

The Problem of the City

The problem of the city Negro is but the accentuated counterpart of the problem of all urban inhabitants. Segregation and the consequence congestion, the evils of bad housing conditions with their inevitable accompaniment of dangerous sanitation and loose morals, the lack of facilities for wholesome recreation and the ill-regulated picture shows and dance halls combine to make conditions which demand instant relief. Add to this a population constantly augmented by Negroes from small towns or rural districts of the South, and the problem of the league is before you.

* * *

The [Urban League] has sought to establish agencies for uplift where needed. If no committee could be found ready to take over and conduct the particular undertaking, the league has handled the movement through its local office staff.

The Sojourner Truth house committee, with Mrs. George W. Seligman as chairman, has undertaken the task of establishing a home for delinquent colored girls under 16 years of age, because of the failure of the State and private institutions to care adequately for these unfortunates. The league made an investigation of this need and formed a temporary committee from which developed the present organization.

The league also inaugurated the movement for the training of colored nursery maids. A committee, of which Mr. Franck W. Barber is chairman, has worked out the details for courses of study in hospital training in care of infants, kindergarten training, child study and household arts.

During the summer of 1911 the league conducted, in Harlem, a playground for boys, for the purpose of demonstrating the need of recreational facilities for the children of Harlem. As a result of this movement, and a continuous agitation for more adequate play facilities, the city has practically committed itself to the operation of a model playground on any plot of ground in the Harlem district, the use of which is donated to the City Parks Department.

The travelers' aid work, in charge of Miss Eva G. Burleigh, has consisted principally in the meeting of the coastwise steamers bringing large numbers of women and girls from Southern ports to New York City, who are without acquaintance with methods of meeting the competition of city life, and who are frequently sent to New York to be exploited by unreliable employment agents or questionable men. The league supports two travelers' aid workers in Norfolk, Va., which is the gateway to the North for hundreds of women and girls from Virginia and the Carolinas.

The preventive or protective work of the league consists of the visiting in the homes of school children who have become incorrigibles or truants, for the purpose of removing the causes of these irregularities. This work is in charge of Mrs. Hallie B. Craigwell and Mr. Leslie L. Pollard.

Probation work with adults from the court of general sessions is done by Mr. Chas. C. Allison, Jr. In connection with this work with delinquents the Big Brother and Big Sister movements are conducted. The league seeks to furnish to each boy or girl passing through the courts the helpful influence and guidance of a man or woman of high moral character.

The league conducts a housing bureau for the purpose of improving the moral and physical conditions among the tenement houses in Negro districts. It seeks principally to prevent the indiscriminate mixing of the good and bad by furnishing to the public a list of houses certified to be tenanted by respectable people. It also seeks to get prompt action of agents and owners or the city departments whenever there is need for correcting certain housing abuses.

Source: *The Crisis* 8 (Sept. 1914).

than twenty-five nursing schools in the country. In Chicago, for example, Provident Hospital was started in 1890 by Dr. Hale Williams as the first integrated teaching hospital in the United States. Created because of the discrimination black doctors and nurses found in white hospitals, under Williams's leadership, Provident's goal of integration was of paramount importance. With financial support from the white philanthropic community, at the turn of the century it boasted both a black and white medical staff and black and white patients.

By 1917, however, the influx of migrants and the increasing segregation had helped to transform the institution into an all-black facility. Its new head, George Cleveland Hall, straddled two ideological camps within the black community, supporting an accommodationist philosophy that viewed racial segregation as a temporary trade-off, but striving toward the ultimate goal of achieving economic independence.

Under the banner of black self-help, a number of social service organizations were founded specifically to aid migrants and, in general, to uplift the community from inside. Notable in Chicago was Ida B. Wells Negro Fellowship organization, and the Wabash Avenue Y's. Many northern churches also established employment offices, recreation centers, and welfare agencies to address the complex needs of the newly arrived migrants. Again, the point of these organizations was not merely to "help" but also to establish an economic foundation.

BLACK CULTURE TRANSFORMED

In the new urban centers, different cultural traditions confronted each other. Poet Imamu Amiri Baraka argues that significant cultural transformations accompanied the new community. The central point is the North represented a place where they could begin again. Music, particularly the classic urban blues, became an important expression of that transformation. One of the first commercial recordings by a black artist was done by Mamie Smith, a singer from Cincinnati with a "heavy voice, heavy hips, a light complexion and wavy brown hair." Her recording "Crazy Blues" sold "tens of thousands of copies in northern black centers." Her words—"I can't sleep at night. I can't eat a bite. Cause the man I love, He didn't treat me right"—captured a despair that cut across ethnic and racial lines. But the music also ushered in an era of production of "race records," a recognition on the part of the recording industry that a significant market existed within the black community. Race records quickly became big business. Friday nights after work, Baraka explains, "Negro working men lined up outside record stores to get the new blues, and as the money rolled in, the population of America, as shown on sales prognostication charts in the offices of big American industry, went up by one-tenth." Mamie Smith, who earned nearly $100,000 in recording royalties, is said to have made so much money she never actually counted it.

Some expressed alarm at the new music. One federal investigator was shocked that migrants enjoyed such suggestive pieces as "He May Be Your Man, But He Comes To See Me Sometimes." But a new consciousness emerged with the music as classic blues singers of the 1920s sang of mature, sexual, and independent women.

The author Richard Wright saw the difference between North and South embodied in their music. While southern music "carried a strain of other-worldly yearning which people called 'spiritual'" the new forms of blues, jazz, swing, and boogie-woogie were "'spirituals' of the city pavements," representing "our longing for freedom and opportunity, an expression of our bewilderment and despair in a world whose meaning eludes us. Our thirst for the sensual is poured out in jazz; the tension of our brittle lives is given forth in swing; and our nervousness and exhaustion are pounded out in the swift tempo of boogie-woogie."

CONCLUSION

Migrants lived in a very restricted economic arena. To survive, they rather quickly had to find a job and earn money. This reality influenced all of their decision making. The world they shaped, as a result, was very pragmatic, limited, and ever changing. Contemporary observers, interviewing participants in the Great Migration, frequently commented on what they called their "economic motivations." Often they would press migrants on such topics as southern exploitation, only to get the response, "I don't care nothing about that."

Recent scholars have challenged these characterizations, suggesting that observers intentionally ignored important noneconomic motivations. Surveys of letters to newspapers, organizations, families, and friends all suggest, on the other hand, that migrants themselves highlighted economic concerns with much greater frequency than anything else. Even when they talked of other things, they did so in an economic context:

> I am the mother of 8 children 25 years old and I want to get out of this dog hold because I dont know what I am raising them up for in this place and I want to go to Chicago where I know they will be raised and my husband crazy to get there because he know he can get more to raise his children.

The decision to leave was no more complicated than this. Participants in the Great Migration shared with many who had come before and with many more who would come after a simple dream, to make it in America.

FOR FURTHER READING

Adero, Malaika, ed. *Up South: Stories, Studies and Letters of This Century's African-American Migrations.* New York: The New Press, 1994.

Baraka, Imamu Amiri [Jones, Leroi]. *Blues People: Negro Music in White America.* New York: William Morrow & Company, 1983.

Clark-Lewis, Elizabeth. *Living In, Living Out: African American Domestics and the Great Migration.* New York: Kodansha International, 1996.

Collins, Patrica Hill. *Black Feminist Thought: Knowledge, Consciousness, and the Politics of Empowerment.* Rev. ed. New York: Routledge, 1999.

Comer, James P. *Maggie's American Dream: The Life and Times of a Black Family.* New York: Plume, 1989.

Giddings, Paula. *When and Where I Enter: The Impact of Black Women on Race and Sex in America.* 2nd ed. New York: William Morrow & Company, 1996.

Gottlieb, Peter. *Making Their Own Way: Southern Blacks' Migration to Pittsburgh, 1916–1930.* Urbana: University of Illinois Press, 1997.

Grossman, James R. *Land of Hope: Chicago, Black Southerners, and the Great Migration.* Chicago: University of Chicago Press, 1991.

Jones, Jacqueline. *Labor of Love, Labor of Sorrow: Black Women, Work, and the Family from Slavery to the Present.* New York: Vintage, 1986.

Kennedy, Louise. The *Negro Peasant Turns Cityward: Effects of Recent Migration to Northern Centers.* New York: AMS, 1968.

Levine, Lawrence W. *Black Culture and Black Consciousness: Afro-American Folk Thought from Slavery to Freedom.* New York: Oxford University Press, 1978.

Marable, Manning. *Black Leadership.* New York: Columbia University Press, 1998.

Marks, Carole C. *Farewell—We're Good and Gone: The Great Black Migration.* Bloomington: Indiana University Press, 1989.

Painter, Nell Irvin, ed. *The Narrative of Hosea Hudson: The Life and Times of a Black Radical.* New York: W. W. Norton & Co., 1993.

Robinson, Armstead L., and Patricia Sullivan, eds. *New Directions in Civil Rights Studies.* Charlottesville: University Press of Virginia, 1991.

Spear, Allan. *Black Chicago: The Making of a Negro Ghetto, 1890–1920.* Chicago: University of Chicago Press, 1969.

Trotter, Joe W. *Black Milwaukee: The Making of an Industrial Proletariat, 1915–1945.* Urbana: University of Illinois Press, 1985.

———. *The Great Migration in Historical Perspective: New Dimensions of Race, Class, and Gender.* Bloomington: Indiana University Press, 1991.

Wright, Gavin. *Old South, New South: Revolution in the Southern Economy since the Civil War.* Baton Rouge: Louisiana State University Press, 1996.

chapter 9

From Booker T. to Malcolm X

Black Political Thought, 1895–1965

Wilson J. Moses

O N FEBRUARY 20, 1895, FREDERICK DOUGLASS, orator, statesman, universal reformer, and reputed spokesman of black America, returned from a speaking engagement to his Washington,
D.C., home, and, as he often did, began to entertain his wife with a humor-
ous reenactment of the day's events. Midway through his performance, Douglass dropped to his knees, gasping for breath; Helen Pitts Douglass suddenly
realized, to her alarm, that he was not acting. Douglass expired on the parlor
floor, within minutes, and with him passed an era in the struggle for African-
American intellectual leadership. Rising to national prominence in the year
of Douglass's death was Booker T. Washington, the new symbolic speaker for
black America, who was fated to be the lonely captain of the foundering ship
of Reconstruction.

THE RISE OF BOOKER T. WASHINGTON

The end of the nineteenth century was a dismal period in the history of black
Americans, as most of the gains they had made as a result of emancipation and
postwar Reconstruction seemed to be slipping away. At the end of the Civil
War, northern philanthropists and liberals had offered substantial assistance
to the black American quest for full participation in American life. By the turn
of the century, however, it was clear that black citizenship was to be sacrificed
to the ideal of white national unity. White Americans were fatigued after the
great internecine struggle, and the passion for social reform was overwhelmed
by the lure of materialism in the nation's response to industrialism. Rayford
W. Logan has characterized the period as one of "betrayal" and as the "nadir"

of African-American history, while John Hope Franklin suggested the spirit of the times in the term "counter-reconstruction."

Booker T. Washington's ideology was shaped largely by his childhood experiences, first in slavery, then in the salt mines and coal mines of Malden, West Virginia. He was influenced profoundly by the Yankee values of Viola Ruffner, for whom, at the age of fifteen, he went to work as a houseboy. Washington later credited Ruffner with teaching him the practical usefulness of honesty, industry, thrift, and abstinence that later figured in his educational and political philosophy. In 1872, he worked his way to Hampton, Virginia, traveling most of the way there on foot. There, he eventually graduated with honors from the Hampton Normal and Agricultural Institute headed by Samuel Chapman Armstrong. During several months at the Wayland Seminary in Washington, D.C., he was exposed to the South's new black middle class, with its crass materialism and petty snobbishness. The experience contributed to his lifelong hostility toward the black bourgeoisie. He wished that "by some power of magic," he might "remove the great bulk of these people into the country districts and plant them upon the soil." Washington returned to Malden, where he taught school for two years, and then returned to Hampton, where he gained two additional years of teaching experience. In 1881, he founded the Tuskegee Normal and Industrial Institute in Alabama.

Patient as a spider, Washington began to construct a network of power and influence, consciously maneuvering himself into the position of spokesman for black America. Then, on September 18, 1895, seven months after the death of Douglass, he capitalized on an opportunity to address the Atlanta and Cotton States Exposition. With stunning brilliance, Washington used the occasion to exploit the white South's legend of the contented slave, which he transformed into a myth of black loyalty during the Civil War. He advised white-controlled business and industry to entrust its destiny to the loyal black population, saying, "Cast down your bucket . . . among the eight millions of Negroes whose habits you know, whose fidelity and love you have tested in days when to have proved treacherous meant the ruin of your firesides." He also exploited the South's xenophobia with respect to European emigrants, promising a loyalty "that no foreigner can approach" and casting suspicion on those "of foreign birth and strange tongue and habits." Washington also called on black Americans to cast down their buckets "in agriculture, mechanics, in commerce, in domestic service, and in the professions."

Contrary to popular belief, Washington's goal was never to consign black Americans to menial occupations, but rather to develop a stratified society, in which the masses would be prosperous farmers and handworkers, led by a managerial elite of college-trained technocrats. He was a missionary to the children of slavery, preaching the "Gospel of Wealth," the "Protestant Ethic," and family values. Tuskegee established extension programs among the agrarian masses, instructing them in such useful skills as crop rotation, animal husbandry, personal hygiene, and the management of household finances.

Washington was contemptuous of education that was not aimed at the creation of material wealth and believed that persons of marginal ability who "wasted" their time studying Greek and Latin were assuring their own economic failure. Tuskegee, nonetheless, had a solid liberal arts curriculum, and students were provided the basic elements of cultural literacy, economics, history, and the arts of communication. The better graduates were encouraged to under-

From the Atlanta Exposition Address

Booker T. Washington

To those of my race who depend on bettering their condition in a foreign land or who underestimate the importance of cultivating friendly relations with the Southern white man, who is their next-door neighbour, I would say: "Cast down your bucket where you are "— cast it down in making friends in every manly way of the people of all races by whom we are surrounded. Cast it down in agriculture, mechanics, in commerce, in domestic service, and in the professions. And in this connection it is well to bear in mind whatever other sins the South may be called to bear, when it comes to business, pure and simple, it is in the South that the Negro is given a man's chance in the commercial world, and in nothing is this Exposition more eloquent than in emphasizing this chance. Our greatest danger is that in the great leap from slavery to freedom we may overlook the fact that the masses of us are to live by the productions of our hands, and fail to keep in mind that we shall prosper in proportion as we learn to dignify and glorify common labour and put brains and skill into the common occupations of life; shall prosper in proportion as we learn to draw the line between the superficial and the substantial, the ornamental, gewgaws of life and the useful. No race can prosper till it learns that there is as much dignity in tilling a field as in writing a poem. It is at the bottom of life we must begin, and not at the top. Nor should we permit our grievances to overshadow our opportunities.

To those of the white race who look to the incoming of those of foreign birth and strange tongue and habits for the prosperity of the South, were I permitted I would repeat what I say to my own race, "Cast down your bucket where you are." Cast down among the eight millions of Negroes whose habits you know, whose fidelity and love you have tested in days when to have proved treacherous meant the ruin of your firesides. Cast down your bucket among these people who have, without strikes and labour wars, tilled your fields, cleared your forests, builded your railroads and cities, and brought forth treasures from the bowels of the earth, and helped make possible this magnificent representation of the progress of the South. While doing this, you can be sure in the future, as in the past, that you and your families will be surrounded by the most patient, faithful, law-abiding, and unresentful people that the world has seen. As we have proved our loyalty to you in the past, in nursing your children, watching by the sick-bed of your mother, and fathers, and often following them with tear-dimmed eyes to their graves, so in the future, in our humble way, we shall stand by you with a devotion that no foreigner can approach, ready to lay down our lives, if need be, in defence of yours, interlacing our industrial, commercial, civil, and religious life with yours in a way that shall make the interests of both races one. In all things that are purely social we can be as separate as the fingers, yet one as the hand in all things essential to mutual progress.

Source: Booker T. Washington, *Up From Slavery* (New York: Doubleday, Page and Co., 1901), pp. 218–21.

take advanced studies at such leading northern universities as Harvard and Cornell.

The "Wizard of Tuskegee" was a Renaissance man—in the Machiavellian sense. Ruthless and cunning, he sought to establish himself as supreme "ward boss" of black America. In the presence of white power, he was a fox, stealthy, covert, and self-obscuring, but, in his dealings with other black leaders, he was a lion who brooked no opposition. The historian Louis Harlan views Washington as a many-layered persona, inscrutable to the core and perhaps lacking in substance. Others see him as a complex individual whose powerful personality left an indelible impact on black American ideology. One need not engage in the sentimentalism promoted by some of Washington's earlier biographers to appreciate the subtlety, as well as the limitations, of his philosophy.

Washington's autobiography, *Up From Slavery*, was a reminder to his audience that, like Frederick Douglass, he was a former slave. It also gave him a place within the broader tradition of the American self-made man, and he was

An enormously prominent individual in his day, Booker T. Washington remains a central, if controversial figure in black intellectual history. From Mary Helm's *The Upward Path* (Atlanta, 1904). Credit: The Library Company of Philadelphia.

sometimes compared to Benjamin Franklin, the philosopher of Yankee enterprise. He encouraged practicality in religion, as in all other things, and ridiculed the otherworldly emotionalism of untrained rural preachers. He was equally unimpressed with the secular enthusiasms of the black masses and their putative love for expensive "gew-gaws" and frivolous ostentation. As a preacher of the "Gospel of Wealth," Washington seemed, in the mind of W. E. B. DuBois, to have assimilated far too thoroughly the "speech and thought of triumphant commercialism, and the ideals of material prosperity." And yet it must be said in Washington's defense that the capitalism he advocated was not the cloying excess of the Gilded Age, but the creative Yankee enterprise represented in the philosophy of Andrew Carnegie, a pragmatic industrialist and socially minded entrepreneur.

In a sense, Washington was a "materialist," an economic determinist, who believed that the progress of black Americans would be best assured by establishing a solid base in the capitalist system. On the other hand, he held the "idealist" belief that the foundation of economic progress must be embedded in moral values. Asserting that economic success could never be achieved by a people who retained the habits of slavery, he set out to eradicate the vestiges of slave culture that he perceived among the African-American masses. He believed that exposure to Anglo-Protestant civilization was a providential by-product of the evil of slavery. Protestantism, properly controlled, could be a source of industrial values and ultimate economic strength. He justified his strategy of temporarily accepting political disfranchisement and working toward economic and industrial power in terms of the exigencies of the times. Indeed, one may ask if anything more could have been accomplished by a rhetoric of militancy. Washington realistically appreciated that the American civilization of the late nineteenth century was hostile to the presence of black persons in politics. This was the reason for his insistence that the best way for black men and women to get ahead was to ignore politics for a season and concentrate on business enterprise.

DISSENTING VOICES

Life was not so simple, in the view of Ida B. Wells, one of Washington's severest critics. Wells, the most militant black American leader of the period, argued that the disabilities of black Americans had little to do with any failure to master the values of contemporary capitalism. She publicized the lynching in Memphis of three black businessmen whose crime had been to establish a successful grocery store at a convenient point on the streetcar line, thereby exploiting an opportunity that white men had lacked the vision to seize. Wells disputed the white southern canard that lynching was a response to unmentionable crimes against white women. She insisted that lynching was simply one of the forms of political and economic terrorism, perpetrated, in many cases, against the most upstanding and enterprising class of black Americans.

Ironically, the three Memphis citizens were punished not for some form of political activism, but for practicing exactly the doctrines that Booker T. Washington preached.

In 1895, Josephine St. Pierre Ruffin convened a meeting of black women's clubs in Boston to form the National Federation of African-American Women (NFAAW). Ruffin was strongly influenced by Ida B. Wells's agitation against lynching and by the slanders against black men and women perpetrated in the press. She also sided with Wells in her opposition to Booker T. Washington. Ruffin was the product of an interracial marriage and an avowed integrationist, whose afternoon teas in Boston featured the social mingling of Harvard and Radcliffe students across racial lines and sexual barriers. Josephine Ruffin absolutely rejected Washington's pronouncement that "in all things purely social," blacks and whites could be "as separate as the fingers of the hand," since she was aware that few elements of human affairs are purely social. Nonetheless, Margaret Murray Washington, the wife of Booker T., was elected president of the NFAAW. Elected to chairmanship of the executive board was Victoria Earle Matthews, who was a Washington admirer, although a vocal opponent of lynching.

The Conservation of the Races

W. E. B. DuBois

If we carefully consider what race prejudice really is, we find it, historically, to be nothing but the friction between different groups of people: it is the difference in aim, in feeling, in ideals of two different races; if, now, this difference exists touching territory, laws, language, or even religion, it is manifest that these people cannot live in the same territory without fatal collision: but if, on the other hand, there is substantial agreement in laws, language, and religion: if there is a satisfactory adjustment of economic life, then there is no reason why, in the same country and on the same street, two or three great national ideals might not thrive and develop, that men of different races might not strive together for their race ideals as well, perhaps even better, than in isolation. Here, it seems to me, is the reading of the riddle that puzzles so many of us. We are Americans, not only by birth and by citizenship but by our political ideals, our language, our religion. Farther than that our Americanism does not go. At that point, Negroes, members of a vast historic race that from the very dawn of creation has slept, but half awakening in the dark forests of its African fatherland. We are the first fruits of this new nation, the harbinger of that black to-morrow which is yet destined to soften the whiteness of the Teutonic to-day. We are the people whose subtle sense of song has given America its only American music, its only American fairy tales, its only touch of pathos and humor amid its mad money-getting plutocracy. As such, it is our duty to conserve our physical powers, our intellectual endowments, our spiritual ideals: as a race we must strive by race organization, by race solidarity, by race unity to the realization of that broader humanity which freely recognizes differences in men, but sternly deprecates inequality in their opportunities of development.

Source: W. E. B. DuBois, *The Conservation of Races* (Occasional Paper of the American Negro Academy, 1897), pp. 11–12.

Discord within the women's group arose in the autumn of 1895 at a meeting of women's clubs in connection with the Atlanta Exposition. Considerable friction was sparked by Ida B. Wells's denunciations of Francis Willard, a white feminist known for racist statements. The following year (1896), when the NFAAW met in Washington, D.C., it merged with the Colored Women's League of Washington, D.C., to become the National Association of Colored Women (NACW), and Mary Church Terrell, a Tuskegee supporter, became the first national president in 1897. Margaret Murray Washington, who always identified herself as Mrs. Booker T. Washington, was elected chairwoman of the executive board. From that point on, it was clear that the NACW was to be under the control of the Tuskegee forces, and that Ida B. Wells and Josephine St. Pierre Ruffin were to be relegated to minor roles in the organization.

Further rumblings of protest about Washington's leadership were heard in 1897, when the venerable black leader Alexander Crummell organized the American Negro Academy. According to its constitution, the academy was to be "an organization of Authors, Scholars, Artists, and those distinguished in other walks of life, men of African descent, for the promotion of Letters, Science, and Art." Crummell delivered two addresses at the first convention of the academy: "Civilization, the Primal Need of the Race" carried an implicit criticism of Washington's gospel of wealth and materialism, and "The Attitude of the American Mind Toward the Negro Intellect" addressed the need for scholarly vindication of the abilities of African Americans.

Crummell's ideology has been called "civilizationism," a belief in the "uplift" and "redemption" of Africa and all her scattered peoples, both in religious and secular terms. He called for a leadership elite, educated in the liberal arts, but willing to descend from the clouds atop Parnassus and to meet the "primal need of the race" by bestowing the blessings of "civilization" on the untutored masses. It was neither "property nor money, nor station, nor office, nor lineage" that gave a people greatness and vitality, he argued, but their absorption in "large, majestic, and abiding things." Thus the need to encourage the production of "letters, literature, science, philosophy, poetry, sculpture, architecture, yea all the arts." The bylaws of the academy included the injunction that all meetings would be opened with prayer.

From its founding in 1897 until its demise in 1928, the American Negro Academy published twenty-two occasional papers, written by its members, in vindication of the race. Its first publication, contributed by Kelly Miller, professor of mathematics at Howard University, was representative. Miller's paper was a scathing review of Frederick L. Hoffman's *Race Traits and Tendencies of the American Negro*, a study sponsored by the American Economic Association. The thesis behind the work was an old one, namely that slavery was the natural state of the black race. Hoffman had marshaled statistics to demonstrate that since emancipation the health and morals of black Americans had dramatically deteriorated. The cause of this deterioration was "not [in] the conditions of life but in the race traits and tendencies" of the black race, namely its mental, physical, and moral inferiority. Furthermore, these "traits and tendencies must in the end cause the extinction of the race." Miller's purpose was to refute Hoffman's arguments by means of systematic analysis and introduction of statistical evidence. In his final paragraphs, Miller invoked the argument that "God is the controlling factor in human affairs," and his belief that, "if the Negro . . . will conform his life to the moral and sanitary laws," the social evils that Hoffman noted would be overcome.

Other members of the academy included Francis J. (Frank) Grimké, a Presbyterian minister and prolific scholar whose sermons and addresses were posthumously published in 1942, and Archibald Grimké, Frank's brother, also a successful author who wrote seven of the academy's occasional papers, biographies of abolitionists William Lloyd Garrison and Charles Sumner, and numerous newspaper and magazine articles. Archibald Grimké also published his own newspaper, *The Hub*, in Boston. John W. Cromwell, who contributed the eighth occasional paper, "The Early Negro Convention Movement," was the author of *The Negro in American History*, as well as editor of *The People's Advocate*. Theophilus G. Steward, a retired army chaplain, selected military themes for his two occasional papers. One of them dealt with black soldiers in the American Revolution, and the other described the Haitian Revolution. William S. Scarborough, a professor of classics at Wilberforce University, used an occasional paper to offer instruction on "The Educated Negro and His Mission."

Among members of the academy, the name of W. E. B. DuBois became almost identical with the mission of the educated Negro when he coined the term "Talented Tenth." DuBois had been born into genteel poverty in Great Barrington, Massachusetts, in 1868, but his native intellect and dogged determination had won him scholarships to Fisk and Harvard Universities and the University of Berlin. Within a week of Washington's Atlanta Exposition address, DuBois had written to congratulate him for his "phenomenal success

"The Talented Tenth"

W. E. B. DuBois

Men of America, the problem is plain before you. Here is a race transplanted through the criminal foolishness of your fathers. Whether you like it or not the millions are here, and here they will remain. If you do not lift them up, they will pull you down. Education and work are the levers to uplift a people. Work alone will not do it unless inspired by the right ideals and guided by intelligence. Education must not simply teach work—it must teach Life. The Talented Tenth of the Negro race must be made leaders of thought and missionaries of culture among their people. No others can do this work and Negro colleges must train men for it. The Negro race, like all other races, is going to be saved by its exceptional men.

Source: W. E. B. DuBois, "The Talented Tenth," in *The Negro Problem: A Series of Articles by Representative American Negroes of To-day* (New York: James Pott. and Co., 1903), p. 75.

at Atlanta," calling the speech "a word fitly spoken." In the next eight years, however, DuBois began to disagree publicly with Washington. In 1903 he published *The Souls of Black Folk*, with its two chapters on black leadership, "Of Booker T. Washington" and "Of Alexander Crummell."

DuBois's attacks on Washington's policies of accommodation were institutionalized in the founding of the Niagara Movement in 1905 when DuBois was joined by William Monroe Trotter, publisher of the Boston *Guardian*, and more than two dozen black business and educational leaders in a convention in Ontario. Trotter and DuBois were disturbed by the same elements of Washington's public demeanor that annoyed Ida B. Wells. Not only did they find him needlessly servile, but justifiably, they felt threatened by his covert political manipulations, which often sabotaged political initiatives or ruined careers. The clash between Washington and DuBois was due partially to a difference in personalities and leadership styles and partially to conflicting political ambitions. Nonetheless, although DuBois advocated a more militant posture in the struggle for civil rights than did Washington, he recognized the validity of Washington's call for industry, thrift, and the building of African-American institutions.

DuBois also recognized the importance of nurturing a distinctly African-American culture and tradition. Influenced, no doubt, by his German training and the concept of *Volksgeist* (soul of the folk, or spirit of the people) that dominated much of German cultural nationalism, he was the first American intellectual to attempt a theory of African-American culture rooted in the folkways of the masses. His "scientific" paper read before the American Negro Academy in 1897, entitled "The Conservation of Races," was flamboyant and mystical, as was most racial theory of the time, and it gave no indication of the proletarian romanticism that would affect his later work. *The Souls of Black Folk* (1903) was, on the other hand, a poetic rhapsody, largely in celebration of black *Volksgeist* or the spirit of African-American peasant culture.

DuBois was elected second president of the American Negro Academy, but with the exception of "The Conservation of Races," his efforts at race vindication would be aimed beyond the audience for the occasional papers. At the time of the academy's founding, DuBois was already concluding *The Philadelphia Negro* (1899), a pioneering work in the field of American sociology. He now proposed a long-term, systematic project to study the life and culture of African Americans. In 1897 DuBois became professor of economics and history at Atlanta University and began to devote the greater part of his energies to what he called "The Laboratory in Sociology at Atlanta." He inaugurated the Atlanta University Studies, a project aimed at gathering information and publishing a series of documents with such titles as *Morality among Negroes in Cities, The Negro in Business, The Negro Church*, and *The Negro American Family*.

As we have seen, not every educated African-American was hostile to Tuskegee policy. Mary Church Terrell, for example, represented the complex relations between Booker T. Washington and the Talented Tenth, the educated black elite that DuBois believed would lead the race forward. She was the daughter of Robert Church, a black entrepreneur who had made his fortune in Memphis real estate, much of it on the notorious Beale Street. He provided Mary with an education at Antioch and Oberlin Colleges, and afterward sent her to travel and study in Europe. In 1919 she addressed the Quinquennial International Peace Conference in Zurich, delivering her speech in English, French, and German. She sided with Washington in his conflict with DuBois, although her admiration for Washington was not without qualification, and she found his "darky stories" distasteful. Nonetheless, whenever she heard criticisms of Washington's policies, Terrell's response was, "But, have you seen Tuskegee?"

Mary Church Terrell's husband, Robert Herberton Terrell, and a fellow Harvard graduate, Richard T. Greener, also found cooperation with Booker T. Washington congenial. Francis J. Grimké, Victoria Earle Matthews, and T. Thomas Fortune, editor of the New York *Age*, were supporters of Washington from the Talented Tenth, and occasionally practiced a militancy that Washington eschewed. Nonetheless, Kelly Miller made clear in his 1908 work, *Radicals and Conservatives*, that it was impossible to reduce black thought at the dawn of the new century to the issue of degrees of militancy in race relations. Miller asserted that Washington had undergone tremendous growth as a result of "adverse criticism, and the growing sense of responsibility." "Even those who continue to challenge his primacy," he wrote, "confess that they are opposing the Washington of long ago rather than the Washington of to-day."

Despite widespread intellectual ferment during the period 1895–1915, there is an unfortunate tendency to reduce black leadership of the era to a succession of giants, from Douglass to Washington to DuBois. Even worse, DuBois is seen as the unchallenged intellectual colossus of black America, standing head and shoulders above all his contemporaries. This approach, which has its roots in the nineteenth-century deification of Frederick Douglass, is condescending and false. Washington, to his credit, never publicized himself as the prime intellectual leader, and in any case, by the time of his death in 1915, a large number of black Americans might have been identified as intellectuals of comparable or greater distinction. DuBois was a man of exceptional genius, and the best-publicized black thinker of his day on racial issues, but he was not an unchallenged intellectual titan, categorically superior to all his contemporaries. Mary Church Terrell was clear-sighted enough to see this, and she was known to tease DuBois in public, figuratively pulling his nose, when she addressed him as "Willie."

AFRICA AND AFRICAN AMERICANS

Understandably, some scholars have been dissatisfied with the tendency to discuss African-American thought during this period solely in terms of the Washington-DuBois conflict. A much neglected strain in African-American thought immediately preceding the First World War was the so-called "African Movement," represented by several black churchmen during the late nineteenth and early twentieth centuries. William H. Heard, a bishop of the African Methodist Episcopal (AME) Church, toured the western coast of the continent and worked to establish his church in South Africa. AME Bishop Henry McNeal Turner had been an advocate of black resettlement in Africa during the Civil War and continued to advocate African migration until his death in 1915. And Rev. Orishatukeh Faduma, born W. J. Davies of Yoruba parents in Barbados, a member of the American Negro Academy and principal of the Peabody Academy of North Carolina, became involved with a movement headed by Alfred C. Sam, a lesser chief of the Akan people of Gold Coast, West Africa, that attempted, unsuccessfully, to establish a steamship line between the United States and Africa.

Far more important to most black intellectuals than back-to-Africa schemes was the movement known as "Pan-Africanism." In 1900 Alexander Walters, a bishop of the African Methodist Episcopal Zion (AMEZ) Church, joined with Trinidad barrister, Sylvester Williams, Anna Julia Cooper, and W. E. B. DuBois to organize a Pan-African Conference in London. The variety of Pan-Africanism represented in this movement was concerned primarily with the universal defense of people of African descent from the effects of slavery, colonialism, and racial prejudice. Nineteenth-century antecedents of this philosophy include such publications as Damic Walker's *Appeal With a Preamble to the Colored Citizens of the World* (1829) and the *Constitution of the African Civilization Society* (1861), the latter of which expressed a devotion to the redemption of Africa, as well as "the welfare of her children in all lands."

In the United States, Pan-Africanism was influenced by Edward Wilmot Blyden, a Liberian scholar of West Indian origins. Blyden's writings and periodic visits to the United States in the late nineteenth century had a crucial influence on African-American intellectual life. He was associated with two important strains in African-American thought, "vindicationism" and "Ethiopianism." Vindicationism was a tradition that sought to demonstrate the humanity of African peoples by proving their contributions to world history, through the civilizations of ancient Egypt and the "blameless Ethiopians." These historical references to Ethiopia must be distinguished from "Ethiopianism," the religious movement for the conversion and civilization of Africa, which was a teleology based on the biblical passage, "Princes shall come out of Egypt; Ethiopia shall soon stretch forth her hands unto God." Blyden's early ideas were clearly buttressed by his Christian training and by his belief that Africa must be redeemed, both spiritually and materially. His historical researches and biblical interpretations led him to the belief that the African race had a noble past and a glorious destiny.

Blyden was among the progenitors of the "Afrocentric" school, as it was later called, with his assertion that the peoples and civilization of ancient Egypt were organically related to the population of the entire African continent. But although Blyden learned many African languages and sought to establish African studies in the University of Liberia, he was unable to overcome the civilizationism of his generation, the view that history was an evolutionary climb from barbarism to progressively higher forms of social, intellectual, and behavioral norms. In one of his later works, *Christianity, Islam, and the Negro Race*, Blyden expressed the belief that traditional African culture and religion must give way before the influences of Christianity and/or Islam. He viewed both of these missionary religions as more conducive to material progress than the religions of the various indigenous ethnic groups.

African civilizationists were future oriented and hoped to produce a sterling civilization in Africa as a vindication of the abilities of the African race. They were also determined to prove that black folk were the progenitors of civilization in ancient times and that black individuals had made significant contributions to human progress throughout history. Civilizationists believed that the vindication of the African races must also involve "uplifting" the masses of black people to a contemporary level of progressive civilization. In the nineteenth century, theories of black progress and civilization were linked to Christian missionary efforts. In the twentieth century, civilizationism sometimes took the form of Marxism; at other times, it adopted the rhetoric of laissez-faire capitalism and constitutional democracy. Nonetheless, Christianity, Marxism, and bourgeois democracy all assumed the existence of universal truths, which had been discovered, not devised, by Europeans, and therefore could not be rightfully appropriated by them. The truths of human progress, currently arrogated to themselves by white supremacists, were just as properly the cultural property of Africans, who should busy themselves with reclaiming their legitimate heritage.

Standing in sharp contrast to the ideology of "civilizationism" in the early twentieth century was the new movement toward "cultural relativism." Emerging in the writings of white American scholars, particularly Franz Boas and his student Melville Herskovits, cultural relativism provided black scholars with a new means of racial vindication. Hitherto, the defense of Africa had relied almost exclusively on the relationship of African culture to Egypt. Now, it became possible to defend West Africa, the historic homeland of African Americans, on its own terms. The "folkways" theory of social Darwinist William Graham Sumner provided an additional building block for the theory of cultural relativism as it allowed black Americans to argue that African manners and customs were intelligent adaptations to the conditions of life in Africa, rather than evidence of genetic or moral inferiority. Furthermore, it allowed social scientists to achieve an aesthetic enjoyment of the arts and folklore of indigenous African peoples.

By the 1920s, many intellectuals were abandoning monistic civilizationism to adopt the emerging ideology of "cultural pluralism" and "cultural relativism." Alain Locke, the influential Howard University scholar, understood correctly that cultural pluralism could be used to buttress democratic and egalitarian ideas and to nurture a tolerance and appreciation for the differences between peoples. What Locke and his cohorts seemed to forget was that nineteenth-century intellectuals had argued no less convincingly for a religious universalism as the basis of democracy and egalitarianism. There can be no denying that the political implications of cultural pluralism, as Locke articulated them, were generous and humane. At the same time it should be recalled that cultural pluralism flourished in the black community *after* white economic and intellectual elites had become interested in jazz and had begun to invest heavily in African modes of art, represented in the primitivism of Modigliani, Picasso, and the German expressionists.

Cultural relativism did have the positive effect of transforming the scholarly treatment of Africa. The relativistic thrust of social science made the study of African culture both fashionable and respectable in intellectual circles of Europe and North America. Simultaneous with the rise of cultural relativism in America, the researches of the German scholar Leo Frobenius had a strong influence on W. E. B. DuBois and other African-American intellectuals. Frobenius's observations, when placed within the conceptual frameworks of Boas, provided an intellectual basis for the appreciation of those cultures of sub-Saharan Africa that had never produced a pyramid.

Carter G. Woodson made contributions to the new African studies when, in 1915, he founded the Association for the Study of Negro Life and History (ASNLH). The following year, Woodson founded the *Journal of Negro History (JNH)*, a "gray-cover" journal whose sedate appearance reflected the scholarly intentions of its author. Unlike the American Historical Association, the ASNLH was not based in colleges and universities but was a grass-roots organization based in local Negro History chapters. Although *JNH* published articles on African history both ancient and modern, Woodson was not obsessed with the African past or with Ethiopian glories. Woodson followed in the tradition of nineteenth-century historians William Wells Brown and George Washington Williams in that his efforts aimed at a fair and factual presentation of the role of black citizens in the history of the United States.

Woodson, like DuBois, remained partially within the tradition of vindicationism that sought to justify the African race in terms of pyramid building. Both men aimed increasingly, however, to find elements of worth in traditional West African cultures. They were joined by a number of other black history pioneers in the United States during the first three decades of the twentieth century. One of these was William H. Ferris, a member of the American Negro Academy who published *The African Abroad*, a wide-ranging collection of essays treating African, Caribbean, and African-American history. Other vindicationists who began to move away from a strict monistic civilizationism were Arthur A. Schomburg and John E. Bruce, who cofounded the Negro Society for Historical Research in 1911.

At the same time black historians were founding learned societies, they appealed to a mass readership with their biographical sketches of famous

"Negro" individuals who were commonly considered white, realizing that American society arbitrarily broadened or narrowed its definition of "Negro" in accord with local custom or legal caprice. An individual might, therefore, legally change his or her race simply by stepping across a state line, or moving to a new neighborhood. Many of the persons identified as black in these popular biographies were of mixed racial ancestry, as, for example, Alexander Pushkin and Alexander Dumas. The vindicationists pointed out that certain of Egypt's pharaohs would have had difficulty obtaining hotel or travel accommodations in the United States during the 1920s.

Joel Augustus Rogers, the most flamboyant representative of this popular vindicationist school, discovered the suppressed black ancestry of numerous historical figures, including Hannibal, Cleopatra, Ludwig van Beethoven, Johann Strauss, Abraham Lincoln, and four other presidents of the United States. The point of Rogers's raciological detective work was that many famous persons might easily have been classified as black if certain ambiguities in their ancestry had been known and acted upon. Rogers's efforts were clearly intended to point up the irrationality and inconsistency of racial classification, but the ironic tone that permeates his work has been lost on many of his readers.

THE HARLEM RENAISSANCE AND BEYOND

Cultural relativism and pluralism continued to gain strength among academically trained intellectuals like Alain Locke, a Rhodes scholar and Harvard Ph.D., who took a skeptical and ambivalent view of the universalist concept of civilization. His anthology, *The New Negro*, has come to be seen as the standard introduction to the "Harlem Renaissance," or, as others prefer to call it, the "Negro Renaissance," or "New Negro Movement." The period is also sometimes referred to as the "Jazz Age," because it seemed to be paced to the erotic rhythms of hot jazz and "gut bucket" blues. The term "jazz" itself had sexual connotations and represented a strident flouting of repressive bourgeois sexual morality in an age that was flushed with the excitement of having discovered Freud. This spirit was reflected in such novels as Claude McKay's *Home to Harlem*, Jessie Fauset's *Plum Bun*, and Wallace Thurman's *Infants of the Spring*.

The poet and critic Sterling Brown, although much involved in developments of the period, was uncomfortable with the term "Negro Renaissance." "The five or eight years generally allotted are short for the life-span of any 'renaissance,'" he wrote:

> The New Negro is not to me a group of writers centered in Harlem during the second half of the twenties. Most of the writers were not Harlemites; much of the best writing was not about Harlem, which was the show-window, the cashier's till, but no more Negro America than New York is America. The New Negro movement had temporal roots in the past and spatial roots elsewhere in America and the term has validity, it seems to me, only when considered to be a continuing tradition.

Brown believed, furthermore, that Jazz Age stereotypes were nothing but a revitalization of old plantation darky myths. He expressed his distaste for the black writers and intellectuals who "helped to make a cult of Harlem [and] set up their own Bohemia, sharing in the nation-wide rebellion from family, church, small town, and business civilization . . . grafting primitivism on decadence." Locke, for his part, warned that "too many of our younger writers . . . are pot-plants seeking a forced growth according to the exotic tastes of a pampered and decadent public." Locke's description of black culture in terms of hothouse exoticism was an obvious borrowing from the language of Alexander Crummell, half a century earlier. Locke was by no means a cultural conservative or a literary traditionalist. He supported the work of young modernist intellectuals. At the same time he had some misgivings with respect to the exotic stereotype. His ambivalence was shared by other black modernists, including Langston Hughes, Jessie Fauset, Wallace Thurman, and James Weldon Johnson.

E. Franklin Frazier, a black sociologist of Marxist leanings, offered even more stringent criticism, when he accused the Harlem literati of being too easily impressed by the white intellectual attack on bourgeois values and too ready in their acceptance of the Marxist critique of the capitalist class. Black folk in America needed to nurture a capitalist class, argued Frazier, for the black businessman was far more independent in spirit than were the black artists who parroted proletarian slogans. At this early stage in his career, Frazier was a champion of the black bourgeoisie, which he hoped would soon produce a true capitalist class, a necessary phase in the evolutionary development of an independent intellectual class, according to his Marxist theory of history.

One strain of bourgeois capitalist culture that would seem to have met Frazier's requirements was embodied in the movement of Marcus Garvey, a flamboyant leader of Jamaican origin. Garvey's Universal Negro Improvement Association (UNIA) arose in Harlem during the First World War and flourished until his imprisonment in 1925 for mail fraud and his deportation in 1927. By 1919 Garvey had built a political movement based on a revitalization of the pan-African ideology that had flourished in the generation of Blyden and Crummell. Marcus Garvey's arrogant and theatrical temperament was reflected in the quarrelsome nature of the UNIA, evident in the month-long convention of August 1923. Garvey was caught up in contradictions between a reverence for the past and a fascination with modernity. As a result, he was torn between a desire to identify himself with tradition and a contradictory impulse to present himself as a total innovator. The UNIA program was, however, more closely associated with the bourgeois aspirations of the working class than with the avant-garde "modernism" of marginalized Jazz Age libertines.

With the coming of the Great Depression in the 1930s, many black intellectuals in the United States became cynical with respect to the values of the Negro Renaissance. The romantic racialism of the Renaissance was continued

by Francophone intellectuals of the Negritude school, especially as transla-
tions of Frobenius's work became available in French. In the United States,
however, black intellectuals relocated their proletarianism in a Marxian
rhetoric and sometimes in actual Communist Party membership. Langston
Hughes, who had been one of the intellectuals most associated with the exoticism of the twenties, refashioned himself as a Marxist, albeit half-heartedly.
Richard Wright, the most successful black writer of the Depression era,
joined the Communist Party for a short time, but later expressed his disillu-
sionment in autobiographical writings and in his novel *The Outsider*. Ralph
Ellison, who never actually became a communist, satirized the racial clumsi-
ness of white Marxists in his novel *Invisible Man*.

DuBois's path after 1930 is confusing and seemingly contradictory to those
lacking the stamina to trace his intellectual odyssey through voluminous publications over a period of seventy years. In the 1940s, DuBois, despite his left-
liberal inclinations, expressed a black nationalist ideology when he called for
voluntary segregation in his *Dusk of Dawn*, a book in which he specifically
endorsed Washington's program of economic self-help and self-separation. In
defecting from the integrationist line, he grudgingly admitted that perhaps
Booker T. Washington had correctly understood the importance of building
an economic and institutional base upon which political activism might more
successfully be grounded.

DuBois's economic theories drifted steadily in the direction of black nationalist separatism. As an economic determinist, he now went a step beyond
Booker T. Washington, embracing at least some aspects of Marxist economic
theory. In 1962, the year before his death, he joined the Communist Party,
although there is some controversy as to whether he ever became a doctrinaire
Marxist. On the other hand, he did become an apologist for Stalinism,
attempting, as did Stalin, to reconcile Marxist internationalism with nationalist multiculturalism. His framework for doing this was the pan-African supra-
nationalism championed by Kwame Nkrumah, president of the Republic of
Ghana. DuBois eventually migrated to Ghana where he died in 1963, a supporter of Nkrumah's increasingly ruthless dictatorial policies.

During this period, other black intellectuals reappraised the doctrines of
Booker T. Washington, although often refusing to acknowledge they were
doing so. Carter G. Woodson denounced the failure of the Talented Tenth to
provide meaningful leadership in the struggle for desegregation. In *The Mise-
ducation of the Negro* (1933), Woodson's criticism of bourgeois insincerity
recalled the position of Washington in *Up From Slavery*. On the other hand,
Woodson was clearly impatient with the accommodation to segregation on the
part of the Booker T. Washington's ideological successors. E. Franklin Frazier likewise became increasingly critical of middle-class venality. In 1947 he
reiterated some of Woodson's points in an article on "The Negro's Vested
Interest in Segregation," accusing the black bourgeoisie of a big-frog/little-
pond mentality. Increasingly, he abandoned his hopes for the black middle

class and the Negro businessman, which he had expressed during the 1920s. Like Washington, Frazier recognized the self-deception of the black middle class, but he bitterly condemned the Tuskegee machine's legacy of political accommodation.

It is often commented that Frazier owed an intellectual debt to Robert E. Park, a distinguished white professor at the University of Chicago. Earlier in his career, Park had been secretary to Booker T. Washington and had served as Washington's interpreter during a European tour. Sincerely admiring Washington as a politician and as a philosopher, Park once said, "I think I learned more about human nature and society in the South under Booker T. Washington than I had learned elsewhere in all my previous studies." Frazier, however, never shared Park's admiration for Washington. Furthermore, he disagreed with Park's position that the personalities and psychologies of individuals might partially be influenced by hereditary racial traits. Frazier did, however, make use of Park's theory that black life had been catastrophically disrupted by slavery. Frazier's obsession with black social pathologies as the result of slavery and segregation was basic to his tendency to identify dysfunctional behavior in almost every black social institution, most notably in the black family.

Unlike Park and DuBois, Frazier was neither ambivalent nor sentimental with respect to the traditional and sacred values associated with small village communities. Frazier believed that the increasing urbanization and secular-

From the Future As I See It

Marcus Garvey
When we come to consider the history of man, was not the Negro a power, was he not great once? Yes, honest students of history can recall the day when Egypt, Ethiopia and Timbuctoo towered in their civilizations, towered above Europe, towered above Asia. When Europe was inhabited by a race of cannibals, a race of savages, naked men, heathens and pagans, Africa was peopled with a race of cultured black men, who were masters in art, science and literature; men who were cultured and refined; men who, it was said, were like the gods. Even the great poets of old sang in beautiful sonnets of the delight it afforded the gods to be in companionship with the Ethiopians. Why, then, should we lose hope? Black men, you were once great; you shall be great again. Lose not courage, lose not faith, go forward. The thing to do is to get organized; keep separated and you will be exploited, you will be robbed, you will be killed. Get organized, and you will compel the world to respect you. If the world fails to give you consideration because you are black men, because you are Negroes, four hundred millions of you shall, through organization, shake down the pillars of the universe and bring down creation, even as Samson brought down the temple upon his head and upon the heads of the Philistines.

Source: A. J. Garvey, ed., *The Philosophy and Opinions of Marcus Garvey* (New York: Humanities Press Inc., 1968), p. 78.

ization of American society would lead to the breakdown of traditional "caste restrictions." Therefore, he sanctioned cosmopolitanism as the best means of promoting human progress. Since in his view black separatism was nothing more than accommodation to racism, his intellectual agenda after 1945 was determined by his uncompromising commitment to social integration and cultural assimilation. He opposed black nationalism as well as the accommodationist forms of racial separatism. This led to his diatribes against black institutions, notably *Black Bourgeoisie* (1957) and *The Negro Church* (1962). These publications, while brutally honest, factual, and courageous in terms of a human rights agenda, failed to explore the question of separate cultural and institutional mechanisms for the improvement of African-American life.

BLACK INTELLECTUAL LIFE AFTER DUBOIS: THE CIVIL RIGHTS ERA

From the mid-1930s to the mid-1960s, black intellectual leadership was overwhelmingly committed to integrationism. Walter White, as head of the NAACP, founded in New York City in 1910, had little patience with DuBois's focus on encouraging improvements within the black community. Charles Hamilton Houston, a Howard University law professor, and his student Thurgood Marshall concentrated their efforts on a legal strategy for the destruction of segregation in the United States. In this they were supported by the direct political efforts of such activists as Mary Church Terrell and Mary McCleod Bethune. The sociological jurisprudence of Thurgood Marshall was grounded in the social and historical studies of such scholars as E. Franklin Frazier, Ralph Bunche, and John Hope Franklin.

Thurgood Marshall on the Role of Law

What is striking is the role legal principles have played throughout America's history in determining the condition of Negroes. They were enslaved by law, emancipated by law, disenfranchised and segregated by law; and, finally, they have begun to win equality by law. Along the way, new constitutional principles have emerged to meet the challenges of a changing society. The progress has been dramatic, and it will continue.

The men who gathered in Philadelphia in 1787 could not have envisioned these changes. They could not have imagined, nor would they have accepted, that the document they were drafting would one day be construed by a Supreme Court to which had been appointed a woman and the descendent of an African slave. "We the People" no longer enslave, but the credit does not belong to the framers. It belongs to those who refused to acquiesce in outdated notions of "liberty," "justice," and "equality," and who strived to better them.

Source: Thurgood Marshall, "Reflections on the Bicentennial of the United States Constitution," *Harvard Law Review* (Nov. 1987), p. 5.

Marshall, who had been head of the NAACP legal staff since 1938, eventually argued before the United States Supreme Court that the "separate but equal" doctrine was unconstitutional. Evidence was presented that in states where segregation was practiced, black institutions were invariably inferior to white institutions. The arguments of Marshall and White, in opposition to those of DuBois, eventually won out and led to the *Brown* v. *Board of Education* decision in 1954, in which the Supreme Court ruled that separate but equal "had no place" in public education. There is continuing controversy among black intellectuals whether the legal strategy of White and Marshall was in every respect well advised, although there is no disagreement that desegregation has mostly benefited black Americans. Nonetheless, many critics have begun to ask whether separate institutions must be categorically and inherently inferior to integrated ones. Ironically, *Brown* v. *Board* has led to the virtual abandonment of the racial mission of several historically black colleges in the South, but it has not always led to a proportional integration of traditionally white institutions.

The *Brown* v. *Board* decision gave encouragement to civil rights advocates throughout the South, and in 1955, Rosa Parks's courageous refusal to relinquish her seat on a bus in Montgomery, Alabama, marked the beginning of the Civil Rights movement. Martin Luther King Jr., one of the leaders of the resulting boycott of public transportation in the city of Montgomery, became recognized as the principal shaper of the movement. Reverend King's philosophy derived from the mainstream American "Social Gospel Movement," particularly from the writings of theologian Walter Rauschenbush. The roots of King's social thought are traceable to other American reformers including Henry David Thoreau, Ralph Waldo Emerson, and Washington Gladden. King was much affected as well by Mohandas Ghandi's philosophy of Satyagraha, a term untranslatable in English but loosely represented by the words "passive resistance." But like many of the major spokesmen for black American rights before him, King also drew considerably from activist black church traditions. The particular "Afro-Baptist" theology and heritage King learned and practiced at home and church directly connected social justice with Christian theology. It combined Jesus' message of brotherly love with the political philosophies of self-help and protest espoused by King's major predecessors, Booker T. Washington, W. E. B. DuBois, and Marcus Garvey.

It was from this broad body of social and ethical theory that King developed during and after the Montgomery boycott a strategy to deliver African Americans from the "nagging injustice" embodied in racial segregation and exploitation. King's plan featured mass action based on the concept of God's love for humanity (*agape* in Greek) and the Ghandian principle of nonviolent protest. King's objective was a just society, a beloved community, characterized by racial integration and equal opportunity. His moral vision emanated from mainly Christian tenets and the democratic creed embodied in America's Declaration of Independence, the Constitution, and the Bill of Rights.

As King skillfully advocated black militancy and interracial amity to secure "first-class citizenship" for African Americans, he rejected the separatist motif of restless black nationalists who espoused voluntary segregation, community autonomy, and sometimes violence. King not only felt the separatist remedy was unrealistic and risky but believed it constituted a form of black supremacy. God, he asserted, was not interested merely in black liberation but freedom of the entire human race and in the creation of a society where all men could live together in harmony. As eloquently enunciated in his speech before the Lincoln Memorial at the 1963 March on Washington, King dreamed of a day when Americans of all colors would ultimately unite across racial lines and finally "transform the jangling discords of our nation into a beautiful symphony of brotherhood."

Following a decade of intense struggle, blacks inspired to mass action by King's powerful words and deeds finally moved the U.S. Congress in the mid-1960s to pass federal laws shaped to dismantle segregation and stimulate racial integration. During this period, 1955–1965, black nationalism—the philosophy of black separatism—was confined almost exclusively to the lower economic classes, mainly in Northern urban centers. Black nationalists of the day tended to be distrustful of King and the liberal intellectuals whom they perceived as too humble and accommodating in the face of white prejudice. They accused King and the left-liberal progressives of discouraging black unity and self-help. The best-known examples of black nationalism in this period were the Moorish Science Temple, organized by Noble Drew Ali, and the Nation of Islam, organized by W. D. Fard and Elijah Muhammad, but not all black nationalists were Muslims. Another classic example of black nationalism flourished among separate black Jewish groups, who called themselves "Black Hebrews," or "Ethiopian Hebrews." Some of these migrated to Israel from Detroit and Chicago during the late 1960s and early 1970s. These groups denounced the secularism and atheism that they identified with left-liberal traditions.

Another tendency in African-American leadership that developed in opposition to the mainstream Civil Rights movement was conservatism. George Schuyler, the best-known black conservative during the early 1960s, was a man of considerable complexity who toyed intellectually with Marxism and with black nationalism at various points in his career. Conservatives have not been ideologically bound either to integrationism or to separatism, but have believed that they can render the black presence in America more useful and acceptable to the society at large by endorsing the traditional religious, economic, and family values of American society. Generally moderate in ideology, they have often taken a dim view of interracial marriage, but their essential integrationism has led them to accept the practice in recent years.

Conservatives do not denounce black separatism when it is associated with capitalist doctrines of self-help, and conservatives have often paid lip service to groups such as the "Black Muslims." This is due to the black conservatives' partiality to economics as the means to improving the black condition in the

United States. They also advocate patriotism and support military service as a means to demonstrating full commitment to the American Way. DuBois expressed an early conservative viewpoint during World War I, when he called on black Americans to temporarily set aside their grievances and rally around the war effort, while Booker T. Washington's conservatism was apparent in his organizing the National Negro Business League.

Under the leadership of Messenger Elijah Muhammad, the Nation of Islam was essentially a conservative black movement. Muhammad's principal spokesman during the civil rights decade was Malcolm Little, Malcolm X, who at the beginning of his career functioned as a mouthpiece for the messenger's self-help doctrines and militant antiwhite philosophy. According to this demonology, Caucasians were a race of devils, who persecuted black Americans purely because of the intrinsic and immutable evil of the white race. The only hope for black Americans was to secede or leave the United States and found their own nation in Africa.

Malcolm X faithfully preached this doctrine throughout much of his public life. A brilliant speaker and a manipulator of white guilt, he began to appear widely before white liberal audiences and was invited to lecture at Harvard and the University of London. In the aftermath of John F. Kennedy's assassination in 1963, when asked what he thought of the Kennedy assassination, he responded that it was a matter of the "chickens coming home to roost." Elijah Muhammad, alarmed by the foreseeable public outcry evoked by such a statement, banned his disciple from speaking publicly. Malcolm submitted for several months but then began to denounce Muhammad, accusing him of numerous sexual improprieties. In 1964, Malcolm made the second of two pilgrimages to Mecca and returned to proclaim that he was now a Sunni Muslim and that he no longer considered all white people to be devils. His pronouncements after the summer of 1966 were universalist, rather than black nationalist, and seemed to be on a line of convergence with the radical leftist universalism of Martin Luther King Jr., especially on such issues as opposition to the war in Vietnam.

The Black Revolution

Address to a Meeting in New York, 1964

This is a real revolution. Revolution is always based on land. Revolution is never based on begging somebody for an integrated cup of coffee. Revolutions are never fought by turning the other cheek. Revolutions are never based upon love your enemy, and pray for those who spitefully use you. And revolutions are never waged singing, "We Shall Overcome." Revolutions are based upon bloodshed. Revolutions are never compromising. Revolutions are never based upon negotiations. Revolutions are never based upon any kind of tokenism whatsoever.

Source: Two Speeches by Malcolm X (New York: Merit, 1965).

Malcolm X was murdered in February 1965, and there continues to be a great deal of controversy over who planned and carried out the assassination. After Malcolm's death, nationalists and socialists began to engage in bitter disputes over the meaning of his intellectual legacy, and posthumous publications of his work became the symbolic battleground for these campaigns. Several of Malcolm's speeches given before the Trotskyist Socialist Labor Forum were edited by the Trotskyist George Breitman, and Breitman's biography of Malcolm argued inaccurately that Malcolm was a socialist practically from the time of his silencing by Muhammad. When pressed in debate by Reverend Albert Cleage, a Christian black nationalist, Breitman admitted, however, that Malcolm had not become an integrationist. No evidence has emerged to support the view that Malcolm ever abandoned black nationalism.

The popular posthumously published *Autobiography of Malcolm X*, actually written by Alex Haley, has become the standard interpretation of Malcolm's significance. The book, together with a highly publicized Hollywood film biography and black youth's appropriation of Malcolm as a political icon, have elevated him to a status in death that he had never known in life. The American public's postmortem fascination with Malcolm continues to grow so that he has gained—with Douglass, Washington, DuBois, Garvey, and King—a preeminent place in the pantheon of black liberation theorists and activists.

CONCLUSION

Black intellectual life in the thirty years since the death of Malcolm X has not been dominated by the nationalistic concerns he identified as primal, but rather has come to define itself increasingly in terms of the ideological interests of African-American academicians. First brought onto the faculties of major universities in modest numbers after Martin Luther King's assassination, black academics, such as the prominent Harvard scholars Cornel West and Henry Louis Gates Jr., now dominate the black intellectual scene. Based at elite colleges and universities, mainstream black scholars generally eschew racially focused ideological terms like "nationalist" or "pan-Africanist," preferring to describe themselves as "leftists," "progressives," or "public intellectuals" committed to grass-roots empowerment. Their thinking usually assumes patterns determined by the New Left agenda of multiculturalism and gender studies and pays subordinate attention to race and class concerns. Meanwhile, the black nationalist position, while mostly out of fashion on elite campuses, is nonetheless flourishing in some public schools and universities.

It is fair to say, however, that in the overall pattern of black American intellectual life in the twentieth century almost every aspect of black thought has been influenced by the question of race. W. E. B. DuBois's perceptive comment at the dawn of the century that "the problem of the Twentieth Century is the problem of the color line" has dominated the thought of black savants and will doubtlessly affect their outlook in the new century. The degree to

220 Wilson J. Moses

which it prevails is the question. In the event that the United States is able to move toward an egalitarian society, in which race no longer imposes limitations on personal fulfillment, black American intellectual life will eventually change to reflect this new ideal. If, however, future generations of black Americans remain marginalized, then we can expect that African-American intellectual life will retain its historically focused identify. In such case, African-American thought will surely continue to center on questions of race.

FOR FURTHER READING

Banks, William M. *Black Intellectuals: Race and Responsibility in American Life*. New York: W. W. Norton & Co., 1998.

Cruse, Harold. *The Crisis of the Negro Intellectual*. New York: William Morrow & Co., 1984.

Douglass, Frederick. *Narrative of the Life of Frederick Douglass*. New York: Viking Penguin, 1997.

DuBois, W. E. B. *Souls of Black Folk*. New York: Dutton, 1995.

Franklin, John Hope, and Alfred A. Moss Jr. *From Slavery to Freedom: A History of African Americans*. 7th ed. New York: McGraw-Hill Publishing Companies, 1997.

Harlan, Louis R. *Booker T. Washington: The Making of a Black Leader, 1856–1901*. New York: Oxford University Press, 1989.

James, Joy. *Transcending the Talented Tenth: Black Leaders and American Intellectuals*. New York: Routledge, 1997.

Lincoln, C. Eric. *The Black Muslims in America*. 3rd ed. Grand Rapids: Wm. B. Eerdmans Publishing Co., 1994.

Locke, Alain L. The *New Negro*. New York: Simon & Schuster, 1997.

Logan, Rayford W. *The Betrayal of the Negro: From Rutherford B. Hayes to Woodrow Wilson*. New York: Da Capo Press, 1997.

Martin, Waldo E., Jr. The *Mind of Frederick Douglass*. Chapel Hill: University of North Carolina Press, 1986.

Meier, August. *Negro Thought in America*. Ann Arbor: University of Michigan Press, 1963.

Moses, Wilson J. The *Golden Age of Black Nationalism, 1850–1925*. New York: Oxford University Press, 1988.

———. *Black Messiahs and Uncle Toms: Social and Literary Manipulations of a Religious Myth*. University Park: Pennsylvania State University Press, 1993.

———. *Alexander Crummell*. New York: Oxford University Press, 1989.

———, ed. *Classical Black Nationalism: From the American Revolution to Marcus Garvey*. New York: New York University Press, 1996.

Walker, David. *David Walker's Appeal*. Rev. ed. New York: Hill & Wang, 1995.

Washington, Booker T. (William L. Andrews and Thomas C. Moser, eds.). *Up from Slavery: An Authoritative Text, Contexts, and Composition History, Criticism*. New York: W. W. Norton & Co., 1995.

Wells, Ida B. (Allreda M. Duster, ed.). *Crusade for Justice: The Autobiography of Ida B. Wells*. Chicago: University of Chicago Press, 1991.

Wintz, Cary D., ed. *African American Political Thought, 1890–1930: Washington, DuBois, Garvey, and Randolph*. Armonk, N.Y.: M. E. Sharpe, 1996.

X, Malcolm, and Alex Haley. *The Autobiography of Malcolm X*. New York: Ballantine Books, 1992.

chapter 10

Rights, Power, and Equality

The Modern Civil Rights Movement

Edward P. Morgan

THE CIVIL RIGHTS CAMPAIGN OF THE 1950S AND 1960S stands as one of the most remarkable liberation movements of modern times. Reflecting a new assertiveness among racial and other marginalized minorities in the post–World War II United States, the civil rights crusade brought the quasi-feudal American South into the liberal-capitalist American mainstream. It did so through the combination of court litigation, federal lobbying, nonviolent direct action in communities throughout the South, brilliant leadership, courageous grass-roots activism, and an American populace finally awakened to the grotesque nature of Jim Crow.

As significant as this accomplishment was by itself, the Civil Rights movement was also the catalyst for a whole era of political activism that convulsed the United States and spread to far corners of the globe. In brief, the civil rights struggle inspired others to struggle for justice. Through voter registration drives and nonviolent direct action, it generated profoundly liberating experiences that gave birth to a student movement that subsequently engulfed American campuses and, still later, the American war in Vietnam. It put equality on the nation's political agenda, evolved into a Black Power movement that revitalized black nationalism, and inspired a variety of egalitarian spin-offs—a Latino movement, the Chicano movement, the American Indian movement, the women's movement, even the gay liberation movement—each an expression of a group that perceived itself as left out of full participation in the American dream. Beyond America's shores, the Civil Rights movement inspired renewed activism within South Africa, Northern Ireland, and mainland China. Its most visible leader, Reverend Martin Luther King Jr., was awarded the Nobel Peace Prize in 1964.

The Civil Rights movement sought a variety of objectives: the application of the Fourteenth Amendment equal protection clause and Fifteenth Amendment voting rights to African Americans in the South, who had been long denied their constitutional rights by the Jim Crow laws promulgated in the post-Reconstruction years; citizen empowerment through community-based participation; personal expression through the embrace of African-American culture; and ultimately the full and equal membership of African Americans in the fabric of American life. Together with the 1964 War on Poverty and the Poor People's campaign of 1968, the Civil Rights movement agitated for equal educational opportunity and the elimination of poverty amidst plenty. Only the first of these several objectives was fully realized during the civil rights era.

These goals, and the strategies utilized to achieve them, reflected two distinct strains of American public life, often present simultaneously. One was grounded in American liberal ideology and the institutions of a constitutional democracy and market economy. The other reflected, at least implicitly, a vision of participatory democracy—of communities of people finding and expressing their political voice by directly confronting their oppressors as well as their own internalized powerlessness. The initial and crucially important litigation strategy fully embraced the liberal model. With the introduction of direct action and community boycotts, however, civil rights activists employed strategies that began to deviate from American "politics as usual" and implicitly contained a more participatory and personally liberating dynamic. In time, especially as significant legislative victories were achieved yet deep-seated inequalities remained, the movement as a whole shifted in a more radical direction, becoming more prone to challenge, rather than to work with, prevailing national institutions. In effect, the initial Civil Rights movement utilized national political institutions to achieve goals fully justified by a national ideology of equal rights, in the process bringing a deviant South into the American mainstream. In its broader manifestations, the civil rights struggle posed a variety of challenges to the American mainstream.

BROWN V. BOARD OF EDUCATION, THE MONTGOMERY BUS BOYCOTT, AND THE BEGINNING OF THE CIVIL RIGHTS MOVEMENT

The post-Reconstruction era of the latter nineteenth century established a rigid, tripartite system of racial segregation and oppression in the South—a system reinforced by periodic waves of terror and the constant threat of violence against any blacks who failed to toe the line. Southern blacks were effectively denied the right to vote and thus a political voice; if they were fortunate enough to be employed, then they remained at the bottom position, dependent on the good graces of their white employers; and they were subjected to humiliating rituals governing everything from interracial and intergender conversation to separate "colored" and "white" drinking fountains, eating establishments, public transportation, and public accommodations. Over the years, thousands of African Americans were violently lynched and assaulted for real and imagined transgressions against the "Southern way of life."

The impact of Jim Crow was devastating—not only in the arbitrary violence perpetrated against any African Americans deemed "uppity" by whites but also in the degree to which thousands more became resigned to the seeming inevitability of their oppressive circumstances. However, just as the abolition of slavery was the culmination of antislavery efforts spanning decades, the successful dismantling of Jim Crow was grounded in almost a century of struggle.

U.S. participation in the Second World War helped to transform the climate of race relations and foster a new assertiveness among African Americans. The struggle against the racist horror of Nazism spawned renewed efforts, particularly among Jewish and black Americans and sectors of the labor movement, to confront state-sanctioned inequities in the United States. Equally important, some five hundred thousand African-American men who fought for the United States in racially segregated units of the armed forces returned from the war to find the "old ways" of the South, including attacks on returning soldiers, doubly offensive. Finally, the war's aftermath brought the decline of European colonialism and a wave of independence movements in Africa, releasing a new assertiveness that spread contagiously back and forth between emergent nations and the American civil rights struggle.

One of the early beneficiaries of these shifts was the National Association for the Advancement of Colored People (NAACP), long the focal point for struggle against racial oppression in America. In 1946, NAACP special counsel Thurgood Marshall created the organization's Legal Defense Fund to accelerate prewar efforts to challenge the "separate but equal" doctrine adopted by the United States Supreme Court in its 1896 *Plessy* v. *Ferguson* decision. With support from Jewish and liberal organizations, the NAACP began to challenge the practice of racial segregation in the schools.

In 1950, a national conference of NAACP lawyers decided to wage an all-out assault on segregated education in the South. The five lawsuits filed in federal courts between 1950 and 1952 culminated in the landmark *Brown* v. *the Board of Education of Topeka, Kansas* decisions in 1954 and 1955 overturning de jure segregation and the notion of "separate but equal" education in the South. In his opinion written for a unanimous Court, Chief Justice Earl Warren asked the central question posed by the challenge to *Plessy*: "Does segregation of children in public schools solely on the basis of race, even though the physical facilities and other tangible factors may be equal, deprive children of the minority group of equal educational opportunities?" Drawing on sociological evidence and reasoning about the fundamental importance of public education in modern society, the Court answered its question unanimously, "We believe it does."

The response to the Court's momentous pronouncement was palpable. Northern liberals were effusive in their praise. A *Washington Post* editorial anticipated that the ruling would have a "wonderfully tonic effect" in ridding the

United States of an embarassing "incubus" and engendering a "renewal of faith in democratic institutions and ideals." Southern whites, however, denounced the ruling as a "mere scrap of paper," in Georgia Governor Herbert Talmadge's phrase, and warned it would "mark the beginning of the end of civilization in the South as we have known it," as South Carolina Governor James F. Byrnes put it. Between 1954 and 1959, whites attacked southern NAACP chapters, states contrived to impose bans on NAACP membership, and "Impeach Earl Warren" billboards began to appear along America's highways.

Despite the forceful language of *Brown*, the Court's follow-up implementation order in 1955 called for states to move ahead on school desegregation "with all deliberate speed," ambiguous phrasing that reportedly reflected Warren's concession to Justice Reed so the Court's decision could be unanimous. It was not clear what the impact of *Brown* would be in its highly politicized wake.

Perhaps the most far-reaching effect of the Court's decision was its impact on Southern blacks. Most were justifiably skeptical of the "paper guarantees" of the American Constitution, yet many also recognized that the *Brown* decision provided them with an institutional ally in the federal government and legitimized their cause in the national arena. The ruling generated a sense that the American political system *might* respond to their petition for an end to segregation and centuries of oppression. This ray of hope became a crucial ingredient in mobilizing popular participation at the local level in the South.

In 1955, a young black teenager, Emmett Till, was brutally killed in Money, Mississippi. A native of Chicago, Till was visiting relatives and, innocent of the norms of Jim Crow and acting on a dare, "talked fresh" to a white store clerk, saying "Bye, Baby" as he left the store. His murder and the subsequent acquittal of his killers were highly publicized in the national black press, providing fresh fuel for efforts to confront racial oppression in the South.

The spark, though, that ignited the movement toward direct action in the South was the nationally visible Montgomery Bus Boycott. The immediate catalyst for the boycott occurred on December 1, 1955, when a local NAACP Youth Council adviser, Rosa Parks, refused to surrender her seat on a city bus to a white man. When he heard of Parks's arrest, E. D. Nixon, head of the local branch of A. Philip Randolph's Brotherhood of Sleeping Car Porters, reasoned that it could be the catalyst that would break down Montgomery's segregated bus system. Meanwhile, the Women's Political Council organized a one-day boycott of the city's buses; with the assistance of her students, council President Jo Ann Robinson distributed 35,000 fliers announcing the boycott.

Local groups coalesced under an umbrella organization called the Montgomery Improvement Association (MIA) and met in Reverend Ralph Abernathy's First Baptist Church. The MIA responded to the brilliantly successful one-day action by organizing a sustained, community-wide boycott of Montgomery buses and filing a complaint against the city in federal court. They selected the twenty-six-year old preacher Rev. Martin Luther King Jr. as their president, in part because, as a local newcomer, he was not saddled with obligations to the white community. King's powerful leadership and impressive speaking and organizational skills soon became apparent at the biweekly meeting of the boycott participants.

The Montgomery bus boycott was sustained with virtually 100 percent cooperation from the black community for thirteen months, despite sabotage efforts by white leaders and bomb attacks on the homes of King and Nixon. In addition to the economic pressure it imposed on the bus system, two factors were crucial to the boycott's eventual success: the community-wide organizing that enabled black citizens to get to and from work, and the rousing mass meetings that sustained the spirits of boycott participants. Aided by those blacks who owned cars, along with a number of sympathetic white women who wanted to keep their maids and babysitters, the MIA organized an efficient transportation system. Meanwhile, every Monday and Thursday night, one of the local churches was filled to the rafters with gatherers singing hymns, spirituals, and freedom songs and responding enthusiastically to the oratory of Martin Luther King Jr., Ralph Abernathy, and other local preachers. The church meetings drew together blacks of all social classes and forged a sense of collective power. As Reverend Abernathy recalled later, "The fear that had shackled us across the years—all left suddenly when we were in that church together." Martin Luther King's blend of Gandhian principles of nonviolent resistance and Christian love convinced his audience that they were on the side of justice and inspired confidence that they would ultimately prevail.

The Montgomery boycott succeeded when the U.S. Supreme Court affirmed a lower court ruling outlawing segregation of the local buses. After December 21, 1956, when blacks in Montgomery boarded the local buses and sat in the front seats, it took whites awhile to adjust to integrated public transportation; in fact, the court decision was followed by an accelerated terror campaign by the Ku Klux Klan. Yet the boycott and its success stimulated

Rosa Parks Begins the Montgomery Bus Boycott, 1955

The next stop was the Empire Theater, and some whites got on. They filled up the white seats, and one man was left standing. The driver looked back and noticed the man standing. Then he looked back at us. He said, "Let me have those front seats," because they were the front seats of the black section. Didn't anybody move. We just sat right where we were, the four of us. Then he spoke a second time: "Y'all better make it light on yourselves and let me have those seats."

The man in the window seat next to me stood up, and I moved to let him pass me, and then I looked across the aisle and saw the two women were also standing. I moved over to the window seat. I could not see how standing up was going to "make it light" for me. The more we gave in and complied, the worse they treated us.

Source: Rosa Parks with Jim Haskins, *Rosa Parks: My Story* (New York: Dial Books, 1992).

positive change. It inspired similar black actions in Birmingham and Mobile, Alabama, and Tallahassee, Florida. It also gave rise to the formation of a new organization, the Southern Christian Leadership Conference (SCLC) with King at its head. Yet its most telling impact may have been local and personal. While the boycott's goals, an end to arbitrary racial segregation, were entirely compatible with American liberal ideology, the tactic of direct action energized a community-based notion of politics. From the perspective of boycott participants, the politics of desegregation were not something abstract and programmatic. They were concrete, deeply felt, and imbued with moral righteousness. The victory in Montgomery was as personally meaningful as anything could be. In Jo Ann Robinson's words, "We felt that we were somebody." A spark had been ignited, both locally and nationally.

THE PEAK CIVIL RIGHTS YEARS: 1960–1965

The years immediately following the Montgomery boycott saw a continuation of the turbulence initiated by *Brown*. National organizations like the NAACP, the Congress of Racial Equality (CORE), and the regionally based SCLC pursued various organizing strategies in the South, including voter education and registration and training young people in the discipline of nonviolence. Simultaneously, the white backlash continued unabated. School desegregation efforts burst into national visibility when the Eisenhower administration was forced to dispatch federal troops to Little Rock, Arkansas, in 1957 to protect nine youngsters from hysterical racist mobs seeking to prevent the integration of Central High School. Although little tangible change occurred in the system of southern segregation between 1956 and 1960, the momentum for change was building, and the nation as a whole was becoming more aware of conditions in the South.

In 1960, the Civil Rights movement experienced a new surge of energy when a generation of young people of college age entered the fray. The students had been exposed at a formative age to the awakening racial consciousness through church youth groups, campus YM/YWCAs, and local NAACP Youth Councils, as well as the increasingly visible leadership of Martin Luther King Jr. and his cohorts in the SCLC. Although isolated sit-ins had occurred in the late 1950s, it wasn't until 1960 that student sit-ins catapulted into public awareness.

Two students in Nashville, Tennessee, Diane Nash and John Lewis, had been attending nonviolence workshops taught by the Fellowship of Reconciliation's James Lawson, and with several others, they organized the Nashville Student Movement and planned to begin a nonviolent campaign to end segregation in Nashville. However, the first student sit-in occurred in Greensboro, North Carolina, on February 1, 1960, when four students at North Carolina Agricultural and Technical College—Ezell Blair Jr., Franklin McCain, Joe McNeil, and David Richmond—sat down at the Woolworth's lunch counter in Greensboro in a direct challenge to southern ordinances prohibiting whites and blacks from eating together in public places. All four had been members of the NAACP Youth Council and had spent much of the previous evening discussing what could be done to break down segregation.

With the aid of national news coverage and the network of SCLC movement centers, the effect of the sit-in was immediate and electric. The original four protesters in Greensboro were joined the next day by hundreds of students from nearby colleges. One week later, the sit-ins had spread to neighboring Winston-Salem and Durham. Through the organizing efforts of the NAACP and CORE, movement activists were contacted throughout North Carolina, South Carolina, and Virginia. By the end of February, sit-ins had spread throughout these states. By the end of March, they had spread to about seventy southern locales, including the deep South cities of Birmingham, Montgomery, Baton Rouge, New Orleans, Tallahassee, and Savannah. National chains like Woolworth's found themselves targeted by picket lines in northern cities such as Boston and New York as well.

In Nashville, while local business leaders railed against "outside agitators" stirring up "our Negroes," young whites attacked the students sitting at the lunch counter. When police intervened, however, they arrested the nonviolent activists, not their attackers, for "disorderly conduct." Following futile efforts to argue their case in courts, the Nashville movement expanded its focus and virtually the entire black community joined in a boycott of downtown stores as the sit-ins continued. Eventually, after a bomb destroyed the home of the black attorney defending the students, Nashville Mayor Ben West conceded that it was not morally right for local merchants to sell goods to black customers yet deny them lunch counter service. In the aftermath of his words, the merchants proceeded with integration, knowing they could shift the responsibility to West.

The sit-ins marked the emergence into the Civil Rights movement of a new, younger generation of activists who tended to be more spontaneous, less cautious, and ultimately more committed to a participatory style of organizing. Compared to community-wide boycotts, sit-ins were a more assertive form of "putting your body on the line," requiring a greater commitment to action on the part of their participants. Caught up in the spirit of collective action and casting aside personal fears, many of the young activists experienced profound levels of personal liberation and empowerment. In fact, with the rapid spread of the sit-ins, people began speaking of "the Movement," as if they were aware they were participating in something profoundly historic.

Members of the more established groups like the SCLC, CORE, and the NAACP provided crucial support for the students, especially as they were assaulted by whites and incarcerated in southern jails. And Martin Luther King Jr.'s teachings on nonviolence and Jim Lawson's training were enormously influential in shaping the young activists's predisposition. At the same time, the civil rights groups, particularly the SCLC, also evolved toward increasingly aggressive, nonviolent direct action campaigns aimed at eliciting strong civil rights enforcement by the federal government. These were to prove crucial in gaining passage of landmark civil rights legislation.

The nascent youth movement quickly reached a crossroads in April, 1960, when Ella Baker, the executive director of the SCLC, helped organize a meeting of SCLC and other civil rights leaders with students from the sit-in campaign. Both Martin Luther King Jr. and Jim Lawson urged the students to mobilize a nonviolent project to spread the "freedom struggle" across the South. Faced with SCLC's hope that they would stay "in the flock" as a youth arm of the SCLC or the NAACP, the students chose, with Baker's support, to remain independent and formed the Student Nonviolent Coordinating Committee (SNCC, or "Snick").

From 1960 to 1965, SNCC grew from a loosely organized network to an alliance of black and white field activists committed to mobilizing poor blacks in the deep South, what Vincent Harding called the "shock troops of the nonviolent movement." It was from the ranks of SNCC that the first cry of "black power" was raised in 1966. Direct confrontation with the most vicious white racism, community organizing among poor rural blacks, growing impatience with delay and an uncooperative federal government, a sense of moral righteousness, and a grass-roots lifestyle—all were the trademarks of SNCC at its peak. SNCC was the only civil rights group that, in effect, "gave up" on the federal government because of its inaction in protecting civil rights workers in the line of fire. Also, SNCC's emphasis on the psychological and community foundations of empowerment helped to push it toward disassociation from white activists. As SNCC migrated toward grass-roots organizing in the deep South, a civil rights agenda gradually began to emerge in national politics.

One factor that contributed to the growing national visibility of civil rights was the presidential candidacy of John F. Kennedy. As a candidate and later as president, Kennedy was drawn to foreign policy, leaving his brother Robert as the administration's chief law enforcement officer in charge of civil rights. As a cautious pragmatist, Kennedy was also extremely wary of jeopardizing the Democratic Party's strong base of electoral votes in the South. However, at numerous points, Kennedy's path intersected that of the Civil Rights movement. During 1960, he met with Martin Luther King Jr. and expressed his belief that action was needed to ensure voting rights. In the course of his campaign, he criticized the Eisenhower administration for inaction on housing segregation and pledged that he would end public legal housing discrimination "with the stroke of a pen," a promise he never quite fulfilled.

Civil rights leaders tended to view John Kennedy as detached, reflecting the distance between his affluent northern background and their struggles in the southern battlefield. At the same time, King was impressed by the young candidate's "forthright and honest manner," and Kennedy's phone call to Coretta Scott King while her husband was jailed (and Robert Kennedy's intercession with the judge for King's release) carried political risks that were appreciated by civil rights activists. More significantly, it was instrumental in swinging the black vote heavily toward Kennedy, thereby helping to ensure his narrow election over Richard Nixon in the 1960 presidential election. However, it remained to civil rights activists to force the civil rights question onto the president's agenda. The first crucial catalyst was provided by the Freedom Rides, organized by CORE and ultimately sustained by SNCC.

THE FREEDOM RIDES

Exactly one year after the first Greensboro sit-in, James Farmer was named the new national director of CORE. In its past, CORE had concentrated on advancing civil rights outside the deep South. However, reflecting a 1947 "Journey of Reconciliation" organized by longtime civil rights advocate Bayard Rustin, Farmer hatched the idea for the Freedom Rides to confront segregation in interstate bus facilities throughout the South, from Washington, D.C., to New Orleans. Farmer intended to "create a crisis" that would require federal intervention. He reasoned accurately that the integrated bus riders would provoke a reaction from white segregationists, thereby drawing northern (and governmental) attention to the harshness of southern segregation.

On May 4, 1961, a biracial group of thirteen embarked from Washington, D.C., and traveled through Virginia, the Carolinas, and Georgia, encountering relatively mild reactions along the way. However, when the two buses left Georgia, heading toward Birmingham, they encountered mob violence in the town of Anniston, Alabama. One bus was attacked as it pulled into the depot. A mob of thirty to forty whites shattered windows, hammered the body of the bus with chains and iron bars, and dragged Freedom Riders from inside the bus and beat them. After police finally rescued the riders and escorted the bus out of town, the attackers followed in their cars. The bus was forced to stop when a tire blew out, and the mob resumed its attack, shattering more windows and throwing a firebomb into the bus. Passengers were beaten as they fled the burning vehicle. The second bus was also stopped and riders were forced to the rear of the bus. Those who refused were beaten; one suffered permanent brain injuries. Although the FBI was tipped off that there would be trouble in Birmingham, no police were visible when the second bus pulled into the depot. The riders were once again attacked by a vicious mob when they disembarked; one rider, William Barbee, was paralyzed for life. Photos of the firebombed bus were carried on the front pages of the nation's newspapers.

When the Greyhound bus company refused to carry the Freedom Riders further, several of the original riders gave up and "completed" their journey by flying to New Orleans. However, SNCC activists felt it was critical that the rides be continued, and Nashville SNCC coordinator Diane Nash organized a group, including ten students, who traveled to Birmingham to complete CORE's itinerary.

The Freedom Rides succeeded in creating a crisis. The Kennedy administration began a series of negotiations with the bus company and Alabama Governor John Patterson. Robert Kennedy sought protection for the Freedom Riders (simultaneously urging them to consider a "cooling off" period), while Patterson denounced federal intervention in support of "rabble-rousers and outside agitators." Through the direct intervention of Kennedy aide John Siegenthaler, it appeared that the bus would have safe passage en route to Montgomery. In fact, police cars and helicopters escorted the bus from Birmingham to the outskirts of Montgomery, where local police were supposed to take over. However, once again, no police presence was visible as the bus arrived at the depot, and once again a hysterical mob attacked the riders. This time, as the crisis in Montgomery intensified, Kennedy sent six hundred federal marshals to the Montgomery area as protection. With an angry mob threatening the marshals and a mass meeting convening at Reverend Ralph Abernathy's church, Governor Patterson was finally forced to declare martial law and mobilize the state police and Alabama National Guard to disperse the crowd.

Subsequently, the Freedom Riders were escorted to the Mississippi border and then, with a Mississippi National Guard escort, proceeded to Jackson. Behind the scenes, Attorney General Robert Kennedy had extracted a promise of no violence against the Freedom Riders from Mississippi officials. In exchange, he agreed he would not enforce federal laws requiring integrated bus terminal facilities. Thus, when they disembarked in Jackson, the Freedom Riders were simply herded through the terminal and into police wagons and thence to jail. Subsequently, they were all found guilty of trespassing by the district judge and sentenced to sixty days in the state's maximum security penitentiary at Parchman.

Freedom Rider Hank Thomas on the Freedom Rides, 1961

The Freedom Ride didn't really get rough until we got down in the Deep South. Needless to say, Anniston, Alabama, I'm never gonna forget that, when I was on the bus that they threw some kind of incendiary device on. . . .

It wasn't until the thing was shot on the bus and the bus caught afire that everything got out of control, and . . . when the bus was burning, I figured . . . [pauses] . . . panic did get ahold of me. Needless to say, I couldn't survive that burning bus. There was a possibility I could have survived the mob, but I was just so afraid of the mob that I was gonna stay on that bus. I mean, I just got that much afraid. And when we got off the bus . . . first they closed the doors and wouldn't let us off. But then I'm pretty sure they realized, that somebody said, "Hey, the bus is gonna explode," because it had just gassed up, and so they started scattering then, and I guess that's the way we got off the bus.

Source: "Freedom Riders," from Howell Raines's *My Soul Is Rested: Movement in the Deep South Remembered* (New York: G. Putnam and Sons, 1977), pp. 113–14.

During the summer, however, more than three hundred additional Freedom Riders traveled through the deep South, trying to force the integration of all interstate transportation facilities. Eventually, at the attorney general's urging, the Interstate Commerce Commission adopted explicit regulations requiring the desegregation of bus terminals. In the interim, Kennedy felt the direct action campaign had forced the administration into the politically untenable position of choosing between the civil rights activists and the Democratic Party's southern base. As an alternative, he began urging civil rights groups to shift their energies to voter registration drives, reasoning that a political voice within local politics would give southern blacks leverage against resistant local officials. Despite their skepticism toward what looked like a self-serving administration effort to deflect growing civil rights momentum, some civil rights leaders began to see voter registration as a potentially effective path of empowering southern blacks. For SNCC, voter registration was a natural focal point for its participatory approach to community organizing, while SCLC leaders saw the potential national appeal of black citizens seeking their voting rights. Many were relieved that the violent confrontations seemed over. However, the path to voter registration would prove at least as dangerous and violent as the direct action campaigns.

The Freedom Rides propelled the struggle for civil rights to the center of the nation's political agenda. While the Kennedy administration may have preferred a quieter process of gradual black voter registration in the South, this was not to be the case. In fact, while the Freedom Rides were occurring, and while SNCC's Bob Moses joined with others to begin a voter registration campaign in McComb, Mississippi, the NAACP's Mississippi field director, Medgar Evers, was helping a black veteran by the name of James Meredith apply to the University of Mississippi. Later, after the university rejected Meredith, a federal court ruling ordered the decision reversed. In response,

---

Robert Moses on Community Organization in Mississippi, 1961–62

I accompanied about three people down to Liberty in Amite County to begin our first registration attempt there. One was a very old man, and then two ladies, middle-aged. We left early morning of August 15, it was a Tuesday, we arrived at the courthouse at about 10 o'clock. . . .

The first person who filled out the form took a long time to do it and it was noontime before he was finished. When we came back, I was not permitted to sit in the office, but was told to sit on the front porch, which I did. We finally finished the whole process at about 4:30; all of the three people had had a chance to register, at least to fill out the form. This was victory, because they had been down a few times before and had not had a chance to even fill out the forms.

Source: Bob Moses, "Mississippi: 1961–1962," *Liberation*, 14 (January 1970).

Mississippi Governor Ross Barnett denounced the court order and called upon white Mississippians to defend white supremacy in the South. Stirred up by Barnett's words, white youths rioted on the "Ole Miss" campus, eventually forcing the Kennedy administration to send army troops to bring the crowd under control—although not until two men, a French reporter and a bystander, were killed in the melee. Meredith subsequently attended the university.

THE ALBANY MOVEMENT, BIRMINGHAM, AND THE MARCH ON WASHINGTON

The violence in Oxford, Mississippi, not only heightened public awareness throughout the nation (it was the subject of the Bob Dylan song, "Oxford Town") but also it was a significant civil rights victory that again placed the Kennedy administration on the side of civil rights enforcement. In 1961, SNCC volunteers began to spread out throughout the deep South in their drive to register and organize black voters. Two veterans of the Freedom Rides, Charles Sherrod and Cordell Reagon, arrived in Albany, Georgia, to open a SNCC office. Their objective was to live and work among the "common people" of Albany, to organize a community-wide movement to confront segregation and register black voters. With the help of students from Albany State College, a sit-in at the "white" bus terminal galvanized the support of the entire black community, leading to the formation of an umbrella organization called the "Albany movement," with Reverend William Anderson as its president. In the wake of student arrests, a mass meeting at the Mount Zion Baptist Church generated a sense of collective strength through song, prayer, and inspirational speech.

Mass arrests and jailings followed. Unknown to SNCC, Police Chief Laurie Pritchett had studied the nonviolent tactics of Gandhi and Martin Luther King Jr. and had determined to avoid the provocative violence exhibited elsewhere. Pritchett planned to defuse quickly the community mobilization by rapidly and nonbrutally arresting the protesters and transporting them to vacant jail space throughout the surrounding countryside. With vast numbers stuffed into overcrowded jails, Pritchett's arrests began to take the steam out of the movement, especially since the absence of police brutality helped to keep the Kennedy administration at bay. The arrival of Martin Luther King Jr. posed the momentary threat of national media exposure, especially when King and Ralph Abernathy were also arrested. However, the white segregationists checked King's tactic by secretly arranging to bail him out of jail and then obtaining a federal court restraining order against further "unlawful" protest. King was unwilling to flout the order of a crucial civil rights ally, the federal courts, and thus was rendered politically impotent. The city held out until the energy and enthusiasm of the movement waned. SNCC worker Bill Hansen observed, "We ran out of people before [Chief Pritchett] ran out of jails."

The Albany movement ignited protracted local activism that continued for years, but it failed to create a spark that would advance the civil rights agenda nationally. It also represented a low point in the personal prestige of Martin Luther King as the movement's most visible and inspiring leader. However, circumstances changed when, learning from its Albany experience, the SCLC leadership decided to locate its next direct action campaign in Birmingham, Alabama. Not only did Birmingham have a long history of racist violence, including the vicious attack on the Freedom Riders two years before, but the SCLC had a strong organizational presence led by the fiery Reverend Fred Shuttlesworth. Birmingham had also recently experienced a division between business leaders seeking a new mayor/council form of government and the forces who led the attack on the Freedom Riders, including Commissioner of Public Safety Eugene "Bull" Connor. Amid confusion over which duly elected government was legitimate, the SCLC campaign came to town.

The Birmingham movement sought the complete elimination of local seg-regation, starting with the integration of downtown lunch counters, and encompassing public facilities, parks, and playgrounds; the establishment of fair hiring procedures in all retail stores; and the creation of a biracial commission and timetable for desegregating the city schools. SCLC leaders developed a three-stage strategy aimed at splitting the white economic elite from political officials and the racist white "rednecks." The first stage involved a boycott of downtown stores, the second revolved around mass marches on City Hall, and the third so-called "project" for confrontation involved students of all ages getting arrested and going to jail in massive numbers.

Phase one began slowly, although arrests were a catalyst for massive turnout at nightly meetings in the city's churches. As was the case in other locales, the church meetings were full of inspiring oratory and rousing singing, and the growing sense of collective confidence and determination. Yet, sensing that the white businesses were not likely to respond without additional pressure, the SCLC leaders gave the green light to phase two, the mass marches. As arrests mounted and the jails began to fill, the boycott gained momentum. Martin Luther King Jr. and Ralph Abernathy led a march in violation of a court injunction obtained by Bull Connor, and both were arrested. In a full-page ad in the *Birmingham News*, eight white clergy labeled King's actions "unwise and untimely." While in jail, King penned his distinguished defense of civil dis-obedience, later published "Letter from a Birmingham Jail." "We know from painful experience that freedom is never voluntarily given by the oppressor," King wrote, "it must be demanded by the oppressed. Frankly, I have yet to engage in a direct-action campaign that was 'well timed' in the view of those who have not suffered unduly from the disease of segregation. For years now I have heard the word 'Wait!' It rings in the ear of every Negro with piercing familiarity. This 'Wait' has almost always meant 'Never.'"

The demonstrations began to lose their steam as King's time in jail dragged on. Finally, King and Abernathy were released on bail and met with other

SCLC leaders to plan "Project C" using black children. After viewing *The Nashville Story*, a film about the student sit-in movement, the children gathered in the Sixteenth Baptist Church to hear Reverend King tell them they were fighting for their parents and the future of America. They proceeded toward downtown where they were met by police who began to arrest them. Still singing and marching in large numbers, the children were soon herded into school buses and dispatched to jail. More than nine hundred were arrested on the first day.

On the second day of Project C, as more than one thousand children stayed out of school, Bull Connor sought to thwart the march by calling out the city's police dogs and firefighters. While dogs attacked several demonstrators, the fire hoses, which packed more than 100 pounds of pressure per square inch, were trained on the youngsters, knocking many off their feet. The attack so enraged the entire black community that it united behind SCLC's campaign. Some blacks were so furious that it took James Bevel, a veteran of the Nashville sit-ins and mastermind of Project C, to quiet them and avoid a riot.

Meanwhile, television, newspaper, and news magazine pictures of the fire hose and police dog attacks carried the Birmingham story across the country and throughout much of the world. The public and the president were shocked. While the SCLC and local business leaders sought to hammer out a desegregation agreement through the mediation of the Justice Department's Burke Marshall, a bomb exploded at King's headquarters at the Gaston Hotel. In response, an angry black mob rampaged through the streets. At his brother's urging, President Kennedy dispatched federal troops to the outskirts of Birmingham and affirmed his determination to preserve order and "uphold the law of the land." Peace was restored. After the Alabama Supreme Court officially recognized the new city government, it, in turn, affirmed the settlement negotiated between business leaders and the SCLC.

In the immediate aftermath of the Birmingham movement, Alabama Governor George Wallace boldly squared off against Deputy U.S. Attorney General Nicholas Katzenbach in a doorway of the University of Alabama. Wallace was defying the court-ordered desegregation of the university. After denouncing the unconstitutionality of the federal court order, Wallace stepped aside and the two black students were allowed to register. The next night, President Kennedy went on national television to call for passage of historic civil rights legislation he was introducing in Congress, the most far-reaching of any since Reconstruction. His words had a new tone of moral urgency: "We are confronted primarily with a moral issue. . . . The heart of the question is whether all Americans are going to be afforded equal rights and equal opportunities; whether we are going to treat our fellow Americans as we want to be treated." Kennedy's bill banned segregation in all interstate public accommodations and enabled the U.S. attorney general to initiate lawsuits to integrate local schools and cut off federal funds to any programs that practiced discrimination.

"I Have a Dream"

... I say to you today, my friends, that in spite of the difficulties and frustrations of the moment, I still have a dream. It is a dream deeply rooted in the American dream.

I have a dream that one day this nation will rise up and live out the true meaning of its creed: "We hold these truths to be self-evident: that all men are created equal."

I have a dream that one day on the red hills of Georgia the sons of former slaves and the sons of former slaveowners will be able to sit down together at a table of brotherhood.

I have a dream that one day even the state of Mississippi, a desert state, sweltering with the heat of injustice and oppression, will be transformed into an oasis of freedom and justice.

I have a dream that my four children will one day live in a nation where they will not be judged by the color of their skin but by the content of their character.

I have a dream today.

I have a dream that one day the state of Alabama, whose governor's lips are presently dripping with the words of interposition and nullification, will be transformed into a situation where little black boys and black girls will be able to join hands with little white boys and white girls and walk together as sisters and brothers.

I have a dream today.

I have a dream that one day every valley shall be exalted, every hill and mountain shall be made low, the rough places will be made plain, and the crooked places will be made straight, and the glory of the Lord shall be revealed, and all flesh shall see it together.

This is our hope. This is the faith with which I return to the South. With this faith we will be able to hew out of the mountain of despair a stone of hope. With this faith we will be able to transform the jangling discords of our nation into a beautiful symphony of brotherhood. With this faith we will be able to work together, to pray together, to struggle together, to go to jail together, to stand up for freedom together, knowing that we will be free one day.

This will be the day when all of God's children will be able to sing with a new meaning, "My country, 'tis of thee, sweet land of liberty, of thee I sing. Land where my fathers died, land of the pilgrim's pride, from every mountainside, let freedom ring."

And if America is to be a great nation this must become true. So let freedom ring from the prodigious hilltops of New Hampshire. Let freedom ring from the mighty mountains of New York. Let freedom ring from the heightening Alleghenies of Pennsylvania!

Let freedom ring from the snowcapped Rockies of Colorado!

Let freedom ring from the curvaceous peaks of California!

But not only that; let freedom ring from Stone Mountain of Georgia!

Let freedom ring from Lookout Mountain of Tennessee!

Let freedom ring from every hill and every molehill of Mississippi. From every mountainside, let freedom ring.

When we let freedom ring, when we let it ring from every village and every hamlet, from every state and every city, we will be able to speed up that day when all of God's children, black men and white men, Jews and Gentiles, Protestants and Catholics, will be able to join hands and sing in the words of the old Negro spiritual, "Free at last! free at last! thank God Almighty, we are free at last!"

Source: Delivered on August 28, 1963, by Martin Luther King Jr. during the March on Washington.

Leaders from the SCLC, CORE, the NAACP, SNCC, and their allies sought to mobilize public pressure for passage of the civil rights bill by organizing a mass march and rally in Washington, D.C. Inspired by A. Philip Randolph's plan for a 1941 fair-employment march, the 1963 march was not at first universally favored by all civil rights leaders. The NAACP's Roy Wilkins and Whitney Young of the Urban League were initially fearful that the march might spawn violence; John Lewis of SNCC and James Farmer of CORE felt the march was a rather docile tactic. However, through the organizing efforts of Randolph, the movement's elder statesman, and Bayard Rustin, the march organizer, the civil rights leaders rallied around a march focusing on passage of the civil rights bill, fair employment, job training, and public school integration.

Concerned that the march might undermine tenuous congressional support for his legislation, President Kennedy initially tried to discourage Randolph and Rustin from moving ahead with their plans. Convinced that the march was going to occur anyway and that it would be peaceful, Kennedy endorsed the "peaceful assembly for the redress of grievances." For its part, SNCC was becoming increasingly skeptical of administration sympathies for the civil rights cause, given the lack of federal attention to SNCC's grass-roots campaign in the deep South. Initially, John Lewis had planned a militant speech for the march, but after the intervention of Randolph himself, he agreed to tone down parts of his speech.

The march on August 28 exceeded even the most optimistic expectations of civil rights leaders. Internal divisions faded from view as more than a quarter of a million people, some 60,000 of them white, descended on Washington via "freedom buses" and "freedom trains" from all over the nation and marched to the rally that spread from the steps of the Lincoln Memorial around the reflecting pool to the Washington Monument. The mass of people listened to gospel and folk music performed by Odetta, Mahalia Jackson, Josh White, Joan Baez, Bob Dylan, and Peter, Paul & Mary; they sang and swayed to the movement anthem, "We Shall Overcome." They were repeatedly aroused to cheers and acclamation by inspiring oratory from A. Philip Randolph, John Lewis, and other leaders, but especially by Martin Luther King Jr.'s "I Have a Dream" speech. Randolph described the march as "the advance guard of a massive moral revolution for jobs and freedom," while King's cadence of "I Have a Dream" and "Let Freedom Ring" rang out over the crowd and television airwaves, powerfully stirring those who heard it. The march was unprecedented spectacle that brought a glimpse of civil justice to millions of Americans.

Nonetheless, civil rights advocates were brought back to harsh reality just eighteen days after the march when a bomb exploded in the Sixteenth Street Baptist Church in Birmingham, killing four children who were attending Sunday school. Once again, white violence had struck, and once again, in the towns and cities of the South, in churches and synagogues in the North, and at a benefit concert at Carnegie Hall, the movement summoned its determination to move ahead. The young president never saw his civil rights bill passed into law as he, too, was struck down by an assassin's bullet less than three months later. It remained for Lyndon Johnson, the nation's first southern president since Reconstruction, to bring historic civil rights legislation to fruition.

MISSISSIPPI AND THE ROAD TO BLACK POWER

From its origins in 1960, SNCC was drawn to grass-roots organizing among local communities in the deep South, with a particular emphasis on voter education and registration. The tactic was classic community organizing: live and work among the local "common people"; provide organizing skills, political education, and the inspiration of courageous personal action; gain the people's trust by respecting their political voice—all with the aim of enabling the people to become a political force in their own right. The courage of SNCC field-workers was matched by the courage of individual poor blacks who rose to the challenge and often risked death in the struggle for their liberation.

For most of its early years, SNCC's political style was the embodiment of the "participatory democracy" ideal that was articulated in the founding *Port Huron Statement* of the other major student group organized in the early 1960s, the Students for a Democratic Society (SDS). In effect, SNCC was simultaneously trying to transform areas of the South—to bring democracy to the South—and to discover and create a more democratic mode of living among SNCC staffers themselves. The early SNCC experience, like that of SDS, was enormously energizing, creative, intimate, and demanding. The fact that black and white students struggled together to break down barriers meant that the SNCC experience was charged with the energy of liberation—what SNCC workers described as a "freedom high." Indeed, SNCC was such a natural draw for college students that several dropped out of college to become full-time SNCC staffers. It was also no coincidence that one of the first expressions of what later became the women's liberation movement emanated from women in SNCC.

It was also no coincidence also that SNCC workers were drawn to the areas where racial oppression was most pronounced—rural parts of Georgia, Lowndes County of Alabama, and the state of Mississippi, known for its virulent "Mississippi justice." With the highest percentage of blacks (45 percent) of any state in the nation, Mississippi also had the most racial lynchings, assaults, and "disappearances." It also had the lowest percentage of registered black voters and was the poorest state in the nation. Several NAACP leaders in Mississippi were killed during the postwar civil rights years, among them George Lee, Gus Courts, and Medgar Evers.

A twenty-six year-old-schoolteacher from New York named Robert Moses had been drawn to the South after seeing a photograph of the Greensboro sit-ins. Traveling through the deep South for SNCC in 1960, Moses met Amzie

Moore, a Mississippi NAACP leader who encouraged Moses to bring SNCC workers to Mississippi. The following summer, Moses brought the SNCC campaign to McComb, located in the impoverished Mississippi Delta. Together with members of the NAACP voter registration campaign, the SNCC workers began to provide weekly voter education classes, traveling door-to-door in the effort to persuade black residents to take Mississippi's registration test. SNCC also trained local teenagers in nonviolent direct action techniques, and a handful held sit-ins at the local Woolworth's lunch counter. Local enthusiasm for the voter project grew, as did the number of SNCC field-workers.

However, white resistance also heated up. Bob Moses was arrested while accompanying three local residents to the registrar's office and later beaten up by the local sheriff's cousin. NAACP worker Herbert Lee was murdered. Arrests mounted. In a pattern that was to repeat itself over the next several years, SNCC appealed to the Justice Department for protection but was rebuffed.

Nonetheless, the voter registration movement grew and spread through Mississippi. In 1962, the diverse civil rights groups combined their forces to form an umbrella organization called the Council of Federated Organizations (COFO) to coordinate the statewide voter registration drive. Under the direction of Bob Moses, and aided by white students recruited from Yale and Stanford Universities, COFO launched its "Freedom Vote" campaign in 1963, designed as an open mock-election alternative to the state's closed gubernatorial election. White violence continued. On the night in June that President Kennedy announced his civil rights bill on national television, NAACP leader Medgar Evers was shot and killed outside his home. During the Freedom Vote campaign, the homes of black residents who registered to vote were shot up and firebombed, and a car carrying Bob Moses and two associates was bombarded by gunfire while driving on a state highway. Nonetheless, the Freedom Vote campaign was a success; 93,000 people "elected" Aaron Henry and Edwin King, the COFO nominees for governor and lieutenant governor.

The Deaths of Goodman, Chaney, and Schwerner— Mississippi Freedom Summer

Como, August 3

About three weeks ago there was a flying rumor that they had been found in a rural jail. Tonight it was said that three graves had been found near Philadelphia. How the ghosts of those three shadow all our work! "Did you know them?" I am constantly asked. Did I need to?

Source: Elizabeth Sutherland Martinez, *Letters from Mississippi* (New York: McGraw Hill, 1965).

In the aftermath of the Freedom Vote, COFO planned an even bigger voter registration drive for the following summer, aided by the recruitment of students from across the nation. This time "Freedom Summer," as it was called, aimed at registering black voters statewide for the 1964 elections, electing an open "Freedom Democratic Party" delegation that would challenge the whites-only regular Mississippi Democratic Party at the 1964 presidential convention, and establishing "freedom schools" to teach reading and math to black children who were neglected by the state's public schools. White politicians promised that they would be ready for the upcoming "invasion" and beefed up their police forces accordingly.

The Freedom Summer volunteers enrolled in an intensive weeklong training and orientation session in Oxford, Ohio. On the day after the first wave of volunteers left for Mississippi, three of them were reported missing while on the road investigating the burning of a black church. The ominous disappearance of Andrew Goodman, James Chaney, and Michael Schwerner—two of whom were white students from the North—aroused the attention of the national media and the Johnson administration. Federal personnel were dispatched to Mississippi to search for the missing men, who were later discovered (along with several other missing black Mississippians) to have been murdered. Despite casting a pall over the beginning of Freedom Summer, the disappearances heightened the determination of the student volunteers. Throughout the summer about one thousand volunteers engaged in door-to-door canvassing, taught in freedom schools, and provided legal and medical assistance in "freedom clinics." By the end of the summer, some eighty thousand black Mississippians had joined the Mississippi Freedom Democratic Party (MFDP), along with a handful of whites.

When the bodies of Goodman, Chaney, and Schwerner were discovered just eighteen days before the start of the national Democratic Party convention, the national media again scrutinized the events in Mississippi, raising the stakes for the Johnson administration. With the support of northern liberals, the MFDP mobilized to challenge the regular state Democratic delegation at the August convention. At the tumultuous Credentials Committee hearing to determine the legitimacy of the MFDP's claims, the American public witnessed the stirring testimony of Fannie Lou Hamer, a Mississippi sharecropper. "Is this America?" she asked. "The land of the free and the home of the brave? Where we have to sleep with our telephones off the hook, because our lives be threatened daily?" Hamer's graphic account of Mississippi violence upstaged the president who preempted live television coverage by calling an impromptu press conference. The administration quickly offered a "compromise" plan that would seat Aaron Henry and Ed King as "at large" delegates along with the regular state delegation. Infuriated that they were being asked to "betray" their constituents back in Mississippi, the MFDP rejected the compromise. As SNCC's Charles Sherrod put it, "we want much more than token positions.... We want power for our people."

Although much of the MFDP worked for the reelection of President Johnson that fall, many in SNCC were alienated by the national Democratic Party's disinterested, detached stance, which compounded their sense of federal abandonment during Freedom Summer. The SNCC field-workers brought a profound moral commitment to their cause, a commitment that was reinforced by their sense of intense solidarity in standing together, by themselves, against racist violence in the deep South. As SNCC's James Forman recalled, "Bob Moses said we had to bring morality into politics. That's what's wrong with the country now. There is no morality in politics, otherwise we wouldn't be here."

While the MFDP challenge cracked opened a crucial door in Democratic Party politics, SNCC was moving in a different direction, more critical of the political system as a whole. Reflecting long-simmering tensions, one SNCC contingent, inspired by the quiet, egalitarian leadership of Robert Moses, held to their belief that SNCC should break free from traditional top-down, centralized politics; the other, including SNCC's James Forman, believed that political power for black people required more effective and centralized organization. The SNCC that continued its community organizing, notably in Alabama's Lowndes County, became essentially an all-black organization attuned to the independence struggles in Africa and influenced by the charismatic Malcolm X. Soon, the chant "Black Power" would emerge from its militant ranks.

Freedom Summer thus marked a major turning point in the southern Civil Rights movement. However, it was also an enormously significant formative experience for hundreds of white student volunteers who came south for the summer. Few had experienced conditions anything like what they observed in Mississippi, not only the Jim Crow discrimination that was readily visible but also the depth of rural sharecropper poverty, the brutal lawlessness of the white power structure, and perhaps most of all the degree of federal complicity in southern racial oppression. It was a stunning awakening that shook their political beliefs to their foundations.

At the same time, the Freedom Summer volunteers experienced the powerful liberating effect of working and struggling together in the "beloved community" of SNCC. Tensions between students who were free to return to their northern campuses and Mississippi fieldhands who would remain behind to continue their struggle, between whites and blacks, and between women and men lay just beneath the surface, only to erupt from time to time in long soul-searching community sessions. Yet many of the volunteers said years later that they found such a profound sense of community and idealistic moral action in their Freedom Summer experiences that they would continue to seek these for the rest of their lives. Indeed, quite a few returned to their college campuses in the fall of 1964 and began to question and challenge the hypocrisies of their college educations. As demonstrated by Berkeley's Free Speech Movement, the seeds of liberation sown during Freedom Summer were soon to prosper on college campuses, especially as the war in Vietnam began to heat up.

SELMA, ALABAMA, AND THE VOTING RIGHTS ACT

Buoyed by passage of the Civil Rights Act of 1964, civil rights leaders turned their attention to voting rights. As Freedom Summer demonstrated, effective black voter registration across the South demanded federal enforcement. Working with liberal allies in Congress, the SCLC began to hatch plans to push for voting rights legislation. For their part, however, Johnson administration officials were advocating a breathing period to demonstrate publicly the impact of the new Civil Rights Act.

SCLC's Birmingham experience had demonstrated that nonviolent direct action was most effective when it stood in visible contrast with violent repression by racist forces in the South. Since Sheriff James Clark of Selma, Alabama, was known for his violent temper in dealing with blacks, Selma seemed like an opportune locale in which to focus a direct action campaign for voting rights. The SCLC campaign could also profit from two years of prior local organizing by SNCC in the Selma's Dallas County and Lowndes County to the South. In fact, while mobilizing the local black population, SNCC had been so brutally harassed by Clark that the federal government had intervened in court to restrain Clark's forces. Martin Luther King Jr.'s instinct that Selma would provide the needed catalyst for federal legislation was, indeed, accurate.

Thus, in 1965, following a direct action protest in St. Augustine, Florida, King and the SCLC brought their new campaign to Selma, where they once again joined forces with SNCC. The Selma campaign was the last large-scale civil rights effort involving both SCLC and SNCC, and it was the last major direct action campaign of the southern Civil Rights movement. The new Nobel Peace Prize winner announced plans to "march by the thousands" to the places of registration. With national attention focused on Selma, Mayor Joseph Smitherman, who was eager to bring new industry to the city, urged Sheriff Clark to avoid violence in handling civil rights protests. At first, he succeeded. A group led by King ate at a white-only restaurant and then marched to the courthouse without arrest. The next day, however, Clark forcefully pushed Selma activist Amelia Boynton away from the courthouse door, and his actions were caught by national news photographers.

With King out of town on speaking engagements, the marchers continued their activities. Black teachers risked disciplinary action by marching to the courthouse door where they, too, were halted by a nightstick-wielding Clark. A subsequent march produced arrests of some three hundred schoolchildren, along with Reverend King. Again, the news media carried photographs of mass arrests and of King kneeling in prayer before being arrested. A visiting congressional delegation issued a call for voting rights legislation at the federal level. Following another attack by Clark's men—this time against C. T. Vivian of the SCLC—blacks marched in nearby Marion after an evening speech by Vivian. With the streetlights suddenly turned off, local and state police and angry whites attacked the marchers. One participant, Jimmie Lee Jackson, was followed into a nearby cafe and shot by police as he tried to defend his mother from a policeman's club. Jackson died a week later.

Following the Jackson shooting, SCLC announced it would take the protest to Montgomery to confront Governor George Wallace. The 50-mile march would begin in Selma, cross the Edmund Pettus Bridge and continue along Route 80 to Montgomery. Wallace announced that the state would not permit the march and put the state highway patrol on alert. While Johnson administration officials conferred with civil rights leaders over language for a new voting rights bill and Reverend King was delivering a sermon in Atlanta, the march began. About six hundred people, led by Hosea Williams of SCLC and SNCC chairman John Lewis, marched in pairs across the Edmund Pettus Bridge, where they were met by a phalanx of Alabama state troopers. The marchers were ordered to disperse in two minutes. The police then charged into the marchers, firing tear gas and swinging billy clubs at anyone they could reach. Police on horseback charged after the fleeing marchers, cracking heads with their billy clubs as they burst through the crowd. News and vivid accounts of "Bloody Sunday," as the event became known, spread instantly across the country. ABC interrupted its broadcast of the movie *Judgment at Nuremberg* with a news flash of the police attack.

Two days later, King led a second march across the bridge, and again state police blocked the path. This time, the marchers were temporarily enjoined by the federal court from marching; so, after being led in prayer by Reverend Abernathy, King turned the marchers around, much to the consternation of many participants. Later an angry white mob attacked and beat three ministers leaving a black restaurant; one of these, James Reeb, a white thirty-two-year-old Unitarian from Boston, died from a blow on the head.

A national outcry followed. White Americans denounced the violence and wrote members of Congress urging federal action. Congressional leaders demanded progress on voting rights legislation. SNCC leaders were embittered by the contrast between the vehement national response to Reeb's death and the lack of response to Jimmie Lee Jackson's death. The situation in Selma remained tense. President Johnson pressured Governor Wallace to help protect the marchers and then went on national television to announce his voting rights legislation, concluding with the movement's own theme. "Their cause must be our cause, too," Johnson urged. "Because it's not just Negroes, but it's really all of us who must overcome the crippling legacy of bigotry and injustice. And, we *shall* overcome."

At a tense church rally the next night, it was announced that federal Judge Frank Johnson had issued an injunction protecting the march to Montgomery from obstruction by state officials. Bolstered by a fresh wave of volunteers arriving from all over the nation, and protected by the federalized National Guard and U.S. army troops, the march proceeded to cover the 50 miles to Montgomery without any violence. Ten years after the culmination of the Montgomery bus boycott, some 25,000 marchers celebrated their arrival in the capitol city with an inspiring rally. Afterward, a white homemaker from Detroit, Viola Liuzzo, was killed by white gunmen while helping to transport people home from the rally.

The Selma march achieved precisely what King had hoped it would: swift passage of strong voting rights legislation. The SCLC had applied its Birmingham lesson in practicing effective protest politics. In effect, the national audience was moved to action by the picture of African Americans marching for the fundamental constitutional right to vote. The universality and dignity of their cause stood in stark contrast to the brutal attacks by Alabama state troopers and redneck racists. President Johnson signed the Voting Rights Act into law in early August 1965. By the following summer, some nine thousand blacks had registered in Dallas County, leading to the subsequent electoral defeat of Sheriff Jim Clark. In the aftermath of the Voting Rights Act, southern blacks in large numbers registered and voted and began to win election to public office. The face of the old South began to change.

BLACK POWER AND THE NORTHERN MOVEMENT

In just more than ten years, the Civil Rights movement had accomplished its most pressing objectives: passage of civil rights and voting rights legislation. Through direct action, voter registration, and eventual federal intervention and enforcement, the courageous actions of thousands of civil rights participants had begun to eradicate Jim Crow oppression throughout the South.

As remarkable as this achievement was, however, it only succeeded in removing the more blatant forms of racism and racial oppression from American life. Its very success—and the violent response it sometimes aroused—inspired a broader struggle against forces that overlapped with race in depriving millions of Americans of full membership in the larger social order. Absent the more overt Jim Crow racism, millions of African Americans were effectively trapped in the inner-city ghettoes of the North—suffering from woefully inadequate schools and crowded, substandard housing; high unemployment rates and little opportunity for meaningful employment; drug trafficking and high levels of criminal activity; and an often oppressive police presence.

These conditions, of course, predated the Civil Rights movement and were exacerbated by the migration of tens of thousands of African Americans in the immediate pre- and postwar years. Civil rights leaders were conscious of the need to address the more intractable conditions and institutional (rather than overt) racism of the northern cities. Martin Luther King Jr. led the SCLC into Chicago in 1966 in an unsuccessful effort to force the federal government to act on the issue of housing desegregation, and in 1968 he helped to mobilize the Poor People's Campaign. The SCLC Chicago effort failed in part because the movement encountered what King termed the "worst racism" he had ever witnessed, in part because the scale of poverty and misery was so overwhelming, and in part because the Johnson administration's "mandate" following the 1964 election had been depleted by Republican gains in the midterm election of 1966. Johnson failed to gain passage of his 1966 Civil Rights Bill which bolstered previous legislation by targeting housing segregation.

However, by placing equality on the nation's agenda, the Civil Rights movement also helped to trigger the wave of poverty-related reforms that emerged from the Johnson administration in 1964 and 1965. These included the various programs within Johnson's "War on Poverty," Head Start, the Job Corps, Community Action, and Title I of the 1965 Elementary and Secondary Education Act, which targeted federal funds for remedial educational programs in low-income school systems. Although these programs later came under fire during the conservative retrenchment of the 1970s and '80s, they succeeded in providing inner-city (and other poor) populations with improvements in their life opportunities. The Community Action Program was the most daring, since it placed federal funds at the disposal of impoverished community activists themselves, at least until their newfound assertiveness caused local political officials too many headaches and the program was collapsed back under the control of city governments.

In this midst of this volatile environment, a newly assertive black voice was emerging in the North. Reflecting the urban scene, it was an angrier voice than that of the nonviolent Civil Rights movement, one less rooted in the stabilizing influence of strong community ties. In fact, part of its anger reflected the lack of the strong community institutions and religious traditions that sustained the movement in the South, for it seemed as if one's racial identity, one's blackness, had to be denied in order to gain access to the white treadmill to success. Witnessing photographs of the violence meted out to the southern civil rights activists only fueled the anger of some young blacks. One outlet for this wounded anger was to withdraw from the struggle and embrace (or seek) one's own culture, drawing wherever possible on non-mainstream roots. Another was to strike out in rage.

The writings and speeches of Malcolm X played a crucial role in enhancing black consciousness, not only throughout the cities of the North but also, after Malcolm addressed the activists gathered in Selma, throughout the ranks of SNCC. Influenced by his ministry in the Nation of Islam, Malcolm's fiery oratory shocked and terrified the white establishment. At the same time, it engendered a sense of selfhood and racial pride in his black audience. Those who had led a lifetime of accommodating to being beaten down by the system were heartened by Malcolm's own transformation from a self-destructive street hustler to a powerful figure who demanded to be dealt with on his terms. Young blacks drawn to activism and self-assertion found in Malcolm an inspiration for their own struggles.

Nonetheless, the growing assertiveness and rising expectations that the times would get better ran into contrary signals from the political system. White violence in the South against civil rights activists had become rampant. And while the Community Action program provided an impetus for local participation, thereby awakening a new awareness of empowerment, federal funding began to fall well short of urban needs—especially with the commitment to war in Vietnam growing exponentially. With control of Community Action funds being withdrawn from local groups and turned over to city halls, the fuse of black frustration grew shorter. In this context, a random act of police harassment or brutality was enough to make the inner cities explode. In 1964, Harlem, Rochester, and North Philadelphia experienced fiery insurrections. The following year, a massive riot erupted in the Watts section of Los Angeles, generating a frenzy of national media attention. Riots broke out in Chicago, Omaha, Cleveland, and several smaller cities in 1966, and then the summer of 1967 saw the two largest eruptions of the decade in Newark and Detroit. Black rage spilled out violently across the country in the wake of Martin Luther King Jr.'s assassination in April 1968.

The "long, hot summers" were only the most dramatic and visible evidence of self-conscious black anger. By 1966 both SNCC and CORE were moving toward excluding white participants to better ensure black self-determination. During a "march against fear" held in Mississippi in 1966—in the aftermath of an assassination attempt against James Meredith—SNCC's Stokely Carmichael and Willie Ricks aroused the marchers with the rousing cry for "black power." The national media instantly picked up on the slogan as an expression of antiwhite sentiment among younger black activists. In reality, black power meant many things to many people. In its tamer version, it simply reflected an age-old American tradition of ethnic solidarity at election time; black voting power could be mobilized just as Irish or Italian voting power were regularly mobilized in city elections. In its more aggressive version, it meant black nationalism—from the embrace of African and African-American cultural expression (music, hairstyle, dress, names, and so forth) to Pan-Africanism and identification with the world's people of color who were exploited by Euro-American imperialism.

Black power also meant community power: direct participation by the black community in running the political institutions that affected their lives. Thus there were calls for "civilian review boards" for mostly white city police departments, and New York City's school system embarked on a turbulent experiment in "community control" of schools. In both cases, community control was an alternative to the apparent futility of trying to integrate city schools or police departments. Schools seemed at best unresponsive, at worst hostile to the particular cultural background and learning needs of inner-city minority populations; to many youngsters, they felt like alien environments that judged them on how well (or badly) they shed the manifestations of home, community, and race. Largely white and often arbitrarily violent, police began to feel like an outside "occupying army" to the young black males who were constantly harassed on street corners of the big cities. The faces of authority were almost always white and often seemingly hostile. Absent real economic and educational opportunities, inner city blacks were as effectively trapped as their counterparts in the South, and the remedy was not as readily apparent.

One group that experimented with various forms of black power was the Black Panther Party for Self-Defense, organized by Huey Newton and Bobby Seale in Oakland, California, in 1966. Drawing on door-to-door canvassing of Oakland residents, Newton and Seale issued a ten-point program of party goals and demands, which included the "power to determine the destiny of our Black community," full employment of black Americans, business reparations and an end to "robbery" of the black community, an end to police brutality and murder, and a call for armed self-defense against the outside occupying power. Using Newton's legal studies, the pair produced an initial strategy that proved highly inflammatory yet effective. Aimed at the common practice of police cruisers arbitrarily stopping and harassing young blacks who gathered on street corners, Newton and Seale created a system of legal "patrol cars" in which Panthers in black berets and leather jackets would follow police cars throughout the inner city, armed with guns and lawbooks to ensure the constitutional rights of young blacks were not violated. The patrol cars infuriated the Oakland police, generating an instantaneous effort to change California's gun laws, but they had a palpable effect on ghetto youth, especially as the incidents of police harassment declined.

A year later, the Panthers dropped the "self-defense" part of their title, a change which not only reflected their broadened political agenda but also their initiation of a variety of community programs: rent eviction protests, welfare rights education, black-history schools, and free breakfasts for children—echoing the spirit of the community control movements in other parts of the nation. Yet the Panther's early embrace of guns to create an intimidating presence against police brutality became a crucial part of their public image both among inner-city youths and in the wider audience of white America. In effect, the party became captive to this image. Some of its recruits were drawn to the party because of the guns and berets, while much of the mainstream media and their audience never saw past the guns and angry rhetoric to the Panther's substantive politics or programs.

In fact, with its systematic counterintelligence program (COINTELPRO) that began in 1968, the federal government began to provoke, undermine, marginalize, and eventually eliminate the more militant expressions of dissent among African Americans, the New Left, and the American Indian movement. Among these groups, the Panthers were a high priority. FBI Director J. Edgar Hoover termed them the "number one threat" in the nation. Wherever a Panther chapter was organized, local police cooperated with federal officials in infiltrating, harassing, and in some cases killing members of the party in a series of violent ambushes and shoot-outs. At least ten Panthers were killed between 1967 and 1969, among them Chicago's charismatic leader Fred Hampton. Eventually, the Black Panther Party faded from view, as did the public agenda for liberating the inner-city populations from the chains of hopelessness.

CONCLUSION

By the end of the 1960s, the South was well on its way toward becoming the "new South" in which black and white Americans mingled freely in the formerly segregated spaces of Jim Crow. The Civil Rights movement had liberated millions of black Americans from the psychological residues of racial oppression. The Civil Rights Act of 1964 and Voting Rights Act of 1965 were historic reforms that unleashed a campaign of effective federal enforcement. In addition, the South shifted away from an agriculture-based economy in which blacks were relegated to dependent poverty. Black Americans of at least middle-class status had far greater access to the rewards of the American political and economic system, and nowhere was this more apparent than in the symbolic arena of popular culture, particularly television and movies.

Yet a subtler form of racism persisted, reflected in everyday black experience. Particularly where prejudiced whites conflate race with class, black Americans regularly find themselves viewed with suspicion, ignored, or even denied service or access available to whites. In fact, as the black middle class became more pervasively visible in mainstream institutions, racial inequality increasingly became class inequality compounded by racism. Meanwhile, in the aftermath of a conservative backlash against the "excesses of the sixties," public officials at best ignore and at worst scapegoat America's poor. Nonetheless, within the history of the Civil Rights movement, one can find an inspiring grass-roots movement that not only spread contagiously to other sectors of society in the 1960s but can continue to inspire struggles to realize the dream of full democratic empowerment for all Americans.

FOR FURTHER READING

Branch, Taylor. *Parting the Waters: America in the King Years, 1954–1963*. New York: Touchstone Books, 1989.

_____. *Pillar of Fire: America in the King Years 1963–65*. New York: Simon & Schuster, 1999.

Carmichael, Stokely, and Charles V. Hamilton. *Black Power: The Politics of Liberation in America*. New York: Vintage, 1993.

Carson, Clayborne. *In Struggle: SNCC and the Black Awakening of the 1960s*. Cambridge: Harvard University Press, 1995.

Evans, Sara. *Personal Politics: The Roots of Women's Liberation in the Civil Rights Movement and the New Left*. New York: Random House, 1980.

Foreman, James. *The Making of Black Revolutionaries*. Seattle: University of Washington Press, 1997.

Garrow, David J. *Bearing the Cross: Martin Luther King, Jr. and the Southern Christian Leadership Conference*. New York: William Morrow & Co., 1999.

_____. *Protest at Selma*. New Haven, Conn.: Yale University Press, 1978.

Halberstam, David. *The Children*. New York: Fawcett Books,1999.

King, Mary. *Freedom Song: A Personal Story of the 1960s Civil Rights Movement*. New York: William Morrow & Co., 1987.

Kluger, Richard. *Simple Justice: The History of Brown v. Board of Education and Black America's Struggle for Equality*. New York: Random House, 1977.

McAdam, Doug. *Freedom Summer*. New York: Oxford University Press, 1990.

Morgan, Edward P. *The Sixties Experience: Hard Lessons about Modern America*. Philadelphia: Temple University Press, 1991.

Morris, Aldon D. *The Origins of the Civil Rights Movement: Black Communities Organizing for Change*. New York: Free Press, 1986.

Powledge, Fred. *Free at Last?: The Civil Rights Movement and the People Who Made It*. New York: Harper Collins, 1992.

Raines, Howell. *My Soul is Rested: Movement Days in the Deep South Remembered*. New York: Viking Press, 1983.

Riches, William T. Martin. *The Civil Rights Movement: Struggle and Resistance*. New York: St. Martin's Press, 1997.

Weisbrot, Robert. *Freedom Bound: A History of America's Civil Rights Movement*. New York: E. P. Dutton, 1991.

Williams, Juan. *Eyes on the Prize: America's Civil Rights Years, 1954–1965*. New York: Penguin USA, 1988.

Wirt, Frederick M. *"We Ain't What We Was": Civil Rights in the New South*. Durham, N.C.: Duke University Press, 1997.

X, Malcolm, and Alex Haley. *The Autobiography of Malcolm X*. New York: Grove Press, 1992.

Zinn, Howard. *SNCC: The New Abolitionists*. Westport, Conn.: Greenwood Publishing Group, 1985.

part 4.

African-American
Identity and Culture

chapter 11

The Sounds of Blackness

African-American Music

Waldo F. Martin Jr.

USIC HAS DEEPLY INFLUENCED and informed the culture of Africans in the Americas from the initial days of New World African enslavement. Throughout the African sojourn in the Americas, enslaved Africans continued to practice music as they had in their various African societies. Music operated in a unified intellectual and emotional world where mind and body were inseparable, where the sacred and the secular were understood as a whole. The enduring power of New World African music can be traced to this belief and the ability of music to integrate function and meaning.

Notwithstanding similarities of form and content, significant differences emerged between native African and diasporan African music. These dynamic processes of cross-cultural influence can be seen across the changing cultures of the interacting peoples of African, European, and indigenous New World descent. And indeed a critical element of the fashioning of New World African cultures was the ongoing tradition of cross-cultural sharing among Africans themselves, which yielded mixed African-American cultures unlike their parent cultures in crucial ways. Music has played a key role in this complicated process of the creation and elaboration of a sense of identity at once American and African-American. Attracted by the beauty of the American ideal while at the same time repelled by the racism of the American reality, Africans have sought to realize the former by ceaselessly struggling to undermine the latter. African-American music vividly captures the powerful dialectic at the center of this continuing struggle.

The African influence in the United States can be illustrated in part by looking at the Americanization of Africans in the New World. This same influence can also be viewed by looking at the Africanization of the Americas. African-American music illuminates, on the one hand, the cultural interpenetration of Africa, Europe, and the New World. On the other hand, and even more crucial for our purposes here, the social history of African-American music sheds much-needed light on African agency and the powerful African impact on the cultural mapping of the Americas. The argument here is that American culture possesses an intrinsic Africanness within its creole complexity. This Africanness is a principal defining quality of American culture as well as African-American culture.

When contrasted with its African roots, African music in the North American colonies and subsequently the United States reveals significant continuities and shifts that can be traced primarily to the critical changes indigenous African music withstood in the New World. First, as slaves coming from different African societies, African Americans created music that resulted in part from the melding of diverse African influences. Notwithstanding the dominance of certain African musical cultures in specific areas, like the Bakongo among the Gullah in coastal South Carolina, African-American music reflected various African traditions. An important consequence of this merging of African musics was the pushing forward of similarities as well as the resolution of differences in the development of African-American music. Second, African-American music developed under the influence of the various types of European music it encountered. Third, Africans also encountered Native-American music in certain areas, and scholars have traced these influences in vocal and instrumental musical traditions. Not surprisingly, however, the evidence of cross-cultural musical influence among Native Americans and Africans is rare compared to that found among European Americans and African Americans.

Despite these influences, several developments gave emerging African-American music unusual resiliency and power. First, where similarities existed among the different traditions—as in certain vocalizing and drum techniques, and the key role of music and dance in rituals and ceremonies—African musical traditions found reinforcement, even enrichment. Second, the traditional African musical openness to outside influences and emphasis on innovation enabled African Americans to incorporate into their own musical practices innumerable outside ones. In effect, they reinterpreted these practices—like the playing of the violin, or the singing of hymns—within their own musical style and repertoire, making these practices their own. Finally, the ubiquitous presence of music within African-American cultures enhanced the music's significance.

THE AFRICAN ROOTS OF AFRICAN-AMERICAN MUSIC

These emphases—upon improvisation, inclusiveness, innovation, and flexibility—were vital to the enduring vitality and impact of African-American music. At the center of this pan-African musical consciousness is rhythmic complexity and a corresponding hypnotic feel. This complicated musical heartbeat—encompassing polyrhythms and cross rhythms—propels and unifies the various elements. Other defining elements include the call-and-response, or antiphony (back-and-forth exchanges between groups/individuals within the music-making event); a social, or collective, setting; an intimate tie to dance and bodily movement, a crucial part of its performance feature; and an emotive, even ecstatic, temper.

In varying combinations, these characteristics make African-American music distinctive and must be understood to originate in the West African and west-central African cultures from which the bulk of the slaves came. The sites of capture and transfer to the slave ships for the forced passage to the New World witnessed terrible scenes of loss, separation, grief, and mourning. The shrieks, groans, moans, and songs were in part strategies of survival and adjustment. These plaintive stirrings often found the captives seeking solace from

Mungo Park Describes African Music in the Eighteenth Century

Of their music and dances, some account has incidentally been given in different parts of my journal. On the first of these heads, I have now to add a list of their musical instruments, the principal of which are,—the *koonting*, a sort of guitar with three strings;—the *korro*, a large harp with eighteen strings;—the *balafou*, an instrument composed of twenty pieces of hard wood of different lengths, with the shells of gourds hung underneath to increase the sound;—the *tangtang*, a drum open at the lower end;—and lastly, the *tabalu*, a large drum, commonly used to spread an alarm through the country. Besides these, they make use of small flutes, bow-strings, elephants' teeth, and bells; and at all their dances and concerts, *clapping of hands* appears to constitute a necessary part of the chorus.

With the love of music is naturally connected a taste for poetry, and fortunately for the poets of Africa, they are in a great measure exempted from that neglect and indigence, which in more polished countries commonly attend the votaries of the Muses. They consist of two classes; the most numerous are the *singing men*, called *Jillikea* mentioned in a former part of my narrative; one or more of these, may be found in every town; they sing extempore songs in honour of their chief men, or any other persons who are willing to give "solid pudding for empty praise." But a nobler part of their office is, to recite the historical events of their country; hence, in war, they accompany the soldiers to the field, in order, by reciting the great actions of their ancestors, to awaken in them a spirit of glorious emulation. The other class are devotees of the Mahomedan faith, who travel about the country, singing devout hymns, and performing religious ceremonies, to conciliate the favour of the Almighty, either in averting calamity, or in insuring success to any enterprize. Both descriptions of these itinerant bards are much employed and respected by the people, and very liberal contributions are made for them.

Source: Travels in the Interior Districts of Africa, Performed Under the Direction and Patronage of the African Association in the Years of 1795, 1796, and 1797, by Mungo Park, Surgeon (New York, 1800).

their traditional gods and ancestors and pleading with, cursing, and condemning their captives and disclosed inter- and intragroup communication among the captured. Various descriptions of these haunting vocal messages noted their musicality as well as their insight into the captives' thoughts and feelings. Furthermore, the musical sounds accompanying the horror of capture and enslavement laid the basis for a cultural memory rooted in resistance, struggle, and hope amid "unspeakable" oppression. That memory found musical remembrance in many ways, perhaps most tellingly in the nineteenth-century crucible of the spirituals and the turn-of-the-century crucible of the blues.

During the dreaded Middle Passage (the hellish slave voyage to the Americas), the practice aboard slave ships of forced merrymaking among the enslaved offers similar evidence of an early site of African-American music making. Serving as entertainment for the slavers (who often got in the act) as well as exercise/recreation for the slaves, "dancing the Negroes" also allowed for the initial reworking of African music and dance, often in concert with European influence. In the course of the slave trade, on the African coast, on the slave ships, and in the Americas, spoken communication and musical wails often employed pidgin languages that combined African and European elements. Nevertheless, this creolized music remained fundamentally African, reinforcing the growth of a pan-African sense of identity among the enslaved.

Once in the Americas, music remained a revealing expression of a distinctive African-American culture. During the eighteenth century, when the bulk of the African slaves were imported, the constant infusion of African cultural influences continually revitalized the music's Africanness. In the nineteenth century, with the abolition of the transatlantic slave trade and the subsequent expansion of the domestic slave trade, memory, tradition, and the continuing practices of music making sustained the Africanness of this most vital African-American cultural framework. In rural and urban settings, North and South, African-American music during slavery revealed an increasingly singular sense of pan-African consciousness, in spite of the differences among African Americans, that reflected common critical elements derived from the African source. These elements included a sacred understanding of the cosmos, a cyclical sense of time, and a reliance on the oral transmission of culture.

These fundamental emphases found expression in African-American musical aesthetics, notably rhythm. Where melody formed the basis of European music, African music was anchored in rhythm. Consequently, rhythm, particularly expressed through drumming, provided a common syntax and grammar. The intense rapid rhythmic pulse of the drum enabled African Americans to evoke and thus to communicate with the ancestral spirits, to delineate musical time, to punctuate cultural events, to provide a foundation for song and dance, and to communicate as with words. Indeed the notion of "talking drums," or "drum language," signified the wide-ranging communicative abilities of skillful players and listeners, permitting multiple uses and complex statements.

The power of the drum and its percussive corollaries united and sustained African Americans politically as well as culturally, and references to its role in slave social life and unrest can be found throughout the colonies. The drum served to draw together African Americans in ways that promoted instances of individual resistance, such as absconding to freedom, and collective resistance, such as uprisings. Increasingly aware of the drum's subversive capacity, especially in the eighteenth century, European Americans throughout the colonies officially banned African-style drumming. (Interestingly, African Americans, slave and free, played drums along with trumpets and fifes in militia bands. The approved style was European, simple and straightforward.) While the ban on African drumming appeared effective, in fact it pushed the practice underground. The rhythmic engine of the music resurfaced in the increased use of other percussion instruments, of nonpercussion instruments played percussively, and of the voice and the body itself used as percussion instruments.

If the drum was in many ways the most powerful of the African instruments to come to North America, the banjo was among the most popular. Accounts of fine banjo playing by African Americans are not hard to find. Similarly, clear evidence exists of African Americans playing a variety of other African instruments, including horns, small flutes, thumb pianos, bells, rattles, and pipes. African Americans also became exceedingly proficient on a variety of European instruments, including flutes, horns, and violins. When playing these instruments, African Americans evinced what observers often characterized as unique techniques or approaches: a distinctive African-derived style.

MUSIC IN THE SLAVE'S WORLD

Both African Americans, free and slave, and European Americans, especially slave masters, appreciated African-American musical virtuosity. Within the black and white communities considerable status and prestige resulted from the demonstration of musical talent. These musicians often had special privileges, such as extra provisions and greater mobility for slaves and more pay for free blacks. Many musicians performed in social gatherings, formal and informal, among both whites and blacks. Whereas African Americans themselves preferred those African-American musicians skilled in African-style music, European Americans favored those skilled in European-style techniques. The experience of music making in both African and European styles enhanced the cross-fertilization of both styles and expanded the musicians' repertoires.

African-American stylistic distinctiveness was evident in vocal as well as instrumental music. The song style of African Americans was highly expressive: more percussive than lyrical. Ample reference is made to the resounding singing of African Americans among themselves, as well as the overpowering vocal might of African Americans drowning out European Americans when both groups sang together in religious as well as secular settings. In addition to great volume and emotional intensity, African-American song style blended vocal gestures—including shouts, falsetto, trills, and slurs—and physical movements like foot stomping, hand clapping, body weaving, and head bobbing. While reinforcing a fundamental rhythmic thrust, this song style also reflected the intimate tie of the music to bodily motion and dance, of music making to performance.

Indeed, African-derived sensibilities and movements have dominated the history of American dance. Like the music of which it is an integral part, dance was a vital social practice binding the group together and projecting a collective sense of identity. Also like the music, dance reflected fundamental cultural ideals: rhythm, flexibility, innovation, spontaneity. The movements themselves reflected a physicality, an earthiness, a comfortableness with the body. Specific features included dragging and gliding steps, pelvic movement, impersonations (notably of animals), little contact between dancers, and numerous gestures—subtle, vigorous, and smooth. Broadly speaking, European dances tended toward the more formal and rigid, African dances toward the more open and expressive. Despite the cross-fertilization between traditions, in the development of both African-American dance and music African styles and movements prevailed.

The significance of the dance-music nexus was evident in sacred as well as secular contexts, playing a central aspect in ritual celebrations and ceremonies ranging from funerals to corn shucking. The Christmas–New Year term was an important season for parties and celebrations showcasing music and dance. Likewise, regional antebellum celebrations such as Election Day and Pinkster Day in New England, the John Canoe festival in eastern North Carolina, and Sunday celebrations in New Orleans's Place Congo were structured around the dance-music dynamic. Throughout those areas with a more pronounced African presence, such as the South Carolina–Georgia Sea Islands, music, dance, and especially ritualized celebrations vividly preserved that influence. Funerals often included libations, grave decorations, and animal sacrifices, evidencing the traditional African emphasis on veneration of the ancestors and a holistic worldview uniting the spirit and physical worlds, while the music and the dance ranged from the somber and reverential to the joyful and ecstatic. Similarly, secular events like corn shucking parties found African Americans singing and dancing, often quite vigorously, as an expression of sociality as well as conviviality. Even with whites present and under the sobering influence of Christianity, African modes of celebration persisted in highly expressive social events both binding the community together and reflecting a collective sensibility.

At least since the nineteenth century, the history of African-American dance—secular and religious—has emphasized the influence of the ring shout and its various permutations. Both informal and formal religious worship services, as well as sacred ceremonies like funerals, might feature variations of this kind of holy dancing. In this African-derived movement, participants sway in a counterclockwise circle propelled by the spirit, going from a slow-motion shuffle to a more rapid rhythmic series of steps, while powerful interlocking singing helped to drive the ritual momentum. Indeed the ring shout has been a vital crucible for countless reworkings of religious tunes. In these intensely charged ritual moments of ecstatic dancing and singing, elements of various religious songs and messages were transformed into African-American sacred music, most notably the spiritual.

Emblematic of the sacred worldview of the slave, the spirituals clearly represent a creole form with deep African roots. Building upon African Americans' religious understandings, the texts of the spirituals—including Biblical stories, psalms, and hymns—emphasize sorrow and optimism, affirmation and deliverance. An intensely moving body of music, the spirituals speak to the life-and-death issues dealt with in sacred music generally. The profundity of the spirituals derives in significant measure from the dialectic between African Americans' search for secular freedom and their deep-seated religious faith. Indeed, this dialectic between liberation struggle and religious commitment shows their interconnectedness; historically, they have informed one another. They have also buttressed a sense of peoplehood, community, or nationality among African Americans.

An important aspect of the world of the spirituals was the personalization of the ties between biblical figures and the African-American community. Religious figures are addressed possessively as "My God," "King Jesus," "Sweet Jesus," "Sister Mary," or "Brother Daniel." Similarly, in the spirituals African Americans likened themselves to the Chosen People, the Jews of Israel, whose destiny it was to overcome persecution and deracination. God had brought the Jews out of bondage and he would do the same for African Americans. Secular as well as spiritual freedom, then, was understood to be a consequence of Christian faith and "Steal Away to Jesus" was an urging for untold numbers of slaves to make the break and run to freedom. This extraordinary sacred music—like much of African-American music—has helped African Americans to transcend their earthly oppression, if only momentarily. This psychic relief has contributed to the deep spiritual reservoirs that strategies of endurance and self-affirmation have demanded.

In light of the holistic worldview of antebellum African Americans, especially slaves, it is not surprising that their secular music making was quite similar to their religious music making in style and power. At social occasions and seasonal ceremonies (like those marking the end of planting and harvesting seasons) music was an essential element of the merrymaking. Lyrically, this music ranged from the political and the satirical to the ordinary and frivolous. Frederick Douglass provides a striking example of the satirical slave song in his autobiography where the speaker complains, "We raise de wheat, Dey gib us de corn. We bake de bread, Dey gib us de crust." Clearly these more subversive lyrics were most likely to be found in those situations where blacks were less constrained by white surveillance.

Work songs were particularly prominent in the secular music repertoire. Song could be heard during housework, field work, industrial work, and work on the wharves and waterways. Certain public forms of secular musical expression were notable for their effectiveness at combining work with song. Street cries were used by itinerant salespersons to draw attention to their wares. Spirited field hollers were observed throughout the plantation South. Water calls were an effective means of communication on the waterways. Those African Americans laboring on the lakes, rivers, and oceans as well as the ports not only developed engaging tunes depicting their lives but also were a vital conduit for the migration of musical influences as black musical styles traveled up and down the Mississippi River.

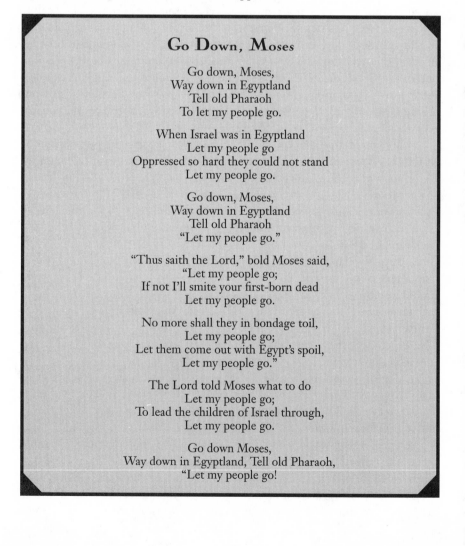

Go Down, Moses

Go down, Moses,
Way down in Egyptland
Tell old Pharaoh
To let my people go.

When Israel was in Egyptland
Let my people go
Oppressed so hard they could not stand
Let my people go.

Go down, Moses,
Way down in Egyptland
Tell old Pharaoh
"Let my people go."

"Thus saith the Lord," bold Moses said,
"Let my people go;
If not I'll smite your first-born dead
Let my people go.

No more shall they in bondage toil,
Let my people go;
Let them come out with Egypt's spoil,
Let my people go."

The Lord told Moses what to do
Let my people go;
To lead the children of Israel through,
Let my people go.

Go down Moses,
Way down in Egyptland, Tell old Pharaoh,
"Let my people go!

Steal Away to Jesus

Steal away, steal away, steal away to Jesus!
Steal away, steal away home,
I ain't got long to stay here.

Steal away, steal away, steal away to Jesus!
Steal away, steal away home,
I ain't got long to stay here.

My Lord, He calls me, He calls me by the thunder,
The trumpet sounds within-a my soul,
I ain't got long to stay here.

Steal away, steal away, steal away to Jesus!
Steal away, steal away home,
I ain't got long to stay here.

Steal away, steal away, steal away to Jesus!
Steal away, steal away home,
I ain't got long to stay here.

Green trees a-bending, po' sinner stand a-trembling,
The trumpet sounds within-a my soul,
I ain't got long to stay here,
Oh, Lord, I ain't got long to stay here.

Many Thousand Gone

No more peck o' corn for me
No more, no more
No more peck o' corn for me
Many thousand gone.

No more driver's lash for me,
No more, no more,
No more driver's lash for me
Many thousand gone.

No more pint o' salt for me
No more, no more,
No more pint o' salt for me
Many thousand gone.

No more hundred lash for me,
No more, no more,
No more hundred lash for me,
Many thousand gone.

No more mistress' call for me,
No more, no more,
No more mistress' call for me,
Many thousand gone.

African-American Music in the Nineteenth Century

[The slaves] would sing, with other words of their own improvising—jargon to others, but full of meaning to themselves. I have sometimes thought, that the mere hearing of these songs would do more to impress truly spiritual-minded men and women with the soul-crushing and death-dealing character of slavery, than the reading of whole volumes of its mere physical cruelties. They speak to the heart and to the soul of the thoughtful. I cannot better express my sense of them now, than ten years ago, when, in sketching my life, I thus spoke of this feature of my plantation experience:

"I did not, when a slave, understand the deep meanings of those rude, and apparently incoherent songs. I was myself within the circle, so that I neither saw nor heard as those without might see and hear. They told a tale which was then altogether beyond my feeble comprehension; they were tones, loud, long and deep, breathing the prayer and complaint of souls boiling over with the bitterest anguish. Every tone was a testimony against slavery, and a prayer to God for deliverance from chains. The hearing of those wild notes always depressed my spirits, and filled my heart with ineffable sadness. The mere recurrence, even now, afflicts my spirit, and while I am writing these lines, my tears are falling. To those songs I trace my first glimmering conceptions of the dehumanizing character of slavery. I can never get rid of that conception. Those songs still follow me, to deepen my hatred of slavery, and quicken my sympathies for my brethren in bonds. If any one wishes to be impressed with a sense of the soul-killing power of slavery, let him go to Col. Lloyd's plantation, and, on allowance day, place himself in the deep, pine woods, and there let him, in silence, thoughtfully analyze the sounds that shall pass through the chambers of his soul, and if he is not thus impressed, it will only be because 'there is no flesh in his obdurate heart.'"

Source: Frederick Douglass, *My Bondage and My Freedom* (Boston, 1855), pp. 193–94.

THE BLUES

Emancipation altered the historical landscape and led African-American music making in new directions. With freedom came increased opportunities for African Americans to make music openly and publicly in proliferating venues, from the juke joints of the rural South to the elegant theaters of the cities. Despite the institutionalization of Jim Crow and the marginalization of black culture, African-American music flowered and sought to give meaning to life under freedom. The most important developments in twentieth-century African-American music—blues, gospel, jazz, and other types of postwar popular music—continue to illustrate efforts by blacks to define themselves as both a distinctive people and as Americans in their ongoing struggle for empowerment and self-definition. In addition, these hybrid yet fundamentally African musical forms demonstrate the continued cross-fertilization among both themselves and with other musics.

These genres had their immediate origins in the postemancipation period and the desire of free and emancipated blacks to substantiate their apparent gains. For untold numbers of former slaves especially, the ability to move from place to place signified freedom. Over time that commitment to migration in search of freedom would transform the African-American landscape, and, in turn, African-American music. In the late nineteenth century, African Americans were overwhelmingly southern and rural. By 1970 they lived mostly in cities outside the South. Similarly, African-American music has gone from pockets of local, regional, and national notoriety in the late nineteenth century to dominance of the world music market in the late twentieth. While African Americans themselves have not always benefited fully from the commercial success of their music, its staying power resides in the fundamental humanism of African-American music: its ability to speak to basic human goals and desires; its willingness to grapple with the complexity of the human condition.

Nowhere is this clearer than in the blues. The origins of the blues date back to the turn of the century and demonstrate the increasing personalization of musical expression, on one hand, and the increasing emphasis on solo artistry, on the other. This growth of the individual voice personifies the postemancipation quest to arrive at a more satisfactory representation of African-American identity and, ultimately, an insightful African-American perspective on the modern existential condition. The blues has most effectively turned inward and explored the complexities of lived experience. Dedicated to a thoroughgoing examination of the thin line between such dichotomies as joy and pain, love and hate, lust and affection, triumph and failure, the blues scrupulously dissects human psychology and emotions. Issues of pleasure and desire animate the music. Sadness is simply one emotion within the wide-ranging emotional palette of the blues, which is ultimately a celebration of the human spirit.

Like the spirituals, the blues is a music of hope and affirmation building upon diverse African-dominated roots. The secular roots of the blues are traceable to minstrel, vaudeville, and ragtime tunes as well as ballads and work music. Religious roots include the spirituals themselves, hymns, and early gospel music. Often characterized as the "devil's music" by those who objected to its unabashed celebration of the pleasures and desires of the flesh, the blues nonetheless prospered in large part because of this sensual and sexual fixation. At the same time, the blues profited enormously from cross-pollination with sacred music. This intense exploration of not just the profound similarities between the sacred and the secular but also the inherent ties between them has been reinforced in African-American music in the course of the twentieth century, and the blues have become a bedrock genre upon which subsequent African-American music, like gospel and soul, has drawn.

The universal appeal of the blues, however, resides primarily in its ability to render the complicated human condition both meaningful and understandable. The form of the blues is the deceptively simple "three-cornered" stanza, with the second line a repetition of the first. Within this uncomplicated structure, the range of vocal and instrumental variations has been impressive. Vocally, the blues has relied heavily upon its folk roots. A favorite blues approach has been the re-creation of emotion through the use of falling pitches. Voices ranging from the smooth to the rough have employed an impressive number of vocal gestures including cries, bends, moans, dips, grunts, and the use of falsetto and vibrato for effect. Instrumentally, blues musicians often accompanied themselves with guitars, banjos, pianos, and harmonicas. As blues musicians have grown in vocal and instrumental dexterity, so too have blues performances. Indeed the emphasis on skilled musical performance, an ability to "bring the house down," has contributed mightily to the influence of all African-American music.

Roughly speaking, there are three widely recognized blues styles: down-home (country); classic women's blues of the 1920s, '30s (and beyond); and urban blues. Needless to say, these divisions often function better as categorical devices instead of analytic ones. While down-home blues styles incubated throughout the early twentieth-century South, the most influential developed in the Mississippi Delta. The most important of these Delta bluesmen was the elusive Robert Johnson, who died violently in 1938 at the age of 28. His slender recorded output belies his enormous impact. Provocative songs like his "Sweet Home Chicago" and "Hellhound on my Trail" attest to a restless, rootless spirit seeking but never quite discovering fulfillment. In addition to a fundamental grittiness and lyrical bite, his music featured a strong delivery, quick bottleneck runs on the guitar, and finely wrought yet earthy vocals.

Ma Rainey, the Mother of the Blues, and Bessie Smith, the Empress of the Blues, exemplified a dazzling blues tradition, which achieved considerable commercial success in the '20s and '30s. In various forms this tradition has tremendously enlivened the whole of African-American music as well as the music of black women vocalists. The huge 1920 hit recording of Mamie

Blues Music

In its origin, modern blues music is the expression of the emotional life of a race. In the south of long ago, whenever a new man appeared for work in any of the laborers' gangs, he would be asked if he could sing. If he could, he got the job. The singing of these working men set the rhythm for work, the pounding of hammers, the swinging of scythes; and the one who sang most lustily soon became strawboss. One man set the tune, and sang whatever sentiments lay closest to his heart. He would sing about steamboats, fast trains, "contrairy" mules, cruel overseers. If he had no home, he sang about that; if he found a home next day, he sang about needing money or being lonesome for his gal. But whatever he sang was personal, and then the others in the gang took up the melody, each fitting it with personal words of his own. If fifty men worked on the gang, the song had fifty verses, and the singing lasted all day through, easing the work, driving rhythm into it. By word of mouth, the songs of these humble, untrained musicians traveled from place to place, wherever the roving workers went, exactly as folksongs always have traveled, all over the world, as expressions of national soul life.

Source: W. C. Handy, "The Heart of the Blues," *Etude Music Magazine* (March 1940), p. 152.

Smith's "Crazy Blues" contributed to a two-pronged craze for the music of blues women and blues music in general. While Ma Rainey's work went in a folk direction, that of Bessie Smith was more influenced by jazz. Nevertheless both singers had powerhouse voices, vigorous deliveries, and commanding performance styles. These blues divas worked in a grand tradition of such earlier pioneers as Victoria Spivey, Sippie Wallace, and Memphis Minnie.

The music of black blueswomen has been an important creative outlet for a compelling expression of black women's concerns and perspectives. At its finest, this music has been about the intricacies and insights of "truth talking." In the post–World War II period, this tradition has spilled over with wonderful effect into other genres and been influenced by them in turn. The 1950s rhythm-and-blues explosion witnessed the revitalization of this tradition with the work of such artists as Big Mama Thornton, Ruth Brown, and LaVern Baker. Soul music divas Etta James, Nina Simone, and Aretha Franklin likewise revivified the blueswoman tradition, joining it with gospel roots. More recently, not to be neglected is the work of those like dynamic Chicago blueswoman KoKo Taylor. For several decades now, she has presented authentic urban blues from a black woman's point of view.

Black bluesmen likewise had a profound impact on black popular music. They, too, spoke with authority and insight about life from an experiential perspective. Pushed by southern poverty and Jim Crow and pulled by the lure of better jobs and opportunities, especially during World Wars I and II, the migration of huge numbers of blacks to large northern cities, especially Chicago, deeply affected black popular music. Rural blues adapted to urban rhythms and sensibilities, and the music increasingly spoke to the black urban experience. The music of Mississippi Delta bluesmen Muddy Waters, Howling Wolf, and John Lee Hooker vividly captures the post–World War II urbanization of the country blues. This was perhaps best represented not just in the growth of rhythm-and-blues offshoots but also in the revitalizing urban energy represented by the growing use of amplified instruments among blues musicians. The stunning electric guitar work of 1940s blues legend T-Bone Walker captivated audiences and influenced the likes of B. B. King, who continues to personify the extremely influential tradition of electric guitar-based blues.

If blues can be seen as "secular spirituals," then gospel can be seen as "spiritual blues." A performance-based music like blues, gospel also seeks an incandescent emotional peak. Gospel, however, relies far more heavily upon the traditional group-based ethos so central to the collective and spontaneous African-American music-making style. The antiphonal cross-currents, therefore, are far stronger, as these encompass call-and-response among musicians— singers and instrumentalists—as well as the musicians and the audience. Gospel arose as a turn-of-the-century response to one of freedom's dilemmas, evidence of the decline in group spiritual life, especially since emancipation. To recapture that fervent emotionalism of yesteryear, gospel updated the spirituals and the stock of traditional religious music with an injection of ardent evangelism.

Gospel developed its strongest roots initially in the fundamentalist churches. As southern rural blacks came increasingly to cities, gospel took on an urban gloss. Unwritten texts gave way to written texts; the holy fire had to accommodate over time to the more tempered conventions of Black Baptist and Methodist congregations. Critical to the growing popularity of gospel were the efforts of composers like Charles A. Tindley, who early in this century wrote down many gospel songs. Similarly, in the 1930s, the efforts of Thomas A. Dorsey—clearly a father of modern gospel—along with those of gospel singers like Sallie Martin and the incomparable Mahalia Jackson were crucial to the growing popularity of the music. They traveled the country bringing the gospel music news and made innumerable converts, at times even winning over those who saw in the sacred music too much influence of the blues and jazz.

In fact, the increasingly popular "gospel blues" style of Dorsey and his growing legion of supporters provided potent doses of secular musical styles, particularly rhythms, beats, and song structures. For much of the 1920s Dorsey had been a blues pianist and composer of considerable achievement, having worked with Ma Rainey and Tampa Red. As with other forms of African-American music, this cross-fertilization of gospel with blues influences immeasurably enhanced its power and appeal. Furthermore, this blurring of the sacred/secular music border reveals a persistent tension within African-American music between "traditionalists" favoring a tighter boundary and "progressives" favoring a more permeable one. Especially since the 1960s, African-American secular music styles, like soul, have benefited tremendously from the creative borrowing of rhythm and blues from gospel, while gospel progressives have continually revivified their music through creative borrowings from secular genres, like soul.

The desired effect of a gospel performance remains to work the audience into a charged state as a way to strengthen religious commitment, or better still, to bring souls to religion. This tradition persists and illustrates the dramatic intensity of an incandescent musical/ritual experience. The best groups and soloists compete to outshine the others in their "church wrecking" ability. The idea is to make the performers and audience one in the service of God. The music is a critical element of a multilevel process including preaching, praying, testifying, and a broad range of physical responses from foot stomping and moaning to shouting and speaking in tongues. The vocal and instrumental music build up to a spiritual peak, sustain it, and then gear it up to higher levels until the spirit has been satisfied. The experience can be overpowering.

Singing preachers, notably those who specialize in the "performed" sermon, are especially effective at propelling this ritual forward. Reverend C. L. Franklin, Aretha's father, was a master. The singing itself is often awesome in its intensity. The vocal repertoire is vast: runs across octaves, note bending, playing with notes and words/phrases, effortlessly taking syllables/words over several notes (melisma), shouts, grunts, whispers, moans, cries, lyrical flourishes and full-throated ones. For maximum effect, highly dramatic vignettes, often employing gripping narratives such as the crucifixion and resurrection of Christ, accompany the singing. This spiritual ecstasy has clear analogues in the kind of secular ecstasy to which the best blues performance aspires. Therein lies a crucial element of the transgressive power and universal appeal of African-American music: its creative blurring of the secular/sacred border.

THE BIRTH OF JAZZ

Jazz owes much of its popular appeal to its fruitful working of this same sacred/secular terrain. A most powerful modern urban musical response to the challenges of freedom, principally in cosmopolitan cities like New Orleans, jazz evolved out of an African-American amalgam of various influences. The roots of this exceedingly hybrid musical form include brass band music, syncopated dance music, dance orchestra music, blues, minstrel/vaudeville tunes, ragtime, and sacred music. The key to jazz is its emphasis on improvisation. In an important sense, this music epitomizes the performance basis of African-American music. Through improvisation, jazz endeavors to re-create itself not merely with each formal/musicological advance of the music but also with each performance as well. This is indeed a most difficult challenge.

The major innovator of early-twentieth-century jazz was trumpeter Louis Armstrong, who emerged from his early days in New Orleans and Chicago to revolutionize American music. Two of his signal contributions were his technical brilliance and his development of a stunningly distinctive style as a soloist, especially in the context of group performance. Armstrong of course had influences, notably trumpeters Buddy Bolden, Bunk Johnson, and King Oliver. What set Armstrong apart, however, was his astonishing and individualized sound. Particularly striking were his tonal range, his octave-leaping runs, his ability to reinvent a melody, his sure-handed rhythmic sense, his feel for the blues, and his ability to swing. These are all basic to the jazz vocabulary. In addition, Armstrong's assertion of a pathbreaking musical voice—like that of blueswomen Ma Rainey and Bessie Smith—epitomized the "New Negro" of the twenties Harlem Renaissance. Although barely glimpsed at the time, Armstrong's signature voice personified that audacious cultural quest for a new, vibrant, and uniquely African-American artistic identity far more vividly than the vast majority of the literary and visual artists most often associated with the movement. In addition, Armstrong was a first-rate entertainer, and from the 1930s until his death in 1971, he was also a major American celebrity. In his most influential music from the late twenties and early thirties, his melodic and rhythmic innovations heralded a fusion of passion and technique in the service of improvisation. From that point on, jazz has never been the same.

As Armstrong expanded the frontier of solo jazz performance, Edward Kennedy "Duke" Ellington challenged the dimensions of jazz orchestra and jazz composition. Building upon the innovations of contemporaries like pianist-composer Jelly Roll Morton and band leaders Fletcher Henderson and

Don Redman, by the early 1930s Ellington had created an exceptional band with a remarkable repertoire. His many achievements included successfully resolving the problems of balancing the often-competing demands of improvisation and composition. Likewise, through a rigorous understanding of his band's group strengths as well as its outstanding solo voices, he fashioned music blending these ensemble and individual talents. The music of Ellington is often lauded for its wide-ranging scope, textures, colors, and beauty. Another aspect of his music's greatness is its successful merger of often quite different forms, notably elite and vernacular styles. An excellent pianist, Ellington was also an extraordinary bandleader and an even more impressive composer, with more than fifteen hundred works to his credit. These include film scores, operas, extended concert works, as well as the popular tunes like "Sophisticated Lady" for which he is so well known.

A music born of innovation, jazz continued to evolve. Armstrong and Ellington pushed the music forward, as did other popularizers like white bandleaders Paul Whiteman and Benny Goodman. In fact, the 1930s swing music craze fed the growth of many first-rate black territory bands, most notably Count Basie's hard-driving group out of Kansas City, which went on to international acclaim. Swing offered Depression America a pleasurable respite amidst the gloom. African-American music since the 1940s has been deeply influenced by the growing political assertiveness of the black liberation insurgency. This expanding commitment to both black self-definition and black consciousness found resonance among exemplars of bebop and free jazz and has continued to influence jazz developments. With the decline of swing and swing bands in the forties, bebop reignited the music with its renewed emphasis on improvisational acuity, harmonic and melodic inventiveness, and the ability to play brilliantly at breakneck speed. While the work of many—including trumpeter "Dizzy" Gillespie, pianist "Bud" Powell, and drummers Kenny Clarke and Max Roach—contributed to the music's evolution, the awe-inspiring work of alto saxophonist Charlie Parker exemplified the challenging world

Drummer Max Roach on the 1940s Scene

When you get down to the music, there was a period when the music moved from uptown to downtown, and they had no name for it. . . . Nobody considered the music as "bop" until it moved downtown. So to derogate the music and make it look like it was one of them things, they started hanging labels on the music. For example, don't give me all that 'jazz,' or that's 'bop' talk, this thing or the other. We argue these points because words mean quite a bit to all of us. What we name our things and what we call our contributions should be up to us so that we can control our own destiny.

Source: Quoted in John Birks "Dizzy" Gillespie and Al Fraser, *To Be or Not to Bop* (Garden City, N.J.: Doubleday, Inc., 1979), p. 209.

of bebop. Not only did he play music of uncommon mastery and beauty but also Parker lived on the edge. Consequently, he influenced countless musicians and artists who admired his risk-taking iconoclasm.

Likewise, the development of free jazz involved innovators of the first order. Of particular note is the highly influential work of saxophonists John Coltrane and Ornette Coleman. Their best work exemplifies the quest for full improvisational freedom within the context of collective music making that is the hallmark of free jazz. Coltrane's mesmerizing and dense aural explorations made him immensely popular, especially among those engaged in issues of black cultural aesthetics. That over time his playing took on probing spiritual qualities, reminiscent of the emotional intensity of gospel music at its peak, only added to his aura. Coleman's pathbreaking work beautifully resolves the problems of playing freely yet coherently outside the received strictures of chord changes, rhythms, and harmony. Like the innovations of Ellington and other great jazz composers operating more squarely within traditional limits, however, Coleman's have inspired those seeking to play jazz seamlessly as solo and ensemble, on the one hand, and composition and innovation, on the other.

Black women in jazz have achieved their greatest acclaim as vocalists. Indeed the tradition of jazz vocals has spawned a stellar array of talents. As within other musical genres, jazz vocalists apply their masterful touch to songs from various genres, including pop and blues. Interpretive ability, emotional depth, and stylistic uniqueness set the best apart. From the gripping poignancy of Billie Holiday to the awe-inspiring technical aplomb of Sarah Vaughn, this music has immeasurably enriched American culture. Equally important, black women vocalists whose work operated within and across various genres—such

Jazz in the 1960s

Bebop is roots, now, just as much as blues is. "Classical" music is not. But "classical" music, and I mean now contemporary Euro-American "art" music, might seem to the black man isolated, trying to exist within white culture (arty or whatever), like it should be "milked" for as many *definitions as* possible, i.e., *solutions* to engineering problems the contemporary jazz musician's life is sure to raise. I mean, more simply, Ornette Coleman has had to live with the attitudes responsible for Anton Webern's music whether he knows that music or not. They were handed to him along with the whole history of formal Western music, and the musics that have come to characterize the Negro in the United States came to exist as they do today only through the acculturation of this entire history. And actually knowing that history, and trying to relate to it culturally, or those formal Euro-American musics, only adds to the *indoctrination*. But jazz and blues *are* Western musics; products of all Afro-American culture. But the definitions must be black no matter the geography for the highest meaning to black men. And in this sense European anything is irrelevant.

Source: Imamu Amiri Baraka, *Black Music* (New York, 1967), p. 70.

as Dinah Washington, who could apparently sing anything well—carved out a vital creative niche for others like them. An important consequence of these developments has been the growing demand that jazz and jazz musicians be accorded the respect and accolades at home that they receive abroad. In the 1990s jazz's growing popularity as well as its increasing recognition by major national cultural institutions, like the Smithsonian and America's principal concert halls, appear to augur well for the music's future.

CONCLUSION

In the 1950s, popular black music became known as rhythm and blues, an increasingly urban, rhythmically dense, hybrid blues-driven music. The concurrent development of rock and roll greatly increased the exposure, appreciation, and acceptance of African-American music. Even more important for the growing recognition and popularity of African-American music was the pervasive impact of the Civil Rights and Black Power movements. The ever-increasing visibility of African Americans and the growing white acceptance of the legitimacy of African-American claims for both full-fledged citizenship and full participation in the American dream spilled over into enhanced appreciation for African-American history and culture. Within this context, '60s soul music—evident in the work of Sam Cooke, Ray Charles, Etta James, Aretha Franklin, and James Brown, to name just a few—married the secular power of the blues to the sacred intensity of a gospel style and found enormous popularity.

In the late twentieth century, two tendencies propel the continuing growth and vitality of African-American music. First, as evident in the work of influential jazz trumpeter Wynton Marsalis, the African-American musical tradition is sufficiently rich and complex to sustain both contemporary revisions as well as repertorial interpretations. Second, the richness and complexity of this diverse tradition reveals a powerful dynamism. More recently, there has been effective borrowing from Brazilian, Caribbean, East Asian, European, and African influences. In effect, the ongoing processes of revision and renewal constitute fertile ground that spawns exciting and significant new forms. The most arresting and influential development of the last two decades has to be rap music, itself a diverse and changing music. As a union of various African-American oral traditions with the latest music-making technology, rap has revitalized earlier black music, especially the soul and funk innovations of artists like James Brown, through its ability to sample virtually unlimited bits and pieces of other work. Similarly, through its emphasis on powerfully spoken/chanted lyrics, it revitalizes black traditions of verbal virtuosity such as boasting, signifying, and storytelling. Also important is its telling commentary on late-twentieth-century America, especially the state of America's black inner cities. The extraordinary popularity of rap music, not only in the black community but among a wide variety of listeners, speaks to the enduring influence of African-American music on mainstream culture.

FOR FURTHER READING

Baraka, Imamu Amiri [Leroi Jones]. *Blues People: Negro Music in White America*. New York: William Morrow & Company, 1983.

Barlow, William. *Looking Up at Down: The Emergence of Blues Culture*. Philadelphia: Temple University Press, 1989.

Chernoff, John M. *African Rhythm and African Sensibility*. Chicago: University of Chicago Press, 1981.

Cone, James H. *The Spirituals and the Blues: An Interpretation*. Maryknoll, N.Y.: Orbis Books, 1992.

Epstein, Dena J. *Sinful Tunes and Spirituals: Black Folk Music to the Civil War*. Urbana: University of Illinois Press, 1977.

Ferris, William R. *Blues from the Delta*. New York: Da Capo Press, 1988.

Giddins, Gary. *Visions of Jazz: The First Century*. New York: Oxford University Press, 1998.

Gioia, Ted. *The History of Jazz*. New York: Oxford University Press, 1997.

Guralnick, Peter. *Sweet Soul Music: Rhythm and Blues and the Southern Dream of Freedom*. New York: Harper & Row, 1986.

Hennessey, Thomas J. *From Jazz to Swing: African-American Jazz Musicians and Their Music, 1890–1935*. Detroit, Mich.: Wayne State University Press, 1994.

Hirshey, Gerri. *Nowhere to Run: The Story of Soul Music*. New York: Penguin Books, 1985.

Keil, Charles. *Urban Blues*. Chicago: University of Chicago Press, 1992.

Levine, Lawrence W. *Black Culture and Black Consciousness: Afro-American Folk Thought from Slavery to Freedom*. New York: Oxford University Press, 1978.

Litweiler, John. *The Freedom Principle: Jazz after 1958*. New York: Da Capo Press, 1990.

Murray, Albert. *Stomping the Blues*. New York: Da Capo Press, 1989.

Oliver, Paul. *Blues Fell This Morning: Meaning in the Blues*. New York: Cambridge University Press, 1990.

Palmer, Robert. *Deep Blues*. New York: Viking Press, 1995.

Rose, Tricia. *Black Noise: Rap Music and Black Culture in Contemporary America*. Hanover, N.H.: University Press of New England, 1994.

Schuller, Gunther. *Early Jazz: Its Roots and Musical Development*. New York: Oxford University Press, 1986.

———. *Swing Era: The Development of Jazz, 1930–1945*. New York: Oxford University Press, 1991.

Small, Christopher. *Music of the Common Tongue: Survival and Celebration in Afro-American Music*. New York: Riverrun Press, 1994

Southern, Eileen. *The Music of Black Americans: A History*. 3rd ed. New York: W. W. Norton & Company, 1997.

Spencer, Jon Michael. *Protest and Praise: Sacred Music of Black Religion*. Minneapolis: Fortress Press, 1997.

Stearns, Marshall W. *The Story of Jazz*. New York: Oxford University Press, 1985.

Stuckey, Sterling. *Slave Culture: Nationalist Theory and the Foundations of Black America*. New York: Oxford University Press, 1988.

Ward, Brian. *Just My Soul Responding: Rhythm and Blues, Black Consciousness, and Race Relations*. Berkeley and Los Angeles: University of California Press, 1998.

chapter 12

Black Voices

Themes in African-American Literature

Gerald Early

I N ONE OF THE ESSAYS IN HIS 1957 BOOK, *White Man, Listen!*, Richard Wright claims, "The Negro is America's metaphor." By this he meant not only that blacks were the symbolic embodiment of the history of America, an outcast people trying to find a new identity in the New World, but also that they were, through the circumstances of being forced to live in a country "whose laws, customs, and instruments of force were leveled against them," constant reminders of the anguish of being without an identity, constant reminders of human alienation. According to Ralph Ellison, Wright's good friend back in the 1930s, "The white American has charged the Negro American with being without a past or tradition (something which strikes the white man with a nameless horror), just as he himself has been so charged by European and American critics with a nostalgia for the stability once typical of European cultures."

But Wright saw in the African-American's quest for an identity, in his struggle against human alienation, against being a symbol of the abyss of estrangement, a deep political and philosophical resonance that, in fact, gave America both an aesthetic—blues music—and crucial forms of social engagement that blacks, and the political culture of the United States itself, used as forms of dissent against the idea of human alienation: first, abolition, then, Reconstruction, and, finally, the Civil Rights movement. "Is it not clear to you that the American Negro is the only group in our nation that consistently and passionately raises the question of freedom?" asks Wright. "This is a service to America and to the world. More than this: The voice of the American Negro is rapidly becoming the most representative voice of America and of oppressed people anywhere in the world today." In effect, Wright is suggesting that black Americans, within the framework of their isolation, had managed to create community and common cause with other victimized peoples in the world (particularly the "colored" world). Wright suggests that black Americans were to construct a penetrating view of the general human condition through the prism of their own localized experience.

Because the quests for a usable community and for identity have shaped black experience itself in America, Wright argues his essay, these quests ultimately inform all of African-American literature.

A QUESTION OF IDENTITY: FROM PHILLIS WHEATLEY TO RICHARD WRIGHT

When one thinks of poet Phillis Wheatley (1753?-1784), the earliest black writer in America to produce an estimable body of work, this observation certainly seems true, not simply about black people generally but about the black writer especially. Wheatley, born in Senegal and brought to America at the age of eight, had to learn both a new language and a new religion, indeed, an entirely new way of life, the same cultural disruption and brutally imposed cognitive dissonance that other Africans experienced as well, except that in some manner, as a child, the adaptation had to be, paradoxically, both easier and harder. Yet she so completely absorbed aspects of her new culture that she was able to write poetry in the leading literary style of the day by the time she was a teenager. Naturally, because of her age, some of her poetry exhibits facility but lacks depth. But the question of identity, while muted in most of her work, still appears here and there, and one must suppose that she thought a great deal about her precarious fate as a favored slave and about the nature of the black community that she was not fully a part of for a good portion of her life in America and which was powerless to support her as a writer. In any case, she never forgot that she was an African. It was hardly likely that she forgot that passage or the circumstances that brought her over to the New World. She wrote in the poem, "To the Right Honorable William Early of Dartmouth, His Majesty's Principal Secretary of State for North America, Etc.":

> Should you, my lord, while you pursue my song,
> Wonder from whence my love of Freedom sprung,
> Whence flow these wishes for the common good,
> By feeling hearts alone best understood,
> I, young in life, by seeming cruel fate
> Was snatch'd from Afric's fancy'd happy seat:
> What pangs excruciating must molest,
> What sorrows labour in my parent's breast?
> Steel'd was the soul and by no misery mov'd
> That from a father seiz'd his babe belov'd
> Such, such my case. And can I then but pray
> Others may never feel tyrannic sway?

In these lines, there is not only a sense of being taken away from the life and culture and from parents who felt concern and cared for their child (concerns seldom attributed to Africans by whites at the time) but also a sense of thwarted justice born from having endured the experience of a disrupted community. Wheatley, who died poverty-stricken, abandoned by both the black and white communities, in some ways both voiced and personified the themes of identity and community that were to be fully developed and elaborated upon by later black writers.

"The radical solitude of human life," wrote José Ortega y Gasset in his 1957 philosophical treatise, *Man and People*, "the being of man, does not, then, consist in there really being nothing except himself. Quite the contrary—there is nothing less than the universe, with all that it contains. There is, then, an infinity of things but—there it is!—amid them Man in his radical reality is alone— alone *with* them." Somehow, this seems to capture Wheatley herself, mastering foreign cultural tools for a self-expression that was never quite her own, a sly and complicated ventriloquism that was both the triumph and the tragedy of her assimilation. By redefining her theft from Africa as a providential plot for placing her in a more transcendent community, she might ultimately find closure for her predicament. Thus, she writes, in "On Being Brought From Africa to America":

> Twas mercy brought me from my Pagan land,
> Taught my benighted soul to understand
> That there's a God, that there's a Saviour too:
> Once I redemption neither sought nor knew.
> Some view our sable race with scornful eye,
> "Their colour is a diabolic die."
> Remember, Christians, Negroes, black as Cain,
> May be refin'd, and join th' angelic train.

In eighteenth-century New England, with the rise of liberalism, Calvinism was forced to retreat before a more humanitarian worldview, before the view that, despite their condition, babies, "idiots," blacks, and others "naturally perverse in their will toward sin" ought not be consigned to hell. This view obviously affected Wheatley in two ways: first, as a product of the new liberalism where her poetry would be appreciated and encouraged as a sign of God's deliverance of the benighted; and second, as a believer in the new liberalism as a way to explain her fate and the form of cultural assimilation that she was experiencing. More important, the idea that blacks could be or had to be, in one way or another, "refin'd" or uplifted as a cure for their alienation or degradation, has been a constant in African-American thought, from the earliest writings in English to the ideas of nationalists like Marcus Garvey (whose organization was called the Universal Negro *Improvement* Association) and Malcolm X. Perhaps one way in which Richard Wright was truly pathbreaking was in his reluctance to think in those terms.

Struck deeply by the alienation described by Ortega y Gasset, Wright was one of the major African-American writers of the twentieth century, a figure so monumental that the era from the late Depression when Wright began publishing through 1960, the year of his death, is often referred to as his epoch. Wright was heavily influenced by Marxism, a philosophy he learned during his days as a Communist writer and editor in Chicago and New York in the early and mid-'30s, and by existentialism, a philosophy he felt intuitively from his youth when it provided a substitute for the Christianity that he abhorred. Wright read deeply about existentialism after World War II, existentialism's heyday. In his major works before his self-imposed exile from America after the Second World War, it was not that Wright introduced new themes to African-American writing. Instead, he concentrated, as had others before him, on the quests for identity and for usable community. However, partly because Wright was born and reared, for the most part, in Mississippi, the most backward and brutal state in the Union on the matter of race, no black writer before him achieved either Wright's visceral intensity in describing black-white relations or displayed as deep a passion for seeking broad philosophical implications in black American life. And no black writer before him saw black life in such stark, often cosmically lonely terms. Finally, no black writer until Wright had become as famous, as accepted in this country, and particularly abroad, as a genuine man of letters and a writer of unquestioned stature.

The works for which Wright became known—*Uncle Tom's Children* (1937), a collection of novellas set in the South, *Native Son* (1940), his grand urban novel of crime and punishment set in Chicago, and *Black Boy* (1945), his autobiographical exploration of black adolescence in the American South— emphasize a deep sense of estrangement in characters unable to connect with a larger aggregate of humanity, characters trying heroically to establish their identities but confounded by incredible forces that manipulate and annihilate their sense of place and belonging, by forces that transform anxiety into impotent rage and turn fear into inexhaustible dread. The stories in *Uncle Tom's Children*, all about black rebellion against the violent white power structure, move from heroes who are unconscious of any political significance in their acts, largely buffeted by the tides and whimsies of a cruel, indifferent world, trying desperately to extricate themselves from a seemingly inescapable fate, to more politically aware heroes (the heroine of the last story is a Marxist as well as a deep believer in black solidarity) whose revolts are self-consciously motivated. But even in the most restricted circumstances, Wright gives his black characters choices. Wright was never to abandon his Marxist/existentialist belief that man makes his world, makes his circumstances, and makes his fate.

In *Native Son*, considered by most critics Wright's masterpiece, the reader is given the most vehement critique against the idea of welfare-state liberalism ever written by a black to this time. In this ideologically driven novel, Wright presents welfare-state liberalism, which for the rich, white Dalton family of the novel, represents a mere mask for exploitative power and for maintaining the status quo of keeping black families like that of Wright's protagonist, Bigger Thomas, poor and huddled in ghettos. Bigger's psychotic attempt at liberation is doomed to failure because he has accepted the terms of blackness that white society has imposed upon him. In other words, he has sought his humanity by becoming the very inhuman thing that white society said he was and, in effect, made him. In *Black Boy*, by looking in an exaggerated and not entirely factual way at his family and rearing in the South, Wright explores exclusively the idea of what black community means. It was in this book that Wright made one of his striking, and, for some, disturbing, statements about the meaning of black community:

> After I had outlived the shocks of childhood, after the habit of reflection had been born in me, I used to mull over the strange absence of real kindness in Negroes, how unstable was our tenderness, how lacking in genuine passion we were, how void of great hope, how timid our joy, how bare our traditions, how hollow our memories, how lacking we were in those intangible sentiments that bind man to man, and how shallow was even our despair. After I had learned other ways of life I used to brood upon the unconscious irony of those who felt that Negroes led so passional an existence! I saw that what had been taken for our emotional strength was our negative confusions, our flights, our fears, our frenzy under pressure.
>
> Whenever I thought of the essential bleakness of black life in America, I knew that Negroes had never been allowed to catch the full spirit of Western civilization, that they lived somehow in it but not of it. And when I brooded upon the cultural barrenness of black life, I wondered if clean, positive tenderness, love, honor, loyalty, and the capacity to remember were native with man. I asked myself if these human qualities were not fostered, won, struggled and suffered for, preserved in ritual from one generation to another.

Wright had two aims in writing this passage: first, despite his own love of sociology, he wanted to lift the level of discourse about the black condition from mere sociology to something philosophical, to something which spoke of the problem of human community. Second, hoping to reverse, harshly and shockingly, a tendency he disliked in earlier black writing, particularly in some of the writing of the Harlem Renaissance, he wanted to de-romanticize and de-exoticize black life.

THE FOUNDATION OF AN AFRICAN-AMERICAN LITERARY TRADITION

To understand fully how an author like Wright shaped his work, it is necessary to go back to the slave narrative, the earliest form of black American writing that formed a coherent body of work, that expressed a plain ideological task and purpose and set forth the themes of identity and community that were to characterize all the black writing that came after. While poet Phillis

Wheatley's work exhibited these themes, almost as a subtext, the antebellum slave narratives sharpened and strengthened these concerns by making the black writer a presence in American life and letters.

One of the antecedents of the antebellum slave narrative was the Indian captivity narrative of the eighteenth century, usually a tale about a white captured and forced to live for some period of time among Indians. Other captivity narratives tell of persons surprisingly impressed in the navy or unfairly or unfortunately seized by the nation's enemy. The earliest black narratives such as *A Narrative of the Uncommon Sufferings and Surprizing Deliverance of Briton Hammon, a Negro Man*, published in 1760, and *A Narrative of the Life of John Marrant of New York, in North America: With An Account of the Conversion of the King of the Cherokees and his Daughter*, published in 1785, were precisely in the captivity narrative mode. Indeed, slavery was scarcely the subject of them in any sort of political way. Built on the captivity narrative model, *The Interesting Narrative of the Life of Olaudah Equiano or Gustavus Vassa, the African* (1791), was the first true slave narrative in that it was a self-conscious and explicit protest against slavery. It was the first self-conscious black or African political literature in English in the Western world.

Although there were important black publications of a political or polemical sort published earlier, works such as *A Narrative of the Black People during the Late Awful Calamity in Philadelphia* (1794) by Richard Allen and Absalom Jones, and *David Walker's Appeal in Four Articles; Together with A Preamble, To the Coloured Citizens of the World, but in Particular, and Very Expressly, To Those of the United States of America* (1829), the full development and enrichment of black literature occurred in the antebellum period of 1830 to 1860. From small tracts and pamphlets to major, polished autobiographies, literally hundreds of slave narratives were published. Sponsored largely by white abolitionist societies in the North, where antislavery had become a major political and social movement in the United States, much of this writing suffered from the same problems as early European-American literature, an imitative or dull style and an overwrought Christian piety. Moreover, because they were unable to appear before the public as guarantors of their own stories, without the aid of a vouching white editor or friend, black authors were at a severe disadvantage. Finally, there was the problem of audience—whom did the slave narrator wish to address and why? Obviously, the slave narrator desired to move white readers to act against slavery. This meant that the literature had to present the black narrator as palatable to whites who were, almost exclusively, committed to white supremacist ideals. But the black narrator, and all black writers since this period, also felt the pressure of being representative of his race and wanted to cast no undue aspersions upon it. That is to say, the slave narratives were meant both to be a protest, crossover literature for whites (to help them understand the true nature of slavery or, one might say, the black American experience) and, in some sense, a "race" literature addressing the needs of black self-esteem and racial community.

The idea or ideal of black community during antebellum America was a difficult one to maintain. First, the black community was a complex set of structures: there were various divisions within slavery, fieldhands versus house servants, artisans versus the unskilled, light-skinned versus dark-skinned, more recent African arrivals versus third-, fourth-, or fifth-generation "detainees." In addition there were the free black communities of both the North and South. Because it was the free blacks who could effectively or at least more visibly agitate for freedom, these free communities, although small, were essential to the much larger slave communities. But the free community was a complex mixture, exhibited many of the same elements that made up the slave communities, and, like the slave communities, was largely at the mercy of the whites who surrounded it. Without a centralized church, any school system worth the name, or any of the normal civic privileges that the average white citizens enjoyed, it was difficult for the free black communities to act as a vanguard for the slave communities.

Second, blacks in antebellum America were experiencing a complex form of cultural syncretism. It must be remembered that a number of ethnically diverse Africans were brought to the New World during the Atlantic slave trade so two simultaneous processes were taking place in the creation of black community. First, the Europeans worked assiduously to remove as many cultural props—language, religion, kinship rituals, rites of passage—that they could to make the Africans a less volatile, less warlike labor presence (which is why, in the end, the African was preferred to the Indian as a slave). Black community was always meant to be, in the eyes of whites, dependent, precarious, impoverished, an area or configuration to be policed and contained. Second, the Africans came to meld or distill the strands of cultural expressions that they were able to maintain to forge a new identity. So, true black community—independent, stabilized, and prosperous—was to become a subversive concept.

The most famous of the slave narratives were Frederick Douglass's 1845 *Narrative of the Life of Frederick Douglass, An American Slave* and his 1855 *My Bondage and My Freedom,* Harriet Jacobs's *Incidents in the Life of a Slave Girl,* published in 1861, *The Narrative of William Wells Brown,* published in 1846, *Running a Thousand Miles for Freedom* by William and Ellen Craft, published in 1860, *The Narrative of Henry Box Brown Who Escaped from Slavery in a Box Three Feet Long and Two Feet Wide; Written from a Statement of Facts by Himself,* published in 1849, *Life of Josiah Henson, formerly a Slave, Now an Inhabitant of Canada, Narrated by Himself,* published in 1849, and *Twelve Years a Slave: the Narrative of Solomon Northup, a Citizen of New York, Kidnapped in Washington City in 1841, and Rescued in 1853, from a Cotton Plantation Near Red River in Louisiana,* published in 1853. All of these works tried in various ways to create a sense of black community in the narratives by talking not only of the slave narrator's sense of connection to his or her own family (family piety was virtually a cliché in this works) but to the larger community of slaves, who often assisted the narrator in his escape. Moreover, the books tried to create a sense of connection through their texts between blacks in the North and South, slave and free. Of these, the works by Douglass, William Wells Brown, and Jacobs are considered by literary critics and African-American literary experts today to have the most value.

Indeed, Douglass and Brown, both escaped slaves who became veteran speakers on the abolition circuit, were true men of letters. Douglass ran a newspaper for many years, and Brown published several other works including the earliest black novel, *Clotel or the President's Daughter*, published in 1853, and *Three Years in Europe*, the first black travel book, published in 1852. Brown was to publish several more books, including some of the earliest full-scale black histories. Other early black novels published before 1860 were Frank J. Webb's *The Garies and Their Friends*, a novel about free blacks in Philadelphia, published in 1857, Martin R. Delany's *Blake: Or, the Huts of America*, a militant, highly polemical novel about black rebellion and emigration, published in 1859, and Harriet E. Wilson's *Our Nig*, an autobiographical novel about a biracial child's indentured servitude in a cruel white household, published in 1859. Most of these novels received little attention, at least from white audiences. Unquestionably, the most significant piece of racial fiction published during this period was written by a white woman. Harriet Beecher Stowe's epochal antislavery novel, *Uncle Tom's Cabin* was published in 1852 and had an influence that extended far beyond the immediate issue of slavery. The name of the title character was to become a hated epithet among blacks, and the long shelf life of the work as popular theater ensured that a number of troubling stereotypes endured as near myths in the American imagination. Novelist James Baldwin, in declaring his literary independence nearly one hundred years later, was to damn, in particular, the burden of this novel on the work of black writers.

TOWARD A BLACK LITERARY AESTHETIC

The slave narratives were, far and away, the most important and most developed black literature in the United States, indeed, in the Western world at that time. They were to establish two major trends in African-American literature: first, a preoccupation with autobiographical and confessional writing that remains to this day; and second, a strong tendency to bind social protest or explicit political consciousness with the aesthetic act of making literature. While the first trend has produced an extraordinarily rich vein of American writing, to Booker T. Washington's *Up From Slavery* to *The Autobiography of Malcolm X*, from Maya Angelou's *I Know Why The Caged Bird Sings* to James Weldon Johnson's *Along This Way*, from Ann Moody's *Coming of Age in Mississippi* to Langston Hughes's *The Big Sea*, the second has been far more problematical.

Black literature has been charged over the years by white critics with being nothing more than social protest, or "mere sociology," or a literature without technique, style, or innovation. It was not until the 1952 publication of Ralph Ellison's *Invisible Man*, nearly one hundred years after the publication of the first African-American novel, that a black fictional work was considered without question to be of superior literary merit, equal to the best white literature. This slow growth of recognition and of true achievement was, in some respects, inevitable. It took nearly two hundred years for white American literature to evolve from sermons and tracts to the works of Whitman, Hawthorne, Melville, and Poe. Black writers who were serious about the craft of making good literature have always been sensitive to the charge from whites of writing second-rate, race-bound works. But they have been equally sensitive to the needs of their black audience and of their group in general, understanding that African Americans would not be interested in a literature that was to given over to "mere aesthetics" or to the idea of art for art's sake, which most would think a frivolous indulgence and not a serious engagement with life and art as they saw those matters. Most black writers saw literature as something that represented their community, that was a force in the ideological and political construction of their community whether or not the literature actually depicted black community as a successfully working enterprise. One aspect of this problem is well captured in James Weldon Johnson's "The Dilemma of the Negro Author," published in the *American Mercury* in 1928 where he raised the issue of different audiences and the inability of the black author to reconcile their expectations, their needs, their perspectives. The reason for the severity of this problem stems in part from the nature of the black community itself and how, historically, it has been forced to function totally for the white community's convenience. The conflict about the purpose of African-American literature—for the question of its content and its craftsmanship comes down to the issue of function—in relation to the formation of community remains of great, even overriding, profundity for black writers and their audience as well as the larger society.

AFRICAN-AMERICAN LITERATURE IN THE AGE OF FREEDOM

Since the Civil War, there have been three crucial periods for African-American literature where the conflict about its purpose became explicit: the New Negro or Harlem Renaissance era, the early Civil Rights era of the 1950s, and the Black Arts movement of the late 1960s. Briefly considered, these periods coincide with certain extraordinary developments within the United States itself: Prohibition, urbanization; false prosperity; a new wave of black political consciousness; a rising interest in and concern about communism during the 1920s and 1930s; the cold war; prosperity; a national policy of racial integration; a new assertiveness among blacks; the rise of youth culture in the 1950s; an intense black militancy; a nation deeply divided over the Vietnam War; a rash of political assassinations; a national policy to wipe out poverty; questions about the extent and future of prosperity; and a sharply influential counterculture on the left during the late 1960s. It is important to note two things about these three eras: each occurred during or immediately after a major American war; and in each instance, as has been the case for African Americans in their struggle in the United States since the end of Reconstruction, the major political concerns about citizenship and community are tied, often expressly so, with the meaning and function of African-American art, generally, and African-American literature, in particular.

The era of the Harlem Renaissance, starting with the black migration to the North in 1915 and ending with the rise of Richard Wright—a southern migrant—in the late 1930s, revived the issue of African-American musical theater and African-American vernacular expression, which originated in the 1890s with the famous comedy team of Williams and Walker and the coon song, on the one hand, and the dialect poetry of Paul Laurence Dunbar, on the other. Indeed, James Weldon Johnson, who was such an important presence in both areas in the 1890s, was to be a prime mover and shaker during the Renaissance. African-American musical theater became very big in the 1920s as did experimentation in vernacular poetry leading, in one direction, to the blues lyrics of the young Langston Hughes, and, in another direction, to the sermonic cadences of Johnson's *God's Trombones*.

In each case, old-fashioned, overly sentimentalized, and crudish dialect was eschewed for something more subtle, richer, closer to the actual power and expressive range of black speech. The Renaissance brought together a number of forces: a large nationalist mass movement spearheaded by Marcus Garvey that made Africa and Pan-Africanism thought about in ways that far exceeded the intensity expressed in the 1890s black nationalist movements; the two large black middle-class organizations, the National Association for the Advancement of Colored People and the Urban League; a revolutionary black music called jazz and, in phonograph records, a new technology with which to hear it; an intense historical consciousness that resulted in the formation of the Association for the Study of Negro Life and History and a number of anthologies on black culture including Alain Locke's *The New Negro*, the most storied of the age. It is no surprise, therefore, that this era saw the publication of Jean Toomer's experimental work *Cane* (1923), Claude McKay's *Home to Harlem* (1928), Countee Cullen's *Color* (1925), Langston Hughes's *The Weary Blues* (1926), Nella Larsen's *Passing* (1929), Zora Neale Hurston's *Their Eyes Were Watching God* (1937), to name only a small number of works by authors who were to become principal names in African-American fiction and poetry. This could only have happened because the black community itself reached a certain level of strength and self-confidence.

Nonetheless, the Renaissance was considered a failure by many black writers and critics, including a number who lived through it. First, it was felt that much of the literature seemed preoccupied with middle-class concerns or with presenting blacks as exotics. This criticism was not entirely deserved, but certainly one of the burning questions of the age was "How Is the Negro to Be Depicted in Literature?" (A version of that question is still a vital concern for

African Americans today.) Many white literary types thought this concern to be somewhere between philistine and infantile, but they hardly understood the sensitivity of a group that had been so viciously and persistently maligned by their culture. Second, compared to the incredible experimentation taking place in the best white literature of the day, from Hemingway to Stein, from Joyce to T. S. Eliot, African-American literature seemed tame, indeed, almost old-fashioned in some of its Victorian flavor. Third, the black community was still weak: no major black publishing houses were produced in this era, nor were there any successful black drama companies, despite black popularity on the Broadway musical stage. Indeed, this last point may be the most telling; for unlike white ethnic enclaves like the Jewish or Irish Catholic communities in the United States, the black community was constantly seen by whites as threatening if it were not rigidly controlled and contained. Whites also used the black community as the venue for their own crimes and vices. In short, the larger white community worked very hard to make sure that the black community could never fully function as a community.

Although Wright continued to produce much important work in the 1950s, including political works, a collection of short stories, and three new novels, the 1950s saw the end of the dominance of this artist, whose works largely ended the Harlem Renaissance by reinventing the black novel as a politically self-aware, proletariat mechanism for social criticism and engagement.

In fact, it ended, at least temporally, a black interest in Marxist-oriented art and sheer naturalistic writing. In the early 1950s came such writers as William Demby (*Beetlecreek*), James Baldwin (*Go Tell It On the Mountain*, *Giovanni's Room*), Ralph Ellison (*Invisible Man*), and Gwendolyn Brooks (*Annie Allen*, *Maud Martha*) who were to garner great critical recognition and respect from the white literary establishment. None of these novels was a purely naturalistic work and Brooks's poetry was demanding in a way unlike any Harlem Renaissance poet (except possibly the highly experimental Jean Toomer). Just a few years after Jackie Robinson integrated professional baseball, in an era of a more sensitive treatment of blacks in films like "Home of the Brave," "No Way Out," "Cry, The Beloved Country," and "Blackboard Jungle," and right around the time of the Supreme Court decision to desegregate public schools, there was a considerable willingness on the part of the liberal white intelligentsia to accept blacks into the American mainstream, not realizing that blacks, as Ralph Ellison was to argue so eloquently in his essays, helped to invent the mainstream that had denied them for so long.

Although much of this work still exhibited the despair, hopelessness, and violence that one found in Wright, some, like Baldwin and Ellison quite critically, muted elements of social protest by going off in new directions, writing more textured, densely complex works about the inner psychological life of black people. The end of the decade saw the rise of novelists Paule Marshall and William Melvin Kelly, poet LeRoi Jones, and playwright Lorraine Hansberry. The criticism of the literature of this period was that it was too assimilationist and far too concerned with technique, although these were, in fact, its strengths in moving black literature into the mainstream of American writing. But the movement was not quite as assimilationist as some critics thought. The black writers of the 1950s came to prominence during the liberation movements taking place in Africa and the concerted attacks against European imperialism by the Third World generally. Writers like Baldwin and Hansberry wrote about Africa as black writers have done since the days of Phillis Wheatley. Nearly all continued to attack racism vehemently. Several black writers of note found America so difficult to live in that they left the country, opting for Europe instead. The writing of this period certainly reflected not simply what the black bourgeoisie wanted but where the black community as a whole wished to go, not into a white world but away from the restrictions of a black one.

BLACK LITERATURE AND THE BLACK COMMUNITY

By the late 1960s, LeRoi Jones, having become a much-read poet (*The Dead Lecturer*, *Preface to a Twenty-Volume Suicide Note*), playwright (*Dutchman* and *The Slave*), and essayist (*Home: Social Essays*), changed his name to Imamu Amiri Baraka and launched the Black Arts movement, first in Harlem, then in Newark, New Jersey, in a period lasting roughly from 1965 to 1975. Partly in response to the strong assimilationist tendencies of the Civil Rights movement, partly in response to a growing and more radical black youth movement, partly in response to black nationalism's finally having, in the figure of the recently assassinated Malcolm X, a martyr upon which to hang myths, the Black Arts Movement invented a black nationalist value system called Kawaida. Inspired, in part, by the African socialist philosophy of Julius K. Nyerere, Kawaida spawned the popular black holiday Kwanzaa and insisted that all black art had to be explicitly political, aimed at the destruction of whites or white values, and preoccupied solely with the liberation of black people. Black art had to be aimed at the masses, thus the rise of black theater and an accessible, nearly didactic black poetry. It had to eschew white technique or an overly white, bourgeois concern with the problems of technique or formalistic meaning and process. Much of this work descended into a kind of black agitprop. Yet there was impressive work accomplished at this time including the establishment of several black publishing companies—Broadside in Detroit and Third World Press in Chicago; *Black Fire*, the epochal anthology edited by Baraka and Larry Neal; work by writers like Don L. Lee (Haki Madhubuti), Sonia Sanchez, Nikki Giovanni, Etheridge Knight, and Eldridge Cleaver. It was the time of the black exploitation movies (which spawned the incredible Melvin Van Peebles's film, "Sweet, Sweetback's Badass Song"), the emergence of black radio as a true force in American culture, and the rise of boxer Muhammad Ali (who had changed his name from Cassius Clay) as a black hero of resistance. Self-absorbed with its dramatic self-presentation, the Black Arts movement produced little fiction. The most important novelist of the period, John A. Williams, who wrote the defining work of the age, *The Man Who Cried I Am*, was not associated with the Black Arts movement, nor were Toni Morrison and Alice Walker, who both began their work at this time.

What might be said about all of these creative periods is that the black community evolved or changed in some vital ways or felt itself in a state of crisis. The literature tended not simply to reflect or merely respond to, but actually to be part of the change or crisis itself. How can writing, or literature, continue to serve the black community or help make it continue to function as community in its present condition? In each instance, innovations were produced. But there was also less dependence on the past, less self-conscious creation of tradition than there could have been. Perhaps in the 1920s or even in the 1950s, this was not possible. But in the 1960s, surely, one of the failures of the Black Arts movement to become what the Harlem Renaissance sought to be—a new black cultural-nationalist movement, a political movement for independence through the reinvention of culture—was the inability to formulate a usable black literary past of sufficient strength and diversity to support an atmosphere that would continue to generate innovation and enrichment. This is slowly but surely happening with African-American literature today, with a greater number of recognized writers than at any time in history.

THE FUTURE OF BLACK LITERATURE

It has been said that since the end of the Black Arts Movement, women have come to dominate African-American literature. Certainly, with the rise of feminism in the 1970s and a growing self-consciousness about gender on the part of black women, women's issues and concerns in African-American literature have received considerable prominence. Toni Morrison (the first black American to receive the Nobel Prize for literature), Alice Walker, Gloria Naylor, and even more recently, Terry McMillan and Bebe Campbell, have all become best-selling authors. Lesser known but equally well-regarded writers such as June Jordan, Audre Lorde, Octavia Butler, Gayle Jones, and Ntozake Shange have had a considerable impact on the present literary scene. Moreover, as more women—black and white—have become university professors and literary critics, there has been a growing intellectual and scholarly interest in the work of black women. Since the end of the Black Arts Movement, however, there have emerged several black male writers as well: Ernest Gaines, Ishmael Reed, James McPherson, David Bradley, Reginald McKnight, Charles Johnson, and Samuel Delany have all received a great deal of attention.

Moreover, the dominant black figures in public intellectual discourse these days, such as Henry Louis Gates Jr., Stanley Crouch, Houston Baker, Stephen Carter, Shelby Steele, Glenn Loury, and Cornell West, are men. The belief that black women and feminist issues dominate African-American literature today has led to a distinct undercurrent of tension between black men and black women, as the former accuse the latter of unfairly attacking and criticizing them, playing into the hands of the white power structure. This debate has been fueled as well by a concern over the survival of black men in American society, which some think has reached a crisis point.

Once again, these developments point to the burden that black literature, fraught with political and social significance, must bear in constructing the idea of black community and the difficulty it faces in trying to do so. These pressures also point to the problem of audience, as more black writers are currently being recognized and rewarded by the white literary establishment, although there is a more powerful black reading audience than ever. There is, finally, the question of precisely what black literature should be about, how much social protest or sociological weight it should carry, and how black people should be depicted in it. Despite these ongoing concerns, contemporary African-American writing is a richly diverse field and a compelling presence on the American literary scene.

FOR FURTHER READING

Angelou, Maya. *I Know Why the Caged Bird Sings*. New York: Bantam Books, 1983.

Asante, Molefi. *The Afrocentric Idea*. Rev. ed. Philadelphia: Temple University Press, 1998.

Baker, Houston A., Jr. *Blues, Ideology and Afro-American Literature: A Vernacular Theory*. Chicago: University of Chicago Press, 1987.

———. *Long Black Song: Essays in Black Literature and Criticism*. Charlottesville: University of Virginia Press, 1990.

———. *Singers of Daybreak: Studies in Black American Literature*. Washington, D.C.: Howard University Press, 1983.

Baraka, Imamu Amiri. *Home: Social Essays*. Hopewell, N.J.: The Ecco Press, 1998.

Braxton, Joanne M., and Andree Nicola McLaughlin, eds. *Wild Women in the Whirlwind: AFRA-American Culture and the Contemporary Literary Renaissance*. New Brunswick, N.J.: Rutgers University Press, 1990.

Carby, Hazel. *Reconstructing Womanhood: The Emergence of the Afro-American Woman Novelist*. New York: Oxford University Press, 1990.

Cooke, Michael G. *Afro-American Literature in the Twentieth Century: The Achievement of Intimacy*. New Haven, Conn.: Yale University Press, 1990.

Fischer, Dexter, and Robert Stepto, eds. *Afro-American Literature: A Vernacular Theory*. New York: Modern Language Association, 1979.

Gates, Henry Louis Jr., ed. *The Classic Slave Narratives*. New York: NAL/Dutton, 1987.

———. *The Signifying Monkey: A Theory of African-American Literary Criticism*. New York: Oxford University Press, 1990.

Gates, Henry Louis Jr., and Sunday Ogbonna Anozie, eds. *Black Literature & Literary Theory*. New York: Routledge, 1990.

Huggins, Nathan I. *The Harlem Renaissance*. New York: Oxford University Press, 1973.

Hughes, Langston. *The Langston Hughes Reader*. New York: George Braziller, 1981.

Hurston, Zora Neale. *Their Eyes Were Watching God*. Reissue Ed. New York: Harper Collins, 1999.

Morrison, Toni. *Playing in the Dark: Whiteness and the Literary Imagination*. New York: Vintage, 1993.

Redding, J. Saunders. *A Scholar's Conscience: Selected Writings of J. Saunders Redding, 1942–1977*. Ed. Faith Berry. Lexington: University of Kentucky Press, 1992.

Smith, Valerie. *Self-Discovery and Authority in Afro-American Narrative*. Cambridge: Harvard University Press, 1991.

Stepto, Robert B. *From Behind the Veil: A Study of Afro-American Narrative*. 2nd ed. Urbana: University of Illinois Press, 1991.

Wright, Richard. *Early Works*. Ed. Arnold Ramersad. New York: Library of America, 1991.

chapter 13

Black Religious Traditions

Sacred and Secular Themes

Gayraud S. Wilmore

I N A CLASSIC ESSAY ON BLACK RELIGION W. E. B. DuBois, probably
the greatest African-American scholar of the twentieth century, wrote:
"Three things characterized this religion of the slave—the Preacher, the
Music, and the Frenzy." Although this brief but suggestive description captures the dynamic of the Africans' earliest appropriation of evangelical Protestantism on both sides of the Atlantic, contemporary studies reveal a more complex and comprehensive pattern of religious development. From a perspective
that includes not only what DuBois called "an adaptation and mingling of heathen rites . . . roughly designated as Voodooism," but also the later institutionalization of early slave worship in black churches of the nineteenth and twentieth centuries, three dominant themes or motifs stand out as foundational
from the first arrival of African indentured servants at Jamestown, Virginia, in
1619, to the present. They are survival, elevation, and liberation.

It is tempting to try to encompass the entire history of black religion in
this country by arranging these motifs in chronological order. In that case par-
adigms of *survival*—the sheer effort to use religion to stay alive or to keep
body and soul together—would characterize the earliest period of clandestine
slave worship in the seventeenth and eighteenth centuries; efforts to make
religion a ladder for the educational, moral, and cultural *elevation* of resource-
ful individuals would represent the second period— from the 1850s, says
Carter G. Woodson, through the "civilizing" efforts of northern white missionaries when they were free to minister to the former slaves during and following the Civil War, to the urban, social service-oriented "institutional
churches" of the first half of the twentieth century; and finally, the paradigm
of *liberation*—direct action on the part of churches to free the slaves, combat

racial discrimination, and garner black political, economic, and moral power—
would represent the third period: from the Civil War to the end of the present century.

On closer scrutiny, however, this neat chronological order breaks down.
One finds these themes entwining and overlapping in various configurations
at several stages. For example, a radical liberationist orientation is seen in the
religiously inspired rebellions led by Denmark Vesey and Nat Turner in 1822
and 1831, while the newly independent African Methodist Episcopal churches
of the North were cooperating with groups like the American Moral Reform
Society, seeking to elevate life in the antebellum ghettoes of the northern
cities through education and cultural refinement. Similarly, in the storefront
Pentecostal churches of the inner city between the two world wars there was
a reversion to the same patterns of emotionalism and other African forms of
religiosity that helped the slaves survive the brutality of plantation life in the
late eighteenth century. Thus, as useful as the chronological sequence is, in
the final analysis, it is more accurate to understand survival, elevation, and liberation as major emphases that emerged simultaneously through the entire
course of African-American religious history.

THE AFRICAN HERITAGE

It seems incontrovertible that religious traditions brought from West Africa
gave comfort and consolation to the slaves as they were slowly acculturated to
the new religion of Christianity in North America. In the beginning African
traditional religions functioned as a survival strategy for the captives as they
struggled to maintain life and sanity under bondage to white people who
regarded them as little more than beasts of burden. The first Africans who
were transported in the seventeenth and eighteenth centuries brought religious beliefs and practices that prevented them from being totally dehumanized by chattel slavery. In their homeland they had shared, within many
cultural and language groups, certain ancient ways of life—rituals, myths, wise
sayings, and ethical teachings—that had been handed down from generation
to generation. Ancient beliefs, folklore, attitudes, and practices provided a
worldview—a holistic view of reality—that made no radical separation
between religion and life. There was in everyday affairs no consciousness that
at one moment one was being religious and at another moment nonreligious
or secular. There was no sense that certain understandings of time, space,
human affairs, or relations between human and divine beings belonged to science or philosophy, rather than to religion, to the life of the mind rather than
to the life of the spirit.

We must proceed carefully here. This is not to claim that the slaves and
those they left behind in Africa did not perceive the difference between sacrificing a chicken to a familial god and hoeing a garden. We are not saying that
Africans did not esteem some men and women more than others because of

the special training and knowledge they possessed that could open up the secrets of nature, man, and God. Precisely so. But there was no absolute disjunction between the holy and the profane. What we must understand is that the African perspective looked upon the work of the intellect and the work of the spirit as a harmonious whole, as being ultimately about the same thing. Presuppositions and experiences of the unity of body and spirit, of heaven and earth, was the common privilege of everyone—not the guarded sinecure of intellectuals called philosophers or religionists called priests or specialists in magic and divination.

It may be almost impossible for modern people to understand fully the way of life out of which the slaves came. To do so we are obliged to change our entire habit of thought about the difference between being and doing, between reflection and action, the commonplace, ordinary affairs of daily experience and what we vaguely call the "spiritual life." Only in this way can we begin to appreciate the comprehensive, unitary character of the African consciousness. Of course, some scholars contend that the past was almost completely obliterated for the slaves who were brought to North America. But let us argue, for the moment, that for those who did remember anything about their former life (and it is unreasonable to suppose that everything was immediately forgotten once they disembarked on the quays of Jamestown or Charleston) there was no separation between religion and life, between the sacred and the secular. Experience was truth, and truth was experience. The single entity— what we might call "life-truth," or "truth-for-living"—comprehended the totality of existence. Reality was, at one and the same time, immanent and transcendent, material and spiritual, mundane and numinous.

It would be naive to assume that such a worldview was a primitive and simplistic stage of humanization. The folklore of Africa, comprising thousands of myths, folktales, and proverbs still being transmitted from one generation to another, is as subtle and complex in its probity as the choicest dialectical ruminations of a Platonic dialogue. As Richard F. Burton writes concerning the excellence of the proverbs of the Yoruba people of Nigeria: "Surely these proverbs are indications of no ordinary perception of moral truths, and are sufficient to warrant the inference that in closeness of observation, in depth of thought, and shrewd intelligence, the Yoruba is no ordinary man."

Nor were Africans so unsophisticated in their ideas of God that the religions preserved by some slaves in America can be dismissed as grossly inadequate compared with the theological presuppositions of the missionaries. Not only had some been already introduced to Islam and to the remnants of Portuguese Catholicism in West Africa but also their traditional religions were not inferior in insight and coherence to those two faiths. The twentieth-century Nigerian author Chinua Achebe captures the keen wit and profundity of the traditional religion in his novel *Things Fall Apart*. In one scene, Akunna, is in a confrontation with Mr. Brown, an English missionary who came to Akunna's village.

"You say that there is one supreme God who made heaven and earth," said Akunna on one of Mr. Brown's visits. "We also believe in Him and call Him Chukwu. He made all the world and the other gods."

"There are no other gods," said Mr. Brown. "Chukwu is the only God and all others are false. You carve a piece of wood—like that one" (he pointed at the rafters from which Akunna's carved Ikenga hung), and you call it a god. But it is still a piece of wood."

"Yes," said Akunna. "It is indeed a piece of wood. The tree from which it came was made by Chukwu, as indeed all minor gods were. But He made them for His messengers so that we could approach Him through them. It is like yourself. You are the head of your church."

"No," protested Mr. Brown. "The head of my church is God Himself."

"I know," said Akunna, "but there must be a head in this world among men. Somebody like yourself must be the head here."

Achebe's deftly drawn picture of Ibo life shows the inseparable connection between the soil in which the ancestors are buried, the community, and God. It calls into question the West's facile assumptions about the childishness of African religion and philosophy. Without it the African arrivals to the New World would have been hollow men and women. With it they were able to survive with their bodies and souls intact for the long and rugged ascent into the twentieth century.

THE CHRISTIANIZATION OF THE SLAVES

Any analysis of African-American religion must begin with two issues of critical importance: the nature of the earliest slave religion and the attitude of white Christians toward the Christianization of slaves and the abolition of slavery. The first recorded baptism of an African in the American colonies occurred in Virginia in 1624, but there was no systematic evangelization until the eighteenth century. Even then, the colonists were in no hurry to introduce their slaves to Christianity. The English rationalized the enslavement of both Africans and Indians because they were both different in appearance to themselves and because they considered both to be heathens. When it became evident that blacks were becoming believers despite widespread neglect by official church bodies, Virginia was the first of the colonies to make short shrift of the matter by declaring in 1667 that "the conferring of baptisme doth not alter the condition of the person as to his bondage or freedom."

It was difficult enough to induce a healthy state of religion among the white population. Attempts by the Society for the Propagation of the Gospel in Foreign Parts, an outpost of the bishops of London, to encourage planters to provide religious instruction for their slaves were largely unsuccessful, but almost from the beginning some blacks attended public worship and requested baptism. By the American Revolution a few had become Anglicans, Baptists, or

Methodists. In South Carolina, one missionary, the Reverend Samuel Thomas of Goose Creek, reported as early as 1705 that he had given religious instruction to at least one thousand slaves, many of whom could read the Bible and were memorizing the Creed.

Taking the gospel to blacks helped to ease the consciences of the colonial establishment about slavery, but it did not solve the problem completely. All of the American churches wrestled with the issue and, with the possible exception of the Quakers, finally compromised their ethical sensibilities. Bitter contention raged between northern and southern churchmen. As early as 1837 there were splits among the Lutherans and Presbyterians. In 1844 the Methodist Church divided North and South over slavery, followed by the Baptists in 1845. The antislavery American Missionary Association virtually split the Congregational Church in 1846. The Presbyterians finally set up northern and southern branches in 1861 and a fissure opening up in the Episcopal Church was aborted in 1862 by the refusal of northern Episcopalians to recognize that any unbrotherly controversy existed. Both the Episcopal and Roman Catholic churches, with some difficulty, were able to maintain structural unity throughout the Civil War.

THE EVOLUTION OF BLACK CHRISTIANITY

While the white churches anguished over slavery, the special nature of black Christianity was secretly asserting itself. We do not know when the first slaves stole away from the surveillance of the masters to worship in their own way. Two conjectures seem reasonable, however. First, it must have been early in the seventeenth century, for Africans would not have neglected practicing their ancestral religion altogether, and the whites did little to induce them to adopt theirs. Secondly, it is unlikely that the worship they engaged in was devoid of transplanted traditions from Africa. Today most scholars accept the position of W. E. B. DuBois and his contemporary, Melville Herskovits, a Jewish anthropologist, that survivals of African religion actually endured the Middle Passage and the "breaking-in" process in North America and reappeared under disguise in the early religious meetings of the "Invisible Institution"—the protochurch of the slaves. Present-day secular scholar John W. Blassinghame writes:

> In the United States, many African religious rites were fused into one—voodoo. From the whole panoply of African deities, the slaves chose the snake god of the Whydah, Fon, and Ewe. Symbolic of the umbilical cord and the rainbow, the snake embodied the dynamic, changing quality of life. In Africa it was sometimes the god of fertility and the determiner of good and ill fortune. Only by worshipping the god could one invoke his protective spirit.

There is scant evidence that Voodoo or some discrete form of reinterpreted African religion synthesized as effectively with Protestantism in the English colonies as it did with Roman Catholicism in the Caribbean and Latin America. Nevertheless, reports of missionaries and slave narratives show that the African conjurer and medicine man, the manipulation of charms and talismans, and the use of drums and dancing were present in the slaves' quarters as survival strategies, even after conversion to orthodox Christianity. Selective elements of African religions were not easily exterminated. A Presbyterian missionary, the Reverend Charles C. Jones, described what he encountered among the slaves as late as 1842:

> True religion they are inclined to place in profession, in forms and ordinances, and in excited states of feeling. And true conversion in dreams, visions, trances, voices—all bearing a perfect or striking resemblance to some form or type which has been handed down for generations, or which has been originated in the wild fancy of some religious teacher among them.

Reverend Jones warned his fellow missionaries that the blacks displayed "sophisticated perversions of the gospel" accountable only to the influence of African survivals. So impressed was he with their covert resistance to white Christianity that he compared their objections to "the ripe scholarship and profound intelligence of critics and philosophers."

THE FIRST BLACK CHURCHES

Although historian Mechal Sobel explains that there was a black congregation on the plantation of William Byrd III, near Mecklenburg, Virginia, as early as 1758, the first black-led churches formed along the Savannah River in Georgia and South Carolina in the 1770s, and in the North at about the same time. Immediately following the American Revolution black versions of white Baptist and Methodist churches appeared in Philadelphia, Baltimore, and New York City. But in the Sea Islands off South Carolina and Georgia coasts, in Louisiana, and on scattered plantations across the Southeast, a distinctive form of black folk religion flourished and infused the adopted white evangelicalism with retentions of African philosophy and spirituality. A new and implacable African-American Christianity was being created, much less puritanical and otherworldly than its white counterpart. In this regard it is significant that the three best-known slave revolts were led by fervently religious men—Gabriel Prosser in 1800, Denmark Vesey in 1822, and Nat Turner in 1831. Studies of the music of the early Black Church show that hidden rebelliousness and a desire for emancipation were often expressed in song. The independent black churches—particularly the African Methodist Episcopal (AME) Church founded in Philadelphia in 1816, and the African Methodist Episcopal Zion Church (AMEZ) founded in New York in 1821—were "freedom churches" in the sense that their latent, if not manifest, concern was *liberation* from slavery and *elevation* from ignorance and degradation to a higher status through education and self-help.

Within this tradition, a number of remarkable preachers emerged. David George, who served as *de facto* pastor of an independent black congregation at Silver Bluff, South Carolina, before 1775; George Liele and Andrew Bryan of the First Colored Baptist Church in Savannah during the same period; Josiah Bishop of Portsmouth, Virginia, and other preachers—from 1760 to 1795— were all former slaves who ministered in hostile territory, sometimes under the sponsorship and encouragement of radical white Baptist preachers. Some among them, like the full-blooded African "Uncle Jack," "Black Harry" Hosier, who served the Methodist bishop Francis Asbury, and the many illiterate preachers mentioned in missionary reports and other sources, are almost legendary. Many of their sermons dealt with the deliverance of Israel from Egyptian captivity, with stories of heroism and faithfulness in the Old Testament, and with the identification of Jesus with the poor and downtrodden masses. Mainly untutored, but rarely artless, they told "many-a-truth in a joke," as the saying goes, slyly philosophizing about how "God don't like ugly," "everybody talkin' 'bout heaven ain't goin' there," and "the freedom train's a-coming," obliquely reassuring their congregations of the ultimate vindication of their suffering. Moreover, many animal tales, adages, and proverbs that make up the corpus of black folklore were repeated from the pulpit as homiletical devices, as one preacher said, to "explain the unexplainable, define the indefinable, and unscrew the inscrutable."

The theological motif of these early preachers was survival by any means possible, but especially by virtue of the supernatural power available to every believer. They were preoccupied with maintaining their people's health, keeping them alive, helping them to retain some semblance of personhood and self-esteem in the face of massive dehumanization. Blassingame writes:

> One of the primary reasons the slaves were able to survive the cruelty they faced was that their behavior was not totally dependent on their masters.... In religion, a slave exercised his own independence of conscience. Convinced that God watched over him, the slave bore his earthly afflictions in order to earn a heavenly reward. Often he disobeyed his earthly master's rules to keep his Heavenly Master's commandments.... Religious faith gave an ultimate purpose to his life, a sense of communal fellowship and personal worth, and reduced suffering from fear and anxiety.

DEVELOPMENT OF THE NORTHERN CHURCHES

A somewhat different tradition developed among black churches in the North. Many of their pastors also came out of slavery and humble rural backgrounds. But in the relatively freer atmosphere of the North the theological content of their religion took another turn. It tended toward the ethical revivalism that characterized white Protestantism during the so-called Second Great Awakening, the phenomenal revival of heartfelt, benevolent religion that swept the nation from 1790 to around 1830. It was more urban, more pragmatic, more appealing to those blacks who were beginning to enjoy a relative measure of the prosperity and greater access to educational opportunities found in the northern cities.

In Philadelphia, Richard Allen and Absalom Jones protested racial segregation by walking out of St. George's Methodist Church in 1787 and founded a quasi-religious community organization called the Free African Society. In Baltimore, New York, Providence, and Boston, similar associations—dedicated to the educational, moral, and religious uplift of Africans—became the scaffolding of the black churches of the North. Immediately following voluntary or forced separation from white congregations, African Americans demonstrated an overarching interest in social, economic, and political advancement by making their new churches centers of civic activities. They were aided by white friends such as Anthony Benezet and Benjamin Rush of Philadelphia in organizing and funding self-help and charitable societies, but their churches were the main engines driving all "secular" enterprise. The primary impulse behind these northern developments was a desire for socioeconomic and religious autonomy, for racial solidarity, self-help, and personal and group elevation in all branches of civilization.

Thus, as Lewis V. Baldwin explains in his work on the early African-American Church, Peter Spencer formed a new denomination, the Union Church of African Members, in Wilmington, Delaware, in 1813; Richard Allen became the first bishop of the African Methodist Episcopal Church in Philadelphia; and James Varick became the first bishop of the African Methodist Episcopal Zion Church in New York. These men, together with Absalom Jones, rector of St. Thomas Episcopal Church of Africans in Philadelphia; John Gloucester, pastor of the First African Presbyterian Church of the same city; Peter Williams Jr., of New York City, the first ordained black priest of the Episcopal Church; and Thomas Paul, founder of the first African Baptist Church, also in New York, were all strong, progressive leaders who, in the first two decades of the nineteenth century, promoted education and social betterment as a religious obligation. They encouraged their laypeople to undertake racial progress programs and activities at a time when public meetings of blacks were forbidden in the South and even preaching was prohibited except under white supervision.

We can speak of these northern church leaders, therefore, as elevationists in the sense that their concerns went far beyond mere survival to racial advancement. The physician and journalist Martin R. Delany of Pittsburgh, Pennsylvania, is a good example of the elevationist orientation found generally among the black middle class, which black churchmen and most black Christian laymen of the period shared. For Delany, education, self-help, a desire for equality and racial progress were rungs on the ladder of black elevation and "the means by which God intended man to succeed." In *The Condition, Elevation, Emigration, and Destiny of the Colored People of the United States*, Delany says:

If, as before stated, a knowledge of all the various business enterprises, trades, professions, and sciences, is necessary for the elevation of the white, a knowledge of them also is necessary for the elevation of the colored man. . . . What we desire to learn now is, how to effect a *remedy*; this we have endeavored to point out. Our elevation must be the result of self-efforts, and work of our own hands. No other human power can accomplish it.

The concept of elevation appears by name in black literature throughout the nineteenth century. Before many of them could properly read and write, black men and women, lay as well as clergy, envisioned a broad horizon of racial uplift or advancement through religion. They were the people who dominated the free black communities of the North and led such causes as the boycotting of goods produced by slave labor, resistance to efforts of the American Colonization Society to return free blacks to Africa, and the promotion of moral reform societies. As the clergy became more distracted by the ecclesiastical responsibilities of their burgeoning new denominations, the secular organizations that they once spawned, such as the American Moral Reform Society and the National Negro Convention movement, gradually became autonomous, although still under the parental influence of the urban churches. The National Negro Convention first met in a church in 1830 and held seven consecutive annual convocations on elevationist issues. Many of these meetings were attended by liberal whites for whom they provided an opportunity to continue to have a fellowship with (and, thereby, to exercise subtle control over) blacks that had been made more difficult by the development of separate black churches.

The regional and national conventions devoted to abolition and moral reform also represented the liberation motif that was nurtured by a growing black educated class anxious for upward mobility. In the antebellum period the themes of liberation and elevation were sponsored by relatively wealthy black laymen like James Forten, Robert Purvis, William Whipper, and William C. Nell. The most influential among them was the journalist David Walker, whose incendiary *Appeal to the Colored Citizens of the World*, published in 1829, inspired former slaves like Frederick Douglass and William Wells Brown, and "freeborn" propagandists like Martin R. Delany, William H. Day, and H. Ford Douglass. The elevation-conscious, progressive middle class extricated itself from the control of the preachers early in the nineteenth century. The impetus for reform was to come from church-related, but intellectually independent laymen and women—like Paul Cuffee, the Massachusetts sea captain of the late eighteenth century, Maria Stewart, the great woman orator and emancipator, Booker T. Washington, the foremost black educator and national spokesperson during the last century, and W. E. B. DuBois, the brilliant sociologist and political activist who opposed Washington's more passive theory of racial advancement.

A COMPARISON OF MOTIFS

There is, obviously, an intricate and dialectical relationship between the survival, liberation, and elevation traditions in the African-American community. All three were seminal in the churches of the nineteenth century and continued into the next century in various configurations and degrees of tension, depending upon differences due to time and place. In the ghetto of Los Angeles, between 1906 and the First World War, the survival-oriented followers of William J. Seymour and other charismatic evangelists produced an unprecedented display of African religious retentions that had lain dormant in the interstices of black rural society for a hundred years. Thus black Pentecostalism matured after having been conceived and nurtured in the "Invisible Institution," but was almost extinguished by the middle-class Negro churches and "civilizing" white missionaries who followed the Union Army into the South during the Civil War.

Holiness or Pentecostalism claimed 34 percent of the black churches in New York City in the mid-1920s. In twelve other northern cities in 1930, 37 percent of the churches were storefront missions that fostered a volatile combination of survival and liberation hermeneutics. During and after the First World War this distinctive strain of lower-class religion, derided and repudiated by the elevation-oriented churches of the established middle class, was radicalized. In the purifying fires of these churches, Pentecostalism metamorphosed into various religio-political sects and cults, including blackenized versions of Judaism and Islam. The black Jews and the Black Muslims of the Depression era were, therefore, unique representations of an indigenous, survival-oriented religiosity seeking a new cultural and nationalistic expression under the duress of American urbanization, industrialization, and racism.

Survival-oriented southern migrants, who found a cool reception for their rural folk Christianity among the elite churches of the urban North, were ripe for the messages of Timothy Drew (Noble Drew Ali), founder of the Moorish Science Temple, Marcus Garvey, leader of the quasi-religious "Back to Africa" mass movement of the present century, and W. D. Fard, the mysterious founder of the Black Muslims of America. Although Garvey's Universal Negro Improvement Association (U.N.I.A.) found its validation in a heterodox form of Christianity that synthesized elements of the ancient churches of Egypt and Ethiopia, Roman Catholicism, and the Anglicanism of the British colonies in the Caribbean, the appeal of the Moorish Science and Black Muslims was basically cultic in the sense that their highly charismatic and autocratic leaders attempted to create what were virtually wholly new religions in the black ghetto.

Into this ferment came Elijah Poole, the son of a Baptist minister and sharecropper in Sandersville, Georgia, who moved to Detroit in 1919 and changed his name to Elijah Muhammad. There, as an ardent follower and successor of Fard, he studied Islam. But the Black Muslims did not seriously challenge the older Negro churches until the rise of Malcolm X Shabazz in the 1960s. Malcolm's appointment as national spokesman and his extraordinary ability as an organizer and interpreter of the faith of Elijah catapulted him into leadership of the disillusioned youth of the black ghetto and the remnants of Garveyism who saw a possibility for the revitalization of black nationalism through connections with his movement. Malcolm's assassination on February 21, 1965, served only to increase his influence among important sectors of the African-American community. In 1975, after the death of Elijah, his son, Wallace D. Muhammad, assumed leadership of the Black Muslims and immediately instituted a radical reversal from the cult of his father to the established religion of orthodox Islam—today a strong competitor of Christianity for the loyalty of the masses of black people.

Today if the mainstream African-American churches are only moderately interested in liberation from all forms of oppression, and are mainly elevationist in their orientation, the black Muslims—now under the leadership of Minister Louis Farrakhan—represent a radicalization of the essentially survivalistic tradition of the underclass that tends in the direction of black nationalism and the goal of pan-African liberation.

Between the First and Second World Wars the attempt was made by organizations such as the National Association for the Advancement of Colored People (NAACP) to realign the survival, elevation, and liberation motifs so as to create the kind of balance and harmony between them that would be conducive for racial progress. It was the experience of black leadership during the era of abolitionism and emigrationism that when one of these themes was either neglected or exaggerated above the other two—such as commitment to the biblical God and a spirit-led, evangelical church, on the one hand, or to black political, economic, and cultural life, on the other hand—the center collapsed. For example, after the Civil War black churches became excessively bourgeois and bureaucratic, and again during the Great Depression they lost ground to the cults, on the one hand, and to secular organizations like the NAACP and the National Urban League on the other, notwithstanding the effort on the part of DuBois and progressive elements in the NAACP to create a balance of cultural and political emphases. On both occasions the consequence was a kind of paralysis that left the masses in moral confusion and the middle classes in a spiritual malaise that was powerless to give leadership when relative calm and prosperity returned, and another realignment and new beginning were called for.

Beginning in 1955, it was the genius of the Reverend Dr. Martin Luther King Jr., that brought the three traditions together again in a history-making, prophetic ministry that wedded the deep spirituality and will to survive of the alienated and impoverished masses with the sophisticated pragmatism and desire for equality and liberation that characterized the parvenu urbanites and the Negro intelligentsia—the "New Negro" of the 1920s and '30s. King embraced all three of these tendencies and created a multidimensional movement, inseparable from the black church, that set in motion social, political, economic, religious, and cultural forces that have not yet run their full course. King stands at the pinnacle of black religious and political development in the twentieth century.

King was not alone in pointing the way to a new future, for the black Muslim minister Malcolm X forced a decisive break between moderate accommodationism that compromised the liberation ideology and a form of protest that was truly revolutionary, a form of protest that ultimately radicalized King. But in King was found the confluence of all the complex and variegated tendencies and orientations that are summed up in the traditions of survival, liberation, and elevation. Other leaders were to come out of the sacred ground upon which he stood, yet beyond him lay unexplored heights that could not have been seen without standing on his shoulders.

The black church in America continues to evolve in the post-King era. The publication in 1969 of *Black Theology and Black Power*, by Union Theological Seminary professor James H. Cone, provided a thunderous challenge to Euro-American theological scholarship, made room for an alternative strategy for the black church and an intrusive new, unruly tenant in the racially segregated halls of academe. This method of theologizing had not been altogether absent during the years before King, but it had brooded in the shadows outside the mainstream black denominations and the ivy-covered walls of their church-related schools and colleges. Cone's first book gave a name to this neglected and ignored stream of African-American religious thought that probably came into existence when the first slave tossed all night on his straw mat, wondering why he was expected to believe in a God who ordained all blacks to perpetual bondage. The name given by Cone to what he found pulsating just beneath the surface of King's more conciliatory Social Gospel, to this religious first cousin to the Black Power philosophy enunciated and popularized by the young civil rights revolutionary Stokely Carmichael and the militant black sociologist Charles V. Hamilton, was "black liberation theology."

Before the end of the 1960s the liberation theme had once again regained ascendancy and proliferated far beyond the black ghettoes of the United States. Liberation theology took root among oppressed campesinos and barrio-dwellers in Latin America, among black Christian leaders in South Africa, and, in the United States, among white feminists and black womanists (the term adopted by black women to differentiate their more lower-class, rebellious, down-to-earth feminism from that of the triumphant white middle-class women who, in many instances, continued to be racist). The liberation theme rapidly became a major topic among theologians on both sides of the Atlantic and in ecumenical circles such as the World Council of Churches. But since 1967 the discussion has not been limited to seminaries and church councils. In that year a small but belligerent movement for black religious power and social transformation broke out under the aegis of a new coalition of African-

American church executives, pastors, and academics that called itself the National Committee of Black Churchmen (NCBC)—a northern version of King's Southern Christian Leadership Conference (SCLC). The watchword in important segments of the African-American religious community was *liberation*—which meant freedom from racism, poverty, powerlessness, and all forms of white domination. Liberation became a theological codeword for the indigenous religious genius of an oppressed community. On their part, African-American theologians, freed from dependence upon priests and preachers, and deference to ecclesiastical politics—even within the black church—began to teach and write a revolutionary Christianity that originated with Jesus, whom they called the Black Messiah. Jesus was the Oppressed Man of God who challenged the hypocrisy of Jewish religion (recapitulated in both white Christianity and a contaminated Negro religion) and the unjust power of the Roman state (recapitulated in the worldwide political and economic hegemony of American capitalism at the end of the twentieth century).

CONCLUSION

Throughout their history African-American churches have struggled to hold racial advancement on the political, economic, and cultural front and "winning souls for Christ" in a precarious balance. Generally they have refused to have one without the other. Social action and evangelism were complementary. This enabled the churches to do three things: first, to help the race survive, that is, to hold body and soul together against the atrocities of white racism; second, to help the race free itself from legal slavery, economic exploitation, and the curse of second-class citizenship; and third, to elevate the young and the masses to a level of moral and spiritual integrity that ennobled both the individual and collective life of the community. Today that community is in crisis partly because material interests—the undisciplined desire for money and pleasure—has overridden the values of the Civil Rights era which deepened spiritual commitments and opened up new material opportunities for the black middle class, and partly because the black church, seduced by an evangelical backwardness that is not native to it but was borrowed from conservative white Christianity, by an anti-intellectual emotionalism, and by a sterile and sometimes exploitative ecclesiasticism, has lost the balance between the historic pillars of black religion—survival, liberation, and elevation. The disequilibrium of these motifs meant the loss of the black church's true external mission and gift to American society and, at the same time, the loss of control over and the trivialization of its internal mission to itself and African-American culture.

In consequence, the holistic character of black religion was fractured after King and Malcolm, and both the black church and black culture, previously inseparable, lost that essential connection they require. Today they find themselves, in the first instance, in the throes of a severe crisis of faith; and in the second instance, in the grip of a crisis of meaning, a disjunction and corruption of worldview and ethos.

These crises cannot be solved by encouraging "the classes and masses" to repudiate religion as anachronistic, or by black scholars like Jawanza Kunjufu pretending that a transient youth culture that glorifies volatility, that disregards serious commitments, and that calls black women whores and bitches, is authentic African-American culture. To undermine black religion by alleging its mystification, and to trivialize African-American culture by denying its historic roots in the black church is only to deepen the crisis, not get rid of it. Historic black faith has nothing to do with the posturings of black preachers who ape white televangelists, any more than hip-hop and New York City lifestyles represent black culture at its best or have much to do with the rich deposits of black folk wisdom in the souls of black folk, African religious retentions, and African-American intellectual traditions from David Walker, for example, to Toni Morrison, the prize-winning novelist of black culture.

Perhaps the time has come for the next generation of African Americans to reassert the great tradition we have been examining; to insert values that are truly Afrocentric; to rescue the inheritance of Martin and Malcolm—the strategies of survival, liberation, and elevation—from moral and spiritual debasement by children who never knew them and who, shamefully, have never been taught the truth about who they are, from whence they come, and how they fell into this sorry plight.

This is one of the goals of black theology. If the church will return to basics and tap once again into that ennobling and enlightened strain of religion that brought African Americans through the Civil Rights period and helped them amass a modicum of Black Power, perhaps the crisis of these closing years of the twentieth century will be surmounted and they can go into the next one with integrity and hope. Martin King anticipated this possibility. Indeed, it was a part of his dream—an embracing of enduring values, a profoundly religious reorientation, a rejuvenation of the spirit of blackness. This seems to be what he envisioned when, at the end of *Where Do We Go From Here? Chaos or Community*, he wrote these words:

> This is our challenge. If we will dare to meet it honestly, historians in future years will have to say that there lived a great people—a Black people—who bore their burdens of oppression in the heat of many days and who, through tenacity and creative commitment, injected a new meaning into the veins of American life.

On the threshold of the twenty-first century, the direction of black religion in America defies any easy prediction, but the dynamism of the African spiritual inheritance, of which it is the historic expression and primary carrier in the West, is likely to preclude its total secularization in the foreseeable future.

FOR FURTHER READING

Baldwin, Lewis V. *The Mark of a Man: Peter Spencer and the African Union Methodist Tradition*. Lanham, Md.: University Press of America, 1987.

Blassingame, John W. *The Slave Community: Plantation Life in the Antebellum South*. 2nd ed. New York: Oxford University Press, 1979.

Carmichael, Stokely, and Charles V. Hamilton. *Black Power: The Politics of Liberation in America*. New York: Vintage, 1992.

Cone, James. *Black Theology and Black Power*. Maryknoll, N.Y.: Orbis Books, 1997.

————. *Martin and Malcolm and America: A Dream or a Nightmare?* Maryknoll, N.Y.: Orbis Books, 1992.

Fulop, Timothy. *African American Religion: Interpretative Essays in History and Culture*. New York: Routledge, 1996.

Grant, Jacquelyn. *White Women's Christ and Black Women's Jesus: Feminist Christology and Womanist Response*. Atlanta: Scholars Press, 1990.

Harding, Vincent. *There Is a River: The Black Struggle for Freedom in America*. New York: Harcourt Brace, 1981.

Hinks, Peter P. *To Awaken My Afflicted Brethren: David Walker and the Problem of Antebellum Slave Resistance*. University Park: Penn State University Press, 1996.

Johnson, Paul E. *African-American Christianity: Essays in History*. Berkeley and Los Angeles: University of California Press, 1994.

King, Martin Luther, Jr. *Where Do We Go From Here? Chaos or Community*. New York: Harper, 1967.

Lincoln, C. Eric. *The Black Church in the African American Experience*. Durham, N.C.: Duke University Press, 1990.

Raboteau, Albert J. *Slave Religion: The "Invisible Institution" in the Antebellum South*. New York: Oxford University Press, 1980.

Sobel, Mechal. *Trabelin' On: The Slave Journey to an Afro-Baptist Faith* [Abridged]. Princeton, N.J.: Princeton University Press, 1988.

Wilmore, Gayraud S. *Black Religion and Black Radicalism: An Interpretation of the Religious History of African Americans*. 3rd ed. Maryknoll, N.Y.: Orbis Press, 1998.

part 5.

Family, Class, and Gender

chapter 14

African-American Family Life in Societal Context

Crisis and Hope

Walter R. Allen

> The contempt we have been taught to entertain for the Blacks makes us fancy many things that are founded neither in reason nor in experience.
>
> —Alexander Hamilton

ESPITE THE VOLUMINOUS RESEARCH on black family life, students of the African-American family are often made uneasy by much of what is written on the subject. This uneasiness is partly caused by continued references to the monolithic notion of "The Black Family." Such references ignore the extensive regional, ethnic, value, and income differences among black families. This uneasiness may also arise from the theoretical and methodological shoddiness apparent in so many published, widely circulated studies of such families. This uneasiness is bred by entrenched, stereotypical portrayals of black families that not only persist, but often dominate many of these studies. This wariness is caused by the frequently demonstrated ignorance of supposed authorities concerning the internal dynamics and motives of black family life in American society.

DIVERSITY AND STEREOTYPES IN THE STUDY OF BLACK FAMILY LIFE

Much that is written about black American families is flawed by the tendency of researchers to gloss over intragroup differences. While prior research has explored black/white family differences, information is relatively sparse regarding differences among African-American families of different incomes, regions, life-cycle stages, and value orientations. As a result, monolithic, stereotypic characterizations of black families abound. The black family headed by a single mother with numerous children and living in a roach-infested tenement is a familiar stereotype. This image has been reinforced in the hallowed halls of universities, on the frenetic sets of movies and television shows, as well as in the august galleries of Congress. That this stereotype represents but a limited slice of black family life in the United States is unfortunate; that it distorts the truth about female-headed households in the black community is worse. Such stereotypes leave the genuinely curious searching for the true faces of black family life in this country.

As a society, the United States is comfortable with stereotypes. Indeed, we Americans revel in them. Stereotypes serve a useful function: they help to reduce the complexity, nuances, and dilemmas of life to manageable proportions. In this respect, Americans are no different from other people. Generally speaking, humans seek to organize reality by extracting neat categories of meaning. Thus we become accustomed to loose usage of terms charged with unstated implications to summarize our day-to-day experiences. Designations such as "liberals," "born-again Christians," "fascists," "feminists," and "racists" are commonplace in our daily discourse. Rarely, in the next breath, are the intricacies of meaning apparent in such terms clarified. Why should they be? We all know what is meant by them . . . or do we?

Race is an area of inquiry in the social and behavioral sciences particularly affected by our willingness to accept simplistic, unsupported, and stereotypic statements at face value. Such confusion may have complex explanations, such as the difficulty of disentangling race from culture and history; or the explanations may be more simple, as in the failure to recognize that race is not a perfect predictor of a person's psyche, values, or even experiences. Therefore race continues to be one of the most widely studied, yet most poorly understood areas of scientific inquiry. As the esteemed sociologist E. Franklin Frazier noted, and as the eminent scholar W. E. B. DuBois had emphasized before him, ours is a society obsessed with color. How we think about and interact with race, therefore, exerts profound influence on the broader realities of black individuals, groups, and institutions. These are topics requiring further study.

Predictably, black family studies share many problems with the related area of race relations research. Writers in the area obscure much of the richness, complexity, and subtleties of African-American family systems through their use of crude categories, poorly defined concepts, and negative stereotypes. Apparent in the literature are abundant references to "family disorganization," the "underclass," "culture of poverty," and "the Black Matriarchy." Such terms are offered, picked up, and repeated as if they effectively summarized the reality of black family life in this society. They do not. Unfortunately, with successive repetition, such concepts and the myths they represent become more palatable and more believable. Equally dissatisfying are terms offered by those seeking to blame social problems on the victims in the ongoing debate over pathology and well-being among black American families. For me, the issue is not wholly over whether black families should be cast as good or bad, positive or negative. Both views pursued to an extreme tamper with reality, become stereotypic, and ultimately dehumanize black families. In its most fundamental sense, life is a collage of good, bad, and indifferent; so, too, is black family life.

This chapter advocates the setting aside of the language of black family wellness or illness. The record of these families in ensuring the survival and development of black Americans and their culture on these shores since 1619 is sufficient evidence of their adaptability and viability. Instead, this piece is concerned with seeing the core of black family life and exploring its essential character. To this extent, the research question is recast, avoiding the charged language of "wellness" or "illness" to examine how black families really live. What are the significant qualities, characteristics, and dimensions of black family life revealed in the research record from 1965 to the present? What environmental and historical conditions determine the tenor of a black family's experiences? What are the distinctive features of African-American family life? In sum, the need is to understand black families for who and what they are.

BLACK FAMILIES: DEFINITIONS AND TRANSITIONS

Before undertaking the examination of the experiences of black American families, it must first decide how best to define these families. The criteria for definition will vary in accordance with the definitions used by authors whose research is being examined. Readers should therefore expect to see, and not be put off by, shifts in the parameters used to define black family life. In some cases, location will be emphasized, thus defining family as coterminous with household. In other cases, blood ties will be relied upon to define the boundaries of a given black family. At still other points, functional ties such as shared emotional support or economic responsibilities will be used to define families. In the thinking of the author, emphasis of shared location over, say, functional ties as the criterion for defining family relationship is an *analytic decision*. Such decisions do not alter the fact that black families are defined by complicated overlaps between location, functional relations, shared values, affiliations, and blood ties. As such, black families represent complex systems of relationships that transcend any one of these areas of life. The accommodation to multiple definitions of black family life simply admits the current limitations in social science theory and the methods requiring that researchers restrict their focus to smaller parcels of the family system they seek to understand. However, a consistent feature across researchers' definitions is the primacy assigned to blood ties. At root, black families are seen as institutions whose most enduring relationships are biological.

Systematic examinations of significant trends and statuses in black American family life offer useful lessons for evaluating scientific research in the area. The history of black Americans, like that of any people, is marked by change. Black Americans have experienced four major transitions in their history, each having left legacies which influence contemporary black family life. The first and most obvious transition involved bringing captured Africans to this country as slaves. For enslaved Africans, this transition involved both gross (e.g., the loss of personal freedom) and subtle (e.g., exposure to plantation agriculture) redefinitions. Out of these redefinitions was created a new people—African Americans—who represented cultural, social, and, yes, biological hybrids. The second major transition in African-American history involved emancipation: blacks were freed from slavery. This status change was accompanied, however, by the equally demeaning and restrictive redefinition of blacks as an "untouchable"-like caste group in American society. It is worth noting that, while over time the terms of reference (e.g., Negro, colored, black, African-American) have changed, the degraded caste status of black people has been an immutable constant. On the heels of this evolution of blacks from slavery to caste status came the geographic, socioeconomic and cultural transitions of black America from a southern, rural, agrarian folk society to a northern, western, and midwestern industrial society. In four generations, or roughly one hundred years, African Americans had moved from agrarian slavery into the industrial and urban heartlands of this country. They had become hybrids, combing the heritages of their African and American experiences.

The fourth major transition for African Americans involved the desegregation of U.S. society. This transition was most notably signaled by the string of presidential orders and Supreme Court decisions banning racial segregation in public life (e.g., the 1949 presidential order desegregating the military, the 1954 court decision outlawing segregated public schools). A major impetus for the desegregation of American society were the activities and actors associated with the Civil Rights movement. However, efforts to desegregate U.S. institutional, corporate, and community life at all levels have so far proven to be only partially successful. Vestiges of past disadvantages and persistent discrimination in the present continue to restrict black equality and participation in this society.

THE EMPIRICAL PICTURE: PATTERNS AND TRENDS

Government statistics convey valuable information about the contemporary faces of black families. Such statistics are admittedly limited in what they reveal concerning the nuances of black family life. However, these statistics do provide valuable insight into the broad pattern characteristic of black families currently. Looking at the wealth of data compiled in the 1990 census, we can roughly sketch some of the parameters of African-American family structure toward the end of the twentieth century. At that time, the black presence in this country had grown to roughly 31 million, representing 13 percent of the total U.S. population and some 7.7 million households. A massive geographic redistribution had also occurred. Since 1945 there has been a sizable drop in the percentages of black residents or born natives of the South (the figure declined from 80 percent to 50 percent); contemporary blacks and their households are overwhelmingly located in urban areas (nearly 85 percent). Recent statistics suggest sizable modifications in historically observed patterns: increasing numbers of blacks will likely return to the South or move to suburbs or small towns.

The trend toward increased numbers of female-headed black households noted by Frazier in the 1930s and Daniel Patrick Moynihan in the 1960s continued. By 1992, 46 percent of all black households had female heads; in addition, the percentage of dual-parent households had declined to 47 percent (respectively, 18 percent and 77 percent in 1940). Consistent with shifts in family headship were declines in the percentage of black children residing with both parents, from 75 percent in 1960 to 36 percent. Black childbearing rates continued their steady drop toward replacement levels, reaching an all-time low total fertility rate of an estimated 2.28 children per woman in 1975 (as compared with 2.62 in 1940). Finally, rates of marital dissolution and lifelong singlehood continued to rise among black Americans during the period. The latter statistic certainly reflected, in part, the great imbalance between men and women in the critical marriage and childbearing years (in 1974, there were 100 men for every 116 women aged 20 to 54, not adjusting for men lost from the pool of eligibles for reasons of imprisonment, interracial preferences, homosexuality, and so forth). This leads to one of the most striking differences between African Americans and other segments of the society. In the early 1990s, fewer than three of four black women would eventually marry compared to nine out of ten white women.

Along with shifts in the geography and structure of family life among blacks came important changes in the socioeconomic status. Median family income levels had been rising since 1947. The real median income of black families in 1991 was $33,310 compared to $41,510 for white families. The real median income for black female-headed households was substantially lower: $11,410. The percentage of black family incomes below the poverty level also had dropped steadily, from 41 percent in 1959 to 15 percent in 1974. Entering the 1990s, the number of black families below the poverty line had risen to 32 percent. Fortunately this has fallen in the course of the decade.

Accompanying changes in family income levels were changes in the educational and occupational attainments of black Americans. Since 1940, the median years of school completed by blacks has doubled and is close to that of whites. More than 80 percent of blacks had four or more years of high school, and one in nine African Americans had four or more years of college. Both of the latter figures represent a sixfold increase from 1940 to 1975. In the world of work, contradictory trends are observed. On the one hand, black representation in higher-status occupations has increased dramatically. From 1960 to 1972, the percentage of black workers in white-collar jobs grew from 16 percent to 45 percent. On the other hand, since 1978 black labor force participation rates have declined steadily, down to 70 percent for men and 58 percent for women by the year 1992. Unemployment rates have continued to rise, reaching crisis levels in many black communities across the country.

When attention is turned to health, morbidity, and mortality statistics, major improvements can again be noted for African Americans since World War II. Life expectancies for black men and black women in the 1990s are 65 and 74 years, respectively, versus 51 and 55 years in 1940. The infant mortality rate has been cut from 80 to 18 per 1,000 live births, while maternal deaths in childbirth have been reduced eightfold (to fewer than .2 per 1,000 live births). Black deaths due to so-called "poverty diseases" (e.g., tuberculosis, venereal disease, cirrhosis of the liver, and contagious disease) have also been drastically curtailed. Moreover, the percentage of black families residing in substandard housing dropped from more than 50 percent in 1940 to less than 25 percent by 1970.

The picture conveyed by this overview of key government statistics is one of gradual but steady improvement in the life circumstances of black families in the last half-century. During the African-American's transition from the rural South into the urban North, significant improvements have occurred in health, education, income, occupation, and housing. Lest a false sense of complacency result, however, it must be pointed out that deprivation and disadvantage are relative concepts. Compared to white families in this society, black families continue to be extremely disadvantaged. Now, as earlier in this country's history, the occupational and educational attainments, health statuses, housing conditions, incomes, and life opportunities of white Americans are far superior to those of their black brethren. When select subcategories of black families (e.g., urban, lower income, aged, and so forth) are compared to black families in the general case, another level of inequality is revealed. Vast differences in resources, opportunities, and quality of life are often found among black families of different incomes, regions, and headship statuses (e.g., two-parent versus single-parent).

The aggregate statistics discussed above conceal a complex array of underlying relationships. For this reason, what a particular statistical pattern reveals about the nature of black family life in this society is not always clear. Undoubtedly poor health, chronic unemployment, teen parenthood, paternal absence, and poverty have potentially negative consequences for black family organization and functions. However, the relative impact of these factors on particular families are mediated by those families' resources, values, and situations. It is thus important to recognize that individual and family characteristics help to determine whether certain conditions are positive or negative in the effects, and to what degree. This essay will now turn to a consideration of the complicated interaction between class and culture in African-American families.

CONCEPTUAL ISSUES:
CLASS, CULTURE, AND BLACK FAMILY LIFE

Researchers have long debated the importance of economics and culture in the determination of black family organization and functions. The sociologist and educator E. Franklin Frazier (1894–1962), profoundly influenced thinking about the interplay of class and race in black family life. Writing in an era of social concern with the consequences of industrialization and rapid urbanization for families, Frazier focused his attention on black families. He rejected explanations attributing high rates of marital instability, desertion, and illegitimacy among urban black families to innate, biological deficiencies. Rather, Frazier believed these disrupted family patterns were caused by a unique historical experience which left some black Americans ill-prepared to cope with the exigencies of life in modern, industrial society. Briefly, he argued that personal and institutional discrimination in society placed blacks at a severe economic disadvantage, with ruinous consequences for their family life. Denied the skills necessary to ensure economic viability, black men fell short in the performance of their provider roles, thereby contributing to the break-up of families. Hence, Frazier largely attributed family disorganization among blacks to economic factors, suggesting in the process that as black families achieved higher economic status, their rates of disorganization would drop.

Certain features in Frazier's research make its application to the analysis of contemporary black family life problematic. First, he failed to specify the societal-level processes thought to determine black family patterns. At best, readers are left with vague impressions of such processes and their causal operation. Second, he consistently denied the legitimacy of aspects of black family life representing departures from normative white family patterns. Third, he implicitly emphasized cultural consequences of economic deprivation, such that he advanced the idea of family disorganization as the result of cultural continuities. Black family disorganization, he argued, derives from a self-perpetuating tradition of fragmented, pathological interaction within lower-class black urban communities. A culture of poverty, if you will, is said to develop. Frazier basically proposed a socioeconomic/cultural deprivation model for interpretation of black family life, as an alternative to then-current biological deficit models. Unfortunately, Frazier's perspective is sometimes equally injurious to the image and understanding of black family life. By treating racial discrimination in vague historic terms, denying the legitimacy of black cultural forms, and fostering deterministic views of poverty and its consequences, his perspective lends itself to interpretations of black families as pathological. Where black families exhibit signs of disorganization, the tendency is to seek internal, rather than external, causes, or, for that matter, to not question the ethnocentric connotations of family disorganization. A vivid illustration of this point is provided in the controversial Moynihan report of 1965, which is closely patterned after Frazier's work. Moynihan portrayed black family life as grim and concluded that:

> At the heart of the deterioration of the fabric of Negro society is the deterioration of the Negro family. It is the fundamental source of weakness in the Negro community at the present time. . . . The White family has achieved a high degree of stability and is maintaining that stability. By contrast, the family structure of lower class Negroes is highly unstable and in many urban centers is approaching complete breakdown.

E. Franklin Frazier, "The Negro Family in 1940"

Because of the extent to which class differentiation has evolved in the large north-ern cities, the organization of Negro family life must be studied in relation to the class structure in these communities. It may be well to begin at the bottom of the class structure, since as one considers the higher levels the effects of urban living from the standpoint of reorganization, of the family in the urban environment become more pronounced. The lower-class families are physically segregated to a large extent in the deteriorated areas where Negroes first secure a foothold in the community. It is among this class that one finds the large proportion of fam-ilies with female heads. This is the result of the economic insecurity of the men and illegitimacy. Because of the precarious hold which women of this class have on men, their attitudes alternate between one of subordination to secure affection and one of domination because of their greater economic security than their spouses. But there is in the lower class a "church centered" core of families that endeavor to maintain stable family relations despite their economic insecurity and other exigencies which make family life unstable. Even during periods of com-parative prosperity the employment of women may prove a disintegrating factor since these families lack a deeply rooted tradition.

The occupational differentiation of the Negro population in the northern city, as we have seen, has made possible the emergence of a substantial middle class. The middle class is comprised largely of clerical workers and persons in the service occu-pations, though there are professional workers and some business persons in this class. But, perhaps, the most important accession to the middle class in the north-ern cities has been the families of industrial workers, especially the skilled workers. It is among the occupational class that the male head of the family has sufficient economic security to play the conventional rôle of provider for his family without the aid of the wife. This was indicated in a study of the industrial employment of Negro men and the employment of Negro married women in 75 northern and southern cities with a total population of 100,000 or more in 1930. It was found that the proportion of married women employed declined as the proportion of employed Negro males in industry increased.

Although the husband or father in the middle-class Negro family is generally recognized as the head of the family, the wife or mother is not completely subor-dinated. There is often a division of labor in the management of the household and a spirit of democracy in the family. The dignified and respected position of the wife and mother is due partly to the tradition of independence among Negro women. The spirit of democracy often springs from the fact that there is consid-erable cooperation in order that the family may purchase a home or that the chil-dren may obtain an education. The education of children means that the family is "getting up" in the world. To be respectable and to "get up" in the world are two of the main ambitions of middle-class families. Therefore, it is not unusual that parents in middle-class families make tremendous sacrifices to enable their chil-dren to get a college education. At the same time the children of the middle class are not as a rule spoiled as are often the children in the upper class. They are gen-erally subjected to strict discipline but they are not treated with the harshness which is often found in the case of children in lower-class families. The boys who begin at any early age to earn money in such jobs as running errands and selling newspapers generally develop a sense of responsibility and habits of industry. Con-sequently, the ambitious and thrifty middle-class families are the mainstay of the Baptist and Methodist churches and other institutions in the Negro community.

"The Negro Family in 1940" (continued)

We come finally to the upper-class families in the large cities of the North. The upper-class Negro families do not derive their support from invested wealth but rather from professional and other kinds of services. Yet because of their class position, their outlook is often that of a wealthy leisure class. Many heads of upper-class families can tell success stories of their *rise* in the world, but these stories are very seldom concerned with becoming heads of business enterprises. As a rule the stories tell of their struggle to achieve a professional education. Moreover, the wives of these upper-class men like upper-class wives in the border cities are sometimes employed in professional occupations.

Source: From E. Franklin Frazier, *The Negro in the United States* (New York: Macmillan, 1949), pp. 328–31.

While criticisms of Moynihan's conclusions were widespread, perhaps the most penetrating and thought-provoking criticism was offered by the psychologist Nathan Hare. In 1976, Hare suggested that Moynihan, by neglecting Frazier's crucial linkage of black family pathologies with racial oppression "had stood Frazier's analysis on its head and made family instability the source of black occupational and economic degradation." Again, African Americans were blamed for their depressed status in society (and for any negative consequences deriving from this status), only in this instance, learned cultural, rather than innate biological, deficiencies were alluded to as causes. During the 1960s several leading scholars concurred with Moynihan's conclusions on the issue of culture and disorganization in black family life. They also saw an intergenerational "tangle of pathology" founded on historic racial oppression that was perpetuated by contemporary destructive, cultural, and interactive patterns within black family life. Some adherents, including sociologists Nathan Glazer and David A. Schulz, explicitly restricted their generalizations to lower-class, urban blacks even more than Moynihan and other supporters of the "sociocultural determinism" perspective.

In contrast to proponents of this model, sociologist Andrew Billingsley and others emphasize facets of Frazier's writings dealing with the economic determinants of black family organization. Writing from the perspective of socioeconomic determinism, Billingsley and others argue that black families—indeed black communities—are economically dependent on and subordinate to the larger society. Recognizing the inextricable dependence of black families on the society for resources linked to their sustenance and survival, Billingsley expands Frazier's original thesis, linking economics with family organization and function. The result is a typology outlining various structural adjustments that black families make in response to economic imperatives threatening their ability to provide for family member needs. The idea of differential susceptibility to economic and social discrimination is integral to

The "Moynihan Report," 1965

There is probably no single fact of Negro American life so little understood by whites. The Negro situation is commonly perceived by whites in terms of the visible manifestations of discrimination and poverty, in part because Negro protest is directed against such obstacles, and in part, no doubt, because these are facts which involve the actions and attitudes of the white community as well. It is more difficult, however, for whites to perceive the effect that three centuries of exploitation have had on the fabric of Negro society itself. Here the consequences of the historic injustices done to Negro Americans are silent and hidden from view. But here is where the true injury has occurred: unless this damage is repaired, all the effort to end discrimination and poverty will come to little.

The role of the family in shaping character and ability is so pervasive as to be easily overlooked. The family is the basic social unit of American life: it is the basic socializing unit. By and large, adult conduct in society is learned as a child. . . .

It may be hazarded that the reason family structure does not loom larger in public discussion of social issues is that people tend to assume that the nature of family life is about the same throughout American society. The mass media and the development of suburbia have created an image of the American family as a highly standardized phenomenon. It is therefore easy to assume that whatever it is that makes for differences among individuals or groups of individuals, it is not a different family structure.

There is much truth to this; as with any other nation, Americans are producing a recognizable family system. But that process is not completed by any means. There are still, for example, important differences in family patterns surviving from the age of the great European migration to the United States, and these variations account for notable differences in the progress and assimilation of various ethnic and religious groups.

But there is one truly great discontinuity in family structure in the United States at the present time: that between the white world in general and that of the Negro American.

The white family has achieved a high degree of stability and is maintaining that stability.

By contrast, the family structure of lower class Negroes is highly unstable, and in many urban centers is approaching complete breakdown.

There is considerable evidence that the Negro community is in fact dividing between a stable middle-class group that is steadily growing stronger and more successful, and an increasingly disorganized and disadvantaged lower-class group. There are indications, for example, that the middle-class Negro family puts a higher premium on family stability and the conserving of family resources than does the white middle-class family. . . .

There are two points to be noted in this context.

First, the emergence and increasing visibility of a Negro middle-class may beguile the nation into supposing that the circumstances of the remainder of the Negro community are equally prosperous, whereas just the opposite is true at present, and is likely to continue so.

Second, the lumping of all Negroes together in one statistical measurement very probably conceals the extent of the disorganization among the lower-class group. If conditions are improving for one and deteriorating for the other, the resultant statistical averages might show no change. Further, the statistics on the Negro family and most other subjects treated in this paper refer only to a specific point in time. They are a vertical measure of the situation at a given moment.

The "Moynihan Report," 1965 (continued)

They do not measure the experience of individuals over time. Thus the average monthly unemployment rate for Negro males for 1964 is recorded as 9 percent. But *during* 1964, some 29 percent of Negro males were unemployed at one time or another. Similarly, for example, if 36 percent of Negro children are living in broken homes *at any specific moment*, it is likely that a far higher proportion of Negro children find themselves in that situation *at one time or another* in their lives.

Source: *The Negro Family: The Case for National Action* (Washington, D.C.: United States Department of Labor, 1965).

Billingsley's argument; thus more severe resource limitations cause low-income black families to display higher rates of disorganization than middle- and upper-income black families. To buttress this point, he presents case studies of middle-class black families and their accomplishments. In each instance, the long-term economic stability of these families enhanced their ability to maintain conventional patterns of organization, to fulfill member needs, and to conform to societal norms. Social scientists Joyce A. Ladner, Hyman Rodman, John H. Scanzoni, and Carol B. Stack share this perspective through their stress on the primacy of immediate, economic factors over historic, cultural factors in the determination of black family organization. This perspective, it should also be noted, views lower-class, urban black family departures—where these occur—from normative family patterns as valid, sensible adaptations to the attendant circumstances of racial and economic oppression.

In summary, two competing perspectives, both derived from Frazier's earlier work, tend to dominate our thinking about relationships between class, culture, and black family life. Sociocultural determinism attributes disorganization in black family life to what were initially adaptive responses to economic deprivation, but over time have become ingrained, self-perpetuating cultural traits. By contrast, socioeconomic determinism views black family disorganization as an outgrowth of immediate economic deprivation. Quite simply, the question concerns the relative importance of class and culture in the determination of black family organization. Are black family organization patterns most effectively explained in terms of current economic circumstances or persistent cultural values? In the view of the author, it is wisest to assume that where rates of family disorganization (measured by conventional indices, e.g., divorce, desertion, illegitimacy, and nonsupport rates) are high among African Americans, it is due more often to economic deprivation than to "ingrained" cultural values.

Both historically and today, the special circumstances that characterize black family life in the United States warrant—indeed require—that these families be examined in relation to their environments. Where this is done, one can expect clearer understandings of black family experiences. African-American families display an incredible diversity of value orientations, goals, behavioral patterns, structural arrangements, geographic locations, and socioeconomic statuses. This is not to ignore the elements that are common to all African-American families—those qualities that join them and distinguish them from other families in the society. Rather than singling out only certain facets, scholarship should seek to identify the varied significant factors that combine to create the essential character of the family life of people of African descent born and raised in the United States in all of its complexity.

IMPLICATIONS FOR SOCIAL POLICY

Black children and their families currently face social and economic crises of such magnitude that their very survival is threatened. Spiraling inflation, soaring unemployment, and changing societal priorities greatly diminish the opportunities and quality of life for black families and their children. Social scientists therefore have a special obligation to offer practical recommendations aimed at alleviating the crises currently experienced by too many black (and minority and poor) families and children in this society. I offer these recommendations not as a disinterested, dispassionate, detached scholar, but rather as an African-American professional who is concerned about the futures of our children and of our communities.

Ironically, this agenda calls for actions that echo a similar call made by Allison Davis and John Dollard in 1940. In the ensuing five decades, much has changed in the lives of black people; unfortunately, much has also remained the same. There are more black millionaires, physicians, professors, private contractors, and attorneys now than ever before. However, there continue to be unacceptably high numbers of black children denied adequate health care, equal educational opportunity, and minimal living standards. The following recommendations suggest an action agenda which will ensure that black (and minority) families who are currently disadvantaged receive their full benefits from this society. These recommendations are not intended to be all-inclusive. Instead, they present my view of key arenas for corrective action.

Poverty

African-American families continue to be disproportionately represented among this country's poor. From generation to generation, blacks—compared to whites—earn less, have fewer capital resources, and are caught in systems of economic deprivation. Poverty conditions the life chances and experiences of black children in a variety of ways. In this society, the basic necessities of life—and any frills—are for sale. Those with limited or nonexistent purchasing power are placed therefore at a great disadvantage. Action is required to improve the economic circumstances of black children and their families. Among the actions to be taken are the following: institution of an adequate guaranteed minimum family income; institution of a program of full employment involving the public and private sectors; and the equalization of worker salaries and earnings potential.

Health Care

African-American children and their families are deprived of adequate health care in this, the world's most medically advanced society. Disproportionate numbers of black children die in infancy, suffer poor nutrition, are not immunized, and die from accidents. Poor access to health care ends many young black lives prematurely and diminishes the quality of existence for others. Action is required to improve the health status and health care access of African-American families. The specific needs include alternative financing of medical and health care services to ensure their availability, regardless of the basis of ability to pay; expansion of health care outlets, including the location of health care facilities in inner-city areas and increased recruitment/training of black physicians and health care professionals; and the establishment of comprehensive, preventive health programs emphasizing early and periodic screening/intervention.

Education

Educational attainment has steadily risen among African Americans. There is reason to believe, however, that the qualitative gains in their education have been less pronounced—certainly the economic returns on the educational gains are lower than for whites. Black children lag behind whites on most objective measures of achievement: their suspension rates are higher, and college entrance rates are lower. The educational experiences of black children are impaired through their enrollment at schools with larger numbers of underachieving students, more frequent violence, fewer experienced teachers, and substandard facilities. In order to improve the school experience and educational outcomes for black children, there is a need for alternative financing approaches to eliminate current economic inequities among school districts; the development and implementation of individualized remedial/instructional programs; and the implementation of school accountability systems that establish target achievement goals and assess progress toward these goals.

Media

The electronic media in the form of television and radio exert an influence on African-American children that at times exceeds the influence of parents. Children spend substantial amounts of time absorbing the content of the most recent television programs and the most popular songs. Yet parents and the black community exert at best minimal control over the content of these messages. Media messages are often detrimental to black children's healthy development. The negative effects include advocacy of violence, sexual indiscriminations, and conspicuous consumerism. Steps must be taken to maximize the positive effects of media and to minimize any negative effects. There is need for parents to regulate their children's media habits and exposure, and for the community to monitor media broadcasts to encourage positive programming.

Child Care

If there was ever a time when the model of a full-time homemaker/wife had applicability in African-American communities, that time has long since passed. The majority of black mothers who can find jobs are employed outside the home. At the same time, the character of extended family involvements has changed in ways which reduce the viability of these as child care alternatives. The result has been an increased need for child care services by black families. Limited availability of child care options, high costs where these are available, and large numbers of black children in foster care make the provision of child care services to black families necessary. When these facts are recognized, the following requirements become clear: the expansion of low-cost/community-based child care programs to serve the needs of working parents; the institution of training programs and referral resources for child care providers; and the revision of guidelines regulating black child placements in foster homes or group care facilities.

CONCLUSIONS AND IMPLICATIONS

Thirty years ago, Daniel Patrick Moynihan issued a call for national action to respond to real threats to African-American family life. Citing the declining fraction of households headed by married couples, he forecast the destruction of African-American family and community life unless the government took dramatic action. The trends identified by Moynihan have continued. In the 1990s nearly half of all black families are headed by a single female. More often than not, these families are mired in poverty and beset by the social problems associated with severe economic deprivation.

Time has proven the trends in African-American family life to be much more complex and elusive than Moynihan predicted. In fact, what has happened since 1965 is a hastening of two trends in black family life and in black communities. On the one hand, many black families have sunk deeper into abject poverty. Associated with their impoverishment is their isolation from the societal mainstream. They and their family members are increasingly outside the educational system, without jobs, consigned to high-crime areas, leading unproductive lives, and facing limited futures. On the other hand, there is the group of black families who were able to escape the cycle of deprivation and destruction forecasted by Moynihan. These families and their members have moved into areas of American life previously off-limits to black people. With their fantastic success and unrestricted access has come unrivaled social and economic mobility. Hence, two contrasting realities are presented for contemporary African-American families. Middle-class blacks require little more than the continued commitment of the society to equal opportunity. Given a fair chance, they are, by virtue of their educational, economic, social, and political resources, able to compete successfully. At the other end of the continuum are the poor, urban black families, whose needs are legion. Denied or deprived of gainful employment, adequate educational preparation, and safe, healthy communities, these families find it challenging to maintain even a semblance of normal family life.

The case for national action on behalf of urban poor African-American families is indisputable. The nation must mobilize its resources and resolve first to ease and then ultimately to erase the frightening deterioration of viable family and community life among poor, urban African Americans. The problems contributing to this deterioration are not of black people's making; therefore, these problems cannot be left solely for black people to solve. Industrial decline, the proliferation of guns and illegal drugs, the failure of the public school system, and massive unemployment loom large in the equation of black family crisis. African-American families face problems of epic proportions and, unless these problems are solved, the negative effects will continue to be felt by the whole nation. Black families have historically nurtured and sustained African Americans under extreme conditions, ranging from enslavement to impoverishment. With critical assistance from government and the rest of society, these families will continue to produce citizens able to help this society advance.

While the case for concerted action concerning research on African-American families is not so sharply drawn, it is nevertheless of weighty importance. The empirical record cries out for correction. Time and time again, it has shown how researchers have distorted black family life and misinformed society about its essential elements. The result of these flawed studies has been to cripple society's understanding of African-American families and to hamstring attempts to address the problems that confront these families. It is imperative that additional, more sensitive empirical studies of African-American families be undertaken. Further, these studies need to employ alternative theoretical, methodological, and ideological approaches that will help to clarify the socioecological (as opposed to the socioeconomic or sociocultural) context within which African-American families function and to illustrate how these families respond to such constraints. A period of revisionist scholarship is required in order to challenge and to supplant a literature that portrays black families as pathological. The strategy will not be to replace this literature with one that says all is well and perfect with black families in America. Instead, the attempt will be to produce studies to illuminate the essential nature of black family life, showing not only its obvious characteristics but also its subtle variations. From such research will come reliable information to guide attempts to shape social policy that improves the circumstances of African-American families.

> Faith is the substance of things hoped for,
> the evidence of things not seen.
>
> —St. Paul

FOR FURTHER READING

Bernard, Jessie. *Marriage and the Family among Negroes.* Englewood Cliffs, N.J.: Prentice, 1966.

Billingsley, Andrew. *Climbing Jacob's Ladder: The Enduring Legacy of African-American Families.* New York: Touchstone Books, 1994.

Davis, Allison, and John Dollard. *Children of Bondage: The Personality Development of Negro Youth in the Urban South.* New York: Harper, 1940.

Farley, W. Reynolds, and Walter R. Allen. *The Colorline and the Quality of Life in America.* New York: Oxford University Press, 1989.

Franklin, Donna L. *Ensuring Inequality: The Structural Transformation of the African-American Family.* New York: Oxford University Press, 1997.

Frazier, E. Franklin. *The Negro Family in the United States.* 1939. Reprint, Chicago: University of Chicago Press, 1966.

Gutman, Herbert G. *The Black Family in Slavery and Freedom, 1750–1925.* New York: Random House, 1977.

Hill, Robert B., et al. *Research on the African American Family: A Holistic Perspective.* Westport, Conn.: Auburn House, 1993.

Jaynes, Gerald D., and Robin M. Williams Jr., eds. *A Common Destiny: Blacks and American Society.* Washington, D.C.: National Academy Press, 1989.

Kelly, Robin D. G. *Yo' Mama's Disfunktional: Fighting the Culture Wars in Urban America.* Boston: Beacon Press, 1997.

Ladner, Joyce. *Tomorrow's Tomorrow: The Black Woman.* Lincoln: University of Nebraska Press, 1995.

Moynihan, Daniel P. *The Negro Family: The Case for National Action.* Washington, D.C.: U.S. Department of Labor, 1965.

Rainwater, Lee. *Behind Ghetto Walls: Black Family Life in a Federal Slum.* Chicago: Aldine, 1970.

Stack, Carol B. *All Our Kin: Strategies for Survival in a Black Community.* New York: Basic Books, 1996.

chapter 15

From Black Bourgeoisie to African-American Middle Class, 1957 to the Present

Robert Gregg

S CHOLARS DISAGREE ABOUT WHETHER the black middle class has received too much or too little attention. Some historians and social scientists suggest that it is lower-class blacks who have been ignored and that most studies of African Americans have focused on a culture that represents a black bourgeoisie. Other scholars, however, maintain that little systematic study of the middle class has actually been undertaken. In fact, a strong case can be made for both positions. In the United States economy and society there have been fundamental transformations that have led to the development of a new African-American middle class very different from the "Black Bourgeoisie" described by E. Franklin Frazier in 1957. Consequently, the older studies of black bourgeois culture, plentiful though they may be, are no longer sufficient to describe this new middle class.

A glance at the collective output of African Americanists reveals that greatest emphasis has indeed been placed on the lives of middle-class intellectuals, politicians, and other leading members of the black communities and on those organizations that they have created or participated in—from protest organizations like the National Association for the Advancement of Colored People and the Urban League, to the churches, the fraternal orders, and the historic black colleges. By contrast, black trade unionists have received little attention and black domestic laborers even less. And yet, a second look at this same literature reveals that many of these institutions are not analyzed in terms of their class but are instead described as "race" institutions. While they do indeed appear to have had "bourgeois" characteristics, what actually made them bourgeois—whether it was the composition of their memberships or just the cultural practices they engaged in—has not been made clear. Indeed, scholars assume, implicitly or explicitly, that these institutions represent the middle class, and the actual nature of the black middle class—its economic, cultural and political bases, its internal divisions, and the degree of its separation from the rest of "the race"—has not received sufficient attention. Consequently, the notion of a black middle class has remained a cultural concept representing almost all black cultural initiatives; it has seldom been used in an economic way to denote a particular socioeconomic grouping.

During roughly the first half of this century, culminating in E. Franklin Frazier's 1957 study, *Black Bourgeoisie*, such a cultural approach was not too inhibiting or inappropriate. Black communities did indeed seem to cohere around a particular culture, which, although divided along the lines of race, class, and gender, maintained bourgeois aspects—promoting self-help, uplift, sobriety, and so on. While this remained true until midcentury, by the 1930s a new and more economically based middle class was already beginning to emerge. At first this class could speak for the community as a whole, in the process making significant contributions to the Civil Rights movement; but soon it became too economically differentiated from other African Americans to continue doing so. The earlier black bourgeoisie was composed of people who, in spite of familial, political, and social ties to other African Americans in the rest of the black community, saw their economic privilege arise from distinct cultural practices. The later class of professionals and civil servants derived their position from their greater incomes, which increased social distance between themselves and the urban poor but which also gave the appearance of a difference in cultural practices. The new threat to this class's viability, which will be outlined below, has led to a renewed emphasis on culture and behavior because, while economic opportunities seemed to account for the growth of the class, those people who manage to retain their position within it will do so, in part, because they follow a particular code of behavior.

Frazier caught the new class in its infancy, and to some extent this explained the harshness of his criticism of it. The class was not large, so that its members' pretensions to status appeared to be nothing more than fanciful or wishful thinking. It was not separate from the remainder of the black community, so its self-image influenced the lives of other African Americans through the organizations that were shared. But in the 1970s and 1980s, an African-American middle class became more distinct, even though it seems again to be vulnerable in ways that Frazier detected almost forty years ago.

To show this transformation from a bourgeois cultural grouping to a more economically defined middle class, this chapter will provide a profile of this middle class as it is today, describing its sources of economic strength. It will then focus on the new suburbs, showing how residential patterns for better-off African Americans have changed since 1957. After this, the political and religious tendencies of this new social group will be examined, followed by a discussion of the concept of "escaping the ghetto." These last two sections reveal that even while the new middle class has established itself, this has not meant that its members have been able to move beyond all the concerns and issues of the old bourgeoisie. Racial discrimination, as well as the differential effect of American economic growth on various elements of the middle class generally, threaten the African-American middle class in ways that force its members to consider the plight of those who remain in the ghetto.

A PROFILE OF THE AFRICAN-AMERICAN MIDDLE CLASS

Precisely locating a middle class among African Americans has always been difficult. Is it located around the middling social group among African Americans or around blacks who fit the income and social profile of the white middle class? For African Americans do not necessarily fit within the same class categories that are used for other Americans. While the white middle class is literally situated between the very wealthy and the working class, the black middle class has incorporated African Americans who, if they were white, might have been differently classified. The very wealthy have not been so numerous among African Americans as to constitute a separate class and they have often had familial and social ties to middle-income blacks; the black laborer who holds steady employment, sometimes but not always of a skilled nature, might be considered middle class because of the large number of blacks who are underemployed and living below the poverty line. But while a strict economic definition is still inadequate, in the last two decades it has become easier to detect a middle class located around particular occupational categories, which also correspond more closely to those among whites than in the past. One of the central determinants of middle class-ness had been cultural, and an individual who adopted "bourgeois" culture might sometimes be able to compensate for deficiencies of income. Today, income levels more clearly determine whether or not someone will be described as upper class, middle class, working class, or underclass.

The rapid growth of the black middle class during and after the 1950s was made possible in part by changes in the United States job market in a number of employment areas: government civil service, the armed forces, industrial labor, and universities. These changes occurred in the immediate aftermath of World War II: local and federal administrations were now forced, either through political pressure from minority communities or civil rights laws, to begin combating discrimination in hiring. They attempted to achieve this goal by pursuing affirmative action policies, whereby whenever two equal candidates vied for a position, the job would be given to the one from the minority community. Under President Harry Truman's leadership, the armed forces established integration and in the process induced the enlistment of many African Americans who believed that their talents would be rewarded more fairly in the military than they would be in other fields; the expanding industrial sector, from the 1940s until the end of the 1960s, provided opportunities for skilled employment for members of previously excluded groups;

and lastly, the universities, in the wake of the *Brown* v. *Board of Education of Topeka, Kansas* decision of 1954, expanded minority representation on their campuses, either in response to the political demands of the more visible minority students who wanted increased numbers of minority faculty or as a result of new curricular initiatives that led to a focus on subjects previously ignored, subjects like African-American or Hispanic American history.

Many of the recent critics of such advances have stressed that given the nature of this transformation and in contrast to the immigrants to America who received no "handouts" and advanced by more "legitimate" means, the growth of this class was not something for which its members themselves were responsible. This is a mistaken assumption. While it is true that the aforementioned areas have contributed greatly to the expansion of the black middle class, they could do so once blatant discrimination was terminated *only* because there existed a large pool of highly trained and educated African Americans ready to fill the positions that began to be opened up to them. The desegregation of major league baseball in 1946 provides us with a model of this process, an appropriate model since the sports leagues have provided many African Americans, although a very small percentage of total black middle-class population, with the opportunity to rise into a black middle and upper classes. While Branch Rickey commenced the first stage of baseball desegregation by bringing Jackie Robinson into the Brooklyn Dodger organization in 1945, he would not have been able to do so, and desegregation could not have been so successful, had not the Negro Baseball League teams nurtured a number of brilliant and often superior black ballplayers. In the same way, the Supreme Court decisions of the 1950s and the civil rights laws of the 1960s could not have had the great impact on black employment patterns had not black colleges and universities like Lincoln, Howard, and Hampton, to name a few, already trained a large number of brilliant professionals who could take advantage of the new climate of antidiscrimination. Furthermore, many of these same black professionals (journalists in the case of baseball and lawyers in the case of the Supreme Court decisions), by bringing pressure to bear on the white establishment, helped create a climate for reform in the first place.

At least until the 1980s, the black middle class underwent a rapid expansion. Between 1960 and 1965 alone, 380,000 African Americans acquired white-collar employment, enlarging the black middle class to about four million—one-fifth of the total African-American population. By 1980, says Harvard political scientist Martin L. Kilson, the percentage of blacks working in white-collar jobs had increased to roughly 40 percent. But around this time, the basis for the growth of the black middle class seemed to come under threat. Whether or not they were racially motivated, calls for smaller government during the Reagan–Bush years were bound to slow the growth of permanent government positions for which educated African Americans could compete. Deregulation and privatization had similar affects, shifting employment opportunities from one section of the economy, where laws about equal hiring were most stringent, to another, where the whims of individual employers could more easily prevail. In addition, as cities deindustrialized, the private sector shift from manufacturing to service left many skilled and semiskilled employees with fewer opportunities to earn more. And lastly, with the ending of the cold war, the closing of many military bases, and the contraction of the number of armed forces' personnel, the U.S. military also witnessed a significant cutback in opportunities for blacks.

Only in the universities have the opportunities remained open to many African Americans, although it has to be noted that attempts to diversify faculties have faced increasing opposition from those who would wish to turn back the clock to a time when universities were not under pressure to increase the number of voices being heard inside academe. In part, this problem was exacerbated by the severe cutbacks in government funding for education during the 1980s, cutbacks which, while not necessarily diminishing the number of positions open to minority faculty, certainly decreased the funding available to those who might come through university graduate schools to fill the positions. Furthermore, if the decisions in California to end affirmative action are taken up elsewhere, this process of retrenchment may be completed. So, even in the universities, the black middle class is likely to have difficulty reproducing itself in the future.

Thus, according to *Business Week*, although the size of the black middle class continued to grow during the 1980s, so that by the end of the decade as many as a third of all black families earned between $25,000 and $50,000—thereby placing them at the low end of the American middle class—the manner in which this increase occurred has not been very promising. As noted by a number of social theorists—Bennett Harrison and Lucy Gorham, in particular—apparent increases reflect not the expanding numbers of high-earning individuals, but rather the consolidation of wages and more effective "repackaging" of income from wages and rent. In many instances, both adults in a family moved into the lower-income levels of the middle class. In fact, according to Harrison and Gorham, the incidence of well-paid black workers actually fell during the 1980s. From one point of view—that of the black women who have seen the significance and size of their wages increase—this change has had some advantages. But from another point of view, it also means that middle-class status no longer depends on the traditional income of the highly skilled (and not-so-easy-to-replace) male head of household. In these circumstances, the tenure of all work within the new black middle class remains uncertain.

At the same time that the position of many within the middle class has become tenuous, the size of the class of people in the inner cities, now commonly called the "underclass," has grown dramatically, and the problems associated with it have become more intense. So, while the number of individuals who, on the basis of earning more than $35,000 or about three times poverty level can be comfortably incorporated into a middle class, declined in one estimate by as much as 22 percent, the proportion of African Americans whose earnings fall below the poverty line increased by one-fifth. Since retention of middle-class status sometimes depends on limiting family size, lower-class blacks reproduce and are forced into more dire economic circumstances by deindustrialization at a greater rate than the black middle class can reproduce itself. African Americans who do climb into the middle class, therefore, do so knowing that there is a strong possibility that they will be pulled back into the ranks of the expanding group hovering around the poverty level.

What members of the black middle class have faced, therefore, is the problem of a shrinking American economy. In this, they have not been alone: the overall proportion of the workforce earning poverty-level wages rose from 25.7 percent to 31.5 percent during the 1980s, while the proportion earning three or more times poverty actually fell, from 14.2 percent to 12.7 percent. African Americans have experienced these problems more intensely than other Americans. Since the black middle class's overall size has not been increasing at the same rapid rate witnessed in earlier years, and since in many ways its position is becoming more tenuous, there is some irony in the increased attention afforded the black middle class at this time. Perhaps the reason for this attention lies in the fact that, like other groups facing external pressures and threats, the members of this class have become more vocal and self-conscious about politics, accentuating a trend, already detectable, toward nationalism.

FROM BREWSTER PLACE TO LINDEN HILLS: RESIDENTIAL PATTERNS

Black middle-class residential patterns have also undergone change over the last twenty years. While earlier "bourgeois" blacks remained close to lower-class blacks and sometimes even continued to live in urban environments like Brewster Place, the fictional setting for Gloria Naylor's first novel, by the 1980s the African-American middle class was to be found living in Linden Hills, the fictional suburb of Naylor's second novel.

The initial impulse of wealthy blacks had been toward racial integration. In the northern cities this impulse preceded the success of the national Civil Rights movement. As the northward migrations of World War I created large urban black communities, the professional elite, who benefited most directly from this expansion, attempted to move into the more attractive residential areas within the cities. As suburban tracts developed along the post–World War II highway system, members of this class endeavored to integrate them also.

The experiences of Sadie Tanner Alexander and Raymond Pace Alexander, members of the Philadelphia black professional class who managed to bring about the integration of the Mount Airy section of Philadelphia, were typical of these early efforts. Sadie was a descendant of the prominent Mossell and Tanner families, who included among their number the founder of Frederick Douglass Hospital, Nathan Mossell, the world-renowned artist Henry O. Tanner, and many leading churchmen in the African Methodist Episcopal

Church. After earning a Ph.D. in sociology from the University of Pennsylvania, Sadie studied law and became a leading figure in Philadelphia's black community as an assistant city counsellor and a member of the city's Committee on Human Relations. Her local prominence was such that she was chosen by Truman to be a member of his Human Rights Commission in 1947. Raymond Alexander came from Virginia Baptists and graduated from Harvard Law School. After establishing a very successful practice in the 1920s, he became a justice on the Court of Common Pleas in 1959. Their successful attempts to integrate Mount Airy in Philadelphia are notable for a number of reasons. First, unlike more recent black suburbanites, they retained their commitment to the city. In doing so, the Alexanders retained the strength of their urban power base. Thus, to the extent that they lived next to white neighbors, their home lives could be integrated while their work lives could remain focused on the increasingly segregated black urban communities. Under these circumstances, they needed to respond to the issues of inner-city dwellers and could benefit from doing so. Moreover, while they moved to the outer reaches of the city, they kept their social ties to the rest of black Philadelphia: Raymond continued to attend Zion Baptist Church in North Philadelphia, while Sadie retained her strong ties to the city's African Methodists. Theirs was a complicated lifestyle, using the power of the newly enlarged black community to their benefit, serving that community while living and working alongside prominent white Philadelphians.

Furthermore, the experience of the Alexanders was not unrepresentative of most black middle-class city dwellers. The history of black urban communities is replete with attempts by better-off members of the community—ministers, attorneys, physicians, teachers, and so on—to move into previously white-only neighborhoods. Often such attempts were met with open violence from the communities, followed by the "white flight" into other white-only areas. In the process, the black middle class would often be drawn back into the surrounding black community, the experience of integration being only temporary.

Contrast this situation with the picture of the black suburb in Prince Georges County, Maryland, provided by David J. Dent in a June 14, 1992, article in *The New York Times Magazine*. Here we find the black middle class living in suburban tracts outside city limits, wishing to develop a new power base around relatively segregated suburbs, seeing themselves as very separate from inner-city blacks who have not had the opportunity to move out of the ghettoes of Washington, D.C. During the 1980s the black suburban population seemed to be an ever-increasing group. According to Dent:

> What some consider the essence of the American dream—suburbia—became a reality for a record number of blacks in the 1980s. In 1990, 32 percent of all black Americans in metropolitan areas lived in suburban neighborhoods, a record 6 percent increase from 1980.... These blacks are moving to black upper- and middle-class neighborhoods, usually pockets in counties that have a white majority.

Furthermore, says Dent, these black suburbs have sprung up all over the United States:

> In the Miami area, there is Rolling Oaks in Dade County. Around St. Louis, black suburbs exist in sections of Black Jack, Jennings, Normandy, and University City in St. Louis County. In the Atlanta suburbs, black majority communities include Brook Glen, Panola Mill and Wyndham Park in DeKalb County. And in the Washington area, Prince Georges County itself has a black majority.

In some instances these segregated suburbs developed as a result of white suburbanites' attempts to exclude blacks from their neighborhoods, but for many African Americans the decision to move into a black suburban neighborhood was the result of the weighing of many factors. By moving they can reap the benefits of middle-class lifestyles, stay connected to African-American cultural traditions promoted by other black suburbanites, and, quite significantly, shield themselves from much of the racial bigotry they would face in white suburbs.

In terms of economic benefits, however, these suburbs have not contributed to the growth of the African-American middle-class in the same way that the growth of suburbs did for other middle-class Americans. They have not provided access to "good jobs at good wages" that has historically been part of the process of white social mobility. While suburbs benefited earlier settlers by giving them access to many of the newly developing labor markets, many of those markets are now disappearing as industrial concerns relocate to areas where there are large pools of cheap labor. Moreover, some of the service-sector employment that can grow in areas surrounding suburbs—at the malls, in particular—have not been forthcoming near black suburbs. Dent notes, for example, that many major department stores have refused to establish outlets in black suburbs. Nordstrom and Macy's have opened stores in Baltimore County, he tells us, "which had a median household income of $38,837, compared with $43,127 in Prince Georges County. But Baltimore County is more than 85 percent white." Since residents of the black county must drive to other counties to do much of their shopping, money that might have stayed in their community ends up elsewhere, while the jobs are to be found in other counties also. This development has a significant impact on the long-term tax base of an African-American county, thus affecting not only present income prospects, but through smaller school appropriations, future prospects also.

MIDDLE-CLASS POLITICS AND RELIGION

The increasingly tenuous position of the middle class in America as a whole has important implications for the politics of the African-American middle class. For as the problems of poverty increase and the number of routes out of the ghetto diminish, the black middle class begins to represent an ever-decreasing proportion of the overall black community. At the same time, however, it is becoming more visible and entrenched in terms of political and cultural consciousness. In addition, as Carol Stack has shown, the kinds of behavior that enable a family to maintain its suburban status—behaviors including limiting family size, owning homes, and saving money—are very different from those that are functional to a ghetto community. Consequently, the middle class is in many ways returning to a situation of being more physically and behaviorally distanced from the ghetto, like the bourgeoisie of Frazier's day. Moreover, because its members feel embattled, they are more reluctant than their predecessors to make strong commitments to lower-class blacks and, thereby, to risk being associated with them.

Nevertheless, even this distance does not lead to complete political detachment on the part of middle-class African Americans. In part, this is because the integrationism of Frazier's day has been replaced by a more nationalistic spirit that pervades even the middle class and assumes an alliance however tentative of middle- and lower-class blacks. Historically, nationalism has been most closely associated with lower-class, urban blacks. Marcus Garvey and Malcolm X were both able to strike chords among an urban poor that was less receptive to the words of Martin Luther King Jr. Now, and especially since Spike Lee's 1992 film version of Malcolm's life, it is members of the black middle class who will point to the lessons to be learned from Garvey and Malcolm and to question King's integrationism. In some ways, though, this new nationalism, which resembles other postcolonial nationalisms described by Frantz Fanon, is a revival of the spirit of Booker T. Washington, pushing for black capitalism and a United States that accepts that blacks and whites can be as separate as the fingers socially and as joined together as the hand economically in the corporate workplace.

In the last ten years there have been continual discoveries and rediscoveries of the black middle class. Black intellectuals questioning the value of what they described as the Civil Rights consensus—people like Thomas Sowell, Shelby Steele, and Stephen Carter, among others—began to be described as representatives of more than just an outlandish strain of conservatism among a small minority of African Americans. They now appear to be spokespersons for a middle class that is undergoing a political shift to the right. Increasingly, the assumption that a member of the black middle class would vote the Democratic ticket has been found to be unreliable. President George Bush's selection of Judge Clarence Thomas for the Supreme Court in 1991, over many more experienced but liberal black judges, represented a recognition of the potential for the Republican Party to increase its support among African Americans. The fact that many African-American church leaders supported Judge Thomas quite vociferously at first, and a little more grudgingly as the Anita Hill allegations were made public, suggests the extent to which Republican political strategists were correct.

To some extent, this black middle-class conservatism has been shaped by the exigencies of suburban life. Perhaps the key difference between the suburban and urban dweller is the difference in family life. Liberal and conservative political positions often revolve around whether the family is a cause or an effect of this difference. Do family values and experiences aid members of the middle class, or does the destruction of families by inner-city experience create this widespread difference in family structures? Whichever it is, the perceived difference orients the focus of political discourse to the nature of the family. As a result, whether or not a member of the black middle class votes Republican, he or she is far more likely than twenty years ago to accept the idea that the problem with inner-city dwellers is founded on the need to develop strong male figures, who can build solid families. In many ways this accounts for the current widespread acceptance of ideas developed by Daniel Patrick Moynihan in 1965 regarding the black family's "tangle of pathology," ideas which had been dismissed as racist throughout most of the 1970s and 1980s and then were ever-present during the "Million Man March" promoted by Nation of Islam leader Minister Louis Farrakhan. Martin Kilson has provided a nuanced view of black middle-class politics. He argues, in the vein of William Julius Wilson's *The Declining Significance of Race*, that there has been a degree of what he calls "deracialization" and that middle- and upper-class blacks have acquired social, professional, and political attitudes that are based more on class than on race. In this they resemble similarly situated whites. The "deghettoization" of the black bourgeoisie's education and job markets, Kilson argues, "disentangles the new black bourgeoisie from the old." "The difference is fundamental," he argues. "[T]he old black bourgeoisie faced a fierce ceiling on its professional and social mobility; the new black bourgeoisie, while still confronting residual racism, takes over much of the professionalization and mobility dynamics of the white bourgeoisie."

At the same time, however, Kilson maintains, there has been an increasing rage among middle-class blacks who resent racism as much as, if not more than before, because, in spite of all they have obtained, they still face the possibility of racial discrimination and bigotry. Consequently, a new nationalism has also emerged among members of the black middle class.

Two events in 1991 helped to cement this new nationalism: the aforementioned nomination of Clarence Thomas to the Supreme Court and the police beating of Rodney King. Judge Thomas's claim that the Senate Judiciary Committee was carrying out a "high-tech lynching" could strike a chord among many wealthier African Americans, who might be, as Thomas was suggesting he was being, unfairly treated because they were both black and successful. An even more powerful symbol of this anger, perhaps, was the Rodney King incident. The arbitrariness of the police brutality in the King case and its clearly racial character, as well as the manner in which the police defendants were acquitted in 1992, led many middle-class African Americans, many of whom had themselves been mistreated by police forces around the country, to feel that they too could be victimized in this manner.

The effect of events of this kind has been the cementing of what Kilson had predicted would become a dual political approach among many black middle-class people. Whether members of the middle class would support conservative or liberal political initiatives would revolve "around whether social and political issues are viewed as class-linked or race-linked. If viewed as class-linked, upper-strata blacks are likely to respond as conservatives. If seen as race-linked, they respond as liberals." In some respects, however, the complexity of black middle-class politics has become yet more complicated. While there are divisions between liberals and conservatives in terms of voting patterns, with the Democrats remaining the greatest beneficiaries, the politics of race have become less easy to characterize along polarities of left and right. Now race can elicit conservative responses where liberal ones prevailed before. The need to provide for role models for young black men, for example, which in the past would have been seen as a conservative or Republican approach to "uplifting" black people, now is often seen as the remedy by black middle-class voters, though more so among men than women. In short, the class and racial attitudes have fused together so that middle-class and nationalist ideas cannot always be separated, as was clear in the support garnered for the Million Man March.

This increasing complexity is particularly apparent where gender plays a central role in a particular issue. The Thomas nomination, for example, received far more widespread criticism from African-American women than from men, even when the issue of race and racism became apparent. It has become increasingly clear during the last twenty years—especially as black women such as Toni Morrison, Alice Walker, bell hooks, and Oprah Winfrey have become vocal—that there is often more than one way of representing "the race," and black middle-class appeals in this area do not always lead to a consensus. The centrality of the family (at the core of all gender analysis) to the life chances of most African Americans places women in a key position to influence black politics. While white middle-class women have historically allied themselves with their husbands and brothers on issues of class, black middle-class women have not always done so. Black women intellectuals seldom propose that the problem with the inner cities is that there are too many single mothers, who are unable to raise young African-American boys properly, though many will argue that black men should be doing more within the family. They are far more likely to argue that this is still a case of "blaming the victims," and, if not racist, is sexist. While black men and women will often argue that they place racial advancement above their own gender aspirations, moreover, because of the significance of gender roles in situating African Americans socially, their definitions of racial advancement may be quite different.

The religious commitments of members of the middle class also appear to have undergone some transformation over the last thirty years. Between the 1930s and 1960s, African-American churches ceded some of their leadership position in black urban communities to the new professional elite, a process of secularization that clearly pleased E. Franklin Frazier. These professionals, while still often churchgoers, used other organizations like fraternities, clubs, and political parties to organize themselves and their constituencies. And, when they remained in the church, they tended to gravitate toward the more elite denominations, like the Presbyterian and Episcopal Churches. African Methodist denominations, which had been able to represent the black community as a whole, now seemed to represent a shrinking section of the overall community.

In the last thirty years there has been a dramatic reversal of this trend. The African Methodist Episcopal Church, in particular, has shown a complete change of fortunes. While still outnumbered by the Baptists, it has taken on a leadership role in the Congress of National Black Churches (CNBC), an organization that was virtually created by the AME Church's initiative, with the financial support of foundations who, in the 1970s, were looking for a more conservative alternative to Black Power.

This new strength comes, in part, from the denomination's highly centralized bureaucracy, allowing it to have more influence in the CNBC than the more decentralized Baptist denomination. But, more important, it derives from the church's theology, which, by marrying together nationalist (African) and European (Methodist) traditions, speaks to the dual political and religious influences of many black suburbanites. Thus, in Prince Georges County, Maryland, the denomination is thriving. The Ebenezer AME Church, which was formerly located in Washington, D.C., has revitalized itself by moving its congregation out of the city. According to Dent, "Membership at the 136-year-old church had dwindled to fewer than 100 members. Since the relocation from Washington in 1983, membership has grown to nearly 7,000 and donations have provided $10 million for the construction of a new church building." The renewed importance of the AME Church is apparent in its frequent appearance in national news: it was recognized for its vocal support for Clarence Thomas, and it was the first black organization President Clinton visited after his election.

CONCLUSION: ESCAPING THE GHETTO

The idea of "escaping the ghetto" has been a powerful one ever since modern black ghettos made their first appearance at the beginning of this century. Paradoxically, as the more economically based middle class has emerged from the black bourgeoisie, the notion of escaping the ghetto has not disappeared. The idea still resonates among members of the African-American middle class largely because the ghetto, or poverty generally, has become so difficult to escape. Except when the problems that lower-class Americans face impinge upon their lives through crime and other social "problems," members of the white middle class are able to forget them and can see no relationship between their own wealth and the poverty of others; black Americans do not have this luxury. In a racially divided society, members of the African-American middle class are constantly pressured to see themselves in relation to poorer African Americans. Even when, in fact, many of them never actually lived in the ghetto, they have managed to "escape," and they must consider the plight of those less fortunate than themselves.

For Frazier the black bourgeoisie had "escape[d] into a world of make-believe," and by putting on the "masks" of the white middle class, its members had found a "sham society" that could only leave them with feelings of "emptiness and futility." This stark judgment was not only harsh; it was also historically inaccurate. While there were times when its members looked scornfully on the poorest members of "the race," the black bourgeoisie had always been forced to focus on and remained willing to champion the cause of all African Americans. What Frazier was seeing in 1957 when he wrote *Black Bourgeoisie* was a change occurring in the ability of blacks to separate themselves spatially from the ghetto by moving into formerly white-only areas of the cities and suburbs. He assumed incorrectly that such migration would, like the "white flight" that preceded it, lead the black bourgeois migrants to forget those that they left behind. The irony is that while white suburbanites did in many respects escape from social reality into a fantasy world that was as temporary as the prosperity brought on by the cold war and America's unchallenged economy, it was black suburbanites who, constantly in fear of losing their social privileges, were being accused of fantasizing.

In addition to the need to escape from poverty, members of the African-American middle class have a need to escape assumptions that are attached to them because they share a racial background and heritage with many of the most visible members of the "underclass." As mentioned previously, because there are now so few avenues by which to escape the ghetto, many social commentators assume incorrectly that a people whose ancestors were slaves, sharecroppers, and ghetto dwellers could only have made it into the middle class as a result of government handouts. For members of the African-American middle class this means that their efforts are constantly being denigrated and that fallacious assumptions about the limited abilities and "cultural deficit" of "the race" are continually being brought to bear upon them. Historically, members of this class have confronted this by contesting these assessments of "the race" and focusing on the contributions and achievements of African Americans in different arenas.

Because of the nature of suburban existence now shared by an increasing number of blacks, the metaphor of escape for the black middle class remains a powerful one. The idea of the suburb is itself one that is very much associated with escaping the turmoils of modern urban society. Whether or not the impulse to own a house and a plot of land goes back to the homesteading, frontier origins of the United States, the impulse to move to a suburb is a more recent phenomenon which coincided both with the rapid expansion of the highway system after World War II and with the arrival of large numbers of African Americans in northern cities before and after World War II. The suburb, then, represents in part an escape from racial conflict. But, given the racial origin of this escapism, African-American suburbanites are constantly confronted by the seemingly contradictory impulses that were found in their politics and religion—the desire to escape and the need to combat the widespread condition of poverty among African Americans.

In the end, the perilous situation for African Americans in today's postindustrial society suggests that the goals of the old black bourgeoisie, the desires to combat discrimination and to uplift the race as a whole, are not significantly different from those of the African-American middle class in the 1990s. For the political and religious aspirations of this latter group highlight the likelihood that the only lasting escape from the ghetto will be achieved by eliminating the inner-city ghettos themselves. As long as industrial decline continues to add to the ranks of the black underclass, and as long as middle-class African Americans are compared unfairly and unfavorably to other middle-class Americans, no escape can be certain and secure.

FOR FURTHER READING

Carter, Stephen L. *Reflections of an Affirmative Action Baby*. New York: Basic Books, 1992.

Feagin, Joe R., and Melvin P. Sikes. *Living with Racism: The Black Middle-Class Experience*. Boston: Beacon Press, 1995.

Frazier, E. Franklin. *Black Bourgeoisie*. 1957. Reprint, New York: Free Press, 1997.

Gates, Henry Louis Jr. *Colored People: A Memoir*. New York: Vintage, 1995.

Gregg, Robert. *Sparks from the Anvil of Oppression: Philadelphia's African Methodists and Southern Migrants, 1890–1940*. Philadelphia: Temple University Press, 1998.

Grier, William H. *Black Rage*. New York: Basic Books, 1992.

Landry, Bart. *The New Black Middle Class*. Berkeley and Los Angeles: University of California Press, 1988.

Naylor, Gloria. *Linden Hills*. New York: Viking Press, 1995.

Oliver, Melvin, and Thomas Shapiro. *Black Wealth/White Wealth: A New Perspective on Racial Inequality*. New York: Routledge, 1997.

Patterson, Orlando. *The Ordeal of Integration: Progress and Resentment in America's "Racial" Crisis*. Washington, D.C.: Counterpoint Press, 1997.

Steele, Shelby. *The Content of Our Character: A New Vision of Race in America*. New York: Harper Collins, 1991.

Wilson, William Julius. *The Declining Significance of Race: Blacks and Changing American Institutions*. Chicago: University of Chicago Press, 1980.

chapter 16

The New Underclass

Concentrated Black Poverty
in the Postindustrial City

John F. Bauman

IDDEN AMONG THE INVISIBLE POOR of the 1950s and occasionally glimpsed during the 1960s by anthropologists studying street corner men, America's underclass suddenly emerged in the consciousness of white America as a social problem in the 1980s. By the 1990s America's black ghetto poor were assailed for the supposed inadequacy of their culture; stripped of any semblance of respectability; and "disentitled" to further public assistance by an increasingly hostile and conservative public sentiment. The president of the United States in 1995, facing an ultraconservative Congress, proffered the nation's neediest a bare remnant of the already badly shredded "safety net." Democrats voted with Republicans to dismantle what little was left of Lyndon Johnson's once heralded "War on Poverty."

Meanwhile day by day both the film and print media barraged the American public with more evidence of underclass violence and immorality. The political assault on the underclass largely ignored a burgeoning mass of sociological, anthropological, and historical evidence about the nature and causes of concentrated urban poverty. Other than an occasional news magazine article and Ken Auletta's 1982 book that popularized the term "underclass," the issue had simmered on a back burner until 1987 when University of Chicago sociologist William Julius Wilson published *The Truly Disadvantaged*.

For Wilson, America's massive post–World War II economic restructuring, not intractable racism or the liberal policies associated with Johnson's "Great Society," best explained underclass formation. Between 1945 and 1975 manufacturing all but disappeared from America's old industrial cities, stranding a growing African-American working class in inner cities bereft of economic opportunity. Wilson's research uncovered a vicious set of collateral explanatory factors including the "Great Society's" success in launching middle-class careers for a generation of upwardly mobile black males. Unfortunately, those males left behind, he argued, too frequently succumbed to drugs, crime, incarceration, or violent death. According to Wilson, the combination of the mobile black middle class that fled the ghetto and those black males killed by street violence, left behind in jail, or without jobs, deprived inner-city black communities of marriageable African-American men. Such communities in Philadelphia, New York, Chicago, Boston, and Detroit changed dramatically, becoming largely peopled by female-headed families often housed in socially stultifying high-rise public housing projects typified by Chicago's notorious Cabrini Green, a design ironically first proposed as a model for urban rejuvenation.

Wilson's sociological tour de force offered a terse, but trenchant definition of the underclass. These were families, he explained, socially and geographically "outside the mainstream of the American occupational system." The underclass included "individuals who lacked training and skills and either experienced long-term unemployment or engaged in street crime or other forms of aberrant behavior and families that experienced long spells of poverty and/or welfare dependency." Although Wilson and many other scholars of inner-city poverty have since repudiated the term "underclass" as too all-encompassing and pejorative, reminiscent of the nineteenth century epithet "undeserving poor," the term possesses a political-historical resonance and is employed here within that framework.

Contemporary ghetto poverty contrasts sharply with late-nineteenth-century urban poverty described by novelists, social workers, and muckraking reporters. The older poverty seemed to have a direct correlation to the wild, exploitative industrialism of the Gilded Age. A complex confluence of historical trends shaped today's urban underclass: firstly, the stage was set by the great cityward migrations of rural blacks beginning around World War I and continuing through World War II and after. These migrations resulted in transformation of this rural-agricultural people into an urban-industrial workforce. Secondly, and most critically, late-twentieth-century deindustrialization rapidly marginalized this new proletariat. The latter process restructured the urban economies of the industrial cities of the northeast from hubs of goods manufacturing into management and technological centers emphasizing finance, information processing, and the delivery of services. In the half century following World War II, this combination of black migration and economic restructuring, plus discriminatory local and federal housing policies, trapped huge numbers of the African-American population in dark ghettos devoid of opportunity.

By raising structural issues such as postindustrialism and the mismatch between black skills and those required in the contemporary urban job market, Wilson attempted to counter conservative claims that the black inner-city neighborhoods' problems derived from federal welfare largesse.

In *American Apartheid: Segregation and the Making of the Underclass*, Douglas S. Massey and Nancy A. Denton modified Wilson's emphatically structural argument. They pleaded that structural forces failed to explain adequately underclass formation in America's aging industrial cities. According to Massey and Denton, racial segregation not only seriously aggravated the economic and social conditions of African-American urban life, but was a primary factor in spawning the modern underclass. The "truly disadvantaged," contend Massey and Denton, are better understood as "truly segregated."

THE ECONOMIC LEGACY OF OPPRESSION

While research like that of Massey and Denton draws attention to a new type of underclass, historians remind us that poverty has long haunted free black families in urban America. The urban poverty uncovered in the 1960s by scholars such as Daniel P. Moynihan, who was then a young Harvard sociologist serving as under-secretary of labor, was deeply rooted in the African-American experience. Black city dwellers in Philadelphia, Chicago, Detroit, and Washington, D.C., knew grinding urban poverty long before recent scholars reported on it. In the eighteenth and early nineteenth centuries Philadelphia blacks, free and slave, crowded into the dank, sunless courts and alleys of the city's Southwark and northern Liberties sections. Prior to World War I, manufacturing firms in Philadelphia, Detroit, Milwaukee, and elsewhere barred most African Americans, relegating what were then fairly modest black working-class populations to the margins of the northern urban-industrial economy. In Philadelphia, according to W. E. B. DuBois's 1899 classic study, blacks toiled primarily as general laborers, hod carriers, carters, cooks, caterers, barbers, laundrymen and -women, porters, bootblacks, and domestics.

The African-American urban population, however, then shared a common poverty and common unsegregated urban space with their immigrant neighbors. In the early twentieth century the singer and actress Ethel Waters, as well as policeman-turned-writer Alan Ballard, recalled Philadelphia childhoods spent in neighborhoods comprising an ethnic and racial mix of Irish, Italians, and Jews. Although blacks in Philadelphia and other cities entered the manufacturing sector during World War I, the first signs of black ghettoization began to appear by 1930 due to the Great Migration northward and the increasing social and residential segregation that characterized the 1920s.

The Great Depression and Franklin D. Roosevelt's New Deal farm policies, which benefited large capital-intensive agriculture, rendered many black tenant farmers and sharecroppers indigent and homeless. World War II, which created economic opportunities for blacks in northern shipyards, aircraft factories, and other war industries, accelerated black migration during the later 1930s and 1940s. By the 1950s these factors had help to establish a thriving black urban culture, but had also paved the way for a segregated, isolated, deprived urban environment that would foster the development of the underclass.

Black population growth in Philadelphia, Chicago, and other cities soared after World War II. Between 1950 and 1970 the percentages of blacks living in northern cities doubled, from 14 percent to 33 percent in Chicago, from 16 percent to 38 percent in Detroit, and from 18 percent to 34 percent in Philadelphia. At the same time, the related forces of deindustrialization and suburbanization transformed American cities socially, economically, and spatially. In the postwar era, city and federal government officials teamed with private corporate executives, bankers, Realtors, and developers to transform gritty downtowns into modern renaissance centers, showplaces for the postindustrial urban economy.

URBAN RENEWAL

Postwar urban redevelopment (after 1954 called urban "renewal") aimed to clear slums, rebuild blighted downtowns, and link cities to growing suburbs and to other cities via dazzling freeways and beltways. Federally funded or underwritten renewal, highway construction, and suburb building created what historian Kenneth T. Jackson dubbed the "Crabgrass Frontier," a whole new postwar world of endless subdivisions, shopping malls, and office and industrial parks. Low-interest federal and veterans' housing administration loans lubricated the process whereby millions of urbanites flocked to the Levittowns, Drexelbrooks, and Park Forests springing up on the cool, green rim of the city. Suburbia unfolded as a white middle-class world, home to that critical segment of managers, engineers, technicians, and professionals who staffed the nation's new service, management, and high technology-oriented economy. Meanwhile, through real estate appraisal tactics, zoning, restrictive covenants, and other devices (some ruled unconstitutional in 1948), federal housing officials and private bankers and Realtors conspired to keep urban blacks walled inside urban ghettos.

The modern postwar black ghetto took shape in the aging inner-city neighborhoods abandoned by fleeing whites. This phenomenon was first described as early as 1948 by a young federal housing official, Robert Weaver, who would later become the first head of the Department of Housing and Urban Development and the first African American in a president's cabinet. Unlike prewar black neighborhoods where clusters of African-American families adjoined nearby concentrations of white residents, the new black ghetto was inhabited exclusively by African Americans. After World War II urban isolation and concentrated poverty arose in tandem for the first time, and an urban underclass materialized as a unique urban phenomenon. Evidence of underclass formation appeared for the first time as early as the 1950s.

Government policy and urban restructuring converged to produce both modern ghettoization and the manifestation of "problem families," an early inkling of the concentrated poverty to come. Postwar urban renaissance, the redesign of dilapidated old commercial-industrial districts into glitzy office canyons of glass and steel, involved both federally underwritten redevelopment and federal public housing. The 1949 Wagner-Ellender-Taft law established government-assisted urban redevelopment linked to the rehousing of those families uprooted in the process. Many of the poor black families displaced by urban redevelopment actions were rehoused in public housing, a low-income shelter program launched in 1937 under the New Deal. Tragically, as the Philadelphia experience indicated, this federal renewal-rehousing policy enabled the kind of concentrated poverty that in the late 1960s and 1970s critics described as characteristic of the underclass. As sociologist Lee Rainwater, journalist Nicholas Lemann, and others have shown, public housing emerged as a crucial and hotly contested site in the postwar black experience.

One of Philadelphia's first three housing projects built under the 1937 Wagner Housing Act, the 1,324-unit Richard Allen Homes—named for the early Philadelphia religious leader—opened for occupancy in 1941 as housing for low-income black families. During World War II the 131-acre sea of red and yellow brick low-rise buildings also housed black families employed in war industries. Wartime project managers enforced strict standards of tenant eligibility, foreclosing any possibility that these "way-stations" for the temporarily submerged middle class might serve the "undeserving poor." Philadelphia housing officials limited eligibility at Allen to American citizens who had resided in the city one year prior to applying for admission. The housing authority also demanded that tenants be part of "natural . . . or cohesive family groups," defined as "working adults known to have regularly lived as an inherent part of a family group whose earnings are an integral part of the family income." While an aunt or uncle might be welcomed in Richard Allen as part of a family, not so for "unrelated persons, or a person living alone." Therefore, lodgers, transient paying guests, or single persons were barred.

THE OTHER PHILADELPHIA STORY

Rising World War II wages and upwardly revised income limits for continued occupancy helped make project communities such as Richard Allen "spic and span places" with a vigorous social life fueled by a host of social organizations. In 1943 couples headed approximately 70 percent of the Allen families. Almost half of these families had three or four members; 40 percent had more than five members. It remained a lively, clean, well-ordered place as late as 1947 when an article in the Philadelphia *Evening Bulletin* described flowers blooming in Allen's front yards, children splashing in the spray pool, adults playing Ping-Pong in the play room. The manager dubbed the project "a family of families [who] are economically and mentally a source of enrichment to one another."

After 1947 several events buffeted project communities such as Richard Allen. Wisconsin Senator Joseph McCarthy unleashed a strenuous campaign to evict all project families whose incomes exceeded the maximum for continued occupancy. By 1950 McCarthy's "over-max" crusade had purged hundreds of solid working-class black families from Allen's tenant rolls. Champions of public housing, forced to rebut accusations that government housing was "communistic," countered by tying the policy to probusiness, urban redevelopment, and to the goal of a "decent" home and environment for all Americans.

Urban renewal, thus, had serious consequences for both public housing and Philadelphia's black community. During the 1950s renewal often was coupled with the demolition of the slums and temporary World War II housing, both of which played an important role in sheltering the widening stream of black migrants arriving into Philadelphia from the South. Many of the thousands of black families dislocated from these areas by urban renewal comprised the "new clientele" for public housing.

Between 1950 and 1956 slum clearance—much of it for public housing projects—uprooted more than 2,000 households in North Philadelphia alone. As elsewhere in urban America, renewal most affected the inner-city black population. Large-scale demolition not only removed a sizable stock of low-rent dwellings but also it often eviscerated the heart of the inner-city economy. In the late 1950s residents of North Philadelphia's huge Poplar Renewal Area complained about abandoned houses, vacant buildings, trash-filled lots, noise, juvenile delinquency, and the proliferation of tap rooms. By 1960 North Philadelphia renewal involved massive clearance operations which dislocated more than 6,250 mainly black families and single persons. Between 1950 and 1970 the number of dwelling units in North Philadelphia declined from almost 114,000 units to under 90,000.

Aside from its effects on dwellings, urban renewal further eroded the delicate economic fabric of the poor inner-city black community by destroying workplaces as well. During two years, 1962–1963, more than six hundred small laundries, repair shops, groceries, garages, ice yards, bakeries, junk shops, and other small businesses, which once dominated the North Philadelphia economic landscape, vanished into rubble. These businesses had provided jobs for neighborhood residents as handymen, washers, stock boys, garage attendants, ice handlers, and junk men—jobs that had historically formed an economic bulwark against the many insecurities of low-income black life.

While businesses and residential structures disappeared from North Philadelphia, people did not. More than 90 percent of displaced families and single persons moved back within a mile of their destroyed residence. Most of these dislocated persons were poor. More than 60 percent of families displaced between 1958 and 1962 had annual incomes under $3,000; a third were divorced, widowed, or separated; 19 percent were single. Another study of 780 families uprooted during the years 1963–1964 found half of these households dependent on welfare, child support, or pensions. Thirty-eight percent of the household heads were not in the labor force; 39 percent were female. Moreover, postwar studies found that a third of the families displaced by renewal had incomes low enough for public housing, and after passage of the 1954

Housing Act, won "first preference" in available units; more than 90 percent of these uprooted North Philadelphia households were black. Increasingly, in the postwar era, these displaced black households constituted the pool of North Philadelphia families seeking shelter in places such as the Richard Allen Homes.

Race infused every aspect of postwar housing and redevelopment policy. Despite the landmark 1948 decision in *Skelly* v. *Kramer*, which outlawed restrictive covenants, and Philadelphia's 1950 City Charter, the city's real estate and home-building industry blatantly pursued policies that contributed to the building of the ghetto. Moreover, despite a commitment to "integrated occupancy" published in 1952, Philadelphia's public housing, like Chicago's, was grossly segregated. Federal Housing Administration real estate appraisal policies helped to consolidate the boundaries of Philadelphia's black ghetto. The guidelines branded black neighborhoods and areas adjoining them as "too risky" for mortgage loans, stymieing private investment in these areas and preventing black movement to better housing on the urban periphery. Public housing in Philadelphia became blacker and poorer largely due to this trend.

DEINDUSTRIALIZATION

The growth of the number of poor black tenants in public housing seemingly defied an overall postwar trend from 1945 to 1973 toward measurable economic progress for all Americans including urban blacks. The process of economic restructuring, however, adversely affected the sizable black population who clung precariously to the edges of the old industrial economy. In effect, as several historians have observed, after World War II many blacks experienced the dissolution of that narrow but vital niche among the working poor, which they had secured in the manufacturing job market between the world wars.

This process, sometimes referred to as "deproletarianization" by social scientists, was plainly visible in postwar Philadelphia, especially among the residents of the Richard Allen Homes. Between 1947 and 1965 employment in the city's basic industries plummeted by a quarter. Philadelphia's once sovereign textile industry was severely weakened in the 1920s, recovered slightly during World War II, and then expired afterward—this time for good. The city's manufacturing sector fared no better. Once the home to giants such as the Baldwin Locomotive Works, which collapsed in the 1930s, Philadelphia lost two-thirds of the jobs in metal manufacturing between 1945 and 1975. By 1963 North Philadelphia's Budd Corporation, producer of truck trailers and railroad passenger cars, trimmed its workforce by almost a half; Midvale Steel cut nearly one-third of its North Philadelphia workforce; Crown Can released more than half of its workers.

The decline in Philadelphia manufacturing was not confined to metals and textiles. Jobs in chemicals fell 20 percent; in food processing 26 percent, and in tobacco manufacturing 76 percent. The latter especially affected black Philadelphia, for companies such as Bayuk Cigar employed many black women—some of whom lived in the Richard Allen Homes.

North Philadelphia, therefore, felt the full brunt of deindustrialization. Between 1928 and 1972, one study estimated, the area lost as many as 50,000 manufacturing jobs. The number of North Philadelphians who reported employment sank from more than 143,000 in 1950 to less than 72,000 in 1970. In 1946, a wide variety of at least 450 businesses and industries crowded North Philadelphia below Allegheny Avenue. These establishments included breweries, hat makers, battery manufacturers, ice cream factories, ice and coal yards, warehouses, and laundries. By 1970, obsolescence, corporate consolidations, buyouts, urban renewal, and suburban relocations expunged these businesses from the city's tax rolls. During the 1950s, North Philadelphia experienced an ominous transformation. The Quaker City's white population declined, while its black population rose by one-third, and its manufacturing base vanished. Where once Irish, German, Polish, and Jewish families built communities around thriving textile and metal-manufacturing enterprises, African Americans now scratched for an existence in an economic wasteland.

Such forces of urban decay operated most destructively on the most vulnerable, those black families whose low incomes and shelter problems qualified them for public housing. In 1945 almost one-quarter of the male workers in Richard Allen Homes held jobs as skilled craftsmen, the majority in Philadelphia's large primary metals industry. Sixty percent of the breadwinners in the project worked in either metal manufacturing or the transportation industry. By 1960 only one-quarter of Allen's gainfully employed labored in manufacturing; a mere 15 percent had jobs in metal-working industries.

The decline in Allen residents' employment in metal manufacturing occurred simultaneously with a growing proportion of Richard Allen women working in the city's dwindling but still extant textile and garment firms. Moreover, an increasing number of household heads labored in the retail, health, and other sectors of Philadelphia's growing service economy. In 1960 more than 60 percent of the breadwinners in the project worked as maids, department stores clerks, or laundresses, orderlies, or aides in city hospitals. By 1965, the year of Moynihan's report on the black family, a clear pattern had emerged in the Richard Allen Homes. Largely populated by working, two-parent families in the 1940s and early 1950s, Allen had already become by the early 1960s a place in which women headed more than 50 percent of the households. Nearly one-quarter of all household heads were not in the labor force, and many barely survived on low paychecks or public assistance.

THE SHIFT IN PUBLIC HOUSING

Faced as early as the mid-1950s with the reality of a "new clientele," public housing managers fought valiantly, but unsuccessfully, to preserve the public image of housing projects as well-managed communities of hardworking families. Policymakers portrayed places such as Richard Allen as publicly owned real estate operations, not welfare hotels. Housing authorities hired managers to collect rent and maintain buildings and grounds; the job never included social work. Public housing managers reluctantly admitted that "broken" or "damaged" families were replacing their "normal" families, thus forcing them to reconsider their stubborn adherence to a strict real estate management role.

By 1955 national estimates placed the welfare population in public housing at from 35 percent to 40 percent. Public housing rents could no longer cover operating costs. To stem the environmental deterioration at Allen, management orchestrated garden and tree planting projects and improved trash collection. But, no matter how luxuriant the flower boxes or the rose arbors that framed the entrance to the management offices, incidents of juvenile delinquency and vandalism escalated. Philadelphia attempted to mobilize city social resources in a campaign called "Plus Values for the Family in Public Housing." City housing officials identified all of the region's public and private agencies available to serve public housing clients, including the Boy and Girl Scouts, the Free Library, several settlement houses, and the YWCA. These agencies would help tenants "understand and accept financial responsibility . . . in a businesslike way," and develop "balanced ways of life [allowing them to] grow into useful, contributing citizens."

The "Plus Values" campaign, like management's crusade to mobilize community agencies to "Keep Allen Beautiful," represented early heroic effort by public housing officials to cure the disease that social epidemiologists labeled "the problem family." The social virus was first identified in Philadelphia in 1952 when the housing authority's Subcommittee on Tenant Selection reported that in addition to low income, many of the families being uprooted from the Poplar urban redevelopment area had "other problems." The committee characterized these families as having "too many children . . . [making] a great deal of noise, quarrel[ing] among themselves, indulge[ing] in hostilities with neighbors . . . [being] chronic alcoholics, narcotics addicts, active T.B. cases, lack[ing] control over their children, tear[ing] up the physical structure," or "engaging in prostitution or random relationships which resemble it." The committee members faced an anguishing dilemma. On the one hand, the multiple social defects of these problem families warranted excluding them from public housing; on the other hand, these were the uprooted households deemed by the housing authority most in need of rehousing. Accordingly, the committee redefined "acceptability" to mean "reasonably stable family groups with some strengths which appeared capable of progress as distinguished from those families with deep, long-term problems which would cause continuous disturbance in a low-rent housing community."

By considerably broadening public housing's responsibility for sheltering uprooted families, the 1954 federal housing legislation made those fine behavioral distinctions used by housing authorities in 1952 moot. Elizabeth Wood, the executive secretary of the Chicago Housing Authority, confessed that the requirement to evict over-maximum-income families and accept families uprooted by urban renewal "has put us in a different kind of business . . . for which we are not prepared." Wood recalled her days as a young Chicago social worker when the intractable case—she used for her example an habitually drunken fictitious client, Mrs. McGee, and her abusive and equally besotted husband—was transferred to the county there to languish on the dole. "My dear brothers and sisters in the public housing business," intoned Wood standing before a large audience at the 1956 annual National Association of Housing and Redevelopment Officials conference, "you are [now] getting the McGees."

PUBLIC HOUSING BECOMES A "PROBLEM"

Between 1956 and 1960 the "problem family" loomed as the number one policy issue in public housing. During these years social work and housing literature brimmed with articles entitled "The Problem Family," "Helping Families in Trouble," and "The Unwed Mother and Public Housing." The realization that public housing had become a haven for broken and dysfunctional families perplexed and further disillusioned liberal intellectuals. Many echoed the *New York Times* writer Harrison Salisbury's 1958 broadside that sheltering dope-abusing dads and sexually loose moms in public housing left them "the same bunch of bastards they always were." "It is now considered more likely," wrote Daniel Seligman the same year in *Fortune*, "that the slums simply attract problem families. And their problems will not be erased by putting these families in public housing projects." Two years later the federal government finally acknowledged that public housing sheltered "troubled families." In 1960 President John F. Kennedy appointed Marie McGuire as commissioner of public housing. Brandishing the slogan "People Oriented Public Housing," McGuire redefined public housing as a mechanism for the delivery of welfare services, rather than as a real estate program.

The odyssey of Philadelphia's Richard Allen Homes and the management's struggle to contend with the "problem family" issue reveals that, in the policy-molded environment of public housing, postwar segregation, urban renewal, and economic restructuring had spawned a new social phenomenon long before social scientists defined it in the 1970s. The Allen experience indicates that in the 1950s these processes created "troubled families" whose profile closely resembled what scholars have called the underclass. Public housing projects such as the Richard Allen Homes did not create the black underclass. However, in conjunction with urban renewal policy, they did function to concentrate and isolate, socially and spatially, a growing segment of the black poor whose many disadvantages—inferior education, unemployment, illegitimacy, crime, alcoholism, and drug abuse—became hallmarks of the underclass.

Public housing's troubled families remained hidden in the 1950s. At the end of the decade social commentators Michael Harrington and Dwight McDonald noted that America's robust postwar economy rendered poverty either invisible or isolated in the rural South or urban pockets like the Richard Allen Homes. After 1973, when the percentage of African Americans in poverty reached its lowest point, the American economy stalled and the twin forces of deindustrialization and persistent racial segregation battered the remnants of the urban-industrial economy, eviscerating the black, inner-city communities. Buffeted by "stagflation" and higher petroleum prices, American manufacturing during the 1970s lost its competitive advantage vis-à-vis foreign producers, yielding rapid disinvestment and a sharp decline in the nation's older industrial centers such as Detroit, Pittsburgh, Cleveland, and Philadelphia. Losses in manufacturing were matched by a sizable growth in the urban service sector, especially in nonproductive business services such as finance, insurance, real estate, law, marketing, accounting, and engineering. By 1988 business services and advanced technology companies represented 61 percent of Philadelphia's regional manufacturing economy. These businesses tended to locate outside of the central city, making them inaccessible to Philadelphia's large pool of African-American workers who, in any case, generally lacked the required skills, having been systematically denied the necessary education. That population concentrated in the city's inner core of neighborhoods became increasingly isolated in an economic wasteland scarred by the empty hulks of abandoned nineteenth-century factories, warehouses, and rows of gutted houses.

THE "DISCOVERY" OF THE UNDERCLASS

Postindustrialism especially devastated the urban world of young unskilled blacks who resided in South Chicago, South-Central Los Angeles, and North Philadelphia. By the 1980s joblessness, hopelessness, and drugs transformed these neighborhoods into a phantasmagoria of disintegrating family life, random violence, and desperation that was captured sometimes brutally and sympathetically in the works of filmmakers such as Spike Lee and John Singleton.

No one disputes the existence of the problem; only the causes are contested. Nationally, in 1987 African Americans constituted 41 percent of all murder victims. Between 1970 and 1984 the number of black households headed by a female increased radically; by 1984 women headed 43 percent of all black families, up from 28 percent in 1970. By 1984, in centers of concentrated black poverty such as Chicago's Robert Taylor Homes, females headed 90 percent of families with children and 83 percent of the project families lived on welfare.

Conservatives blamed rising crime and dependency rates in the inner city on morally injurious federal and state welfare policies and on the "coddling" of criminals. Liberals and others rejected the welfare thesis, pointing out that the value of government transfer payments actually declined in the 1970s and

1980s while the number of female-headed families rose. In explaining the underclass, they focused instead on urban restructuring and also on the operation of "historic discrimination" that erected seemingly insurmountable obstacles to the kind of bootstrap entrepreneurship that sustained and undergirded the mobility of many earlier immigrants. These scholars pointed to the corrosive effect of urban isolation, a negative consequence of black and white middle-class flight from the inner city, which rendered black neighborhoods devoid of functional middle class role models and job networks.

The work of Douglas Massey and Nancy Denton added the final crucial element to the underclass equation by introducing the concept of "hypersegregation." Ghettoized blacks, they argue, endured not only high levels of concentrated poverty but also segregation. In hypersegregated neighborhoods, one-third or more of families were poor. Such poverty-compounded segregation concentrated and exaggerated all the maladies of ghetto living: disproportionately large numbers of female-headed households, crime, drugs, housing dilapidation, abandoned and boarded-up buildings, even fires. In fact, hypersegregation has bred the "oppositional culture" described eloquently by Elijah Anderson in *Streetwise*, which shows how ghetto youth erected a set of behaviors and values diametrically opposed to the norms of the wider society to counter the harsh, violent reality of the street. The street youth he studied derided hard work, sobriety, steady employment, financial security, marriage, and family as "acting white" and, thus, irrelevant. According to Anderson, Philadelphia's alienated underclass youth completely divorced themselves from these conventional values. Streetwise young black men and women engage in a vicious, highly exploitative game, in which men prize women not for love, but as booty; women are objects to be claimed and controlled. Women, like men, reject meaningful stable relationships and seek gratification not in the sexual conquest, but in pregnancy and childbirth itself. The "gift child" becomes the prize, a requisite for membership in the neighborhood baby club.

CONCLUSION

The late twentieth-century urban underclass may be, as I have suggested, nothing more than the latest version of the *residium*. Historians of poverty agree that Western societies have traditionally defined a lowest, ignominious category of the poor and branded it "undeserving." But such labeling ignores the profound impact that global economic forces have exerted in shaping contemporary poverty. Since the dawn of industrialization, economic structures—the size of the workplace, the organization of work, the level of technology—have significantly shaped the profile of the poor and helped determine whether society regarded them as morally worthy or unworthy of assistance.

Structural forces loom especially large in any attempt to comprehend modern concentrated poverty and the peculiar dilemma of the hypersegregated poor. Deindustrialization demolished the opportunity structure erected during two hundred years in such hubs of manufacturing as Philadelphia, Boston, and New York. It decimated the complex infrastructure of hat factories, warehouses, machine shops, railroad yards, docks, breweries, and junkyards that were the economic foothold for generations of white immigrants seeking a niche in urban America. Postindustrialism not only redefined productivity by replacing goods manufacturing with information processing. It also suburbanized work sites and devised and imposed a new and more rigorous set of educational and behavioral standards for labor participation and employment success. While postindustrialism's toll included steelworkers in Pittsburgh and autoworkers in Detroit, it struck hardest at America's newest proletariate, the huge black migrant workforce that between 1917 and 1945 had battled job discrimination and gained for the first time a foothold in the world of urban industrialism.

The Richard Allen Homes case study clearly illustrates how segregation has been the principle ingredient in the making of the underclass. Black migrants flooding into wartime and post–World War II urban America faced open hostility from their white ethnic neighbors. Postwar segregation patterns hardened at the same time deindustrialization eroded the basis for black opportunity. The process intensified after 1973, producing hypersegregated black ghettos and the blossoming of an oppositional culture. Postwar ghetto life featured not the dynamic density described in James Weldon Johnson's *Black Manhattan*, but for black youth in particular, despair and a militant rejection of all of the values of the "outside" society.

Gilding the modern ghetto with "enterprise zones" or enhancing welfare programs hardly addresses the source of the underclass dilemma. Most modern, inner-city neighborhoods are segregated islands of concentrated poverty isolated from the rest of the postindustrial urban world. Opportunity for participation in the burgeoning economy of silicon chips, corporate finance, and global marketing rarely knocks at the ghetto's door. Inner-city communities, whether in Philadelphia, Detroit, Chicago, or Washington, D.C., lack the social, economic, and political resources to combat hopelessness and promote social and economic restructuring. Indeed, isolated, segregated neighborhoods are anachronisms in global economies, which prize open markets and value most the mobility of ideas, goods, and people. Ghetto walls must come down, and the social and cultural isolation must end before the modern underclass can be eradicated.

FOR FURTHER READING

Auletta, Ken. *The Underclass*. Rev. ed. New York: Penguin USA, 1999.

Borchert, James. *Alley Live in Washington: Family, Community, Religion & Folklife in the City 1850–1970*. Urbana: University of Illinois Press, 1980.

Clark, Kenneth B. *Dark Ghetto: Dilemmas of Social Power*. 2nd ed. Middletown, Conn.: Wesleyan University Press, 1989.

Conley, Dalton. *Being Black, Living in the Red: Race, Wealth and Social Policy in America.* Berkeley and Los Angeles: University of California Press, 1999.

DuBois, W. E. B. *The Philadelphia Negro: A Social Study.* Centennial ed. Philadelphia: University of Pennsylvania Press, 1999.

Harrington, Michael. *The Other America: Poverty in the United States.* New York: Simon & Schuster, 1997.

Jenks, Christopher, and Paul E. Peterson, eds. *The Urban Underclass.* Washington, D.C.: Brookings Institution, 1991.

Katz, Michael, ed. *The Underclass Debate: Views from History.* Princeton, N.J.: Princeton University Press, 1993.

Ladner, Joyce A. *Tomorrow's Tomorrow: The Black Woman.* Lincoln: University of Nebraska Press, 1995.

Lane, Roger. *Roots of Violence in Black Philadelphia, 1860–1900.* Cambridge: Harvard University Press, 1989.

Lemann, Nicholas. *The Promised Land: The Great Black Migration and How It Changed America.* New York: Vintage, 1992.

Liebow, Elliot. *Tally's Corner: A Study of Streetcorner Men.* Boston: Little, Brown & Co., 1999.

Massey, Douglas S., and Denton, Nancy A. *American Apartheid: Segregation and the Making of the Underclass.* Cambridge: Harvard University Press, 1993.

Moynihan, Daniel Patrick. *The Negro Family: The Case for National Action.* Washington, D.C.: Department of Labor, 1965.

Murray, Charles. *Losing Ground: American Social Policy, 1950–1980.* Tenth Anniversary ed. New York: Basic Books, 1995.

Oliver, Melvin L., and Thomas M. Shapiro. *Black Wealth/White Wealth: A New Perspective on Racial Inequality.* New York: Routledge, 1997.

Rainwater, Lee. *Behind Ghetto Walls: Black Families in a Federal Slum.* Chicago: Aldine, 1970.

Stack, Carol B. *All Our Kin: Strategies for Survival in a Black Community.* New York: Basic Books, 1997.

Wilson, William Julius. *The Truly Disadvantaged: The Inner City, the Underclass, and Public Policy.* Chicago: University of Chicago Press, 1990.

———. *When Work Disappears: The World of the New Urban Poor.* New York: Alfred A. Knopf, 1996.

chapter 17

Black Feminism
in the United States

Beverly Guy-Sheftall

T HE BLACK FEMINIST MOVEMENT, which began to emerge in the mid-1960s, is a continuation of both an intellectual and activist tradition that began more than a century and a half ago. The argument that African-American women confronted both a "woman question and a race problem" captured the essence of black feminist thought at the turn of the century and would reverberate among intellectuals, academics, activists, writers, educators, and community leaders, both male and female, for generations. While feminist perspectives have in fact been a persistent and important component of the African-American literary and intellectual tradition since slavery, scholars until fairly recently have focused primarily on the racial perspectives of blacks. This tendency to ignore long years of political struggle aimed at eradicating the multiple oppressions black women experience resulted in erroneous notions about the relevance of feminism to the black community during the second wave of the women's movement. Revisioning black history with a gender analysis, however, should render obsolete the notion that feminist thinking is alien to African Americans or that they have been misguided imitators of white women.

While black feminism is not a monolithic, static ideology and there has been considerable diversity of thought among African Americans with feminist consciousness going back to the 1800s, certain premises characterize what came to be labeled black feminism: (1) black women experience a special kind of oppression and suffering in this country that is both racist and sexist because of their dual racial and gender identity; (2) this "double jeopardy" has meant that the problems, concerns, and needs of black women are different in many ways from those of both white women and black men; (3) black women must struggle for gender equality *and* black liberation; (4) there is no inherent contradiction in the struggle to eradicate sexism and racism as well as the other "isms" such as classism and heterosexism that plague the human community; (5) black women's characterisitic struggles with respect to racial and sexual politics, their poverty, and marginalized status have given them a unique view of the world.

EARLY BLACK FEMINISTS

A historical perspective on the evolution of feminist consciousness among African-American women is usually thought to have begun with abolition since the catalyst for the emergence of the women's rights movement in the mid-nineteenth century was the movement to abolish slavery. However, for two hundred years enslaved African females struggled for their freedom and protested beatings, involuntary breeding, sexual exploitation by white masters, family separation, debilitating work schedules, substandard living conditions, bringing slave children into the world, and demeaning stereotypes. A few of their life stories called attention to the peculiar plight of black women and their strategies for resistance. In her antebellum autobiography, *Incidents in the Life of a Slave Girl: Written by Herself* (1861), Harriet Jacobs publicized her sexual vulnerability and stated unequivocally that "slavery is terrible for men; but it is far more terrible for women. Superadded to the burden common to all, *they* have wrongs, and sufferings, and mortifications peculiarly their own." Covert use of contraceptives, the practice of abortion, and desperate attempts to control the fate of their children, including infanticide, provided slave women some measure of control over their bodies and their reproductive capacity. The most well-documented case of infanticide concerns Margaret Garner who escaped slavery in Kentucky in 1856; during her capture in Cincinnati she killed her baby daughter rather than have her returned to her master. This event was the inspiration for Toni Morrison's award-winning novel *Beloved*, which was published in 1987.

Manifestations of their race and gender consciousness are also to be found in the sex-segregated, self-help organizations free black women formed in the early 1800s, because it was difficult for them to become leaders in organizations with black men or because they were denied membership in white women's groups. It was also easier for black women to attend to their own political, cultural, or intellectual agendas with the establishment of separate literary, debating, abolitionist, or other reform organizations. Located primarily in the Northeast, one of the earliest of these organizations was the Afric-American Female Intelligence Society of Boston, founded in 1831. Free women of color were also responsible for organizing in 1832 the first female abolitionist group the Salem Massachusetts Female Antislavery Society. The racially mixed Philadelphia Female Anti-Slavery Society, founded in 1833, included several women from the famous Forten family. Although often ignored by historians attempting to document the development of feminism in the mid-nineteenth century, black women's self-help, abolitionist, and other reform activities also contributed to a climate of female discontent that anticipated the historic women's rights gathering at Seneca Falls in 1848.

In 1832 Maria W. Stewart, a free black from Connecticut with abolitionist and feminist impulses, delivered four public lectures in Boston, the first at the Afric-American Female Intelligence Society. She was probably the first African-American woman to speak publicly in defense of women's rights, though she is remembered primarily as the first American-born woman of any race to lecture publicly to racially mixed audiences of women and men. She spoke on a variety of issues relevant to the black community—literacy, self-determination, abolition, economic empowerment, and racial unity—but she admonished black women in particular to break free from stifling gender definitions and reach their fullest potential by pursuing formal education and careers outside the home, especially teaching; she was also adamant in her belief that black women should assume leadership roles within their communities, all of which were familiar themes in what we would now identify as a black feminist agenda during the nineteenth century. Passionate in her defense of black womanhood, she queried: "How long shall the fair daughters of Africa be compelled to bury their minds and talents beneath a load of iron pots and kettles. . . . Possess the spirit of independence. . . . Sue for your rights and privileges."

Stewart was probably also the first to call for a school by and for black women during a time when education for black men assumed a greater priority. Discouraged by criticism from black men about her inappropriate female behavior (political activism and lecturing in public), however, Stewart left the lecture circuit a year later in 1833, but not without defending her sex in the most glowing terms by alluding to historical and biblical precedents in a "Farewell Address to Her Friends in the City of Boston": "What if I am a woman. . . . Did St. Paul but know of our wrongs and deprivations, I presume he would make no objections to our pleading in public for our rights . . . in the 15th century . . . we might then have seen women preaching and mixing themselves in controversies. Women occupying the chairs of Philosophy and Justice; women writing in Greek, and studying in Hebrew. Nuns were poetesses, and women of quality Divines. . . . Why cannot we become divines and scholars?" She also warned against a paradoxical problem that would plague the black community for generations—preaching against prejudice in the white community but being discriminatory in their own backyards: "Let us no longer talk of prejudice, till prejudice becomes extinct at home. Let us no longer talk of opposition, till we cease to oppose our own." Stewart continued her activism, however, after leaving the lecture circuit by publishing a collection of her work in 1835 (*Productions of Mrs. Maria W. Stewart*), attending the 1837 Women's Anti-Slavery Convention, and joining a black female literary society in New York.

THE STRUGGLE FOR EQUAL RIGHTS

During the 1830s and 1840s other American women, like Stewart, began lecturing against slavery and found that in so doing they had to defend their own
right to speak in public, which in turn led them to demand their own emancipation. At the Convention of the American Anti-Slavery Society in 1839,
doubt was cast upon women's right to participate in the convention, so a resolution was proposed that hereafter women delegates would have votes like
the men. A majority of the male delegates were opposed, but the women present insisted on voting, and their votes gave the resolution a majority. In 1840
the American delegates to the World's Anti-Slavery Convention arrived in
London to find the women delegates among them again excluded from participation. While seated in the gallery behind a curtain with the rest of the
women, Elizabeth Stanton and Lucretia Mott felt the striking similarity
between white women like themselves and black slaves, a common theme in
early white feminist discourse. During the ten days of frustration that followed, they became friends and agreed to hold a women's rights convention
on their return to America. Eight years later in 1848 the Seneca Falls Convention was held, attended mainly by abolitionists. This historic event is considered the beginning of the women's movement in the United States.

While Frederick Douglass, the most prominent black abolitionist and male
women's rights advocate, believed that the antislavery movement was doing
much for the elevation and improvement of women, he understood fully the
need for an independent, organized movement to achieve equal rights for
women. On July 14, 1848, his *North Star* carried the announcement of the
Seneca Falls Convention. A constant reminder to his readers of his commitment to the rights of women was the slogan "Right is of No Sex," which
appeared in an early issue of the *North Star*. At the 1848 Seneca Falls Convention, when it appeared that Elizabeth Cady Stanton's resolution for woman
suffrage was headed for defeat, Douglass at a critical juncture asked for the
floor and delivered an eloquent plea on behalf of women's right to vote. The
resolution was then put to a vote carried by a small margin.

Involvement on the part of black women in women's rights struggles goes
back to Sojourner Truth, perhaps the most frequent black female attendee at
women's rights conventions in the nineteenth century and the most revered
early black feminist. In 1850 she attended the second women's rights convention in Salem, Ohio (as did Douglass), and spoke at the third women's rights convention in Worcester, Massachusetts. Her now controversial "A'n't I A
Woman" speech, delivered at the Akron, Ohio, women's rights convention in
1851, is an eloquent statement of black feminist thought. Some of the delegates
to the convention, according to Frances Gage, describing the gathering some
twelve years later, urged that Sojourner be prohibited from speaking, fearing that
abolitionists in their midst would harm their cause. When she seized the platform, Sojourner directed her remarks against the previous speaker, a clergy-

man who had ridiculed the weakness and helplessness of women, who should, therefore, not be entrusted with the vote. While their first interest was the anti-slavery struggle, two other abolitionist black women were active in the women's rights movement during these early years. They were Frances E. W. Harper, a novelist, poet, and journalist, and Sarah Remond, sister of abolitionist orator Charles Remond, who sat in the balcony with the women at the World's Anti-Slavery Convention meeting in London to protest sexism.

Tensions arose within the equal rights movement. In 1866, Douglass and Remond were among the vice presidents chosen for the newly formed Equal Rights Association (ERA) and later in the year at an Albany meeting, Douglass warned the ERA that it was in danger of becoming an advocate for women's rights alone. At the first annual meeting of the ERA in 1867, Sojourner Truth spoke twice. During one of these talks, she addressed herself to the rights of women, especially black women: "There is a great stir about colored men getting their rights, but not a word about the colored women; and if colored men get their rights, and not colored women . . . there will be a bad time about it. . . . I want women to have their rights." The actual split in the women's movement took place in 1869, a crucial turning point in its history. At the proceedings of the American Equal Rights Association Convention in New York in 1869, the famous debate between Frederick Douglass and the white feminists present took place. Here he argued for the greater urgency of the race issue and defended the positions of abolitionists that now was the Negro hour and women's rights could wait. The great danger was that linking woman suffrage with Negro suffrage at this point would seriously lessen the chances of securing

Sojourner Truth's Address

Akron, May 1851

"Wall, chilern, whar dar is so much racket dar must be somethin' out o' kilter. I tink dat 'twixt de nigger of de Souf and de womin at de Norf, all talkin' 'bout rights, de white men will be in a fix pretty soon. But what's all dis here talkin' 'bout?

"Dat man ober dar say dat womin needs to be helped into carriages, and lifted ober ditches, and to hab de best place everywhar. Nobody eber halps me into carriages, or ober mudpuddles, or gibs me any best place!" And raising herself to her full height, and her voice to a pitch like rolling thunder, she asked, "And a'n't I a woman? Look at me! Look at my arm! (And here she bared her right arm to the shoulder, showing her tremendous muscular power.) I have ploughed, and planted, and gathered into barns, and no man could head me! And a'n't I a woman? I could work as much and eat as much as a man—when I could get it—and bear de lash as well! And a'n't' I a woman? I have borne thirteen chilern, and seen 'em mos' all sold off to slavery, and when I cried out with my mother's grief, none but Jesus heard me! And a'n't I a woman?

Source: Elizabeth C. Stanton, Susan B. Anthony, Matilda J. Gage, eds., *History of Woman's Suffrage* (New York, 1881), vol. I, p. 16.

the ballot for black men, and for the Negro, he reiterated, the ballot was an urgent necessity. When asked whether this was true also about black women, he quickly responded, "Yes, yes, yes ... but not because she is a woman, but because she is black." Frances E. W. Harper supported Douglass, while Sojourner Truth supported the white feminist position, believing that if black men got the vote they would continue to dominate black women.

Following this contentious meeting, Stanton and Anthony organized the National Woman Suffrage Association (NWSA) for women only. They did so in the belief that it was largely due to the male leadership of the suffrage movement that women's interests had been betrayed. In November 1869 in Cleveland, a second organization called the American Woman Suffrage Association (AWSA) was organized with Lucy Stone as chair. By the fall of 1873, even though the resentment over the failure of the Fifteenth Amendment to enfranchise women was still being felt, the leaders of the woman suffrage movement were anxious to reconcile their differences with Douglass. Peace was restored at the 1876 convention of the NWSA during which Douglass was told that his help was needed in the continuing struggle for women's rights. Although he was still somewhat bitter about racist remarks aimed at black men during the battle over the Fifteenth Amendment, he announced that he was still willing to work for the cause. Once the reconciliation had taken place, Sojourner Truth was again a familiar figure at women's rights conventions.

An examination of the extraordinary saga of black women authors during this period provides another mirror on their feminist vision. The pioneering publishing efforts in the 1850s of Mary Shadd Cary, the first black female newspaper editor in North America, mark the beginning of black women's leadership role in journalism. Shadd, known primarily for her advocacy of the political and economic autonomy of blacks, was a writer, teacher, editor, lawyer, nationalist, abolitionist, and suffragist. Born to free abolitionist parents in Delaware, the young Mary was raised in a political household and spent her entire life struggling for the rights of blacks and women. She migrated to Canada with her brother after the passage of the Fugitive Slave Act in 1850 and published *A Plea for Emigration, or Notes on Canada West, in its Moral, Social and Political Aspect* (1852), a guide for fugitive slaves in the United States about what to expect in Canada. A year later she embarked upon a journalism career and solicited the help of Samuel Ringgold Ward, abolitionist and fugitive slave, in the founding of the *Provincial Freeman* whose motto was "Self Reliance Is the True Road to Independence." Critical of the antislavery tactics of some black male leaders, she also accused them of sexism and unethical behavior. After the death of her husband she returned to the United States in 1863, started a school for black children in Washington, D.C., wrote for Frederick Douglass's *The New National Era*, and became an outspoken abolitionist on the lecture circuit. Cary also became the first black woman lawyer in the U.S., graduating from Howard Law School in 1870. Shortly thereafter, she won a case before the House of Representatives Judiciary Committee and was granted the right to vote, a privilege few women during Reconstruction had in federal elections. In 1880 she founded The Colored Women's Progressive Franchise Association in Washington, D.C., one of the earliest women's rights organization for African-American women. Although gaining suffrage for black women was the major objective, the association's twenty-point agenda included broadening occupations for black women and establishing newspapers which black women would control.

THE WOMEN'S CLUB MOVEMENT

The black women's club movement, which emerged on the national level in the 1890s and has been treated by scholars primarily within the context of racial uplift, must be analyzed as well as a manifestation of race and gender obligations on the part of black women. These clubs were established not only because outside of New England white women's clubs prohibited their membership, but also because black women felt they had unique problems to solve. When the First National Conference of Colored Women convened in Boston on July 29, 1895, the agenda included temperance, higher education, domestic questions, morality, and education for girls and boys.

The women's club movement was given fuel as a result of a letter that Florence Belgarnie, an officer of the Anti-Lynching Committee in London, received from John Jacks, American newspaper editor and president of the Missouri Press Association. Angry over Belgarnie's antilynching activities, which had been encouraged by the crusade of black activist Ida Wells-Barnett during her speaking tours in England, Jacks wrote Belgarnie a letter in which he defended the white South by maligning black women for their immorality. Belgarnie in turn sent a copy of the letter to Josephine St. Pierre Ruffin, a member of the largely white New England Women's Club and founder of Woman's Era Club for black women. In 1895 she convened a group of black women at the Charles Street AME Church in Boston, resulting in the formation of the National Federation of African-American Women. Later she distributed the letter to black women's clubs throughout the nation and called for a national conference which eventually led to the formation of the National Association of Colored Women (NACW). In 1896 the association was established when the National Federation of African-American Women, whose president was Margaret Murray Washington, and the National League of Colored Women, whose president was Mary Church Terrell, combined, with Terrell becoming NACW's first national president.

At the historic first gathering of the NACW, Mrs. Mahammitt, a delegate of the Omaha Women's Club, stressed the importance of vindicating the honor of black women and denouncing Jacks. The illustrious group of women present included Margaret Murray Washington, second wife of Booker T. Washington; Anna G. Brown, widow of the well-known writer William Wells Brown; Selena Sloan Butler of Atlanta, Georgia, who some years later would organize the black Parent Teachers Association; and Victoria Earle Matthews, journalist, who in 1897 founded the White Rose Industrial Mission for the purpose of assisting black females who migrated to New York from the South.

A pivotal moment in black women's publishing history and the coming of age politically for clubwomen occurred with the founding of *Woman's Era*. In 1893 Josephine St. Pierre Ruffin had founded the New Era Club in Boston and initiated a monthly publication, *Woman's Era*, the most conspicuous work of the organization and eventually designated the official organ of the NACW. The first issue came out March 24, 1894, and twenty-four issues were published through January 1897. Since it was founded, edited, and published by Ruffin, who was active in the Massachusetts woman suffrage movement, it is not surprising to find the publication a strong advocate of woman suffrage, especially for black women.

It is apparent from its first issue that the editors wanted to make their readers aware of the importance of black women's right to vote. There was also strong advocacy for black women entering the public arena in order to solve their unique problems. An awareness of the dilemma that black women faced as a result of the "double jeopardy" of race and sex is apparent throughout *Woman's Era*, the most significant outlet for the expression of their political views and aspirations during the "Progressive" era.

In 1892, clubwoman Anna Julia Cooper published *A Voice From the South by a Black Woman of the South*, the first book-length feminist analysis of the condition of African Americans. This collection of essays, many of which were speeches delivered to black organizations, is also an enlightened and progressive discussion of the oppressed status of black women. Not content with simply describing the plight of black females, she argued that they needed to speak out for themselves and stop allowing others, including black men, to speak for them. "Only the Black Woman," wrote Cooper, "can say 'when and where I enter, in the quiet, undisputed dignity of my womanhood, without violence and without special patronage, then and there the whole *Negro race enters with me.*'" Commenting on the black woman's unique position, she advanced the argument of "double jeopardy," since black women were confronted by both a woman question and a race problem.

Cooper continued throughout her life to write about women's rights in general, but her major focus was always black women's liberation. She was especially concerned about the accessibility of higher education for black women. She also felt that elevating the status of black women would uplift the entire black race, a persistent theme in the writings of Fannie Barrier Williams, Josephine St. Pierre Ruffin, and Mary Church Terrell, all of whom consistently espoused black feminist ideas in their speeches and articles. Cooper was critical of black men who were unsupportive of the struggle for black female equality and she frequently spoke at black male gatherings about the importance of women in the struggle for racial uplift. In fact, she believed that women, because of their special qualities, should be in the forefront of the fight for racial equality. Although she was aware of the double burden of race and sex which was peculiar to black women, she also felt that black women shared many problems with black males, because of racial oppression, that white women did not share with their men. Cooper's analysis of relationships between black men and women, and the problematic nature of that relationship, links her to contemporary black feminists.

In the 1920s and '30s, Nannie Burroughs, who founded the National Training School for Women and Girls in Washington, D.C., in 1909, continued to espouse the cause of black women in a number of ways. Her concern for the plight of black working-class women, particularly domestic servants, resulted in her organizing the National Association of Wage Earners in 1920. Her intense feelings of racial pride were manifested in her rejection of black emulation of white standards of beauty, and she accused her sisters of "color phobia" if they used hair straighteners and skin bleachers. She is perhaps best known for her leadership in the Woman's Convention (WC) Auxiliary to the National Baptist Convention (NBC), the largest membership organization of black women in the United States. An outspoken advocate of black and women's empowerment and the rights of black Baptist women, she was particularly outraged about women's disenfranchisement and argued that woman suffrage would help to eradicate male dominance and sexual exploitation. After the Nineteenth Amendment was passed in 1919, Burrough's continued her political activism for black women's empowerment and helped to organize the National League of Republican Colored Women in 1924 and became its first president.

During this same period the International Council of Women of the Darker Races, which sometimes met in Washington, D.C., at Nannie Burroughs's school, was spawned by the racial uplift impulses of the black women's club movement. Organized by several black women, most notably Margaret Murray Washington, founding mother of the national black women's club movement and president of NACW from 1914 to 1918, its purpose was to study the condition and status of women of color and children throughout the world. Like Cooper, who wrote about Muslim harems and the Chinese practice of foot-binding on the opening page of *A Voice from the South*, these club-women were aware of cultural differences throughout the world where women were concerned. This forward-looking organization is reminiscent of recent attempts by contemporary black feminists to establish linkages with other women of color internationally and to struggle for the elimination of sexism and racism on a global level.

WHAT BLACK WOMEN WANTED

A frequently overlooked aspect of black women's activism during this period, especially within the context of Pan-Africanism or nationalism, was their battle against gender oppression. The explicitly feminist and visionary writing of Amy Jacques Garvey, Marcus Garvey's second wife, is particularly important in this regard because of her potential impact on thousands of working-class urban blacks involved with the Universal Negro Improvement Association (UNIA), which her husband organized in 1914. As editor from 1924 to 1927 of the Women's Page of the *Negro World*, UNIA's weekly newspaper, Amy wrote passionately in her column "Our Women and What They Think" about the evils of imperialism, materialism, racism, capitalism, and the interlocking race, class, and gender oppression that black and other women experienced globally, particularly in colonial contexts. She believed that the women's movement was one of the most significant struggles in human history and that the emancipation of women was imperative. She critiqued the patriarchal family throughout the world and called for women to participate in all spheres of public life despite their important duties as mothers. She also felt that women were central to the success of black liberation struggles both in the United States and internationally and that they must fight to end imperialist domination as well as their own oppression within their communities. She was especially confident that black women, because of the internal strengths they had developed as a result of perpetual hardships, would be crucial to racial progress, although she lamented their devaluation.

A woman of courage, Garvey was very critical of black men's tyrannical and sexist treatment of women, especially within the UNIA. Echoing Sojourner Truth and Anna Julia Cooper, she espoused a revolutionary, feminist vision of the world in which women would set things right because of their more humane inclinations: "You [men] had your day at the helm of the world, and a pretty mess you have made of it . . . and perhaps women's rule will usher in the era of real brotherhood, when national and racial lines will disappear, leaving mankind in peace and harmony one with another." She also had a special warning for black men: "Watch your step! Ethiopia's queens will reign again and her Amazons protect her shores and people. Strengthen your shaking knees and move forward, or we will displace you and lead on to victory and glory." Concerned about the status of women globally, particularly in Asia and Africa, she applauded Egyptian women's removal of the veil and women's political gains in India, Russia, and China.

Advocating for birth control was another item of the black feminist agenda during the 1920s and '30s, though it would remain controversial given the black community's concern about genocide. It is important to point out that the covert use among slave women of contraceptives and abortifacients was perhaps the earliest manifestation of black women exercising reproductive freedom, a major demand of contemporary feminism. Limiting the size of families was a deliberate strategy of some women for improving the economic viability and standard of living in the black community, and by 1900, black women had significantly lowered their birthrate as well as infant mortality. Black women also had a feminist perspective on excessive childbearing, linking it to burdensome physical and mental problems. The Women's Political Association of Harlem, founded in 1918, was the first black organization to advocate birth control. Although the National Urban League and the NAACP supported family planning, this issue sparked controversy within the black community (among Garveyites, for example) as nationalist concerns about racial extinction and traditional male notions about women's primary role as mothers clashed with feminist demands for sexual autonomy among black women. There was a range of attitudes among black men on this issue, however, including William E. B. DuBois, who argued in "The Damnation of Women (1925)" that women must be free to choose motherhood. Many black women in Harlem also supported Margaret Sanger's establishing a birth control clinic there, although in the 1980s Angela Davis would charge her with racism.

A BLACK FEMINIST AGENDA IN THE '60s AND '70s

In the 1960s, black feminist struggle came to the forefront in a much more conscious manner. The movement coalesced mainly as a result of the successive failures of the civil rights, black nationalist, and women's rights organizations to address the special needs and concerns of black women as well as a heightened consciousness about sexism experienced within the Civil Rights movement. Some black women in the Student Non-Violent Coordinating Committee (SNCC) were angered by the sexist behavior of SNCC men and came to realize that they must battle both racism and gender oppression. In 1964 a group of black and white women led by Ruby Doris Smith Robinson, a former Spelman student, Freedom Rider, and eventually SNCC executive secretary until her untimely death of cancer in 1967, wrote a position paper on the movement's sexist treatment of women. Known as SNCC Position Paper No. 24, "Women of the Movement," it is considered one of the earliest manifestations of the modern women's movement. Septima Clark, the director of education for the Southern Christian Leadership Conference, later criticized the sexist behavior of the male leadership in SCLC, having been influenced by the National Organization for Women (NOW), which she joined in 1968 because she resented southern men's control of women. Clark's autobiography *Ready From Within* (1986), written many years later, revealed that though she was oblivious to their sexism while she was a staff member, SCLC men "thought that women were sex symbols and had no contributions to make."

The simultaneous publication in 1970 of Toni Cade's *The Black Woman: An Anthology*, Shirley Chisholm's autobiography, *Unbought and Unbossed*, Toni Morrison's *The Bluest Eye*, and Audre Lorde's *Cables to Rage* signaled a literary awakening among black women and the beginning of a clearly defined black women's liberation movement which would have different priorities than those of white feminists and generate considerable debate, even hostility, within the black community. Cade's antiracist, antisexist, anti-imperialist agenda captures the essence of black feminism. She proposed black women conduct a comparative study of women's roles in the Third World; debunk myths of the black matriarch and "the evil black bitch"; study black women's history and honor woman warriors such as Harriet Tubman and Fannie Lou Hamer; do oral histories of ordinary black women (migrant workers, quilters, UNIA grandmothers); study sexuality; and establish linkages with other women of color globally.

Cade's anthology includes former SNCC activist Frances Beale's now classic essay on the "double jeopardy" of black women, which highlights their sexual and economic exploitation, the inappropriateness of white models of womanhood, black male sexism, sterilization abuse of women of color globally, and abortion rights. She also voices her disapproval of black nationalist demands that women be subordinate to men and their assumption that women's most important contribution to the revolution is having babies. "To assign women the role of housekeeper and mother while men go forth into battle is a highly questionable doctrine to maintain."

In 1973 the National Black Feminist Organization (NBFO) would emerge, in part as a reminder to the black liberation movement that "there can't be liberation for half a race." Activist-lawyer Flo Kennedy and Margaret Sloan, one of the founding editors of *Ms.* magazine, decided to convene a small gathering of black feminists to discuss their experiences within the racist women's movement and what it meant to be black, female, and feminist. In their statement of purpose, they objected to the perception of the women's movement as solely white and their involvement in it as disloyal to the race. Emphasizing black women's need for self-definition, they identified racism from without and sexism from within as destructive to the black community. This small gathering in May 1973 consisted of thirty women—lawyers, welfare rights workers, housewives, domestics, leaders of various organizations, and other professional women. Plans for a national conference included counteracting negative media portrayals of the women's movement and correcting erroneous assertions about the lack of black women's interest in feminism.

"A Black Feminist Statement"

Combahee River Collective

One issue that is of major concern to us and that we have begun to publicly address is racism in the white women's movement. As Black feminists we are made constantly and painfully aware of how little effort white women have made to understand and combat their racism, which requires among other things that they have a more than superficial comprehension of race, color, and black history and culture. Eliminating racism in the white women's movement is by definition work for white women to do, but we will continue to speak to and demand accountability on this issue.

Source: "A Black Feminist Statement," by the Combahee River Collective, a group of black feminists formed in 1974.

Following the May meeting a coordinating council of seven women was established with Margaret Sloan and Jane Galvin-Lewis assuming the major leadership role. The National Black Feminist Organization (NBFO) officially began November 30, 1973, at an Eastern Regional Conference in New York City at St. John the Divine Church. This was an historic gathering of the first explicitly black feminist organization committed to the eradication of sexism, racism, and heterosexism. Workshops focused on a variety of issues—child care, the church, welfare, women's liberation, lesbianism, prisons, education, addiction, work, female sexuality, and domestic violence. Among those present were Shirley Chisholm, Alice Walker, Eleanor Holmes Norton, Flo Kennedy, and Margaret Sloan, NBFO's first and only president. Unfortunately, the organization was short-lived because of limited financial resources, inadequate staff, internal strife, and inability to attract large numbers of mainstream black women.

A year after the founding meeting, the Boston chapter of NBFO decided to form a more radical organization, according to lesbian feminist writer Barbara Smith, and named itself in 1975 the Combahee River Collective after Harriet Tubman's "military campaign" in South Carolina (1863) which freed nearly eight hundred slaves. After meeting informally for three years and doing intense consciousness raising (the major strategy for feminist organizing in the '70s), a black feminist manifesto was issued in 1977, which foregrounded sexuality and asserted that "sexual politics under patriarchy is as pervasive in black women's lives as the politics of class and race." Emphasizing the "simultaneity" of racial, gender, heterosexual, and class oppression in the lives of black and other women of color, they affirmed their connection to an activist tradition among black women going back to the nineteenth century as well as to black liberation struggles of the sixties. However, they were painfully aware of the failure of progressive movements to make the eradication of black women's oppression a major priority and believed that "the only people who care enough about us to work consistently for our liberation is us."

Although they refer unashamedly to themselves as feminists and lesbians, they also objected to the lesbian separatism of radical white feminists. While affirming their solidarity with progressive black men, they also acknowledged their struggles with them around the issue of sexism. It was also apparent to the collective that many black men were opposed to feminism, believing it to be divisive and a distraction from their own struggles. While embracing the feminist principle that the personal is political, they also called attention to the critical importance of race and class in feminist theorizing, which white women avoided. It would take another decade for these insights to be taken seriously by mainstream feminist theorists.

Despite the difficulty of sustaining a socialist black feminist organization with lesbian leadership for six years, they worked untiringly on a variety of "revolutionary" issues—pro-choice, rape, prison reform, sterilization abuse, violence against women, health care, and racism within the white women's movement. They also understood the importance of coalition building and worked with other women of color, white feminists, and progressive men. The seven retreats they organized provided a safe space for black feminists throughout the country to interact. As important was their breaking the silence about homophobia within the black community and providing opportunities for black women with different sexual orientations to work together.

Michelle Wallace's 1975 article for the *Village Voice* entitled "A Black Feminist's Search for Sisterhood," furthered this debate, as did the publication of *Black Macho and the Myth of the Superwoman* (1978), which caused a storm of controversy among black academics and activists. Wallace attempted to analyze sexism within the black community and the Civil Rights movement, and argued that the new black movement, a struggle for black men's lost manhood, asserted black male rights at the expense of black women and was in the grips of a misogynist "black Macho." She also described black women's invisibility in the Civil Rights movement and the pressure to refute the women's liberation movement in order not to alienate black men.

Echoing Wallace, the August 27, 1979, issue of *Newsweek* chronicled a new black struggle, which underscored intraracial tensions based on gender: "It's the newest wrinkle in the black experience in America—a growing distrust, if not antagonism, between black men and women that is tearing marriages apart and fracturing personal relationships." This "wake-up call" came on the heels of Ntozake Shange's award-winning Broadway play *for colored girls who have considered suicide/when the rainbow is enuff* (1976), which, like Wallace's controversial *Black Macho*, was demonized among large segments of the black community for its assertive tone and for exposing rights in the African-American community along gender lines.

The issue of sexual politics within the African-American community became a hotly debated topic also in black publications such as *The Black Scholar*, *Freedomways*, and *Black Books Bulletin*, and provided the catalyst for the founding of a short-lived bimonthly magazine, *Black Male/Female Relationships* by Nathan and Julia Hare. *Black Scholar* would provide the most important outlet for the articulation of ideas about the explosive subject of sexism within the black community which Wallace and Shange had unmasked in their controversial writings. The April 1973 issue of *Black Scholar* on "Black Women's Liberation" led the way, followed by the March 1975 issue on "The Black Woman," the 1979 "Black Sexism Debate" issue, and the 1986 "Black Women and Feminism" issue. Robert Staples's essay "The Myth of Black Macho: A Response to Angry Black Feminists," which appeared in the March/April 1979 issue, was a feminist-bashing response to Wallace and Shange, whom he accused of black male bashing; it stimulated a flood of reader's responses in the subsequent May/June 1979 issue, and the battle lines were drawn. The editorial for this special issue acknowledged in very strong terms a crisis in black male/female relationships and the need to understand its origins and dynamics as well as struggle for reconciliation: "Black feminists have raised just criticisms of black male sexism," the editors wrote. "We believe that the effort to clarify the nature of black male/female relationships is an important step in the process of re-uniting our people and revitalizing the struggle against oppression.... The problems of black male/female relationships are neither new nor solely the creation of the white media."

RECENT DEBATES

A decade later, the controversy continued and grew more virulent, the most obvious manifestations of which were loud and angry litanies, especially among black professional men, about the portrayal of black male characters in the fiction of contemporary black women writers. Alice Walker's novel *The Color Purple* (1982) and Steven Spielberg's film adaptation with their depictions of male sexual violence against women sparked the most vitriolic responses. Shahrazad Ali's self-published *The Blackman's Guide to Understanding the Black-woman* (1990), which tended to blame black women for the problems faced by black men, was one of the most disturbing publications during this decade-and-a-half-old family battle.

Amid this rancorous debate within the black community about the relevance of the contemporary women's movement and its feminist agendas for black women, several explicitly black feminist publications were significant. One of the most important black feminist intellectuals to emerge was bell hooks, whose pioneering monograph, *Ain't I A Woman: Black Women and Feminism* (1981), delineated the impact of sexism on the lives of black women; analyzed the devaluation of black womanhood, both historically and contemporaneously; and discussed the persistence of racism in the women's movement. The book highlighted the involvement of black women in struggles to achieve equality for women even when they were discouraged from doing so by various

bell hooks, "Black Women"

Black women with no institutionalized "other" that we may discriminate against, exploit, or oppress often have a lived experience that directly challenges the prevailing classist, sexist, racist social structure and its concomitant ideology. This lived experience may shape our consciousness in such a way that our world view differs from those who have a degree of privilege (however relative within the existing system). It is essential for continued feminist struggle that black women recognize the special vantage point our marginality gives us and make use of this perspective to criticize the dominant racist, classist, sexist hegemony as well as envision and create a counterhegemony. I am suggesting that we have a central role to play in the making of feminist theory and a contribution to offer that is unique and valuable.

Source: bell hooks, *Feminist Theory: From the Margin to the Center* (Boston: South End Press, 1984), pp. 14–15.

segments of the white and black communities. The chapter on "Sexism and the Black Female Experience," advanced the new thesis that slavery, a reflection of a patriarchal *and* racist social order, not only oppressed black men but defeminized slave women. In the next decade and a half hooks would become the most prolific among a group of black feminist writers, which included Audre Lorde, Barbara Smith, Alice Walker, and Gloria Joseph, publishing on a broad range of issues. Hooks would also help to redefine feminism as a broad political movement to end all forms of domination: "Feminism is not simply a struggle to end male chauvinism or a movement to ensure that women have equal rights with men," hooks wrote. "It is a commitment to eradicating the ideology of domination that permeates Western culture on various levels—sex, race, and class, to name a few—and a commitment to reorganizing U.S. society so that the self-development of people can take precedence over imperialism, economic expansion, and material desires."

The first explicitly black feminist periodical devoted elusively to the experiences of women of African descent in the United States and throughout the world was founded in Atlanta, Georgia, in 1984 and hosted by Spelman College's Women's Research and Resource Center. *SAGE: A Scholarly Journal on Black Women* would provide a major outlet for black feminist perspectives on a variety of issues including mother-daughter relationships in the black community, health, science and technology, and the situation of women in rural Africa. And Kitchen Table: Women of Color Press was founded for the purpose of publishing mainly feminist works by women of color.

Despite their commitment to the ideals of feminism, however, some black women continued to be alienated by the term. As an alternative to "feminist," the term "womanist" came to be preferred by many in the early 1980s following its introduction in Alice Walker's *In Search of Our Mothers' Gardens* (1983) as a more culturally appropriate way to refer to black feminists or feminists of color. This new label recalled a black folk expression of mothers admonishing their daughters to refrain from "womanish" behavior. Womanists, according to Walker, love other women and men (sexually or nonsexually), prefer women's culture, are committed to the survival of the entire group, are serious, responsible, and "loves struggle, *loves* the folk, and loves herself." Wanting to differentiate themselves from mainstream feminists, Africana women scholars, although critical also of patriarchy and sexism, advocated a broader-based "feminism," which took into consideration profound differences among women and their experience of gender because of race, ethnicity, culture, class, and a number of other variables.

More recently President George Bush's 1991 nomination of Judge Clarence Thomas to the Supreme Court and Professor Anita Hill's subsequent allegations of sexual harassment, which resulted in televised hearings for three days in October 1991, sparked perhaps the most profound intraracial tensions around sexual politics that the modern African-American community had ever experienced. Despite Hill's allegations that Thomas had sexually harassed her while she worked under him at the Department of Education and the Equal Employment Opportunity Commission (EEOC), on October 16 the Senate confirmed, 52–48, Clarence Thomas as associate justice of the Supreme Court in the position vacated by Thurgood Marshall.

A month later, an historic statement opposing the racist and sexist treatment of Anita Hill appeared in the November 17, 1991, issue of *The New York Times*, reminiscent of the media events surrounding the 1895 gathering of black women in Boston. In a piece called "African-American Women in Defense of Ourselves," 1,642 black women reminded the nation of Thomas's persistent failure, despite his own racial history and professional opportunities, to respond to the urgency of civil rights for disadvantaged groups in this country. Furthermore, the statement called attention to a long history of sexual abuse and stereotyping of black women as "immoral, insatiable, perverse," and the failure of Congress to take seriously Hill's sexual harassment charges as an attack on the collective character of black women. Although black female voices were conspicuously absent as commentators during the Thomas/Hill hearings, a number of important statements by progressive black women, many of whom are feminists, found their way in print in the aftermath of the controversial hearings. These included a forum on the hearings in a special issue of *SAGE: A Scholarly Journal on Black Women*; Toni Morrison's edited a collection of essays, entitled *Race-ing Justice, Engendering Power*; and a broad range of essays and documents published by *The Black Scholar* collective entitled *Court of Appeal: The Black Community Speaks Out on the Racial and Sexual Politics of Thomas vs. Hill* (1992).

Although the Thomas/Hill saga provoked unprecedented anger within the black community, perhaps its most significant outcome, according to historian Paula Giddings, is that a mandate on gender, particularly a "sexual discourse unmediated by the question of racism," occurred for the first time among the black masses. In other words, Hill's public disclosure of a black-on-black sexual crime provided the catalyst for a broad-based, enlightened discussion of gender issues which has enormous potential for resolving a number of problems relating to sexual politics, male privilege, and unequal power relations within the black community. Hill's example was a challenge to black women to no longer remain silent under the guise of racial solidarity about the abuse they suffer from black men.

More than any other episode in recent memory, the Thomas/Hill saga unmasked problematic gender attitudes within the black community and in some cases outright misogyny. Because Hill had violated a deeply held cultural taboo—that racial dirty linen shouldn't be aired in public—she came to epitomize black female treachery in breaking the silence about objectionable black male behavior. For more than a decade black women had been labeled traitors among some segments of the community because of their advocacy of feminism or associations with white feminists, and this was the case with Hill. Despite the criticism, contemporary black feminists, like their nineteenth-century counterparts, mobilized for struggle with the hope that eradicating the twin evils of racism and sexism would become a battle cry within the entire community.

In January 1994, the largest gathering of black feminist scholars and activists took place at MIT during a national conference on "Black Women in the Academy: Defending Our Name, 1894–1994." One hundred years after black women had come under attack in many public forums for their supposed immorality, more than two thousand mostly black women came again to Boston. In the 1990s black women also found themselves the targets of public attack, much of which was generated by the Thomas/Hill hearings and propaganda associated with the issue of welfare reform and "family values." In addition, two prominent black academic women with liberal politics, Johnnetta Cole and Laini Guinier (both of whom were keynoters at MIT), had been subject to vicious attacks by the Right which resulted in both of them being abandoned as political appointees of the Clinton administration. In the aftermath of the Thomas/Hill hearings, black women witnessed rancorous public dialogue about their character and points of view, which sparked the formation of an organization, African-American Women in Defense of Ourselves. Reminiscent of the 1890s, black feminism, which foregrounds the intersection of race, gender, class, and sexuality, would provide a context around which Africana women could again rally.

CONCLUSION

Black feminism would come out of the shadows in the 1990s and provide useful insights for analyzing not just the situation of black women but also important aspects of the broader community as well. It would also move from the margins to the center of mainstream feminist discourse just as Anita Hill had provided a shot in the arm for the women's movement. Patricia Hill Collins's ground-breaking theoretical analysis *Black Feminist Thought* (1990), a major text for understanding contemporary black feminism, argues that the fusion of activism and theory is its distinguishing characteristic. Its four core themes include the interlocking nature of race, class, and gender oppression in black women's personal, domestic, and work lives; the need for black women to internalize positive self-definitions and reject the denigrating, stereotypical, and controlling images (mammy, matriarch, welfare mother, whore) of others, both within and without the black community; and the need for active struggle among black women in order to resist oppression and realize individual and group empowerment. This text would establish, along with hooks' *Ain't I A Woman* published a decade earlier, the existence of a strong black feminist intellectual tradition going back to the publication of Cooper's *A Voice from the South* one hundred years earlier.

The evolution of black feminism in the United States illustrates that neither race nor gender alone can explain the complexity of the black female experience. Like Sojourner Truth in the nineteenth century, black women continue to fight on two fronts against race and gender inequality and inspire generations yet unborn to make the world better for black women. The struggle continues.

FOR FURTHER READING

Carby, Hazel. *Reconstructing Womanhood: The Emergence of the Afro-American Novelist.* New York: Oxford University Press, 1990.

Chrisman, Robert, and Robert L. Allen, eds. *Court of Appeal: The Black Community Speaks Out on the Racial and Sexual Politics of Clarence Thomas vs. Anita Hill.* New York: Ballantine, 1992.

Clark, Septima. *Ready from Within: A First Person Narrative.* Lawrenceville, N.J.: Africa World Press, 1990.

Collins, Patricia Hill. *Black Feminist Thought: Knowledge, Consciousness, and the Politics of Empowerment.* Rev. ed. New York: Routledge, 1999.

Cooper, Anna Julia. *A Voice from the South.* New York: Oxford University Press, 1990.

Foner, Philip, ed. *Frederick Douglass on Women's Rights.* New York: Da Capo Press, 1992.

Gates, Henry Louis, Jr., ed. *Schomburg Library of Nineteenth Century Black Women Writers.* 30 vols. New York: Oxford University Press, 1988.

Giddings, Paula. *When and Where I Enter: The Impact of Black Women on Race and Sex in America.* 2nd ed. New York: William Morrow & Co., 1996.

Guy-Sheftall, Beverly. *Daughters of Sorrow: Attitudes Toward Black Women, 1880–1920.* Brooklyn, N.Y.: Carlson, 1990.

Hansberry, Lorraine. *To Be Young, Gifted and Black: Lorraine Hansberry in Her Own Words.* New York: Vintage, 1995.

Hine, Darlene Clark, ed. *Black Women in America: An Historical Encyclopedia.* 2 vols. Bloomington: Indiana University Press, 1994.

————, ed. *Facts on File Encyclopedia of Black Women in America.* 11 vols. New York: Facts on File, 1997.

hooks, bell. *Ain't I A Woman: Black Women and Feminism.* Boston: South End Press, 1981.

————. *Feminist Theory from Margin to Center.* Boston: South End Press, 1984.

Hull, Gloria T., Patricia Bell Scott, and Barbara Smith, eds. *All the Women Are White, All the Blacks Are Men, but Some of Us Are Brave: Black Women's Studies.* Old Westbury, N.Y.: Feminist Press, 1982.

Jacobs, Harriet A. *Incidents in the Life of a Slave Girl Written by Herself.* Ed. Jean Fagan Yellin. Cambridge: Harvard University Press, 1987.

James, Stanlie, and Abena P. A. Busia, eds. *Theorizing Black Feminisms: The Visionary Pragmatism of Black Women.* New York: Routledge, 1994.

Jones, Jacqueline. *Labor of Love, Labor of Sorrow: Black Women, Work, and the Family from Slavery to the Present.* New York: Vintage, 1995.

Kraditor, Aileen S. *The Ideas of the Woman Suffrage Movement, 1890–1920.* New York: W. W. Norton & Co., 1981.

Lerner, Gerda, ed. *Black Women in White America: A Documentary History.* New York: Vintage, 1992.

Lorde, Audre. *Sister Outsider: Essays and Speeches.* Trumansburg, N.Y.: Crossing Press, 1984.

Morrison, Toni, Nellie McKay, and Michael Thelwell. *Race-ing Justice, En-gendering Power: Essays on Anita Hill, Clarence Thomas, and the Construction of Social Reality.* New York: Pantheon, 1992.

Richardson, Marilyn, ed. *Maria W. Stewart, America's First Black Woman Political Writer: Essays and Speeches.* Bloomington: Indiana University Press, 1987.

Smith, Barbara, ed. *Home Girls: A Black Feminist Anthology.* New York: Kitchen Table, 1983.

Smith, Jessie Carney, ed. *Notable Black American Women.* Detroit, Mich.: Gale Research, 1992.

Smith, Valerie. *Not Just Race, Not Just Gender: Black Feminist Readings.* New York: Routledge, 1998.

Truth, Sojourner. *The Narrative of Sojourner Truth.* Ed. Margaret Washington. New York: Vintage, 1993.

Walker, Alice. *In Search of Our Mother's Gardens.* San Diego, Calif.: Harcourt Brace, 1984.

part 6.

The Postwar
Agenda

chapter 18

African Americans and Education since the Brown Decisions

A Contextual View

Stephen N. Butler

S INCE THE 1954 SUPREME COURT DECISION in *Brown v. Board of Education of the City of Topeka, Kansas,* which declared segregation in the public schools unconstitutional, the education of African Americans has generated continued debate and controversy. Desegregation, integration, educational opportunity, and affirmative action have been the main issues for the public and for policymakers concerned with black intellectual empowerment. But other questions have been raised recently, generating much confusion and controversy. Many African Americans, previously committed to school integration, have now begun to challenge the merit of mixed schools and common curricula to advocate Afrocentric approaches and all-black academies for young men.

The problems faced by African Americans as the twentieth century draws to a close are quite different than those of fifty years ago. Massive demographic change and equally important restructuring of the American economy have produced a totally different historical context that has given rise to a host of new questions about black education in the United States. The fact that the inclusionist principles embraced and enshrined in the original *Brown* decision are no longer accepted without qualification and that positive values are increasingly associated with separate black schools relates to changes in the context of black life in the forty years between the passage of the *Brown* decisions and the present day. A review of the progress in black education since 1954 and African-American perceptions of contemporary conditions explain this curious transition.

THE SOCIAL CONTEXT OF THE *BROWN* DECISIONS

Segregation in itself is a matter of law, and that law can be changed at once, ... I think in every community there is some segregation that can be changed at once, and the area of higher education is the most favorable for making the change.

—Robert Redfield in *Sweatt v. Painter*

The end of World War II marked the beginning of profound changes in American society; nowhere more than in the revolution in education. Soldiers, returning home to resume their civilian lives, received support from the federal G.I. Bill of Rights enabling unprecedented numbers of ordinary Americans to enter the world of higher education, previously the preserve of the wealthy. At the time of Pearl Harbor, the average American had an eighth-grade education. Fifty years later, fourteen million Americans would be enrolled in America's colleges and universities. Public school facilities were vastly expanded.

As they had following the Civil War, the Spanish-American War, and World War I, black soldiers returned to their families and communities determined to attain the freedom long denied them. After having fought to defeat racist regimes abroad, the veterans of World War II were confronted with the frustrating reality of continued domestic racism. Few adapted easily to the old conventions and practices, and many took up directly or indirectly the battle for first-class citizenship, many ultimately becoming part of black community action programs initiated to desegregate public schools in the South, becoming part of what historian/theologian Vincent Harding calls the "Great Tradition of Protest."

Black communities, especially in the rural South, were faced at the time with chronic problems related to education. At the beginning of World War II, three-quarters of all African Americans still lived in the states of the old Confederacy. There, a large majority lived in rural areas and were involved in agriculture, economically bound in various states of dependency. Schools at all levels were not only segregated but also "undernourished and inadequate" in almost every way. According to the Swedish sociologist Gunnar Myrdal, who published his classic *An American Dilemma* in 1944, "The insufficient support of Negro schools in the South is reflected in a complete lack of schools in more rural areas, an insufficient number of schools in other areas, a grave lack of equipment, a lack of enforcement of truancy laws for Negroes, an inferior quality of teacher training, differential payment of teachers, and miserably poor standards all around."

Although Myrdal commented that "the usual measures of school efficiency" were inadequate to plumb the depths of the problem, he did use them to sketch the general outlines. While the average African-American had less than a sixth-grade education, the condition of rural-farm blacks was worse: 15 percent had no education at all and nearly two-thirds never reached fifth grade.

Brown v. Board of Education of Topeka, Kansas

These cases come to us from the States of Kansas, South Carolina, Virginia, and Delaware. They are premised on different facts and different conditions, but a common legal question justifies their consideration together in this consolidated opinion.

In each of the cases, minors of the Negro race. through their legal representatives, seek the aid of the courts in obtaining admission to the public schools of their community on a nonsegregated basis. In each instance, they had been denied admission to schools attended by white children under laws requiring or permitting segregation according to race. This segregation was alleged to deprive the plaintiffs of the equal protection of the laws under the Fourteenth Amendment. In each of the cases other than the Delaware case, a three-judge federal district court denied relief to the plaintiffs on the so-called "separate but equal" doctrine announced by this Court in *Plessy* v. *Ferguson*. . . . Under that doctrine, equality of treatment is accorded when the races are provided substantially equal facilities, even though these facilities be separate. In the Delaware case, the Supreme Court of Delaware adhered to that doctrine, but ordered that the plaintiffs be admitted to the white schools because of their superiority to the Negro schools.

The plaintiffs contend that segregated public schools are not "equal" and cannot be made "equal," and that hence they are deprived of the equal protection of the laws. Because of the obvious importance of the question presented, the Court took jurisdiction. Argument was heard in the 1952 Term, and reargument was heard this Term on certain questions propounded the Court.

In *Sweatt* v. *Painter* . . . , in finding that a segregated law school for Negroes could not provide them equal educational opportunities, this Court relied in large part on "those qualities which are incapable of objective measurement but which make for greatness in a law school." In *McLaurin* v. *Oklahoma State Regents* . . ., the Court, in requiring that a Negro admitted to a white graduate school be treated like all other students, again resorted to intangible considerations: ". . . his ability to study, to engage in discussions and exchange views with other students, and, in general, to learn his profession." Such considerations apply with added force to children in grade and high schools. To separate them from others of similar age and qualifications solely because of their race generates a feeling of inferiority as to their status in the community that may affect their hearts and minds in a way unlikely ever to be undone. The effect of this separation on their educational opportunities was well stated by a finding in the Kansas case by a court which nevertheless felt compelled to rule against the Negro plaintiffs:

> Segregation of white and colored children in public schools has a detrimental effect upon the colored children. The impact is greater when it has the sanction of the law; for the policy of separating the races is usually interpreted as denoting the inferiority of the negro group. A sense of inferiority affects the motivation of a child to learn. Segregation with the sanction of law, therefore, has a tendency to [retard] the educational and mental development of negro children and to deprive them of some of the benefits they would receive in a racial[ly] integrated school system.

Whatever may have been the extent of psychological knowledge at the time of *Plessy* v. *Ferguson*, this finding is amply supported by modern authority. Any language in *Plessy* v. *Ferguson* contrary to this finding is rejected.

We conclude that in the field of public education the doctrine of "separate but equal" has no place. Separate educational facilities are inherently unequal. Therefore, we hold that the plaintiffs and others similarly situated for whom the actions have been brought are, by reason of the segregation complained of, deprived of the equal protection of the laws guaranteed by the Fourteenth Amendment. This disposition makes unnecessary any discussion whether such segregation also violates the Due Process Clause of the Fourteenth Amendment.

Source: 347 U.S. 483 (1954).

"Only 5.5 percent of rural-farm Negroes ... [in the South]," according to Myrdal, "have received any high school training whatsoever." The figures for the nation as a whole were slightly better, but still only one out of fourteen African Americans completed high school and a mere 1.2 percent graduated from college at a time when 5.4 percent of whites did. At each grade a larger number of blacks than whites dropped out; the black school year was shorter than that for whites; the teachers were overworked and undereducated; and, as a result, African Americans scored "far below the national average in scholastic achievement." Yet, African Americans showed a zeal for education that exceeded their white countrymen's optimistic faith that education would continue to guarantee success for whites.

Education had been seen as the key to success for African Americans from the time of emancipation. For years African-American parents had extolled their children with the value and importance of education, a "good" that, once attained, belonged to one for life. Many accepted the idea that "the race" would prosper through education. Whether one agreed with the trade school orientation of Booker T. Washington or espoused W. E. B. DuBois's vision of the "Talented Tenth," African Americans generally viewed education as their best chance for improving their situation. Throughout the era of segregation, African Americans worked through their own separate institutions to be assimilated eventually into the American social fabric. They took seriously the simple notion of "one people, with liberty and justice for all" and firmly believed that change through the institutions of law and education would remove the obstacles and stigmas that denied them the benefits of first-class citizenship.

It was the post–WWII initiatives of blacks in law and education that first effectively tested the doctrine of "separate but equal" that legalized racial segregation. Enunciated in 1896 in *Plessy* v. *Ferguson*, this decision addressed separate accommodations on railways, but its provisions were rapidly extended during the era of Jim Crow to support the entire edifice of segregation including education. For more than half a century, the decision had stood as the prime premise of American apartheid. It was not until the era of the Depression that lawyers of the National Association of Colored People (NAACP) mounted a serious attack on the doctrine of "separate but equal," and it was not until a decade after the victory over fascism that its attorneys were able to overturn *Plessy*.

The NAACP experienced its first successes, ironically, in desegregating the nation's law schools; in 1950 it won a case before the Supreme Court in *Sweatt* v. *Painter*, which overruled the attempt by the state of Texas to circumvent earlier rulings. It was in this case that Thurgood Marshall, head of the NAACP's Legal Division, first introduced expert testimony from social scientists to support the NAACP's case. Subsequently, social science research became an integral part of the NAACP's legal argument in the fight against segregation.

The same year that the Court ruled in *Sweatt* v. *Painter*, Marshall and his staff challenged local school boards in Prince Edward County, Virginia, in Clarendon County, South Carolina, and in the city of Topeka, Kansas. Earlier cases had been prosecuted under the idea that separate schools were not provided with equal facilities as required by the law. NAACP lawyers gradually shifted their strategy, and their assaults on segregation in primary and secondary schools increasingly included not only evidence that the facilities of the black schools were inferior to those in white schools, but also the broader assertion that the fact of separation itself violated the equal protection clause of the Fourteenth Amendment.

After hearing the arguments in five related cases in 1952 and 1953, the Supreme Court called for reargument in which the lawyers addressed a series of historical questions concerning the original intent of the Fourteenth Amendment. Finally, on May 17, 1954, the Supreme Court under the leadership of Chief Justice Earl Warren declared in its first *Brown* decision, "that in the field of public education the doctrine of 'separate but equal' has no place. Separate educational facilities are inherently unequal." In the second *Brown* decision the following year, the Court remanded the cases "to the District Courts to take such proceedings and enter such orders and decrees consistent with this opinion as are necessary and proper to admit to public schools on a racially nondiscriminatory basis with all deliberate speed the parties to these cases."

Although these two decisions "dismantled" legal justification of school segregation, the phrase "with all deliberate speed," designed to give judges discretion to find appropriate modes of compliance for each community, offered an opportunity for the "massive resistance" movement among southern whites that fused racism with traditional states' rights arguments to hold off effective integration of southern schools for more than a decade. Across the South, white communities and local boards of education supported religious leaders and elected officials who opposed desegregation. Old cultural patterns proved resistant to modification. Southern social and political institutions were permeated with racism. In the face of the growing Civil Rights movement, many whites embraced a clear and simple formula: maintain segregation and fight integration. Meanwhile, for blacks the battle became more intense as they resolved to gain the political and educational rights so long denied them.

The post–WWII Supreme Court decisions gave legitimacy to the growing conviction that segregation could no longer be tolerated. In 1956, Autherine Lucy attempted to enter the University of Alabama. Nine African-American students tested the law in 1957 at Central High School in Little Rock, Arkansas. Governor Orville Faubus placed the city of Little Rock forever on the American map of racial intolerance by his refusal to integrate the high school. President Eisenhower believed that "Negroes . . . must be patient" and not move "too fast" in their pursuit of racial equality, but white behavior forced him to federalize the National Guard to prevent "anarchy" in Arkansas.

BLACK PROGRESS IN EDUCATION

The years between WWII and the passage of the Civil Rights Act in 1964 witnessed a slow but positive increase in the educational position of American blacks. Illiteracy continued to decline, the average number of years completed increased to nine, and the gap between blacks and whites narrowed. The proportion of African Americans graduating from high school had tripled since 1940. In part these improvements were due to the higher levels of enrollment of the school-age population, which by 1961 was about the same as that for white children. It was also due to the sizable demographic shift in the African-American population that was moving out of the South during these years. Although blacks faced prejudice and discrimination in the North, they had always fared better in the northern schools. In the cities that drew most of the black migrants the rates of high school graduation for blacks were twice what they were in southern cities. By 1960 two-fifths of the black population lived outside the South, and the exodus was increasing.

The quality of African-American education still suffered when compared to that available to whites. Half the black population left school before completing the eighth grade, and more than one-third of those entering high school in 1960 dropped out. The vast majority of black students continued to attend segregated schools with inadequate facilities and poorly trained teachers. A decade after the Court ordered the southern states to desegregate, practically no headway had been made. As late as 1962 only 1.2 percent of the black students in the southern states attended mixed schools, and most of those were in Texas. There were only twelve blacks in schools with whites in Florida and nine in Georgia; there were none in Mississippi, Alabama, or South Carolina. Eight of the most powerful men in the United States Senate introduced an amendment to the Constitution that would preserve to the states the right to control public education and maintain segregation.

THE EDUCATIONAL SCENE

The launching of the Sputnik unmanned satellite by the Soviet Union in 1957 took professional educators by surprise. The Soviet foray into space raised harsh questions about the quality and standards of American education, particularly in mathematics and science. Thus international developments, which would exert increasing pressure on American society, intruded into what many saw as a domestic issue. Although African Americans emphasized integration and eventual assimilation as a solution to the nation's racial ills, the connection between their educational achievement and larger social forces had not yet become a major topic of debate among professional educators.

During the 1960s American education became the focus of an intense debate about both the quality of education and its social impact. Much of the discussion shifted from questions defined by integration in the South to those directly related to urban education in the North and the West where de facto segregation was becoming an increasing problem. The proportion of blacks living outside the South grew from one-third in 1950 to one-half by 1970, and residential segregation in these regions increased with the continued movement of whites from the central cities to the suburbs.

Slums and Suburbs, by the former president of Harvard University, James Bryant Conant, had already used the term "social dynamite" to describe out-of-school and out-of-work urban youth, when Frank Riessman articulated a new view of urban education, introducing, in 1962, the concepts of "culturally deprived" and "culturally disadvantaged" to describe African Americans. At the same time, Columbia University's Teachers College, taking the lead in addressing problems of urban education, created the Institute of Urban Education. Two years later, the institute helped the State Education Commissioner's Advisory Committee on Human Relations and Community Tensions produce a report for the New York City Board of Education, "Desegregating the Public Schools of New York City." Although the report offered a clear blueprint, the state's board of education pursued its own agenda, according to unwritten rules that included "do not bargain with militant civil rights leaders over desegregation" and "do not question the ability of headquarters professionals to make meaningful innovations and evaluations of programs."

Jonathan Kozol, Herbert Kohl, and James Herndon, among others, argued in widely read books that African Americans' education, indeed American education in general, was suffering from a crisis of major proportions. Kozol, perhaps the most consistent critic of American education in the latter half of the twentieth century, emphasized particularly the educational deprivation of African Americans and portrayed the racism endemic to the Boston public schools in *Death at an Early Age* (1967). In the same year, Elliot Liebow published *Talley's Corner*, a sensitive study of black street corner men that echoed Conant's earlier view of "social dynamite." Still, terms like "culturally deprived" and "educationally disadvantaged" served as rallying points for professional educators and helped to create career opportunities for often well-meaning educators of all stripes and colors who located the educational "problems" of African Americans in their "culture."

Kenneth Clark, the prominent African-American psychologist who had given crucial and dramatic testimony in the *Brown* case, considered deficient schooling of African Americans a result of larger social dynamics. He identified power relationships, economics, psychological factors, and social class as the components of a social pathology that contributed to the existence of "ghetto schools, separate and unequal." Clark believed that Riessman's conception of African-American students as "culturally disadvantaged" could be used as an excuse for denying them an adequate education. He described a pattern of growing segregation in urban areas across America—a trend that would continue through the early 1990s.

In the two decades from 1970 to 1990 the nature of the educational problems facing black America changed dramatically. From the mid-1960s into the early 1970s most of the school districts in the South were successfully integrated. By the end of the decade, nearly every indicator of educational improvement signaled that a revolution in schooling had taken place in black America. The median years completed by African Americans was twice what it had been at the time of World War II and only slightly different than that of whites. More than half of all black adults were high school graduates. In 1980 the proportion of black college graduates (8.4 percent) was higher than the proportion of high school graduates in 1940, four times the proportion of black college graduates in 1950, and well above the percentage of whites who graduated from college in 1960. The proportion of black high school graduates enrolled in college (28.3 percent) had moved close to that for whites (32.4 percent).

As one detailed study pointed out, however, "while it may appear that blacks and whites are receiving comparable educations, the actual facts may be the opposite." The educations of whites and blacks differ in relative quality and the contrasting educational experiences of African Americans and Americans in general are reflected in the outcomes of standardized tests like the California Achievement Test for grade school children and the Scholastic Aptitude Test, which is required for entrance into most colleges. These differences are clearly related to racial segregation in central cities with deteriorating school systems. White representation in urban school districts has been rapidly declining since the mid-1960s. In just a decade from the late 1960s to the late 1970s, the white student population in cities like Detroit, San Francisco, Washington, and Atlanta decreased by 60 percent or more as the urban core of the country's major metropolitan areas has become increasingly black and populated by a growing "underclass."

THE TUMULTUOUS '60s

In his inaugural address John F. Kennedy sparked the idealism of a new generation with the admonition: "Ask not what your country can do for you, but what you can do for your country." Despite political pressure from southern Democrats, he took a strong moral position on segregation. In his June 11, 1963, television address to the nation, against a backdrop of civil rights demonstrations across the South, he supported first-class citizenship for African Americans. With Kennedy in charge, it seemed as though both national and international crises could be dealt with effectively, and African Americans looked forward to a new day under the leadership of a young and dynamic president. But his thousand-day reign ended in Dallas on November 22, 1963.

A southerner from Texas, Lyndon Johnson, became president after Kennedy's assassination, but he proved a greater ally to African Americans than his predecessor, pushing both the Civil Rights Act of 1964 and the Voting Rights Act of 1965 through Congress and then mounting his "War on

Poverty." Growing involvement in the war in Vietnam, however, sapped the vitality of Johnson's domestic program and drained the necessary funds to make his "Great Society" a reality. Meanwhile, the movement emerging in opposition to the war called into question the nation's integrity and ultimately resulted in Johnson's decision not to seek a second term in office.

During the Civil Rights movement of the 1950s, Martin Luther King Jr. emerged as the moral leader of African Americans. As the movement advanced, King sought to expand its scope. In addition to desegregation and voting rights, he identified poverty, housing, and unemployment as critical problems. In this respect, King's views came to complement the ideas of the black nationalist leader Malcolm X, whose message to the urban masses focused on improvement of their social conditions. Neither leader, however, had much time to develop or implement his plans for black economic advancement. Both were assassinated as were John and Robert Kennedy. By 1968, when King was gunned down in Memphis, white and black America were devastated emotionally. It appeared that violence and death were tearing the nation apart at its seams. That fear was intensified by the riots of the late 1960s.

URBAN RIOTS

> Police! Police!
> Come and get this man!
> He's trying to ruin the government
> and overturn the land!
>
> —Langston Hughes

The riots of the late 1960s in major American cities—Atlanta, Cincinnati, Detroit, Tampa, and Newark—awakened America to the seriousness of the nation's urban problems and led to the establishment of a presidential commission to study the subject. To Kenneth Clark this seemed an exercise in futility. He told the commission he had recently reread the report on the 1919 riots:

> And it is as if I were reading the report of the investigating committee on the Harlem riot of '35, the report of the investigating committee on the Harlem riot of '43, the report of the McCone Commission on the Watts riot. I must again in candor say to you members of this commission, it is a kind of Alice in Wonderland, with the same moving picture reshown over and over again, the same analysis, the same recommendations, and the same inaction.

When it appeared in 1968, the *Report of the National Advisory Commission on Civil Disorders* acknowledged, "What white Americans have never fully understood—but what the Negro can never forget—is that white society is deeply implicated in the ghetto. White institutions created it, white institutions maintain it, and white society condones it." High unemployment rates for African Americans, spreading drug addiction, a rising number of single-parent, female-headed households, and the poor academic performance of students in urban areas were brought into sharp focus by the urban riots.

Despite the ambitious government "War on Poverty" and the efforts of institutions like Columbia University's Teachers College, the Center for Urban Education, civil rights organizations, and local community groups, education in the cities deteriorated steadily. Slightly more than one-fifth of African Americans were two years behind their grade level; a larger proportion dropped out of high school than enrolled in college; and black parents constantly complained that among those graduating far too many were functionally illiterate. The trends that Conant, Clark, and the Center for Urban Education had noted were exacerbated by the lack of job opportunities in the cities and by the increasing departure of the black middle class from urban ghettoes.

While America's political leaders started belatedly to pay attention to the growing problems of the cities, major corporations had already begun their

---

Report of the National Advisory Commission on Civil Disorders (1968)

Education in a democratic society must equip children to develop their potential and to participate fully in American life. For the community at large, the schools have discharged this responsibility well. But for many minorities, and particularly for the children of the ghetto, the schools have failed to provide the educational experience which could overcome the effects of discrimination and deprivation.

This failure is one of the persistent sources of grievance and resentment within the Negro community. The hostility of Negro parents and students toward the school system is generating increasing conflict and causing disruption within many city school districts. But the most dramatic evidence of the relationship between educational practices and civil disorders lies in the high incidence of riot participation by ghetto youth who have not completed high school.

The bleak record of public education for ghetto children is growing worse. In the critical skills—verbal and reading ability—Negro students are falling further behind whites with each year of school completed. The high unemployment and underemployment rate for Negro youth is evidence, in part, of the growing educational crisis.

We support integration as the priority education strategy; it is essential to the future of American society. In this last summer's disorders we have seen the consequences of racial isolation at all levels, and of attitudes toward race, on both sides, produced by three centuries of myth, ignorance, and bias. It is indispensable that opportunities for interaction between the races be expanded.

We recognize that the growing dominance of pupils from disadvantaged minorities in city school populations will not soon be reversed. No matter how great the effort toward desegregation, many children of the ghetto will not, within their school careers, attend integrated schools.

If existing disadvantages are not to be perpetuated, we must drastically improve the quality of ghetto education. Equality of results with all-white schools must be the goal.

Source: Report on the National Advisory Commission on Civil Disorders (Washington, D.C.: United States Printing Office, 1968), pp. 425–26.

exodus to the suburbs which increasingly separated white suburbia from inner-city black ghettoes. This further contributed to the wide variation in property tax revenues supporting public schools, an issue that would become acute in the late 1980s and early 1990s and would give rise to new court and legislative battles. These developments forced Americans to acknowledge the relationship between major social forces and the deficient educational experience of African Americans.

INTEGRATION AND THE BUSING WARS

In the 1970s the courts ordered busing as the way to achieve integration as the Nixon administration withdrew executive support from the enforcement by the Justice Department. Across America transporting black children to predominantly white schools and white children to predominantly black schools reminded Americans of the desegregation/integration struggles of the late 1950s and early 1960s. When violence erupted in Boston, television brought the "busing wars" into the living rooms of America. Resistance to "racial balance" and "forced busing" quickly became national in scope. Antibusing protests occurred in New York City, San Francisco, Pontiac, Michigan, and various cities and towns across the South.

In fact, busing of American schoolchildren was and has continued to be a common experience for Americans in all parts of the country. In 1970 two-thirds used either school buses or public transportation every day. At the time of the *Brown* decision, one-third of American schoolchildren took school buses, and by the time of the Boston crisis in 1973 that proportion increased to 45 percent, but relatively little of this (only 3 percent of the *increase*) was related to desegregation plans. No president publicly protested when black children were bused to enforce segregation. An NAACP study pointed out that there was no "massive" use of busing to counteract residential segregation and that the actual positive uses of school buses helped improve the quality of education. Quite obviously the general response was part of the white backlash against the Civil Rights movement and the gains of African Americans in the 1960s and 1970s. Insensitive judges, a cowardly Congress, and an unscrupulous president combined to make a difficult situation worse and to heighten racial animosities.

While busing was relatively successful in most major cities and medium-sized towns, private academies for white students sprang up in much of the South to thwart these efforts to achieve integration. In the face of strenuous resistance from whites, some African-American parents began to question busing as a remedy. Providing high-quality education in local African-American communities—an idea that was to gain force and intensity in ensuing years—began to appear more desirable. Many Americans, black and white, were torn between the belief in integration and the recognition that pushing it in this fashion might do more harm than good.

In suburban areas in the North and in the West, white Americans fought to preserve the chimera of the "neighborhood school" although this meant maintaining residential segregation. Consequently, because school districts relied on property taxes for funding, they provided sufficient financial support only for largely white suburban schools while furnishing, at best, minimal maintenance for those in the inner cities whose students were predominately black. Jonathan Kozol later commented in his devastating analysis of American urban education, *Savage Inequalities* (1991), that because students are required to attend school in their own district "the state, by requiring attendance but refusing to require equity, effectively requires inequality."

ISSUES IN HIGHER EDUCATION

The War on Poverty programs designed to prepare "culturally deprived" students for higher education helped to bring new perspectives to the nation's colleges and universities. "Upward Bound" proved successful in preparing poor African-American, white, and other "disadvantaged" students for college. Some predominantly white institutions, responding to the temper of the times, modified their admission policies or formulated new standards to encourage the admission of students from these groups.

African-American students who had grown up during the struggle for desegregation and integration witnessed the 1963 March on Washington; the assassinations of the Kennedys, Malcolm X, and King; the reemergence of black nationalism; and the 1968 Black Power demonstration by Tommie Smith,

Other Ways of Knowing

A symbol "revolution" was initiated by the Civil Rights Movement of the '60s and maintained by campaigns against the Viet Nam war. There were, of course, problems of focus. We were articulating a perspective about education that was radical even as we argued that Black Studies was not simply the study of black people but the study of African people from an Afrocentric perspective. This movement was to inaugurate an entire system of thinking about social sciences and criticism, and pointed to the inherent problems of Eurocentric theory when applied to the black literary or rhetorical movements. The intrinsic problem in Western discourse theory were revealed as systemic because even those who were sympathetic to "civil rights" often used a Eurocentric framework to speak of "agitative rhetoric," "protest literature," and so forth, when we should never have forced ourselves to take that position. Thus, even in that situation the European center was assumed and the burden of proof rested with those called dissenters, dissidents, the disturbers of myths. What the symbol revolution has attempted to show is that the hallowed concepts of Western thought—rationality, objectivity, progress—are inadequate to explain all of the ways of knowing.

Source: Molefi K. Asante, *The Afrocentric Idea* (Philadelphia: Temple University Press, 1987), p. 163.

Lee Evans, and John Carlos at the summer Olympics in Mexico City. They brought a new agenda to institutions of higher education, one that would shake cherished ideas about the nature of knowledge and of social reality. Colleges and universities did not yet understand the subcultures and worldviews of different classes of African Americans—particularly the students from urban areas—and were naive in their belief that simply bringing African-American students to campus would be sufficient. On the whole, the academy was ill-prepared for the impact of these students.

As the proportion of African Americans graduating from high school grew dramatically, black students flooded into American colleges and universities. A little remembered fact is that in 1940 a larger proportion of blacks than whites who graduated from high school went on to graduate from college! From fewer than 50,000 in 1950 the number of black college students more than tripled by the early 1960s and passed the half-million mark in the early 1970s. Three-quarters of these students attended colleges and universities that were neither traditionally nor predominantly black.

Donald H. Ogilvie on Black Studies

Black students have thought about what we are missing in our university experience and we see a black curriculum as giving us the opportunity to find direction. Within the present available framework we cannot readily apply the tools of a scholastic discipline to the experience, the problems, the wisdom or the expression of black people. We are saying that this condition must be changed—radically. There is no justification for delay. It is true the bodies of knowledge of which we speak have been criminally ignored by the majority of the intellectual community. Yet no matter how poorly documented some of those areas within the social sciences and humanities that touch on the black perspective may be, or how limited in number and scope some of the analyses and interpretations are, an initial exposure to this existing material is possible *now*.

We want an opportunity to learn about things that are relevant to our existence and we want to learn in the best possible ways, experiencing the expertise of all those who have something to offer. This means exposure in the classroom to men of controversial qualification—on the one hand, eminently qualified to instruct because of what they know; yet, on the other hand, grossly underqualified because of how they came to know it. Perhaps faculties and administrations will view demands for such men as less of a dilemma if they realize this one central fact: as much as black students repudiate those "academically qualified" purveyors of the traditional white racist perspective, they do not want to see the void which is perpetuated by these "scholars'" existence filled with black charlatans who have little to offer besides their "front." We look for no pedants, either black or white, with magic formulas; instead we look for men who can offer a range of information and insight that effectively provides alternatives from which *we* can choose.

Source: Armstead L. Robinson, Craig C. Foster, and Donald H. Ogilvie, eds., *Black Studies in the University* (New Haven, Conn.: Yale University Press, 1969), pp. 81-82.

The arrival of this new population on the campuses posed serious challenges to higher education. African-American students demanded the hiring of more black professors and administrators and the inclusion in the curriculum of courses relevant to the African-American experience. Borrowing protest tactics from the Civil Rights movement, these students took over college buildings and presented their lists of demands to college authorities. African-American students also sought relationships with local black communities, something new to the college scene. Misunderstandings abounded. White professors often assumed that all black students were needy and lacked the educational preparation necessary for college success. This characterization did not go unnoticed by those to whom it referred, and these students, in turn, questioned how whites could adequately study, teach, and understand things they had not experienced. Epistemological issues—"How do we know what we know?"—were crystallized at a Yale symposium in 1969, and a "new" discipline, Black Studies, was introduced.

At the same time, historically black private colleges and state supported institutions generally located in the South, institutions that together had produced the vast majority of African-American college graduates, grew in popularity among the expanding black middle class that was the primary beneficiary of the federal government's programs. No doubt encouraged by television's popular "Cosby Show," African Americans saw these institutions as places that offered nurturing academic and social environments, and from 1980 to 1990 their enrollments grew 15 percent—from 186,000 to 214,000 students. These colleges had long had black faculty and administrators and taught courses such as African and African-American history essential to Black Studies.

With this increase in popularity, however, came new questions concerning these historically black colleges. Do they prepare African-American students to cope in a multicultural society? Should state-supported predominantly black institutions be merged with predominantly white state universities and effective integration extended from primary and secondary schools to undergraduate education? Were African Americans exchanging psychological comfort for inferior education and the perpetuation of the known deficiencies of a segregated society?

Persistent unemployment and underemployment and the growing "underclass" called for a more complex interpretation of American society. But the college students of the late 1980s and early 1990s had missed the Civil Rights movement and the tumultuous '60s. They had spent their adolescence listening to the economic ideology of the Reagan and Bush administrations, which championed free enterprise, deplored "big government," and tacitly supported those who blamed African Americans for their social and economic disadvantages. It became increasingly acceptable for whites to denounce "affirmative action" with claims of "preferential treatment" and "reverse discrimination" although African-American students still faced problems encountered by their predecessors.

CHALLENGES TO AFFIRMATIVE ACTION

The 1978 Supreme Court decision in *Regents of the University of California* v. *Bakke* brought a new challenge to affirmative action. In a complex opinion that reflected a divided court, the case was fought and won on the popular notion of "reverse discrimination." The *Bakke* case made it more difficult for African Americans to take full advantage of opportunities created by federal legislation and programs. Those who opposed affirmative action found refuge in the decision and justified the status quo in education and employment. More sophisticated educational institutions found they could hire token African Americans who would not push for change. While these institutions were producing African-American professionals who mirrored their view of things, many white Americans were rallying to the unspoken word from the nation's Capitol. The message they heard was that the injustices faced by African Americans had been rectified and no longer needed to be taken seriously.

Regents of the University of California v. Bakke (1978)

This case presents a challenge to the special admissions program of the Petitioner, the Medical School of the University of California at Davis, which is designed to assure the admission of a specified number of students from certain minority groups. The Supreme Court of California held the special admissions program unlawful, enjoined petitioner from considering the race of any applicant, and ordered Bakke's admission. For the reasons stated in the following opinion, I believe that so much of the judgment of the California court as holds petitioner's special admissions program unlawful and directs that respondent be admitted to the Medical School must be affirmed.

In summary, it is evident that the Davis special admissions program involves the use of an explicit racial classification never before countenanced by this Court. It tells applicants who are not Negro, Asian, or "Chicano" that they are totally excluded from a specific percentage of the seats in an entering class. No matter how strong their qualifications, quantitative and extracurricular, including their own potential for contribution to educational diversity, they are never afforded the chance to compete with applicants from the preferred groups for the special admission seats. At the same time, the preferred applicants have the opportunity to compete for every seat in the class. The fatal flaw in petitioner's program is its disregard of individual rights as guaranteed by the 14th Amendment. Such rights are not absolute. But when a State's distribution of benefits or imposition of burdens hinges on the color of a person's skin or ancestry, that individual is entitled to a demonstration that the challenged classification is necessary to promote a substantial state interest. Petitioner has failed to carry this burden. For this reason, that portion of the California court's judgment holding petitioner's special admissions programs invalid under the 14th Amendment must be affirmed.

Source: 438 U.S. 265 (1978).

Thurgood Marshall on Race-based Legal Remedies

In my separate opinion in *Bakke* . . . [I] stated: because of a legacy of unequal treatment that we now must permit the institutions of this society to give consideration to race in making decisions about who will hold the positions of influence, affluence, and prestige in America. For far too long, the doors to those positions have been shut to Negroes. If we are ever to become a fully integrated society, one in which the color of a person's skin will not determine tile opportunities available to him or her, we must be willing to take steps to open those doors." Those doors cannot be fully opened without the acceptance of race-conscious remedies. As my Brother Blackmun observed in *Bakke*, "in order to get beyond racism, we must first take account of race. There is no other way." . . .

Source: Fullilove v. Klutznick, 448 U.S. 448 (1980).

Among whites hostile to African Americans' advancement, affirmative action became equated with "preferential treatment" and with the rejection of merit as the basis for employment and promotion. Such people devalued African Americans' achievement in colleges, government, and the professions; and, in response, some African Americans shied away from requesting racially based consideration.

The conservative African-American scholar Thomas Sowell, argued that affirmative action "policies set in motion complex reactions which pit minority and non-minority students against each other, and generate stresses and reactions among faculty, administrators, and outside interests." African Americans faced hostility from whites who assumed that they had benefited from "preferential treatment" and racial conflict at colleges and universities, including Princeton, the University of Rhode Island, the University of Arizona, the University of Nebraska, and the University of Michigan—whose Institute for Social Research had foreseen such events. In 1985, the popular African-American magazine *Ebony* described the academic and social discrimination that plagued black students on predominantly white campuses where the response to their concerns ranged from minimal support to indifference and outright hostility. African-American students came to see themselves as outsiders—at best, marginalized and, at worst, victims of a racist America.

NEW PARADIGMS FOR AFRICAN AMERICANS

Educators and academics grappling with the growing complexity of the times and influenced by neo-Marxist "critical theory" and the perspective of "postmodernism" sought new ways to understand social life. Peter Berger and Bernard Luckmann's *The Social Construction of Reality* set the stage for multiple ways of understanding social problems; in the 1980s and 1990s black scholars adopted its mode of analysis. Black feminist Audrey Lorde's widely circulated article "The Master's Tools Will Never Dismantle the Master's House" echoed the insight of the African-American historian and educator Carter G. Woodson who, writing forty-five years earlier, called for new forms of analysis. Patricia Hill Collins's article "Learning From the Outsider Within: The Sociological Significance of Black Feminist Thought," which followed a similar intellectual strategy, quickly became the most widely cited article in the field of Black Studies. Martin Bernal created a stir in the scholarly community with his book *Black Athena*, which emphasized the importance of Africa in the development of Western civilization, while Molefi Asante provided a new paradigm that encouraged African Americans to replace Eurocentric approaches with Afrocentrism, placing themselves at the center of scholarly discourse. In popularized form, this paradigm easily took hold in communities that had responded to the oratory of Malcolm X. In *Countering the Conspiracy to Destroy Black Boys*, Jawanza Kunjufu caught the attention of those who have attempted to give voice to the "underclass."

By the end of the 1980s, a confusing array of solutions was offered. Conservatives promoted the ideal of individual achievement; older liberals and civil rights leaders continued to emphasize integration; black nationalists demanded separatism. Meanwhile, middle-class African Americans continued their flight from the inner city, leaving the poor to face the pathologies spawned by increasing racial and social-class isolation and the disintegration of the social fabric.

THE NEGLECT OF CITIES

Reagan's victory, which originated in the rise of the "Sunbelt" and the shift of southern whites to the Republican Party in response to the victories of Civil Rights movement, signaled the further marginalization of African Americans and their concerns within the government of the United States. Bush, who had begun his career in opposition to the civil rights legislation of the 1960s, made race the core of his first election campaign with the infamous "Willie Horton" television advertisement that exacerbated white America's fears of black male sexuality and criminality. Playing the "race card" served to obscure the twelve-year policy of neglect of urban America in favor of more affluent white suburbs, where the wealthiest 2 percent of the country multiplied their riches at the expense of the huge majority of the American people.

African Americans of all classes suffered from the federal government's neglect of the cities. This neglect was fueled by the economic Darwinism of the Reagan and Bush administrations, which led Kevin Phillips, a former Republican political strategist and assistant attorney general under Reagan, to write in his polemic against the effects of Republican tax policy, *The Politics of Rich and Poor*:

Regions, neighborhoods and people without capital, skills or education were losing their identities. Impoverished small cities definitely became more noticeable during the 1980's. Forgotten municipalities like East St. Louis, Illinois, Benton Harbor, Michigan, and Camden, New Jersey, all largely black, sank below stereotypical big-city slums like the South Bronx, eliciting attention as America's new version of apartheid.... [A] number of major cities—Newark, Atlanta, Miami, Baltimore and Cleveland—had counted at least 20 percent of their population living below the poverty line.... [T]he gap between the big city slums and the rest of metropolitan America was getting bigger.

The economic policies of the Reagan and Bush administrations had a far greater impact on inner-city education and the nation than most people realized. The retreat of the federal government from the urban scene, tax policies that favored the rich, and rhetoric from the White House that denied the existence of racial problems and championed private enterprise, contributed to the devastation of the nation's urban centers. The infrastructure of cities, from roads and bridges to housing, schools, and health care facilities, deteriorated. Urban schools continued to decline as suburbs prospered. While the Reagan and Bush administrations asked Americans to return to the values and simplicity of the past, the social pathologies Kenneth Clark had identified grew in the nation's cities to an extent unimaginable in the 1950s. Urban problems grew despite the election of African-American mayors in cities like Atlanta, Birmingham, Chicago, Detroit, Flint, Newark, and New Orleans. Increasing racial, geographical, and social isolation of the underclass resulted in high unemployment, proliferation of gangs, mounting drug use, rising crime rates, growing rates of teenage pregnancy and occurrence of female-headed households, and homeless families and individuals. African-American mayors could not overcome greater political, social, and economic forces that contributed to inadequate education in the nation's cities. African-American theologian and social critic Cornel West told a *Newsweek* interviewer:

> Economic desperation coupled with social breakdown now threatens the very existence of impoverished communities in urban areas—with growing signs of the same forces at work in rural and suburban America. The drug and gun cultures among youth are the most visible symptoms of this nihilism. If we are to survive as a nation, the 1990s must be a decade in which candid and critical conversation takes place about race and poverty, rights and responsibilities, violence and despair.

CONCLUSION

In the 1954 *Brown* decision, the United States Supreme Court proclaimed "separate educational facilities inherently unequal" and ruled, "To separate [African Americans] from others of similar age and qualifications solely because of their race generates a feeling of inferiority as to their status in the community that may affect their hearts and minds in a way unlikely ever to be undone." Fourteen years later, the riot commission's *Report* stated, "Our nation is moving toward two societies, one black, one white—separate and unequal" and accurately predicted the decline of urban America accompanied by decreasing job opportunities and the deterioration of the public schools with the end result of increasing segregation. Ironically, in July 1993, the Supreme Court let stand a federal appeals court ruling that Topeka, Kansas, had failed to desegregate its schools.

Forty years after the first *Brown* decision, while the educational attainment of African Americans has improved immensely, segregation of African-American students remains a problem, particularly in the decaying urban schools of the North, and has caused thoughtful critics to raise troublesome questions. Was school integration possible? Did curriculums adequately address the African-American experience? Could white teachers ever learn how to teach black students? Have talented African-American students intentionally not achieved in school because their peers would accuse them of "acting white"? Why should African Americans have to deny their experiences in order to be successful in white America? Questions like these brought up a long-standing problem, namely this: Could African Americans be honest about their experiences without being ignored, stigmatized, or viewed as radical by white Americans?

Whether or not black academies and Afrocentrism flourish in the next century, one thing remains clear. African-Americans value their children's education and will persist in promoting programs to advance black learning. They appreciate that knowledge is the key to self-esteem, independence, and positive social transformation. They agree, in essence, with the opinion of the noted black social critic and novelist James Baldwin, who poignantly explained in 1963:

> The purpose of education, finally, is to create in a person the ability to look at the world for himself, to make his own decisions, to say to himself this is black or this is white, to decide for himself whether there is a God in heaven or not.

Baldwin expresses concern that, in a society that does not really value such persons, preferring instead "a citizenry which will simply obey the rules," institutions are unlikely to pursue this purpose. Responsible people, says Baldwin, have an obligation to fight for change, to demand genuinely liberating education for all members of society.

FOR FURTHER READING

America 2000: An Education Strategy. Washington, D.C.: U.S. Department of Education, 1991.
Asante, Molefi K. *The Afrocentric Idea*. Philadelphia: Temple University Press, 1987.
Bernal, Martin. *Black Athena: The Afroasiatic Roots of Classical Civilization*. Volumes I & II. New Brunswick, N.J.: Rutgers University Press, 1989–1991.

Clark, Kenneth B. *Dark Ghetto: Dilemmas of Social Power*. 2nd ed. Middletown, Conn.: Wesleyan University Press, 1989.

Herndon, James. *The Way It Spozed To Be*. Portsmouth, N.H.: Heinemann, 1997.

Kluger, Richard. *Simple Justice: The History of Brown v. Board of Education and America's Struggle for Equality*. New York: Random House, 1977.

Kozol, Jonathan. *Savage Inequality: Children in America's Schools*. New York: Harper Collins, 1992.

Kunjufu, Jawanza. *Countering the Conspiracy to Destroy Black Boys*. Chicago: African American Images, 1986.

Liebow, Elliot. *Talley's Corner: A Study of Negro Streetcorner Men*. Boston: Little, Brown & Co., 1999.

Martin, Waldo E., ed. *Brown v. Board of Education: A Brief History with Documents*. New York: St. Martin's Press, 1998.

Morris, Aldon D. *The Origins of the Civil Rights Movement: Black Communities Organizing for Change*. New York: Free Press, 1986.

National Commission on Excellence in Education. *A Nation At Risk: The Full Account*. Portland, Ore.: USA Research, Inc., 1992.

Nieli, Russell, ed. *Racial Preference and Racial Justice: The New Affirmative Action Controversy*. Washington, D.C.: Ethics and Public Policy Center, 1991.

Robinson, Armstead L., et. al., eds. *Black Studies in the University: A Symposium*. New Haven, Conn.: Yale University Press, 1969.

Rogers, David. *110 Livingston Street: Political and Bureaucracy in the New York City Schools*. New York: Random, 1968.

Ryan, William. *Blaming the Victim*. Rev. ed. New York: Vintage, 1976.

Sarat, Austin. *Race, Law and Culture: Reflections on Brown v. Board of Education*. New York: Oxford University Press, 1997.

Thernstrom, Stephan A., and Abigail M. Thernstrom. *America in Black and White: One Nation, Indivisible*. New York: Simon & Schuster, 1997.

Wilson, William J. *The Truly Disadvantaged: The Inner City, the Underclass, and Public Policy*. Chicago: University of Chicago Press, 1990.

Woodson, Carter G. *The Mis-Education of the Negro*. Trenton, N.J.: Africa World Press, 1990.

chapter 19

After the Movement

African Americans and Civil Rights since 1970

Donald G. Nieman

URING THE FIRST HALF OF THE 1960s, a rising tide of African-American protest forced the nation to dismantle the legal edifice of segregation and disfranchisement. Spurred on by the moral claims of civil rights leaders, the growing insistence of African Americans, and fear of the consequences of inaction, Congress passed landmark civil rights legislation. The Civil Rights Act of 1964 committed the national government to end segregation in public places and outlawed employment discrimination. The Voting Rights Act, passed a year later, destroyed the barriers southern states had established to prevent African Americans from voting. These measures dramatically altered race relations, especially in the South. By the beginning of the 1970s, "whites only" signs were relics of the past, and African Americans enjoyed service in restaurants, theaters, hotels, parks, and sports arenas that previously had been closed to them; significant school desegregation occurred, making southern schools the most integrated in the nation by 1972; and African Americans registered and voted in large numbers, becoming a significant force in southern politics.

By the late 1960s, however, support for civil rights reform had waned. As debate over the war in Vietnam raged in the years after the 1965 civil rights agenda lost much of the salience it had enjoyed. Even more important, support among northern whites—which had been critical to the victories of the mid-1960s—quickly declined. The emergence of a militant Black Power movement, a series of eruptions in America's inner cities in the years following the Watts riot of 1965, and growing mass protest against segregation and discrimination in the North produced a white backlash and a shift to the right in American politics that helped Richard M. Nixon win the presidency in

1968. In the face of mounting white resistance, the Civil Rights movement itself appeared to be in disarray by the end of the decade. Groups like the Student Non-Violent Coordinating Committee (SNCC) and the Congress of Racial Equality (CORE), which had provided the movement's shock troops, were torn apart by internecine struggles. And the assassination of Martin Luther King Jr., in 1968, deprived the movement of its most charismatic and unifying leader.

Although the Civil Rights movement appeared to expire with the 1960s, during the following decades civil rights leaders were surprisingly successful. Relying on lobbying and litigation, rather than on mass protest, they not only held the ground they had won during the 1960s but also made significant gains. Civil rights advocates pushed beyond the demand for simple nondiscrimination that had characterized the movement in the halcyon days of the mid-1960s. Recognizing that the effects of a centuries-old caste system continued to disadvantage African Americans and well aware that discrimination could take subtle forms, they demanded that government take affirmative action to undo the effects of slavery and segregation. Yet despite these gains, the victories won in the 1970s and 1980s produced more ambiguous results than the triumph over segregation and disfranchisement in the 1960s. They also generated a powerful reaction that gathered force in the 1980s and by the mid-1990s threatened to roll back many of the advances won during the Indian summer of the Civil Rights movement.

FIGHTING SEGREGATION IN PUBLIC SCHOOLS

School desegregation remained high on the civil rights leaders' list of concerns in the early 1970s. Although by 1972 there had been substantial progress toward integration in rural areas and small cities in the South, urban schools remained highly segregated. In rural areas, where there was little residential segregation, assignment of students to the schools nearest their homes produced considerable integration. In towns and small cities, which encompassed limited areas, school attendance zones could easily be drawn to achieve integration. But large cities often sprawled over dozens of square miles and had highly segregated residential patterns. Consequently, no matter how school attendance zones were drawn, most neighborhood schools would remain highly segregated. Meaningful desegregation was possible only if children attended schools outside their neighborhoods.

Given this reality, civil rights attorneys pressed federal courts to use busing, arguing that without it, segregated schools would remain a part of the urban landscape, perpetuating racial polarization. School officials demurred, insisting that while the Fourteenth Amendment banned racial discrimination, it did not mandate integration. In *Swann* v. *Charlotte-Mecklenburg Board of Education* (1971), brought by the National Association for the Advancement of Colored People (NAACP) Legal Defense and Education Fund, Inc., the

United States Supreme Court rejected this position and gave the green light to busing. In a unanimous decision, the Court ruled that where states had established segregation by law, they had a positive duty to undo the results of their past policies and achieve integration. Transportation of students to schools outside their neighborhoods, the justices concluded, was a permissible means to accomplish this.

Swann provided an effective tool for dismantling segregation in the urban South, where state laws had required black and white children to attend separate schools. Its implications for highly segregated northern urban schools were less certain, however. In 1962, for example, two-thirds of the African-American students in Gary, Indiana, attended schools that were 99 percent black. Conventional wisdom held that northern school segregation was a product of residential patterns and had not been imposed by law. In fact, few northern states had enacted school segregation laws, and many had explicitly banned segregation. Nevertheless, in most northern cities school officials had chosen school sites, drawn school attendance zones, and adopted pupil transfer policies in ways calculated to promote racially segregated schools.

The United States Supreme Court soon subjected northern schools to similar scrutiny with its decision in *Keyes* v. *School District No. 1, Denver, Colo.* (1973), another case initiated by the NAACP. If school officials were shown to have adopted policies that promoted segregation, the Court ruled, federal judges could impose desegregation plans. And those plans might include busing if that were necessary to dismantle segregation and achieve integrated school systems.

Swann and *Keyes* triggered a flurry of desegregation activity by federal courts in the North as well as in the South. Predictably, as busing spread northward, white opposition mounted and became a powerful force on Capitol Hill. In 1972, legislation drastically restricting the federal courts' authority to order busing gained broad support in Congress, and only a filibuster by Senate liberals prevented passage. Two years later, similar legislation was defeated by one vote in the Senate. In the face of these defeats, antibusing sentiment became more powerful, and congressional opponents of busing redoubled their efforts. Although ultimately they were unable to end the federal courts' authority to order busing, in early 1976 the antibusing forces enacted legislation stripping the Department of Health, Education, and Welfare (HEW) of authority to cut off federal aid to school districts which refused to adopt busing plans to achieve integration. As a result, the agency lost its authority to invoke the power of the purse—which had been crucial in desegregating schools in the rural South— to achieve integration in the nation's cities.

As antibusing pressure grew in Congress, the Supreme Court itself imposed a significant restriction on the tools available to remedy segregation. Because of white movement to the suburbs in the decades after World War II, by the 1970s most urban schools had become heavily black while the surrounding suburban districts were predominantly white. Therefore, in most cities meaningful desegregation required busing of students between city school districts and suburban districts. In *Milliken* v. *Bradley* (1974), however, a sharply divided Court severely restricted the federal courts' authority to order busing across school district lines. Unless plaintiffs demonstrated that suburban districts intentionally adopted policies designed to promote segregation, the majority ruled, they could not be included in metropolitan busing plans.

Although it did not preclude the use of busing, *Milliken* was a severe setback for proponents of school desegregation. In cities with metropolitanwide school districts (such as Charlotte, which had a countywide school district) *Milliken* did not pose a barrier to desegregation. And in cities such as Louisville, Kentucky, and Wilmington, Delaware, where civil rights attorneys could show that school district boundaries had been drawn with segregative intent or that the policies of suburban districts sustained segregation in the city, federal courts ordered students bused between city and suburban schools.

Nevertheless, *Milliken* meant that in most of the nation's large cities, judges' options were limited. When they ordered citywide desegregation plans, they often merely spread a few white students among predominantly black schools, in the process speeding white flight to the suburbs. They could—as they did in Kansas City and Chicago—devise plans that compensated for past discrimination by enhancing the quality of inner-city schools. But this seemed like a reversion to *Plessy* v. *Ferguson*'s separate but equal doctrine rather than a fulfillment of the dream of achieving integration. By devising plans which called for establishing schools with special curricula (so-called "magnet schools"), judges could attract white as well as black students to select inner-city schools, thereby creating pockets of integration in a sea of predominantly African-American schools. However, in the absence of cross-district busing, the federal courts lacked the tools to desegregate schools in most cities. Consequently, the rapid progress toward school integration that had occurred during the late 1960s and early 1970s came to a halt; by the early 1990s, schools in most of the nation's large cities, where a majority of blacks lived, were more segregated than they had been in 1968.

FIGHTING FOR EQUAL EMPLOYMENT OPPORTUNITIES

Civil rights advocates turned their efforts as well to winning more effective remedies against employment discrimination. Deeply rooted discrimination in the North as well as the South had relegated most African Americans to unskilled, low-paying jobs and contributed to an extremely high rate of poverty among African Americans. Discrimination and poverty (not to mention inferior schools in black neighborhoods) undermined young African Americans' incentive and ability to finish high school, thereby locking them into low-paying, dead-end jobs. Title VII of the Civil Rights Act of 1964 had attempted to deal with the economic problems of African Americans, prohibiting discrimination by private employers and creating the Equal Employment Opportunity Commission (EEOC) to monitor compliance. The Civil Rights Act and changing attitudes generated by the Civil Rights movement had eliminated much of the most blatant ("no colored need apply") discrimination and had contributed to significant gains in employment and earnings among African Americans during the late 1960s and early 1970s. Yet discrimination did not disappear; instead, it became more subtle, harder to detect, and more difficult to prove. Even more troubling, those for whom past discrimination denied education, job training, and employment experience continued to find the promise of economic opportunity and a better life elusive.

The 1970s proved a less propitious time than the 1960s to tackle these difficult problems. Not only had the conservative political tide deprived civil rights leaders of allies in the White House, but the economic climate militated against further efforts to redress the effects of past discrimination. The dynamic economic growth of the 1960s slowed during the 1970s, and sharply rising inflation alarmed most Americans, convincing them that it was harder to make ends meet and to maintain their standard of living. Afraid that the pie was no longer growing, many whites felt threatened by programs that promised a bigger piece to African Americans. Consequently, like busing, the issue of employment discrimination promised to become highly charged and hotly debated.

Nevertheless, civil rights advocates, working closely with supporters of the resurgent women's movement, scored important victories. In 1972, Congress adopted the Equal Employment Opportunity Act, considerably strengthening the EEOC. The Civil Rights Act of 1964 had given the agency authority to investigate complaints of employment discrimination, but had denied it real power to move against offenders. The 1972 law remedied this defect, authorizing the EEOC to initiate lawsuits against employers or unions that refused to end discriminatory employment practices. Equally important, during the 1970s the agency's budget increased dramatically, allowing it to expand the size of its staff. By 1977, the EEOC's Office of General Counsel employed more than three hundred attorneys, giving the agency adequate personnel to use its newly won powers.

Civil rights advocates also secured legal changes that facilitated lawsuits by victims of discrimination. In 1976, Congress authorized the federal courts to award attorneys' fees to victorious parties in civil rights suits, thereby removing one deterrent to private claims. The same year the Supreme Court opened the way for employment discrimination suits under a federal statute first adopted during Reconstruction. Although the law required proof of intentional discrimination, it authorized federal courts to award monetary damages beyond those available under the Civil Rights Act of 1964, which limited remedies to instatement in the position denied with back pay. This offered a potent remedy to victims of discrimination and encouraged private attorneys to take employment discrimination cases.

These changes resulted in a fivefold increase in employment discrimination cases between 1970 and 1981. This surge in litigation helped break down barriers that African Americans and women had encountered. Employers, eager to avoid the expense of lawsuits, had an additional incentive to open their doors to minorities and follow equal employment guidelines promulgated by the EEOC.

Civil rights attorneys also succeeded in broadening the definition of employment discrimination under the Civil Rights Act of 1964, making it easier to win lawsuits initiated under that act. In *Griggs* v. *Duke Power*, a 1971 case argued by attorneys from the NAACP Legal Defense and Education Fund, Inc., the Supreme Court held that job requirements that had an adverse impact on African Americans could only withstand scrutiny if the employer could prove that they were job related. Requirements that disproportionately excluded African Americans (e.g., requiring prospective employees to have a high school diploma or to pass an aptitude test) were suspect and the *Griggs* rule freed plaintiffs in employment discrimination cases from having to prove that employers intentionally discriminated against them, something that was very difficult to establish. It also provided remedies to blacks who were denied employment and job advancement on the basis of arbitrary policies that were ostensibly nondiscriminatory but which, in actual practice, gave the edge to whites. Equally important, it encouraged employers to remove unnecessary employment criteria that excluded African Americans.

THE AFFIRMATIVE ACTION DEBATE

By the early 1970s, affirmative action programs also offered a potentially effective—if highly controversial and frequently misunderstood—remedy for discrimination in the workplace. Developed in the late 1960s by the Department of Labor to guarantee nondiscrimination by firms doing business with the federal government, affirmative action principles were adopted by the EEOC during the early 1970s. The commission warned employers that the equal employment opportunity guaranteed by the Civil Rights Act of 1964 required more than adoption of nondiscriminatory hiring practices. Rather, it demanded that employers work actively to increase the number of minorities in their workforce by developing recruiting strategies, setting goals for hiring minorities, and establishing timetables to reach those goals. Given the EEOC's newly won authority to sue employers and the rapid growth of employment discrimination cases, many employers took notice, adopting and even implementing affirmative action programs as a hedge against litigation.

Like busing, affirmative action generated passionate argument. Critics charged that it gave special preferences to African Americans and women and amounted to "reverse discrimination." Moreover, they argued that by assigning rights on the basis of race, affirmative action violated the principle of color-blind citizenship established by the Fourteenth Amendment and threatened the most important accomplishment of the Civil Rights movement. Discrimination was wrong, the critics argued, whether it worked against African Americans or in their favor.

Defenders of affirmative action responded that rules which were seemingly equal often served to perpetuate discrimination and inequality. Although it generally took more subtle forms, they asserted, discrimination against African Americans and women continued to be a reality. White men generally controlled hiring decisions in business, government, and education. Even when not consciously prejudiced, they frequently felt most comfortable with applicants who were like themselves, believed that they would "fit in" better than blacks and women, and thus subtly slanted hiring decisions in favor of white males. According to its defenders, affirmative action would serve as a check against subtle forms of discrimination that were still all too prevalent.

Proponents of affirmative action also argued that while a color-blind society was a laudable goal, it was essential to take color into account to remedy the continuing effects of past discrimination. Generations of white men, they pointed out, had benefited from a de facto affirmative action program that had reserved the choicest jobs for them and relegated blacks mainly to low-paying and menial positions. Moreover, they argued that the legacy of segregation, unequal education, and poverty made it difficult for African Americans to overcome the historic advantages enjoyed by whites and threatened to leave them stuck at the bottom of the economic ladder. The temporary special protection afforded by affirmative action, its defenders concluded, was designed to achieve meaningful equality and therefore was fully in keeping with the spirit of the Fourteenth Amendment and the Civil Rights movement.

Opponents countered that affirmative action penalized persons who themselves were not guilty of discrimination in order to rectify wrongs committed by previous generations. By giving special consideration to African Americans, they argued, affirmative action meant that better qualified white males were passed over for jobs and promotions. Consequently, they would suffer a loss, not because of wrongful behavior on their part, but because of their race. Concomitantly, individual black applicants would benefit, not because they themselves had been the victims of discriminatory acts, but because members of their race had been subject to discrimination. Moreover, critics pointed out that for many lower-class whites who came from severely disadvantaged backgrounds, affirmative action would be one more obstacle to overcome. Indeed, middle-class blacks would reap the benefits of affirmative action programs, even though they were not disadvantaged, while whites would be penalized, regardless of their background.

To claim that special treatment for blacks inflicted wrongs on innocent whites, proponents of affirmative action responded, was only half the story. Even if blatant, systematic discrimination against African Americans had ended, they argued, its effects continued to burden young blacks who had never known the harshness of segregation. High rates of poverty, unemployment, illiteracy, and broken homes in the African-American community were the legacy of centuries of discrimination. As a result, young African Americans all too frequently lacked the supportive home environment that was crucial to success in school; grew up without role models to encourage success; found schools frustrating places that were irrelevant to them and dropped out; and lived in urban ghettos where high unemployment made it difficult to obtain essential work experience. Refusing African Americans special assistance would only condemn them to compete in a game whose rules were stacked against them and perpetuate injustice in the name of policies that were formally neutral but actually gave decided advantages to whites. Moreover, while defenders of affirmative action admitted that there were disadvantaged whites, they pointed out that, as a group, African Americans labored under a heritage of discrimination that was far more severe than that whites had ever known. Indeed, it was so severe and so pervasive that policymakers were justified in giving special treatment to African Americans as a group.

Questions of justice aside, opponents charged that affirmative action subverted the principle of reward according to merit and thus threatened to bury American society in mediocrity. Although they admitted that most affirmative action programs did not establish formal quotas, critics contended that they put almost irresistible pressure on employers to hire blacks and women regardless of their qualifications. They argued that this made race, rather than merit, the crucial factor in hiring decisions. At a time when American firms were coming under increasingly sharp competition from abroad, the critics argued, the nation could ill afford to promote mediocrity.

Defenders of affirmative action strenuously denied these charges. Pointing to the *Griggs* case, they argued that employers frequently established arbitrary qualifications that were irrelevant to job performance but which effectively screened out African Americans and women. Moreover, proponents charged that the critics had created a largely imagined golden age, before the onset of affirmative action, when employment decisions were made solely on the basis of merit. They pointed out that employment decisions frequently had been based on race and gender (excluding blacks and women from consideration regardless of their qualifications) or on family influence and personal connections, rather than merit. Indeed, plenty of mediocre and incompetent white men had found their way into jobs without raising the hue and cry that greeted affirmative action. By encouraging the hiring and promotion of African Americans and women, proponents argued, affirmative action would help break down the "old boy" networks that had long worked in favor of white males.

Not surprisingly, the debate soon found its way before the Supreme Court. Although often sharply divided, the Court was generally supportive of affirmative action. In *Regents of the University of California* v. *Bakke* (1978), it struck down a state medical school program that set aside a specified number of spots for minority candidates. But even though the Court held that it was impermissible for states to establish racial quotas, a majority ruled that schools might take race into account in the admissions process in order to create a more diverse student body, thereby opening the door to affirmative action programs.

The Court looked more favorably upon voluntary affirmative action programs established by private employers. In *Weber* v. *United Steel Workers* (1979), it upheld a plan—agreed to by an employer and a labor union—setting aside half the places in a training program for African Americans. In deciding the case, the majority emphasized that the plan did not involve discriminatory state action (prohibited by the Fourteenth Amendment), was temporary, and had been adopted to redress a long history of discrimination that had excluded African Americans from well-paid skilled jobs. *Weber* was significant, signaling that the Court would not block the momentum building among private employers for affirmative action.

Although civil rights advocates built on the successes of the '60s and won surprising victories against employment discrimination in the 1970s and early 1980s, many wondered whether they were winning the battles but losing the war. To be sure, affirmative action had helped open avenues of opportunity to African Americans in business, labor, education, government, and the professions. Many observers pointed to a growing black middle class as proof that African Americans were slowly but surely moving into the mainstream. African-American students were graduating in greater numbers than ever before from colleges and professional schools. And after graduation they were being recruited by businesses, universities, law firms, and government. Indeed, in 1978, the black sociologist William Julius Wilson published a prize-winning study suggesting *The Declining Significance of Race* in American life.

Yet Wilson and many others who applauded the growth of the black middle class were not sanguine about the future. Paradoxically, while some blacks were reaping the fruits of the Civil Rights movement and entering the middle class, unemployment and poverty rates among African Americans actually grew during the late 1970s and early 1980s. The nation's inner cities contained a large black population beset by joblessness, poverty, single-parent families, low levels of educational achievement, crime, drugs, and despair. Affirmative action, which helped open opportunities for those who had the basic qualifications for employment, could do little for those who had no work experience or skills and little education. Moreover, the changing structure of the economy locked these people—Wilson called them "the truly disadvantaged"—into poverty. The drift of businesses to the suburbs put many jobs beyond their reach. More important, the decline of the automobile, steel, and other basic industries during the 1970s and early 1980s denied unskilled and semiskilled blacks access to jobs that paid well and offered hope of economic mobility. New jobs opened primarily in the service industries, where those without skills could expect to earn low wages and live close to or even below poverty level.

AN INCREASING ROLE IN THE POLITICAL PROCESS

Although their efforts to achieve equal employment opportunity had mixed results, civil rights advocates were more successful in expanding African Americans' access to political power. This effort focused principally on the South, where Africans Americans had been systematically excluded from the political system. Although the Voting Rights Act of 1965 opened the ballot box to black southerners, they confronted continued barriers to effective use of the ballot. Given the prevalence of voting along racial lines, African-American candidates could usually hope to win elections only in districts with a majority or near-majority of African-American voters. White politicians sought to minimize the number of black officials—and thereby reduce the effect of black votes—by establishing multiseat electoral districts and at-large elections. In a city with a five-member city council and a black population of 40 percent, for example, African Americans would be likely to have majorities in two wards and elect two black members. However, if members were elected at-large, with voters throughout the city casting ballots for all five seats, the white majority could preserve a white council.

There was sharp debate over whether the Voting Rights Act prohibited such electoral changes. In states and counties with a history of discrimination, the act required preclearance by the Justice Department or the federal district court for the District of Columbia for any change in "voting qualification or prerequisite to voting, or standard, practice, or procedure with respect to voting." The change would be permitted only if the attorney general or the court were satisfied that neither its purpose nor its effect was discriminatory. Civil rights advocates contended that laws establishing at-large elections or otherwise diluting the effect of black votes were not only subject to preclearance but were illegal because of their discriminatory effect. Conservatives disagreed, arguing that while the Voting Rights Act prohibited laws and regulations designed to prevent individuals from registering and voting, it did not apply to all changes in the electoral process. Indeed, they charged civil rights advocates with attempting to transform a measure that had been adopted to guarantee the right to vote into one that would guarantee proportional representation for African Americans. Like affirmative action, they contended, the Voting Rights Act would give African Americans special privileges and violate the Fourteenth Amendment's equal protection clause.

The Supreme Court quickly swept aside arguments for a narrow interpretation of the law. In *Allen* v. *State Board of Elections* (1969), a case brought by the NAACP Legal Defense Fund, it held that a law replacing single-member districts with multiseat districts and at-large elections was subject to preclearance and should not be allowed to take effect if it diluted black votes. The Voting Rights Act, the Court concluded, gave "a broad interpretation to the right to vote, recognizing that voting includes 'all action necessary to make a vote effective.'" Procedures diluting the votes of African Americans would "nullify their ability to elect the candidate of their choice just as would prohibiting some of them from voting" and therefore came within the act's purview. Four years later, in *Georgia* v. *United States* (1973), the Court ruled that a state's plan for reapportioning seats in the legislature was covered by the preclearance requirement. Moreover, the majority suggested that any plan that made it more difficult for African Americans to elect candidates of their choice should be rejected. These holdings enabled civil rights advocates to block redistricting and reapportionment measures that diluted African-American voting strength and thus contributed to a steady increase in the number of African-American elected officials during the early 1970s.

The Voting Rights Act's rigorous preclearance process, however, applied only to newly adopted laws and procedures, not to those already in force in 1965. During the 1970s blacks began to challenge pre-1965 laws establishing at-large elections and multiseat districts, many of which had been enacted around the turn of the century as part of the campaign to disfranchise African Americans. Initially, the Supreme Court proved receptive to claims that these laws were discriminatory and therefore violated the Voting Rights Act and the Fourteenth and Fifteenth Amendments. In *City of Mobile v. Bolden* (1980), however, the Court reversed course, ruling that plaintiffs who challenged existing laws and procedures had to prove that they were adopted with intent to dilute African Americans' voting strength, a very difficult matter at best.

Rebuffed by the Supreme Court, civil rights advocates turned to Congress for a remedy, even though the political climate in Washington, D.C., was chillier in the wake of Ronald Reagan's landslide victory in the 1980 presidential election. Despite facing a more conservative Congress and sharp opposition from the Reagan administration, in 1982 civil rights advocates won passage of legislation extending the life and expanding the coverage of the Voting Rights Act. The new measure not only renewed the preclearance provision of the Voting Rights Act (which was to have expired in 1982) for twenty-five years. It also prohibited existing electoral laws and procedures that gave minorities less opportunity than whites to elect candidates of their choice. The effect was to sweep aside *Bolden's* intent requirement.

The 1982 legislation had a dramatic effect. It made challenges to at-large elections easier to win and compelled state legislatures to redraw legislative and congressional districts to maximize the number of districts with African-American majorities. The result was a dramatic increase in the number of African-American elected officials—from school boards and county commissions to state legislatures and the U.S. House of Representatives. Between 1982 and 1992, for example, African-American representation in Congress jumped from twenty to thirty-nine members.

SETBACKS IN THE REAGAN ERA

Civil rights advocates' success helped fuel a powerful reaction as the 1980s progressed. The Reagan administration, which relied heavily on support from conservative southern whites and northern Democrats who had left that party because of its liberal policies, led the way. The president, who had been at odds with civil rights leaders since the mid-1960s, sharply criticized busing and affirmative action. And he appointed persons who shared his views to such crucial positions as attorney general, assistant attorney general for civil rights, chair of the EEOC, and chair of the U.S. Civil Rights Commission.

Shortly after Reagan entered office, his administration mounted a powerful albeit unsuccessful campaign against broadening coverage of the Voting Rights Act. They also targeted affirmative action, denouncing it as establishing racial quotas and sanctioning "reverse discrimination." Although equating affirmative action with quotas was inaccurate, it was a rhetorical masterstroke. The term struck a responsive chord among many white Americans who were fearful that in a zero-sum economy African Americans' gains would come at their expense. And it helped reassure the president's middle- and working-class white supporters that he was standing up for them, even though his economic policies resulted in a significant transfer of wealth to upper-income Americans.

The administration's attack on affirmative action went beyond mere rhetoric. During the 1980s, Justice Department attorneys regularly filed briefs on behalf of white male plaintiffs who challenged affirmative action programs. Despite these efforts, the Supreme Court continued to support voluntary affirmative action programs as long as they did not establish quotas, were temporary, did not unduly burden whites, and did not disregard the seniority rights of white workers when layoffs were involved. By the end of the 1980s, however, it appeared that the administration's efforts were not in vain. Reagan's judicial appointments transformed the federal district courts and courts of appeals, shifting them sharply to the right. Moreover, by 1988, with the appointment of Justice Anthony Kennedy, the president appeared to have secured a conservative majority on the Supreme Court.

During the 1988–1989 term, the new majority clearly signaled its hostility to many of the innovations in civil rights law that had occurred during the previous two decades. In *Patterson* v. *McLean Credit Union* (1989) the Court sharply restricted its interpretation of the Reconstruction-era civil rights measure that enabled parties who could prove intentional discrimination to sue employers for monetary damages. It also dealt a severe blow to the use of consent decrees (i.e., court orders enforcing agreements reached out of court by parties to a lawsuit) to settle employment discrimination cases. In *Martin* v. *Wilks* (1989) the Court ruled that affirmative action plans embodied in such decrees were not immune to legal challenge. White employees had the right to challenge them, the majority ruled, even if they had ample opportunity to do so before the decree was announced. By leaving employers who entered consent decrees vulnerable to continued litigation, the decision reduced their incentive to settle employment discrimination suits out of court, thereby making the work of civil rights lawyers more time consuming and expensive. Finally, the new conservative majority undermined the *Griggs* ruling of 1971. In *Ward's Cove Packing Company* v. *Atonio* (1989), it held that even when plaintiffs demonstrated that company policies had an adverse effect on hiring and promotion of minorities, the burden remained on the plaintiffs to prove that these policies were unnecessary. ˙

The Court also dismantled state and local programs requiring that a certain percentage of the funds spent on publicly financed construction projects be awarded to minority-owned firms. Such programs were designed to redress the historic exclusion of African Americans from the construction business. Writing for the majority in *Richmond* v. *Croson* (1989), Justice Sandra Day O'Connor held that the Richmond, Virginia, set-aside program at issue established a racial classification and therefore was inherently suspect under the Fourteenth Amendment's equal protection clause. Moreover, she denied that the city's desire to overcome general societal discrimination against African Americans constituted the compelling interest the city was required to show to justify the program. Only if the city could demonstrate that actual discrimination had occurred against the minority contractors who benefited from the set-asides would the program pass constitutional muster. That, she concluded, the city had not done. *Croson* not only led to the demise of state and local minority set-aside programs, but O'Connor's analysis cast a long shadow over other affirmative action programs.

The Court also appeared poised to strike down creation of black majority electoral districts under the Voting Rights Act. In *Shaw* v. *Reno* (1993), it considered a challenge to a North Carolina congressional district that had been drawn to create a black voting majority and therefore to send an African American to Congress, something that had not happened in the state since 1900. The district, drawn by the state legislature, was strangely configured, snaking along Interstate 85 for more than 160 miles, linking heavily black communities in Charlotte, Greensboro, Durham, and Winston-Salem. While the Court ultimately returned the case to the trial court for further hearings, Justice Sandra Day O'Connor's opinion charged that the North Carolina district bore "an uncomfortable resemblance to political apartheid" and suggested that it was inherently suspect because it was based on racial classification. *Shaw* led to a flood of cases challenging other black majority districts, in the process threatening many of the political gains African Americans had made during the 1980s and early 1990s.

While it remains unclear how far the Court will go in dismantling the victories civil rights advocates won in the 1970s and 1980s, the conservative majority that has emerged will probably continue to control the Court's civil rights jurisprudence in the near future. The appointment of four new justices (Clarence Thomas, David Souter, Ruth Bader Ginsburg, and Stephen Breyer) who have joined the Court since 1989, appears not to have altered the balance on civil rights. Even if Souter (who dissented in *Shaw*) and Breyer (a Clinton appointee) hew to the line of William Brennan and Harry Blackmun, the liberals they replaced, and even if Ginsburg is more liberal than her predecessor Byron White, the conservative majority will remain because Justice Thomas, an outspoken conservative, sits in the seat once occupied by Thurgood Marshall, the father of the modern civil rights revolution in American law.

As the Supreme Court became less receptive to their arguments, civil rights advocates looked to Congress to redress some of the setbacks dealt them by the Court. In 1989, following the Court's assault on remedies against employment discrimination, Senator Edward M. Kennedy and Representative Augustus Hawkins introduced legislation that reversed the Court's decisions in *Martin v. Wilks, Patterson v. McLean Credit Union*, and *Ward's Cove*. President George Bush repeatedly attacked the measure as a "quota bill" and vetoed it in 1990. One year later, however, as supporters of the measure appeared to pick up enough Republican supporters to override a veto, the president acquiesced and signed into law the Civil Rights Restoration Act of 1991, which undid much of the damage of the 1988–1989 rulings.

CONCLUSION

This legislative victory may have been a kind of last hurrah of civil rights activists. The elections of 1994 made Republicans the majority party in both houses of Congress for the first time since 1954. Conservative Republican leaders, many of whom had entered politics or had emerged to positions of leadership during the "Reagan Revolution" of the 1980s, held a special hostility for affirmative action. Moreover, they were well aware that opposition to affirmative action was smart (if divisive) politics.

Not surprisingly, the only serious civil rights initiatives that emerged from Capitol Hill in the late 1990s were measures to end federal affirmative action programs. Opposition to affirmative action also gathered momentum outside of Congress. The federal courts continued to use the doctrine of strict scrutiny as a weapon against color-conscious programs designed to rectify past discrimination. In 1995, the United States Supreme Court struck down a federal procurement program giving preferences to minorities who had historically been denied access to government contracts and the United Court of Appeal for the Fifth Circuit appeared to sound the death knell of affirmative action in higher education, ruling that the University of Texas School of Law could not use race as a factor in determining admissions (*Hopwood v. Texas*). The United States Supreme Court declined to hear an appeal, thus allowing the Fifth Circuit's ruling to stand, and Hopwood gained acceptance in other circuits, suggesting that it was the shape of things to come. Hostility to affirmative action also grew stronger at the grass-roots level. In 1996, Californians passed Proposition 209, which amended the California Constitution, prohibiting the state from granting "preferential treatment to any individual or group on the basis of race, sex, color, ethnicity, or national origins." As voters elsewhere followed California's lead, adopting their own antiaffirmative action measures, it appeared that the days of affirmative action were numbered.

As the nation neared the end of the century, the Indian summer of the Civil Rights movement seemed to be over. The victories of the 1960s were truly monumental achievements, ending the state-imposed segregation and disfranchisement that had for so long made a mockery of the nation's promise of equality. However, centuries of slavery, segregation, and disempowerment had left many African Americans without the education, skills, experience, social connections, and, in some cases, hope to enjoy the fruits of the Civil Rights movement. At the moment the Civil Rights movement broke down legal barriers to African-American advancement, the deindustrialization of the American economy limited economic opportunity for persons without skills and education. Moreover, although it usually took more subtle forms, racism remained a reality of American life. During the 1970s and 1980s, African-American leaders and their white allies attempted to overcome these barriers and realize the promise of the Civil Rights movement. In an unfavorable political climate, they achieved remarkable success, creating some of the tools necessary to remove the obstacles. Yet by the 1990s, a powerful reaction had built, dividing the nation along racial lines, rolling back the modest victories of the 1970s and 1980s, and threatening yet again to deny African Americans the full enjoyment of the civil rights guaranteed to every American.

FOR FURTHER READING

Bell, Derrick. *Faces at the Bottom of the Well: The Permanence of Racism*. New York: Basic Books, 1993.

Belz, Herman. *Equality Transformed: A Quarter-Century of Affirmative Action*. New Brunswick, N.J.: Transaction Publications, 1990.

Davidson, Chandler, and Bernard Grofman. *Quiet Revolution in the South: The Impact of the Voting Rights Act, 1965–1990*. Princeton, N.J.: Princeton University Press, 1994.

Formisano, Ronald P. *Boston against Busing: Race, Class, and Ethnicity in the 1960s and 1970s*. Chapel Hill: University of North Carolina Press, 1991.

Graham, Hugh Davis. *The Civil Rights Era: Origins and Development of a National Policy, 1960–1972*. New York: Oxford University Press, 1990.

Hacker, Andrew. *Two Nations: Black and White, Separate, Hostile, Unequal*. Rev. ed. New York: Ballantine Books, 1995.

Katz, Michael B. *Improving Poor People: The Welfare State, the "Underclass," and Urban Schools as History*. Princeton, N.J.: Princeton University Press, 1997.

Kousser, J. Morgan. *Colorblind Injustice: Minority Voting Rights and the Undoing of the Second Reconstruction*. Chapel Hill: University of North Carolina Press, 1999.

Lawson, Steven F. *In Pursuit of Power: Southern Blacks and Electoral Politics, 1965–1982*. New York: Columbia University Press, 1987.

Nieman, Donald G. *Promises to Keep: African Americans and the Constitutional Order, 1776 to the Present*. New York: Oxford University Press, 1991.

Oliver, Melvin, and Thomas M. Shapiro. *Black Wealth/White Wealth: A New Perspective on Racial Inequality*. New York: Routledge, 1997.

O'Neill, Timothy J. *Bakke and the Politics of Equality*. Middletown, Conn.: Wesleyan University Press, 1985.

Thernstrom, Abigail M. *Whose Votes Count? Affirmative Action and Minority Voting Rights*. Cambridge: Harvard University Press, 1989.

Urofsky, Melvin I. *A Conflict of Rights: The Supreme Court and Affirmative Action*. New York: Scribner's, 1991.

Wilkinson, J. Harvie. *From Brown to Bakke: The Supreme Court and School Integration, 1954–1978*. New York: Oxford University Press, 1981.

chapter 20

The Quest for Black Equity

*African-American Politics
since the Voting Rights Act of 1965*

Lawrence J. Hanks

T HE VOTING RIGHTS ACT OF 1965 was a milestone in the modern struggle for black equality. Its passage paved the way for testing a long-held theory of black power that perceives politics as the path to extensive African-American empowerment. A consequence of black leaders' views since slavery on the attainment of political, social, and economic equity, the theory is derived from four basic assumptions: through continued agitation Americans from Africa would gain access to the ballot; enfranchised, African Americans would elect to public office black officials or other politicians sensitive to their interests; elected officials concerned with black needs would enact progressive public policy; as a result of this policy, the socioeconomic status of the African-American collective would ultimately gain parity with the white majority.

This chapter examines efforts to optimize black political power in America since the Voting Rights Act. From the origins of the theory of black political empowerment, through the impact of the 1965 law on the American political system in the 1990s, I'll examine here recent changes in black political activity, the development of African-American elected officials, the influence of black interest groups, shifting ideologies, and the viability of electoral politics as a strategy to achieve black equity at large.

THE EVOLUTION OF THE THEORY
OF BLACK POLITICAL EMPOWERMENT

A belief in the power of political agency can be traced throughout African-American history. The twenty Africans originally brought to Jamestown in

1619 came not as chattel slaves but as indentured servants. However, with the gradual recognition that success of the colony depended on permanently unfree labor, Virginia's planters increasingly treated black servants as lifetime workers even before laws establishing slavery had been passed. While some Africans in British America acquired free status and property, by 1664 permanent bondage, limited to Africans, had been legalized in six of England's American colonies.

For the first African Americans, the sanctioning of racial slavery provided dramatic testimony of the power of policymakers and furnished the basis of a nascent theory of black political empowerment—the view that if politics can be used as a means of oppression, it could also be used as an instrument of liberation. During the colonial period and after, Americans from Africa appealed repeatedly to lawmakers for the amelioration of the dark race's oppressed condition, most notably through suppression of the slave trade, abolition, and citizenship rights leading to black political empowerment.

An instrumentalist approach to American politics, the belief that political power can be used to achieve specific goals, has dominated black thought throughout U.S. history. Despite despair and doubts at times about legislators' will to enact and enforce progressive race laws, black leaders have generally viewed political participation as the most effective strategy for advancement. This assumption is reflected in the actions of African Americans in the major historical periods following the abolition of slavery in 1865: Reconstruction, 1865–1877; the nadir, 1877–1909; the era of the NAACP, 1909–1954; the Civil Rights movement, 1955–1968; and the struggle for political, social, and economic equity, 1968 to the present.

The era of Reconstruction provided major impetus to the instrumentalist strategy. With the passage of the Thirteenth, Fourteenth, and Fifteenth Amendments to the Constitution, black Americans were formally freed from bondage, granted citizenship, and permitted to vote. In tandem with the disenfranchisement of certain classes of Confederate officials, African Americans gained access to political offices in considerable numbers in the South. The progressive politics black lawmakers pursued aided fellow blacks as well as poor whites. They abolished property requirements for voting, eliminated imprisonment for debt, established statewide public schools, and suspended cruel and unusual punishment such as public whippings.

The political achievements of African Americans, however, proved to be transient. As Thomas Wentworth Higginson, the white abolitionist and officer of a black Civil War regiment noted, "Revolutions May Go Backwards." Even as African Americans were making progress, a series of events were coming together to undermine Reconstruction and return the white Democrats to power in the states of the Confederacy.

White southerners fought fiercely—and often violently—throughout Reconstruction to regain control of state affairs from the blacks, scalawags, and carpetbaggers they felt had gained power. At the same time, by the mid-

1870s, many northerners had grown weary of the intersectional tension caused by Congress's Reconstruction program. The death of Thaddeus Stevens and Charles Sumner, the major leaders of the Radical Republicans, who were the force behind Reconstruction, and a racist backlash that returned control of Congress to the Democrats after the elections of 1874, significantly undermined the progress made by blacks. It was undermined further by a Supreme Court that had grown increasingly hostile to the postwar civil rights legislation and eventually sharply restricted the scope of the Reconstruction amendments. When Republicans reached a compromise with Democrats during the presidential elections of 1876 and agreed to remove federal troops from the South, southern blacks in the South had been essentially abandoned by the rest of the nation.

From 1877–1909, the southern states erected new barriers to black advancement, and virtually all of the gains of Reconstruction were lost. During the 1890s, the Jim Crow system of racial segregation was established throughout the South producing the post–Civil War nadir of the African-American experience. It was in this context of intensified racial oppression that Booker T. Washington, the most influential leader of this period, gained the support of whites nationally by urging blacks to suspend their demands for social and political rights and to focus on economic empowerment.

From the time the National Association for the Advancement of Colored People (NAACP) was founded on Lincoln's birthday, February 12, 1909, to the mid-1950s, the NAACP revitalized black protest activity among African Americans, mainly in the North, and spearheaded the movement in the first half of the twentieth century for black equity. The organization protested against southern segregation and discrimination in the federal government and carried out an ultimately fruitless effort to obtain a national antilynching law. More successful was its vigilant legal fight against discrimination and segregation that reached its culmination with the decision in the school desegregation case of *Brown* v. *The Board of Education of Topeka, Kansas* (1954). Overturning *Plessy* v. *Ferguson* (1896), the court ruled that separate facilities were inherently unequal and thus that segregation was unconstitutional. This ruling set the stage for the post–World War II Civil Rights movement.

Between 1955 and 1968, African Americans fought vigilantly to secure their constitutional rights. The major strategy was utilization of the courts and direct action, specifically the theory of nonviolent protest. Although the views of black nationalists such as Muslim leaders Elijah Muhammad and Malcolm X, the Black Panthers and others affected the outcome of public policy, Martin Luther King Jr. was the decisive black leader and strategist of the era. The key events that produced the restoration of lost ground spanned a decade of intense struggle, beginning with the *Brown* decision of 1954 in which the U.S. Supreme Court undermined the entire system of Jim Crow and placed the federal government in support of the Civil Rights initiatives. Following the Court's ruling, mass mobilization on behalf of black rights escalated with the Montgomery Bus Boycott in December 1955 and continued with the Freedom Rides, sit-ins in numerous southern cities, the March on Washington, the Mississippi Freedom Summer Project, and marches in support of "freedom now" for black citizens all over the nation.

These activities contributed to the enactment of three major pieces of legislation: the Civil Rights Act of 1964; the Voting Rights Act of 1965; and the Fair Housing Act of 1968. The Civil Rights Act hastened into law, aided by the unfortunate assassination of John F. Kennedy, provided African Americans with access to places of public accommodation. The Voting Rights Act, whose passage gained impetus from the brutal police assault of civil rights demonstrators in Selma, Alabama, provided access to the ballot. Finally, the Fair Housing Act, following the murder of Martin Luther King Jr., assured African Americans a legal right to purchase homes in neighborhoods of their choice. Ironically, while by the time of King's assassination African Americans had regained precious political rights they had lost following the Reconstruction, his death brought an end to a major phase of the African-American struggle for equity. Blacks now had the legal rights that had been systematically denied them since the onset of slavery.

As a result of the Voting Rights Act of 1965, for the first time in American history, *all* adult African Americans, males and females in all geographic locations, had the right to the ballot. With the elimination of literacy tests and other disqualifying strategies, registration was the only requirement for voting. For African Americans, the ballot had long been held as the great equalizer but never had there been more systemic opportunities to turn theory into action. The period from 1965 through 1995 would see unprecedented progress in the procurement of black political power, even while many blacks lost ground economically.

AMERICAN POLITICS TRANSFORMED

Since the end of Reconstruction, blacks had been essentially excluded from the political process in the South where white superiority prevailed through law, custom, and force. White politicians there were sensitive to a shared racial prejudice and often sought to outdo their opponents with antiblack diatribes and warnings of the need to prevent black suffrage.

With the passage of the 1965 Voting Rights Act, however, African Americans assumed a permanent place in American politics. Whereas there had been no national black electorate previously, African-American voters now constituted a nationwide political force. A new strategy involving the language of racial moderation and the consideration of black interests emerged. Political pragmatism now dictated that overt racism and manipulation of traditional prejudices were no longer acceptable. In face of the changed political climate, campaign rhetoric would become more civil, genteel, and issue oriented. The South had been transformed from a place where nonparticipant blacks were demeaned to a place where attempts were overtly made to win their votes.

The result, especially in the South, was the gradual shift of the African-American agenda from protest to participation. The Voting Rights Act enabled blacks to elect individuals who would strongly advocate their own interests. While they became powerful "balance-of-power" actors in many areas where they did not have sufficient numbers, blacks dramatically increased their numbers in elective offices, especially in predominantly black areas. While national black registration rose from less than 31 percent in 1965 to approximately 66 percent by 1984, the number of black elected officials rose from approximately five hundred in the early 1970s to more than eight thousand by the early 1900s. African Americans have served as mayors of major cities such as Atlanta, Baltimore, Birmingham, New Orleans, Cleveland, Detroit, New York, Philadelphia, San Francisco, Seattle, Los Angeles, and Washington, D.C. Following the election of 1992, the Congressional Black Caucus was forty strong, with thirty-nine representatives and America's first black female senator, Carol Mosely Braun of Illinois.

Braun's election to the U.S. Senate in 1992 belies the paucity of black officials at the state and national levels where the limits of black politics are most pronounced. There have been no other black senators and L. Douglas Wilder of Virginia, elected governor of Virginia in 1989, has been the only African-American to serve in that office. Of the nation's one hundred senators, only one is African-American. Moreover, despite the rather pronounced increase in participation of blacks at the state and national levels, one can reasonably question the extent of its impact. The Reagan-Bush era revealed that black political power is limited in the face of unified popular white support. When the majority white vote is split fairly evenly between the major parties, however, the black vote tips the balance and in effect selects the winning candidate. (The balance-of-power strategy operates better at the local and state levels where the size of the black minority is more significant.) Even under this scenario, transforming support at the polls into public policy is often challenging.

The passage of the Voting Rights Act of 1965 gave the empowerment theorists the long-awaited opportunity to test their theory that political rights led to policy gains. Now that blacks had access to the ballot, would they be able to elect blacks and other candidates of their choice? The answer is that when blacks possess sufficient numbers, leadership, organization, and resources, they have been fairly successful at gaining political offices. This can be clearly seen when one examines black elected officials at the local, state, and national levels.

A major factor in electing black officials is the percentage of the voting-age population that is black. Local areas, cities, counties, county commission districts, and city council districts have the largest concentration of African Americans, and it is at the local level that you will find the greatest percentage of black elected officials. These officials include mayors, county commissioners, city councilmen, and other municipal and county governing boards.

According to the 1993 volume of the Joint Center for Political and Economic Studies *Roster of Black Elected Officials*, the 5,709 black local officials constitute approximately 70 percent of the 8,015 black elected officials.

State senators and representatives make up the second largest group of black officials. In the period from 1965 to 1992, there has been a dramatic increase in the proportion of black legislators elected to state houses, primarily in southern states. There are now 533 black state officials, approximately 7 percent of the 8,015 black elected officials. During the '70s, approximately 84 percent of the black legislators represented predominantly black districts while the figure increased to 90 percent during the 1980s.

The election of L. Douglas Wilder as governor of Virginia is especially significant. Given the reluctance of whites to support black candidates, his victory was held as a progressive breakthrough although he did not receive a majority of the white vote. As is the case in all of the states, African Americans constituted a minority of the voters in Virginia and could not deliver the election for Wilder on the strength of their votes alone. However, given the strong support in the white community, the black electorate became the balance of power in this historic election.

National representatives and senators constitute the smallest cohort of black elected officials even though, as a result of the 1992 elections, they reached an all-time high. But their capacity to influence national policy makes them arguably the most far-reaching minority voting bloc. Although they have not been uniformly successful, their influence on the Clinton administration has been at times clearly felt, particularly in the question of stabilization in Haiti.

An examination of black elected officials at the local, state, and national levels reveals that the theory of black political empowerment has borne fruit. When leadership, organization, resources, and numbers are present, the black electorate is capable of electing a candidate of their choice. Although areas in the rural black South have the requisite number of black voters, they have generally lacked the leadership, organization, and resources that are required to elect African-American candidates to office. It is also important to note that while blacks comprise approximately 12 percent of the U.S. population, they hold fewer than 2 percent of all elected offices. The election of black officials, however, pushed the theory of black political empowerment to another level. Once African Americans gained a significant number of political offices, they were faced with the task of influencing public policy in such a way that black people as a whole would benefit. It is in this area—the translation of votes and offices into a wide-ranging policy agenda—where the theory of black political empowerment has been found wanting.

BLACK POLITICAL POWER AND PUBLIC POLICY

As they struggled to secure black voting rights, black leaders such as Aaron Henry, Martin Luther King Jr., and Stokely Carmichael predicted that once blacks gained access to the ballot, they would elect black officials who would promote public policies that would eventually raise the collective black socioeconomic status to parity with white socioeconomic status. In fact, the impact of black political participation has been mixed. While there has not been a socioeconomic revolution, the benefits of black political empowerment have been considerable.

One cannot overemphasize the impact in the African-American communities when the first blacks gained elective offices. On the national level, 1967 marked the year when Carl Stokes and Richard Hatcher became the mayors of Cleveland, Ohio, and Gary, Indiana, respectively. By 1970, African Americans had been elected in such numbers that the Congressional Black Caucus was organized. Moreover, as the number of blacks increased at the local level, great pride was taken merely in the symbolic victory of having African Americans in heretofore inaccessible positions of power. However, this novelty would soon wear off, and cries for substantive public policies would be heard.

The material benefits from black political empowerment have indeed been substantial, including greater access to elected officials, a decline in police brutality, additional resources for job training, improvement of municipal water systems, better medical services, more low-income houses, improved basic services, and greater access to government jobs. In brief, most of the benefits of black political power have been in a more equitable share of the benefits distributed by the public sector. But while the distribution of these rewards is far more equitable now, blacks have not been able to make their power felt as effectively in the private sector, business and industry, especially in predominantly black urban areas. As business and industry move to the suburbs, black mayors find themselves crippled by the lack of a tax base that had heretofore been provided by these businesses. From the businesses that remain, black elected officials have generally been less than effective in garnering support for efforts that would benefit the predominantly black residents of the inner city. And efforts to woo businesses back into the city have usually ended in failure.

On the positive side, many black mayors have instituted set-aside programs for major city contracts. Thus, black businesses are guaranteed a minimal proportion of city contracts. Maynard Jackson, the first black mayor of Atlanta, was especially artful with his affirmative action efforts: he threatened to move all city accounts from local white banks unless they developed affirmative action programs, and he held up construction on Hartsfield International Airport, the world's largest, until black contractors were guaranteed a considerable share of the contracts.

Black political power has had a far greater impact in rural areas then in urban ones. Many predominantly underdeveloped black rural areas sorely lacked basic services, and the introduction of street lights, paved roads, water treatment facilities, low-income housing, and more access to public resources were immediate gains. These political plums were taken for granted in urban areas where there was a more urgent need for jobs and other remedies that would chip away at poverty and inequality, but those goals challenged entrenched white interests. As predominantly black rural communities have become more accustomed to the accoutrements of modern living, they are also making more wide-ranging demands on their elected officials.

Although the increased political participation and office holding proved not to be enough to attain the highest hopes of black political empowerment theorists—black socioeconomic parity with whites—a number of developments have taken place that highlight the continued importance of black involvement in political participation. Chief among these developments are the increased political prominence of the Congressional Black Caucus, the black electorate's participation in presidential politics, and the Jesse Jackson presidential candidacies.

The Congressional Black Caucus was organized in 1970 with thirteen members, all representing primarily urban constituencies outside of the South, especially in the Midwest, Northeast, and California. While these officials represented a national voice for black America, they did not wield any appreciable degree of power, and President Reagan's refusal to meet with them is indicative of their lack of bargaining leverage. All of this was to change in the election of 1992, however, when the size of the Congressional Black Caucus doubled from twenty representatives to thirty-nine representatives and one senator. This expansion resulted from the Justice Department's efforts to create predominantly black districts primarily in areas where white racial bloc voting had produced a situation in which blacks faced insurmountable odds in their efforts to get elected to Congress. The redistricting that took place after the 1990 created black majorities who in turn voted for black candidates. These victories moved the Congressional Black Caucus from the status of being "the conscience of the House," primarily using moral suasion, to a voting bloc with the capacity to play hardball politics.

During the Nixon and Carter years, the Congressional Black Caucus did not have the numbers to have a major impact on legislation. During the Reagan and Bush eras, loyal Republican support for the administration was enhanced by conservative "boll weevil" Democrats from the South. As conservative "boll weevil" support weakened under Clinton, the Congressional Black Caucus's bargaining power has grown. With their high degree of solidarity and the current Democratic dissension, the Congressional Black Caucus have proven to be a significant voting bloc, because they have maintained unity on several closely fought pieces of legislation.

PARTY LOYALTIES IN THE PRESIDENTIAL PROCESS

When Republican President Abraham Lincoln issued the Emancipation Proclamation on January 1, 1863, he laid the foundation for loyal black support for his party. Frederick Douglass once said, "The Republican Party is the deck, all else is the sea." Thus the Republican Party garnered the lion's share of the African-American vote until blacks shifted to the Democratic Party in response to Franklin Roosevelt's New Deal legislation. During the Eisenhower years blacks divided their votes rather evenly between the two parties, but since 1964 they have voted in much larger numbers and have given their overwhelming support to the Democratic Party. In fact today they remain the most loyally Democratic element of the electorate.

This trend was encouraged in 1960 when John F. Kennedy made the first overt appeal to black voters, using his influence to secure the release of Martin Luther King Jr. from Georgia's Reidsville State Prison. Rev. Martin Luther King Sr., a powerful figure in his own right, switched his support from Nixon to Kennedy, and millions of other black voters followed. Black voters provided the margin of victory for the Massachusetts Democrat in crucial northeastern precincts, and in return expectations rose concerning his advocacy of civil rights. Once in office, as Kennedy had to concern himself with the southern opposition in the Senate, he deprioritized civil rights to the chagrin of the black electorate. Thus, when the Civil Rights Act of 1964 was passed after Kennedy's assassination in 1963, largely as a tribute to his civil rights leanings, some analysts were prompted to write that he did more for civil rights in death than he did in life.

Lyndon B. Johnson, Kennedy's southern vice president who had initially been opposed by civil rights leaders, received overwhelming support from the black community at the polls when he turned out to be a major advocate of civil rights. Johnson would eventually sign the three most important pieces of major civil rights legislation since Reconstruction: the Civil Rights Act of 1964, the Voting Rights Act of 1965, and the Fair Housing Law of 1968. His War on Poverty programs created a social service structure that greatly benefited poor blacks, while he also signed an omnibus bill that included a mandate for implementing school desegregation. Thus it was apparent that overwhelming support for the Democratic Party was justified, and Johnson's Republican presidential opponent, Barry Goldwater, received less than 10 percent of the black vote in 1964.

The conservative law-and-order campaign of Richard Nixon did not attract an appreciable increase in black support for the Republican Party in the 1968 election. When Gerald Ford ran against Jimmy Carter in 1972, it was the black vote that provided Carter with the winning margin of victory in seven states with a total of 117 electoral votes. Thus expectations were high that Carter would develop programs to help black Americans in their quest for socioeconomic equity inasmuch as they played a crucial role in his election. Nonetheless, given his thin margin of victory, Carter, like Kennedy in 1960, focused on repositioning himself so as to attract more broad-based white support for his administration. Carter eventually set a new ceiling for senior-level black appointees, created the job-training Comprehensive Employment and Training Act (CETA), and passed a diluted version of the Humphrey-Hawkins

Bill, a legislative effort to create more jobs and economic development. While blacks were somewhat disappointed in the degree of Carter's support for black issues, their level of registration increased, and African Americans solidly supported Carter in his losing effort against Ronald Reagan in 1980.

The Reagan-Bush era was a twelve-year period of extreme black frustration with presidential power. Both men had opposed the civil rights legislation of the 1960s and threatened many of the gains that were made at that time. While the popular Republican president promised economic growth that would "trickle down" to the black community, he was more immediate in his efforts to retreat from the enforcement of civil rights laws. Social welfare efforts were reduced; the Equal Opportunity Commission and the U.S. Commission on Civil Rights were filled with appointees who opposed an aggressive civil rights agenda; and courts were packed with conservative federal judges. Moreover, the Justice Department ceased vigorous enforcement of busing orders and affirmative action laws, while the solicitor general argued against their constitutionality before the Supreme Court. Although Bush's rhetoric had a more conciliatory tone, his domestic agenda did not differ enough from Reagan's to convince African Americans to take his promise for a "kinder and gentler America" seriously.

As the black electorate provided Clinton with overwhelming support, the 1992 election was the fourth time since 1960 that the black vote was critical to the Democratic victory. On two of these occasions, 1960 and 1976, black issues were deprioritized to gain white support because of their paper-thin victories. In 1964, issues of civil rights had national support and gained priority status. While Clinton has set a new record for black senior-level appointees, programs that are likely to help the black masses exclusively are probably not forthcoming although African Americans stand to be major beneficiaries of any policies that will help the poor.

This analysis of the black electorate's involvement in presidential politics reveals a dilemma. The black electorate plays a pivotal role in presidential elections only when the white vote is evenly split. While this pivotal role encourages blacks to expect political payoffs, it also creates a political situation for the new president in which white support is not sufficiently strong to sustain a commitment to issues of importance primarily to the black electorate. Alternatively, when African-American voters give monolithic support to the losing candidate, they are ignored. Thus it appears that the black electorate at the national level is powerless in either case. It also appears that black public policy preferences get attention only when they are embraced by a majority of the white electorate. Certainly, this was the case in 1964 when Johnson received more than 60 percent of the vote and went on to sign the major civil rights legislation of the post–World War era.

Within this context, Jesse Jackson's 1984 campaign for the Democratic nomination for the presidency was the first campaign effort of an African-American to be taken seriously. Although Shirley Chisholm had previously sought the nomination of the Democratic Party in 1972, several factors helped to deny her the status of a serious challenger. Chief among them were her shortage of funds and other resources. Moreover, her lack of nationwide name recognition made it difficult for her to overcome opposition from black and feminist leaders. Although her campaign was groundbreaking, she received only 7 percent of the total number of black delegates at the 1972 Democratic Party National Convention.

In 1984 Jackson's campaign was an attempt to gain leverage within the Democratic Party. Jackson generated 3.3 million votes (18 percent of those cast; 77 percent of the African-American voters) and received 384 delegates. Despite the fact that he created new enthusiasm among blacks, he was unable to get the concessions that he sought: to lower the 20 percent threshold needed to get delegates; to end the runoff primary system which splits delegates; and to gain more minority representation on the Mondale campaign staff. Nonetheless, the 1984 campaign had generated newfound interest in political participation for African Americans. Ultimately, the Jackson campaign produced largely symbolic results and revitalized the discussion regarding the ability of political participation to create substantive and measurable change that has an impact upon the socioeconomic status of blacks.

Jackson was not deterred, and his 1988 campaign was more successful. He doubled his primary vote from 3.3 million in 1984 to 6.7 million, receiving approximately 29 percent of the primary vote, and his delegate count of 1,122 nearly tripled his 1984 count. Several factors were responsible for his success: the endorsements of black officials were more numerous and increased his support among blacks from 77 percent to 92 percent; a broader range of issues allowed him to gain 13 percent of the white Democrats; he was not running against an established national Democrat; the threshold for winning had been reduced from 20 percent to 15 percent; and both he and his campaign managers benefited from their previous experience running his campaign.

Jesse Jackson's Speech to the Democratic Convention, 1984

Tonight we come together bound by our faith in a mighty God, with genuine respect for our country, and inheriting the legacy of a great party—a Democratic Party—which is the best hope for redirecting our nation on a more humane, just and peaceful course.

This is not a perfect party. We are not a perfect people. Yet, we are called to a perfect mission: our mission, to feed the hungry, to clothe the naked, to house the homeless, to teach the illiterate, to provide jobs for the jobless, and to choose the human race over the nuclear race.

Source: Thomas A Frazier, ed., *Afro-American History: Primary Sources* (Chicago: Dorsey Press, 1988), pp. 443–44.

Because of his stronger organization and greater success, Jackson was able to win more concessions from the party regarding its platform. The Democrats increased "set-asides" for minority contractors in federal contracts, urged D.C. statehood, and supported same-day voter registration. These concessions, however, did not do much for the status of rank-and-file African Americans. Thus, although there was a good deal of renewed interest in presidential politics in black America with Jackson's candidacy, the black electorates' lack of influence in 1984 and 1988 created a sense of disenchantment even though the black vote was crucial in helping the Democrats keep control of Congress. The two failed Jackson candidacies highlighted the fact that even unprecedented levels of black political participation could not, by themselves, sway a national election.

THE FUTURE OF BLACK POLITICS

After examining the impact of black elected officials at the local, state, and national levels, it becomes clear that the theory of black political empowerment overestimated the power of elected officials, in general, and that of black elected officials, in particular. While political activity is not the predicted panacea for the ills of the black community, it is a resource that has benefited the black community. The battle for equality cannot be fought without an arsenal of political activity and office holding. However, there is a growing understanding that the goal of socioeconomic parity cannot be addressed solely within the confines of electoral politics. Strategies for economic empowerment must be developed independently of the political process, a philosophy that was espoused decades earlier by Booker T. Washington.

Washington publicly argued that African Americans should focus their activities on developing their economic resources and forgo efforts to attain political and social rights. He argued that political and social rights would eventually flow from the acquisition of skills and economic resources. Although this view was the dominant black strategy during his life, it was challenged by W. E. B. DuBois and the NAACP and abandoned upon Washington's death.

DuBois had always challenged Washington's emphasis on economic resources while accommodating whites on the issue of political and social equality. Between 1909 and 1954, he pursued strategies for political and social equality, paving the way for the post–World War II Civil Rights movement. By the 1960s African Americans had gained access to places of public accommodation and to the ballot box. Thus political and social equality had arrived in the legal sense, insofar as the U.S. government no longer sanctioned discrimination. The lack of economic power, however, severely limited the benefits of this political and social victory. Fear of reprisal and economic intimidation continues to keep many blacks from voting; a lack of economic resources continues to hamper the campaigns of black candidates; and a lack of money continues to keep a large majority of blacks from patronizing many places of public accommodation. These factors, coupled with the constraints on black elected officials, have convinced practitioners and scholars that political empowerment is not sufficient to secure economic empowerment.

This conviction has given a new impetus to the black economic empowerment movement. Black leaders, from all points on the political-ideological spectrum are calling for black Americans to develop the economic resources of their community. The new economic empowerment theorists argue that to the extent that African Americans can start to provide jobs for themselves, economic disparity will be lessened. Black consumers, entrepreneurs, and capitalists must develop a group consciousness with respect to economic development, ensuring that "the black dollar" remain in the black community longer than it presently does. While there is appreciation for the role of government in the black political empowerment process, there is a growing consensus that the ultimate answer to black economic inequality must come from within the black community. There is also a growing acceptance that racism, which lies behind many obstacles to political and economic parity, may be a permanent feature of American society.

Racism is a moral and pragmatic problem. It is a moral problem simply because it is wrong to judge individuals based on group membership. These judgments can be choices that some individuals make, and they are protected constitutionally as part of their individual civil liberties. However, the state itself cannot embrace these views. Racism is a pragmatic problem because it keeps African Americans from living the good life—it denies learning and advancement opportunities which provide the foundation for security and happiness. The advocates of black economic empowerment argue that if somehow African Americans could develop their own economic institutions and have the capacity to hire a large segment of the black collective, then racism would cease to be a pragmatic problem. In other words, if African Americans could develop their own institutions, which would meet their human needs, then despite the existence of racism, African Americans could live productive lives. While still supporting strong enforcement of political and social rights, this view de-emphasizes political participation as the major tool of black empowerment.

Thus, the goal of integration at the expense of dissolving black institutions has little credence in the present era. While blacks will continue to demand political access to the mainstream like all other ethnic groups, black pluralism argues that blacks must develop and maintain their own political, social, and economic institutions. Thus, while politics alone cannot increase the socioeconomic status of the black community, it is now believed that political activity supplemented by strong social and economic institutions can. As opposed to expecting socioeconomic conditions to change because of political activity, there will be an increased emphasis on independent movements that will focus on the economic and social condition of African Americans. Hard lessons have been learned, and new strategies are being born.

FOR FURTHER READING

Button, James W. *Blacks and Social Change: Impact of the Civil Rights Movement in Southern Communities*. Princeton, N.J.: Princeton University Press, 1993.

Clay, William L. *Just Permanent Interests: Black Americans in Congress, 1870–1992*. New York: Amistad Press, 1992.

Davidson, Chandler, and Bernard Grofman, eds. *Quiet Revolution in the South: The Impact of the Voting Rights Act, 1965–1990*. Princeton, N.J.: Princeton University Press, 1994.

Hanks, Lawrence J. *The Struggle for Black Political Empowerment in Three Georgia Counties*. Knoxville: University of Tennessee Press, 1987.

Jennings, James. *The Politics of Black Empowerment: The Transformation of Black Activism in Urban America*. Detroit, Mich.: Wayne State University Press, 1992.

Lawson, Steve. *Running for Freedom: Civil Rights and Black Politics in America since 1941*. 2nd ed. New York: McGraw-Hill College Publishers, 1996.

Marable, Manning. *Black Leadership*. New York: Columbia University Press, 1998.

Persons, Georgia A., ed. *Dilemmas of Black Politics: Issues of Leadership and Strategy*. New York: Harper Collins, 1993.

Reed, Adolph L., Jr. *The Jesse Jackson Phenomenon: The Crisis of Purpose in Afro-American Politics*. New Haven, Conn.: Yale University Press, 1986.

Swain, Carol. *Black Faces, Black Interests: The Representation of African Americans in Congress*. Cambridge: Harvard University Press, 1995.

Tate, Katherine. *From Protest to Politics: The New Black Voters in American Elections*. Cambridge: Harvard University Press, 1994.

Walters, Ronald W. *Black Presidential Politics in America: A Strategic Approach*. Albany: State University of New York Press, 1988.

———. and Robert C. Smith, eds. *African American Leadership*. Albany: State University of New York Press, 1999.

chapter 21

Black Internationalism

African Americans and Foreign Policy Activism

William R. Scott

> No other group [African Americans] as a whole should be more sensitive to the aspirations of African peoples for freedom, equality, and recognition, more understanding of the underlying factors of motivation, and more determined that the United States make a significant contribution to Africa's uplifting.
>
> —Charles C. Diggs Jr., June 1959

AFRICA CONSCIOUSNESS, CONNECTIONS, AND CONCERNS

INSPIRED BY STRONG BONDS OF ALLEGIANCE to their ancestral homeland, ethnic groups in the United States have exerted considerable influence on America's policy toward their countries of national origin. From the founding of the American nation to the present, as political theorists observe, immigrants of diverse overseas origins have organized to pressure the U.S. government to pursue foreign policy advantageous to kinfolk abroad. American ethnic groups, states Alexander DeConde, traditionally have operated as special interest lobbyists on foreign policy, often affecting government decisions involving countries with significant numbers of immigrants in the United States. These nationalities would include the Irish, Germans, Jews, and most recently Albanians who have pressed Washington to intervene militarily in the Kosovo crisis to defend ethnic Albanians against Serbian domination. The response of policymakers to ethnic group pressure has varied, but the views of Americans from Europe have consistently influenced aspects of American diplomacy.

Unlike European ethnic groups, African Americans have rarely been a force in the formation of America's relations with Africa, the black motherland. Exclusion until the last quarter of the twentieth century from effective participation in all facets of government produced the preoccupation among American blacks with the attainment of domestic rights long denied them. Constricted constantly by the color line, most severely in the country's southern states, African Americans generally had little reason to be concerned with the conditions of blacks beyond America's borders. In addition, pejorative stereotypes of Africa, pervasive in American society since the Atlantic slave trade, had created a marked resistance to an African identity and interest in African affairs among numerous Americans of African descent. White racism and the rationalization of racial slavery had spawned widespread negative images of Africa and Africans. "These stereotypes," explains Robert Weisbord, "enjoyed wide currency among whites and not infrequently were ingrained in black minds." Africanness became a source of shame to many African Americans constantly subjected to society's racist defamation of Africa and African peoples.

Despite the prevalence of negative perceptions of Africa and Africans among Americans from Africa, there has always been a stratum of American blacks that consciously embraced an African identity and espoused Africa's progress. For instance, blacks in eighteenth-century America preferred the name "African" over the other racial appellations then applied to them, names such as the Portuguese-derived term "negro" that the Iberians and gradually other Europeans imposed on enslaved Africans. It was the designation they commonly gave themselves and their organizations, as witnessed in the Free African Society, the African Methodist Episcopal Church, the African Lodge of Prince Hall Masons, and the African Grove Playhouse. During and after the colonial period, observes Sterling Stuckey, "the term African held pride of place among black leaders in the North, to say nothing of the preferences of the black masses."

Some early proponents of an African identity established programs to promote the welfare of African nations through black emigration, enterprise, and evangelism. Paul Cuffee, the devout Quaker and prosperous Massachusetts trader, proposed a selective Africa return of African Americans. In 1811, the black sea captain and shipbuilder sailed to the West African colony of Sierra Leone, newly formed by British abolitionists as a sanctuary for freed blacks in England, to inspect the prospects there for repatriation. As a Christian, successful entrepreneur, and member of the "African race," Cuffee believed he could convert his benighted brethren from paganism and participation in the slave trade into disciples of the Cross and capitalism. Content with the conditions he found in Sierra Leone, Cuffee returned there four years later, taking largely at his own expense thirty-eight free blacks who settled there and made the British colony their home. The black Yankee planned subsequent ventures in West Africa, but his untimely death in 1817 abruptly ended those undertakings.

Other black men of substance—Daniel Coker, Lott Carey, John Russwurm, Martin Delany, and Henry H. Garnet—also moved by beliefs in black brotherhood, emerged in the antebellum period as prominent advocates of African emigration and generation. A religious leader in Baltimore's black community, Coker aligned himself with the American Colonization Society (ACS), an organization that was formed in 1816 by whites devoted to the wholesale deportation of free blacks to Africa, in the newly formed colony of Liberia. Carey, a Baptist preacher in Richmond, and Russwurm, editor of America's first black newspaper, *Freedom's Journal*, also cooperated with the ACS and settled in Liberia under its sponsorship. Delany and Garnet, on the other hand, dissociated themselves from the society. They independently sought to settle African Americans among the Yoruba in the Niger River valley where they felt blacks could develop their own culture and institutions outside the dominance of white men.

"Pan-Negro nationalism," however, never succeeded in creating a major return to Africa or a persistent contact with African communities. Most articulate northern blacks before the Civil War opposed colonization, insisting that they were no longer Africans but the descendants of Africans. Two centuries of acculturation in America, they argued, had melded them into a new people—Americans from Africa whose appropriate name was "colored American." Africa was the land of their ancestors, but America had become their home. Among free blacks adamantly opposed to white-led repatriation, however, adopting an American nationality and rejecting an African identity did not mean that African Americans had severed all ties with Africa.

Between 1850 and 1900, in the years of Europe's penetration and partition of Africa, a segment of America's Africa-conscious black bourgeoisie began to employ diplomacy as a means of advancing the welfare of overseas Africans. The initial focus of these efforts was the fragile republic of Liberia. Founded in 1822 by freed African Americans repatriated in West Africa by the American Colonization Society, Liberia had been troubled throughout Europe's takeover of the continent by the threat of French and British encroachment. African Americans posted in Monrovia, the Liberian capital, as U.S. emissaries, such as J. Milton Turner, John H. Smyth, and Henry Highland Garnet, struggled to press Washington to protect Liberia's sovereignty from ambitious European powers. As diplomatic scholar Elliott Skinner has written, a critical problem for Liberia's African-American advocates was that the overthrow of Reconstruction had whittled away any political clout U.S. blacks had obtained after the civil war.

By the end of the century, the foreign policy initiatives of African Americans—led by the noted educators Booker T. Washington and W. E. B. DuBois—extended beyond Liberia to the Congo Free State, the Union of South Africa, and Abyssinia in the Horn of Africa. These were areas where African rights had been brutally abused or where valiant armed resistance to European rule continued. Early in the next century, black diplomacy was prominently reflected initially in a series of Pan-African conferences organized by DuBois with other elite blacks from Africa and in the diaspora to ameliorate through congresses and conventions the abuses of colonial rule. The plan of the mass-based Universal Negro Improvement Association (UNIA), led in the 1920s by the charismatic Jamaican immigrant, Marcus Garvey, went beyond practical appeals to reform systems of imperial control. The UNIA's petitions to the Powers, issued from its New York headquarters, sought Africa's full freedom from foreign rule based on the principle of "Africa for the Africans at home and abroad." But all the Garveyites' demands produced was alarm in European capitals that militant African Americans were seeking to subvert white rule over the "dark continent." It would take another devastating world war to actually loosen Europe's grip on its African colonies.

In the mid-1940s, global conflict produced strong currents of internationalism among American black leaders of diverse political doctrines and provided a strong impetus toward anticolonialist agitation. At the center of this activity was a band of black activists led by the actor Paul Robeson and scholars W. E. B. DuBois and Alphaeus Hunton. The group adopted what historian Penny Von Eschen has called "diaspora identities" and coordinated anticolonial actions under the umbrella of the Council on African Affairs (CAA), a black leftist organization with communist connections. The organization operated until the early 1950s when the U.S. attorney general charged that CAA was directed by communists and used its record of solidarity with emergent African liberation groups as proof of sedition.

Following CAA's demise, during the McCarthy era, the politics of the African diaspora was eclipsed by the accent of black leaders, intellectuals, and journalists on "differences between African Americans and Africans rather than on the bonds that had been so forcefully pronounced during and after World War II." But by the advent of the Civil Rights Movement, the actions of African nationalists to free their nations from foreign rule had revived the active interest of U.S. black leaders in anticolonial agitation.

Rarely, however, did African-American ventures into international affairs reflect coordinated cooperation of the black elite and the rank and file. Whatever the issue—whether it was Africa's partition, Belgian atrocities in the Congo, the Anglo-Boer War, African self-determination, Liberian aid, decolonization, or majority rule—action to affect U.S. policy toward Africa was generally limited to Africanists among the black intelligentsia. As Congressman Charles Diggs observed on the eve of sub-Saharan Africa's liberation from colonialism, very few African Americans "below a select leadership" appreciated the important implications of America's relations with Africa. The imposition during slavery of ideas of African inferiority based on an imputed lack of cultural heritage and group achievement, he explained, had trained the black masses to disdain Africa and dismiss America's duty to advance Africa's development.

Only twice in the history of U.S.–Africa relations were Africanists able to organize broad interclass action around America's Africa policies. The first time African Americans organized extensively across class lines to lobby Washington on behalf of an African nation was in 1935, when both the black masses and leadership mobilized around the defense of invaded Ethiopia. It was not until fifty years later, at the height of antiapartheid struggle in South Africa, that similarly large coaction was coordinated to pressure the White House to advance human rights in South Africa. Aside from these two instances of foreign policy activism, American blacks have not organized extensive interclass action on behalf of African causes.

The mass response of African Americans to the Italo-Ethiopian crisis and the mobilization of U.S. blacks against South African apartheid are historic landmarks. In the modern era, the events mark milestones of the reclamation of an African identity among Americans of African ancestry. Both constituted the continuation and consequence of major black nationalist movements, movements with distinctive international dimensions and launched by influential race-first ideologues in the 1920s and 1970s. They also demarcate the extended time it took—from the advent of Garveyism to the aftermath of Black Power—for African Americans to acquire the amount of African awareness and public influence required to affect America's relations with Africa and other parts of the black world.

THE ETHIOPIAN DEFENSE MOVEMENT

Momentous events in the Horn of Africa shortly before Pearl Harbor precipitated the process that would ultimately "Africanize" and internationalize modern black American politics. It was in November 1934 that an Anglo-Ethiopian commission surveying the contested boundary between Ethiopia and Italian-ruled Somaliland found itself faced by a force of Italian colonial soldiers at Walwal, a tiny oasis in the Ogaden desert near the disputed border. The two forces were soon plunged into battle, with casualties suffered on both sides. It was the clash of arms at Walwal that precipitated a major diplomatic crisis between Italy and Ethiopia and provided Benito Mussolini, the Italian premier, with just the excuse he needed for a war to avenge Italy's defeat in battle in Ethiopia in 1896.

Although faced with abject indigence and rampant racism, America's deprived black multitudes were deeply stirred by Italian militarism's threat to the freedom of the East African kingdom of Ethiopia. For two years—through the diplomatic crisis of 1935 that preceded fascist Italy's invasion to Ethiopia's occupation in 1936—sectors of the African-American population struggled to defend and aid the ancient black monarchy ruled by His Majesty Hayle Selasse I. The mass character of the campaign is reflected in the scope and constituency of pro-Ethiopian activism. In their first major foray into foreign affairs, blacks from all geographical regions and socioeconomic backgrounds participated in antifascist activity. In small- and large-scale demonstrations, both spontaneous and organized, aroused sectors of the black privileged and poor prayed, petitioned, and protested for Abyssinian rights, albeit without success.

Pro-Ethiopian activists included an array of elites from the African-American establishment. Leaders of the major civil rights, church, and civic associations actively participated in or contributed to Ethiopian defense actions. Prominent black figures such as the NAACP's Walter White, Adam Clayton Powell Jr., pastor of Harlem's Abyssinian Church, and Mary Church Terrell, an influential figure in the black women's club movement, were ardent champions of Abyssinian justice. So were the distinguished black scholars of the day. The noted historians W. E. B. DuBois, Carter G. Woodson, and Charles Wesley propagandized vigorously in black publications for Ethiopian rights. Leaders outside the black mainstream, such as the heads of the nationalist and socialist associations who stressed the power of mass politics, were also deeply involved in pro-Ethiopian agitation. A. L. King, a principal Garveyite, and the Communist James W. Ford became central figures in the grass-roots mobilization of African Americans around the Ethiopian cause.

African-American secular and spiritual organizations heeded the calls of their leaders and vowed their allegiance to Ethiopia's freedom, on essentially racial grounds. The NAACP, the Urban League, and the National Association for Colored Women published statements supporting Ethiopia's position against Italy. They also lobbied the White House to oppose the territorial encroachment of Ethiopia and urged African Americans to send contributions to Addis Ababa. Varied black church denominations depicted the African kingdom of Ethiopia as an ancient Christian state and declared U.S. blacks were bound by race and faith to aid their Abyssinian brethren.

The African-American press acted similarly. Aware of the news value and racial symbolism of the Ethiopian dispute, black newspaper editors devoted extensive coverage to the Abyssinian crisis. The Pittsburgh *Courier*, the Chicago *Defender*, the California *Eagle*, and other black papers carried scores of pictures, reports, and commentaries on the war. In pro-Ethiopian articles and editorials, leading black journalists such as Roi Ottley and Joel Rogers contended that African Americans had a racial duty not only to defend Ethiopia but also to have an effective voice in policy affecting Negro nations.

At times African-American radicals and racialists worked jointly and with other black grass-roots groups in coalitions such as the Provisional Committee for the Defense of Ethiopia (PCDE). A black united front, the PCDE was headed by Garveyites and communists based in New York. The organization raised funds for Ethiopia's defense, requested the Vatican's intervention in the dispute, and chastised Franklin Roosevelt for America's neutral stand on the Abyssinian crisis before it dissolved in late 1935 and was replaced by support groups formed for war relief—the Friends of Ethiopia, the United Aid for Ethiopia, and the Ethiopian World Federation. These extensions of the PCDE were black-led and mass oriented. Through the dispute, they operated as the spearhead in America of the Abyssinian defense and relief effort.

Underlying most black agitation and mobilization were the sentimental ties of ordinary African Americans with venerable Abyssinia. American blacks generally felt a far greater sense of racial identity with Ethiopia than they felt with the rest of Africa. It was rooted in the tradition of Ethiopianism, which peaked when Tafari Makonnen was crowned as Emperor Hayle Selasse I. Tafari's coronation in 1930 as king of kings implied to African Americans nurtured on Ethiopian symbology that the promised day of global black redemption was imminent. The fascist menace to Ethiopia seemed, therefore, to threaten the last great hope for African salvation everywhere.

Of great import was the relation African Americans perceived between Italian fascism and American racism. The masses of American blacks typically identified neo-Roman imperialism with "Red-neck" racism. They equated the lynchings of blacks in the American South with the slaughter of Africans in Abyssinia. In the South, the parallels were accentuated by the terrorist actions of the Blackshirts, white vigilante groups whose name coincided with the fascist militia that forced Benito Mussolini into power in Rome and led to the bloodbath in Ethiopia.

Black American concern for Ethiopia's freedom had no impact on U.S. foreign policy or on the war's outcome. Appeals of Ethiopianists to the black public for relief funds produced meager results. The efforts of race patriots to enlist in the Ethiopian military were thwarted by U.S. law. And pleas sometimes made with white liberals and leftists to Washington and Geneva for antifascist sanctions were rejected by the Powers. It was the policy of the White House, under great pressure from the powerful isolationist lobby, to avoid involvement in the conflict, and the League of Nations was far more concerned with appeasing Rome than with protecting the safety of a small African nation.

The state of black America in the 1930s impeded black ambitions in foreign affairs. African Americans were wretchedly poor during the Depression years. Furthermore, they were politically impotent. There was only one black in Congress, Arthur B. Mitchell, a Democrat from Illinois. Nowhere, not even in the North where they could freely vote, had blacks obtained political power sufficient to wield influence over government policy, domestic or foreign. They constituted no electoral threat. The only lobbying apparatus at the time was the NAACP which, although committed to Ethiopia's freedom, was naturally preoccupied with domestic rights. The Ethiopian societies had no experience in foreign affairs and no access to policymakers. There were also the problems of general U.S. disinterest in Africa, the "dark continent," and the American public's widely held isolationist outlook. It would take fifty years before Africanists could cultivate a critical Africa constituency among blacks and generate public awareness and pressure around America's Africa policy.

THE FREE SOUTH AFRICA MOVEMENT

The issue that galvanized broad segments of the black community again around foreign affairs was major race conflict in South Africa. Township unrest, sparked by the exclusion of the African majority from the newly created tricameral parliament, erupted in a people's war in 1984 against the apartheid state. The insurgency was widely covered in the foreign press as was the Italo-Ethiopian War many years earlier. Until official bans were placed on the media, reports of the rebellion and repression in South Africa, especially televised images of the unrest, brought the issue of apartheid into the homes of most African Americans. The press reports of the battle inside South Africa inspired and incensed American blacks. The news of black repression and resistance pushed black American emotions to almost a fever pitch, producing widespread demands for punitive measures against South Africa. In the 1930s, reports from the press, radio, and newsreels of Ethiopian valor and the ruthless Italian assault had essentially the same effect on black Americans.

American blacks first became conscious of South Africa at the same time they became aware of modern Ethiopia. Their knowledge of the people and polities at Africa's southern extremity dates from the end of the last century when Reverend Magena Makone, the leader of an "Ethiopianist" secessionist movement from the Wesleyan Church, came to the United States to affiliate the native sect with the African Methodist Episcopal Church. The ensuing associations that the black preacher from Pretoria formed between South Africans in the church independency movement and African Americans in the AME denomination during the era of expanding race segregation extended into the new century.

The formation of these transatlantic ties coincided with wars in Ethiopia and South Africa. An event covered extensively in African-American newspapers, the Ethiopian conflict of 1896 ended in the defeat of an invading Italian army at Adwa, raising hopes of black freedom everywhere and symbolizing ascendant black power globally. British might prevailed over Afrikaner nationalism in the other conflict, the Anglo-Boer War—the so-called "white man's war." The victory in South Africa of a British expeditionary force over Boer soldiers also lifted black hopes around the world. But the conciliatory peace the Crown made with the Boer generals at Vereeniging paved the way for the decline of black rights in South Africa. After creation of the country's new political union, its race policies increasingly resembled segregation in America's new South.

It was not until about a century later that white supremacy in South Africa became a priority of the African-American public and politicians. Through the decades of disfranchisement and dispossession that followed the Anglo-Boer War and preceded the Nationalist Party's election victory of 1948, American blacks attentive to African affairs sympathized with oppressed blacks in South Africa. But black leaders imbued with the "romance of Africa," such as Paul Robeson, chairman of the Council on African Affairs, America's leading Africanist organization at the time of the triumph of Afrikaner nationalism, were unable to generate serious opposition to expanding white power overseas. African Americans, with the exception of the council's members, rarely linked the black American struggle with African liberation. Even after the imposition of apartheid rule, South Africa remained a remote issue for most American blacks, who were becoming increasingly absorbed in the mounting domestic struggle for racial equality.

From the Eisenhower to the Kennedy administrations, apartheid was mainly the concern of the predominantly white American Committee on Africa, a private policy-oriented group formed in 1953. In the 1960s, however, the decade of African decolonization, notions of common cause with African nations expanded among African Americans. Martin Luther King Jr., and other members of the civil rights establishment showed through the American Negro Leadership Conference (ANCL), a coalition of the Negro vanguard, heightened interest in African affairs, including South Africa. They issued affirmations of African kinship, urging African Americans to identify with black liberation movements overseas, and appealed to the Kennedy and Johnson administrations to associate America with the aspirations of Africans under apartheid. These actions advanced awareness among African Americans of their African ancestry and America's adoption of a South African arms embargo. Even so, at the time of Dr. King's murder in Memphis in 1968 most U.S. blacks still remained disinterested in white supremacy in faraway Africa.

The gospel of black separatism, as preached by the Black Muslim Malcolm X and later popularized by Black Power ideologues such as the grass-roots activist Stokely Carmichael and the radical poet LeRoi Jones, produced a wave of Afrocentric sentiments and styles in the 1970s. A pan-African ethos surged through black communities inspiring popular conceptions of global black identity and unity. Just as Ethiopianists had drawn from the Garveyite philosophy to generate pro-Abyssinian activism, militant and moderate black organizations were inspired by neonationalist ideas in the civil rights aftermath to advance assorted African support action. The Congress of African Peoples, the National Black Political Convention, and the Congressional Black Caucus were among the varied black interest groups that sponsored pro-Africa resolutions and rallies signaling to Washington expanding African-American support of African causes and of action to affect America's Africa policies.

But it would take another decade, after the Nixon, Ford, and Carter administrations, before apartheid would become a central concern of African Americans. It was only when brutal white repression of the black revolt in South Africa revealed the depth of African despair and President Reagan responded to the escalating crisis with a policy of "constructive engagement" with the government of P. W. Botha, whose intent was to reform white politics but retain at all costs white power, that numerous U.S. blacks were finally moved to antiapartheid action. It had taken almost forty years—after the Sophiatown removals, the Sharpeville shootings, and the Soweto uprisings—before American blacks had embraced South Africa as a cause célèbre and assumed a vanguard role in the American antiapartheid movement.

Black denunciation of Italian aggression in Ethiopia had been mainly a protest of white abuse of black rights. It also represented dissent with American foreign and public policy pertaining to Africans and African Americans. The reasons for black American mobilization around South Africa were similar. In the 1980s, African Americans also organized against external and inter-

nal black subjugation. Antiapartheid activism was inspired by Afrikaner persecution of Africans and by American policy that was perceived to prevent black
liberty abroad and black dignity at home.

The reelection in 1984 of Ronald Reagan, a longtime leader of Republican
conservatives, who had won the presidency four years earlier in a landslide
victory, caused civil rights leaders grave concern. Black rights advocates feared
that the agenda of the conservative coalition the president headed was to
reverse the civil rights gains of the 1970s. They complained that the president,
in his first term in office, had "retreated from well established bipartisan civil
rights policies." The Civil Rights Task Force of the Washington Council of
Lawyers claimed that the Reagan administration had failed to implement
cohesive and consistent civil rights policies. In its opinion, the president had
even encouraged resistance to further black progress. Moreover, there was evidence that he was insensitive to the problems of minorities and the poor,
aggravated in the recession of the early 1980s by spiraling inflation and
soaring unemployment. The economic recovery plan of the Reagan administration featured major federal cuts of social programs for the poor at a time
when life for disadvantaged Americans sometimes resembled conditions in the
dark days of the Depression. The result was widespread alienation from
the White House—an estrangement that had not been so strongly experienced and expressed since the Nixon years when the White House had
retreated from vigorous enforcement of civil rights policy set by the Lyndon
Johnson administration.

Black estrangement was underscored by White House policies on South
Africa. To many articulate African Americans, the administration's view that it
could best promote change by cooperating with the white oligarchy and by
retaining trade with Pretoria represented complicity in white minority rule
and indifference to legitimate black aspirations. Also, the increase in the
regime's aggressive and repressive security activity in black townships seemed
to have been a consequence of Washington's permissive policy. Black leaders
charged that, expecting no criticism from the United States, Pretoria had acted
with "draconian impunity." America had sent wrong signals to the apartheid
state and the world. Constructive engagement with the Afrikaner minority and
containment of communism among radicals in the African majority disparaged
black rights and defended white privilege. U.S. policy toward South Africa, it
was contended, revealed the oval office's cold-war philosophy and preference
for white over black power.

There was no specific incident that initiated pro-Ethiopian activism. Black
antifascist action evolved in response to each act of Italian aggression taken
after the skirmish at Walwal in 1934 and culminated with broad protests
against the actual invasion several months later. There was, however, a particular event that ignited extensive antiapartheid action. It was the demonstrations launched in 1984 on Thanksgiving eve at the South African Embassy in
Washington, D.C. The arrests, a sophisticated media ploy, of three noted

African Americans—D.C. Congressman Walter Fauntroy, Mary Frances Berry of the Civil Rights Commission, and Randall Robinson, executive director of TransAfrica, the black lobby for Africa and the Caribbean—sparked a national campaign against apartheid and U.S. policy known as the Free South Africa Movement (FSAM).

Within a week public demonstrations against South African consulates, Krugerrand coin dealers, and corporations tied to South Africa spread throughout the nation under the banner of FSAM, which became a national multiracial front against apartheid under essentially black leadership. Every state, major religious denomination, ethnic group, and occupation was represented in the new coalition. For two years and in more than forty U.S. cities, operating mainly within the FSAM structure, ordinary blacks and professionals marched, rallied, sat-in, picketed, and petitioned for justice in South Africa. Other blacks unattached to the alliance, such as student advocates of university divestment from American companies operating in South Africa, aided its aims through independent antiapartheid action. By the end of 1985 a mass Free South Africa Movement had emerged involving large-scale coordinated, and spontaneous action on the part of thousands of Americans, black and white, across the country. Turmoil in South Africa and tolerance in the White House of the domination and disadvantage of blacks there and at home had finally catalyzed African Americans into widespread protests against apartheid and administration policy.

FSAM drew a black constituency that reflected elements active in the pro-Ethiopian movement. It attracted support from the black bourgeoisie and rank and file. Trade unionists, office workers, religious forces, student groups, scholar activists, and civil rights leaders responded to its calls to protest South African racism and U.S. policy. In addition, but in contrast to the 1930s when there was no black politician of national prominence, FSAM derived support from the constituency formed by Jesse Jackson in his run in 1984 for the presidency. The broad organization in the multiracial Rainbow Coalition of blacks around Jackson's candidacy, which highlighted the issue of apartheid, constituted a bridge to mobilization against apartheid.

Through the enforcement of the Voting Rights Act of 1965, African-American politicians had won election by the mid-1980s to a critical number of seats in local, state, and national legislative assemblies, including the U.S. House of Representatives. In 1985, black elected officials numbered about six thousand. The Congressional Black Caucus, formed in 1969 to build power through collective voting, had grown from its original sixteen members to twenty. Because of their increased numbers at various levels of government, African Americans now had expanded bureaucratic access to policymakers and enhanced means, albeit still limited, to affect American foreign policy.

It was the Black Caucus that carried popular antiapartheid agitation from the streets and campuses of America into the halls of Congress. In 1985, a leading member of the caucus, Representative Ronald Dellums of California, introduced legislation in Congress to end most U.S. trade with South Africa. Although defeated in the Senate, after having passed the House of Representatives, the Dellums Bill publicized and propelled FSAM's push for comprehensive sanctions against the apartheid state.

African Americans from the arts, entertainment, and sports participated in FSAM actions. This was a stratum of black society that had taken no prominent part in the Ethiopian campaign. The voices of black celebrities were rarely heard in the outcry against fascist aggression—muted in the Depression by personal, professional, and political considerations. Prominent athletes and artists felt sufficiently secure to speak out, however, against apartheid and American policy. Arthur Ashe, Harry Belafonte, Dick Gregory, Stevie Wonder, and Alfre Woodward, who portrayed Winnie Mandela on film, were among the many African-American personalities who helped publicize the free South Africa campaign.

The main factor motivating black antiapartheid activism was the perception of the affinity of struggle in South Africa with the battle for black American rights and protection of the law against white violence. For many African Americans, South Africa was a clear-cut case of racist immorality and white complicity that extended to the White House. Apartheid-rule represented an overseas version of Jim Crow that the conservative powers in Washington supported. The persistence of exclusive white power in South Africa was perceived as unfinished business in the continuing struggle of American blacks against white supremacy.

This was also the case in the 1930s, when black Americans equated fascist aggression in Africa with white terrorism in America's "tar and feather belt." African Americans in the 1980s viewed apartheid from the perspective of their own history of race oppression. It had only been twenty years since Birmingham and Selma. Many could personally remember the humiliation of segregation and readily recognized in the vivid television scenes of police brutality connections between Afrikaner apartheid and the American caste system of Jim Crow.

The black elite at the forefront of the antiapartheid movement made much of the connection and the common experiences of blacks under lynch law and minority domination. Randall Robinson argued that U.S. blacks were uniquely concerned about America's reaction to apartheid. One reason was that African Americans were bound to Africa by race and heritage. Another was that they had acquired through their own struggle for racial equality a frame of reference for empathetically understanding the pain of black South Africans.

Another element present in both the 1930s and 1980s was the perception of charismatic leadership of African resistance to racist domination. Nelson Mandela had been lionized as the heroic icon of the black freedom struggle, not only in South Africa but also worldwide. The jailed leader of the banned

African National Congress epitomized the long battle against apartheid and racism in general. Mandela's stature among African Americans, heightened by his long years of principled opposition to white domination, matched in many ways an earlier generation's reverence of Hayle Selasse. In the Depression era, Ethiopia's king represented the figurehead of global African redemption. In contemporary times, the Xhosa patrician Nelson Mandela became the world's preeminent symbol of race emancipation. According to Howard University professor Ronald Walters, the vast majority of African Americans marveled at Mandela's integrity and his consistency in the long pursuit of democracy in South Africa.

A similar stimulus to African-American identification with the South African struggle was the significance black Americans attached to South Africa. A free Azania, the preferred name of black nationalists for South Africa, symbolized the black race's new Zion, its new promised land. Before, Abyssinia represented Africans' last great hope for race resurgence. South Africa, a country of vast wealth, the continent's most industrialized nation, constituted revived hope in Africa's global renascence. It signified for contemporary American blacks a potential center of worldwide black power, the place where, as the South African sociologist Mamphela Ramphele has commented, African Americans felt they might come to win battles and gain opportunities they had given up for lost in the United States.

There are other relevant parallels. African Americans were acutely conscious in the 1980s of a positive African identity. The rise of Black Power after the Civil Rights movement effectively advanced identification with Africa. This had been true of the African heritage movement led by Marcus Garvey in the years preceding the Ethiopian crisis. The modern Africanist spirit, evidenced in the philosophy of the martyred Malcolm X, remained a potent force through the '70s and '80s. Advanced by Maulana Karenga and other cultural nationalists devoted to the recovery of an African identity and aided by the emergence of the Black Studies movement in the American academy, it inspired black and white collegians to explore and embrace the aspirations of the African world—from Selma to as far away as Soweto. Because of the black revolution of the '70s, African Americans had become especially aware of their links to Africa.

There were also critical differences between the 1930s and 1980s. The passions of Ethiopian patriots ran deeper than the emotions of modern Africanists. So intense were antifascist and pro-Abyssinian sentiments that riots erupted between African and Italian Americans. There were also violent clashes with police in New York City and its environs. The distinctly radical and racialist dimension of Ethiopian activism encompassed the extensive, although failed, recruitment of black combat troops for service in Ethiopia. FSAM's antiapartheid activism was mainstream, moderate, and multiracial. Civil disobedience was its most militant form of protest, which made the movement easy to support in liberal circles.

No persistent or permanent black lobby for African causes existed during the Depression. The black world had no voice at the time on Capitol Hill. The pro-Ethiopian societies were ad hoc groups organized to halt Italian militarism or provide Ethiopian medical relief. They also operated out of Harlem, the focus of Ethiopian activism, instead of Washington—the center of national power and diplomacy. The organizational base of the Ethiopian aid societies was mainly an impoverished black rank and file, and their mostly black nationalist or socialist leadership had no access to the nation's power structure.

Conceived at an African-American leadership conference held by the Congressional Black Caucus, TransAfrica was organized in 1977 as a permanent organization with funding from liberal religious groups and the Ford Foundation. Its main constituency was the black middle and upper classes which by the 1980s had gained substantial affluence and access to the nation's power centers. The economic and political power gained by African Americans by the time of South African crisis contrasted sharply with the desperate plight of blacks during the Ethiopian War. The educational, economic, and political empowerment in the post–Civil Rights era of a critical mass of African Americans who were prepared to work as partners with whites explains much of the success of the antiapartheid movement.

The White House and Congress had become especially sensitive by late 1985 to the strong opposition of the U.S. public, black and white, to apartheid rule and American policy. Faced with South Africa's defiant rejection of calls for change and foreign banks' suspension of credit to Pretoria, President Reagan issued an executive order in September placing limited trade and financial sanctions against Pretoria in an unsuccessful move to preempt stronger measures by Congress. In response to the intransigence of the South African government and the wave of FSAM protests, Congress, with the support of liberal Republicans, overrode a presidential veto and passed in October 1986 the Comprehensive Anti-Apartheid Act, which imposed strident selective sanctions against South Africa. For the first time, African Americans had played a major part in shaping U.S. policy toward Africa. And, for the first time, African Americans had shown that they comprised a potentially powerful foreign-policy constituency.

FSAM constituted the kind of interracial network the Ethiopianists were never able to organize. Strong impulses toward white racism and black nationalism prevented the formation of a broad coalition of Ethiopian support groups with a black organization at the vanguard. FSAM was a classic example of how interracial but decentralized coaction could be successfully coordinated around foreign-policy issues. The movement also demonstrated the importance of interracial struggle. As was the case with the Civil Rights movement, liberal white allies played an integral role in the Free South Africa Movement. The alliance's success showed as well how basic American values, such as human rights and majority rule, could be effectively used to affect liberal and even conservative public opinion.

THE FUTURE OF MASS FOREIGN AFFAIRS ACTIVISM

The broad organization of African Americans against fascist aggression and racist rule during severe economic depression and recession pose important tactical questions for Africanists inspired to galvanize U.S. blacks in the interest of future African causes. For instance, how likely is it that broad action can be generated around other Africa crises and policy disputes? What is the probability, when officials reject the policy preferences of African Americans, that mass pressure can be organized to influence policymakers? Should pro-Africa lobbies, when all else has failed, be sanguine about possibilities of mobilizing the African-American elite and masses in public protest?

Black politics in the United States has now been sufficiently internationalized to ensure continued concern, in the future, for the welfare of overseas black communities. As Francis Kornegay, a Washington expert on African affairs, has stated, the black American connection with Africa has come into its own as a permanent asset and influence in U.S.–Africa relations. The linkage has increased in importance since the reemergence of pan-African consciousness among key sectors of the African-American population in the late 1960s and will doubtlessly contribute to efforts to ensure that "Africa is more than an after-thought on the U.S. foreign policy agenda." However, mass mobilization of African Americans around African issues, whether in autonomous or in cooperative action with allied groups, seems unlikely.

The critical force generating mass black activism around Italian fascism and South African apartheid was white supremacy. It was the the parallel African Americans saw between expressions of white racism in Africa and in America that captured the minds of African Americans and motivated their protests. It was mainly the extraordinary power that race exerted on African-American attitudes that moved blacks in the United States to confront imperialism in Ethiopia and racism in South Africa. In the case of apartheid, notes journalist Okey Nibe, South Africa's racist philosophy and practice struck a raw nerve among people who had made considerable strides toward racial equality but were themselves just emerging from the depths of racial segregation and discrimination. Because of its affinity with white supremacy in modern America, apartheid represented a deeply resented moral and psychic affront that black Americans felt compelled to attack.

Nonracialism has officially defeated racialism in South Africa. Apartheid has now been repealed. Two Africans, Nelson Mandela and Thabo Mbeki, have been elected to the state presidency. And settler domination has been abolished throughout Africa, but with the end of white supremacy on the African continent, the emotive relation between racism in America and in Africa, the relation that Trans-Africanists and Ethiopianists exploited to organize broad pro-African action, has ceased to exist. Crises caused by conflict across the color line are not now as likely anywhere in Africa as are catastrophes caused by poverty, famine, ethnic antagonisms, and civil war. However,

African destitution and devastation—sometimes involving the loss of millions of lives—seemingly lack the power to provoke African-American passions and protests in ways that racial suppression has.

The tragedy in Rwanda of 1994 is telling. With the exception of elite blacks in the Congressional Black Caucus, TransAfrica, and other Africanist organizations, the bulk of American blacks were publicly silent about the mass murder of Africans by Africans. In sharp contrast to the strong reaction of African Americans to Afrikaner racism, no public demonstrations were mounted by black special interest groups to protest the massacre or pressure U.S. policymakers to prevent the human rights disaster in Rwanda. The destruction in three weeks of a million Tutsis and moderate Hutus by extremist Hutus in the Rwandan military and militia may have appalled—but prompted no major action from—African Americans. Rwandan genocide, one of the great human rights disasters of modern time, produced no considerable outpouring of concern from American blacks, in particular, or from Americans in general.

Black inaction on the Rwandan crisis underscores the point that pro-Africa mobilization has only occurred during crises involving major interracial conflict, crises that coincided in critical ways with the racial suppression of African Americans. It has only been where racial strife in Africa has produced potent parallels with racist practices in modern America—practices such as segregation, police violence, and lynching—that African Americans have been aroused en masse. The implication of the fact that black mobilization has depended on the recognition of commonalities between the domestic and foreign struggles of African people against racist rule is that, in the postapartheid era, Africanists will be hard-pressed to mount broad solidarity action in support of African causes.

Whether they view mass mobilization as the ultimate pressure tactic or as a strategy of last resort, Africanists will have to discern and deploy powerful inducements other than antiracism to arouse elite and grass-roots African Americans to concerted action. Their success in organizing massive foreign policy activism around African issues will depend on how well Africanists employ the expanding Afrocentric tendencies of African Americans and demonstrate that people of African descent have a political part to play in Africa's salvation beyond the substitution of white dominance with black governance.

FOR FURTHER READING

Campbell, James T. *Songs of Zion: The African Methodist Episcopal Church in the United States and South Africa*. Chapel Hill: University of North Carolina Press, 1998.

DeConde, Alexander. *Ethnicity, Race and American Foreign Policy*. Boston: Northeastern University Press, 1995.

Frederickson, George M. *Black Liberation: A Comparative History of Black Ideologies in the United States and South Africa*. New York: Oxford University Press, 1996.

Gordon, David F., David C. Miller, and Howard Wolpe. *The United States and Africa: A Post–Cold War Perspective*. New York: W. W. Norton & Co., 1998.

Harris, Joseph E. *African-American Reactions to the War in Ethiopia, 1936–1941*. Baton Rouge: Louisiana State University Press, 1994.

Love, Janice. *The U.S. Anti-Apartheid Movement: Local Activism in Global Politics*. Westport, Conn.: Praeger Press, 1985.

Magubane, Bernard M. *Ties that Bind: African American Consciousness of Africa*. Trenton, N.J.: Africa World Press, 1988.

Plummer, Brenda Gayle. *Rising Wind: Black Americans and U.S. Foreign Affairs, 1935–1960*. Chapel Hill: University of North Carolina Press, 1996.

Scott, William R. *The Sons of Sheba's Race: African Americans and the Italo-Ethiopian War*. Bloomington: Indiana University Press, 1993.

Von Eschen, Penny. *Race against Empire: Black Americans and Anti-colonialism, 1937–1957*. Ithaca, N.Y.: Cornell University Press, 1997

Walters, Ronald W. *Pan-Africanism in the African Diaspora: An Analysis of Modern Afrocentric Political Movements*. 2nd ed. Detroit, Mich.: Wayne State University Press, 1995.

The Future
of African Americans

Charles V. Hamilton

I T IS SAFE TO SAY THAT THERE HAS NOT BEEN A TIME in the struggle of African Americans in the United States when the strategies and
tactics of that struggle have not been intensely debated. While most
fair-minded persons, blacks and whites, could agree that the general goal of
improvement of the condition of blacks was the goal, there have been many
different views on precisely how to bring that about. This perennial debate
predates the Civil War, gained increased attention after emancipation, accelerated during the era of the New Deal, leaped to absolute prominence at the
height of the Civil Rights movement in the 1960s, and is still of immediate
concern in the 1990s and beyond. It is reasonable to expect the discussion to
continue into the future.

Always, the debate centers on *what* policy to concentrate on (broadly
described universal economic development in which everyone would share or
specific race-oriented advancement for blacks), or on *how* to pursue those
goals (protest action, litigation, electoral politics, even emigration). At times,
the debates become condensed to rather simplistic dichotomies such as race
versus class, integrationist alliances versus nationalist mobilization.

This discussion of the future of African Americans will suggest that
although the issues are not new, the coming years will present an environment
where both the goals of the struggle *and* the strategies pursued need not be in
conflict, but, indeed, may be seen as complementary. In fact, one might argue
that the debates in the past have been exaggerated and that there has always
been room for different emphases and multiple strategies. But certainly, as we
move toward the twenty-first century, the complementarity of goals and
strategies will be even more manifest. Neither should one be surprised to find

that while other groups (namely, European ethnic immigrants) have faced similar intracommunal debates, these issues, for various historical and racial reasons, have been most public and persistent among and about African Americans. Whatever the current state of political-civic concern for other groups (ethnic groups, women, gays and lesbians, the disabled), the fact is that when one refers to America's "dilemma," the historical reference is to race and African Americans in American society. It has been the struggle of blacks that has fueled the long concern over interpretation of the Constitution's Civil War amendments. It has been the traditional black-oriented Civil Rights movement that has served as a catalyst to other groups to seek civil rights protections for themselves.

Thus, in many ways, the African-American struggle has been in the vanguard of transforming the United States from a parochial, closed, castelike society to a more open, egalitarian one. It has been that struggle that has, in the realm of citizenship and human relations, been the critical barometer to measure the country's commitment and capacity to achieve a viable democratic polity. Therefore, in a precise sense, a discussion about the future of African Americans is a discussion about the future of the United States of America.

In the closing years of the 1990s, as we watched dramatic changes in a post–cold war world, our attention understandably was turned to such foreign locales as Eastern Europe, the former Soviet Union, the Middle East, and South Africa. But the thrust of this afterword is that the United States is faced no less urgently with its own internal challenges of adapting to a new era.

THE DUAL AGENDA

Going back only to the 1930s, there seems to have been no annual conference of the National Association for the Advancement of Colored People (NAACP) where at least one speaker did not admonish the black delegates to be sure to concern themselves not only with the plight of African Americans but with that of "all" Americans. The refrain became a familiar one: granted, blacks faced serious problems of racial segregation and discrimination, but in economic terms, they were more likely to advance if they thought and acted in concert with the majority society, irrespective of race. A rather typical observation is found in the address in 1933 by Dr. Paul H. Douglas (future senator from Illinois, and then a professor of economics at the University of Chicago):

> As I see it, Negroes face two sets of problems—one set of problems peculiar to themselves, and one set of problems they face in common with all mankind. . . . When you think of the Negro race and how we can benefit them, we must think how we can benefit them as poor farmers and as poor wage-earners. . . . I believe the reconciliation of the Negro and white races . . . is going to come through our being partners in a common enterprise; and so I say to you as a friend, along with all the noble work which you are doing to protect your position as Negroes do something also to protect your position as common members of the human race.

It was not as if such admonitions were falling on deaf ears or were not heeded by civil rights organizations. In fact, historical records amply reveal that the NAACP and the National Urban League (NUL), two of the oldest and largest groups formed to assist blacks, spent more than a small amount of time specifically attempting to push *both* a civil rights agenda that would protect blacks from racial abuses and a broader social welfare agenda that would provide economic security and development for everyone. On more than a few occasions, the NAACP had to remind others that it was indeed mindful of and active in both arenas. When an Ohio congressman misread a letter sent to him from Walter White of the NAACP in 1937, White responded laconically, "My letter to you of October 21 was not about the anti-lynching bill but regarding the passage of a nondiscriminatory wages and hours bill at the next session of Congress. I am not surprised that you assumed that my communication had reference to the anti-lynching bill since that has been the subject of our correspondence for so long a time. But you can see from my letter of the twenty-first that after all I can write about other matters."

This concern for "other matters," that is, broader socioeconomic issues in addition to civil rights, has characterized the position of many African-American organizations over the decades. They have always understood the necessity to pursue what can best be described as a dual agenda. Thus, they supported proposed full employment legislation in the 1940s even though no attention in the proposed bill was paid to racial discrimination in employment. Similarly, they agreed *not* to link civil rights demands to their support for progressive legislation on health, education, and housing.

For a time in the 1950s, however, the patience of African-American organizations ran out, and the strategy of subordinating civil rights to broader liberal social legislation was changed. The NAACP vigorously supported the so-called "Powell Amendment" (named after the sponsor, Congressman Adam Clayton Powell Jr., of Harlem, New York) proposing that no federal funds should be appropriated to any institution, agency, or local or state government that practiced racial segregation and discrimination. This caused an intense debate within liberal, progressive circles, with blacks and whites lining up on both sides. The liberal opponents of the amendment argued that such a provision would lose votes for the broader social legislation because southern democrats and northern conservatives would reject the attempt to enforce civil rights protections in such a manner. The proponents, on the other hand, insisted that both goals—liberal social legislation *and* protection of civil rights—should be combined and pursued simultaneously. To do otherwise, they argued, would reinforce the old "separate but equal" doctrine, which the Supreme Court was already declaring unconstitutional in the historic school desegregation cases.

Finally, in 1964, with the passage of Title VI of the Civil Rights Act outlawing segregation, the two agendas were no longer theoretically in conflict. After that point, the civil rights groups pursued the two agendas in a complementary, not oppositional, manner. They supported measures to end de jure segregation and discrimination, while at the same time pushing for liberal, progressive legislation on socioeconomic issues: the antipoverty programs of the 1960s and 1970s; an expanded version of the proposed Family Assistance Plan of the early 1970s; a meaningful Humphrey-Hawkins bill for full employment; adequate aid to urban areas. All these measures were seen as applicable not only to African Americans but also to all Americans.

And yet, critics of the civil rights groups persisted into the 1990s in claiming that such organizations were overlooking economic issues or were narrowly focused on racial discrimination and racism. These charges came from both blacks and whites, and from conservatives and liberals. African-American columnist William Raspberry pointedly chastised civil rights advocates in 1991 for putting so much effort into passage of a civil rights bill that focused on the means of establishing proof of racial and gender discrimination in employment. To be sure, the bill should be passed, but, he and others wondered, would it really deal with the immense problems of joblessness, family dissolution, crime, drugs, and "the economic marginality of our people." He concluded, "The Civil Rights Act of '91 won't do a blessed thing about these problems." What was needed was to put priority on the economic issues, and this, in turn, would probably avoid aggravating racial tensions sure to result from race-specific remedies.

Similarly, sociologist William Julius Wilson wrote in 1987: "Politicians and civil rights organizations . . . ought to shift or expand their definition of America's racial problems and broaden the scope of suggested policy programs to address them. They should, of course, continue to fight for an end to racial discrimination. But they must also recognize that poor minorities are profoundly affected by problems in America that go beyond racial considerations."

Countering such sentiments was a statement in 1991 by the president of the National Urban League, John E. Jacob, that was laced with a frustration and pique reminiscent of Walter White's letter. Responding to an article in the *New York Times* that suggested lack of adequate attention by civil rights groups to economic issues, Jacob wrote:

> Those who accuse civil rights groups of ignoring the crucial economic problems of African Americans or who condemn them for not transcending black concerns, conveniently choose to ignore the National Urban League's Urban Marshall Plan proposal. . . . We object to articles that misinform the public into believing that civil rights and social problems represent an either/or choice for the Civil Rights movement. Both need to be pursued and both are being vigorously pursued.

One might ask, in the face of clear evidence to the contrary, why the critics of civil rights groups continue raising the issue of failure or at least reticence on the part of black civil rights groups to address economic problems. The answer very likely lies, paradoxically, in the record of success of those groups on the agenda of civil rights, per se, but the persistent and increasing economic problems of large numbers of blacks in terms of the social welfare agenda. There is no denying that a vibrant Civil Rights movement in the United States has achieved enormous victories overcoming de jure racial segregation and, especially, obtaining the right to vote over discriminatory racial denials of the franchise. This is, indeed, a success story. But economic conditions of blacks have only improved substantially for some and have deteriorated for many others.

The conclusion, however, that this situation results from earlier inattention to economic problems is unwarranted. African Americans accomplished through diligent struggle what they could in a most reluctant sociopolitical system. To assume that *more* emphasis earlier on universal, economic issues would have yielded more substantive gains for masses of blacks flies in the face of long-standing political and economic realities. Blacks were not unaware of the transformation of the productive sector of the economy, or of the importance of developing marketable skills to fit a changing labor market. They raised these issues over the decades, but they were certainly in no position on their own to overcome the dire consequences of these developments. In the 1930s and 1940s, for example, the failure to include two-thirds of the black labor force (agricultural and domestic workers) under initial social insurance coverage in the Social Security system severely restricted economic security of blacks decades later. This was a consequence foreseen by the NAACP and the NUL, but their potential liberal allies were insufficiently responsive to the warnings.

Historical data attest to the efforts of African-American groups to enlist enlightened allies in the struggle, but the social welfare agenda clearly did not have the same support as the civil rights agenda at critical times, especially in the mid-1960s. With pursuit of the civil rights agenda, there was no real economic cost to be borne by the larger society. In fact, as legal racial barriers were removed, many whites stood to gain economically from blacks who were then able to spend their money in nonsegregated markets—in such places, for example, as business establishments, schools, colleges. In an ironic sense, the end of legal racial segregation created new markets for white Americans! Even as civil rights gains were made, very many people—liberals and conservatives, blacks and whites—erroneously assumed that all groups would benefit equitably from an expanding economy.

After the 1960s, when many white Americans began to experience harsh economic realities—modernized production and business practices that could maximize profits with fewer employees, loss of job security, layoffs, inflation, lowering standard of living with rising prices and stagnant wages, need for higher educational skills, vulnerability to soaring health care costs—problems that were common, long-standing experiences of blacks became part of the daily lives of many other Americans as well. Not until those actual, painful facts of life were broadly shared could there be any real prospect for effective widespread political mobilization. But dealing with problems of increasing economic insecurity not only among blacks and other minorities but among whites as well presented a very different circumstance.

PROSPECTS: SOCIAL POLICY AGENDA

Given the problems facing the country in the 1990s and beyond, there is every reason to believe that the pressing issues of economic growth and social welfare, broadly defined, will be top priorities. Health care, welfare reform, and job creation are, of course, obviously high on the list. African Americans have always been concerned about these issues and have supported progressive reforms to deal with them. Their organizations are not latecomers to these interests precisely because these problems have always plagued a majority of blacks. Even in the best of times, especially during the period of greatest economic growth after World War II, African Americans have lagged behind other Americans in reaping the benefits of prosperity. Therefore, one would not be surprised to find sustained interest in social welfare policies in the African-American community.

The critical point is that these issues will have to be dealt with in an environment of economic austerity and devastating budget deficits, along with increasing economic competition from foreign countries. Such circumstances always produce clashes between contending economic theories about how best to support a market economy *and* commit to social welfare protection. For too long, African Americans have been effectively locked out of access to the resources and benefits of a market economy, and it is not surprising that an enormous amount of energy has been devoted to breaking down those barriers. This struggle will continue. It will require joining the continuing American debate on the most appropriate role of the government in fiscal and monetary policies, subsidies, and investment in human capital.

There will continue to be the perennial debate in American society regarding how far the national government should go in committing resources to education, and, indeed, regarding what form those commitments should take—loans, scholarships, tax credits, vouchers. The policy options are numerous, each carrying its own ideological stamp of justification—from the Left and the Right. This is no less the case with issues of chronic unemployment, health care, and affordable housing, not to mention the always vexing questions of taxes and how to finance the programs so many need.

Through their established organizations and growing numbers of elected and appointed officials, blacks have indicated a particular liberal-progressive orientation on all these issues. But if such an orientation is to prevail in the long run, it will need broad political support requiring allies and coalitions. It is equally evident that these coalitions will be based on shifting perceptions of self-interest among the component parts that cut across racial/ethnic lines. The appeal for allies is predicated on the assumption that there are some issues—for example, health care, jobs, education, housing—that affect many people, not just African Americans. To be sure, blacks are disproportionately disadvantaged, and, therefore, would benefit greatly, but not exclusively, by progressive social-economic legislation. There is, in other words, a possibility for a political strategy of "deracialization," a strategy that identifies common interests among as wide a spectrum of interest groups as possible. Such interests ought to be the targets of specific coalitions, with no naive expectation that such alliances can or ought to be *all* encompassing or even permanent. The old political adage: There are no permanent enemies, no permanent friends, only permanent interests—is appropriate here.

As African Americans increase their political mobilization, they will be more adept at playing in that classic American political pluralist game. Those groups best equipped to participate in that process are those groups best able, *over the long run*, to maximize their victories and minimize their defeats. And, it should be said, they are the very groups that ultimately gain the *respect* of others.

PROSPECTS: CIVIL RIGHTS AGENDA

Paying attention to economic and social welfare issues should not be understood as sufficient to deal with persistent problems of racial discrimination. Clearly, an argument has been made—normally articulated in terms of race versus class—that poverty, not racism, was the major reason for the lowly status of many African Americans. Tend to matters of eradicating poverty, proponents claimed, and in time the effects of racism would substantially, if not entirely, disappear. As indicated earlier, this has been a theme, from liberals and conservatives, for several decades.

While many African Americans have understood the importance of the social welfare agenda, they have not been sanguine that this by itself is enough in a race conscious society. A society with a legacy of centuries of slavery, segregation, and discrimination based on race should not be naive in believing that racist beliefs and practices could be easily eradicated. The dual agenda recognizes the need to continue to struggle against denial of basic civil rights. The passage of important legislation in the 1960s ending de jure segregation could not be expected to have completed the task of achieving racial equity. That racism remains a prominent factor in American life should not be difficult to document. Indeed, such evidence is available, especially in the areas of employment and housing.

A continuing responsibility of those so inclined is to push vigorously the civil rights agenda, to ferret out acts of discrimination, and to seek the most appropriate means of remediation and punishment. It should also be clear that at times remedies might call for the most firm implementation of *measurable* affirmative action policies. This is as clear a value in a democratic polity as is the achievement of economic development. It should also be clear that pursuit of the civil rights agenda, of necessity, must be race- (and gender-) specific precisely because the obstacles to be overcome are embedded in racial and gender prejudices. A social welfare agenda addresses problems shared across race lines. A civil rights agenda confronts head-on problems of discrimination faced by specific, identifiable, ascriptive groups. While pursuit of the social welfare agenda can and ought to be deracialized, that is understandably not the case with the civil rights agenda.

This fact got confused in the 1960s when liberals prematurely announced the death of racism in the brief, euphoric period of passage of the Civil Rights Act of 1964 and the launching of the Great Society's War on Poverty. Many changes were taking place on the civil rights front along with the enactment of significant new social legislation in education, Medicare, and Medicaid. At the same time, beginning in 1964, the country began to experience riots in the inner cities among blacks, stemming from many causes economic and social, that occurred with such rapidity every year that journalists began to refer prospectively to the "long hot summer." Poverty became associated with race relations and civil rights. Analysts combined the two.

In 1965, Vice President Hubert H. Humphrey was designated by President Lyndon B. Johnson to serve as honorary chairman of the National Advisory Council to the Office of Economic Opportunity, a group to advise on implementing the various War on Poverty programs. In his initial remarks to the council, Johnson stated:

> I consider the poverty and the civil rights assignments part of one objective—the opening up of real opportunities for all of our people. Civil Rights victories as such will be meaningless unless we give people the education and the jobs and the housing that will permit them to have genuinely equal opportunities. All of you in this Council have served the cause of equal rights; now you can help obtain equal opportunities for the victims of discrimination.

Given the times and the politics, such a linkage of poverty and civil rights was understandable, even if somewhat simplistic and overly optimistic, and many people held similar views at that time.

But over time, it has become clearer that while the two agendas are certainly related, they nonetheless present quite different policy options and political challenges. In recognizing the distinction between the two agendas, it is important to understand that different political coalitions will be available for different goals. The coalitions possible for achieving *full* employment might well not be the same coalitions amenable to achieving *fair* (nondiscriminatory) employment, especially when achieving the latter involves certain policies calling for preferential hiring. A viable national health care system for all, which is by no means race-specific, is one thing. Effective remedy against racial discrimination in hospital employment—for example, affirmative action—is another matter. The social policy agenda, of necessity, must consider class differentiations. The civil rights agenda is aimed at overcoming race differentiations. Achieving success in one arena will not ipso facto produce success in the other. Therein lies the need to understand that these are importantly related, but they are at the same time distinct areas of operation. It may well be that more emphasis will have to be put on one agenda for *political* reasons. That is, the political coalitions may be stronger and more easily built. In a sense, this was the case regarding the earlier civil rights success in the courts and Congress in overcoming legal segregation in the 1950s and 1960s. But this should be understood as a matter of political calculation, as a matter of the need to make pragmatic political choices. It is hardly a matter of one agenda being intrinsically more important than the other. African Americans have economic *and* racial obstacles, and it would be inadvisable to conclude that either set of problems ultimately should be subordinated to the other.

CONCLUSION

Charting strategies in the future to deal with both a social policy and a civil rights agenda will be the essential challenge for African Americans and their allies. If coalitions will shift based on the particular policies pursued, then it is also clear that strategies will include reliance on different political institutions at different times. For a long time, the United States Supreme Court was the major institution in moving the civil rights agenda forward. In the near future, that institution is not likely to be as responsive as the Warren Court was in the 1950s and 1960s. Initiation of effective policies may require more attention to Congress, where African Americans are increasing their presence and influence, and to the executive branch.

Political regimes change, and political strategies must be adaptable. This has obvious implications for political mobilization, which must recognize that litigation, electoral politics, and protest action are all viable means for pursuing one's political objectives. It is clear that over the years African Americans have not been remiss in taking advantage of both the complicated check-and-balance structures of the three branches of government and the federalist nature of the system. The future will require no less attention to this frustrating but at the same time potentially rewarding reality. But if any group in the United States has understood and engaged the protracted political struggle in the face of seemingly insurmountable obstacles, African Americans have demonstrated that capacity.

FOR FURTHER READING

Diawara, Manthia, Clyde Taylor, and Regina Taylor, eds. *Black Genius: African American Solutions to African American Problems.* New York: W. W. Norton & Co, 1999.

Hamilton, Dona C., and Charles V. Hamilton. *The Dual Agenda: Race and Social Welfare Policies of Civil Rights Organizations.* New York: Columbia, 1997.

Jaynes, Gerald D., and Robin M. Williams Jr., eds. *Common Destiny: Blacks and American Society.* Washington, D.C.: National Academy Press, 1989.

Myrdal, Gunnar. *An American Dilemma: The Negro Problem and Modern Democracy.* New Brunswick, N.J.: Transaction Publications, 1996.

Ture, Kwame [Stokely Carmichael], and Charles V. Hamilton. *Black Power: The Politics of Liberation.* Rev. ed. New York: Vintage, 1992.

Turner, Margery, Michael Fix, and Raymond Struyk. *Opportunities Denied, Opportunities Diminished: Racial Discrimination in Hiring.* Washington, D.C.: Urban Institute Press, 1991.

Wilson, William Julius. *The Truly Disadvantaged: The Inner City, The Underclass, and Public Policy.* Chicago: University of Chicago Press, 1990.

Notes on Contributors

Walter R. Allen is currently Professor of Sociology at the University of California at Los Angeles. He holds degrees in the field of sociology from Beloit College (B.A., 1971) and the University of Chicago (M.A., 1973; Ph.D., 1975). Dr. Allen has held teaching appointments at the University of Michigan (1979–1991), the University of North Carolina, Chapel Hill (1974–1979), Howard University, Duke University, the University of Zimbabwe, and Wayne State University. Dr. Allen's research and teaching focus on family patterns, socialization and personality development, race and ethnic relations, health inequality, and higher education. His numerous publications have appeared in scholarly journals. He has coauthored *The Colorline and the Quality of Life in America* (with Reynolds Farley), coedited two books, *Beginnings: The Social and Effective Development of Black Children* (with Geraldine Brookins and Margaret Spencer), and *Black American Families, 1965–1984* (with Richard English and JoAnne Hall), and coauthored a third, *College in Black and White: African American Students in Predominantly White and Historically Black Public Universities* (with Edgar G. Epps and Nesha Z. Haniff).

John F. Bauman earned his Ph.D. from Rutgers University in 1969. Since then, he has been a Professor of History at California University of Pennsylvania and since 1975 a Research Adjunct at the University of Pittsburgh. His research interest has focused mainly on contemporary urban history especially urban housing, urban planning, and the history of African-American poverty. He has authored and coauthored several books on contemporary America including *Public Housing, Race and Renewal: Urban Planning in Philadelphia, 1920–1974*.

Stephen N. Butler earned his B.S. from New York University and his M.A. and Ed.D. from Columbia's Teachers College. In the 1960s he taught in junior high schools in New York City and served as codirector of the Upward Bound Program at Queens College. He has also held positions as Associate

Professor of Sociology and Director of the Social Science Division of Essex Community College in Newark, New Jersey, and Associate Dean of the College and lecturer in Sociology at Wesleyan University. After teaching at Sarah Lawrence College, he became a faculty member at Earlham College, where he is currently Associate Academic Dean and Professor of Sociology. He regularly advises colleges on methods for achieving racially inclusive campus environments, the subject of his present research.

Gerald Early is the Merle S. Kling Professor of Modern Letters in Arts and Sciences and Director of the African and Afro-American Studies Program at Washington University in St. Louis. He has edited a collection of Countee Cullen's work as well as *Speech and Power* and *Lure & Loathing: Essays on Race, Identity, and the Ambivalence of Assimilation*. He is the author of *Tuxedo Junction; Daughters: On Family and Fatherhood*; and a book of poetry, *How the War in the Streets Is Won: Poems on the Quest for Love and Faith*. His most recent book is *One Nation Under a Groove: Motown and American Culture*. *The Culture of Bruising: Essays on Prize Fighting* won the 1994 National Book Critics Circle award. Early is the recipient of a Whiting Writer's Award, a General Electric Foundation Award, and the Washington University Distinguished Faculty Award. In 1995, he organized the first conference on Miles Davis and American Culture.

William H. Gray III has been President and Chief Executive Officer of the College Fund/UNCF since September 11, 1991. Prior to his selection as president of UNCF, Mr. Gray served in the U.S. Congress, elected to the House of Representatives in 1978. He has been a faculty member and professor of history and religion at St. Peter's College, Jersey City State College, Montclair State College, Eastern Baptist Theological Seminary, and Temple University. Mr. Gray attended Franklin and Marshall College, where he earned a B.A. in 1963. He received a master's degree in divinity in 1966 from Drew Theological Seminary, and a master's degree in theology in 1970 from Princeton Theological Seminary. He has also been awarded more than fifty honorary degrees from America's leading colleges and universities.

Robert Gregg is Assistant Professor of History at the Richard Stockton College of New Jersey. He earned his Ph.D. from the University of Pennsylvania in 1989 and has held teaching positions at Princeton University, Mount Holyoke College, and the University of Pennsylvania. He is the author of *Sparks from the Anvil of Oppression: Philadelphia's African Methodists and Southern Migrants, 1890–1940*.

Charles V. Hamilton is presently Wallace S. Sayre Professor of Government at Columbia University. He has held teaching positions at numerous U.S. colleges and universities including Roosevelt University, Lincoln University, and Rutgers University. Among his many scholarly publications are *Adam Clayton Powell, Jr.: The Political Biography of an American Dilemma*; *American Government*; *The Black Preacher in America*; *The Bench and the Ballot: Southern Judges* *and the Right to Vote*; *The Black Experience of American Politics*; and *Black Power*, with Stokely Carmichael. Dr. Hamilton holds M.A. and Ph.D. degrees from the University of Chicago, a J.D. degree from Loyola University School of Law, and a B.A. from Roosevelt University. He is the recipient of the Honorary Doctor of Laws degree from Tuskegee University, a Guggenheim Fellowship, and a host of other prestigious scholarly awards and fellowships.

Lawrence J. Hanks is presently Dean of African-American Affairs and Associate Professor of Political Science at Indiana University at Bloomington. He received his B.A. in political science from Morehouse College and his M.A. and Ph.D. in government from Harvard University. He is the former chair of political science at Tuskegee University. He is the author of *Black Political Empowerment in Three Georgia Counties* and was a contributor to *A Common Destiny: Blacks and American Society*.

Gerald D. Jaynes is Professor of Economics and Chair of the Program in African and African-American Studies at Yale University. He previously taught at the University of Pennsylvania. He earned a B.A. from the University of Illinois where he also obtained a Ph.D. He has served as an adjunct fellow of the Joint Center for Political and Economic Studies and as Chair of the Minority Business Development Agency for the City of New Haven, Connecticut. He is the author of *Branches without Roots* and coeditor of *A Common Destiny: Blacks and American Society*.

Norrece T. Jones Jr. is Associate Professor in the Department of History at Virginia Commonwealth University where he holds a joint position in the African-American Studies Program. He received a Ph.D. in American History from Northwestern University (1981) and a B.A. in history from Hampton University (1974). He has taught at the College of Holy Cross and received fellowships from the National Endowment for the Humanities, the Ford Foundation, and the National Fellowships Fund. He is the author of *Born a Child of Freedom, Yet a Slave: Mechanisms of Control and Strategies of Resistance in Antebellum South Carolina*.

Carole C. Marks is Black American Studies Program Director at the University of Delaware. She holds a joint appointment in the Sociology Department, received her Ph.D. from New York University, and has held a National Institute of Mental Health Post-Doctoral Fellowship at Duke University, and a Research Fellowship at the W. E. B. DuBois Institute at Harvard University. The author of numerous publications and professional papers, Professor Marks is well known for her 1989 book, *Farewell, We're Good and Gone: The Great Black Migration*. She served as a member of the Board of Managers of Haverford College in Pennsylvania for twelve years, is President of the National Association of Black Sociologists, and has been appointed to the State of Delaware Human Relations Commission.

Waldo F. Martin Jr. is Professor of History at the University of California at Berkeley where he teaches courses in African-American and Modern U.S.

History. He is the author of *The Mind of Frederick Douglass*; editor of *The Brown Decision and the Enduring Dilemma of Race*; and coeditor with Julian Bond and Patricia Sullivan of the *Encyclopedia of Civil Rights in the United States*.

Joseph C. Miller received his Ph.D. from the University of Wisconsin-Madison in 1972 and has taught since then at the University of Virginia, where he is now the T. Cray Johnson Jr. Professor of History. He has published widely on the African history of Angola and on the history of the slave trade from Angola to Brazil. His most recent monograph, *Way of Death: Merchant Capitalism and the Angolan Slave Trade, 1730–1820*, won the 1988 Herskovits Prize of the African Studies Association for the best work in English in any field of African studies. He has compiled a continuing series of bibliographies on slavery and the slave trade, worldwide, now totaling nearly 15,000 titles. He has also served as Dean of the College of Arts and Sciences at the University of Virginia and is currently President of the American Historical Association.

Edward P. Morgan is Professor of Political Science of Lehigh University. He was educated at Oberlin College (A.B. 1968) and Brandeis University (M.A. 1973, Ph.D. 1976). He has taught at the University of Massachusetts, Boston, Oberlin College, and the University of Nottingham, England. He has received teaching awards at Lehigh University and grants from NEH, NSF, and the Mellon Foundation and was Spencer Fellow twice. His main fields of interest are propaganda and mass communications, political sociology and the 1960s. He has published extensively in scholarly journals and published three books including *The Sixties Experience: Hard Lessons about Modern America*.

Wilson J. Moses is Professor of History at Pennsylvania State University, and has taught at the University of Iowa, Southern Methodist University, Brown University, Boston University, Harvard University, the Free University of Berlin, and the University of Vienna. Professor Moses received his Ph.D. from Brown University in 1975. He has lectured at the University of Cambridge and the University of Hull in England, Chancellor College in Malawi, Cuttingon College in Liberia, the University of Liberia, Fourah Bay College in Sierra Leone, the National Academy in Hungary, and the University of Graz in Austria. He is the author of *The Golden Age of Black Nationalism*, *Black Messiahs and Uncle Toms*, *Alexander Crummell: A Study of Civilization and Discontent*, and *The Wings of Ethiopia*. He has edited *Destiny and Race: Sermons and Addresses of Alexander Crummell* and *Classical Black Nationalism from the American Revolution to Marcus Garvey*. He has written numerous essays, reviews, and scholarly articles and has held fellowships from the National Endowment for the Humanities, Andrew W. Mellon Foundation, Ford Foundation, the American Council of Learned Societies, and the American Philosophical Society.

Donald G. Nieman is Professor of History and Chair of the History Department at Bowling Green State University. He received his Ph.D. from Rice University in 1975 and has taught at Kansas State University, Hunter College,

Clemson University, and Brooklyn College of the City University of New York. Nieman's research has focused on law and race in American history. His books include *To Set the Law in Motion: The Freedmen's Bureau and the Legal Rights of Blacks, 1865–1860*; *Promises to Keep: African Americans and the Constitutional Order, 1776 to the Present*; *The Constitution, Law, and American Life: Critical Aspects of the Nineteenth Century Experience*; and *African American Life in the Post-Emancipation South, 1861–1900: A Twelve Volume Anthology of Scholarly Articles*.

Armstead L. Robinson was Associate Professor of History, Corcoran Department of History, the University of Virginia, in Charlottesville; was born in 1947 in New Orleans, Louisiana; and died in 1995 in Charlottesville, Virginia. He received a B.A. with Honors and Distinction from Yale University in 1969 and a Doctorate with Honors from the University of Rochester in 1977. He served as Assistant Professor at SUNY-Stony Brook, 1970–1971; SUNY-Brockport, 1971–1973; and UCLA 1973–1980. From 1980 to 1995, he served as an Associate Professor at the University of Virginia. Dr. Robinson was the Director of the University of Virginia's Carter G. Woodson Institute for Afro-American and African Studies. He specialized in the study of the Civil War, particularly in the role slaves and free blacks played in the conflict and Confederacy's demise. He was still polishing the crowning achievement of his own life's work when he died: a three-volume history of slaves and women during the Civil War titled *Bitter Fruits of Bondage*.

William R. Scott is Professor of History at Lehigh University, where he also serves as Director of African Studies. He holds degrees from Lincoln, Howard, and Princeton Universities. He has taught at the University of Wisconsin, Wellesley College, Harvard University, Oberlin College, Clark Atlanta University, and Georgia Institute of Technology. He has served as Associate Dean at Wellesley College and Oberlin College as well as Dean of Arts and Science at Clark Atlanta University, Director of the United Negro College Fund and Andrew W. Mellon Minority Fellowship Program, and consultant to the Educational Opportunities Council in Johannesburg, South Africa. His other published works include *The Sons of Sheba's Race: African Americans and the Italo-Ethiopian War, 1935–1941*.

William G. Shade is Professor of History and Director of American Studies, Lehigh University. He was formerly a member of the Advisory Board to the Secretary of Interior for National Parks, Historic Sites, Buildings, and Monuments and is on the Academic Advisory Council of the Black Institute for Ethnic Studies. Professor Shade has taught at Temple University, Lafayette College, the University of Virginia, University College Galway of the National University of Ireland, and the University of Nottingham. He is the author or editor of twelve books on American social and political history including *Seven on Black: Reflections on the Negro Experience in America*, and has published more than thirty articles in scholarly journals. His most recent book, *Democratizing the Old Dominion*, deals extensively with slavery and abolition in

Virginia. Professor Shade received the Avery O. Craven Prize of The Organization of American Historians in 1998.

Beverly Guy-Sheftall is founding director of the Women's Research & Resource Center and Anna Julia Cooper Professor of Women's Studies at Spelman College, and founding coeditor of *Sage: A Scholarly Journal on Black Women*. Her publications include *Sturdy Black Bridges: Visions of Black Women in Literature* (coedited with Roseann P. Bell and Betty Parker); *Daughters of Sorrow: Attitudes of Black Women 1880–1920*; and *Words of Fire: An Anthology of African American Feminist Thought*.

Jean R. Soderlund is Professor and Chair of the Department of History at Lehigh University and Co-Director of the Lawrence Henry Gipson Institute of Eigtheenth-Century Studies. She received her Ph.D. from Temple University and was a post-doctoral fellow at the Philadelphia Center for Early American Studies at the University of Pennsylvania. Her book, *Quakers and Slavery: A Divided Spirit*, won the Alfred E. Driscoll Publication Prize for the New Jersey Historical Commission. Soderlund was an editor of three volumes of the Papers of William Penn (1981–1983) and co-authored *Freedom by Degrees: Emancipation in Pennsylvania and Its Aftermath*. She is a council member of the Philadelphia Center for Early American Studies, the Pennsylvania Historical Association, and the David Library of the American Revolution, and served as a committee chair for the American Historical Association.

Gayraud S. Wilmore is Professor Emeritus of Church History at the Interdenominational Theological Center in Atlanta, Georgia. He was educated at Lincoln University, the University of Florence, Italy, Temple University School of Religion, and Drew Theological Seminary. He has served as Academic Dean and Professor of African-American Religious Studies at the New York Theological Seminary, Martin Luther King Jr. Professor of Black Church Studies at Colgate Rochester Divinity School, and Martin Luther King Jr. Professor of Social Ethics at Boston University School of Theology. He is the author of *Black Religion and Black Radicalism* and has written or edited nineteen other books that include *Black Theology: A Documented History*.

Peter H. Wood is a graduate of Harvard and a former Rhodes Scholar who teaches Early American History at Duke University. He is the author of the prize-winning book, *Black Majority: Negroes in Colonial South Carolina from 1670 through the Stono Rebellion*. In 1996 he published *Strange New Land: African Americans, 1617–1776* and he is also the author, with Karen Dalton, of *Winslow Homer's Images of Blacks: The Civil War and Reconstruction Years*. Dr. Wood has served on the editorial board of the *Journal of Southern History*, *Ethnohistory*, and the *William and Mary Quarterly* and has served on the board of the Highlander Center, the Menil Foundation, the Africa News Service, and Harvard University.